The Botanical Garden II

Perennials and Annuals

The Botanical Garden II

Perennials and Annuals

The definitive reference with more than 2000 photographs

By

Roger Phillips

&

Martyn Rix

FIREFLY BOOKS

A FIREFLY BOOK

Published by Firefly Books Ltd., 2002

Copyright © 2002 Roger Phillips and Martyn Rix

First Printing

National Library of Canada
Cataloguing in Publication Data

Phillips, Roger
   The botanical garden

Includes bibliographical references and index.
Contents: v.1. Trees and shrubs – v. 2. Perennials and
annuals.

ISBN 1-55297-591-6 (v. 1).– ISBN 1-55297-592-4 (v. 2)

1. Plants, Ornamental. 2. Gardening. 3. Plants,
Ornamental–Pictorial works. I. Rix, Martyn II. Title.

SB450.97.P48 2002   635.9   C2002-900216-8

Publisher Cataloging-in-Publication Data (U.S.)

Phillips, Roger.
   The botanical garden volume II : perennials and
annuals / Roger Phillips ; and Martyn Rix. – 1st ed.
[540] p. : col. photos. ; cm.
Includes bibliographic references and index.
Summary: 510 genera of non-woody garden plants
with full details of how they are related, their origins and
their uses.

ISBN 1-55297-592-4

1. Annuals (Plants) – Encyclopedias. 2. Perennials –
Encyclopedias. I. Rix, Martyn. I. Title.

635.9/ 32/ 097 21   CIP   SB422.P53 2002

Published in Canada in 2002 by
Firefly Books Ltd.
3680 Victoria Park Avenue
Willowdale, Ontario M2H 3K1

Published in the United States in 2002 by
Firefly Books (U.S.) Inc.
P.O. Box 1338, Ellicott Station
Buffalo, New York 14205

Color reproduction by Speedscan
Printed and bound in Great Britain by Bath Press

Acknowledgments

DESIGNER: Jill Bryan
ASSISTANT DESIGNERS: Gill Stokoe,
Debby Curry, and Gaia Chaillet Giusti
EDITOR: Candida Frith-Macdonald
PROOF READER: Jonathan Edwards
PRODUCTION: Chris Gibson and Lee Bekker

Most of the specimens came from the
following gardens, and we would like to
acknowledge the generous help we had from
them and their staff:

Marwood Hill Gardens, Dr Jimmy Smart and
Malcolm Pharoah; The Royal Horticultural
Society's Gardens at Rosemoor and Wisley,
Jim Gardiner, Jenny Holloway, and John
Chesters; Gorwell House, Dr John Marston;
Eccleston Square Garden, Kathryn Maule;
The Chelsea Physic Garden, Sue Minter and
Fiona Crumley; The University Botanic
Garden, Cambridge; The Royal Botanic
Gardens Kew, Jessica Begon, Rosmena
Brown, and Helen Long in the Gardens
Development Unit.

We would also like to thank the following
individuals and gardens for their help,
encouragement, or for providing specimens
to photograph:

Harry and Yvonne Hay; Roger Clark at
Greenway Gardens; Guy and Emma Sissons
at The Plantsman Nursery; Mary Anne and
Alastair Robb at Cothay Manor;
John d'Arcy at the Old Vicarage, Edington;
George Llewellyn; Carolyn Hardy;
Sheila Bryan; Sara and George Sibannac;
Mark Duffy; Alison Rix; Nicky Foy;
Geoffrey Goatcher; and Dr James Compton.

Contents

Due to the number of plants covered, listings given here cannot be comprehensive but instead cover the major groups of plants

GLOSSARY BIBLIOGRAPHY INDEX

Introduction

Our aim in this book is to provide new information and a new way of looking at plants and gardening from a more botanical viewpoint. The plant families are covered systematically, and the relationships between them are discussed; readers will be able to put the knowledge they have acquired piecemeal into a framework, and understand the botanical groups and the similarities and differences between them.

DNA studies in plants

The discovery of the structure of DNA by Watson and Crick in 1953 opened up a whole new method for studying the relationships between living things; much more recently, the use of computers to compare large amounts of simple data has revealed new evidence for the ancestry of plants. These new studies have not proved to be a Rosetta Stone that will reveal all, but they have provided some important new information to help solve old problems. Hitherto unsuspected relationships have been suggested, and interesting variations within a single species have also been shown up. The details of the method are complex, but depend on studying the behaviour of three different bodies within the plant cell. The DNA in two of these, the mitochondrion (involved in respiration) and the chloroplast (involved in photosynthesis), is inherited maternally, while the DNA of the third, the nucleus, is derived from both parents. The genes of mitochondria are too unstable to be of use in these studies, but fortunately the genes of chloroplasts are very stable; rearrangements of their DNA sequences are rare enough to be used to indicate major evolutionary groups, but frequent enough to be interesting and worth looking for. Research since the 1980s is now beginning to be used to describe new relationships between genera and families, and new arrangements have been published. These sometimes confirm the classical view based on the morphology of plants, and sometimes bring surprises.

Major groupings

The main division of the flowering plants into monocotyledons and dicotyledons is upheld by DNA studies, with the exception of a few primitive plants that fall outside both categories; this indicates that the monocotyledons arose as a group within the primitive dicotyledons, rather than separately. Some of the important groupings of monocotyledons are described below. Within the main body of the dicotyledons, around six groups are shown to be rather isolated. Two of these are the Saxifragales and the Caryophyllales, while two others, the Ranunculales and the Proteales, respectively include the largely herbaceous Ranunculaceae (see pp.38–59), Berberidaceae (see pp.60–63), and Papaveraceae (see pp.64–71), and a diverse group related to *Protea*, which includes the familiar genera *Platanus* and *Nelumbo*: this superficially crazy association of the waterlily-like *Nelumbo*, the sacred lotus, with totally different-looking trees and shrubs, must rank as one of the great surprises of DNA research. The rest of the main body of dicotyledons fall into two large clades, the Rosids and Asterids, a clade being a group of families or genera with a common ancestor, an evolutionary lineage. The artificiality of several previously recognised families of plants has been shown up by DNA studies. In particular, traditional Scrophulariaceae has been found to be a diverse assemblage, and although the traditional name has been retained here, the plants have been arranged as they naturally fall (see pp.250–63, pp.268–69, and p.277).

Unanswered questions

The key question of what the first flowering plant looked like is still unanswered, but we are left with a number of interesting speculations. The modest water plant *Ceratophyllum* (see p.385), for example, appears to be a very early offshoot from the flowering plant ancestry, but its exact position still remains uncertain; could this be what the first flowering plant was like?

Hellebore, Epimedium, poppy, and Corydalis

This group of families, which includes the buttercup family, Ranunculaceae (see pp.38–59), was traditionally considered primitive, as many had very simple flowers, with indefinite numbers of separate stamens and carpels. Recent studies have confirmed this, as well as the close relationship of the Berberidaceae (see pp.60–63), which includes several distinct herbaceous genera. Poppies, the Papaveraceae (see pp.64–71), and *Corydalis*, both of which often have a milky sap, are related to this group. The beautiful Japanese *Glaucidium*, which was of doubtful affinity, has been shown to fall within Ranunculaeae, but the rather similar *Paeonia* is now thought to be closer to Saxifragaceae (see pp.98–108).

Corydalis flexuosa

Dianthus, cactus, polygonum, and mesembryanthemum

Pinks and carnations, *Dianthus*, and *Silene* are the main garden genera of their family, the Caryophyllaceae (see pp.74–81); several garden weeds from this family, such as chickweed and mouse-ear chickweed, are almost universal. Related to this group are the mainly succulent families Cactaceae (see p.87), which is so characteristic of the American deserts, and the Aizoaceae or Mesembryanthemaceae (see p.86), which takes its place in southern Africa; both of these families have an unusual metabolism that enables them to withstand extreme drought conditions. Other families of this group, the Caryophyllales, are edible and furnish such vegetables as beet, spinach, and rhubarb, and such diverse ornamentals as *Limonium*, *Mirabilis*, *Drosera*, and *Tamarix*.

Paeonia caucasica

Saxifrage, Sedum, and peony

The group called Saxifragales, as identified by DNA studies, is unusually diverse. The Saxifragaceae (see pp.98–108), many of which are mountain plants, are close to the usually succulent Crassulaceae (see p.109), which includes *Sedum*, the stonecrop. *Paeonia*, a remarkably isolated genus, whose affinities have long been in dispute, probably belongs here, although here Paeoniaceae (see pp.58–59) is listed in its traditional position next to Ranunculaceae; it appears to be closest to *Daphniphyllum*. The woody plants (see Volume 1) traditionally placed in Hamamelidaceae, such as *Liquidambar*, *Cercidiphyllum*, and *Itea*, are now thought to belong here, as does *Ribes*, the gooseberry and currant.

Geranium and Francoa

The important horticultural family Geraniaceae (see pp.112–15) includes the hardy *Geranium*, found all over the world, and the tender *Pelargonium*, which is mainly South African. Both of these genera have a large number of species with attractive characteristics, such as scented leaves and brightly coloured flowers, as well as large seeds that are dispersed far from the parent plant, by a spring in the case of *Geranium* (or rarely as a burr), or by wind, with a silky tail, in the case of *Pelargonium*. DNA indicates that the southern hemisphere plants *Melianthus* and *Francoa* are related to *Geranium*.

Geranium lambertii

Impatiens tinctoria

Sarracenia, Primula, Phlox, and Impatiens

The family Primulaceae (see pp.198–205), though small in number of genera, is important in temperate gardens, mainly because *Primula* itself has undergone such an explosion of beautiful species in the Himalayas and the Alps. The family also includes *Anagallis* and *Lysimachia*. Closely related to *Primula* is the mainly American *Phlox*, *Polemonium*, and the climbing *Cobaea*, in the Polemoniaceae (see pp.196–97). These are shown by DNA studies to fall within the Asterids, and within that to belong to the Ericales, a large group that includes *Impatiens* and the pitcher plants *Sarracenia*, as well as shrubs such as *Styrax*, *Camellia*, and *Rhododendron* (see Volume 1).

Peas, beans, Lathyrus, and Polygala

Peas, beans, and vetches, in the family Leguminosae (see pp.124–37), are shown to be a distinct group within the Rosids. This huge family is mainly tropical and mostly woody, but the temperate Leguminosae are important in gardens, providing sweet peas and many other ornamental species of *Lathyrus*, as well as peas and beans, which are vital to us for their protein-rich seeds. The capacity to fix atmospheric nitrogen is well developed in Leguminosae, and also appears to have arisen independently in a few other families. Milkwort, *Polygala*, in the Polygalaceae (see p.123), a dwarf herb in the northern hemisphere but often tall and shrubby in the south, is related to Leguminosae.

Lathyrus vernus
'Spring Melody'

Foxglove, Mimulus, and Salvia

The Lamiales, grouped around *Lamium*, the dead nettle, mostly have characteristic 2-lipped, tubular flowers. The largest families are Labiatae (see pp.278–99), mostly aromatic plants including mints and sage, and Scrophulariaceae (see pp.250–263, pp.268–269, and p.277). DNA studies show that most of the genera of traditional Scrophulariaceae, such as *Antirrhinum*, *Digitalis*, *Mimulus*, and *Nemesia*, are distinct from a second group, containing *Verbascum*, *Scrophularia*, *Sutera*, and some other small South African genera, which are thought to be closer to Gesneriaeae and Lentibulariaceae (see pp.264–65). Partially parasitic members of the former Scrophulariaceae, such as *Rhinanthus*, are now put in with the fully parasitic Orobanchaceae (see p.276). Even more surprisingly, *Veronica* is shown to be closest to *Campsis* and *Catalpa* (see Volume 1). *Salvia* and the rest of the Labiatae are associated with the shrubs *Callicarpa* and *Clerodendrum* (see Volume 1), formerly in the Verbenaceae (see pp.266–67).

Salvia forsskaolii

Daisies and Campanula

The daisy family, Compositae (see pp.336–81) have long been considered the most advanced of the flowering plants in evolutionary terms. The flowerhead, with its numerous small, 1-seeded flowers, the outer ones resembling petals, has proved very successful, especially in dry, semi-desert climates. Many species also have a parachute to disperse the seeds on the wind. In Campanulaceae (see pp. 324–31), which is associated with Compositae in the Asterales, evolution has gone in different directions: the seeds are very small and simple, and the flowers may be large and few, as in *Canarina*, which has just one flower at the end of each branch, or very small and crowded in a daisy-like head, as in *Jasione*. In *Lobelia*, very close to *Campanula*, the flowers have become 2-lipped for more specialised pollinators, such as hummingbirds in the red-flowered American species.

Nymphaea alba

Nymphaea and the most primitive flowering plants

DNA studies suggest that the most primitive of the flowering plants are a mixed group of herbs and woody plants, which include magnolias, *Laurus,* and *Drimys* (see Volume 1). Primitive herbaceous plants include *Chloranthus, Aristolochia, Asarum,* and *Peperomia*, with Nymphaeaceae (see pp. 282–83) and *Ceratophyllum* the most primitive of all. Many of these plants must have survived unchanged for millions of years, while the rest of the flowering plants continued to evolve. Fossil flowers similar to *Nymphaea* have been found in early Cretaceous deposits in Portugal; they are around 120 million years old. The reduced flowers of *Peperomia* and the simple 3-petalled *Saruma* lead into the monocotyledons, with similarities to *Acorus* and *Sagittaria*.

Paris lancifolia

Lilium, Trillium, Alstroemeria, and Colchicum

In traditional classifications Liliaceae (see pp.416–29), the lily family, included hundreds of genera — almost any plant with six perianth segments, six stamens, and a superior ovary. More detailed studies, aided by DNA, have enabled smaller groupings to be recognised and the new, more narrowly defined Liliaceae is restricted to *Lilium, Tulipa, Calochortus, Tricyrtis, Prosartes,* and *Scoliopus* and their close relatives. *Smilax, Trillium, Alstroemeria,* and *Colchicum* are related and come within the Liliales, but most of the other former Liliaceae come within a widely designated Asparagales.

Orchids, Iris, Narcissus, and Allium

The major group Asparagales now encompasses the old families Orchidaceae (see pp.430–33), Iridaceae (see pp.438–55) and Amaryllidaceae (see pp.464–73), as well as Alliaceae (see pp.474–81) and Convallariaceae (see pp.498–503). Relationships within the group show Orchidaceae, with its complex and advanced pollination and fungus-dependent seeds, to be closest to the simple-flowered *Astelia* and *Rhodohypoxis*. The closeness of Amaryllidaceae and Alliaceae is confirmed, while Iridaceae is shown to be rather isolated.

Grasses, sedges, and rushes

Grasses, sedges, and rushes were traditionally put together by lovers of wild flowers, and DNA studies have confirmed their closeness, along with the burr reed *Sparganium*, and *Xyris*, a rush-like plant with coloured petals. A more surprising member of this group is the Bromeliaceae (see p.512), familiar to Europeans in the pineapple or as "air plants" but very frequent in the warmer parts of both North and South America, where many species are common, forming moss-like grey tufts on trees and even telephone wires. Spanish moss, *Usnea tillandsioides*, is a conspicuous feature of the scenery in the southern United States and Mexico.

Briza maxima

Sphagnum

Sphagnum L. (1753), the sphagnum or bog moss, in the family Sphagnaceae, contains about 320 species throughout the world.

Description Perennial mosses, 15–20cm, with stems growing from the tip, without roots or rhizome. Stem with spreading or drooping branches, and a terminal head of both short and longer branches. Leaves small, oval, 1 cell thick, more or less clasping the stem. Sexual reproduction of mosses is very different from that of seed plants or even ferns. Mosses produce male organs (antheridae), delicate sacs that contain the spermatozoides, and flask-shaped female organs (archegonia) that contain usually 1 egg cell. Spermatozoids swim into the archegonia and fetilize the egg. This develops into a small sporophyte, a plantlet that lives on the female shoot, producing a long-stalked capsule containing spores. The spores are dispersed and form new moss plants.

Key Recognition Features The terminal head of short branches and the spongy texture.

Ecology and Geography In bogs, marshes, wet woods and banks, worldwide in cool temperate conditions.

Comment Instantly recognisable mosses, *Sphagnum* species are the main constituent of moss peat. They can be introduced to a bog garden. *Sphagnum capillifolium* was used by North American Indians as scourers, insulating material, and an absorbent filling in nappies; other species were used as dressings in World War I, being almost sterile and highly absorbent.

Sphagnum palustre
tip of shoot, 2 × life size
October 11th

Sphagnum palustre
life size, October 11th

Sphagnum capillifolium
(below) ¾ life size

Sphagnum auriculatum
var. *inundatum*
just under life size
August 4th

Sphagnum papillosum
(left) showing capsules
¾ life size, June 15th

Polytrichum

Polytrichum J. Hedwig (1801), the hair moss, in the family
Polytrichaceae, contains about 10 species throughout the world.
Description Perennial mosses to 25cm, sometimes robust, with
erect, wiry stems growing from branched underground rhizoids to
form large clumps or patches. Leaves awl-shaped, spreading, deep
green, with fine, parallel plates (laminae) along the central part of the
upper surface. Male plants bear a terminal, flower-like, reddish rosette
of leaves. For reproduction see *Sphagnum*. Spores borne in a small
oblong or oval capsule, sometimes square in section, the tip covered
with a densely hairy, conical cap, the calyptra, which comes off when
the spores are shed. The capsule has a ring of 32 or 64 teeth around
the top, with a whitish membrane attached to them, the spores
escaping through the gaps between the teeth.
Key Recognition Features Prominent capsules with
conspicuous hairy calyptra, flower-like male organs, and the
laminae on the upper surface of the leaves, visible under the
microscope.
Ecology and Geography In woods, often on banks, on loose
soil, in peat bogs, and on moors, generally on acidic soils. About 10
species in Britain; the others are found throughout the world.
Comment One of the more robust and distinctive moss genera,
with several species fairly easy to encourage in gardens on sandy,
acid soils. They are often a conspicuous element in Japanese moss
gardens. The spore release mechanism resembles that of poppies
(*Papaver* see pp.68–69).

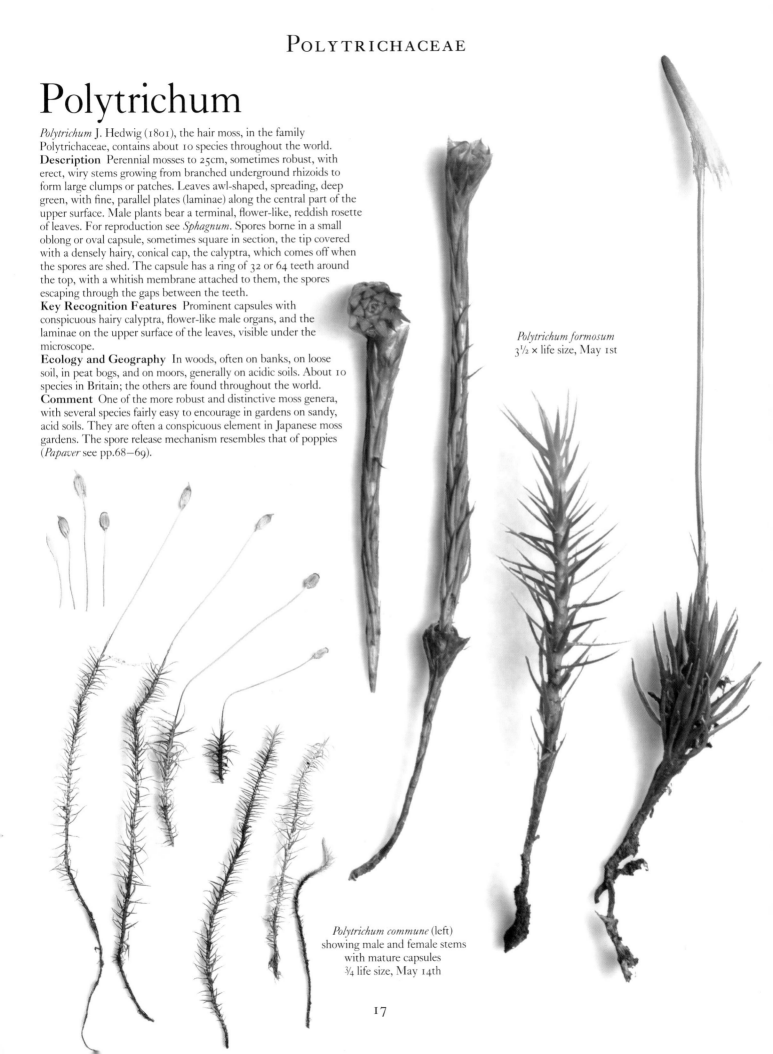

Polytrichum formosum
3½ × life size, May 1st

Polytrichum commune (left)
showing male and female stems
with mature capsules
¾ life size, May 14th

17

Equisetum

Equisetum L. (1753), the horsetail, the only genus in the family
Equisetaceae, contains about 30 species almost throughout the world.
Description Perennials to 5m, those cultivated to 2m, with extensive
rhizomes, often running deep underground. Stems evergreen or
herbaceous, hollow, jointed, usually green, usually with a whorl of
jointed branches, themselves sometimes further branched, at each of
the upper joints. Leaves minute, reduced to brownish, triangular
scales around each stem joint. Spores borne in a cone-like, black or
brown strobilus at the tip of the stem. In several species, including
E. arvense L., the common horsetail of Eurasia and North America,
the cones are borne on distinct pinkish stems without chlorophyll that
appear in early spring, the green stems coming in early summer. The
gametophyte generation that grows from these spores is seldom seen;
indeed in most species it is very rare. It is a green, liverwort-like mass
of cells, up to 1cm across, attached to the ground by rhizoids. Most
species spread vegetatively, and the colonies are very long-lived.
Key Recognition Features The jointed stems, the terminal
"cone", and the whorls of branches.
Ecology and Geography In open grassy places, cultivated land,
woods, ditches, and shallow ponds; 10 species in Europe, the others
throughout the world except for Australasia.
Comment Among the oldest living vascular plants, dating perhaps
to the Carboniferous. The abrasive stems of *E. hyemale* L. and related
species have rows of silica crystals on the ridges of the stems. These
have been used for polishing wood carvings, notably those of Grinling
Gibbons (1648–1721), and metals such as pewter. Although some
horsetails are very elegant, most are too invasive for the garden, apart
from the tiny *E. scirpoides* Michx. — even that is best confined to
a trough. *Equisetum telmateia* Ehrh. is a robust species with
whitish stems, forming handsome stands in wet areas.

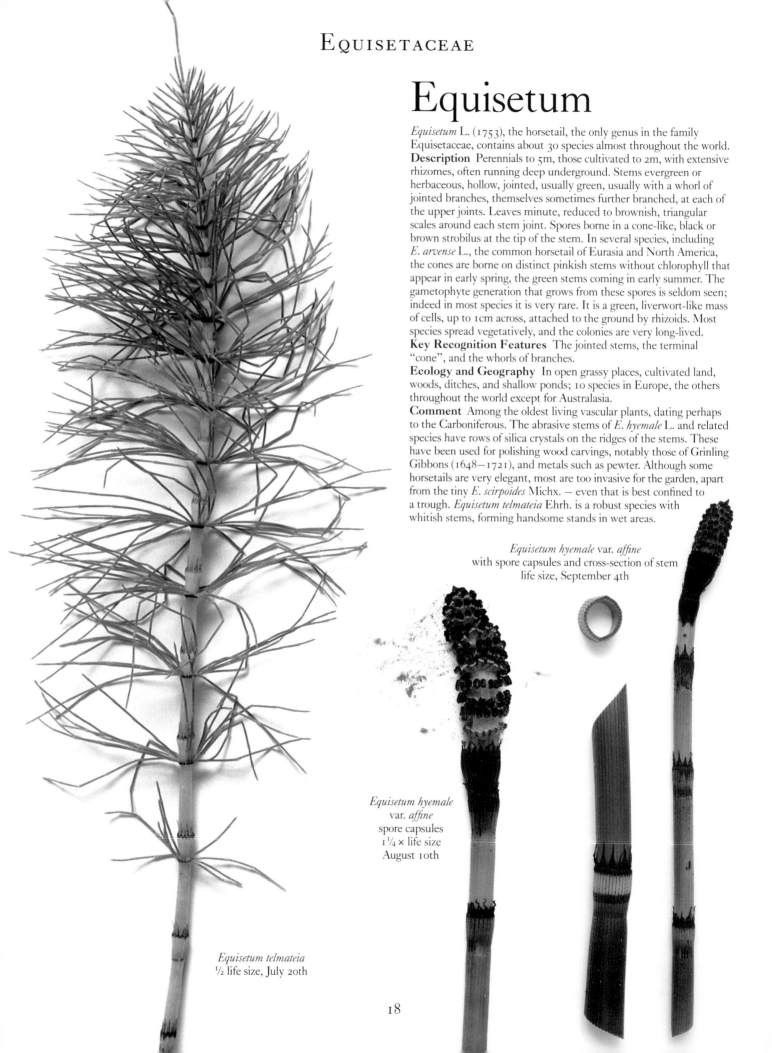

Equisetum hyemale var. *affine*
with spore capsules and cross-section of stem
life size, September 4th

Equisetum hyemale
var. *affine*
spore capsules
1 ¼ × life size
August 10th

Equisetum telmateia
½ life size, July 20th

Equisetum arvense
just under life size, July 11th

Selaginella

Selaginella Beauv. (1805), the spike moss, in the family Selaginellaceae, contains at least 700 species, mostly in the tropics.
Description Small perennials, those in cultivation to 30cm, with long, slender rhizomes, bearing branched leafy stems. Leaves tiny and scale-like or larger and awl-shaped, usually evergreen. For reproduction detail see *Sphagnum*, p.16. Megaspores (female) and microspores (male) are usually borne on small, cone-like strobili, consisting of several leaf-like sporophylls each producing 1 type of spore.
Key Recognition Features The somewhat moss-like stems with small leaves, and often cone-like strobili.
Ecology and Geography On damp rock, epiphytic on trees in moist forests, a few in open mountain habitats. Common and widespread in the tropics; few species in temperate regions, including 3 in Europe.
Comment Attractive moss-like perennials, but not always easily grown. Species such as the fairly hardy *S. helvetica* (L.) Spring and the tender *S. kraussiana* (G. Kunze) A. Braun are sometimes grown for their bright green mats of foliage.

Selaginella martensii
½ life size
September 10th

Selaginella uncinata
½ life size, September 10th

Equisetum telmateia
just under life size, March 20th

Selaginella kraussiana 'Aurea'
⅓ life size, September 10th

Osmunda

Osmunda L. (1753), the royal fern, in the family Osmundaceae, contains 12 species in Europe, North America, and eastern Asia.
Description Perennials to 2m, with a short, often massive rhizome. Fronds deciduous, large, pinnate to 2-pinnate, young stalks often covered with soft hairs. Spores borne on modified pinnae, which may be at the tip of the frond (*O. regalis* L.), in the centre of the frond (*O. banksiifolia* (Presl) Kuhn and *O. claytoniana* L.), or on distinct fertile fronds (*O. cinnamomea* L.). For reproduction see *Onoclea* (p.27).
Key Recognition Features The distinctive arrangement of the spore-bearing parts of the fronds.
Ecology and Geography Moist or wet woods and river banks, with 1 species in Europe, 3 in North America, and the others in temperate and tropical eastern Asia.
Comment A handsome fern for damp or wet places in shade or sun, *O. regalis* will form massive clumps, colouring well in autumn. *Osmunda* has been used as a growing medium for orchids.

Onychium

Onychium Kaulf. (1820), the carrot fern, in the family Adiantaceae, contains about 6 species in the tropics and warm temperate regions of Asia and Africa.
Description Perennials to 35cm, with slender, creeping rhizomes. Fronds evergreen or deciduous, ovate, on slender stalks, very finely dissected (3- or 4-pinnate) into narrowly lance-shaped or linear segments. Spores borne in a continuous row along each margin, and covered by the reflexed margin of the segment, but with no true indusium. For reproduction see *Onoclea* (p.27).
Key Recognition Features The very finely divided fronds, a little like carrot foliage, arising from creeping rhizomes.
Ecology and Geography In woods in warm temperate and tropical Asia.
Comment A very beautiful fern, *O. japonicum* (Thunb.) Kunze is the only species commonly grown in gardens. It is fairly hardy in cool temperate regions, and may become invasive in warmer areas; *O. contiguum* (Wall.) Hope, from the Himalayas and China, is even more finely divided, and is also occasionally grown.

Osmunda regalis
part of fertile frond
1¼ × life size, July 3rd

Osmunda regalis
young stem (left)
½ life size
June 12th

Onychium japonicum
spore-bearing
branchlet
2 × life size
July 23rd

Osmunda regalis
⅓ life size, July 4th

Onychium japonicum
½ life size, July 23rd

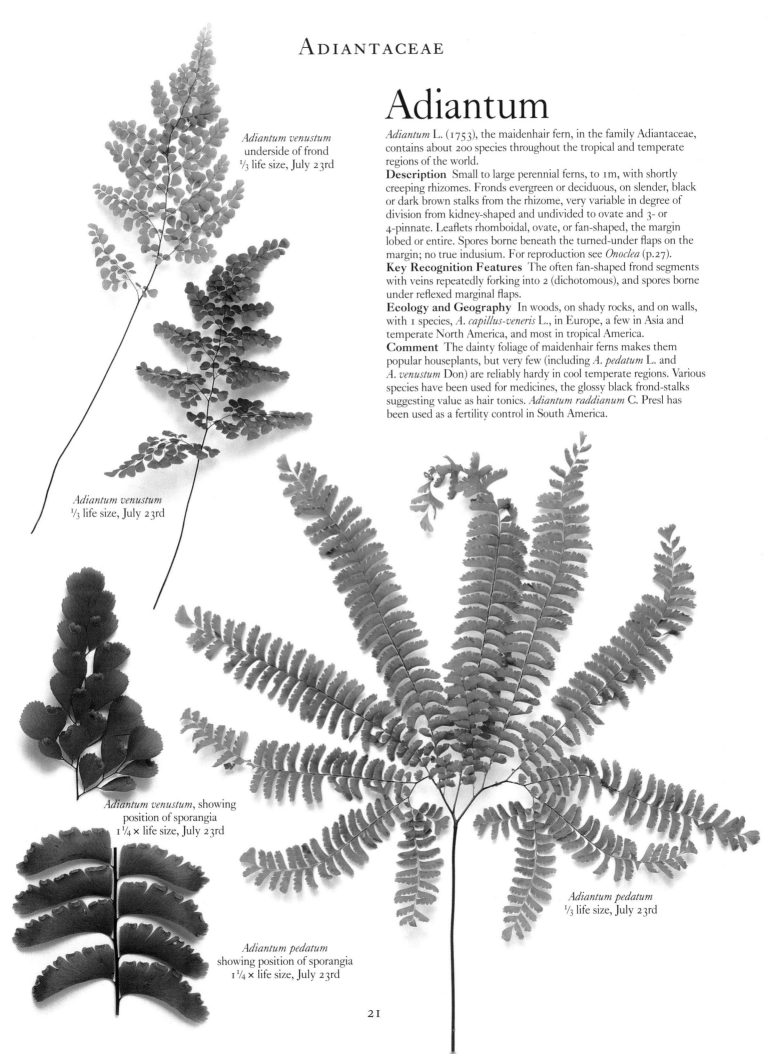

ADIANTACEAE

Adiantum

Adiantum L. (1753), the maidenhair fern, in the family Adiantaceae, contains about 200 species throughout the tropical and temperate regions of the world.

Description Small to large perennial ferns, to 1m, with shortly creeping rhizomes. Fronds evergreen or deciduous, on slender, black or dark brown stalks from the rhizome, very variable in degree of division from kidney-shaped and undivided to ovate and 3- or 4-pinnate. Leaflets rhomboidal, ovate, or fan-shaped, the margin lobed or entire. Spores borne beneath the turned-under flaps on the margin; no true indusium. For reproduction see *Onoclea* (p.27).

Key Recognition Features The often fan-shaped frond segments with veins repeatedly forking into 2 (dichotomous), and spores borne under reflexed marginal flaps.

Ecology and Geography In woods, on shady rocks, and on walls, with 1 species, *A. capillus-veneris* L., in Europe, a few in Asia and temperate North America, and most in tropical America.

Comment The dainty foliage of maidenhair ferns makes them popular houseplants, but very few (including *A. pedatum* L. and *A. venustum* Don) are reliably hardy in cool temperate regions. Various species have been used for medicines, the glossy black frond-stalks suggesting value as hair tonics. *Adiantum raddianum* C. Presl has been used as a fertility control in South America.

Adiantum venustum
underside of frond
⅓ life size, July 23rd

Adiantum venustum
⅓ life size, July 23rd

Adiantum venustum, showing
position of sporangia
1¼ × life size, July 23rd

Adiantum pedatum
showing position of sporangia
1¼ × life size, July 23rd

Adiantum pedatum
⅓ life size, July 23rd

Davallia canariensis
showing cup-shaped sori and sporangia
1½ × life size, October 23rd

Pteris wallichiana
part of a frond
½ life size, October 23rd

Pteris

Pteris L. (1753) in the family Pteridaceae, contains around 250 species throughout the world, mainly in the tropics.

Description Perennials to 1.8m, with usually short, tufted rhizomes. Fronds usually evergreen, pinnae undivided, pinnate, or 2-pinnate, fertile and sterile fronds sometimes distinct. Sori continuous, on the margin of the frond and covered by the edge, which forms the indusium. For reproduction see *Onoclea* (p.27).

Key Recognition Features The leaves with few divisions and the lowest pinnae of the frond deeply forked or divided into 3.

Ecology and Geography On walls and moist rocks, mainly in Africa and southern Asia, with 3 species in southwestern Europe.

Comments Several species are cultivated in greenhouses, where *P. cretica* L. is among the toughest of ferns. *Pteris wallichiana* Agardh. from Japan and China is a large, bracken-like plant, but has a short, erect rootstock.

Pteris wallichiana
with marginal sori
life size, October 23rd

Davallia

Davallia Sm. (1793), the hare's foot fern, in the family Davalliaceae, contains around 34 species, mainly in Africa, Asia, and Australia.

Description Perennials to 1m, those in cultivation to 45cm, with scaly, far-creeping rhizomes. Scales peltate at the base. Fronds evergreen or deciduous, usually triangular, finely divided, rather tough and shiny, usually glabrous. Sori on the tips of the branchlets, at the end of a distinct nerve, covered by a vase-shaped indusium. Spores kidney-shaped. For reproduction see *Onoclea* (p.27).

Key Recognition Features The creeping surface rootstocks and the finely divided fronds with cup-shaped sporangia on the tips.

Ecology and Geography Epiphytic on trees, and on shady cliffs and rocks. *Davallia canariensis* (L.) Sm. extends from Spain, Portugal, and Morocco to the Canaries and Madeira. Other species are found in the warmer parts of Africa, Asia, and eastwards across the islands of the Pacific to Tahiti, with 3 in eastern Australia.

Comments Many species are cultivated in hanging baskets, with the creeping rootstock covering the outside. The scaly rhizomes have given it the common name hare's foot fern. Some species are deciduous in dry weather. The tropical *D. divaricata* Blume from southeast Asia has fronds over 1m long, but most species are smaller.

Polypodium

Polypodium L. (1753), the polypody, in the family Polypodiaceae, contains about 75 species throughout the world.

Description Small to medium perennials, to 60cm, the rhizome creeping over the surface on trees or rocks. Fronds entire or simply pinnate, with entire or finely toothed margins to the segments. Spores often bright yellow, borne in large, rounded sori, with no indusium. For reproduction see *Onoclea* (p.27).

Key Recognition Features The creeping rhizome, pinnate fronds, and large yellow or orange sori.

Ecology and Geography In woods, on rocks and walls, sometimes epiphytic on trees; 3 species in Europe, the others across the world, mainly in northern temperate regions.

Comment Easily grown ferns, some of which are quite resistant to dry conditions when established. A great many tropical species formerly included in Polypodium are now placed in other genera. Both Welsh polypody, *P. cambricum* L. syn. *P. austr_ale* Fée, and *P. vulgare* L. have numerous beautiful cultivars with crested or plumose fronds; *P. interjectum* Shivas is derived from a hybrid between these two.

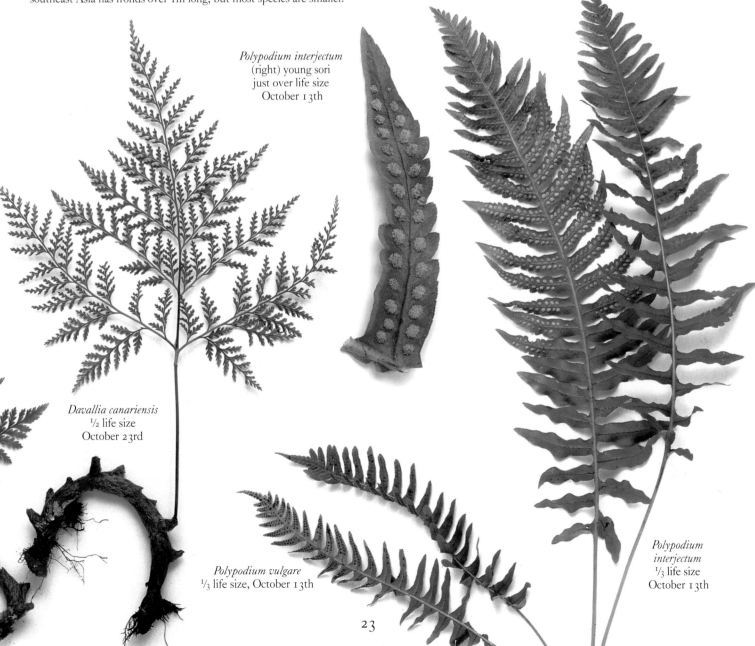

Polypodium interjectum
(right) young sori
just over life size
October 13th

Davallia canariensis
½ life size
October 23rd

Polypodium vulgare
⅓ life size, October 13th

Polypodium interjectum
⅓ life size
October 13th

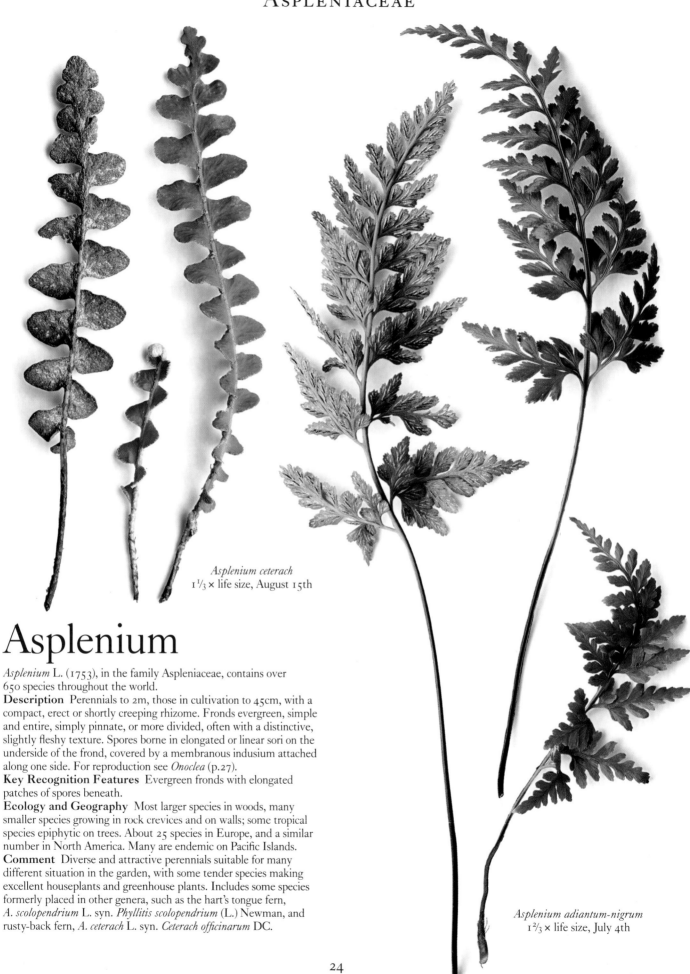

Asplenium ceterach
1⅓ × life size, August 15th

Asplenium

Asplenium L. (1753), in the family Aspleniaceae, contains over 650 species throughout the world.

Description Perennials to 2m, those in cultivation to 45cm, with a compact, erect or shortly creeping rhizome. Fronds evergreen, simple and entire, simply pinnate, or more divided, often with a distinctive, slightly fleshy texture. Spores borne in elongated or linear sori on the underside of the frond, covered by a membranous indusium attached along one side. For reproduction see *Onoclea* (p.27).

Key Recognition Features Evergreen fronds with elongated patches of spores beneath.

Ecology and Geography Most larger species in woods, many smaller species growing in rock crevices and on walls; some tropical species epiphytic on trees. About 25 species in Europe, and a similar number in North America. Many are endemic on Pacific Islands.

Comment Diverse and attractive perennials suitable for many different situation in the garden, with some tender species making excellent houseplants and greenhouse plants. Includes some species formerly placed in other genera, such as the hart's tongue fern, *A. scolopendrium* L. syn. *Phyllitis scolopendrium* (L.) Newman, and rusty-back fern, *A. ceterach* L. syn. *Ceterach officinarum* DC.

Asplenium adiantum-nigrum
1⅔ × life size, July 4th

24

Asplenium scolopendrium
life size, May 3rd

Asplenium ruta-muraria
1 ¾ × life size, July 4th

Asplenium viride
1 ¼ × life size, July 4th

Matteuccia

Matteuccia Tod. (1866), the ostrich plume fern, in the Woodsiaceae, contains about 4 species, all from the temperate northern hemisphere.

Description Medium to large perennials, to 1.2m, with short, erect rhizome or stock, *M. struthiopteris* (L.) Tod. spreading by elongated stolons. Sterile fronds in neat "shuttlecocks", bright green in early summer, lance-shaped or narrowly elliptic to broadly ovate, almost 2-pinnate. Spores borne on shorter, more erect, modified, bead-like fronds in the centre of the rosette. For reproduction see *Onoclea*.

Key Recognition Features The bead-like fertile fronds are characteristic: those of *Onoclea* are similar.

Ecology and Geography In open woods, with 1 species in Europe and North America, 2 or 3 in eastern Asia.

Comment *Matteuccia* will hybridize with *Onoclea*, in which *M. orientalis* (Hook.) Trev. is sometimes included. *Matteuccia struthiopteris* is popular in gardens, forming extensive colonies by means of the slender rhizomes; young frond-tips, called croziers, are eaten in North America and Japan. *Matteuccia orientalis* is equally hardy and of very different habit, with more robust and clump-forming growth, striking in early summer.

Matteuccia struthiopteris
part of fertile frond, 2 × life size
September 25th

*Matteuccia
struthiopteris*
dry, fertile fronds
²/₃ life size
September 13th

Matteuccia struthiopteris
(left) ¾ life size
April 8th

Matteuccia struthiopteris
part of dying sterile frond
just under life size
November 10th

Onoclea

Onoclea L. (1753), the sensitive fern or bead fern, in the family Woodsiaceae, contains 1 species in North America and eastern Asia.

Description Perennial to 60cm, with a creeping rhizome. Sterile fronds deciduous, bright green, broadly triangular-ovate, pinnate, with the divisions lobed or wavy-edged. Spores borne on erect, blackish, bead-like modified fronds. Fern spores generally germinate on the ground, growing into a thin, liverwort-like mass of cells (prothallus), which produces the male and female sex cells (gametes). On fertilisation, which must occur in water, a new fern plant grows from the edge of the thallus.

Key Recognition Features The shape of the fronds is distinctive, and the bead-like fertile fronds resemble only those of *Matteuccia*.

Ecology and Geography In moist, open or partially shady places, ditches, and wet meadows in eastern North America and much of northeastern Asia.

Comment A distinctive, very hardy and easily grown fern for a moist position, where it will form an extensive colony. Close to *Matteuccia*, and *M. orientalis* is also placed in *Onoclea* by some recent authorities. The name sensitive fern may refer to the brittle frond stalks, or to its dying down with the first frosts.

young fern showing the liverwort-like thallus and the small plant, 5 × life size
November 15th

Onoclea sensibilis
sterile frond with autumn colour
²/₃ life size, October 23rd

Cystopteris fragilis
½ life size
May 24th

Cystopteris

Cystopteris Bernh. (1805) in the family Woodsiaceae, contains around 12 species, mainly in the northern hemisphere.

Description Small perennials, to 30cm, with creeping rhizomes. Fronds small, usually deciduous, pinnae 2-pinnate, the fertile and sterile not markedly different. Sori in rounded groups, with a membranous indusium that shrivels by the time the spores mature. For reproduction see *Onoclea* (p.27).

Key Recognition Features The creeping rhizomes and the small, 2-pinnate, usually rather narrow fronds, deciduous in winter.

Ecology and Geography On walls and moist rocks and in shady places in the mountains; 6 species in western Europe, others mainly in Africa and southern Asia. *Cystopteris fragilis* (L.) Bernh. is found across the northern hemisphere and extends as far as south as Chile.

Comments A few species are cultivated by specialists. The American *C. bulbifera* (L.) Bernhardi often has bulblets on the fronds.

Woodsia fragilis (below)
detail showing sori
1 ¼ × life size
September 4th

Woodsia fragilis
⅓ life size
September 4th

Woodsia polystichoides
(right) detail
showing sori
1 ¼ × life size
September 4th

Woodsia polystichoides
(left) ⅓ life size
September 4th

Woodsia

Woodsia R. Br. (1810), in the family Woodsiaceae, contains about 25 species, mostly in the temperate northern hemisphere.

Description Perennials to 30cm, with a short rhizome. Fronds tufted, lance-shaped or oblong, rather small, pinnate to 2-pinnate, sometimes covered with hair-like scales, deciduous or semi-evergreen, the stalks often jointed so the fronds fall to leave part of the stalk. Spores borne in small, circular sori on the underside of the frond, surrounded by a globose indusium, which opens to become cup shaped. For reproduction see *Onoclea* (p.27).

Key Recognition Features The small size and cup-shaped indusium.

Ecology and Geography In rock crevices in sun or shade, sometimes at high altitudes, in Europe, North America, and central and eastern Asia.

Comment Small ferns suitable for the rock garden or alpine house. *Woodsia polystichoides* D.C. Eaton from northeastern Asia is attractive and easily grown. *Woodsia fragilis* (Trev.) Moore, from the Caucasus, growing to 45cm, is one of the larger species.

Gymnocarpium

Gymnocarpium Newman (1851), the oak fern, in the family Woodsiaceae, contains 6 species in the northern hemisphere.

Description Perennials to 35cm, with a slender, black, creeping rhizome, forming extensive colonies. Fronds on long, slender stalks from the rhizome, broadly triangular, of delicate texture, triangular to ovate, often bright or grey-green, and pinnately to 2-pinnately divided. Spores borne in small, rounded sori on the undersides of the fronds, with no indusium. For reproduction see *Onoclea* (p.27).

Key Recognition Features The thin-textured, triangular fronds arising at intervals from a slender rhizome.

Ecology and Geography In woodland in temperate regions, often forming very extensive patches; *G. robertianum* (Hoffm.) Newman grows on limestone substrates, sometimes in the "grikes" of limestone pavement. Two species, *G. dryopteris* (L.) Newman and *G. robertianum* (Hoffm.) Newman) are found in Europe and North America; others in Asia. The Japanese *G. oyamense* (Bak.) Ching is sometimes semi-evergreen in cultivation.

Comment The oak ferns are very pretty groundcover plants for a cool, shady, leafy soil, well-suited to growing under shrubs or in woodland.

Gymnocarpium dryopteris
²/₃ life size, July 23rd

Deparia

Deparia Hook. & Greville (1829–30) in the family Woodsiaceae, contains around 50 species, mainly in eastern Asia.

Description Perennials, usually less than 30cm, with creeping rhizomes. Fronds deciduous or evergreen, pinnae entire, pinnate, or 2-pinnate, the fertile and sterile sometimes distinct. Sori in divergent rows along the mid-veins, linear, and straight or curved. For reproduction see *Onoclea* (p.27).

Key Recognition Features The long, straight or curved sori in divergent rows along the mid-veins, and the creeping rhizomes.

Ecology and Geography In moist woods, from Japan to Australia, with 1 species, *D. acrostichoides* (Swartz) M. Kato, in eastern North America.

Comments Many of the ferns now placed in *Deparia* may also be found in *Asplenium* (see p.24) in older books, then in *Athyrium* (see p.30), *Diplazium* Swartz & Schrad., or *Lunathyrium* Koidz.; in recent Japanese floras *Lunathyrium* is considered a section of *Deparia*, which demonstrates the difficulty of the differentiating between genera in this group of ferns. We have tentatively identified the species shown as *D. japonica* (Thunb.) M. Kato, although most accounts do not mention the distinct prostrate sterile fronds and the stiffly upright fertile fronds. Several species of *Deparia* are edible.

Deparia conilii
front and back of pinnule
just over life size
September 24th

Deparia conilii
fertile frond (right)
and sterile (below left)
¹/₃ life size, September 24th

Athyrium filix femina
back of pinnules showing sori:
young (left) and mature (below left)
1 ⅓ × life size, July 23rd

Dryopteris affinis
½ life size, September 4th

Athyrium

Athyrium Roth (1799), the lady fern, in the
Woodsiaceae, contains around 200 species
throughout the world.
Description Small to large perennials, to 1.2m, with short,
erect or somewhat creeping rhizomes. Fronds deciduous or
evergreen, often in a tuft, lance-shaped or elliptic, 2- to
3-pinnate, often thin-textured, the margins toothed.
Spores borne on the underside of the frond in small, oblong or
U-shaped, rarely rounded sori, in most species covered by a
membranous indusium attached along one side. For reproduction
see *Onoclea* (p.27).
Key Recognition Features The temperate species mostly have
thin-textured, often light green fronds that die down early in winter.
Ecology and Geography In woods; many species in the tropics,
several in temperate eastern Asia, and 1 in Europe and North America.
Comment Attractive and easily grown ferns; *Athyrium filix-femina* L.
has given rise to hundreds of cultivars varying greatly in frond shape
and size. The beautiful Japanese painted fern, *A. niponicum* var. *pictum*
has grey-green, semi-evergreen fronds flushed with purple. Close to
Deparia (see p.29).

Athyrium filix-femina
½ life size, July 23rd

Dryopteris affinis
(left) back of pinnule
life size, September 4th

Dryopteris dilatata
¹/₂ life size
September 4th

Dryopteris affinis
(right) and
Dryopteris dilatata
(far right)
young fronds
¹/₂ life size
May 4th

Dryopteris

Dryopteris Adanson (1763), including the male and buckler ferns, in the Dryopteridaceae, contains at least 150 species throughout the world.
Description Medium to large perennials, to 1.5m, with stout, erect or decumbent rhizomes. Fronds deciduous or evergreen, borne in medium-sized or large rosettes, lance-shaped, oblong, ovate or triangular, pinnate to 3-pinnate, with toothed or almost entire divisions. Spores borne in small, rounded sori, at first covered with a kidney-shaped indusium. For reproduction see *Onoclea* (p.27).
Key Recognition Features The kidney-shaped indusium.
Ecology and Geography In woods, among rocks on mountains, on roadside banks, and occasionally on walls. Found mostly in the temperate northern hemisphere, with about 15 species in Europe, rather more in North America, and many in northeastern Asia (over 100 in China and 60 in Japan).
Comment Among the most easily grown ferns, European species such as *D. dilatata* (Hoffm.) A. Gray and *D. affinis* (Lowe) Fraser-Jenkins have given rise to some cultivars with crested and other variations. Many fine species, such as *D. shiroumensis* Sa. Kurata & T. Nakamura, have been introduced from Japan and China.

DRYOPTERIDACEAE

Polystichum setiferum
Acutilobum Group
½ life size, July 28th

Polystichum polyblepharum
½ life size, July 28th

Polystichum munitum
½ life size
July 28th

Polystichum setiferum
'Bevis', ½ life size
July 28th

Polystichum rigens
½ life size, July 28th

Polystichum setiferum
'Divisilobum Densum'
½ life size, July 28th

Polystichum aculeatum
detail of frond showing sori
2 × life size, November 15th

Polystichum lonchitis
life size, August 12th

Cyrtomium

Cyrtomium Presl (1836), the Japanese holly fern, in the Dryopteridaceae, contains 20 species in the Americas, Africa, Asia, and Hawaii.

Description Small to medium perennials, to 90cm, with a short, erect rhizome. Fronds evergreen, medium to large, tufted, more or less leathery, simply pinnate, with broadly or narrowly sickle-shaped pinnae. Spores borne in rounded sori scattered over the underside of the fronds, each covered with a circular indusium when young. For reproduction see *Onoclea* (p.27).

Key Recognition Features The leathery, sickle-shaped fronds, and the scattered sori.

Ecology and Geography In woods, on shady rocks in eastern Asia, Central and South America, Hawaii, and southern Africa. Sometimes included in *Polystichum*.

Comment The Japanese holly fern, *C. falcatum* (L. f.) Presl is a popular houseplant, valued for its rich green, glossy fronds, although it is fairly hardy. *Cyrtomium fortunei* J. Sm. is hardier, with more erect, rather dull green fronds.

Cyrtomium fortunei
detail of frond
showing sori
just over life size
July 23rd

Polystichum

Polystichum Roth (1799), the shield fern, in the family Dryopteridaceae, contains about 180 species throughout the world.

Description Small to large perennials, to 1.5m, with a stout, erect, scaly rhizome. Fronds usually evergreen, linear, lance-shaped, or oblong, pinnate to 3-pinnate, the ultimate divisions usually with a thumb-like lobe on 1 side at the base, margins often spiny. Spores in small, rounded sori with a round indusium attached by its centre. *Polystichum andersonii* L.S. Hopk., *P. lepidocaulon* (Hook.) J. Sm., and a few cultivars of *P. setiferum* (Forssk.) Woyn. bear bulbils on the fronds. For reproduction see *Onoclea* (p.27).

Key Recognition Features The evergreen fronds, with a thumb-like lobe at the base of each segment in many species.

Ecology and Geography In woods and rock clefts and on mountains. There are 4 species in Europe, a few in North America, South Africa, and Australasia, but most are in northeastern Asia, with about 30 in Japan.

Comment Among the most handsome of garden ferns. Most of the larger species are easily grown in woodland conditions; the smaller ones are suitable for an alpine house or partly shaded rock garden. *Polystichum acrostichoides* (Michx.) Schott is the North American Christmas fern.

Cyrtomium fortunei
⅓ life size, July 23rd

Blechnum

Blechnum L. (1753), the hard fern, in the family Blechnaceae, contains around 220 species throughout the world.

Description Small to large perennials, to 1.5m, with short or elongated rhizomes, forming a short trunk in a few species. Sterile fronds evergreen, simply pinnate, giving a ladder-like effect. Fertile fronds usually more erect, with narrower segments; spores borne in elongated sori between the segment's midrib and an indusium attached by one edge. For reproduction see *Onoclea* (p.27).

Key Recognition Features The evergreen, pinnate fronds and distinct fertile fronds.

Ecology and Geography In woods and other shady places, usually on acidic soils, with *B. spicant* (L.) Roth in Europe and North America, the others throughout the world, mostly in the southern hemisphere.

Comment The hard ferns are popular for their evergreen foliage and characteristic appearance. Small species like *B. penna-marina* (Poir.) Kuhn from South America and Australasia are suitable for a rock garden; larger ones such as *B. chilense* (Desv.) Hieron. make a large and handsome colony in moist ground. The tender *B. gibbum* (Labill.) Mett. forms a trunk up to 90cm.

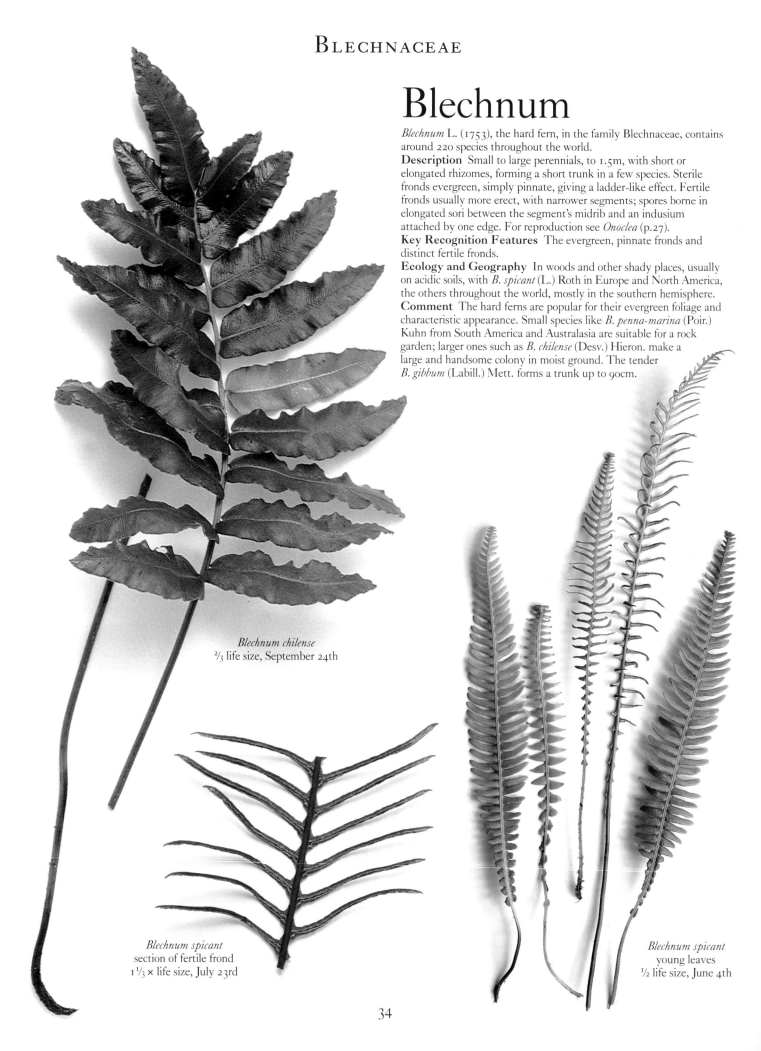

Blechnum chilense
²⁄₃ life size, September 24th

Blechnum spicant
section of fertile frond
1 ¹⁄₃ × life size, July 23rd

Blechnum spicant
young leaves
¹⁄₂ life size, June 4th

Woodwardia unigemmata
²/₃ life size, September 24th

Woodwardia unigemmata
detail of frond showing sori,
1 ¹/₃ × life size, July 23rd

Woodwardia unigemmata
detail of frond showing
sori, ¹/₂ life size
July 23rd

Woodwardia unigemmata
young frond, ¹/₃ life size
July 23rd

Woodwardia

Woodwardia J.E. Sm. (1793), the chain fern, in the family
Blechnaceae, contains 12 species in the northern hemisphere.
Description Large perennials, to 1.8m, with short, erect or shortly
creeping rhizomes. Fronds deciduous or evergreen, large, pinnate, the
pinnae deeply divided into narrow lobes. Spores borne in a series of
short, linear, dash-like sori on either side of the midrib, with the
indusium attached on the side away from the midrib. *Woodwardia
radicans* (L.) Sm. and *W. unigemmata* (Mak.) Nakai reproduce by
plantlets borne on the upper surface of the frond; for sexual
reproduction see *Onoclea* (p.27).
Key Recognition Features The distinctive arrangement of the sori
and, in some species, the plantlets on the upper surface of the fronds.
Ecology and Geography In woods: 1 species, *W. radicans*, in
Europe, others in North America, and most in Asia eastwards to Japan.
Comment Handsome, large ferns, sometimes with pink or red-
flushed young fronds, as in *W. unigemmata*.

Pteridium aquilinum
detail of frond showing sori
1 ¹/₂ × life size, October 23rd

Pteridium aquilinum
autumn fronds
¹/₃ life size, October 23rd

Pteridium

Pteridium Gleditsch ex Scop. (1760), the bracken fern, in the family Dennstaedtiaceae, contains 1 species, *P. aquilinum* (L.) Kuhn, found almost throughout the world.

Description Perennial to 2.5m, with deep, long-creeping rhizome. Fronds large, usually solitary, long-stalked, triangular, 2- or 3-pinnate, deciduous, somewhat hairy beneath. Spores borne in linear sori, protected by the inrolled margin of the segment and the opposed indusium. For reproduction see *Onoclea* (p.27).

Key Recognition Features The large, triangular fronds to 2m or more tall, forming very extensive colonies.

Ecology and Geography In open woods and on hillsides in sun or light shade, often invading and devaluing grazing; occurs almost throughout the temperate parts of the world, sometimes covering vast areas, especially on poor, acidic, upland soils.

Comment Far too invasive for most gardens, but a handsome fern nevertheless. The unfurling young frond tips (croziers) are eaten in Japan. The fronds are carcinogenic, however, and pose some danger to livestock. The rhizome has been used to produce dyes.

Pteridium aquilinum
¹/₃ life size, October 23rd

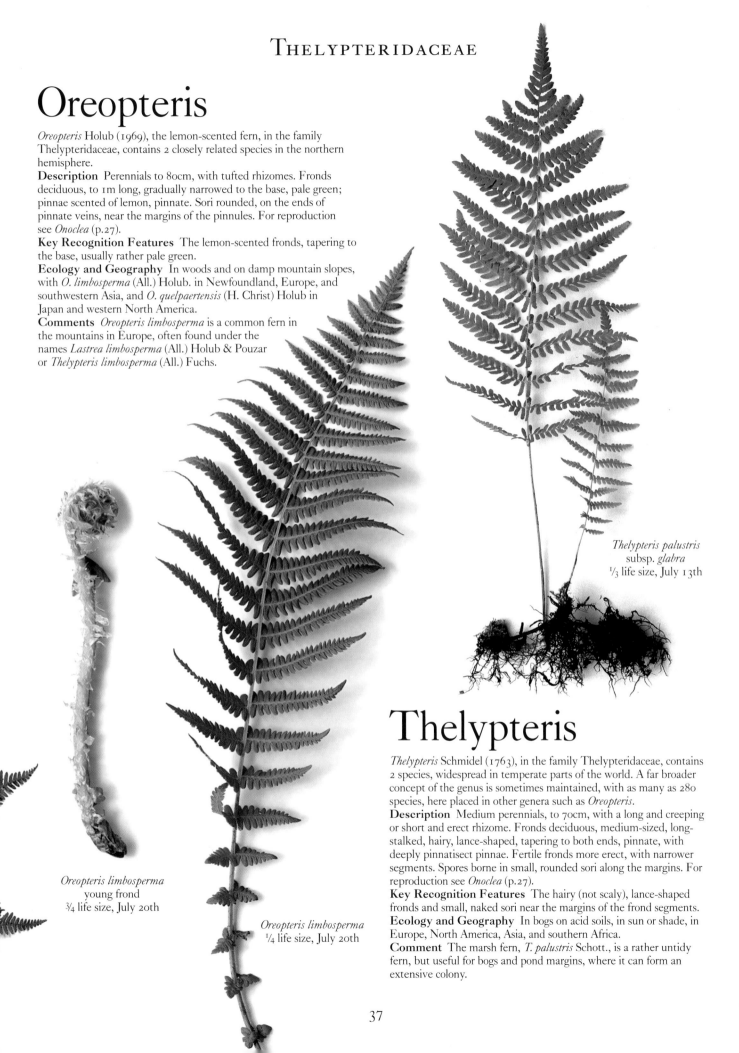

Oreopteris

Oreopteris Holub (1969), the lemon-scented fern, in the family Thelypteridaceae, contains 2 closely related species in the northern hemisphere.

Description Perennials to 80cm, with tufted rhizomes. Fronds deciduous, to 1m long, gradually narrowed to the base, pale green; pinnae scented of lemon, pinnate. Sori rounded, on the ends of pinnate veins, near the margins of the pinnules. For reproduction see *Onoclea* (p.27).

Key Recognition Features The lemon-scented fronds, tapering to the base, usually rather pale green.

Ecology and Geography In woods and on damp mountain slopes, with *O. limbosperma* (All.) Holub. in Newfoundland, Europe, and southwestern Asia, and *O. quelpaertensis* (H. Christ) Holub in Japan and western North America.

Comments *Oreopteris limbosperma* is a common fern in the mountains in Europe, often found under the names *Lastrea limbosperma* (All.) Holub & Pouzar or *Thelypteris limbosperma* (All.) Fuchs.

Thelypteris palustris
subsp. *glabra*
1/3 life size, July 13th

Oreopteris limbosperma
young frond
3/4 life size, July 20th

Oreopteris limbosperma
1/4 life size, July 20th

Thelypteris

Thelypteris Schmidel (1763), in the family Thelypteridaceae, contains 2 species, widespread in temperate parts of the world. A far broader concept of the genus is sometimes maintained, with as many as 280 species, here placed in other genera such as *Oreopteris*.

Description Medium perennials, to 70cm, with a long and creeping or short and erect rhizome. Fronds deciduous, medium-sized, long-stalked, hairy, lance-shaped, tapering to both ends, pinnate, with deeply pinnatisect pinnae. Fertile fronds more erect, with narrower segments. Spores borne in small, rounded sori along the margins. For reproduction see *Onoclea* (p.27).

Key Recognition Features The hairy (not scaly), lance-shaped fronds and small, naked sori near the margins of the frond segments.

Ecology and Geography In bogs on acid soils, in sun or shade, in Europe, North America, Asia, and southern Africa.

Comment The marsh fern, *T. palustris* Schott., is a rather untidy fern, but useful for bogs and pond margins, where it can form an extensive colony.

Thalictrum delavayi
'Hewitt's Double'
flowers, 1¾ × life size
May 5th

Thalictrum flavum
flowers, just under life size
July 14th

Thalictrum flavum
⅓ life size, July 14th

Thalictrum delavayi
fruits, 1½ × life size
September 14th

Thalictrum delavayi
'Hewitt's Double'
¼ life size, May 5th

Thalictrum delavayi
fruits, ⅓ life size
September 14th

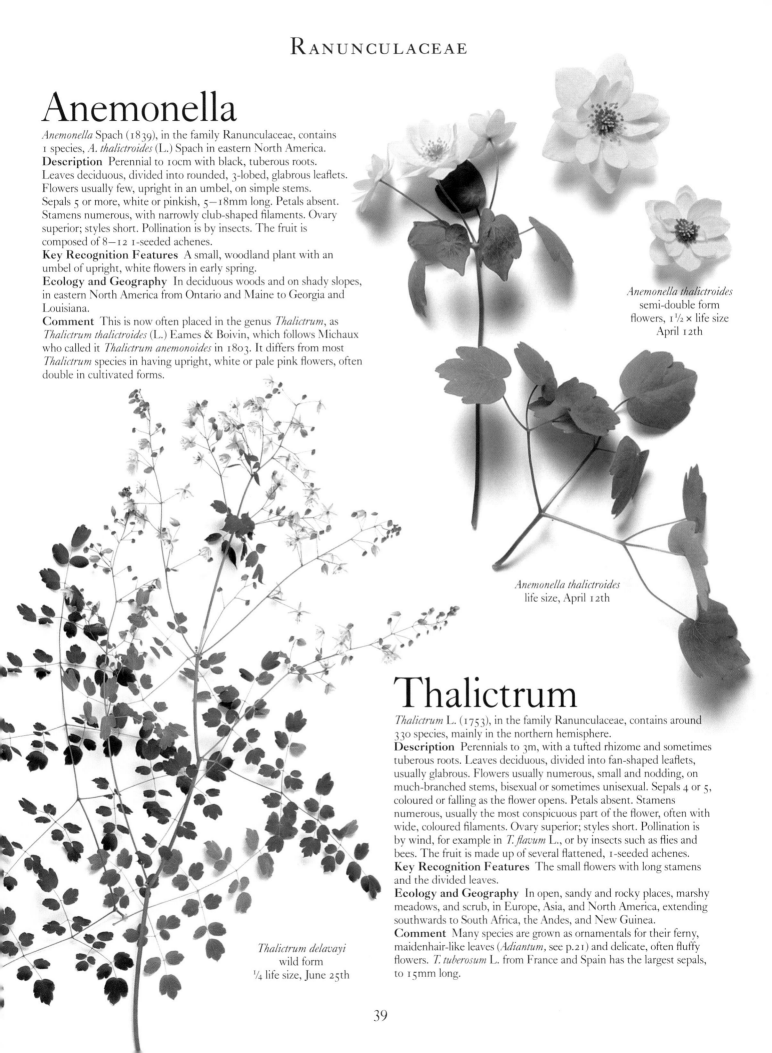

Anemonella

Anemonella Spach (1839), in the family Ranunculaceae, contains
1 species, *A. thalictroides* (L.) Spach in eastern North America.
Description Perennial to 10cm with black, tuberous roots.
Leaves deciduous, divided into rounded, 3-lobed, glabrous leaflets.
Flowers usually few, upright in an umbel, on simple stems.
Sepals 5 or more, white or pinkish, 5–18mm long. Petals absent.
Stamens numerous, with narrowly club-shaped filaments. Ovary
superior; styles short. Pollination is by insects. The fruit is
composed of 8–12 1-seeded achenes.
Key Recognition Features A small, woodland plant with an
umbel of upright, white flowers in early spring.
Ecology and Geography In deciduous woods and on shady slopes,
in eastern North America from Ontario and Maine to Georgia and
Louisiana.
Comment This is now often placed in the genus *Thalictrum*, as
Thalictrum thalictroides (L.) Eames & Boivin, which follows Michaux
who called it *Thalictrum anemonoides* in 1803. It differs from most
Thalictrum species in having upright, white or pale pink flowers, often
double in cultivated forms.

Anemonella thalictroides
semi-double form
flowers, 1½ × life size
April 12th

Anemonella thalictroides
life size, April 12th

Thalictrum

Thalictrum L. (1753), in the family Ranunculaceae, contains around
330 species, mainly in the northern hemisphere.
Description Perennials to 3m, with a tufted rhizome and sometimes
tuberous roots. Leaves deciduous, divided into fan-shaped leaflets,
usually glabrous. Flowers usually numerous, small and nodding, on
much-branched stems, bisexual or sometimes unisexual. Sepals 4 or 5,
coloured or falling as the flower opens. Petals absent. Stamens
numerous, usually the most conspicuous part of the flower, often with
wide, coloured filaments. Ovary superior; styles short. Pollination is
by wind, for example in *T. flavum* L., or by insects such as flies and
bees. The fruit is made up of several flattened, 1-seeded achenes.
Key Recognition Features The small flowers with long stamens
and the divided leaves.
Ecology and Geography In open, sandy and rocky places, marshy
meadows, and scrub, in Europe, Asia, and North America, extending
southwards to South Africa, the Andes, and New Guinea.
Comment Many species are grown as ornamentals for their ferny,
maidenhair-like leaves (*Adiantum*, see p.21) and delicate, often fluffy
flowers. *T. tuberosum* L. from France and Spain has the largest sepals,
to 15mm long.

Thalictrum delavayi
wild form
¼ life size, June 25th

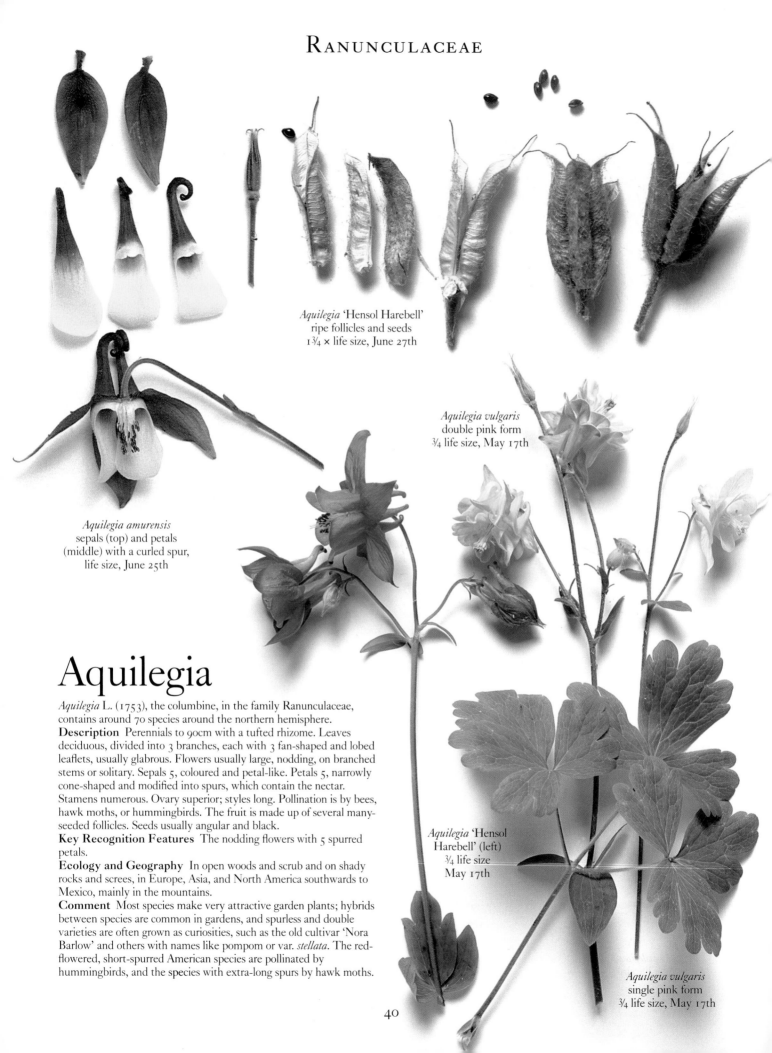

Aquilegia 'Hensol Harebell'
ripe follicles and seeds
1¾ × life size, June 27th

Aquilegia vulgaris
double pink form
¾ life size, May 17th

Aquilegia amurensis
sepals (top) and petals
(middle) with a curled spur,
life size, June 25th

Aquilegia

Aquilegia L. (1753), the columbine, in the family Ranunculaceae, contains around 70 species around the northern hemisphere.
Description Perennials to 90cm with a tufted rhizome. Leaves deciduous, divided into 3 branches, each with 3 fan-shaped and lobed leaflets, usually glabrous. Flowers usually large, nodding, on branched stems or solitary. Sepals 5, coloured and petal-like. Petals 5, narrowly cone-shaped and modified into spurs, which contain the nectar. Stamens numerous. Ovary superior; styles long. Pollination is by bees, hawk moths, or hummingbirds. The fruit is made up of several many-seeded follicles. Seeds usually angular and black.
Key Recognition Features The nodding flowers with 5 spurred petals.
Ecology and Geography In open woods and scrub and on shady rocks and screes, in Europe, Asia, and North America southwards to Mexico, mainly in the mountains.
Comment Most species make very attractive garden plants; hybrids between species are common in gardens, and spurless and double varieties are often grown as curiosities, such as the old cultivar 'Nora Barlow' and others with names like pompom or var. *stellata*. The red-flowered, short-spurred American species are pollinated by hummingbirds, and the species with extra-long spurs by hawk moths.

Aquilegia 'Hensol
Harebell' (left)
¾ life size
May 17th

Aquilegia vulgaris
single pink form
¾ life size, May 17th

Semiaquilegia

Semiaquilegia Makino (1902), in the family Ranunculaceae, contains around 6 species in eastern Asia.

Description Differs from *Aquilegia* in having petal-like sepals and erect petals, usually pouched at the base, and longer than the sepals.

Key Recognition Features Small *Aquilegia*-like plants with small, pinkish-purple flowers without spurs.

Ecology and Geography In open woods and scrub, mainly in the mountains, in eastern China and Korea.

Comment An attractive, modest plant for a cool position. *Isopyrum thalictroides* L. from southern Europe has *Aquilegia*-like leaves, but simple, upright, whitish flowers with petal-like sepals, and very small petals, less than 2mm long. *Enemion* Raf. from North America is similar, but the petals are absent. *Paraquilegia* Drummond & Hutchinson, a genus of beautiful dwarf alpines that grow on mountain cliffs from central Asia to western China, has small, *Aquilegia*-like leaves and large, cup-shaped flowers with 5 sepals and 5 small petals.

Aquilegia 'Hensol Harebell'
flower parts, 1⅓ × life size
May 17th

Semiaquilegia ecalcarata
triangular petals and
rounded sepal
2 × life size, April 12th

Semiaquilegia ecalcarata
just under life size, April 12th

Ranunculaceae

Anemone coronaria
De Caen Group
fruit and seeds
$1\frac{2}{3}$ × life size, June 1st

Anemone hupehensis
flower, $1\frac{1}{2}$ × life size
September 10th

Anemone fanninii
flowers, just over life size
April 10th

Anemone coronaria
De Caen Group
$\frac{1}{2}$ life size
March 13th

Anemone hupehensis
$\frac{1}{2}$ life size
September 10th

Anemone fanninii
$\frac{1}{3}$ life size
April 10th

Anemone blanda
just under life size
March 10th

Anemone blanda
flower parts, 2 × life size
March 10th

Anemone blanda
tuber, life size
September 16th

Anemone

Anemone L. (1753), in the family Ranunculaceae, contains around 144 species throughout the world.

Description Tufted, tuberous or rhizomatous perennials to 1m Leaves usually deeply 3-lobed and often further divided and toothed, often hairy. Flowering stems with 3 short leaves some way beneath the flower. Flowers usually white, sometimes blue, pinkish, red, or yellow. Sepals petal-like, 5 or more. Petals absent. Stamens numerous. Ovary superior; styles short with capitate stigmas. Pollination is by insects, especially bees. Fruits many, 1-seeded, often with silky hairs. Seeds often fluffy and wind-dispersed, sometimes green when ripe and dispersed by ants, occasionally with a long, hooked beak for dispersal on animals.

Key Recognition Features The simple flowers with petal-like sepals, and the group of reduced leaves on the stem below the flower.

Ecology and Geography In woods, alpine meadows, bogs, scrub, or dry hills. Worldwide, but only on mountains in the tropics.

Comment Many species are grown as ornamentals. Forms and hybrids of the Mediterranean A. coronaria L. and A. pavonina Lam. have been cultivated since the 16th century, and are popular cut flowers. Most species are poisonous when fresh and some, such as A. narcissiflora L. were used medicinally to aid blood clotting. The African A. fanninii Marsters, from boggy streams in the Drakensberg, has leaves around 30cm across from a huge, irregular corm. Anemone hupehensis Lem. belongs to a group of autumn-flowering species common in China and eastern Asia and frequently cultivated, the so-called Japanese anemones. Anemone blanda Schott & Kotschy is a common species in the mountains of the eastern Mediterranean.

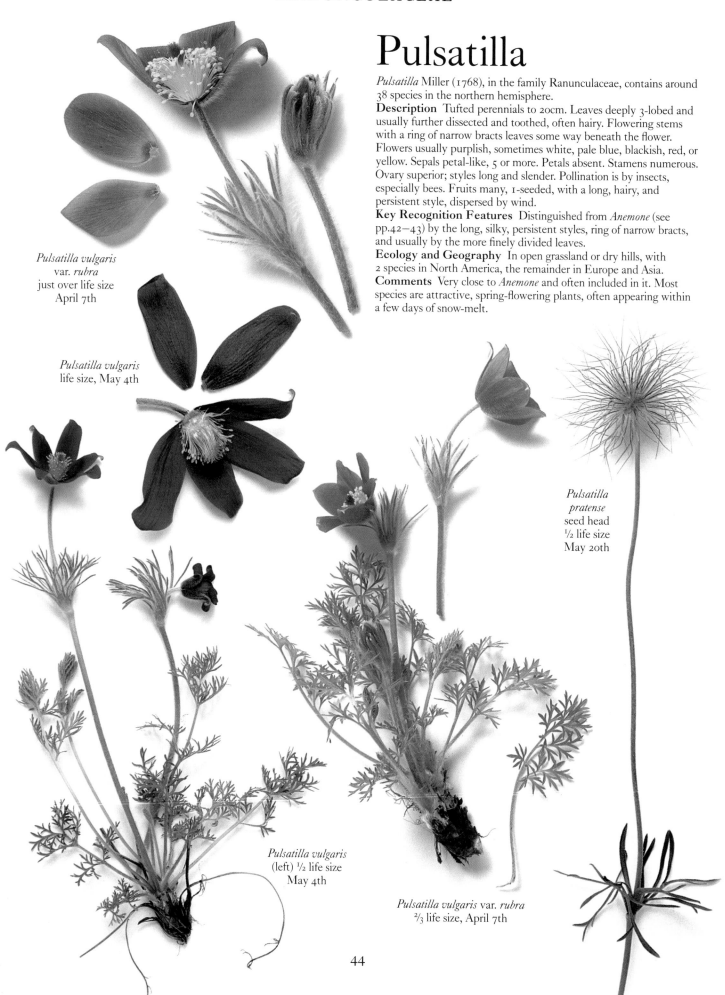

Pulsatilla

Pulsatilla Miller (1768), in the family Ranunculaceae, contains around 38 species in the northern hemisphere.

Description Tufted perennials to 20cm. Leaves deeply 3-lobed and usually further dissected and toothed, often hairy. Flowering stems with a ring of narrow bracts leaves some way beneath the flower. Flowers usually purplish, sometimes white, pale blue, blackish, red, or yellow. Sepals petal-like, 5 or more. Petals absent. Stamens numerous. Ovary superior; styles long and slender. Pollination is by insects, especially bees. Fruits many, 1-seeded, with a long, hairy, and persistent style, dispersed by wind.

Key Recognition Features Distinguished from *Anemone* (see pp.42–43) by the long, silky, persistent styles, ring of narrow bracts, and usually by the more finely divided leaves.

Ecology and Geography In open grassland or dry hills, with 2 species in North America, the remainder in Europe and Asia.

Comments Very close to *Anemone* and often included in it. Most species are attractive, spring-flowering plants, often appearing within a few days of snow-melt.

Pulsatilla vulgaris
var. *rubra*
just over life size
April 7th

Pulsatilla vulgaris
life size, May 4th

Pulsatilla
pratense
seed head
½ life size
May 20th

Pulsatilla vulgaris
(left) ½ life size
May 4th

Pulsatilla vulgaris var. *rubra*
⅔ life size, April 7th

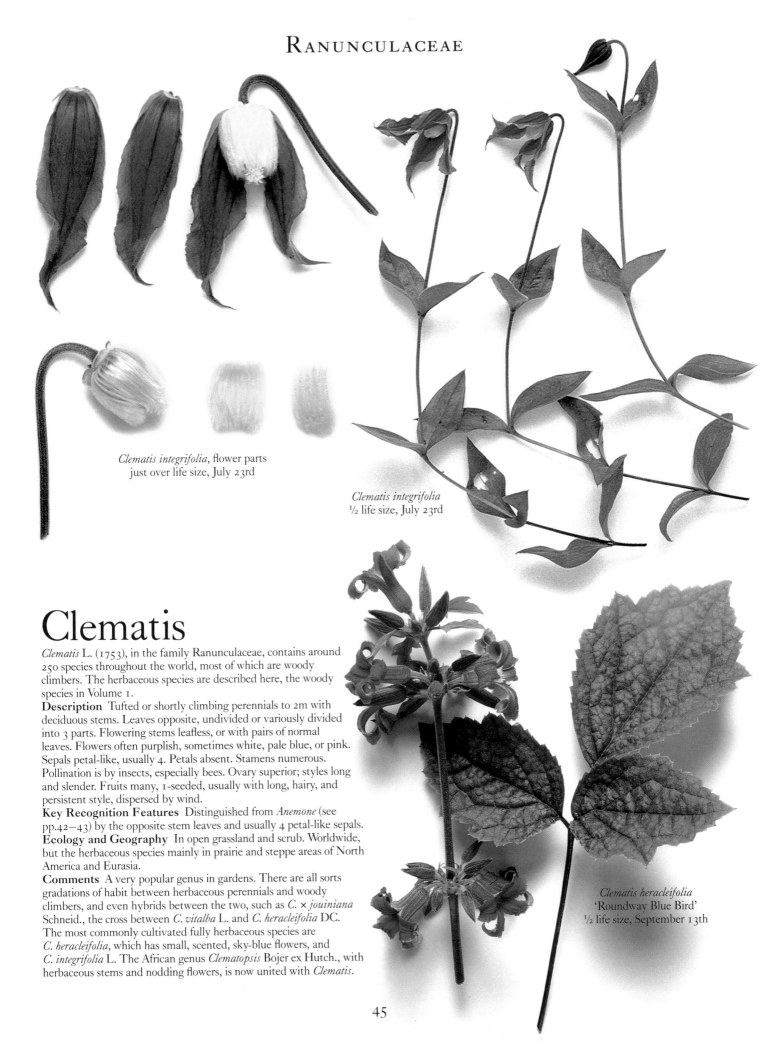

Clematis integrifolia, flower parts
just over life size, July 23rd

Clematis integrifolia
½ life size, July 23rd

Clematis

Clematis L. (1753), in the family Ranunculaceae, contains around
250 species throughout the world, most of which are woody
climbers. The herbaceous species are described here, the woody
species in Volume 1.

Description Tufted or shortly climbing perennials to 2m with
deciduous stems. Leaves opposite, undivided or variously divided
into 3 parts. Flowering stems leafless, or with pairs of normal
leaves. Flowers often purplish, sometimes white, pale blue, or pink.
Sepals petal-like, usually 4. Petals absent. Stamens numerous.
Pollination is by insects, especially bees. Ovary superior; styles long
and slender. Fruits many, 1-seeded, usually with long, hairy, and
persistent style, dispersed by wind.

Key Recognition Features Distinguished from *Anemone* (see
pp.42–43) by the opposite stem leaves and usually 4 petal-like sepals.

Ecology and Geography In open grassland and scrub. Worldwide,
but the herbaceous species mainly in prairie and steppe areas of North
America and Eurasia.

Comments A very popular genus in gardens. There are all sorts
gradations of habit between herbaceous perennials and woody
climbers, and even hybrids between the two, such as *C. × jouiniana*
Schneid., the cross between *C. vitalba* L. and *C. heracleifolia* DC.
The most commonly cultivated fully herbaceous species are
C. heracleifolia, which has small, scented, sky-blue flowers, and
C. integrifolia L. The African genus *Clematopsis* Bojer ex Hutch., with
herbaceous stems and nodding flowers, is now united with *Clematis*.

Clematis heracleifolia
'Roundway Blue Bird'
½ life size, September 13th

45

Hepatica nobilis
flower, 2 × life size
February 17th

Hepatica

Hepatica Miller (1768), in the family Ranunculaceae, contains around 7 species in the northern hemisphere.

Description Tufted perennials to 10cm with wiry roots. Leaves usually 3-lobed and untoothed. Flowers usually blue, pinkish, or white. Sepals 3, small and green. Petals usually 5, often more, without a nectary. Stamens numerous. Ovary superior; styles short with capitate stigmas. Pollination is by insects. Fruits many, 1-seeded. Seeds green when ripe, dispersed by ants.

Key Recognition Features The simple flowers with 3 small sepals at the base and the 3-lobed leaves.

Ecology and Geography In dry woods, with 2 species in eastern North America, 2 in Europe, 2 in northern Asia and Japan, and 1 recently discovered in China.

Comment The genera *Hepatica* and *Pulsatilla* (see p.44) are often included in *Anemone* (see pp.42–43). *Hepatica* differs mainly in having no stem leaves, but 3 sepals, or possibly sepal-like bracts, close below the flower. If the sepals are interpreted as bracts, the petals may be interpreted as coloured sepals. Numerous varieties of *H. nobilis* Mill. are cultivated in Japan. The name *Hepatica* was given to the plant because the blotched leaves resembled a diseased liver to ancient herbalists.

Hepatica nobilis
life size
February 17th

Ranunculus aconitifolius
⅓ life size, May 16th

Ranunculus ficaria
'Flore Pleno'
1¼ × life size
April 12th

46

Ranunculus

Ranunculus L. (1753) the buttercup or crowfoot, in the family Ranunculaceae, contains around 600 species in temperate climates throughout the world.

Description Annuals or perennials to 1m, sometimes aquatic, sometimes with tuberous roots. Leaves usually lobed and toothed, sometimes with rounded blades, and sometimes with finely divided, submerged leaves in the aquatic species. Flowers usually yellow or white. Sepals 3–7, usually 5, small and greenish. Petals usually 5, often more, usually with a small nectary at the base. Stamens numerous. Ovary superior; styles short with capitate stigmas. Pollination is usually by insects. Fruits usually many, 1-seeded achenes. Seeds flattened, sometimes winged.

Key Recognition Features The simple flowers with small nectaries at the base of the petals and the 1-seeded fruits.

Ecology and Geography In many habitats from arctic lakes and rivers to meadows, woods, and bare, summer-dry hills and alpine screes. Worldwide, but only on mountains in the tropics.

Comment A large and diverse genus, with most species in the northern hemisphere, but a group of spectacular alpines in New Zealand. The red or white-flowered *R. asiaticus* L. from the eastern Mediterranean has been cultivated since the 16th century, and double-flowered varieties are still popular in gardens. *Adonis* L., with 20 species form Europe to Japan, has much-divided, feathery leaves, red, white, or yellow flowers, and 1-seeded achenes.

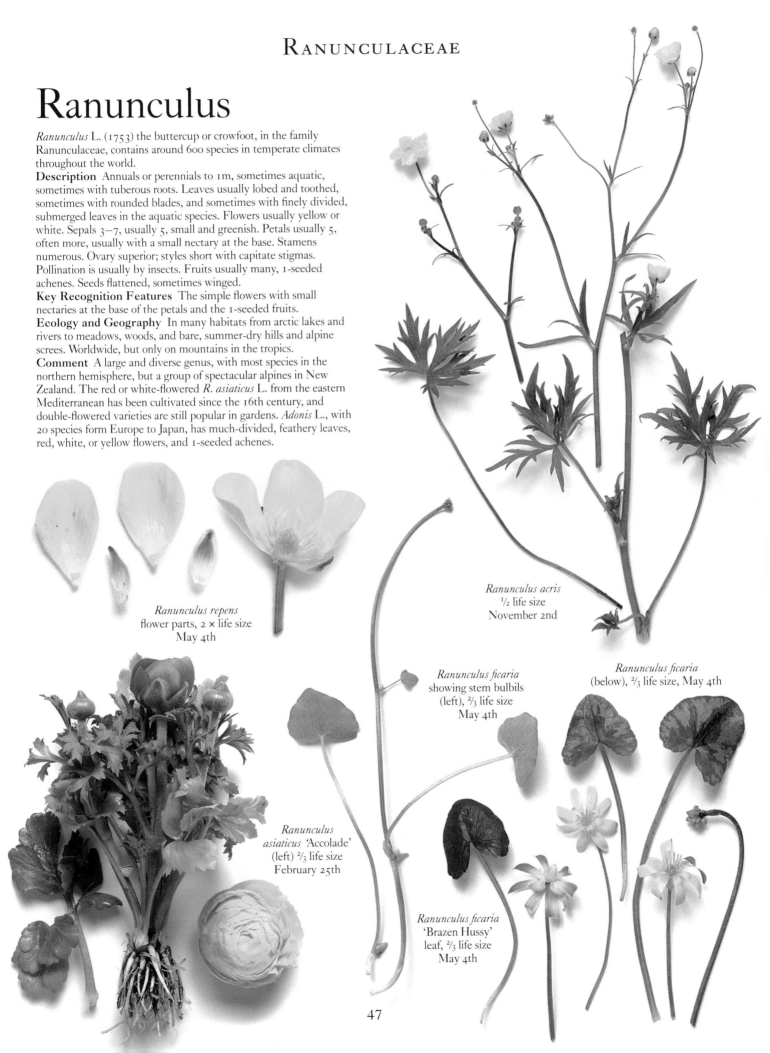

Ranunculus repens
flower parts, 2 × life size
May 4th

Ranunculus acris
½ life size
November 2nd

Ranunculus ficaria
showing stem bulbils
(left), ⅔ life size
May 4th

Ranunculus ficaria
(below), ⅔ life size, May 4th

Ranunculus asiaticus 'Accolade'
(left) ⅔ life size
February 25th

Ranunculus ficaria
'Brazen Hussy'
leaf, ⅔ life size
May 4th

47

Caltha

Caltha L. (1753), in the family Ranunculaceae, contains around 20 species, in temperate areas throughout the world.

Description Perennials to 40cm with tufted rhizomes, sometimes with creeping and rooting stems. Leaves deciduous, usually with a rounded blade with a deep sinus, but sometimes with pointed lobes. Flowers usually few, in a branching inflorescence, yellow or white. Sepals 5–9 or more, petal-like. Petals absent. Stamens numerous. Ovary superior; styles long. Pollination is by insects, probably mainly bees and flies. The fruit is made up of many several-seeded follicles, with a short beak. Seeds usually green or black.

Key Recognition Features The upright, yellow or white flowers and rounded leaves; the plants are soft and fleshy.

Ecology and Geography In wet woods and marshes and by rivers, from lowlands into the mountains.

Comment *Caltha palustris* L., the kingcup or marsh marigold, is a familiar early spring flower in northern Europe, across Siberia and in much of North America; its flowers are usually yellow. The white-flowered *C. leptosepala* DC is found in the Rockies and coast ranges of western North America northwards to Alaska. *Caltha natans* Pallas is an aquatic with white or pinkish flowers, growing in lakes and ponds in northwestern North America and Siberia.

Trollius

Trollius L. (1753), in the family Ranunculaceae, contains around 30 species in the northern temperate regions.

Description Perennials to 50cm with tufted rhizomes. Leaves deciduous, usually with a rounded blade, which is deeply dissected. Flowers usually few, upright, in a simple or few-branched inflorescence, yellow or orange. Sepals 5–20 or more, petal-like, often incurved. Petals 5–15, with a small nectary at the base, usually very small, but sometimes narrow and longer than the sepals. Stamens numerous. Ovary superior; styles short. Pollination is by insects, probably mainly bees. The fruit is made up of many several-seeded follicles. Seeds usually black.

Key Recognition Features The upright, yellow or orange flowers and rounded, deeply cut leaves.

Ecology and Geography In wet woods and marshes and by rivers, from lowlands into the mountains, from Scotland and Portugal eastwards, with 3 species in North America.

Comment *Trollius europaeus* L. is frequent in the mountains from Scotland to the Alps and western Asia, and has incurved sepals, which give it the name globeflower. Other species have more open, buttercup-like flowers. In *T. chinensis* Bunge the ring of narrow, upright petals is conspicuous.

Caltha palustris, flower parts
1½ × life size, March 20th

Caltha palustris
⅓ life size
March 20th

Caltha palustris
follicles and seeds
1¼ × life size
June 10th

RANUNCULACEAE

Trollius chinensis (above) and *Trollius* × *cultorum* (below)
flower parts (from left to right): sepals, stamens, petals
1¼ × life size, June 12th

Trollius × *cultorum*
½ life size, June 12th

Trollius chinensis
½ life size
June 12th

Trollius × *cultorum*
'Lemon Queen'
½ life size, May 4th

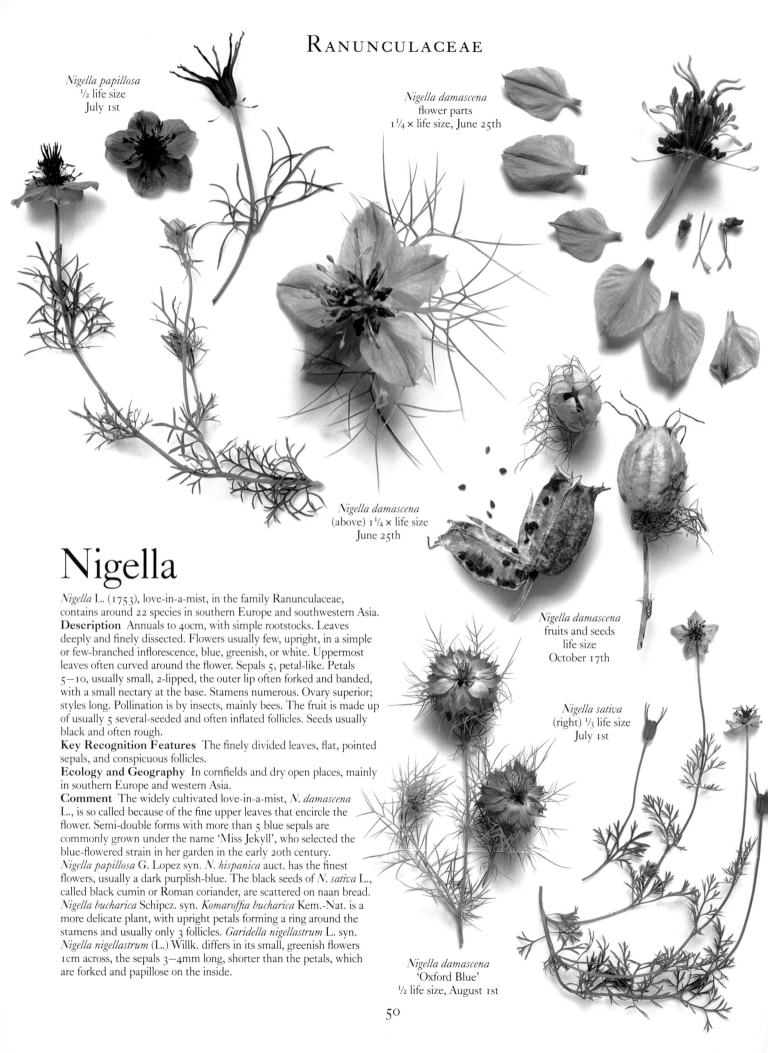

Nigella papillosa
½ life size
July 1st

Nigella damascena
flower parts
1¼ × life size, June 25th

Nigella damascena
(above) 1¼ × life size
June 25th

Nigella damascena
fruits and seeds
life size
October 17th

Nigella sativa
(right) ⅓ life size
July 1st

Nigella damascena
'Oxford Blue'
½ life size, August 1st

Nigella

Nigella L. (1753), love-in-a-mist, in the family Ranunculaceae, contains around 22 species in southern Europe and southwestern Asia.

Description Annuals to 40cm, with simple rootstocks. Leaves deeply and finely dissected. Flowers usually few, upright, in a simple or few-branched inflorescence, blue, greenish, or white. Uppermost leaves often curved around the flower. Sepals 5, petal-like. Petals 5–10, usually small, 2-lipped, the outer lip often forked and banded, with a small nectary at the base. Stamens numerous. Ovary superior; styles long. Pollination is by insects, mainly bees. The fruit is made up of usually 5 several-seeded and often inflated follicles. Seeds usually black and often rough.

Key Recognition Features The finely divided leaves, flat, pointed sepals, and conspicuous follicles.

Ecology and Geography In cornfields and dry open places, mainly in southern Europe and western Asia.

Comment The widely cultivated love-in-a-mist, *N. damascena* L., is so called because of the fine upper leaves that encircle the flower. Semi-double forms with more than 5 blue sepals are commonly grown under the name 'Miss Jekyll', who selected the blue-flowered strain in her garden in the early 20th century. *Nigella papillosa* G. Lopez syn. *N. hispanica* auct. has the finest flowers, usually a dark purplish-blue. The black seeds of *N. sativa* L., called black cumin or Roman coriander, are scattered on naan bread. *Nigella bucharica* Schipcz. syn. *Komaroffia bucharica* Kem.-Nat. is a more delicate plant, with upright petals forming a ring around the stamens and usually only 3 follicles. *Garidella nigellastrum* L. syn. *Nigella nigellastrum* (L.) Willk. differs in its small, greenish flowers 1cm across, the sepals 3–4mm long, shorter than the petals, which are forked and papillose on the inside.

Eranthis

Eranthis L. (1753), the winter aconite, in the family Ranunculaceae, contains around 8 species in Europe and across Asia.

Description Perennials to 10cm with tuberous rhizomes. Leaves deciduous, basal, stalked, and usually rounded and deeply lobed, sometimes pinnate. Flowers usually solitary. Sepals 5–8, petal-like, yellow or white. Petals modified into 2-lipped, tubular nectaries. Stamens numerous. Ovary superior; styles long. Pollination is by insects, probably mainly bees and flies. The fruit is made up of few or many several-seeded follicles. Seeds scaly.

Key Recognition Features The upright flowers produced in early spring on short stems, with a whorl of bract-leaves below the flower.

Ecology and Geography In woods, scrub in the lowlands, and open rocky places in the mountains, from southern Europe across Asia and Siberia to China and Japan.

Comment *Eranthis* are among the earliest flowers of spring, opening soon after the first thaw. Species from Europe and western Asia are yellow; those from eastern Asia are white-flowered and particularly delicate; both grow best on limestone soils.

Eranthis 'Guinea Gold'
flowers with sepals removed
1 ¾ × life size, February 14th

Eranthis 'Guinea Gold'
1 ¼ × life size, February 14th

Eranthis 'Guinea Gold' (left to right): young follicles, stamens, and
modified petals, 2 ¼ × life size, March 5th

Eranthis 'Guinea Gold'
flower section
2 × life size, March 5th

Eranthis 'Guinea Gold',
2 × life size, March 5th

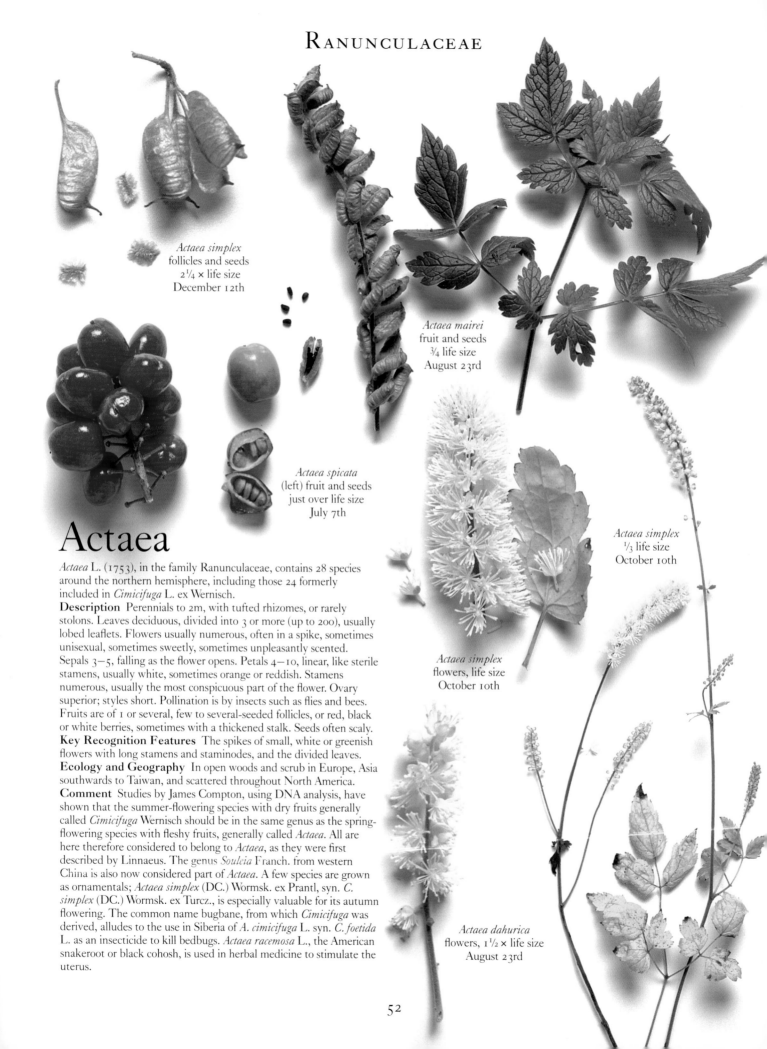

Actaea simplex
follicles and seeds
2¼ × life size
December 12th

Actaea mairei
fruit and seeds
¾ life size
August 23rd

Actaea spicata
(left) fruit and seeds
just over life size
July 7th

Actaea simplex
⅓ life size
October 10th

Actaea simplex
flowers, life size
October 10th

Actaea dahurica
flowers, 1½ × life size
August 23rd

Actaea

Actaea L. (1753), in the family Ranunculaceae, contains 28 species around the northern hemisphere, including those 24 formerly included in *Cimicifuga* L. ex Wernisch.

Description Perennials to 2m, with tufted rhizomes, or rarely stolons. Leaves deciduous, divided into 3 or more (up to 200), usually lobed leaflets. Flowers usually numerous, often in a spike, sometimes unisexual, sometimes sweetly, sometimes unpleasantly scented. Sepals 3–5, falling as the flower opens. Petals 4–10, linear, like sterile stamens, usually white, sometimes orange or reddish. Stamens numerous, usually the most conspicuous part of the flower. Ovary superior; styles short. Pollination is by insects such as flies and bees. Fruits are of 1 or several, few to several-seeded follicles, or red, black or white berries, sometimes with a thickened stalk. Seeds often scaly.

Key Recognition Features The spikes of small, white or greenish flowers with long stamens and staminodes, and the divided leaves.

Ecology and Geography In open woods and scrub in Europe, Asia southwards to Taiwan, and scattered throughout North America.

Comment Studies by James Compton, using DNA analysis, have shown that the summer-flowering species with dry fruits generally called *Cimicifuga* Wernisch should be in the same genus as the spring-flowering species with fleshy fruits, generally called *Actaea*. All are here therefore considered to belong to *Actaea*, as they were first described by Linnaeus. The genus *Souleia* Franch. from western China is also now considered part of *Actaea*. A few species are grown as ornamentals; *Actaea simplex* (DC.) Wormsk. ex Prantl, syn. *C. simplex* (DC.) Wormsk. ex Turcz., is especially valuable for its autumn flowering. The common name bugbane, from which *Cimicifuga* was derived, alludes to the use in Siberia of *A. cimicifuga* L. syn. *C. foetida* L. as an insecticide to kill bedbugs. *Actaea racemosa* L., the American snakeroot or black cohosh, is used in herbal medicine to stimulate the uterus.

Anemonopsis

Anemonopsis Sieb. & Zucc. (1846) in the family Ranunculaceae, contains 1 species, *A. macrophylla* Sieb. & Zucc., from Japan.

Description Perennial to 80cm with tufted rhizome. Leaves deciduous, 3-pinnate, divided into lobed and sharply toothed leaflets. Flowers usually few, in a branching inflorescence. Sepals 3, pale mauve. Petals 8–10, purple, shorter and forming a cup. Stamens numerous. Ovary superior; styles long. Pollination is by insects, probably mainly bees. The fruit is made up of 2–4 several-seeded follicles, with a long beak. Seeds scaly.

Key Recognition Features The nodding, purplish, waxy flowers on dark stems.

Ecology and Geography In deep woods in the mountains in Honshu, on the Pacific coast side.

Comment A very elegant and attractive plant for a shady garden. In many characteristics, particularly leaf and fruit, as well as in DNA, *Anemonopsis* is very close to *Actaea*.

Anemonopsis macrophylla
1⅓ × life size, June 25th

Anemonopsis macrophylla
seeds, 2 × life size
August 10th

Anemonopsis macrophylla
½ life size
June 25th

Anemonopsis macrophylla
follicles, life size
August 10th

Anemonopsis macrophylla
flower parts
1⅓ × life size
June 25th

Anemonopsis macrophylla
flower backs
½ life size
June 25th

53

Helleborus argutifolius
follicles and seeds
(left and below)
²/₃ life size
June 18th

Helleborus foetidus
'Wester Flisk'
flower parts (below left)
just over life size
April 10th

*Helleborus
foetidus*
'Wester Flisk'
¹/₂ life size
April 10th

Helleborus × ballardiae
stamens and tubular petals
(above) just over life size
March 1st

Helleborus

Helleborus L. (1753), in the family Ranunculaceae, contains around 15 species in Europe, western Asia, and China.

Description Perennials to 80cm, often with tufted rhizomes. Leaves deciduous or evergreen, usually with a rounded blade, which is deeply dissected into 3, 5, or many lobes. Flowers usually nodding, in a few-branched inflorescence, greenish, white, or purple, often spotted. Sepals 5, petal-like and leathery, persisting until the flowering stems die. Petals 5–15, usually very small, tubular and flattened, green or purple. Stamens numerous. Ovary superior; styles long. Pollination is by insects, mainly by bees. The fruit is made up of many several-seeded follicles; seeds usually black, often with a fleshy, white appendage, which attracts ants for dispersal.

Key Recognition Features The nodding flowers and tubular petals, combined with an acrid smell if the leaves are crushed.

Ecology and Geography In dry woods and scrub from England and Spain (2 species), to the Balkans (8 species), Turkey, and the Caucasus; 1 species, *H. thibetanus* Franch., has recently been introduced to cultivation from the mountains of western China.

Comment Numerous species and hybrids, such as *H. × ballardiae* (*H. niger × H. lividus* Ait. ex Curtis, backcrossed to *H. niger*) are cultivated in gardens, where they are among the earliest flowers to open, hence the names Christmas rose for *H. niger* L. and Lenten rose for *H. orientalis* Lam. and its hybrids. The plants are very poisonous, and were used medicinally in the past: *H. foetidus* L., the stinking hellebore, was used to cure coughs and wheezing in horses, or for humans as a drastic emetic, according to Gerard, for "mad and furious men". In medieval medicine the black-rooted *H. niger* was called the black hellebore to distinguish it from the white hellebore, *Veratrum album* L. Both were used as rat poisons. *Helleborus vesicarius* Auch. from southern Turkey is summer-dormant, the leaves emerging in autumn, the flowers in spring; the seed pods are inflated and papery, and probably dispersed by wind; the seeds are hard and round, and only 1 or 2 ripen in each follicle.

Helleborus argutifolius
¹/₂ life size, March 1st

RANUNCULACEAE

Helleborus lividus
¾ life size
February 25th

Helleborus orientalis, folicles and seeds
(right) life size, June 6th

Helleborus × ballardiae
⅓ life size, March 1st

*Helleborus
orientalis*
a collection of
cultivars
½ life size
March 1st

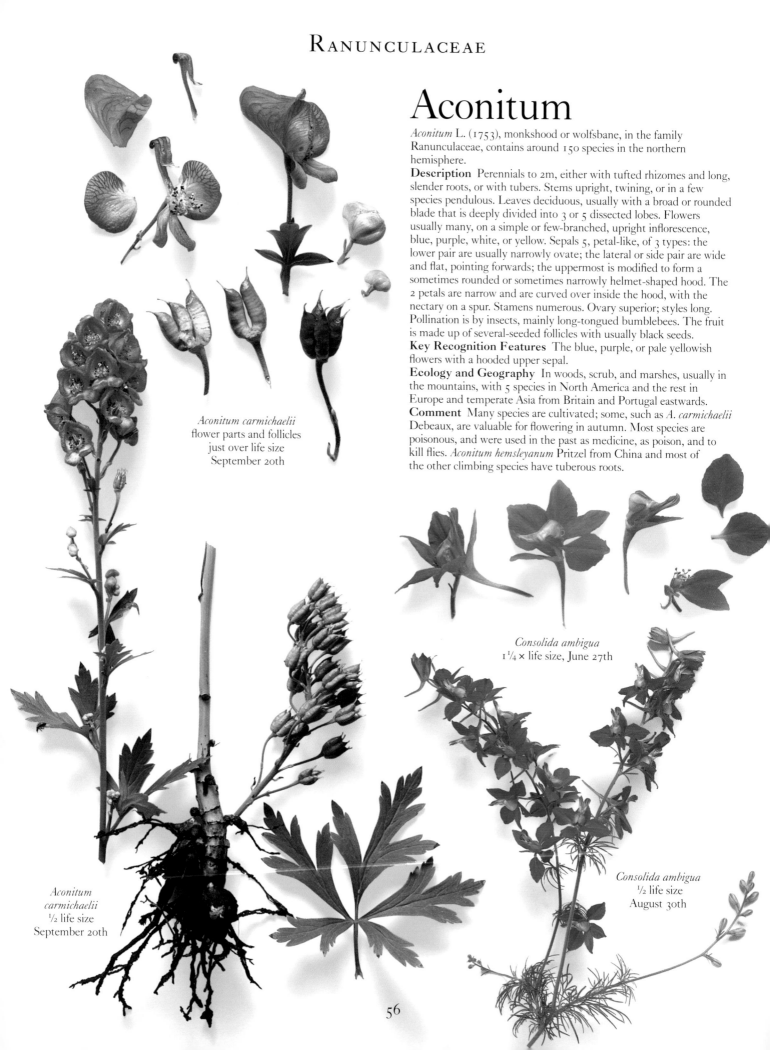

Aconitum

Aconitum L. (1753), monkshood or wolfsbane, in the family
Ranunculaceae, contains around 150 species in the northern
hemisphere.

Description Perennials to 2m, either with tufted rhizomes and long,
slender roots, or with tubers. Stems upright, twining, or in a few
species pendulous. Leaves deciduous, usually with a broad or rounded
blade that is deeply divided into 3 or 5 dissected lobes. Flowers
usually many, on a simple or few-branched, upright inflorescence,
blue, purple, white, or yellow. Sepals 5, petal-like, of 3 types: the
lower pair are usually narrowly ovate; the lateral or side pair are wide
and flat, pointing forwards; the uppermost is modified to form a
sometimes rounded or sometimes narrowly helmet-shaped hood. The
2 petals are narrow and are curved over inside the hood, with the
nectary on a spur. Stamens numerous. Ovary superior; styles long.
Pollination is by insects, mainly long-tongued bumblebees. The fruit
is made up of several-seeded follicles with usually black seeds.

Key Recognition Features The blue, purple, or pale yellowish
flowers with a hooded upper sepal.

Ecology and Geography In woods, scrub, and marshes, usually in
the mountains, with 5 species in North America and the rest in
Europe and temperate Asia from Britain and Portugal eastwards.

Comment Many species are cultivated; some, such as *A. carmichaelii*
Debeaux, are valuable for flowering in autumn. Most species are
poisonous, and were used in the past as medicine, as poison, and to
kill flies. *Aconitum hemsleyanum* Pritzel from China and most of
the other climbing species have tuberous roots.

Aconitum carmichaelii
flower parts and follicles
just over life size
September 20th

Consolida ambigua
1¼ × life size, June 27th

Aconitum
carmichaelii
½ life size
September 20th

Consolida ambigua
½ life size
August 30th

56

Consolida

Consolida (DC.) Gray (1821), in the family Ranunculaceae, contains around 40 species, mainly in Europe and Asia but naturalised elsewhere.

Description Annuals to 1.5m with upright or wide-branching stems. Leaves usually finely divided into narrow lobes. Flowers usually many, on a simple or branched inflorescence, blue or purple. Sepals 5, petal-like, the uppermost with a backwards pointing spur. Petals 2, fused into a single nectary. Ovary superior; styles long. Stamens in 5 spiral series. Pollination is by insects, mainly bumble-bees. The fruit is 1 several-seeded follicle. Seeds dark brown or black.

Key Recognition Features The blue or purple flowers with a long-spurred upper sepal, combined with the very finely divided leaves.

Ecology and Geography In cornfields and on dry hills, with 12 species in Europe and the rest mainly in southwestern and central Asia.

Comment Many species are cultivated as ornamental annuals, and *C. ajacis* (L.) Schur syn. *C. ambigua* Ball & Heywood is widely naturalised in North America and other wheat-growing areas of the world.

Delphinium

Delphinium L. (1753), in the family Ranunculaceae, contains around 300 species, mainly in the northern hemisphere.

Description Perennials to 2.5m, either with tufted rhizomes or with tubers; sometimes biennials or annuals. Stems upright, often wide-branching. Leaves deciduous, usually with a broad or rounded blade, which is deeply divided into 3 or 5 dissected lobes. Flowers usually many, on a simple or few-branched, upright inflorescence, blue, purple, pale yellow, white, or red. Sepals 5, petal-like, the uppermost with a backward- or upward-pointing spur. Petals 4, often blackish and hairy, the uppermost 2 with projections that extend into the spur and produce nectar, the lower 2 smaller than the sepals. Stamens numerous. Ovary superior; styles long. Pollination is by insects, mainly long-tongued bumblebees, or by hummingbirds in the case of the red-flowered American species. The fruit is made up of 3–5 several-seeded follicles. Seeds usually black.

Key Recognition Features The blue, purple, or pale yellowish flowers with a long-spurred upper sepal.

Ecology and Geography Woods, scrub, meadows, and dry hills, with 61 species in North America, 26 in Europe, and the rest in Asia; 1 or 2 species extend into the mountains of Africa southwards to Malawi.

Comment Many species are cultivated, and *D. elatum* L. from Europe and western Asia is the basic species for the large, blue delphiniums popular in herbaceous borders. The newer red, pink, and yellow colours have been bred by hybridisation with the red-flowered *D. cardinale* Hook. and *D. nudicaule* Torr. & Gray from North America and the yellow-flowered *D. semibarbatum* Bienert ex Boiss. from Afghanistan and central Asia.

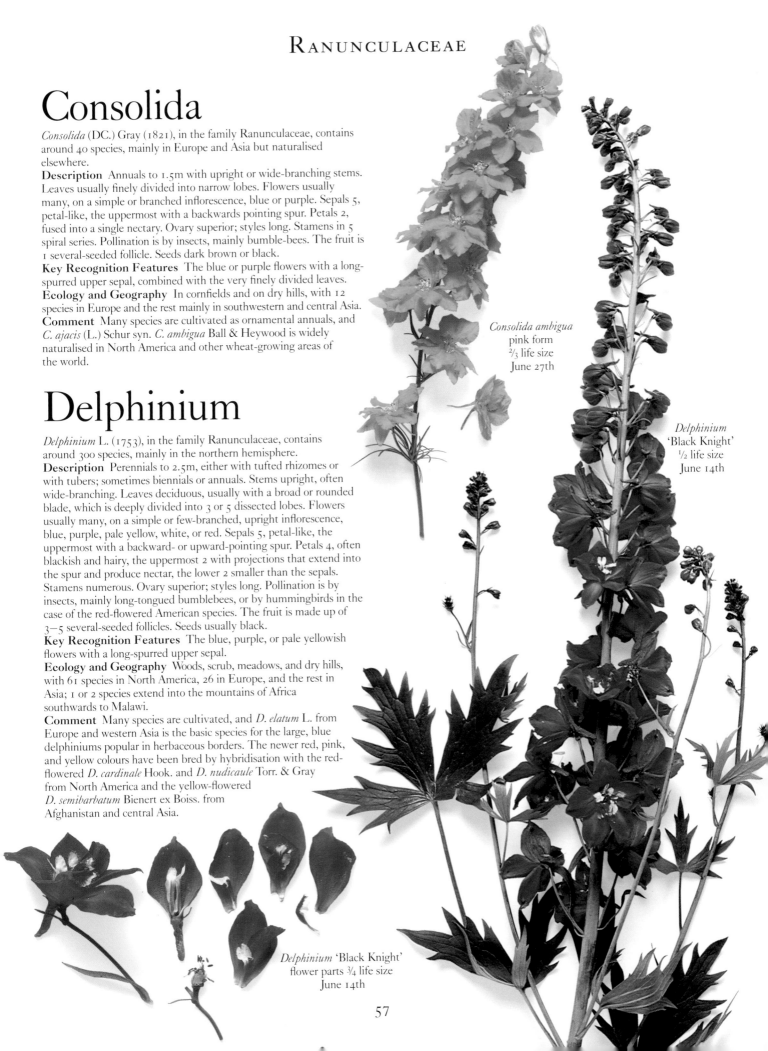

Consolida ambigua
pink form
²/₃ life size
June 27th

Delphinium
'Black Knight'
¹/₂ life size
June 14th

Delphinium 'Black Knight'
flower parts ¾ life size
June 14th

Glaucidium

Glaucidium Sieb. & Zucc. (1845), in the family Ranunculaceae, contains 1 species, *G. palmatum* Sieb. & Zucc., in Japan.

Description Perennial to 20cm with a tufted rhizome and black roots. Leaves deciduous, 7- to 11-lobed, and toothed. Flowers large, 5–10cm across, upright, pale purple or white, in the axils of leaf-like bracts. Sepals 4, coloured and petal-like. Petals absent. Stamens numerous. Ovary superior; styles short with capitate stigmas. Pollination is by bees. The fruit is made up of usually 2 several-seeded follicles. Seeds flat and winged.

Key Recognition Features The rounded, lobed, and toothed leaves and the 4-sepalled flowers.

Ecology and Geography In low alder scrub (*Alnus*, see Volume 1) in the mountains, usually where avalanches keep the ground open, in Honshu and Hokkaido.

Comment *Glaucidium* has often been considered sufficiently distinct to belong in a family of its own, but DNA studies suggest that it is a primitive member of the *Ranunculaceae*. It is a most beautiful plant for a cool garden, flowering in early spring. *Hydrastis* L., with 2 species, *H. canadensis* L. in northeastern North America and another in northeastern Asia, is also considered primitive within the *Ranunculaceae*. It has rather similar leaves, flowers without petals, sepals that fall as the flower opens, and 12 or more carpels that ripen into scarlet berries.

Paeonia

Paeonia L. (1753) in the family Paeoniaceae, contains around 30 species, in Europe, across Asia, and in western North America. The herbaceous species are described here; for the few woody species see Volume 1.

Description Perennials to 1.5m with thick, often tuberous roots, sometimes with stolons. Leaves deciduous, alternate on the stems, divided into 3 or more entire or coarsely toothed leaflets or ovate to narrowly linear lobes. Flowers to 15cm across, cup-shaped, white to pinkish-purple or red, solitary or up to 3 on the stem. Sepals 6, unequal, and variably leafy. Petals 5–9. Stamens numerous; anthers opening by slits. Ovary superior, of 1–8 separate carpels, each with numerous ovules; style absent, the stigmatic surfaces along the upper edge of the carpel. Pollination is by insects, especially beetles. Fruits of swollen follicles with numerous seeds, a few black and fertile, but mostly red, sticky, and infertile, to attract birds, which distribute the fertile seeds.

Key Recognition Features The leaves divided into 3 and the large flowers with carpels with a crest-like, stigmatic surface.

Ecology and Geography In scrub and woods, often in rocky places or on cliffs. Most species in eastern Europe, others in the Caucasus, central Asia, the Himalayas, and Japan, mainly on limestone, and 2 species in dry parts of California.

Comment Peonies have long been cultivated for their spectacular flowers as well as for their medicinal properties, particularly in China from the 7th century. The large-flowered cultivars of *P. lactiflora* Pallas, originally imported from China, were particularly popular in Edwardian herbaceous borders; many, such as 'Sarah Bernhardt', have huge double flowers; others have large petals surrounding a mass of sterile petaloid stamens. The evolutionary relationships of *Paeonia* have long been the subject of speculation; traditionally it has been linked with the Ranunculaceae, especially with *Glaucidium*. Others have considered it close to Dilleniaceae, but DNA studies now suggest that it is an isolated family within the order Saxifragales, nearest to *Daphniphyllum*, *Cercidiphyllum* and *Liquidambar* (see Volume 1).

Glaucidium palmatum
½ life size, autumn leaves
October 13th

Paeonia caucasica
⅓ life size, April 2nd

Paeoniaceae

Paeonia 'Kelway's Brilliant' (left)
⅓ life size, June 24th

Paeonia 'Mr G. F. Hemerick' (above) ⅓ life size
June 24th

Paeonia 'Sir Edward Elgar'
⅓ life size, June 24th

Paeonia emodi
⅓ life size, May 25th

Paeonia triternata fruit
showing red sterile seeds
and 1 black fertile seed
1⅓ × life size, August 8th

Paeonia 'Kansas'
autumn leaf
⅓ life size
September 25th

Paeonia emodi
flower parts
⅔ life size, May 25th

Diphylleia cymosa
¹/₃ life size, May 25th

Diphylleia cymosa
flower parts, 1¹/₄ × life size
May 25th

Diphylleia

Diphylleia Mich. (1803), in the family Berberidaceae, contains 3 species in eastern North America and eastern Asia.
Description Perennials to 1m with thick rhizomes. Leaves deciduous, the basal leaves peltate, the stem leaves with a central sinus and several pointed lobes. Flowers small, to 2cm across, white, and slightly cup-shaped, with up to 70 in an umbel. Sepals 6, soon falling. Petals 6, more or less flat. Stamens 6, anthers opening from the base by flaps. Ovary superior; style very short with a flat stigma. Pollination is by insects. The fruit is a dark blue berry with 1 or 2 red seeds.
Key Recognition Features The large, paired leaves and the umbels of flowers.
Ecology and Geography In woods by mountain streams. *Diphylleia cymosa* Mich. is confined to the Blue Ridge Mountains from Virginia to Georgia; *D. grayi* is found in Japan, growing in cool places in the mountains, often associated with *Glaucidium* (see p.58); *D. sinensis* was found by Handel-Mazzetti in rainforest in Yunnan.
Comment *Diphylleia cymosa* is an attractive plant for a woodland garden, grown for its bold leaves and dark blue berries. The Asian species are more delicate, and seldom cultivated.

Diphylleia cymosa
flowers, life size
May 25th

Podophyllum

Podophyllum L. (1753) in the family Berberidaceae, contains around 10 species in eastern North America and eastern Asia.

Description Perennials to 30cm with thick, often creeping rhizomes. Leaves deciduous, in pairs on the stems, peltate or with a central sinus and several pointed and jagged or blunt and finely toothed lobes. Flowers to 7.5cm across, cup-shaped, white to pinkish, dark purplish-brown, or pale yellow, upright and solitary, nodding and solitary, or up to 15 in a hanging umbel beneath the leaves. Sepals 6, soon falling. Petals 6 or 9. Stamens 12–18, anthers opening by slits. Ovary superior; style very short with a rounded stigma. Pollination is by insects. The fruit is a large, fleshy, red berry with many seeds.

Key Recognition Features The large, paired leaves and the flowers solitary and upright or in nodding umbels.

Ecology and Geography In meadows and woods. *Podophyllum peltatum* L. forms wide, spreading mats of leaves in deciduous woods in eastern North America, *P. hexandrum* Royle forms tight clumps in meadows and scrub in the Himalayas, and the remaining species are found in woods in China.

Comment A few species are cultivated as ornamentals and also have potential as anti-cancer drugs. The genus is sometimes divided into 3, with *Podophyllum* restricted to the American species *P. peltatum* L., *Sinopodophyllum* Ying containing *P. hexandrum* and 1 or 2 other Asian species, and the remainder of the genus separated as *Dysosma* Woodson; most of the species put into *Dysosma* have peltate leaves and nodding umbels of brown flowers. These Chinese species are rare in the wild, but often seen in the gardens of old monasteries.

Podophyllum hexandrum
flower parts, 1⅓ × life size, May 16th

Podophyllum hexandrum
flower back and front
1¼ × life size, May 16th

Podophyllum hexandrum
fruit, ½ life size
August 8th

Podophyllum hexandrum
⅔ life size, May 16th

Podophyllum hexandrum
fruit and seeds, life size
August 8th

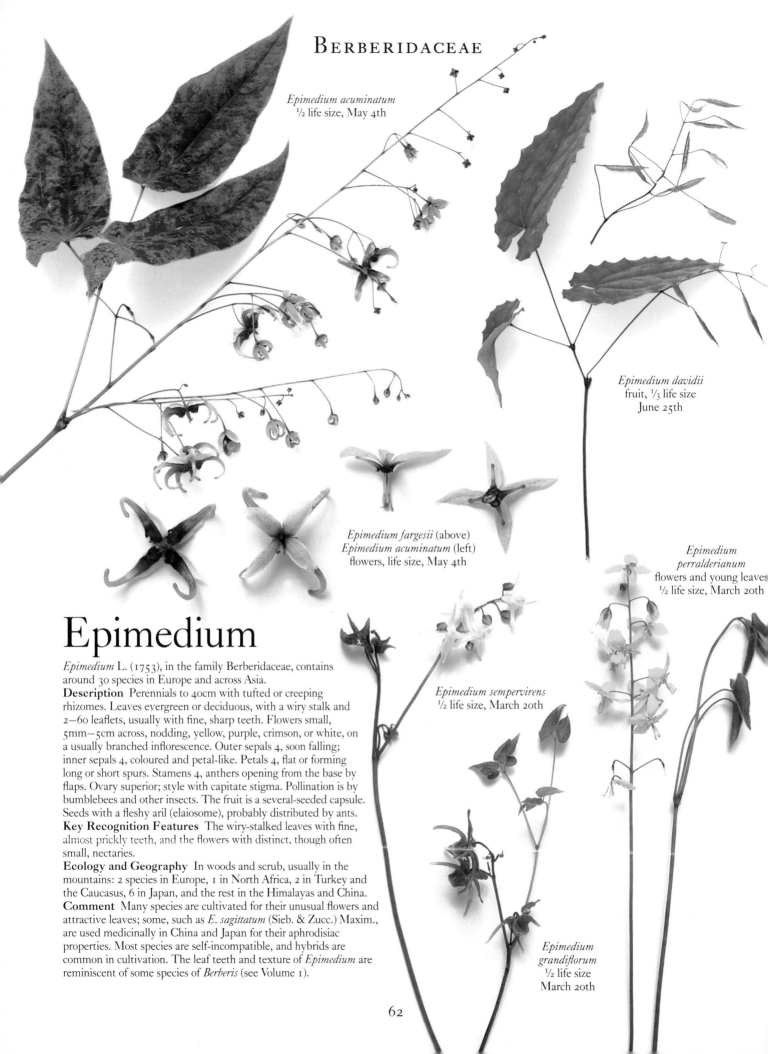

Epimedium acuminatum
½ life size, May 4th

Epimedium davidii
fruit, ⅓ life size
June 25th

Epimedium fargesii (above)
Epimedium acuminatum (left)
flowers, life size, May 4th

*Epimedium
perralderianum*
flowers and young leaves
½ life size, March 20th

Epimedium

Epimedium L. (1753), in the family Berberidaceae, contains around 30 species in Europe and across Asia.

Description Perennials to 40cm with tufted or creeping rhizomes. Leaves evergreen or deciduous, with a wiry stalk and 2–60 leaflets, usually with fine, sharp teeth. Flowers small, 5mm–5cm across, nodding, yellow, purple, crimson, or white, on a usually branched inflorescence. Outer sepals 4, soon falling; inner sepals 4, coloured and petal-like. Petals 4, flat or forming long or short spurs. Stamens 4, anthers opening from the base by flaps. Ovary superior; style with capitate stigma. Pollination is by bumblebees and other insects. The fruit is a several-seeded capsule. Seeds with a fleshy aril (elaiosome), probably distributed by ants.

Key Recognition Features The wiry-stalked leaves with fine, almost prickly teeth, and the flowers with distinct, though often small, nectaries.

Ecology and Geography In woods and scrub, usually in the mountains: 2 species in Europe, 1 in North Africa, 2 in Turkey and the Caucasus, 6 in Japan, and the rest in the Himalayas and China.

Comment Many species are cultivated for their unusual flowers and attractive leaves; some, such as *E. sagittatum* (Sieb. & Zucc.) Maxim., are used medicinally in China and Japan for their aphrodisiac properties. Most species are self-incompatible, and hybrids are common in cultivation. The leaf teeth and texture of *Epimedium* are reminiscent of some species of *Berberis* (see Volume 1).

Epimedium sempervirens
½ life size, March 20th

*Epimedium
grandiflorum*
½ life size
March 20th

Gymnospermium

Gymnospermium Spach (1839), in the family Berberidaceae, contains around 6 species, in Europe and Asia.

Description Small perennials with round tubers. Leaves deciduous in summer, basal and on the stem, with 4–7 narrow leaflets. Flowers small, to 2.5cm across, nodding, yellowish, often with red lines, on a simple or branched inflorescence, opening in hot sun. Sepals 6, coloured and petal-like. Petals 6, shorter than the sepals, tubular, producing nectar. Stamens 6, anthers opening from the base by flaps. Ovary superior; style long with a very small stigma. Pollination is by insects. The fruit is a few-seeded capsule, which opens before the seeds are ripe. Seeds hard and round.

Key Recognition Features The rounded leaves with narrow leaflets and the small, yellowish flowers.

Ecology and Geography In open scrub and on dry hills. One species in eastern Europe, the rest across central Asia to China.

Comment *Gymnospermium* is one of 3 tuberous genera of Berberidaceae found in the dry parts of eastern Europe and Asia. They grow in bare ground and arable fields, flowering in early spring, becoming dormant in summer. Of the other two, *Leontice* L. has pinnate leaves with many divided leaflets, while *Bongardia* Meyer has pinnately divided leaves with purple-blotched leaflets; both have yellow flowers and papery, inflated capsules.

Vancouveria

Vancouveria Morren & Decne. (1834), the insideout flower, in the family Berberidaceae, contains 3 species in western North America.

Description Perennials to 30cm with creeping rhizomes. Leaves evergreen or deciduous, with a wiry stalk and 3–27 leaflets, usually with wavy edges, without spines. Flowers small, 6–14mm across, nodding, white or yellow, on a branched inflorescence. Outer sepals 6–9, soon falling; inner sepals 6, coloured and petal-like, reflexed. Petals 6, with a hooded or flat lip, producing nectar. Stamens 6, forming a tight cone, anthers opening from the base by flaps. Ovary superior; style with capitate stigma. Pollination is by bumblebees, which hang upside-down to reach the nectaries, and perhaps other insects. Fruit is a several-seeded capsule. Seeds with a fleshy aril, distributed by ants.

Key Recognition Features The wiry-stalked leaves with small, wavy-edged leaflets, and the flowers with 6 sepals and petals and distinct, though small nectaries.

Ecology and Geography In woods and scrub, often in dense redwood forest; *V. chrysantha* Greene on serpentine. Found in coastal hills in California, Oregon, and Washington.

Comment *Vancouveria* is closely related to *Epimedium*. It is named after Captain George Vancouver (1757–98), who mapped the Pacific coast of North America in 1791–95; Archibald Menzies (1754–1842) was the surgeon-botanist on this expedition.

Gymnospermium albertii
2/3 life size
February 28th

Vancouveria chrysantha
flower parts and leaf
(above) 1 1/4 × life size
June 2nd

Vancouveria chrysantha
1/3 life size, June 2nd

Gymnospermium albertii
flower parts, 1 1/3 × life size, February 28th

Gymnospermium albertii
flower, 1 1/3 × life size
February 28th

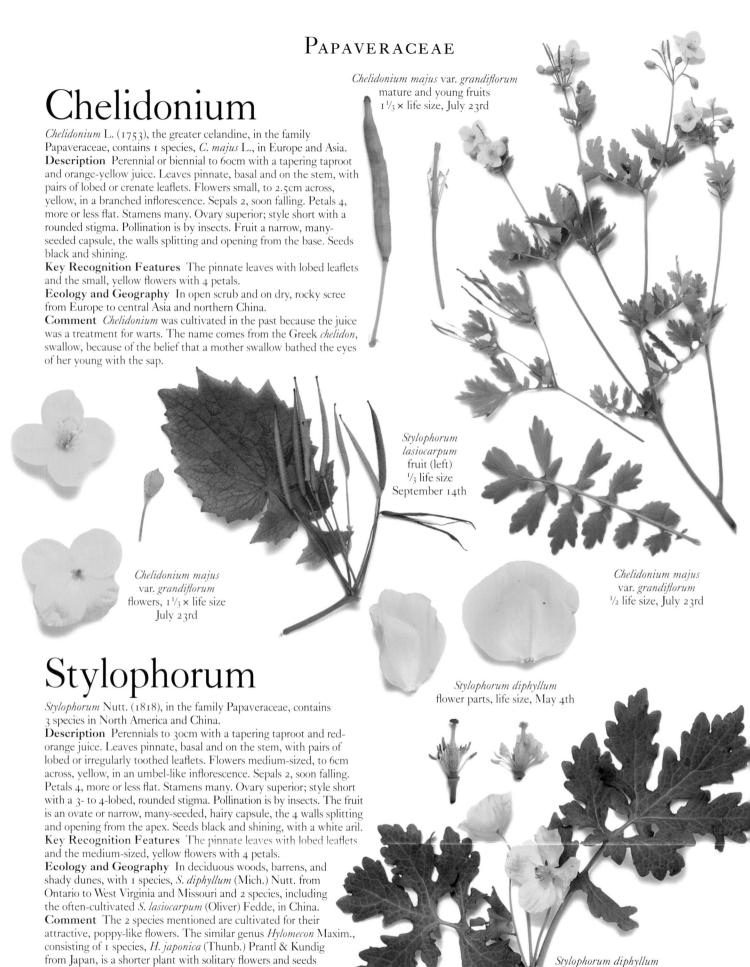

Chelidonium

Chelidonium L. (1753), the greater celandine, in the family Papaveraceae, contains 1 species, *C. majus* L., in Europe and Asia.
Description Perennial or biennial to 60cm with a tapering taproot and orange-yellow juice. Leaves pinnate, basal and on the stem, with pairs of lobed or crenate leaflets. Flowers small, to 2.5cm across, yellow, in a branched inflorescence. Sepals 2, soon falling. Petals 4, more or less flat. Stamens many. Ovary superior; style short with a rounded stigma. Pollination is by insects. Fruit a narrow, many-seeded capsule, the walls splitting and opening from the base. Seeds black and shining.
Key Recognition Features The pinnate leaves with lobed leaflets and the small, yellow flowers with 4 petals.
Ecology and Geography In open scrub and on dry, rocky scree from Europe to central Asia and northern China.
Comment *Chelidonium* was cultivated in the past because the juice was a treatment for warts. The name comes from the Greek *chelidon*, swallow, because of the belief that a mother swallow bathed the eyes of her young with the sap.

Chelidonium majus var. *grandiflorum*
mature and young fruits
1⅓ × life size, July 23rd

Stylophorum lasiocarpum
fruit (left)
⅓ life size
September 14th

Chelidonium majus
var. *grandiflorum*
flowers, 1⅓ × life size
July 23rd

Chelidonium majus
var. *grandiflorum*
½ life size, July 23rd

Stylophorum

Stylophorum Nutt. (1818), in the family Papaveraceae, contains 3 species in North America and China.
Description Perennials to 30cm with a tapering taproot and red-orange juice. Leaves pinnate, basal and on the stem, with pairs of lobed or irregularly toothed leaflets. Flowers medium-sized, to 6cm across, yellow, in an umbel-like inflorescence. Sepals 2, soon falling. Petals 4, more or less flat. Stamens many. Ovary superior; style short with a 3- to 4-lobed, rounded stigma. Pollination is by insects. The fruit is an ovate or narrow, many-seeded, hairy capsule, the 4 walls splitting and opening from the apex. Seeds black and shining, with a white aril.
Key Recognition Features The pinnate leaves with lobed leaflets and the medium-sized, yellow flowers with 4 petals.
Ecology and Geography In deciduous woods, barrens, and shady dunes, with 1 species, *S. diphyllum* (Mich.) Nutt. from Ontario to West Virginia and Missouri and 2 species, including the often-cultivated *S. lasiocarpum* (Oliver) Fedde, in China.
Comment The 2 species mentioned are cultivated for their attractive, poppy-like flowers. The similar genus *Hylomecon* Maxim., consisting of 1 species, *H. japonica* (Thunb.) Prantl & Kundig from Japan, is a shorter plant with solitary flowers and seeds without an aril.

Stylophorum diphyllum
flower parts, life size, May 4th

Stylophorum diphyllum
⅓ life size, May 4th

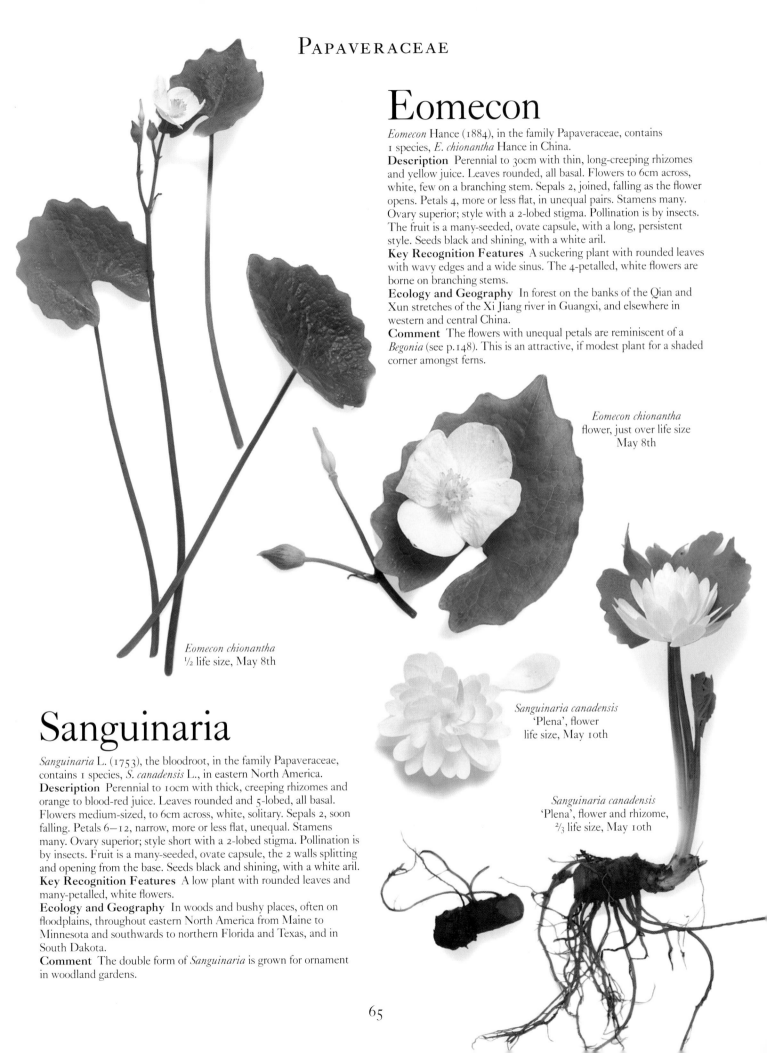

Eomecon

Eomecon Hance (1884), in the family Papaveraceae, contains
1 species, *E. chionantha* Hance in China.

Description Perennial to 30cm with thin, long-creeping rhizomes
and yellow juice. Leaves rounded, all basal. Flowers to 6cm across,
white, few on a branching stem. Sepals 2, joined, falling as the flower
opens. Petals 4, more or less flat, in unequal pairs. Stamens many.
Ovary superior; style with a 2-lobed stigma. Pollination is by insects.
The fruit is a many-seeded, ovate capsule, with a long, persistent
style. Seeds black and shining, with a white aril.

Key Recognition Features A suckering plant with rounded leaves
with wavy edges and a wide sinus. The 4-petalled, white flowers are
borne on branching stems.

Ecology and Geography In forest on the banks of the Qian and
Xun stretches of the Xi Jiang river in Guangxi, and elsewhere in
western and central China.

Comment The flowers with unequal petals are reminiscent of a
Begonia (see p.148). This is an attractive, if modest plant for a shaded
corner amongst ferns.

Eomecon chionantha
flower, just over life size
May 8th

Eomecon chionantha
½ life size, May 8th

Sanguinaria

Sanguinaria L. (1753), the bloodroot, in the family Papaveraceae,
contains 1 species, *S. canadensis* L., in eastern North America.

Description Perennial to 10cm with thick, creeping rhizomes and
orange to blood-red juice. Leaves rounded and 5-lobed, all basal.
Flowers medium-sized, to 6cm across, white, solitary. Sepals 2, soon
falling. Petals 6–12, narrow, more or less flat, unequal. Stamens
many. Ovary superior; style short with a 2-lobed stigma. Pollination is
by insects. Fruit is a many-seeded, ovate capsule, the 2 walls splitting
and opening from the base. Seeds black and shining, with a white aril.

Key Recognition Features A low plant with rounded leaves and
many-petalled, white flowers.

Ecology and Geography In woods and bushy places, often on
floodplains, throughout eastern North America from Maine to
Minnesota and southwards to northern Florida and Texas, and in
South Dakota.

Comment The double form of *Sanguinaria* is grown for ornament
in woodland gardens.

Sanguinaria canadensis
'Plena', flower
life size, May 10th

Sanguinaria canadensis
'Plena', flower and rhizome,
⅔ life size, May 10th

Macleaya

Macleaya R. Br. (1826), in the family Papaveraceae, the plume poppy, contains 2 species in China and Japan.

Description Perennials with stems to 2m, creeping rhizomes, and orange juice. Leaves rounded and lobed, greyish-green and hairy beneath. Flowers very small, to 1cm long in bud, many on a much-branched stem. Sepals 2, falling as the flower opens. Petals absent. Stamens 8–30, the filaments sometimes as long as the anthers. Ovary superior; style short, with a 2-lobed stigma. Pollination is by wind. The fruit is a few-seeded, flattened capsule. Seeds black and shining, with a small, white aril.

Key Recognition Features A very tall, clump-forming plant with rounded leaves and plume-like masses of coral-pink or yellowish flowers on branching stems.

Ecology and Geography In openings in forest, on hills, and along roadsides throughout China and Japan.

Comment The genus is named after Alexander Macleay (1767–1848), a Scottish botanist and entomologist, secretary to the Linnean Society and later colonial secretary of New South Wales. Its leaves are distinctive and beautiful, and its tall flowering stems are striking at the back of herbaceous borders in late summer. The hybrid between the 2 species, *M.* × *kewensis* Turrill, is most commonly cultivated; it is sterile. The juice of *Macleaya* is used as an antiseptic in traditional Chinese medicine. *Bocconia* L., a genus of around 9 species of trees or shrubs fron Central America, has in the past been confused with *Macleaya*; its fruits have 1 seed.

Macleaya cordata,
fruit (left) and flowers (right)
1 ¾ × life size, June 25th

Macleaya cordata
⅓ life size, June 25th

Macleaya cordata
flowers, 1 ½ × life size
June 25th

66

Meconopsis cambrica
seed capsule, life size
July 12th

Meconopsis betonicifolia
flower and capsule
2/3 life size, June 12th

Meconopsis cambrica
1/2 life size, May 3rd

Meconopsis betonicifolia
1/2 life size, June 12th

Meconopsis

Meconopsis Viguier (1814), in the family Papaveraceae, contains around 50 species in western Europe, the Himalayas, and China.
Description Biennials or perennials to 3m with yellow juice. Leaves undivided to 2-pinnate, basal and on the stem, usually hairy. Flowers to 13cm across, yellow, red, white, or blue. Sepals 2, soon falling. Petals 4—10, more or less flat. Stamens many. Ovary superior; style short with several lobes. Pollination is by insects. Fruit a many-seeded, usually hairy capsule, opening by flaps just below the apex. Seeds black and dull, without an aril.
Key Recognition Features Poppy-like plants with rather narrow capsules opening by flaps.
Ecology and Geography In alpine meadows, on screes, and in openings in coniferous and deciduous woods. One species, *Meconopsis cambrica* (L.) Viguier, the Welsh poppy, is found in western Europe, the rest from the Himalayas eastwards to northwestern China.
Comment Many species are cultivated for their beautiful flowers, especially the famous blue-flowered species *M. betonicifolia* Franch., *M. grandis* Prain, and their hybrid *M.* × *sheldonii* G. Taylor. The alpine species grow best in cool-summer climates such as Scotland. Many species are monocarpic, spending 2 or more years forming a large rosette of leaves on the ground, before growing up into a tall stem 2m or more tall with numerous flowers; this then seeds and dies.

Meconopsis cambrica
seed capsules and seeds
1 1/3 × life size, July 2nd

Papaver

Papaver L. (1753), in the family Papaveraceae, contains around 70 species, worldwide in temperate areas.

Description Annuals, biennials, or perennials to 1.2m with yellow or white juice. Leaves undivided to 2-pinnate, basal and on the stem, usually hairy. Flowers to 16cm across, usually red or orange, less often yellow, purplish, or white. Sepals 2, sometimes 3, soon falling. Petals usually 4, rarely 6, more or less flat. Stamens many. Ovary superior; styles forming radiating velvety lines on top of the ovary. Pollination is by insects, often by beetles eating the pollen. The fruit is a many-seeded capsule, opening by pores just below the apex. Seeds black and dull, without an aril.

Key Recognition Features The usually 4 red petals and the capsule with radiating, velvety stigmatic rays.

Ecology and Geography On cold, stony steppes, on screes and rocks, and in meadows and openings in forests. Many species are common weeds of arable fields, and have followed wheat cultivation throughout the world. Most are from the northern hemisphere, but 1 species, *P. aculeatum* Thunb. is native of South Africa and Australia.

Comment Many species are cultivated for their beautiful flowers. The opium poppy, *P. somniferum* L., is the source of most of the world's heroin and morphine, as well as opium; it is grown mainly in Afghanistan and southeastern Asia and is an ancient cultivated plant, unknown in the wild. The perennial Turkish species *P. orientale* L. and *P. bracteatum* Lindl. (sometimes found as *P. orientale* var. *bracteatum*) and their hybrids are widely grown herbaceous perennials. *Papaver croceum* Ledeb. from Mongolia is the original species from which the cultivated Iceland poppies, now generally found under *P. nudicaule*, have been developed. Shirley poppies, selections of the red-flowered *P. rhoeas* L., are now grown in shades of pink, grey and mauve; they all originate from a single pale mutant of *P. rhoeas* spotted by the Reverend William Wilkes in a field near his rectory garden at Shirley, near Croydon, Surrey, in around 1880.

Papaver dubium
⅓ life size
August 16th

Papaver nudicaule 'Constance
Finnis' strain (right)
⅓ life size, May 15th

Papaver rhoeas
'Reverend Wilkes'
⅓ life size
July 15th

Papaver glaucum
½ life size
August 16th

Papaver commutatum
½ life size, August 16th

Papaveraceae

Papaver bracteatum
'Beauty of Livermere'
½ life size, June 25th

Papaver bracteatum
'Beauty of Livermere'
section of fruit
½ life size
June 25th

Papaver bracteatum
stamens (left)
1 ¼ × life size, June 25th

Papaver bracteatum
⅓ life size, June 25th

Papaver bracteatum
sections of ovary and
stigmatic ridges (above)
1 ¼ × life size, June 25th

Papaver somniferum
single mixed, ½ life size
August 8th

Papaver somniferum
capsules and seeds
¾ life size, July 24th

69

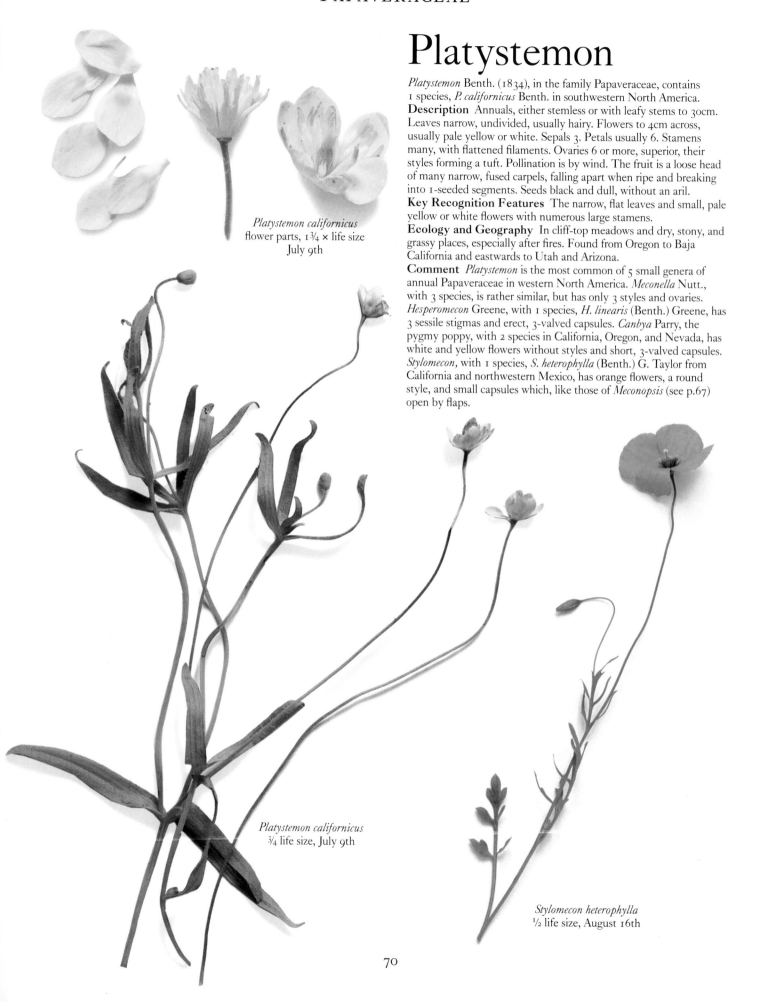

PAPAVERACEAE

Platystemon

Platystemon Benth. (1834), in the family Papaveraceae, contains 1 species, *P. californicus* Benth. in southwestern North America.

Description Annuals, either stemless or with leafy stems to 30cm. Leaves narrow, undivided, usually hairy. Flowers to 4cm across, usually pale yellow or white. Sepals 3. Petals usually 6. Stamens many, with flattened filaments. Ovaries 6 or more, superior, their styles forming a tuft. Pollination is by wind. The fruit is a loose head of many narrow, fused carpels, falling apart when ripe and breaking into 1-seeded segments. Seeds black and dull, without an aril.

Key Recognition Features The narrow, flat leaves and small, pale yellow or white flowers with numerous large stamens.

Ecology and Geography In cliff-top meadows and dry, stony, and grassy places, especially after fires. Found from Oregon to Baja California and eastwards to Utah and Arizona.

Comment *Platystemon* is the most common of 5 small genera of annual Papaveraceae in western North America. *Meconella* Nutt., with 3 species, is rather similar, but has only 3 styles and ovaries. *Hesperomecon* Greene, with 1 species, *H. linearis* (Benth.) Greene, has 3 sessile stigmas and erect, 3-valved capsules. *Canbya* Parry, the pygmy poppy, with 2 species in California, Oregon, and Nevada, has white and yellow flowers without styles and short, 3-valved capsules. *Stylomecon,* with 1 species, *S. heterophylla* (Benth.) G. Taylor from California and northwestern Mexico, has orange flowers, a round style, and small capsules which, like those of *Meconopsis* (see p.67) open by flaps.

Platystemon californicus
flower parts, 1¾ × life size
July 9th

Platystemon californicus
¾ life size, July 9th

Stylomecon heterophylla
½ life size, August 16th

70

Eschscholtzia californica
'Ballerina Mixed'
just under life size
August 10th

Eschscholtzia californica
'Cherry Ripe' (left), just under life size
August 10th

Eschscholtzia californica
bud and young capsule
(left) 1⅓ × life size
August 10th

Eschscholtzia californica
'Purple Violet'
just under life size
August 10th

Eschscholtzia californica
'Milky White'
just under life size
August 10th

Eschscholtzia californica
flower and sepal cap
(right) 1¼ × life size
August 10th

Eschscholtzia

Eschscholtzia Chamisso (1820), the California poppy, in the family Papaveraceae, contains around 12 species in western North America and northwestern Mexico.

Description Annuals, biennials, or perennials to 60cm across with a simple taproot. Leaves mostly basal, finely divided, grey-green, and hairless. Flowers to 16cm across, usually red or orange, less often yellow, purplish, or white. Sepals 2, forming a pointed cap over the bud and splitting as the flower opens, with a ring around the base in *E. californica* Cham. Petals usually 4. Stamens many, with short, often blackish filaments. Ovary superior; styles 4–8, slightly recurved, forming radiating velvety lines on top of the ovary. Pollination is by insects. The fruit is a cylindrical, 2-valved capsule, opening from the base, often explosively. Seeds black and dull, often ridged and pitted.

Key Recognition Features The cap-like sepals and flowers with usually 4 orange or yellow petals; white, pink, or purplish flowers are common in cultivated forms.

Ecology and Geography In cliff-top meadows and dry, stony, and grassy places inland, especially after fires; many species in desert sands and washes. From Washington and Oregon to Baja California and eastwards to Utah, Arizona, and Texas. Commonly naturalised in other parts of the world.

Comment *Eschscholtzia californica* is commonly cultivated, usually as an annual, though individual plants will survive for a few years in suitable climates. *Eschscholtzia caespitosa* Benth. with smaller flowers is always annual, and sometimes sold with the name 'Sundew'. *Hunnemannia* Sweet, from Mexico is superficially close to *Eschscholtzia*, but has separate sepals and a flat stigma. It is sometimes cultivated.

Eschscholtzia californica
⅓ life size, August 10th

71

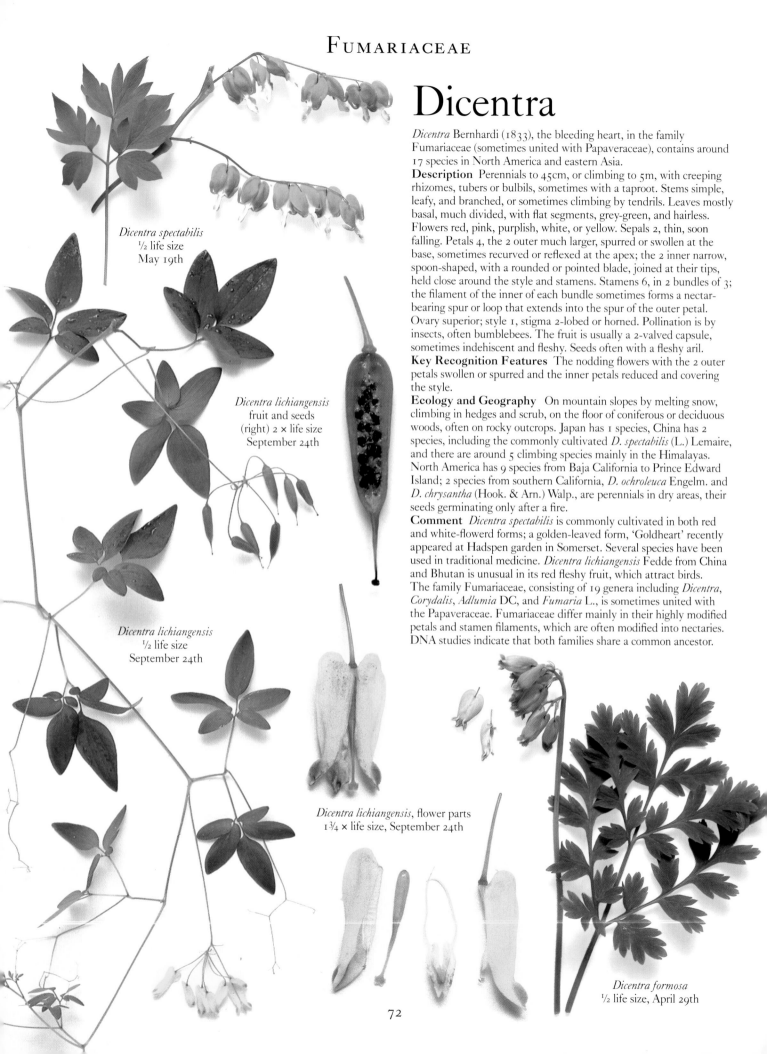

Dicentra

Dicentra Bernhardi (1833), the bleeding heart, in the family Fumariaceae (sometimes united with Papaveraceae), contains around 17 species in North America and eastern Asia.

Description Perennials to 45cm, or climbing to 5m, with creeping rhizomes, tubers or bulbils, sometimes with a taproot. Stems simple, leafy, and branched, or sometimes climbing by tendrils. Leaves mostly basal, much divided, with flat segments, grey-green, and hairless. Flowers red, pink, purplish, white, or yellow. Sepals 2, thin, soon falling. Petals 4, the 2 outer much larger, spurred or swollen at the base, sometimes recurved or reflexed at the apex; the 2 inner narrow, spoon-shaped, with a rounded or pointed blade, joined at their tips, held close around the style and stamens. Stamens 6, in 2 bundles of 3; the filament of the inner of each bundle sometimes forms a nectar-bearing spur or loop that extends into the spur of the outer petal. Ovary superior; style 1, stigma 2-lobed or horned. Pollination is by insects, often bumblebees. The fruit is usually a 2-valved capsule, sometimes indehiscent and fleshy. Seeds often with a fleshy aril.

Key Recognition Features The nodding flowers with the 2 outer petals swollen or spurred and the inner petals reduced and covering the style.

Ecology and Geography On mountain slopes by melting snow, climbing in hedges and scrub, on the floor of coniferous or deciduous woods, often on rocky outcrops. Japan has 1 species, China has 2 species, including the commonly cultivated *D. spectabilis* (L.) Lemaire, and there are around 5 climbing species mainly in the Himalayas. North America has 9 species from Baja California to Prince Edward Island; 2 species from southern California, *D. ochroleuca* Engelm. and *D. chrysantha* (Hook. & Arn.) Walp., are perennials in dry areas, their seeds germinating only after a fire.

Comment *Dicentra spectabilis* is commonly cultivated in both red and white-flowerd forms; a golden-leaved form, 'Goldheart' recently appeared at Hadspen garden in Somerset. Several species have been used in traditional medicine. *Dicentra lichiangensis* Fedde from China and Bhutan is unusual in its red fleshy fruit, which attract birds. The family Fumariaceae, consisting of 19 genera including *Dicentra*, *Corydalis*, *Adlumia* DC, and *Fumaria* L., is sometimes united with the Papaveraceae. Fumariaceae differ mainly in their highly modified petals and stamen filaments, which are often modified into nectaries. DNA studies indicate that both families share a common ancestor.

Dicentra spectabilis
½ life size
May 19th

Dicentra lichiangensis
fruit and seeds
(right) 2 × life size
September 24th

Dicentra lichiangensis
½ life size
September 24th

Dicentra lichiangensis, flower parts
1¾ × life size, September 24th

Dicentra formosa
½ life size, April 29th

Corydalis

Corydalis DC (1805), in the family Fumariaceae (sometimes united with the Papaveraceae), contains around 400 species in the northern hemisphere.

Description Annuals, biennials, or perennials to 80cm with creeping or compact rhizomes, stolons, tubers, or bulbils, sometimes with a simple taproot. Stems usually leafy. Leaves much divided, with flat segments. Flowers red, pink, blue, purplish, white, or yellow. Sepals 2, thin, persisting or soon falling. Petals 4, the 2 outer much larger, the upper spurred or swollen at the base, the lower simple at the base, often expanded into a lip at the apex; the 2 inner petals narrow, joined at their tips, held close around the style and stamens. Stamens 6, in 2 bundles of 3; the filament of one stamen forms a nectary which extends into the spur. Ovary superior; style 1, stigma 2-lobed or horned or with 4–8 protruding papillae. Pollination is by insects, often bumblebees, though many species are normally self-pollinated. The fruit is usually a 2-valved capsule, usually dehiscent and often explosive. In 1 or 2 species from high screes in the Pamirs and Kashmir the fruits are swollen and bladder-like and presumably dispersed by wind. Seeds of most species have a fleshy aril.

Key Recognition Features The flowers with a single spur and the inner petals reduced, covering the style; fruit a capsule.

Ecology and Geography On stony mountain slopes and in scrub, in coniferous or deciduous woods, often on rocky outcrops, on cliffs or by springs and stony streams, for example *C. mucronata* Franch. The tuberous species, such as *C. solida* (L.) Clairv., are most diverse in woodland in eastern Europe and in the mountains of western and central Asia; the herbaceous species, such as *C. flexuosa* Franch., are most diverse in China and the Himalayas.

Comment Several genera are closely related to *Corydalis*. The biennial *Adlumia* DC has 2 species, of which *A. fungosa* (Ait.) Britt. from North America is often cultivated; it has tall, climbing stems with tendrils and pink flowers with their petals fused at the base, persisting on the plant after they have become brown. *Fumaria* L. has around 50 species, mostly weeds of cultivation; the flowers are similar to *Corydalis*, the fruits are round and single-seeded. The familiar *C. ochroleuca* Koch and *C. lutea* (L.) DC are now often put in the genus *Pseudofumaria* Medik., and the delicate climber *C. claviculata* (L.) DC is now in the genus *Ceratocapnos* Lidén. *Corydalis sempervirens* (L.) Pursh is now in the genus *Capnoides* Mill.. Many *Corydalis* species, especially the tuberous *C. cava* (L.) Schweigger & Koerte, have been used for medicine, as a muscle relaxant and sedative; some are reported to be mildly hallucinogenic. Other species are used in China and Tibet.

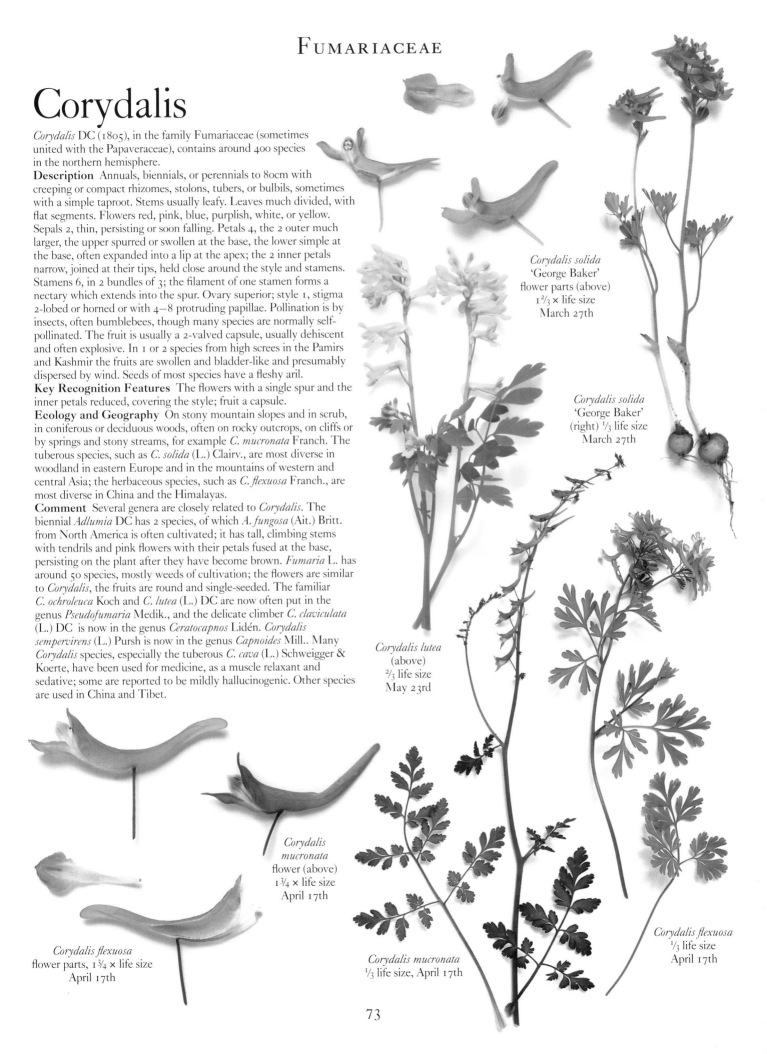

Corydalis solida
'George Baker'
flower parts (above)
1²⁄₃ × life size
March 27th

Corydalis solida
'George Baker'
(right) ¹⁄₃ life size
March 27th

Corydalis lutea
(above)
²⁄₃ life size
May 23rd

Corydalis flexuosa
flower parts, 1¾ × life size
April 17th

Corydalis mucronata
flower (above)
1¾ × life size
April 17th

Corydalis mucronata
¹⁄₃ life size, April 17th

Corydalis flexuosa
¹⁄₃ life size
April 17th

Silene

Silene L. (1753), the catchfly or campion, in the Caryophyllaceae, contains around 500 species throughout the world.

Description Annuals, biennials, or perennials to 60cm, sometimes shrubby at the base. Stems usually leafy and branched. Leaves usually opposite, undivided. Flowers red, pink, purplish, white, or yellow, often scented and opening at night, males and females sometimes on different plants. Sepals 5, joined to form a tubular calyx with 5 short teeth. Petals 5, usually with a long, narrow lower part, the claw, and a broad blade, which is often deeply lobed and also often has a pair of small scales at the throat. Stamens 10. Ovary superior; styles 3, or rarely 5. Pollination is by insects, often butterflies and moths, or by hummingbirds in the red-flowered American species. The fruit is a capsule of fused carpels, opening by 6 or 10 teeth, twice as many as there are styles. Seeds usually kidney-shaped, attached to a central placenta, so-called free-central placentation.

Key Recognition Features The opposite leaves and the flowers with the sepals joined into a tube and petals often forked and uncurling at night; c.f. *Zaluzianskya* in the Scrophulariaceae.

Ecology and Geography On dry slopes and mountain rocks and in open woods. Found in temperate areas throughout the world, but mostly in Europe, with 166 species, and western Asia. A group of species in the high Himalayas have nodding flowers with a swollen calyx and very small petals.

Comment According to DNA evidence, the family Caryophyllaceae is associated with the families Phytolaccaceae, Nyctaginaceae, Amaranthaceae, Aizoaceae, Cactaceae, and Portulacaceae (see pp.82–89 for these), in the order Caryophyllales; the Caryophyllales are associated with the order Polygonales, discussed under *Persicaria* (see p.90). *Silene* itself is one of the largest and most complex temperate genera, and includes such familiar wild flowers as pinkish-flowered European red campion *S. dioica* (L.) Clairv. and the American red-flowered *S. virginica* L.. *Silene coeli-rosa* (L.) Godron is a popular and easily grown annual in gardens. Many species, such as *S. nutans* L., have flowers that open and become sweetly scented at night, and have symbiotic relationships with their own species of moth. *Silene* is very close to *Lychnis*, but *Lychnis* always has 5 styles and capsules that open by 5 teeth.

Lychnis

Lychnis L. (1753), in the family Caryophyllaceae, contains around 15 species in temperate regions of the northern hemisphere.

Description Biennials or perennials to 40cm. Stems usually leafy and branched. Leaves opposite, undivided. Flowers red, pink, or purplish, sometimes white. Sepals 5, joined to form a tubular calyx with 5 short teeth. Petals 5, similar to *Silene*. Stamens 10. Ovary superior; styles 5. Pollination is by insects, usually butterflies. The fruit is a capsule, opening by 5 teeth. Seeds usually kidney-shaped, attached to a central placenta, so-called free-central placentation.

Key Recognition Features Similar to *Silene*, but with 5 styles and capsule teeth. *Lychnis* species are sometimes included in *Silene*.

Ecology and Geography On arctic and mountain rocks, in bogs, and in open woods. *Lychnis alpina* L. is found all round the arctic, and on high mountains elsewhere, particularly on serpentine soils. Around half the species are found in Europe, most of the rest in Asia, and a few in North America.

Comment Several *Lychnis* species are familiar old garden flowers, grown since the 16th century. *Lychnis coronaria* (L.) Desr. has solitary red, pink, or white flowers with stiff coronal scales; *L. chalcedonica* L. has up to 50 scarlet flowers in a flat head; *L. flos-cuculi* L. is ragged robin, common in bogs and wet meadows throughout Europe and Siberia.

Silene dioica
1 1/3 × life size, May 15th

Silene armeria
1/2 life size, July 20th

Silene armeria
1/3 life size
July 20th

Lychnis flos-cuculi
flower parts
1 1/2 × life size
June 22nd

Lychnis flos-cuculi
section through
capsule, 1 1/2 × life size
June 22nd

Lychnis flos-cuculi
1/3 life size
June 22nd

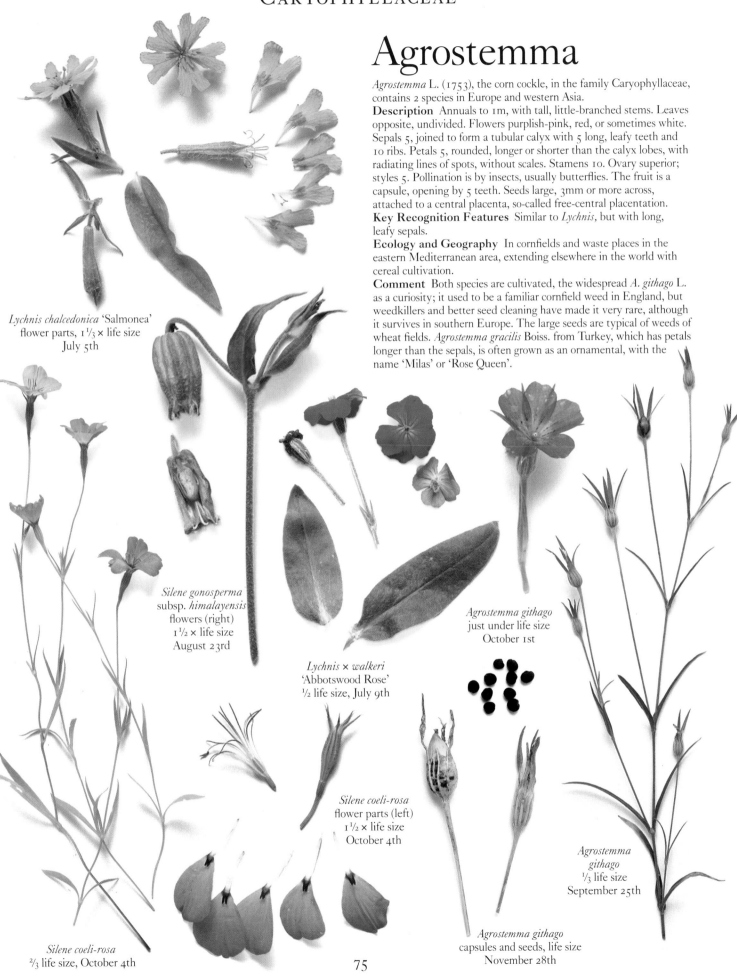

Agrostemma

Agrostemma L. (1753), the corn cockle, in the family Caryophyllaceae, contains 2 species in Europe and western Asia.

Description Annuals to 1m, with tall, little-branched stems. Leaves opposite, undivided. Flowers purplish-pink, red, or sometimes white. Sepals 5, joined to form a tubular calyx with 5 long, leafy teeth and 10 ribs. Petals 5, rounded, longer or shorter than the calyx lobes, with radiating lines of spots, without scales. Stamens 10. Ovary superior; styles 5. Pollination is by insects, usually butterflies. The fruit is a capsule, opening by 5 teeth. Seeds large, 3mm or more across, attached to a central placenta, so-called free-central placentation.

Key Recognition Features Similar to *Lychnis*, but with long, leafy sepals.

Ecology and Geography In cornfields and waste places in the eastern Mediterranean area, extending elsewhere in the world with cereal cultivation.

Comment Both species are cultivated, the widespread *A. githago* L. as a curiosity; it used to be a familiar cornfield weed in England, but weedkillers and better seed cleaning have made it very rare, although it survives in southern Europe. The large seeds are typical of weeds of wheat fields. *Agrostemma gracilis* Boiss. from Turkey, which has petals longer than the sepals, is often grown as an ornamental, with the name 'Milas' or 'Rose Queen'.

Lychnis chalcedonica 'Salmonea'
flower parts, 1⅓ × life size
July 5th

Silene gonosperma
subsp. *himalayensis*
flowers (right)
1½ × life size
August 23rd

Lychnis × walkeri
'Abbotswood Rose'
½ life size, July 9th

Agrostemma githago
just under life size
October 1st

Silene coeli-rosa
flower parts (left)
1½ × life size
October 4th

Agrostemma
githago
⅓ life size
September 25th

Silene coeli-rosa
⅔ life size, October 4th

Agrostemma githago
capsules and seeds, life size
November 28th

Saponaria

Saponaria L. (1753), soapwort, in the family Caryophyllaceae, contains around 20 species, mainly in the mountains of southern Europe and in southwestern Asia.

Description Annuals or perennials to 90cm, with upright, spreading, or trailing and branching stems; sometimes dense cushion plants. Leaves usually opposite, flat and undivided. Flowers pale pink, reddish, or pale yellow. Sepals 5, joined to form a narrow, tubular calyx with 5 short teeth. Petals 5, not or scarcely notched, with or without coronal scales. Stamens 10. Ovary superior; styles 2. Pollination is by insects. The fruit is a capsule, opening by 4 teeth. Seeds large, subglobose, to 2.5mm across.

Key Recognition Features Close to *Gypsophila*, but usually with larger flowers and the bands on the calyx absent or very narrow and pale. Differs from *Lychnis* (see pp.74–75) in the number of styles and capsule teeth.

Ecology and Geography Mountain rocks, screes, dry slopes, open woods, and meadows: 18 species in Turkey, 10 spread across Europe.

Comment *Saponaria officinalis* L., the common soapwort, has been used for cleaning and strengthening delicate fabrics. At Uppark in Sussex it was used successfully on the ancient hangings and curtains. It is often found on roadsides or by abandoned cottages; double reddish or pale pink forms and white forms are known; the flowers are sweetly scented. Other dwarf species are grown in rock gardens.

Saponaria officinalis
flowers, ¾ life size, July 5th

Vaccaria hispanica
'Pink Beauty'
¾ life size
August 30th

Vaccaria hispanica 'Pink Beauty'
flowers, 1⅓ × life size
August 30th

Saponaria officinalis
½ life size, July 5th

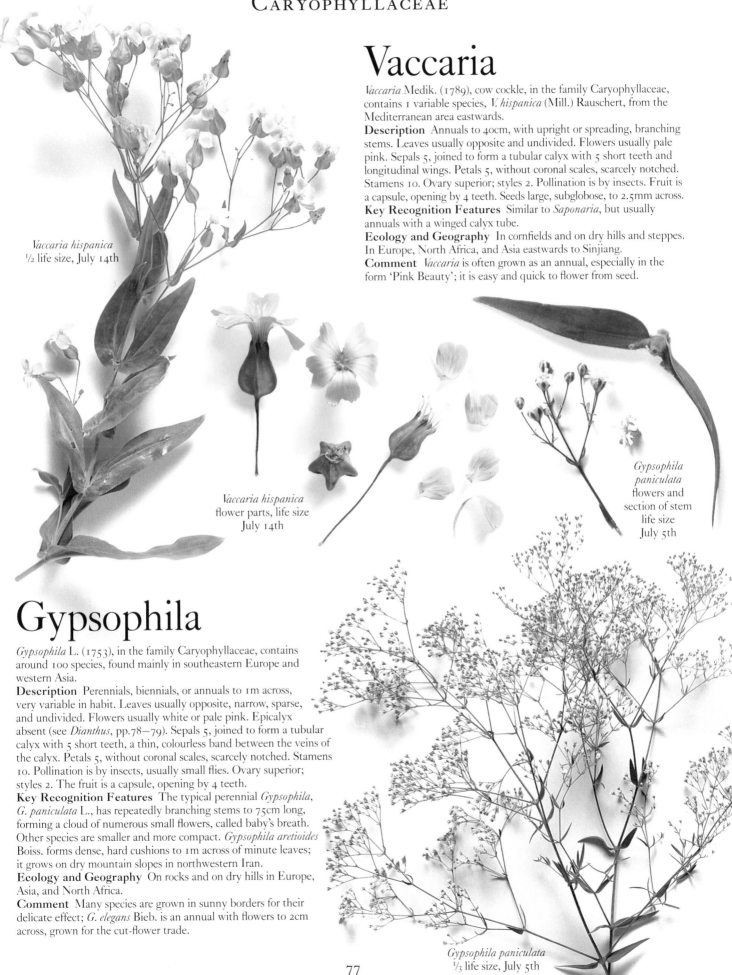

Vaccaria hispanica
½ life size, July 14th

Vaccaria

Vaccaria Medik. (1789), cow cockle, in the family Caryophyllaceae, contains 1 variable species, *V. hispanica* (Mill.) Rauschert, from the Mediterranean area eastwards.

Description Annuals to 40cm, with upright or spreading, branching stems. Leaves usually opposite and undivided. Flowers usually pale pink. Sepals 5, joined to form a tubular calyx with 5 short teeth and longitudinal wings. Petals 5, without coronal scales, scarcely notched. Stamens 10. Ovary superior; styles 2. Pollination is by insects. Fruit is a capsule, opening by 4 teeth. Seeds large, subglobose, to 2.5mm across.

Key Recognition Features Similar to *Saponaria*, but usually annuals with a winged calyx tube.

Ecology and Geography In cornfields and on dry hills and steppes. In Europe, North Africa, and Asia eastwards to Sinjiang.

Comment *Vaccaria* is often grown as an annual, especially in the form 'Pink Beauty'; it is easy and quick to flower from seed.

Vaccaria hispanica
flower parts, life size
July 14th

*Gypsophila
paniculata*
flowers and
section of stem
life size
July 5th

Gypsophila

Gypsophila L. (1753), in the family Caryophyllaceae, contains around 100 species, found mainly in southeastern Europe and western Asia.

Description Perennials, biennials, or annuals to 1m across, very variable in habit. Leaves usually opposite, narrow, sparse, and undivided. Flowers usually white or pale pink. Epicalyx absent (see *Dianthus*, pp.78–79). Sepals 5, joined to form a tubular calyx with 5 short teeth, a thin, colourless band between the veins of the calyx. Petals 5, without coronal scales, scarcely notched. Stamens 10. Pollination is by insects, usually small flies. Ovary superior; styles 2. The fruit is a capsule, opening by 4 teeth.

Key Recognition Features The typical perennial *Gypsophila*, *G. paniculata* L., has repeatedly branching stems to 75cm long, forming a cloud of numerous small flowers, called baby's breath. Other species are smaller and more compact. *Gypsophila aretioides* Boiss. forms dense, hard cushions to 1m across of minute leaves; it grows on dry mountain slopes in northwestern Iran.

Ecology and Geography On rocks and on dry hills in Europe, Asia, and North Africa.

Comment Many species are grown in sunny borders for their delicate effect; *G. elegans* Bieb. is an annual with flowers to 2cm across, grown for the cut-flower trade.

Gypsophila paniculata
⅓ life size, July 5th

Dianthus

Dianthus L. (1753), the carnation or pink, in the Caryophyllaceae, contains around 300 species, mainly in Europe and Asia.

Description Perennials or biennials to 60cm, sometimes shrubby at the base, often dwarf and cushion-forming. Leaves usually opposite, narrow, crowded, undivided, and pointed. Flowers usually pink or purplish, sometimes red, white, or pale yellow, usually sweetly scented of cloves. Bracts or epicalyx of 1–3 pairs, often broad and surrounding the stem. Sepals 5, joined to form a tubular calyx with 5 short teeth. Petals 5, the blade often "pinked", toothed or finely divided, without coronal scales, but often hairy in the throat. Stamens 10. Ovary superior; styles 2, often long and recurved. Pollination is by insects, usually butterflies. The fruit is a capsule, opening by 4 teeth. Seeds usually flattened on 1 side, attached to a central placenta, so-called free-central placentation.

Key Recognition Features The narrow, pointed leaves and the scented flowers with 2 styles.

Ecology and Geography On rocks, mostly in the mountains and on dry hills. Around 120 species in Europe, 1 in arctic North America; others mainly in Asia and in the mountains of Africa southwards to the eastern Cape.

Comment Several species of *Dianthus* are familiar as garden plants; the carnation, *D. caryophyllus* L., has been cultivated since the Roman era, so that its natural distribution in the Mediterranean area, possibly in North Africa, is obscure. The Romans used it medicinally and to flavour wine. Later, carnations were much grown and further developed by the Persians, Turks, and Arabs, before being re-introduced to northern Europe in the 13th century. Pinks were raised from *D. plumarius* L. from central Europe, later crossed with carnations and other dwarf species. The old "laced" pinks, with circles of contrasting colour, date from the 18th century, and were grown especially by the weavers of Paisley. The word pink, used since the 16th century, refers to the toothed edge of the flowers. As far back as the 8th century, the Chinese and Japanese cultivated their native species, *D. superbus* L. and *D. chinensis* L., and their hybrids both for medicine and for ornament. They aimed not for the biggest, roundest flowers, but for the most elegant. At their most extreme, the flowers had hanging, thread-like petals, like a witch's wig, varying in colour from deep red to white. *Dianthus barbatus* L., sweet william or stinking billy, is a biennial grown for its flat heads of many tightly packed flowers and their clove scent.

Petrorhagia

Petrorhagia (DC) Link (1831), in the family Caryophyllaceae, contains around 25 species, mainly in Europe and Asia.

Description Perennials or biennials to 15cm. Leaves usually opposite, narrow, crowded, undivided, and pointed. Flowers usually pale pink, sometimes with darker lines. Bracts or epicalyx usually 2 pairs. Sepals 5, joined to form a tubular calyx with 5 short teeth. Petals 5. Stamens 10. Ovary superior; styles 2. Pollination is by insects, usually small flies. The fruit is a capsule, opening by 4 teeth. Seeds like *Dianthus*.

Key Recognition Features Very like small-flowered, much-branched *Dianthus*, but differing in having a thin, colourless band between the veins of the calyx.

Ecology and Geography On rocks and dry hills in Europe, Asia, and North Africa.

Comment *Petrorhagia saxifraga* (L.) Link is sometimes cultivated in both single- and double-flowered forms. The plant is also found under the name *Tunica saxifraga* (L.) Scop..

Dianthus barbatus
just under life size
June 15th

Petrorhagia saxifraga
½ life size, July 20th

Petrorhagia saxifraga
2½ × life size, July 20th

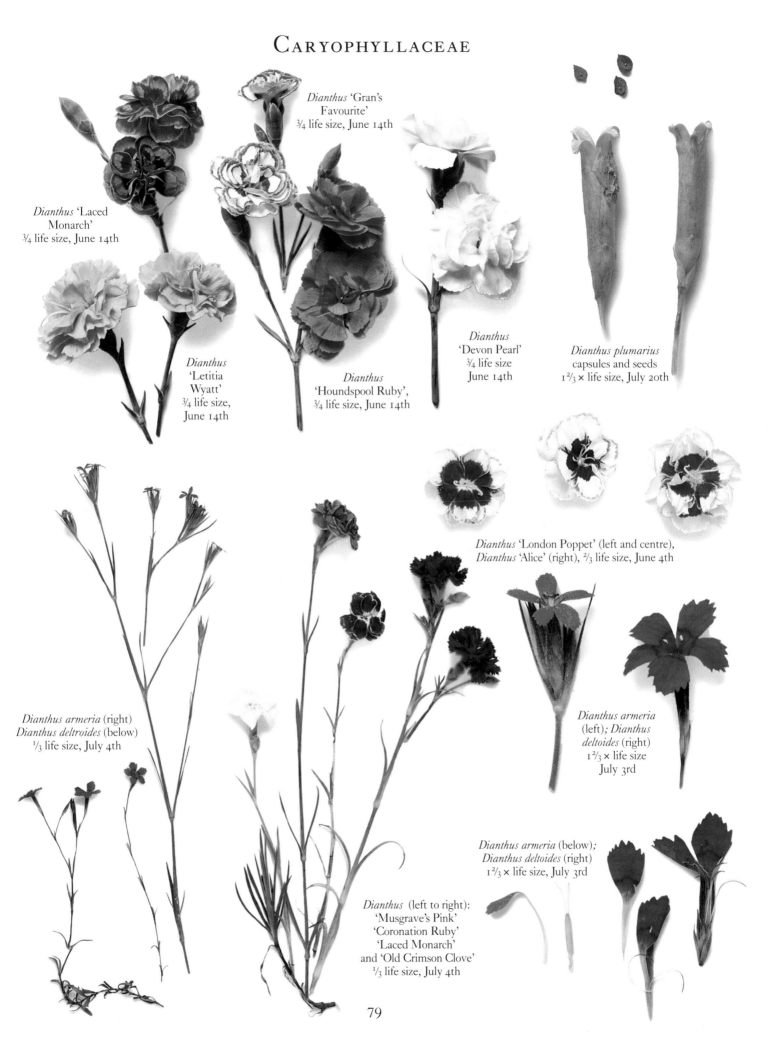

CARYOPHYLLACEAE

Dianthus 'Gran's
Favourite'
¾ life size, June 14th

Dianthus 'Laced
Monarch'
¾ life size, June 14th

Dianthus
'Letitia
Wyatt'
¾ life size,
June 14th

Dianthus
'Houndspool Ruby',
¾ life size, June 14th

Dianthus
'Devon Pearl'
¾ life size
June 14th

Dianthus plumarius
capsules and seeds
1⅔ × life size, July 20th

Dianthus 'London Poppet' (left and centre),
Dianthus 'Alice' (right), ⅔ life size, June 4th

Dianthus armeria (right)
Dianthus deltroides (below)
⅓ life size, July 4th

Dianthus armeria
(left); *Dianthus
deltoides* (right)
1⅔ × life size
July 3rd

Dianthus armeria (below);
Dianthus deltoides (right)
1⅔ × life size, July 3rd

Dianthus (left to right):
'Musgrave's Pink'
'Coronation Ruby'
'Laced Monarch'
and 'Old Crimson Clove'
⅓ life size, July 4th

79

Cerastium

Cerastium L. (1753), the mouse-ear chickweed, in the family
Caryophyllaceae, contains around 100 species, mainly in the northern
hemisphere.

Description Usually sprawling perennials or small annuals to 15cm.
Leaves usually opposite and undivided, often silvery. Flowers usually
white. Sepals 5, not joined. Petals 5, without coronal scales, deeply
divided and tapering gradually towards the base. Stamens usually 10.
Ovary superior; styles usually 5. Pollination is by insects, usually small
flies, or probably by self-pollination. The fruit is a capsule, opening by
10 teeth.

Key Recognition Features Small, usually hairy plants with white
flowers with deeply divided petals.

Ecology and Geography On high mountain screes, cliffs, and
sunny rocks, in dry meadows, and on sand dunes. Found around the
northern hemisphere.

Comment A few species are grown in gardens; *C. tomentosum* L. and
related species and hybrids, called snow-in-summer, are commonly
grown on walls and dry banks. Other species are common weeds.

Arenaria

Arenaria L. (1753), in the family Caryophyllaceae, contains around
160 species, mainly in northern hemisphere.

Description Usually small perennials, biennials, or annuals, to
15cm, very variable in habit. Leaves usually opposite and undivided.
Flowers usually white, rarely pale purple. Sepals 5, not joined. Petals
usually 5, without coronal scales, rounded, and tapering gradually
towards the base. Stamens 10. Ovary superior; styles usually 3.
Pollination is by insects, usually small flies, or probably by
self-pollination. The fruit is a capsule, opening by twice as many
teeth as there are styles.

Key Recognition Features Small plants with flat leaves and small,
white flowers with rounded petals.

Ecology and Geography On high mountain screes, shady rocks
and cliffs, and in dry pine forests. Around the northern hemisphere,
particularly at high latitudes and in mountains; 1 species in the
southern Andes.

Comment A few species are grown in rock gardens: *A. balearica* L.
covers damp rocks with its minute creeping stems and leaves;
A. montana L. from Spain and Portugal has the largest flowers,
around 4cm across; *A. tetraquetra* L. is a high-alpine cushion
plant with stiff leaves in 4 rows and flowers with 4 petals.
Closely related to *Arenaria* is *Minuartia* L., which usually has
linear leaves and capsules with as many teeth as the styles; *M. verna*
(L.) Hiern, has flowers around 12mm across; it is most common on
serpentine rocks and limestone areas with high lead content. Even
smaller-flowered than *Minuartia* is *Sagina* L. which has fine, narrow
leaves joined at the base, forming mossy tufts and mats in damp
lawns and on rocks. *Sagina nodosa* L. Fenzl. has groups of short
leaves up the stem and flowers around 1cm across, while the
commonly cultivated *S. subulata* (Swartz) Presl 'Aurea' forms mossy
tufts of golden leaves.

Cerastium tomentosum
flowers, 1½ × life size
May 15th

*Cerastium
tomentosum*
¾ life size
May 15th

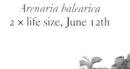

Arenaria balearica
2 × life size, June 12th

Spergularia

Spergularia (Pers.) J. & C. Presl (1819), sea spurry, in the family Caryophyllaceae, contains around 25 species, mainly in Europe.
Description Usually creeping perennials or small annuals to 15cm across. Leaves usually opposite, narrow, fleshy, and undivided, with papery stipules. Flowers usually pinkish, opening in the sun. Sepals 5, not joined. Petals 5, without coronal scales, undivided. Stamens 1–10. Ovary superior; styles usually 3. Pollination is by insects, usually small flies, or perhaps by self-pollination. The fruit is a capsule, splitting into 3.
Key Recognition Features Small, often glandular-hairy plants with narrow, fleshy leaves and pink flowers with pointed petals.
Ecology and Geography On coastal rocks and cliffs and in dry sandy places and salt marshes, with 17 species in Europe, the rest scattered around the world, including Hawaii and southern South America.
Comment These are attractive small plants, most common near the sea. The largest-flowered species in Europe, *S. fimbriata* Boiss, has petals to 6mm long.

Stellaria holostea
½ life size, May 20th

Stellaria media
flowers, life size, May 3rd

Spergularia rupicola
(above and below)
2 × life size, July 23rd

Stellaria

Stellaria L. (1753), stitchwort or chickweed, in the family Caryophyllaceae, contains 150–200 species, mainly in the northern hemisphere.
Description Usually sprawling perennials, or annuals to 30cm. Leaves usually opposite and undivided. Flowers white. Sepals 5, not joined. Petals 5, without coronal scales, divided almost to the base. Stamens 5–10. Ovary superior; styles 2 or 3. Pollination is by insects, or probably by self-pollination. The fruit is a round capsule, opening by twice as many teeth as there are styles.
Key Recognition Features Small or spreading, usually hairless plants with white flowers and very deeply divided petals.
Ecology and Geography In hedges, meadows, and marshes. Chickweed, *S. media* (L.) Vill., is a common garden weed around the world, appropriately named as young chickens adore it. Other species are found across Europe and Asia and throughout North America; 1 species, *S. debilis* D'Urv., is found in Patagonia.
Comment Species of *Stellaria* are seldom deliberately grown in gardens, but *S. holostea* L., the greater stitchwort, is a common hedgerow flower in spring; the developing capsules make a satisfying pop when squashed. *Moehringia trinervia* (L.) Clairv. syn *Arenaria trinervia* L. is very like chickweed, but has undivided petals and leaves with 3 strong veins; it is often found in shady gardens and hedgerows.

Mirabilis

Mirabilis L. (1753), in the family Nyctaginaceae, contains around 60 species from the Americas, but widely naturalised elsewhere.

Description Perennials or annuals to 1m, with upright, branching stems. Leaves opposite, the lower usually stalked. Flowers often scented, usually white, yellow, red, or reddish-purple, surrounded by 5 sepal-like bracts, which sometimes form a cup. Petals 5, joined to form a tubular or trumpet-shaped corolla with a long tube and spreading mouth. Stamens 3–5. Ovary 5-celled; styles 1. Pollination is by insects, in many species by moths. The fruit is usually a many-seeded, 5-angled capsule.

Key Recognition Features Branching plants with opposite leaves and tubular flowers, with 5 or even 10 lobes.

Ecology and Geography By roadsides and in sandy places, mainly in tropical and subtropical America. *Mirabilis jalapa* L. is naturalised in warm areas around the world. It has red, yellow, white, or striped, *Convulvulus*-like flowers on branching stems from a thick, tuberous rootstock.

Comment The Nyctaginaceae, associated with Phytolaccaceae and Amaranthaceae (see pp.83–85) in the Caryophyllales, is mainly tropical and is familiar in the spectacular climber *Bougainvillea* A. Juss. from Brazil, with its usually bright purple bracts and small, white flowers. *Mirabilis jalapa* may be grown in frosty areas if the tuberous roots are protected in winter.

Mirabilis jalapa
²/₃ life size
September 29th

Mirabilis jalapa
life size, September 12th

Phytolacca acinosa
fruit, 1¼ × life size
September 18th

Phytolacca acinosa
¹/₃ life size, July 21st

Phytolacca acinosa, fruit
1²/₃ × life size
September 18th

Phytolacca

Phytolacca L. (1753), pokeweed, in the family Phytolaccaceae, contains around 25 species worldwide.

Description Upright perennials to 2m, from a thick, woody rootstock, or thick-trunked trees. Leaves alternate and undivided, usually stalked. Flowers usually white, greenish, or pinkish-red, in dense or open, upright or drooping spikes. Sepals 5, petal-like, rounded and often becoming thick and fleshy in fruit. Petals absent. Stamens 5–30, in 1 or 2 whorls. Ovary superior; styles 5–16. Pollination is by insects, mainly flies. The fruit is a shining, blackish-purple berry with deep red juice, of 5–16 fused carpels.

Key Recognition Features Tall plants with often reddish, rather fleshy leaves and spikes of flowers.

Ecology and Geography By roadsides and in rough places, the herbaceous species in eastern Asia and eastern North America. *Phytolacca dioica* L., the ombu tree, is the characteristic tree of the pampas in South America. It is commonly planted in the Mediterranean area, being a fast-growing, drought-resistant, and valued for its shade; it fruits in winter.

Comment *Phytolacca* is closely related to *Ercilla* A. Juss. (see Volume 1). A few of the species are grown in gardens. The young shoots of *P. acinosa* Roxb. syn. *P. esculenta* Van Houtte, which has upright flower spikes, are edible if cooked; those of *P. americana* L., which has nodding spikes, are poisonous when fresh, but edible after boiling and discarding the water. The juice from the fruits was used to colour wine and as ink. Some species were used against rheumatism and cancer, particularly leukemia, and others contain saponins which can be used to kill snails.

Atriplex

Atriplex L. (1753), orache, in the family Amaranthaceae, contains around 300 species worldwide.

Description Perennials or annuals to 2.5m, with upright, branching or simple stems, rarely shrubs to 3m; whole plant sometimes coloured, or dusted with mealy powder. Leaves alternate or opposite. Flowers unisexual, small, usually greenish, in loose, upright spikes, solitary or clustered, males and females sometimes on separate plants. Male flowers have 3–5 sepals and stamens. Female flowers usually lack sepals, but have 2 large bracteoles. Ovary 1-celled; styles 3. Pollination is presumed to be by wind. The fruit is usually 1-seeded with enlarged bracteoles.

Key Recognition Features Tall plants with often triangular, stalked leaves, and seeds with circular, heart-shaped or triangular enlarged bracteoles, joined at the base.

Ecology and Geography By roadsides and in rough places. Found worldwide, often in sandy or salty soils.

Comment Silver-leaved, shrubby species, such as *A. canescens* (Pursh) Nutt. and *A. halimus* L., are often used as hedging, especially near the sea. The annual *A. hortensis* L., which is often all red, is grown as a vegetable and can be eaten like spinach. True spinach, *Spinacia oleracea* L., also in the Amaranthaceae, is an annual with bracteoles joined almost to the apex, and hardened in fruit.

Atriplex hortensis
1½ × life size
August 1st

Atriplex hortensis
⅓ life size, August 1st

Amaranthus caudatus
flowers, 1⅓ × life size
August 30th

Amaranthus caudatus
½ life size
August 30th

Amaranthus hypochondriacus
½ life size, May 2nd

Amaranthus

Amaranthus L. (1753), in the family Amaranthaceae, contains around 60 species, mainly in the Americas but widely naturalised elsewhere.

Description Annuals to 3m, with upright, branching or simple stems; whole plant often coloured. Leaves alternate. Flowers unisexual, very small, usually white, greenish, brown, or red, massed in very dense, upright or drooping, cylindrical or rounded spikes. Bracts small and solitary; bracteoles 2, petal-like. Sepals 1–5, transparent, dry and papery. Petals absent. Stamens 1–5. Ovary 1-celled; styles 3. Pollination is presumed to be by wind. The fruit is usually a 1-seeded capsule; seeds less than 1mm, and round.

Key Recognition Features Tall plants with often reddish leaves and upright or arching and hanging spikes of minute flowers.

Ecology and Geography By roadsides and in rough places, mainly in tropical Asia and tropical and subtropical America.

Comment Formerly genera with thin or fleshy sepals and separate stamens were considered to belong to the Chenopodiaceae, while Amaranthaceae had dry and papery sepals and stamens joined at the base. The family Chenopodiaceae is now considered to be part of the Amaranthaceae. Many of those formerly considered to belong to Chenopodiaceae are also halophytes; that is, they grow in salty soils, such as by the sea or in inland desert areas where soils have become saline. *Salicornia* L., the glasswort or sea asparagus, is common in estuarine mud, and is an excellent vegetable, with succulent, leafless stems. Many species of Amaranthus are grown for food: some, such as *A. caudatus*. L. and *A. hybridus* L., are important grain crops, in the Andes since pre-Columbian times and more recently in the Himalayas. Others such as *A. tricolor* L. are eaten like spinach, particularly in China and India. Coloured forms of several species are grown for ornament, of which the most common is *A. caudatus*, or love-lies-bleeding.

Beta

Beta L. (1753), in the family Amaranthaceae, contains around 6 species in southern Europe, but widely grown elsewhere.

Description Perennials, biennials, or annuals to 2m, with upright, branching or simple stems; whole plant sometimes coloured. Leaves alternate. Flowers small, usually greenish, clustered in loose, upright spikes. Bracts 2, small. Sepals 5, thickening in fruit. Petals absent. Stamens 5. Ovary 1-celled, half-inferior, joined to the base of the thickened sepals in fruit; styles 2 or 3. Pollination is presumed to be by wind. The fruit is usually 1-seeded; seeds glossy.

Key Recognition Features Large plants with stalked lower leaves and thickened ovary and sepals in fruit.

Ecology and Geography By roadsides and in rough, stony places. The wild species originated around the Mediterranean, but are now grown worldwide.

Comment Many vegetables, such as beetroot, sugar beet, Swiss chard, and perpetual spinach beet, have been derived from *B. vulgaris* L., sea beet, which is common on rocky and pebbly seashores around Europe. The wild form is sometimes called subsp. *maritima* (L.) Arcangeli, the tuberous-rooted beets subsp. *vulgaris*, and forms grown for their leaves and stems subsp. *cicla* (L.) Arcangeli.

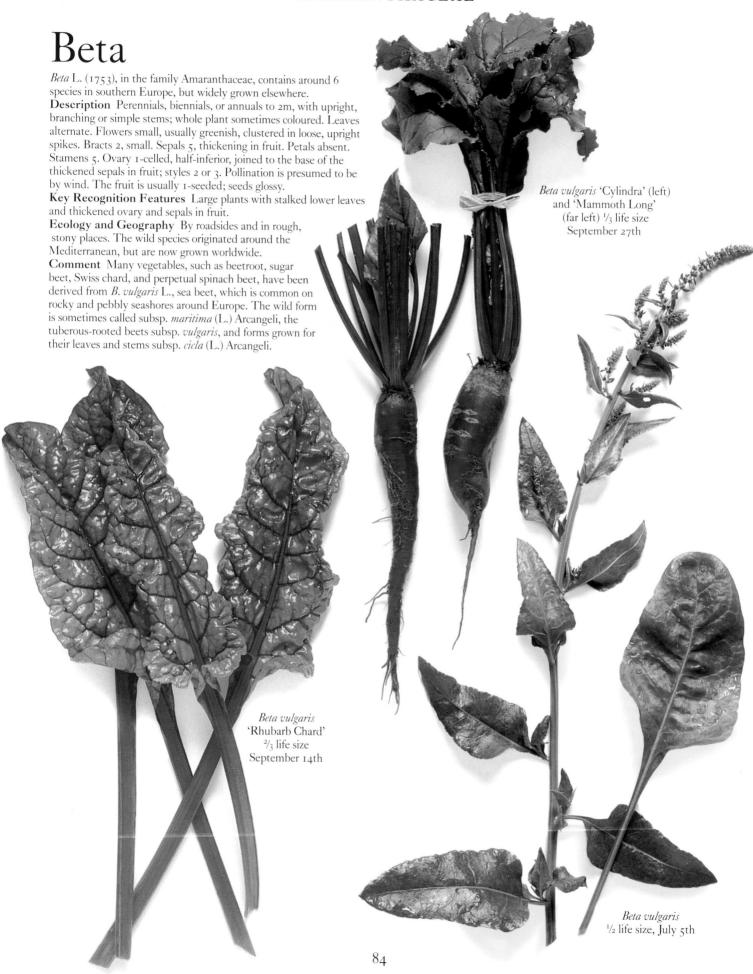

Beta vulgaris 'Cylindra' (left) and 'Mammoth Long' (far left) ⅓ life size September 27th

Beta vulgaris 'Rhubarb Chard' ⅔ life size September 14th

Beta vulgaris ½ life size, July 5th

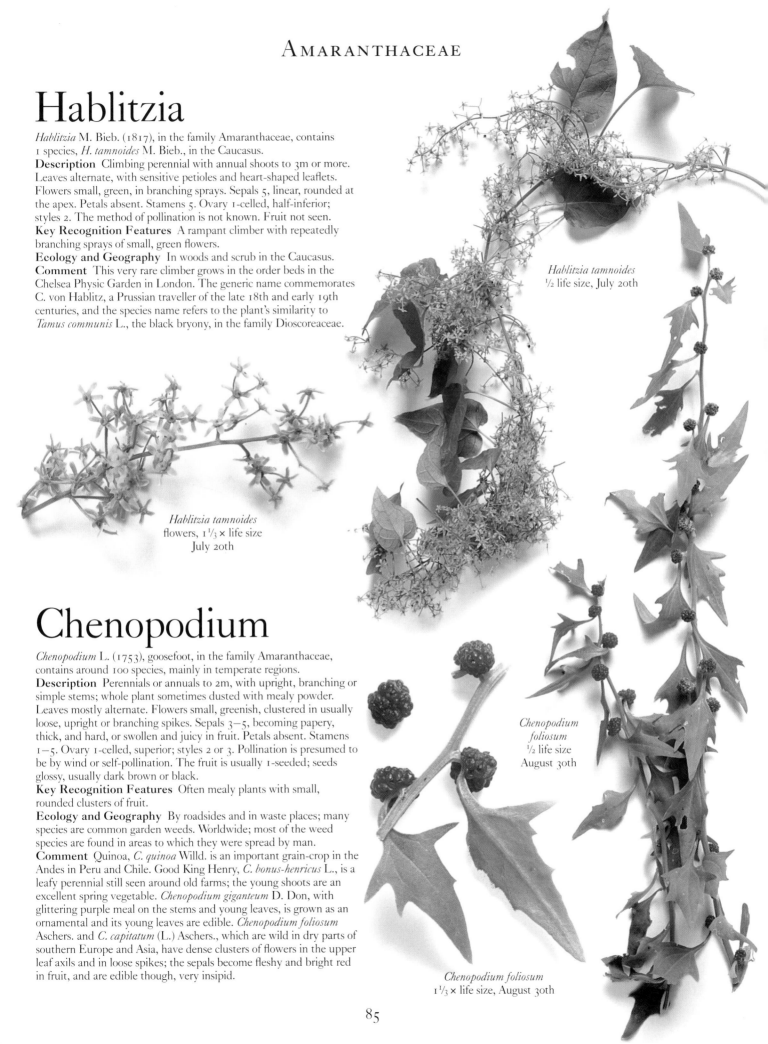

Hablitzia

Hablitzia M. Bieb. (1817), in the family Amaranthaceae, contains 1 species, *H. tamnoides* M. Bieb., in the Caucasus.

Description Climbing perennial with annual shoots to 3m or more. Leaves alternate, with sensitive petioles and heart-shaped leaflets. Flowers small, green, in branching sprays. Sepals 5, linear, rounded at the apex. Petals absent. Stamens 5. Ovary 1-celled, half-inferior; styles 2. The method of pollination is not known. Fruit not seen.

Key Recognition Features A rampant climber with repeatedly branching sprays of small, green flowers.

Ecology and Geography In woods and scrub in the Caucasus.

Comment This very rare climber grows in the order beds in the Chelsea Physic Garden in London. The generic name commemorates C. von Hablitz, a Prussian traveller of the late 18th and early 19th centuries, and the species name refers to the plant's similarity to *Tamus communis* L., the black bryony, in the family Dioscoreaceae.

Hablitzia tamnoides
½ life size, July 20th

Hablitzia tamnoides
flowers, 1⅓ × life size
July 20th

Chenopodium

Chenopodium L. (1753), goosefoot, in the family Amaranthaceae, contains around 100 species, mainly in temperate regions.

Description Perennials or annuals to 2m, with upright, branching or simple stems; whole plant sometimes dusted with mealy powder. Leaves mostly alternate. Flowers small, greenish, clustered in usually loose, upright or branching spikes. Sepals 3–5, becoming papery, thick, and hard, or swollen and juicy in fruit. Petals absent. Stamens 1–5. Ovary 1-celled, superior; styles 2 or 3. Pollination is presumed to be by wind or self-pollination. The fruit is usually 1-seeded; seeds glossy, usually dark brown or black.

Key Recognition Features Often mealy plants with small, rounded clusters of fruit.

Ecology and Geography By roadsides and in waste places; many species are common garden weeds. Worldwide; most of the weed species are found in areas to which they were spread by man.

Comment Quinoa, *C. quinoa* Willd. is an important grain-crop in the Andes in Peru and Chile. Good King Henry, *C. bonus-henricus* L., is a leafy perennial still seen around old farms; the young shoots are an excellent spring vegetable. *Chenopodium giganteum* D. Don, with glittering purple meal on the stems and young leaves, is grown as an ornamental and its young leaves are edible. *Chenopodium foliosum* Aschers. and *C. capitatum* (L.) Aschers., which are wild in dry parts of southern Europe and Asia, have dense clusters of flowers in the upper leaf axils and in loose spikes; the sepals become fleshy and bright red in fruit, and are edible though, very insipid.

*Chenopodium
foliosum*
½ life size
August 30th

Chenopodium foliosum
1⅓ × life size, August 30th

Lampranthus

Lampranthus N.E. Br. (1930), in the family Aizoaceae, contains around 216 species, mainly in southern Africa.

Description Succulent perennials or dwarf shrubs to 1m. Leaves opposite, cylindrical, semi-cylindrical, or 3-angled, without papillae. Flowers usually stalked, magenta, yellow, red, orange, or white. Sepals 5. Petals many, in 2 or 3 rows. Stamens many, erect to inward-leaning. Ovary 4- to 7-celled, more or less flat, inferior; stigmas 4–7. Pollination is by insects. The fruit is a capsule with 4–7 cells. Seeds pear-shaped, blackish.

Key Recognition Features Usually shrubby with internodes visible, and with stalked flowers.

Ecology and Geography Dry hills and rocks in Cape Province in South Africa; 1 species *L. tegens* (F.Muell.) N.E.Br. also in Australia.

Comment The family Aizoaceae, sometimes also called the Mesembryanthemaceae, contains around 128 genera and 1850 species, most of which are found in the Cape region of South Africa. They have succulent leaves and daisy-like flowers with shining petals that open in the sun. Many genera show extreme adaptations to aid survival in hot and dry conditions. The stone plants *Lithops* N.E. Br. and a few other genera have no leaves and cone-shaped stems with a slit across the middle, which remain underground except for a window on the top – quite literally a transparent, colourless area of the surface that lets in light. They live in otherwise bare areas of quartz and dark brown pebbles. *Lampranthus* is one of the genera most tolerant of temperate conditions, and can be grown outdoors in mild areas, surviving a few degrees of frost; *L. glaucus* (L.) N.E. Br. is naturalised along the coast in southern Europe. The most common genus outside South Africa is *Carpobrotus* N.E. Br. with coarse leaves, usually triangular in section, and large flowers with 10–16 cells. A few species are naturalised in both California and western Europe, forming spreading carpets on coastal rocks and sand. Their fruits are edible, known as hottentot fig or sour fig.

Dorotheanthus bellidiformis 'Magic Carpet' ⅔ life size August 30th

Lampranthus glaucus ⅔ life sizee, May 15th

Lampranthus glaucus flower parts, 1½ × life size, May 15th

Dorotheanthus bellidiformis 'Magic Carpet' just over life size August 30th

Dorotheanthus

Dorotheanthus Schwantes (1927), in the family Aizoaceae, contains around 5 species in South Africa. They are often included in the large genus *Mesembryanthemum* L..

Description Creeping or tufted annuals to 6cm. Leaves opposite or alternate, fleshy, flat or almost cylindrical, with a crystalline surface. Flowers usually short-stalked, magenta, yellow, red, orange, or white, generally solitary. Sepals 5, unequal. Petals many, in 2 rows. Stamens many, usually erect. Pollination is by insects. Ovary 5-celled, inferior, placentation parietal; stigmas 5. The fruit is a capsule with 5 cells. Seeds pear-shaped.

Key Recognition Features Annuals with shining, daisy-like flowers and leaves with crystalline cells.

Ecology and Geography On dry hills and rocks, often near the sea in South Africa and Namibia, mostly in the Western Cape.

Comment *Dorotheanthus bellidiformis* (Burm. fil.) N.E. Br. is the Livingstone daisy or iceplant, commonly cultivated in a wide range of colours. *Delosperma* N.E. Br. with around 140 species are dwarf shrubs or mat-forming perennials, with smooth, not glistening, fleshy leaves, mainly in the Cape. The flowers are smaller than *Dorotheanthus*, but in the same range of colours. The genus contains some of the hardiest members of the Aizoceae, which will survive frost and rain in winter; 1 or 2 species reach 2900m in the high Drakensberg; others are found in the Rift Valley and as far north as the Arabian Peninsula.

Opuntia

Opuntia Mill. (1754), in the family Cactaceae, contains around 200 species in North and South America.

Description Trees, shrubs, and spreading perennials to 7m. Leaves small and soon falling; stems jointed, flattened or cylindrical, with tufts of spines or glochids (small, stiff hairs which are easily detached and stick into the skin). Flowers usually without stalks, pinkish, yellow, red, orange, or white, with spines on the base. Sepals and petals numerous, not clearly differentiated. Stamens many. Ovary 1-celled, inferior; placentation parietal; style 1, with lobed stigmas. Pollination is by insects. The fruit is an often juicy capsule with a depression on the top. Seeds numerous, small.

Key Recognition Features Usually branching plants with flattened or cylindrical segments; the small leaves produced soon fall.

Ecology and Geography On dry hills and rocks, from British Colombia, Alberta, and Massachusetts to southern Argentina, and naturalised in other areas, including Bhutan and western China, the Canary Islands, Africa, and Australia, and *O. compressa* (Salisb.) Macbride, and 2 other species in dry valleys in Switzerland.

Comment The family Cactaceae is almost exclusively American, and is often dominant in dry areas. Only 1 species, the epiphytic *Rhipsalis baccifera* (Mill.) Stearn, occurs naturally in Africa, Madagascar, and Sri Lanka as well as South America. Many cacti can tolerate a few degrees of frost if dry; a few experience extreme cold in their natural habitat, usually combined with drought. Many species show extreme adaptations to aid survival in hot and dry conditions, and a few live mainly underground. The fleshy stems store water and have a thick, waxy cuticle. Their metabolism has altered so that the stomata can remain closed during the day, and open at night to take in carbon dioxide, which is then stored as malic acid and used for photosynthesis during daylight. *Opuntia* are among the hardiest of the genera, occurring high, to 3300m in the mountains of California and to 4000m in the Andes. Some of the larger species, such as *O. ficus-indica* (L.) Mill. are used for stockproof hedging in dry areas and for their edible fruit. *Opuntia cochenillifera* (L.) Mill. was grown as host for the cochineal insect, especially in the Canary Islands, and persists in many areas. *Opuntia bigelovii* Engelm., from the deserts of California, Nevada, and Arizona, is the jumping cholla; the cylindrical segments with their sharp, barbed spines detach themselves so easily that they appear to jump out at you.

Mammillaria bocasana
¾ life size, June 26th

Opuntia ammophila (above) life size June 26th

Mammillaria bocasana
1¼ × life size, June 26th

Delosperma nubigenum
¾ life size
June 6th

Delosperma nubigenum
flower and section
2 × life size, June 6th

Mammillaria

Mammillaria Haw. (1812), in the family Cactaceae, contains around 150 species in North and South America.

Description Low, spherical or clump-forming perennials to 20cm. Leaves absent; stems cylindrical, not jointed, with tufts of sometimes hooked spines, hairs, or glochids (small, stiff hairs which are easily detached and stick into the skin), on the tip of nipple-like tubercles, hence the name *Mammillaria*. Flowers without stalks, pinkish, yellow, red, orange, or white, produced between the tubercles, or on the tubercles at the base of a groove. Sepals and petals numerous, similar. Stamens many. Ovary 1-celled, inferior; placentation parietal; style 1, with lobed stigmas. Pollination is by insects. The fruit is an oblong or club-shaped, smooth, red berry, with numerous black or brown seeds.

Key Recognition Features Small cushion-forming cacti with tubercles topped by a rosette of hairs or spines.

Ecology and Geography On dry hills and rocks, often in very shallow soil. Most species originate in Mexico; a few are found in Arizona, California, the West Indies, and northern South America.

Comment *Mammillaria* are among the most popular of dwarf cacti, with over 70 species and many more named forms in cultivation, and surviving long periods of neglect; most flower freely in spring after a dry winter.

Portulaca

Portulaca L. (1753), in the family Portulacaceae, contains around 40 species, mainly in the tropics.

Description Usually prostrate annuals to 30cm across, with alternate or opposite, fleshy leaves. Flowers solitary on the ends of the branches. Sepals 2. Petals 6 or 7. Stamens 7 or more. Ovary 1-celled, half-inferior; styles 1, with 3–9 stigmas. Pollination is by insects, or in the case of *P. oleracea* L. by selfing. The fruit is a many-seeded capsule, the top splitting away from the persistent sepals.

Key Recognition Features Creeping plants with flat or cylindrical, fleshy leaves, and flowers with shining petals.

Ecology and Geography By roadsides and in rough, stony places. *P. oleracea* L. a worldwide weed and pot herb.

Comment The family Portulacaceae is very close to Cactaceae. Many genera are largely succulent, and are most diverse in the Americas, though with 1 genus in Europe (*Montia fontana* L., other *Montia* species having been reclassified as *Claytonia*) and 1 in Africa (*Anacampseros* L). Current interpretation of the parts of the flower in this family is that the 2 so-called sepals are originally bracteoles, that the coloured "petals" are sepals, and that true petals are absent; in the absence of petals, coloured sepals are often called tepals or perianth segments. *Portulaca grandiflora* Hook. from Brazil and Uruguay is a beautiful plant with flowers that open in hot sunlight; it is often grown as an annual, especially in the tropics.

Lewisia

Lewisia Pursh (1814), in the family Portulacaceae, contains around 20 species in western North America.

Description Perennials to 10cm, often with tuberous roots, with rosettes of fleshy leaves. Flowers solitary or many on branching stems, sometimes with pairs of bracts. Sepals usually 2. Petals 4–18, sometimes unequal, often shining, pink, white, or yellow. Stamens 5 or more. Ovary 1-celled, half-inferior; style 1, with 3–8 stigmas. Pollination is by various insects. The fruit is a many-seeded capsule, the top splitting away from the base and opening by 3–8 flaps. In some species the seeds have an aril and are spread by ants.

Key Recognition Features Rosette plants with flat or cylindrical, fleshy leaves, and flowers with many narrow, shining petals.

Ecology and Geography In stony places and rock crevices from British Columbia and Washington to California and Mexico.

Comment *Lewisia* commemorates Captain Merriweather Lewis (1774–1809). *Lewisia rediviva* Pursh, the bitterroot, after which Lewis named the Bitterroot mountains between Montana and Idaho in 1805, was first recorded during Lewis and Clark's expedition to cross North America to the Pacific. It was called *rediviva* because a dried plant from Lewis's herbarium was revived and grown successfully, and a specimen received at Kew was still able to grow after both boiling water treatment and being dry for 18 months. The Flathead tribes of the region ate the roots after soaking off the bitter bark. The most spectacular modern cultivars are hybrids between *L. cotyledon* (Wats.) Robinson and other species.

Portulaca oleracea
½ life size
September 29th

Lewisia tweedyi
just under life size
March 17th

Lewisia cotyledon
¾ life size,
March 17th

Portulaca grandiflora
flowers
¾ life size
August 10th

Lewisia cotyledon
½ life size, March 17th

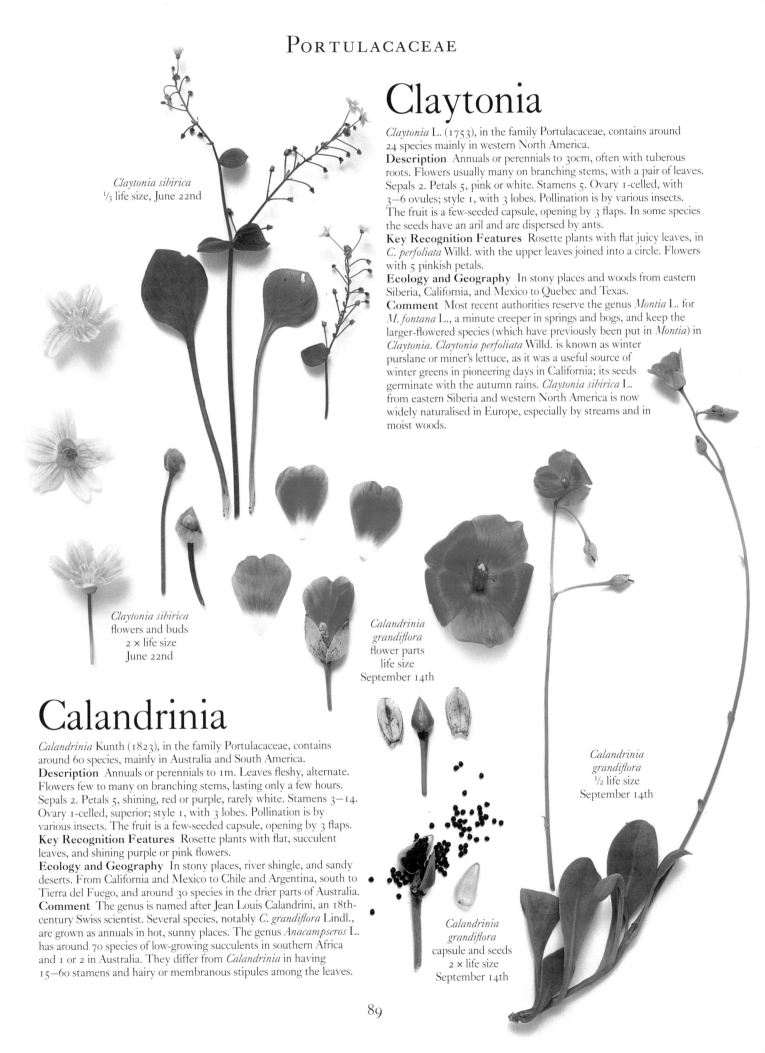

Claytonia

Claytonia L. (1753), in the family Portulacaceae, contains around 24 species mainly in western North America.

Description Annuals or perennials to 30cm, often with tuberous roots. Flowers usually many on branching stems, with a pair of leaves. Sepals 2. Petals 5, pink or white. Stamens 5. Ovary 1-celled, with 3–6 ovules; style 1, with 3 lobes. Pollination is by various insects. The fruit is a few-seeded capsule, opening by 3 flaps. In some species the seeds have an aril and are dispersed by ants.

Key Recognition Features Rosette plants with flat juicy leaves, in *C. perfoliata* Willd. with the upper leaves joined into a circle. Flowers with 5 pinkish petals.

Ecology and Geography In stony places and woods from eastern Siberia, California, and Mexico to Quebec and Texas.

Comment Most recent authorities reserve the genus *Montia* L. for *M. fontana* L., a minute creeper in springs and bogs, and keep the larger-flowered species (which have previously been put in *Montia*) in *Claytonia*. *Claytonia perfoliata* Willd. is known as winter purslane or miner's lettuce, as it was a useful source of winter greens in pioneering days in California; its seeds germinate with the autumn rains. *Claytonia sibirica* L. from eastern Siberia and western North America is now widely naturalised in Europe, especially by streams and in moist woods.

Claytonia sibirica
1/3 life size, June 22nd

Claytonia sibirica
flowers and buds
2 × life size
June 22nd

Calandrinia grandiflora
flower parts
life size
September 14th

Calandrinia grandiflora
1/2 life size
September 14th

Calandrinia grandiflora
capsule and seeds
2 × life size
September 14th

Calandrinia

Calandrinia Kunth (1823), in the family Portulacaceae, contains around 60 species, mainly in Australia and South America.

Description Annuals or perennials to 1m. Leaves fleshy, alternate. Flowers few to many on branching stems, lasting only a few hours. Sepals 2. Petals 5, shining, red or purple, rarely white. Stamens 3–14. Ovary 1-celled, superior; style 1, with 3 lobes. Pollination is by various insects. The fruit is a few-seeded capsule, opening by 3 flaps.

Key Recognition Features Rosette plants with flat, succulent leaves, and shining purple or pink flowers.

Ecology and Geography In stony places, river shingle, and sandy deserts. From California and Mexico to Chile and Argentina, south to Tierra del Fuego, and around 30 species in the drier parts of Australia.

Comment The genus is named after Jean Louis Calandrini, an 18th-century Swiss scientist. Several species, notably *C. grandiflora* Lindl., are grown as annuals in hot, sunny places. The genus *Anacampseros* L. has around 70 species of low-growing succulents in southern Africa and 1 or 2 in Australia. They differ from *Calandrinia* in having 15–60 stamens and hairy or membranous stipules among the leaves.

Persicaria

Persicaria Mill. (1754), in the family Polygonaceae, contains around 150 species worldwide.

Description Annuals or perennials to 2m; stems with ocrae (or ochreae), thin sheaths often ending in wispy threads. Leaves alternate, simple. Flowers small, usually many on branching stems or in dense spikes. Sepals and petals 5, red, pink, white, or green. Stamens 5–8. Ovary 1-celled, superior, with 2 or 3 stigmas. Pollination is by various insects. The fruit is a 1-seeded, triangular nutlet, surrounded by the persistent remains of the sepals and petals.

Key Recognition Features Soft perennials with usually triangular or ovate leaves and small, pinkish flowers.

Ecology and Geography In moist meadows, on mountain slopes and rocks, and in open woods; many species are annual weeds of damp fields and bare ground. A few, such as *P. amphibia* (L.) Gray, are aquatic, with floating leaves and emerging flower spikes at high water; upright with narrow leaves when the water has dried in summer. Most of the ornamental species originate in the mountains of Europe or the Himalayas.

Comment The genus *Polygonum* L. is now restricted to the weed knotgrass, *Polygonum aviculare* L., the related *Polygonum maritimum* L., and a few other species. *Persicaria* contains most of the ornamental herbaceous species, many of which may also be found in the genus *Bistorta* Adans. In the alpine *Persicaria vivipara* (L.) Ronse Decr., many of the flowers are replaced by bulbils. The genus *Eriogonum* Mich. contains around 150 species, mainly in western North America. Some species are grown in rock gardens, and often have showy masses of yellow or reddish flowers. Modern work, backed up by DNA studies, suggests that the order Polygonales is close to Caryophyllales, and covers the familiies Polygonaceae, Plumbaginaceae (see pp.94–96), Droseraceae (see p.97), and the tropical carnivorous family Nepenthaceae.

Fallopia

Fallopia Adans. (1763), in the family Polygonaceae, contains around 8 species in eastern Europe and Asia.

Description Annuals or large perennials to 3m or more; stems with ocrae (or ochreae), thin sheaths often ending in wispy threads. Leaves alternate, usually heart shaped. Flowers small, often effectively unisexual, usually many on branching stems or in dense spikes. Sepals and petals 5, red, pink, white, or green, the outer 3 larger, with keels or wings. Stamens 8. Pollination is by various insects or perhaps by wind. Ovary 1-celled, superior, with 3 styles and capitate or divided stigmas. The fruit is 1-seeded triangular nutlet, surrounded by the persistent and enlarged remains of the sepals and petals.

Key Recognition Features Very tall, robust perennials or climbers with stalked, usually sagittate leaves and small, pink, white, or green flowers and 3-angled nutlets.

Ecology and Geography In open woods and on mountain slopes; the large, herbaceous species in Japan and eastern Asia, and the climbing species in central Asia and westwards to Europe.

Comment *Fallopia* is often included in *Polygonum*, or divided between other genera, but is at present recognised as a genus which includes the mainly climbing plants sometimes put in *Bilderdykia* and the giant, invasive, herbaceous perennials also found under *Reynoutria*, including that potent pest, Japanese knotweed, *F. japonica* (Houtt.). Hybrids between *F. japonica* and the even larger *F. sachalinensis* (F. Schmidt ex Maxim.) Ronse Decr. are frequent in Britain. *Fallopia convolvulus* (L.) A. Löve is a common weed in gardens and cornfields.

Persicaria mollis
⅓ life size
September 16th

Persicaria campanulata
flowers, 1⅓ × life size
September 24th

Persicaria campanulata
⅓ life size
September 24th

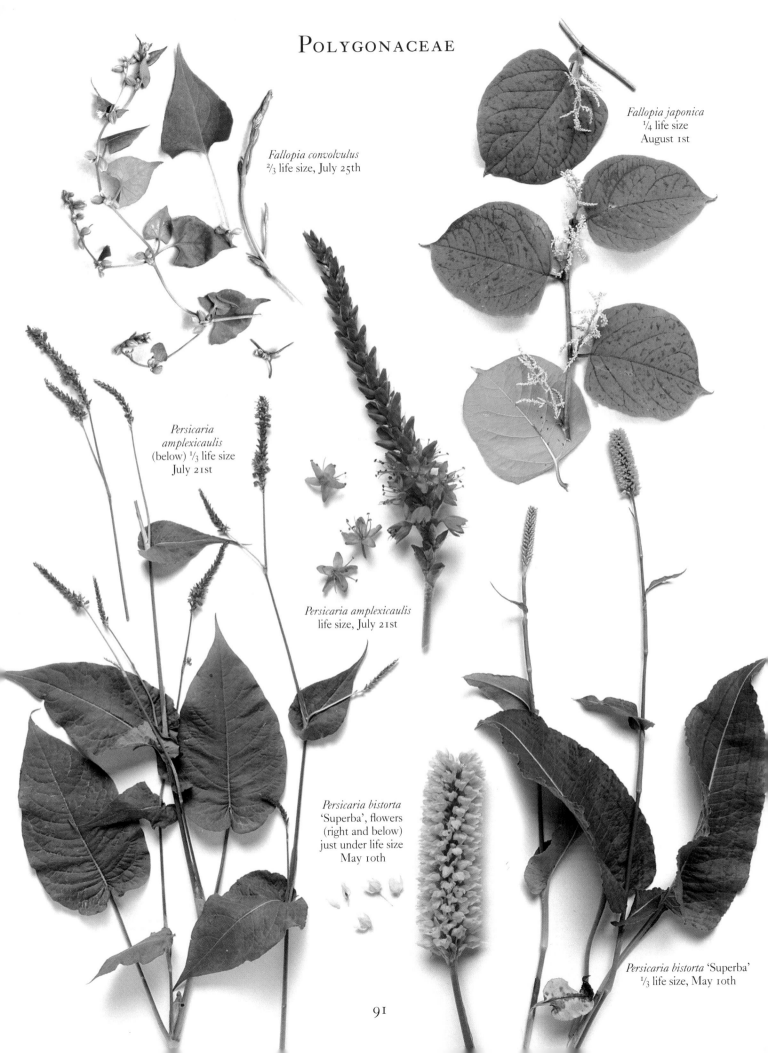

Fallopia convolvulus
⅔ life size, July 25th

Fallopia japonica
¼ life size
August 1st

Persicaria
amplexicaulis
(below) ⅓ life size
July 21st

Persicaria amplexicaulis
life size, July 21st

Persicaria bistorta
'Superba', flowers
(right and below)
just under life size
May 10th

Persicaria bistorta 'Superba'
⅓ life size, May 10th

Fagopyrum

Fagopyrum Mill. (1754), buckwheat, in the family Polygonaceae, contains around 8 species in eastern Asia and Africa.

Description Annuals or perennials to 2m; stems with ocrae (or ochreae), thin sheaths often ending in wispy threads. Leaves alternate, sagittate. Flowers small, usually many, on branching stems. Sepals and petals 5, pink, white, or green, not enlarging in fruit. Stamens 8. Ovary 1-celled, superior, with 3 stigmas. Pollination is by various insects. The fruit is a 1-seeded triangular nutlet, longer than the remains of the sepals and petals.

Key Recognition Features Tall plants with stalked, sagittate leaves and small, pink, white, or green flowers and nutlets 5–8mm long.

Ecology and Geography In mountain meadows and on bare ground as a weed, or as a crop. All the species probably originated in the mountains of Asia.

Comment *Fagopyrum esculentum* Moench. is the buckwheat, long a popular grain from the Ukraine to China, and nowadays in parts of North America. It has a long history of cultivation and is not known as a wild plant, though it probably originated from *F. dibotrys* (D. Don) H. Hara, a tall perennial from eastern Asia, which is sometimes grown in gardens.

Rumex

Rumex L. (1753), docks and sorrels, in the family Polygonaceae, contains around 200 species mainly the northern hemisphere.

Description Perennials to 2m, and usually with deep roots; stems with loose ocrae (or ochreae), thin sheaths often ending in wispy threads. Leaves alternate, with a small blade, triangular, round, or narrow. Flowers small, many, on branching stems, sometimes unisexual. Sepals and petals 6, in 2 whorls of 3, green or pinkish, enlarging in fruit. Stamens 6. Ovary 1-celled, superior, with 3 feathery stigmas. Pollination is by wind. The fruit is a 1-seeded, 3-angled nutlet, enclosed by the inner whorl which becomes enlarged, papery and often toothed or spiny on the margins.

Key Recognition Features The small, pink or green flowers and the seeds with 3 enlarged sepals.

Ecology and Geography In rough ground, meadows, and coastal shingle or by rivers. Most species in Europe and Asia, a few in temperate parts of the southern hemisphere.

Comment *Rumex acetosa* L., sorrel or sour dock, and its cultivated equivalent, *R. rugosus* Campdera, may be used as vegetables, as may *R. scutatus* L. with bluish leaves, called French or buckler leaf sorrel. Most other species are persistent weeds. *Rumex crispus* L. a common weed, can be used for treatment of arthritis and as a laxative. *Rumex pseudoalpinus* Hoefft, usually called *R. alpinus* L. (a muddled species) is often found by old farms in Scotland and northern Europe; its leaves are edible and said to have been used for wrapping butter.

Fagopyrum dibotrys
life size, July 28th

Rumex scutatus
½ life size, July 5th

Fagopyrum esculentum
½ life size, July 14th

Fagopyrum esculentum
flowers, 2½ × life size
July 14th

Fagopyrum esculentum
young fruits, 2½ × life size, July 14th

Rumex acetosa
young fruit
1¹/₂ × life size
July 5th

Rumex scutatus
flowers (right)
1¹/₄ × life size
July 5th

Rumex acetosa
¹/₃ life size
July 5th

Rheum × hybridum
flowers, (right)
1¹/₄ × life size, May 8th

Rheum × hybridum
ripe fruit, ³/₄ life size, July 20th

Rheum

Rheum L. (1753), rhubarb, in the family Polygonaceae, contains around 50 species, mainly in Asia.

Description Stout perennials to 3m, and usually with a thick rootstock; stems with loose ocrae (or ochreae), thin sheaths, often ending in wispy threads. Leaves mostly basal, with a triangular or round blade and thick, edible stalk. Flowers small, many on usually tall, branching stems. Sepals and petals 6, pink, white, or green, not enlarging in fruit. Stamens 9. Ovary 1-celled, superior, with 3 stigmas. Pollination is mostly by wind. The fruit is a 1-seeded, 3-winged nutlet, longer than the remains of the sepals and petals.

Key Recognition Features Usually tall, stout plants with wide leaves and masses of small, pink, white, or green flowers.

Ecology and Geography In mountain meadows and rocky places. One species, *R. tartaricum* L. fil. extends westwards to European Russia, the rest are found across Asia to China.

Comment The vegetable rhubarb, *Rheum × hybridum*, is a complex hybrid involving *R. rhabarbum* L. from Mongolia and other species. It was a particularly valuable crop as it could be forced to give fresh, fruit-like shoots in late winter. The leaves, though generally considered poisonous because of the oxalic acid they contain, were used as a pot herb in Elizabethan times, and later to adulterate tobacco. A few species are grown as ornamentals, notably red-leaved forms of *R. palmatum* L. from northwestern China. *Rheum ribes* L. from Turkey and central Asia, grows in dry gorges; the prickly young leaf stalks are collected and eaten by the locals; the dry leaves become stiff in summer and rattle as they blow around the rocks. *Rheum nobile* Hook. & Thoms. from around 4000m in eastern Nepal, Sikkim, and Bhutan, has a single tall stem with the flowers protected from the monsoon by wide, white, overlapping, translucent bracts. The dried roots of *R. officinale* Baillon, from western China and Tibet, were an important article of trade first brought to Europe by Marco Polo, used medicinally as a purgative.

Rheum × hybridum
'Early Victoria' (right),
'Stockbridge Cropper' (below)
and 'The Sutton' (below right)
¹/₄ life size, April 10th

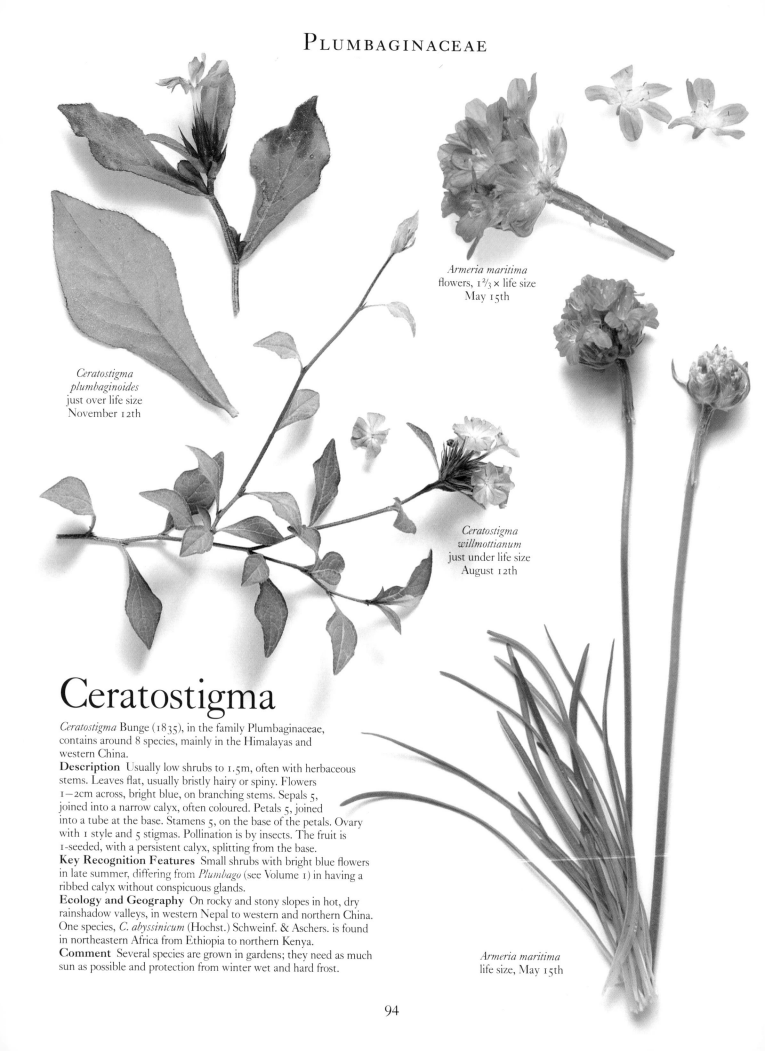

Ceratostigma
plumbaginoides
just over life size
November 12th

Armeria maritima
flowers, 1⅔ × life size
May 15th

Ceratostigma
willmottianum
just under life size
August 12th

Ceratostigma

Ceratostigma Bunge (1835), in the family Plumbaginaceae, contains around 8 species, mainly in the Himalayas and western China.

Description Usually low shrubs to 1.5m, often with herbaceous stems. Leaves flat, usually bristly hairy or spiny. Flowers 1—2cm across, bright blue, on branching stems. Sepals 5, joined into a narrow calyx, often coloured. Petals 5, joined into a tube at the base. Stamens 5, on the base of the petals. Ovary with 1 style and 5 stigmas. Pollination is by insects. The fruit is 1-seeded, with a persistent calyx, splitting from the base.

Key Recognition Features Small shrubs with bright blue flowers in late summer, differing from *Plumbago* (see Volume 1) in having a ribbed calyx without conspicuous glands.

Ecology and Geography On rocky and stony slopes in hot, dry rainshadow valleys, in western Nepal to western and northern China. One species, *C. abyssinicum* (Hochst.) Schweinf. & Aschers. is found in northeastern Africa from Ethiopia to northern Kenya.

Comment Several species are grown in gardens; they need as much sun as possible and protection from winter wet and hard frost.

Armeria maritima
life size, May 15th

Armeria

Armeria Willd. (1809), thrift or sea pink, in the family Plumbaginaceae, contains around 80 species, mainly in southern Europe.

Description Soft or spiny, cushion-forming shrubs or perennials. Leaves narrow, usually soft. Flowers usually small, around 1cm across, in spikelets packed in dense, rounded heads, on simple, leafless stems. Sepals 5, joined into a papery, 5-nerved calyx. Petals 5, white, pink, or reddish. Stamens 5, on the base of the petals. Ovary with 5 styles and feathery stigmas. Pollination is by insects, often butterflies. The fruit is indehiscent, 1-seeded, with the persistent, papery calyx.

Key Recognition Features The often tight clumps of soft leaves and the tight, rounded heads of flowers.

Ecology and Geography In rocks and shingle near the sea, in grassy steppes and high in the mountains; most species (54) in Spain and Portugal, others across Europe. The common thrift, *A. maritima* Willd., is found in Europe, North America from Newfoundland to California, and South America southwards to Tierra del Fuego.

Comment A few species are grown in gardens, but the plants are often a conspicuous and beautiful feature of cliffs along the northwestern coasts of Europe.

Acantholimon

Acantholimon Boiss. (1846), in the family Plumbaginaceae, contains around 120 species, mainly in southwestern Asia.

Description Usually spiny, cushion-forming, shrubby perennials. Leaves narrow, stiff, spine-tipped and crowded. Flowers usually small, around 1cm across, on simple elongating or branching stems, subtended by 3-pointed bracts. Sepals 5, joined into a papery, 5-nerved calyx, which enlarges in fruit. Petals 5, white or pinkish. Stamens 5. Ovary with 5 styles and capitate stigmas. Pollination is by insects. The fruit is indehiscent, 1-seeded, with the persistent, papery calyx acting as a parachute.

Key Recognition Features The clumps of prickly leaves and the papery calyx enlarging in fruit.

Ecology and Geography On dry mountain steppes and rocky areas. Together with spiny *Astragalus* L. and *Minuartia* L., it is often a major constituent species of the hedgehog steppe, dominated by prickly cushion plants, found in Mediterranean mountains in North Africa, Turkey, the eastern Mediterranean region, Iran, and central Asia.

Comment The family Plumbaginaceae includes the pale blue South African *Plumbago auriculata* (see Volume 1) as well as *Limonium* (see p.96), the familiar sea lavender. DNA studies confirm the position of the family within the Polygonales, although in the past it was often associated with Primulaceae (see pp.198–205). A few species of *Acantholimon* are grown in gardens, on walls or in dry rock gardens, but in wet areas they need to be grown in greenhouses where they can be kept dry in both winter and summer.

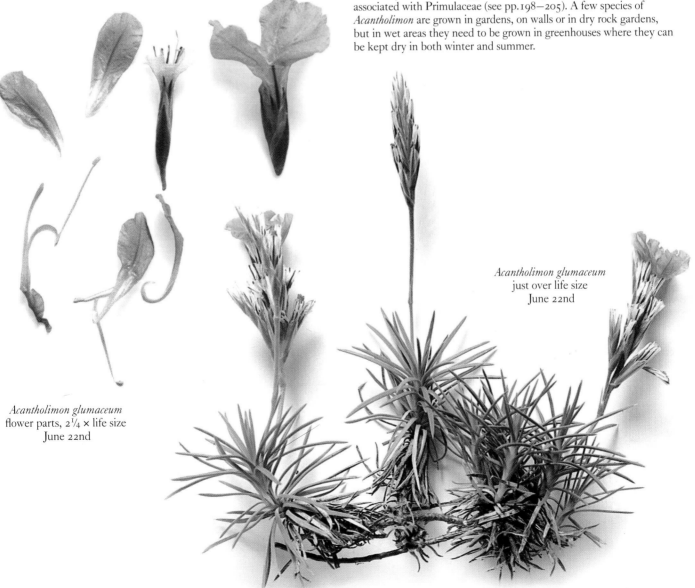

Acantholimon glumaceum
just over life size
June 22nd

Acantholimon glumaceum
flower parts, 2¼ × life size
June 22nd

Limonium binervosum
¾ life size
July 29th

Limonium sinuatum
⅓ life size, July 15th

Limonium sinuatum
flowers and stem section
1½ × life size, August 30th

Limonium

Limonium Mill. (1768), sea lavender or statice, in the family Plumbaginaceae, contains around 300 species, mainly in temperate regions of the world.

Description Usually herbaceous perennials, but a few annuals or low shrubs to 1m. Stems sometimes winged. Leaves flat, usually leathery. Flowers usually small, less than 1cm across, in 1- to 5-flowered spikelets on branching stems. Sepals 5, joined into a papery, 5-nerved calyx, often coloured. Petals 5, bluish, white, pink, or yellow. Stamens 5, on the base of the petals. Ovary with 5 styles and thin, thread-like stigmas. Pollination is by insects. The fruit is indehiscent, 1-seeded, with the persistent, papery calyx.

Key Recognition Features The branching, wiry or winged stalks, and spikelets of few flowers with a papery calyx. *Goniolimon* Boiss. differs in its knob-like stigmas and spikelets with pointed tips to the bracts.

Ecology and Geography Rocky areas and mud flats near the sea, and sandy and salty areas inland. Found from western Europe and the Canaries across Asia to northern China, and on the coasts of Japan, eastern and western North America, and South America.

Comment The common name statice was the name given by Linnaeus. Florist's statice, from the Mediterranean coasts, is now *L. sinuatum* (L.) Mill. It was originally blue, but is now grown in many colours; the calyx retains its colour when dry. *Limonium latifolium* (J. E. Smith) Kuntze, from eastern Europe, is a popular plant for sunny herbaceous borders. The dried flowers of *L. vulgare* Mill., a common salt-marsh species, were sold by gypsies on the streets of Cambridge as "lucky white heather". There are many very similar species of rock sea lavender, *L. binervosum* agg., of very restricted distribution on sea cliffs around the coasts of western Europe; most are apomictic, producing seed without normal fertilisation, so that small differences become stabilised, and specialists can recognise the different microspecies.

Goniolimon tataricum
flower parts
2 × life size
July 21st

Goniolimon tataricum
½ life size, July 21st

Drosera

Drosera L. (1753), sundew, in the family Droseraceae, contains around 100 species, mainly in Australia, with a few through Asia, Africa, and Europe.

Description Carnivorous perennials to 15cm, rarely annuals, trapping small insects on sticky hairs. Leaves in a basal rosette or alternate up the stem, with a small, rounded or narrow, often forked blade, uncoiling as they grow. Flowers usually small, around 1cm across, solitary to many on branching stems, lasting only 1 day. Sepals 4 or 5. Petals 4 or 5, white, red, or pinkish. Stamens 4 or 5. Ovary with 3 or 5 styles, variously branched. Pollination is by insects. The fruit is a capsule with very small seeds, dust-like or to 1mm.

Key Recognition Features The coiling leaves, covered on the upper side with long hairs with a sticky dew-like drop on the tip.

Ecology and Geography In bogs and wet, sandy places, often in shallow water. There are around 100 species in Australia, mainly in Western Australia; 3are also found in Europe, 18 in South Africa, and others in New Zealand and around the tropics.

Comment Sundews entrap insects, which are caught on the sticky hairs. The leaf then coils over the insect and slowly digests it with shorter, glandular hairs near the centre of the leaf. The hairs usually move slowly, but in *D. burmannii* Vahl they move very fast. The largest flowers, to 5cm across, are found in the South African *D. cistiflora* L., in which colour varies from pink and purple to white and yellow or scarlet, often with a black centre. *Drosera indica* L., which is common in tropical Africa, Asia, and Australia, is an annual with threadlike stems to 30cm and small, round, stalked leaves. The family Droseraceae contains 4 genera: *Drosera*, *Drosophyllum* Link, the minute aquatic *Aldovandra vesiculosa* L., and the Venus' fly trap, *Dionaea muscipula* Ellis, a native of pine barrens in eastern North America. *Drosophyllum lusitanicum* (L.) Link is found only in wet sunny places in southwestern Spain, Portugal, and northern Morocco. It is an almost shrubby perennial to 30cm tall with long, narrow, sticky leaves, yellow flowers 4cm across, and pear-shaped seeds around 2mm long.

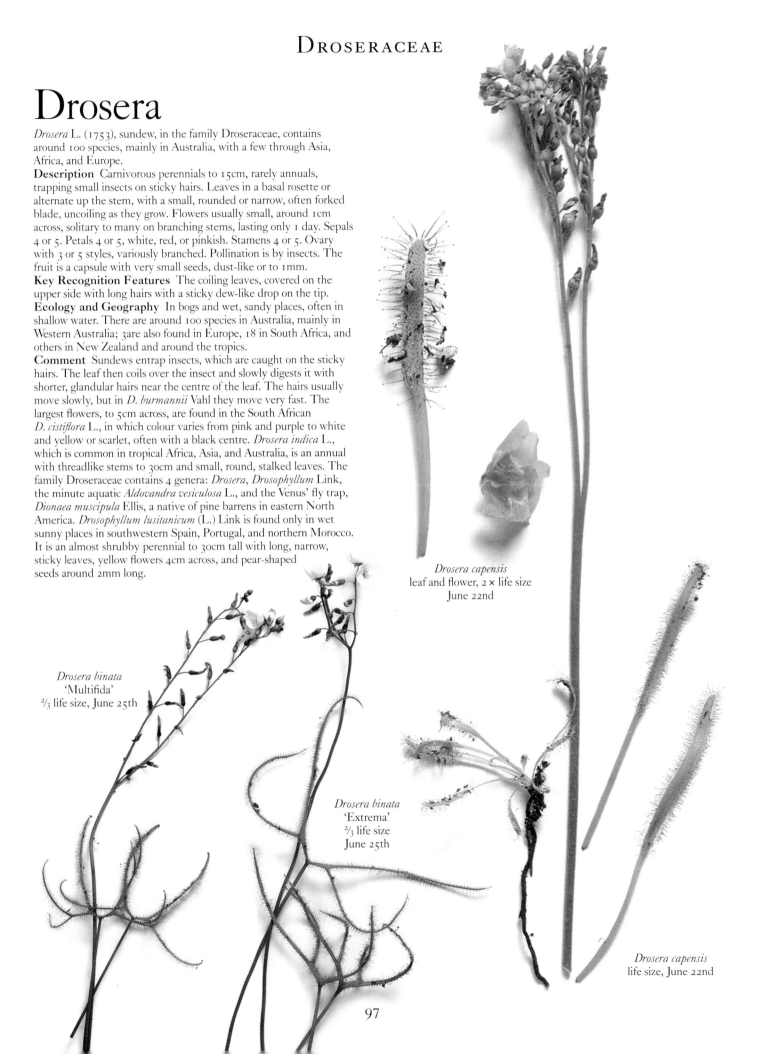

Drosera capensis
leaf and flower, 2 × life size
June 22nd

Drosera binata
'Multifida'
2/3 life size, June 25th

Drosera binata
'Extrema'
2/3 life size
June 25th

Drosera capensis
life size, June 22nd

Saxifraga

Saxifraga L. (1753), in the family Saxifragaceae, contains around 440 species throughout the world but mostly in northern temperate areas.

Description Small to medium-sized annuals or perennials to 30cm. Leaves often in a rosette, rather leathery, and with encrustations of calcium. Flowers to 4cm across, white, pink, yellow, or red. Sepals 5. Petals 5, not joined at the base. Stamens usually 10, rarely 8. Ovary superior to mostly inferior, of 2 carpels, each with 1 style. Pollination is by insects. The fruit is a many-seeded, pointed, 2-lobed capsule. Seeds usually very small.

Key Recognition Features Plants with simple, 5-petalled flowers with 2 stigmas, and a rosette of short-stalked leaves.

Ecology and Geography On rocks and cliffs and in meadows, mainly in the mountains. Around 125 species in Europe, others principally in Asia, North America, along the Andes, and as far south as Thailand and Ethiopia.

Comment Many species are popular garden plants in northern Europe. The genus is very diverse, and has been divided into 15 sections, based mainly on differences in flowers and fruits. Familiar examples of the different sections include London pride, *S. × urbium* D.A. Webb, in Section Gymnopera, a group with relatively large leaves and small flowers; mossy saxifrages, such as *S. × shraderi* Sternberg, in Section Ceratophyllae; meadow saxifrage *S. granulata* L. in Section Saxifraga; and the dwarf, silvery rock-garden species and alpine cushions with leaves encrusted with lime, also called the kabshias, such as *S.* 'Boston Spa', in Section Porphyrion. In the light of DNA studies, the order Saxifragales has been redefined, and is now considered to include the following, mainly woody families (for all see Volume 1); Cercidiphyllaceae, Altingiaceae, Hamamelidaceae, Iteaceae, Daphniphyllaceae, and Grossulariaceae. Among herbaceous plants the largest family to be incorporated in Saxifragales is the Crassulaceae; the Paeoniaceae (see pp.58–59) may also belong here, although it has until now been placed with the Ranunculaceae (see pp.38–58) or Dillenaceae. The shrubby genera *Philadelphus, Deutzia,* and *Hydrangea,* formerly considered part of Saxifragaceae, are now thought close to Cornaceae (for all see Volume 1), and *Parnassia* L. is now considered close to *Celastrus*.

Saxifraga rotundifolia
flowers (above) and capsules
(below) 2 × life size
June 12th

Saxifraga × urbium
½ life size, May 17th

Saxifraga fortunei
life size, November 6th

Saxifragaceae

Saxifraga
'Phoenix'
just over life size
March 17th

Saxifraga × *schraderi*
²⁄₃ life size, June 22nd

Saxifraga cymbalaria
subsp. *cymbalaria*
3 × life size, June 12th

Saxifraga cymbalaria
subsp. *huetiana*
(left) ²⁄₃ life size
.June 12th

Saxifraga cymbalaria
subsp. *cymbalaria*
²⁄₃ life size, June 12th

Saxifraga 'Boston Spa' (left)
1¼ × life size, March 17th

Darmera

Darmera Voss (1899), in the family Saxifragaceae, contains 1 species, *D. peltata* (Torr.) Voss, formerly called *Peltiphyllum peltatum* (Torr.) Engler, in western North America.

Description Large perennial to 1.5m, with long, spreading rhizomes. Leaves deciduous, long-stalked, peltate, to 40cm across. Flowers 9–14mm across, pink or white, in large, dense heads, produced before the leaves. Sepals 5, joined at the base. Petals 5, not joined at the base. Stamens 10. Ovary partly inferior, of 2 carpels, each with 1 style. Pollination is by insects. The fruit is a purplish, many-seeded, 2-lobed capsule. Seeds very small.

Key Recognition Features A large plant with long-stalked, round leaves with a 9- to 15-lobed margin.

Ecology and Geography In marshes and by mountain streams in the forest, from British Columbia to northern California.

Comment Commonly found in large gardens, and often becoming more or less wild in suitable places, covering large areas with its round leaves. Very closely related to *Saxifraga* (see pp.98–99).

Bergenia

Bergenia Moench (1794), in the family Saxifragaceae, contains around 9 species, mainly in the Himalayas and western China.

Description Large perennials to 50cm, with shortly spreading rhizomes. Leaves evergreen, short-stalked, broadly oval to round, to 20cm across. Flowers to 3cm across, purplish-red, pink, or white, in large, branching heads, produced before the new leaves. Sepals 5, joined at the base. Petals 5, not joined at the base. Stamens 10. Ovary mostly inferior, of 2 carpels, each with 1 style. Pollination is by insects. The fruit is a many-seeded, 2-lobed capsule.

Key Recognition Features Large, clump-forming plants with long-stalked, round, floppy leaves and masses of flowers in early spring.

Ecology and Geography On wet rocky areas and cliffs, in Siberia and in the Himalayas from Afghanistan and Kashmir eastwards to Yunnan and Sichuan.

Comment Commonly grown in gardens, where many hybrids have been raised. The plants are very tolerant, thriving both in cold climates and in shade in Mediterranean areas. The genus is named after Carl von Bergen (1704–59), author of *Flora Francofurtana* (1750).

Darmera peltata
½ life size, May 10th

Darmera peltata, flowers
just under life size, May 10th

Saxifragaceae

Bergenia purpurascens
var. *delavayi*, flower parts
2 × life size, May 8th

Bergenia purpurascens
var. *delavayi*
½ life size, May 8th

Bergenia 'Brahms'
(left) ½ life size
April 28th

Bergenia 'Ballawley'
½ life size, April 3rd

Bergenia 'Ballawley'
2 × life size, April 3rd

Boykinia

Boykinia Nutt. (1834), in the family Saxifragaceae, contains around 9 species in North America and Japan.

Description Small, tufted perennials to 30cm. Leaves evergreen, short-stalked, more or less round, lobed and toothed, to 15cm across. Flowers small, white or yellowish. Sepals 5, joined to form a rounded calyx with 5 teeth. Petals 5, not joined at the base. Stamens 5. Ovary inferior, of 2 fused carpels, each with 1 style. Pollination is by insects. The fruit is a many-seeded, rounded capsule.

Key Recognition Features Small, clump-forming plants with short-stalked leaves and branched sprays of small flowers.

Ecology and Geography Woods and damp places in the mountains; 3 species in California, 1 in Japan, the rest in eastern North America.

Comment *Boykinia aconitifolia* Nutt. is often grown in gardens in Europe; it is found wild from Virginia to Georgia. *Sullivantia* Torr. & Gray, with around 4 species in central North America, differs from *Boykinia* mainly in having persistent petals. *Lithophragma* Nutt., the woodland-star, with around 12 species in western North America, is closely related; it has flowers with unequal, toothed or divided petals, 3- to 5-lobed leaves, and bulbils along the rhizomes which become dormant in summer.

Peltoboykinia

Peltoboykinia Hara (1937), in the family Saxifragaceae, contains 2 species in Japan.

Description Medium-sized perennials to 50cm, with short rhizomes. Leaves deciduous, long-stalked, broadly oval to round, 7- to 13-lobed or deeply divided, to 25cm across. Flowers to 1cm across, creamy-white or yellowish, in branching heads. Sepals 5, joined at the base to form a tube. Petals 5, not joined at the base, 8–12mm long, toothed and glandular. Stamens 10. Ovary mostly superior, of 2 nearly fused carpels, each with 1 style. Pollination is by insects. The fruit is a many-seeded, 2-lobed capsule, enclosed in a somewhat enlarged calyx.

Key Recognition Features Plants with long-stalked, lobed, and fleshy leaves and greenish-yellow flowers with toothed petals in summer.

Ecology and Geography In woods in the mountains in central and southern Japan.

Comment Both species of *Peltoboykinia* are sometimes grown in gardens. *Mukdenia* Koidz. syn. *Aceriphyllum* Engelm., with 2 species, including *M. rossii* (Oliv.) Koidz. in Korea and northeastern China, has deeply divided leaves and flowers with pointed white petals shorter than the sepals.

Boykinia occidentalis flowers and fruit 1⅔ × life size August 10th

Boykinia occidentalis ¾ life size August 10th

Peltoboykinia watanabei fruit, 1¾ × life size August 10th

Peltoboykinia watanabei ⅓ life size, August 10th

Chrysosplenium

Chrysosplenium L. (1753), the golden saxifrage, in the family Saxifragaceae, contains around 60 species, mainly in the northern hemisphere.

Description Low, mat-forming perennials to 10cm. Leaves evergreen, almost round, opposite or alternate, stalked, sometimes with shallow lobes. Upper leaves yellowish. Flowers to 4mm across, yellow, greenish, or white, in flat-topped heads. Sepals 4, joined at the base. Petals absent. Stamens usually 8, sometimes 4. Pollination is by small insects. Ovary mostly inferior, with 1 carpel and 2 short styles. The fruit is a many-seeded capsule, splitting into 2 sections. Seeds dispersed by raindrops.

Key Recognition Features Small, creeping plants with bright yellow-green upper leaves and small flowers, giving the effect of a dwarf spurge or *Euphorbia* (see pp.116–17).

Ecology and Geography In wet places by streams and in mossy woods. Mainly in China and Japan, but with several species in Europe and a few in North and South America.

Comment The common European *C. oppositifolium* L. is one of the first wild flowers to open in spring. The more showy Chinese *C. davidianum* Maxim., with hairy leaves, is sometimes cultivated.

Mitella

Mitella L. (1753), in the family Saxifragaceae, contains around 20 species in North America and northern Asia.

Description Low, clump-forming perennials to 20cm, sometimes with creeping rhizomes. Leaves evergreen, mostly rounded, and sometimes with shallow lobes. Flowers small, green or white, in spikes on leafless, slender stalks. Sepals 5, joined at the base. Petals absent or 5, slender and deeply divided, with 3–9 narrow, thread-like lobes. Stamens 5 or 10, short. Ovary superior or partly inferior, with 1 carpel and 2 short styles. Pollination is by small insects. The fruit is a many-seeded capsule, splitting into 2 sections at the top, like a bishop's mitre. Seeds minute.

Key Recognition Features Plants forming clumps or mats of dark green leaves, with spikes of minute, green flowers.

Ecology and Geography In moist woods and wet places, with 6 species in California, 13 in Japan, and the others scattered in eastern North America and in eastern Asia southwards as far as Taiwan.

Comment Various species are occasionally grown for their decorative leaves.

Chrysosplenium oppositifolium
flowers, 1½ × life size
May 31st

Mitella breweri
flowers, 3¼ × life size
May 3rd

Mitella breweri
1½ × life size, May 3rd

Chrysosplenium oppositifolium
life size, May 31st

Astilbe

Astilbe L. (1753), in the family Saxifragaceae, contains around 14 species in eastern Asia and North America.

Description Usually large, clump-forming perennials to 1.5m, sometimes with stolons. Leaves deciduous, ternate, and usually further divided into many toothed and sometimes 3-lobed leaflets. Flowers small, white, pink, or purplish-red, in spikes or pyramidal, branching heads. Sepals 4 or 5, joined at the base into a short calyx. Petals 4 or 5, small and narrow, rarely absent. Stamens 5 or 10. Ovary superior, with 2 or 3 carpels fused at the base and 2 or 3 styles. Pollination is by small insects. The fruit is a many-seeded capsule. Seeds often minutely spiny.

Key Recognition Features Plants forming clumps of divided leaves, with loose, pyramidal heads of very small flowers.

Ecology and Geography In moist woods and damp places, with 12 species in the Himalayas to China and Japan and 2 species in eastern North America in the Appalachians.

Comment Many species and hybrids are grown in bog gardens and by streams. *Aruncus* L. in the Rosaceae is superficially very similar to *Astilbe biternata* (Vent.) Britton, from eastern North America.

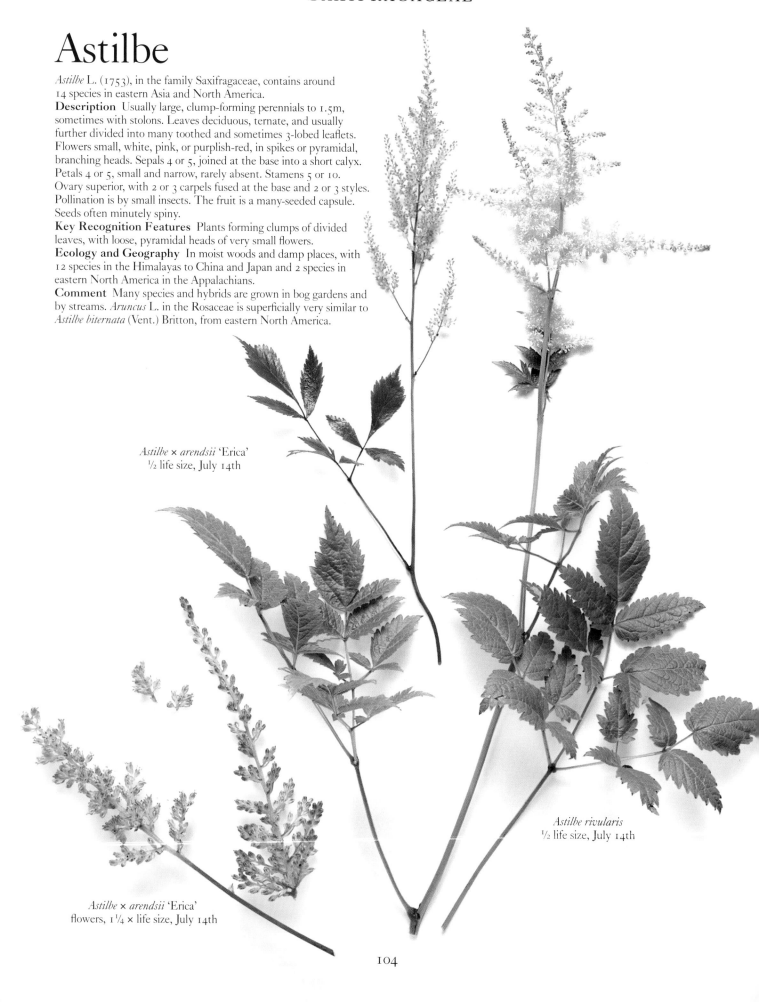

Astilbe × *arendsii* 'Erica'
½ life size, July 14th

Astilbe rivularis
½ life size, July 14th

Astilbe × *arendsii* 'Erica'
flowers, 1¼ × life size, July 14th

Rodgersia

Rodgersia A. Gray (1858), in the family Saxifragaceae, contains around 6 species in eastern Asia.

Description Usually large, clump-forming perennials to 1m, with spreading rhizomes. Leaves mainly basal, deciduous, divided into 5–10 narrow, toothed, veined leaflets. Flowers small, in branching heads. Sepals 5, joined at the base into a short calyx, green, whitish, pink, or red. Petals absent. Stamens 5. Ovary superior, with 2 carpels fused at the base and 2 styles. Pollination is by small insects. The fruit is a many-seeded capsule. Seeds small.

Key Recognition Features Plants forming spreading clumps of bold leaves, with branching heads of small flowers.

Ecology and Geography In moist woods and damp places by streams in the Himalayas from Nepal to China.

Comment Many species are grown in bog gardens and by streams. *Astilboides tabularis* (Hemsl.) Engler syn. *Rodgersia tabularis* (Hemsl.) Kom. is closely related; the leaves are large and peltate, and the inflorescence is taller than the leaves, with masses of small, whitish flowers with 4 or 5 petals. The genus is named after Admiral John Rodgers of the US navy (1812–1882.)

Rodgersia aesculifolia
flowers, 2 × life size
August 17th

Rodgersia aesculifolia
fruits, life size
October 7th

Rodgersia aesculifolia
½ life size, August 17th

Tolmiea

Tolmiea Torrey & Gray (1840), in the family Saxifragaceae, contains 1 species, *T. menziesii* (Pursh) Torrey & Gray, in western North America.

Description Clump-forming perennial to 80cm. Leaves evergreen, lobed, toothed, and hairy. Flowers small, brownish-green, with a narrow tube, in loose spikes on slender stalks with a few leaves. Sepals 5, unequal. Petals 4, rarely 5, brown, slender, and recurved. Stamens usually 3, sometimes 2, with broad filaments. Ovary inferior, with 1 carpel and 2 short styles. Pollination is perhaps by small insects. The fruit is a many-seeded capsule, splitting into 2 sections. Seeds minute.

Key Recognition Features Plants forming clumps of dark green leaves, with spikes of green flowers with a long, narrow tube and long, filiform, reflexed petals.

Ecology and Geography In moist woods from northern California to Alaska.

Comment The genus is named after Dr William Fraser Tolmie (1812–86), physician at the Hudson Bay Company's Fort Vancouver and later with the Canadian Geological Survey, a pupil of W.J. Hooker and amateur botanist. 'Taff's Gold', a particularly ugly form with heavily yellow-spotted leaves, is a popular houseplant.

Tolmiea menziesii
flowers, 2 × life size
May 3rd

Tolmiea menziesii
²⁄₃ life size, May 3rd

Tellima grandiflora
¹⁄₂ life size, April 5th

Tellima grandiflora
flowers, 2 × life size
April 5th

Tellima

Tellima R. Br. (1823), in the family Saxifragaceae, contains 1 variable species, *T. grandiflora* (Pursh) Dougl., in western North America.
Description Clump-forming perennial to 80cm. Leaves mostly evergreen, 3- to 7-lobed, toothed, and hairy, often with a young plant formed where the leaf joins the stalk. Flowers pale green, with a short, wide tube, in loose spikes on slender stalks with a few leaves. Sepals 5, ovate, erect. Petals 5, pinnately divided, recurved. Stamens 10, with short filaments. Ovary inferior, with 1 carpel and 2 short styles. Pollination is perhaps by small insects. The fruit is a many-seeded capsule, splitting into 2 sections. Seeds minute.
Key Recognition Features Plants forming clumps of dark green leaves, with spikes of green flowers with wide, cup-shaped tubes and divided petals.
Ecology and Geography In moist woods and rocky areas from central California to Alaska.
Comment Occasionally grown as an ornamental, and becoming naturalised in many places in western Europe.

Tiarella

Tiarella L. (1753), in the family Saxifragaceae, contains around 5 species in North America and Asia.
Description Clump-forming perennials to 60cm. Leaves mostly evergreen, toothed, 3- to 7-lobed or of 3 leaflets, hairy. Flowers small, white, pink, or green, in spikes on slender stalks, sometimes with a few leaves. Sepals 5, joined at the base, forming a cup-shaped calyx tube. Petals 5, small and simple. Stamens 10, long and slender. Ovary nearly superior, with 2 fused carpels and 2 long styles. Pollination is perhaps by small insects. The fruit is a many-seeded capsule, splitting into 2 very unequal sections. Seeds minute.
Key Recognition Features Plants forming clumps of often purple-veined leaves, with spikes of small flowers with narrow petals, and capsule with 2 unequal parts.
Ecology and Geography In moist woods and on shady mountain slopes, with 4 species in North America from Alaska to California and from Nova Scotia to Georgia, and 1 species, *T. polyphylla* D. Don, from the Himalayas to western China and Japan.
Comment These modest plants are popular in woodland gardens. Many species have attractively marked leaves and fluffy white or pale pink flowers. They have been crossed with *Heuchera* (see p.108) to form the very pretty × *Heucherella alba*, with several named cultivars.

Tiarella polyphylla
pink form, ½ life size
May 4th

Tiarella polyphylla capsules
2 × life size, November 22nd

Tiarella polyphylla
pink form, flowers
2 × life size, May 4th

Heuchera

Heuchera L. (1753), alum-root, in the family Saxifragaceae, contains around 50 species in North America.

Description Clump-forming perennials to 70cm. Leaves mostly evergreen, toothed or lobed, often purplish or silvery. Flowers small, white, pink, red, or green, in spikes or branching heads on slender stalks, usually without leaves. Sepals 5, often unequal, joined at the base, forming a cup-shaped calyx tube. Petals 5, small and simple, sometimes absent. Stamens 5. Ovary half inferior, with 2 fused carpels and 2 styles. Pollination is by small insects, or by hummingbirds in the red-flowered species. The fruit is a many-seeded capsule. Seeds often minutely spiny.

Key Recognition Features Plants forming clumps of often purple or silver, hairy leaves, with spikes of small flowers.

Ecology and Geography In moist woods and on dry, shady mountain slopes, usually among rocks; sometimes on cliffs near the sea. There are 16 species in California, others in the Rockies and in the eastern states from Ontario to Louisiana.

Comment Purple and pewter-leaved species and varieties are now highly fashionable. Hybrids of *H. sanguinea* Engelm. from New Mexico and Arizona have attractive flowers in shades of red and pink. The genus is named after Johann Heinrich Heucher (1677–1747), professor of medicine at Wittenberg University in Germany.

Heuchera 'Chocolate Ruffles'
flowers, 2 × life size
May 25th

left to right: *Heuchera sanguinea*
'Alba', *Heuchera sanguinea*, and
Heuchera 'Edge Hill'
¾ life size, June 3rd

Heuchera
'Chocolate Ruffles'
½ life size, May 25th

Umbilicus

Umbilicus DC (1801), in the family Crassulaceae, contains around 18 species, mainly in Europe and the Mediterranean.

Description Fleshy perennials to 30cm, with tuberous roots. Leaves mainly in a basal rosette, alternate, deciduous, peltate. Flowers small, tubular, in upright spikes, usually greenish or yellow. Sepals 5, not joined. Petals 5, joined into a tube. Stamens usually 10, sometimes 5. Ovary superior, with 5 fused carpels. Pollination is by small insects. The fruit is a many-seeded capsule, splitting into 5 sections. Seeds small.

Key Recognition Features Plants with round, fleshy leaves, which appear in autumn and have often withered before the small, tubular flowers appear.

Ecology and Geography On rocks, walls, and hedgebanks, or in dry woods. From western Europe and around the Mediterranean eastwards to western Iran.

Comment *Umbilicus rupestris* (Salisb.) Dandy, the wall pennywort, is a familiar wild plant in western and southern Europe. Many other genera of Crassulaceae are frost-tender, but familiar as house plants or as rock plants in warm, dry gardens; all have fleshy leaves and usually 5-parted, starry or tubular flowers with usually 10 stamens.

Sedum

Sedum L (1753), stonecrop, in the family Crassulaceae, contains around 280 species mainly in northern temperate regions.

Description Fleshy perennials to 90cm. Leaves mainly on the stem, alternate, opposite, or whorled, deciduous or evergreen, flat to cylindrical. Flowers small, in branching heads, usually starry. Petals, sepals, and carpels usually 5, but sometimes 4 or up to 9. Stamens usually twice the number of petals, with long, slender filaments. Ovary superior, with slender styles. Pollination is by small insects or butterflies. The fruit is a many-seeded, starry capsule. Seeds small.

Key Recognition Features Plants with fleshy leaves and branching heads of small, starry flowers.

Ecology and Geography On rocks and dunes, in woods, and in bogs. From western Europe through Asia to Japan, and in North America southwards to Mexico.

Comment Many species are cultivated; the large, herbaceous ones such as *S. spectabile* Boreau, *S. telephium* L., and their hybrids, provide valuable late nectar for butterflies. Most species of Crassulaceae and many other succulent plants have an unusual metabolism, called crassulacean acid metabolism, associated with tolerance to drought, which means that they can open their stomata only at night. Many are resistant to the weedkiller paraquat, and many, such as *S. acre* L., tolerate salt and become naturalised along stony verges of main roads.

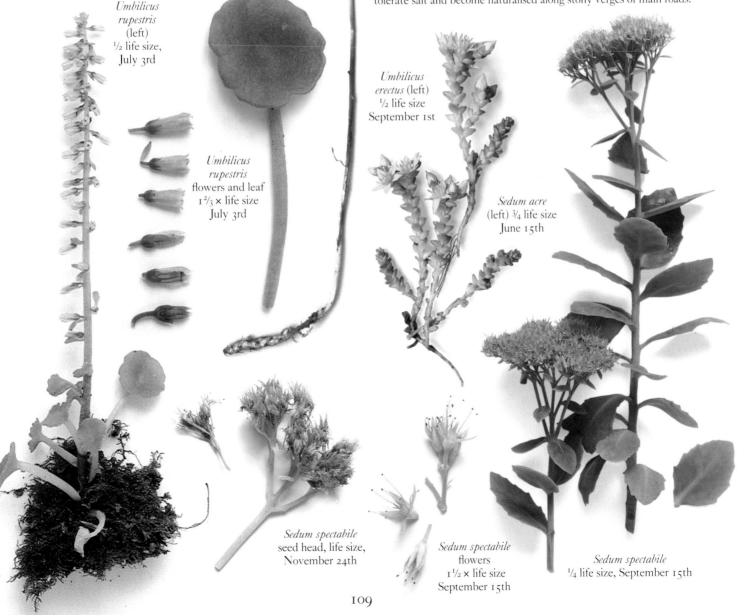

Umbilicus rupestris (left) ½ life size, July 3rd

Umbilicus rupestris flowers and leaf 1⅔ × life size July 3rd

Umbilicus erectus (left) ½ life size September 1st

Sedum acre (left) ¾ life size June 15th

Sedum spectabile seed head, life size, November 24th

Sedum spectabile flowers 1½ × life size September 15th

Sedum spectabile ¼ life size, September 15th

Gunnera manicata
½ life size, April 28th

Gunnera

Gunnera L. (1767), in the family Gunneraceae, contains around 40 species, mainly in the southern hemisphere.

Description Often huge, clump-forming perennials with leaf stalks to 2m or more, but sometimes dwarf, creeping plants, with feathery stipules on the rhizome. Leaves mainly basal, usually deciduous, rounded or ovate, and toothed. Flowers usually green or yellow, very small, in branched spikes, with male, female, and bisexual types usually on the same plant. Sepals 2 or 3 or absent. Petals 1, 2, or absent. Stamens 1 or 2. Ovary inferior, with 1 carpel and 2 feathery styles. Pollination is probably by wind. The fruit is a 1-seeded berry, usually red, orange, or yellow, rarely white, when ripe.

Key Recognition Features Plants forming spreading clumps of bold leaves, with branching heads of small flowers. The male flowers are usually at the tip of the spike, bisexual flowers in the middle, and female flowers at the base.

Ecology and Geography In moist woods and damp places by streams and in swamps, in Australia, New Zealand, South Africa, and South America; also northwards to Hawaii and Malaysia.

Comment This genus contains some very small and some huge herbs; the leaves of *G. manicata* Lindl. ex André from Brazil can be 3m across, on stalks over 2m tall; those of *G. arenaria* Cheesm. from New Zealand are around 1cm across and form a low mat. *G. tinctoria* (Molina) Mirb., smaller and with more lobed leaves than *G. manicata*, is naturalised on the shores of loughs and by streams in Connemara in Ireland and on Achil Island. Many species have symbiotic infections of bacteria, blue-green algae (*Nostoc* and *Chlorococcus*), or fungal mycorrhiza. The genus is named after Ernst Gunnerus (1718–73), a Norwegian bishop and botanist. Although the big gunneras are sometimes called giant rhubarb, they are not closely related to true rhubarb; the stems are, however, edible.

Gunnera manicata
young leaf
½ life size
April 28th

Gunnera manicata
branch of inflorescence
in flower, male flowers
at the top, females
below, life size
May 3rd

Gunnera tinctoria
whole inflorescence
in fruit, ⅓ life size
October 3rd

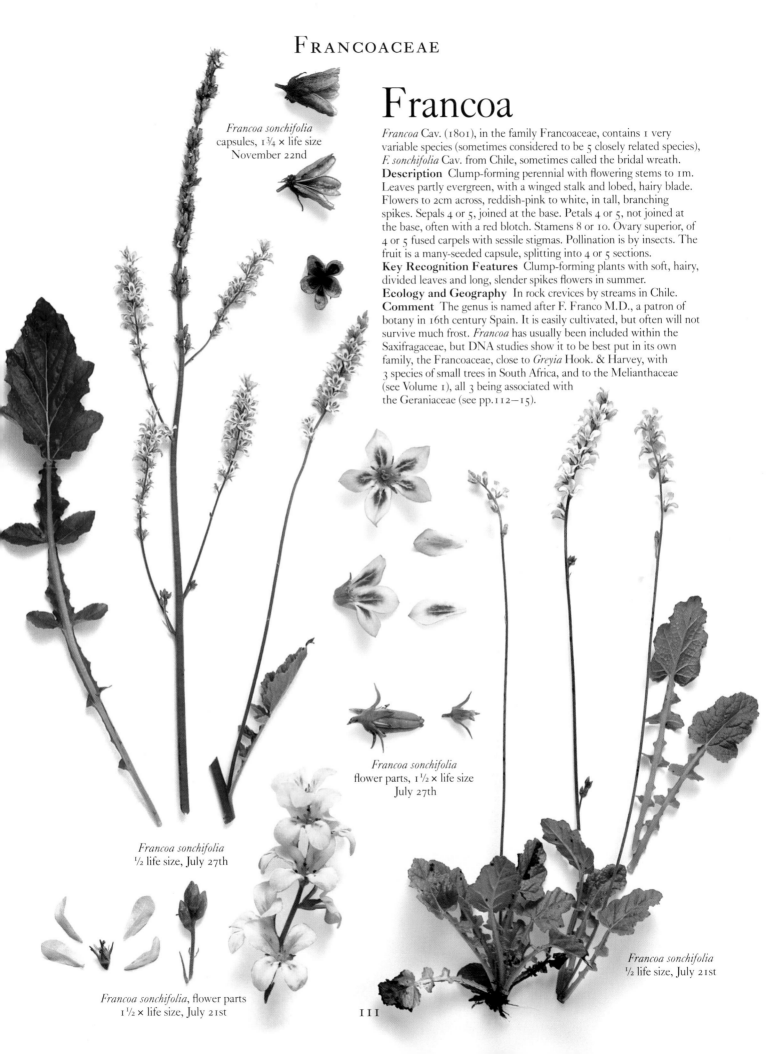

Francoa sonchifolia
capsules, 1¾ × life size
November 22nd

Francoa

Francoa Cav. (1801), in the family Francoaceae, contains 1 very variable species (sometimes considered to be 5 closely related species), *F. sonchifolia* Cav. from Chile, sometimes called the bridal wreath.

Description Clump-forming perennial with flowering stems to 1m. Leaves partly evergreen, with a winged stalk and lobed, hairy blade. Flowers to 2cm across, reddish-pink to white, in tall, branching spikes. Sepals 4 or 5, joined at the base. Petals 4 or 5, not joined at the base, often with a red blotch. Stamens 8 or 10. Ovary superior, of 4 or 5 fused carpels with sessile stigmas. Pollination is by insects. The fruit is a many-seeded capsule, splitting into 4 or 5 sections.

Key Recognition Features Clump-forming plants with soft, hairy, divided leaves and long, slender spikes flowers in summer.

Ecology and Geography In rock crevices by streams in Chile.

Comment The genus is named after F. Franco M.D., a patron of botany in 16th century Spain. It is easily cultivated, but often will not survive much frost. *Francoa* has usually been included within the Saxifragaceae, but DNA studies show it to be best put in its own family, the Francoaceae, close to *Greyia* Hook. & Harvey, with 3 species of small trees in South Africa, and to the Melianthaceae (see Volume 1), all 3 being associated with the Geraniaceae (see pp.112—15).

Francoa sonchifolia
flower parts, 1½ × life size
July 27th

Francoa sonchifolia
½ life size, July 27th

Francoa sonchifolia
½ life size, July 21st

Francoa sonchifolia, flower parts
1½ × life size, July 21st

Geranium phaeum
1½ × life size, May 3rd

Geranium phaeum
flowers with petals
removed, 2 × life size
May 3rd

Geranium

Geranium L. (1753), in the family Geraniaceae, contains around 300 species worldwide.

Description Tuberous, tufted, or creeping perennials or annuals to 1.5m. Leaves alternate, stalked, usually deeply lobed, sometimes aromatic. Flowers blue, purple, white, red, magenta, pink, grey, or black, solitary or paired. Sepals 5, equal, not joined. Petals 5, equal, not joined at the base. Stamens 10, in 2 whorls, the anthers ripening before the styles. Ovary superior, of 5 carpels, and a 5-lobed stigma. Pollination is by insects, usually by bees, very rarely by birds. The fruit is 5-seeded, each carpel with a long beak that curls up like a spring, flinging the seed away from the parent plant. In some species, such as *G. biuncinatum* Kokwaro from the Yemen and northeastern Africa, the beaks of the fruits are modified into hooks to catch in the hair of passing animals.

Key Recognition Features The regular flowers with all petals similar, and the peltate leaves with deep divisions.

Ecology and Geography In woods and meadows, by streams, in rocky areas, and on mountain slopes. Around 40 species in Europe, others worldwide, on high mountains in the tropics. The red-flowered *G. arboreum* A. Gray from Hawaii is the only bird-pollinated species.

Comment The Geraniaceae is an isolated family, closely associated with 4 other small families – Greyiaceae, Francoaceae (see p.111), Melianthaceae (see Volume 1), and Vivianaceae – all from the southern hemisphere, and particularly South Africa. Families such as Oxalidaceae (see p.122) and Balsaminaceae (see pp.206–207), previously thought close to Geraniaceae, are now considered to belong elsewhere. *Geranium* species are very popular in temperate gardens, being mostly hardy, easy to grow, and long-flowering.

Geranium lambertii
flowers (right)
life size
September 24th

*Geranium
tuberosum*
⅓ life size
May 15th

Geranium phaeum
½ life size, May 3rd

Geranium lambertii
½ life size
September 24th

GERANIACEAE

Geranium endressii flower parts
(above) 1 1/3 × life size, June 15th

Geranium wallichianum
magenta form
fruits and seeds (below)
and flower (left)
1 1/3 × life size
September 10th

Geranium wallichianum
'Buxton's Variety'
1/2 life size
September 24th

Geranium endressii
1/2 life size, June 15th

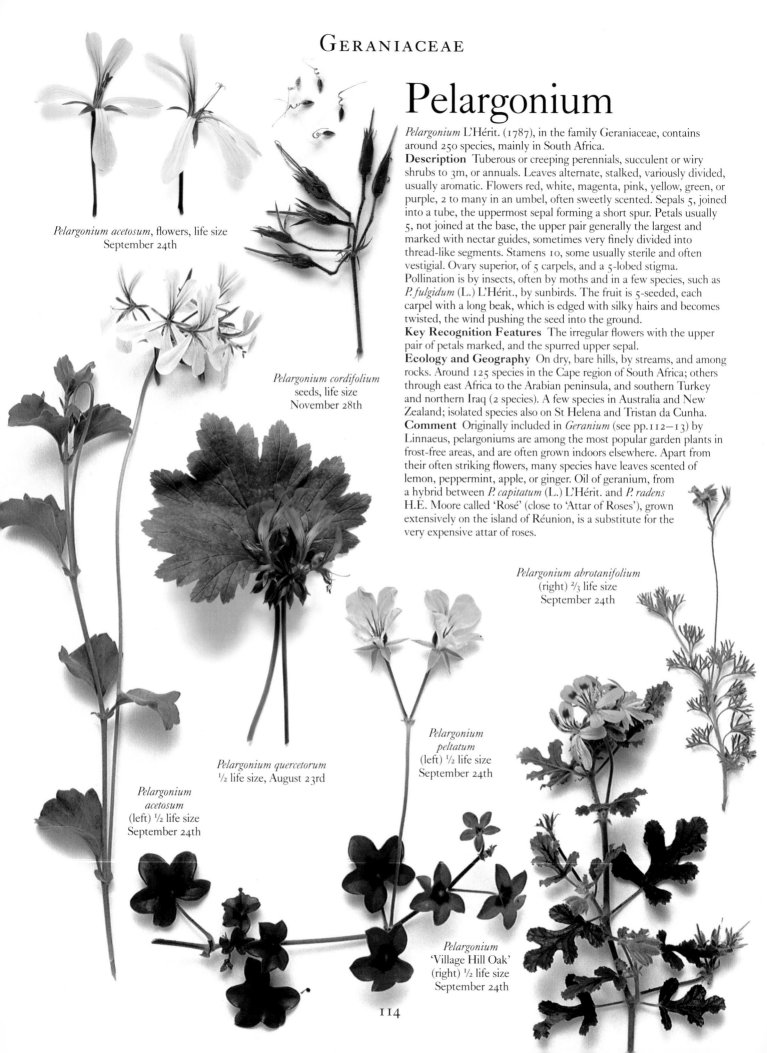

GERANIACEAE

Pelargonium

Pelargonium acetosum, flowers, life size
September 24th

Pelargonium L'Hérit. (1787), in the family Geraniaceae, contains around 250 species, mainly in South Africa.

Description Tuberous or creeping perennials, succulent or wiry shrubs to 3m, or annuals. Leaves alternate, stalked, variously divided, usually aromatic. Flowers red, white, magenta, pink, yellow, green, or purple, 2 to many in an umbel, often sweetly scented. Sepals 5, joined into a tube, the uppermost sepal forming a short spur. Petals usually 5, not joined at the base, the upper pair generally the largest and marked with nectar guides, sometimes very finely divided into thread-like segments. Stamens 10, some usually sterile and often vestigial. Ovary superior, of 5 carpels, and a 5-lobed stigma. Pollination is by insects, often by moths and in a few species, such as *P. fulgidum* (L.) L'Hérit., by sunbirds. The fruit is 5-seeded, each carpel with a long beak, which is edged with silky hairs and becomes twisted, the wind pushing the seed into the ground.

Key Recognition Features The irregular flowers with the upper pair of petals marked, and the spurred upper sepal.

Ecology and Geography On dry, bare hills, by streams, and among rocks. Around 125 species in the Cape region of South Africa; others through east Africa to the Arabian peninsula, and southern Turkey and northern Iraq (2 species). A few species in Australia and New Zealand; isolated species also on St Helena and Tristan da Cunha.

Comment Originally included in *Geranium* (see pp. 112–13) by Linnaeus, pelargoniums are among the most popular garden plants in frost-free areas, and are often grown indoors elsewhere. Apart from their often striking flowers, many species have leaves scented of lemon, peppermint, apple, or ginger. Oil of geranium, from a hybrid between *P. capitatum* (L.) L'Hérit. and *P. radens* H.E. Moore called 'Rosé' (close to 'Attar of Roses'), grown extensively on the island of Réunion, is a substitute for the very expensive attar of roses.

Pelargonium cordifolium
seeds, life size
November 28th

Pelargonium abrotanifolium
(right) ²/₃ life size
September 24th

Pelargonium quercetorum
½ life size, August 23rd

Pelargonium peltatum
(left) ½ life size
September 24th

Pelargonium acetosum
(left) ½ life size
September 24th

Pelargonium 'Village Hill Oak'
(right) ½ life size
September 24th

114

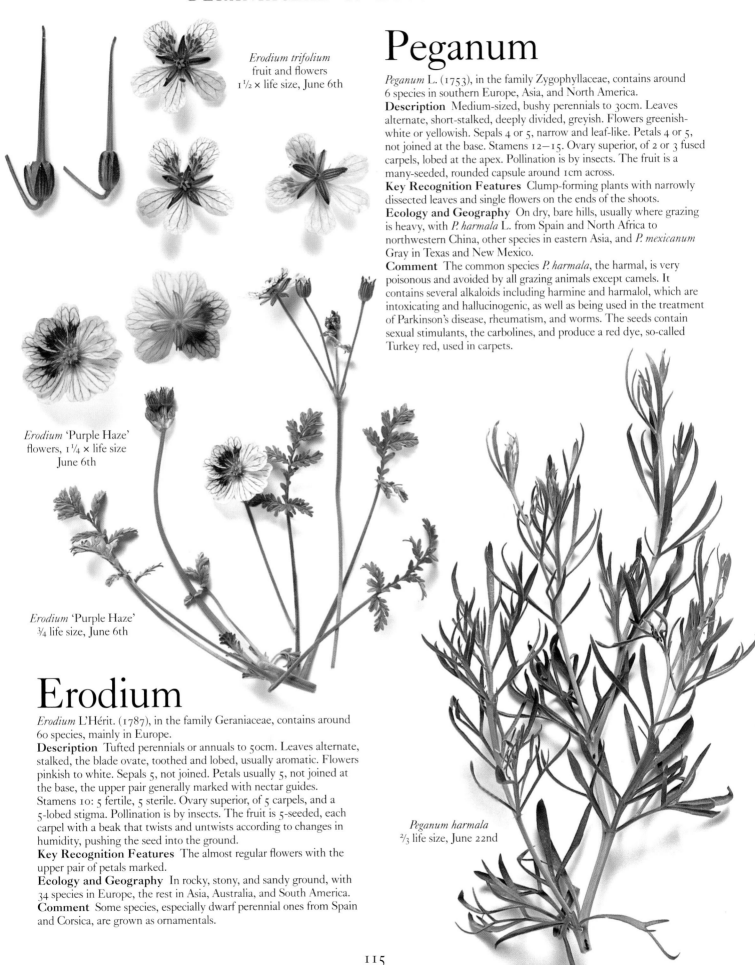

Erodium trifolium
fruit and flowers
1½ × life size, June 6th

Erodium 'Purple Haze'
flowers, 1¼ × life size
June 6th

Erodium 'Purple Haze'
¾ life size, June 6th

Peganum

Peganum L. (1753), in the family Zygophyllaceae, contains around 6 species in southern Europe, Asia, and North America.

Description Medium-sized, bushy perennials to 30cm. Leaves alternate, short-stalked, deeply divided, greyish. Flowers greenish-white or yellowish. Sepals 4 or 5, narrow and leaf-like. Petals 4 or 5, not joined at the base. Stamens 12–15. Ovary superior, of 2 or 3 fused carpels, lobed at the apex. Pollination is by insects. The fruit is a many-seeded, rounded capsule around 1cm across.

Key Recognition Features Clump-forming plants with narrowly dissected leaves and single flowers on the ends of the shoots.

Ecology and Geography On dry, bare hills, usually where grazing is heavy, with *P. harmala* L. from Spain and North Africa to northwestern China, other species in eastern Asia, and *P. mexicanum* Gray in Texas and New Mexico.

Comment The common species *P. harmala*, the harmal, is very poisonous and avoided by all grazing animals except camels. It contains several alkaloids including harmine and harmalol, which are intoxicating and hallucinogenic, as well as being used in the treatment of Parkinson's disease, rheumatism, and worms. The seeds contain sexual stimulants, the carbolines, and produce a red dye, so-called Turkey red, used in carpets.

Erodium

Erodium L'Hérit. (1787), in the family Geraniaceae, contains around 60 species, mainly in Europe.

Description Tufted perennials or annuals to 50cm. Leaves alternate, stalked, the blade ovate, toothed and lobed, usually aromatic. Flowers pinkish to white. Sepals 5, not joined. Petals usually 5, not joined at the base, the upper pair generally marked with nectar guides. Stamens 10: 5 fertile, 5 sterile. Ovary superior, of 5 carpels, and a 5-lobed stigma. Pollination is by insects. The fruit is 5-seeded, each carpel with a beak that twists and untwists according to changes in humidity, pushing the seed into the ground.

Key Recognition Features The almost regular flowers with the upper pair of petals marked.

Ecology and Geography In rocky, stony, and sandy ground, with 34 species in Europe, the rest in Asia, Australia, and South America.

Comment Some species, especially dwarf perennial ones from Spain and Corsica, are grown as ornamentals.

Peganum harmala
⅔ life size, June 22nd

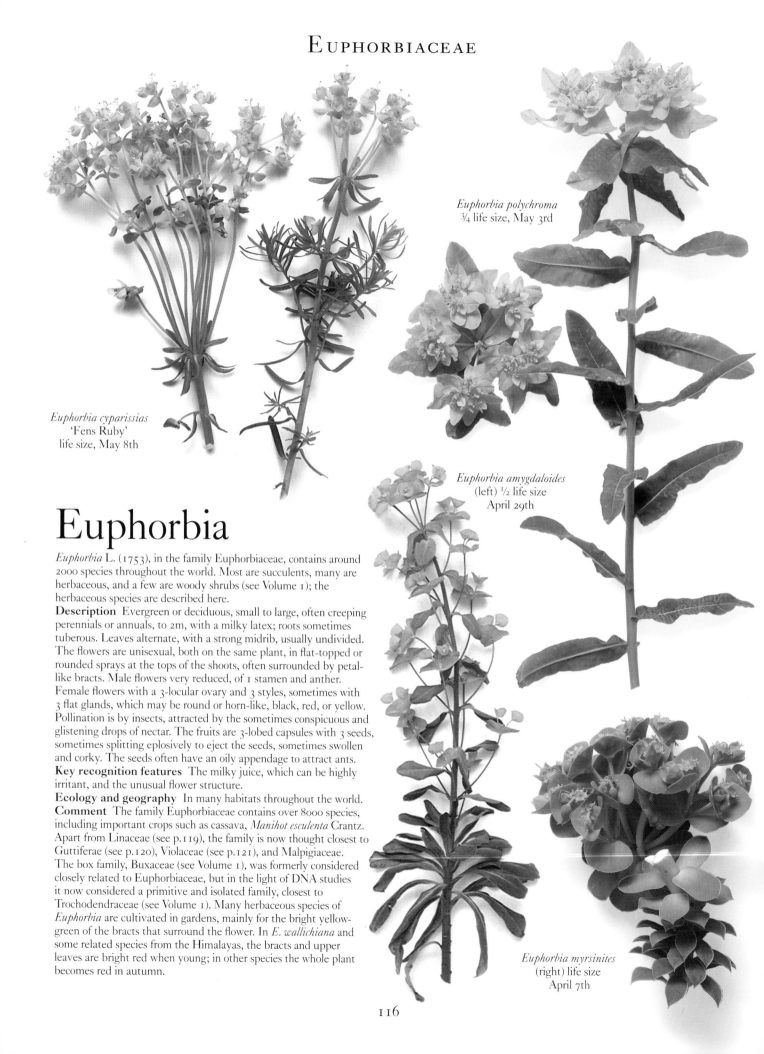

Euphorbia polychroma
¾ life size, May 3rd

Euphorbia cyparissias
'Fens Ruby'
life size, May 8th

Euphorbia amygdaloides
(left) ½ life size
April 29th

Euphorbia

Euphorbia L. (1753), in the family Euphorbiaceae, contains around 2000 species throughout the world. Most are succulents, many are herbaceous, and a few are woody shrubs (see Volume 1); the herbaceous species are described here.

Description Evergreen or deciduous, small to large, often creeping perennials or annuals, to 2m, with a milky latex; roots sometimes tuberous. Leaves alternate, with a strong midrib, usually undivided. The flowers are unisexual, both on the same plant, in flat-topped or rounded sprays at the tops of the shoots, often surrounded by petal-like bracts. Male flowers very reduced, of 1 stamen and anther. Female flowers with a 3-locular ovary and 3 styles, sometimes with 3 flat glands, which may be round or horn-like, black, red, or yellow. Pollination is by insects, attracted by the sometimes conspicuous and glistening drops of nectar. The fruits are 3-lobed capsules with 3 seeds, sometimes splitting explosively to eject the seeds, sometimes swollen and corky. The seeds often have an oily appendage to attract ants.

Key recognition features The milky juice, which can be highly irritant, and the unusual flower structure.

Ecology and geography In many habitats throughout the world.

Comment The family Euphorbiaceae contains over 8000 species, including important crops such as cassava, *Manihot esculenta* Crantz. Apart from Linaceae (see p.119), the family is now thought closest to Guttiferae (see p.120), Violaceae (see p.121), and Malpigiaceae. The box family, Buxaceae (see Volume 1), was formerly considered closely related to Euphorbiaceae, but in the light of DNA studies it now considered a primitive and isolated family, closest to Trochodendraceae (see Volume 1). Many herbaceous species of *Euphorbia* are cultivated in gardens, mainly for the bright yellow-green of the bracts that surround the flower. In *E. wallichiana* and some related species from the Himalayas, the bracts and upper leaves are bright red when young; in other species the whole plant becomes red in autumn.

Euphorbia myrsinites
(right) life size
April 7th

EUPHORBIACEAE

Euphorbia myrsinites
fruit and seeds, 2 × life size, June 6th

Euphorbia characias
subsp. *wulfenii*
flowers, 1 ½ × life size
May 3rd

Euphorbia myrsinites
½ life size, April 7th

Euphorbia characias
subsp. *wulfenii*
½ life size, May 3rd

Euphorbia myrsinites
fruit and flowers
2 × life size, June 1st

Ricinus communis 'Impala', seeds
just over life size
February 20th

Ricinus communis 'Carmencita'
flowers, female (left) and male (right)
2 × life size, July 2nd

Ricinus communis 'Carmencita'
flowers, male (above) and female (top)
with some males still in bud
1 ⅓ × life size, July 2nd

Ricinus

Ricinus L. (1753), in the family Euphorbiaceae contains of 1 species,
R. communis L., the castor oil plant, now found throughout the world.
Description A fast-growing annual or perennial, becoming shrubby
at the base and reaching around 4m. Leaves alternate, peltate, usually
deeply lobed, and often purplish in cultivated forms. The flowers are
unisexual, both on the same plant, in short spikes with the males at
the base and the females at the apex. Male flowers reduced to 1
much-branched stamen. Female flowers with a 3-locular ovary and
3 forked and feathery styles. Pollination is by insects and perhaps by
wind. The fruits are prickly capsules with 3 seeds.
Key recognition features The deeply lobed leaves and prickly
fruits.
Ecology and geography In waste places and on open ground, now
found throughout the world in the tropics and subtropics, but possibly
native of northeastern Africa and the Middle East.
Comment A very poisonous plant, but containing useful oils.
Ricinus is particularly poisonous when introduced into the
bloodstream, and was used by the Bulgarian secret service on a
sharpened umbrella ferrule to kill the dissident Georgi Markos in
London in 1978. The gray, speckled seeds are also very poisonous,
2–6 seeds being fatal. Castor oil has been much used as a purgative,
but historically also in Egypt for lighting. It is also used in soap and
paint, and for waterproofing leather and fabrics. It remains fluid at
low temperatures.

Ricinus communis 'Carmencita'
½ life size, July 2nd

Linum

Linum L. (1753), in the family Linaceae, contains around 180 species throughout the world but mostly in the Mediterranean area.

Description Annuals, perennials, or low shrubs to 60cm. Leaves flat, simple, without stalks, usually lanceolate, with a distinct midrib. Flowers to 4cm across, white, pink, blue, yellow, or red, usually lasting a day or less, on branching stems. Sepals 5, sometimes joined at the base. Petals 5, usually not joined at the base. Stamens 5, widened and joined at the base, alternating with 5 tooth-like staminodes. Ovary with 5 styles. Pollination is by insects. The fruit is a many-seeded, pointed capsule, splitting into 10 sections. Seeds flattened, brown or black, becoming mucilaginous when wetted.

Key Recognition Features Plants with simple leaves and 5 thin, rounded, and shining petals, which open in the sun.

Ecology and Geography In dry, sunny places among rocks, on cliffs, and in open scrub. Around 36 species in Europe, others in North America, eastern Asia, Australia, and New Zealand.

Comment Several species of *Linum* are grown in gardens, especially the spectacular annual *L. grandiflorum* Desf. from North Africa, which may have red, white, white with a red centre, or purple flowers; all need as much sun as possible and well-drained soil. *Linum usitatissimum* L. is cultivated flax, grown both for its fibre (the source of linen) and for its seed (the source of linseed oil). Flax has been cultivated since 8000 BC, and linen was used for wrapping Egyptian mummies. The dainty *L. catharticum* L., common on chalk and limestone grassland in northern Europe, was said to have been used as a purgative. It is now naturalised in many parts of the world. Many species of *Linum* are heterostylous (see also Primula, pp.198–99), with short-styled flowers needing pollen from long-styled flowers in order to be fertilised. *Reinwardtia indica* Dum. has yellow, flax-like flowers with twisted petals and stalked leaves; it is common in subtropical areas of eastern Asia, and is often cultivated. DNA studies show that Linaceae is related to Euphorbiaceae (see pp.116–18).

Linum grandiflorum
flower parts, 1 ½ × life size, August 1st

Linum grandiflorum
½ life size, August 1st

Hypericum

Hypericum L. (1753), St John's wort, in the family Hypericaceae, (sometimes joined with the Clusiaceae in the Guttiferae), contains around 400 species, in temperate regions and tropical mountains. For shrubby species, see Volume 1.

Description Annuals, perennials, shrubs, or small trees to 8m. Leaves opposite, stalkless, usually rounded or narrow and undivided, often with small, pale or dark spots or glands. Flowers yellow or reddish on the outside. Sepals 4 or 5, not joined, or joined only at the base, often glandular. Petals usually 5, not joined at the base, more or less equal and rounded. Stamens many, in bundles opposite the petals. Ovary superior, usually 3- to 5-celled, with 3–5 styles. Pollination is by insects, mainly bees. The fruit is a many-seeded capsule, splitting into 2–5. Seeds many, small, usually narrow and curved.

Key Recognition Features The yellow flowers with usually 5 petals, the numerous stamens, and the opposite leaves, showing as it were pin-pricks if held up to the light; often with square stems.

Ecology and Geography In many different habitats in temperate and montane zones: mountain rocks, bogs, heathland, grassy places, and woods. There are tree species in the mountains of Africa, many shrubby species in the Himalayas and China, but mostly herbaceous species in Europe, northern Asia, and North America.

Comment The family Hypericaceae is now considered close to the weird aquatic family Podostemaceae and to the Clusiaceae, a mainly tropical family. Recently St John's wort, particularly the common *H. perforatum* L., has become valued as a herbal remedy, especially to treat depression. In the past it was used as a cure for almost anything, and especially dissolved in olive oil for treating infected wounds. It was associated with the Hospitallers of St John of Jerusalem, an order of knights that flourished in the 12th century. It is now a pest of meadows in northwestern California, where it is known as Klamath weed. Many species, especially the shrubby ones and some alpines such as *H. olympicum* L., are grown as ornamentals. *Hypericum canadense* L. is one of those interesting few plants which are common in North America and found in Europe only in western Ireland and southwestern England.

Hypericum perforatum
just under life size
July 1st

*Hypericum
humifusum*
life size
August 20th

Hypericum polchrum capsules
2 × life size, December 1st

Viola

Viola L. (1753), the pansy and violet, in the family Violaceae, contains around 400 species, mainly in Europe, Asia and the Americas.

Description Annuals, perennials, and very small shrubs to 10cm, usually with conspicuous and sometimes leafy stipules at the leaf bases. Leaves alternate, stalked, the blade often heart-shaped, ovate, toothed and lobed, sometimes deeply and repeatedly divided. Flowers blue, yellow, purple, pinkish to white, rarely reddish-magenta, often sweetly scented; violets often produce cleistogamous flowers, minute and with reduced petals, which set seed without opening. Sepals 5, not joined, often with appendages. Petals usually 5, not joined at the base, the upper pair generally rather upright, the side pair smaller, the lowest the largest, forming a lip which is often veined and may be spurred. Stamens 5, joined around the ovary; the 2 lower stamens spurred, secreting nectar into the ovary. Ovary superior, with 1 style, often bent near the base, and often club-shaped or beaked at the tip. Pollination is by insects, mainly bees. Fruit a many-seeded capsule, splitting into 3. Seeds large, pear-shaped, often with an oily aril.

Key Recognition Features The irregular flowers with 5 petals, the lowest petal spurred and the most heavily veined.

Ecology and Geography In temperate and montane zones, in many different habitats, often high alpine screes: violets are often woodland plants, but the ancestors of pansies grow in mountain meadows and open stony ground. There are 92 species in Europe; the rest in are found in Asia, Australia, and the Americas.

Comment The Violaceae contains 22 genera, mostly shrubby and in the tropics, but with a few dwarf shrubs in New Zealand (see *Melicytus,* Volume 1). *Viola* has 2 main divisions, violets and pansies. Violets have narrow stipules, bluish or white flowers with the side petals inclined downwards, and cleistogamous flowers in summer. Pansies have leafy stipules, bluish or yellow flowers with the side petals inclined upwards, and no cleistogamous flowers. Cultivated pansies and violas have been selected since the mid-19th century, from hybrids between the very variable heartsease, *V. tricolor* L., and the Russian alpine *V. altaica* Ker.-Gawl. Other perennial species such as the Pyrenean *V. cornuta* L. entered into the parentage of the more perennial violas. Large, round flowers with heavy markings, in colours that include blue, black, pink, crimson, and apricot-orange, are features of modern pansies. Two remarkable sections of the genus are rare and difficult to cultivate. The so-called rosulate violas from the high Andes, such as *V. cotyledon* Ging., have fleshy, greyish or brownish rosettes of stalkless, overlapping leaves, like a saxifrage (see pp.98—99) or a houseleek (*Sempervivum*), and large numbers of small flowers. There are 3 species from limestone rocks in southeastern Spain and the Balkan mountains that have almost shrubby stems, very narrow leaves, and flowers with narrow petals and a long, thin spur, up to 3cm long in *V. cazorlensis* Gand. from the Sierra de Cazorla near Jaen, shorter in *V. delphinantha* Boiss. from Mount Olympus and nearby mountains in Greece and Bulgaria.

Viola tricolor
capsules and seeds
$1\frac{1}{2}$ × life size
September 24th

Viola tricolor, 2 colour
variations, $\frac{2}{3}$ life size
September 24th

Viola tricolor, life size
September 24th

Viola F1 pansy (right)
$\frac{3}{4}$ life size
September 25th

Viola riviniana
$\frac{2}{3}$ life size, April 10th

Viola riviniana
$1\frac{1}{3}$ × life size
April 10th

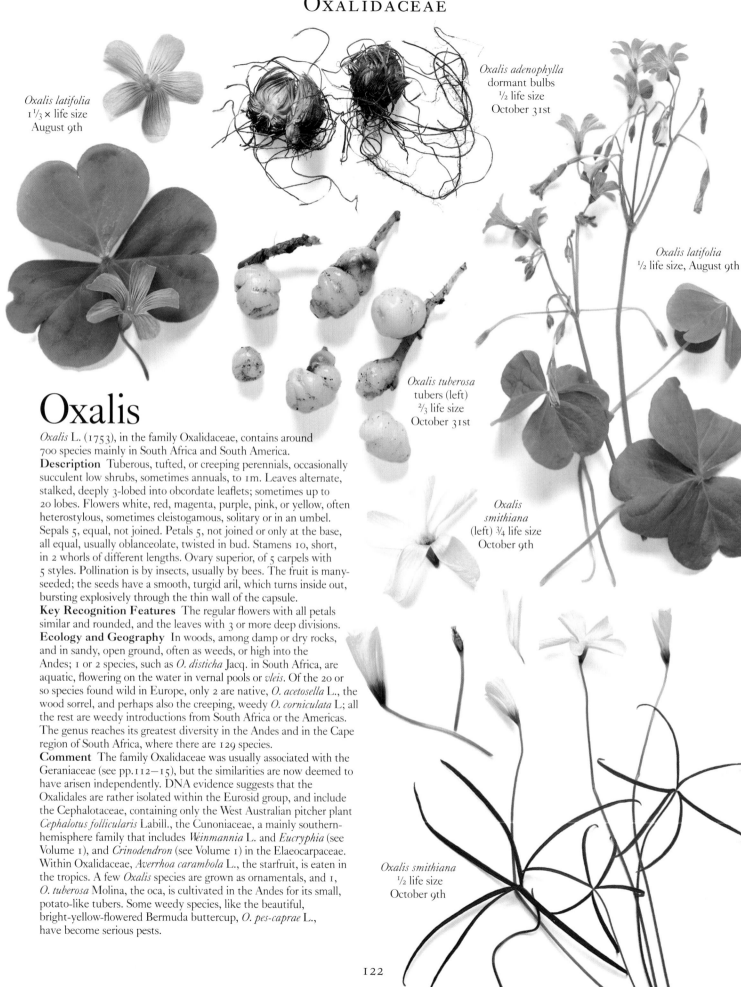

Oxalis latifolia
1 1/3 × life size
August 9th

Oxalis adenophylla
dormant bulbs
1/2 life size
October 31st

Oxalis latifolia
1/2 life size, August 9th

Oxalis tuberosa
tubers (left)
2/3 life size
October 31st

Oxalis smithiana
(left) 3/4 life size
October 9th

Oxalis smithiana
1/2 life size
October 9th

Oxalis

Oxalis L. (1753), in the family Oxalidaceae, contains around
700 species mainly in South Africa and South America.

Description Tuberous, tufted, or creeping perennials, occasionally
succulent low shrubs, sometimes annuals, to 1m. Leaves alternate,
stalked, deeply 3-lobed into obcordate leaflets; sometimes up to
20 lobes. Flowers white, red, magenta, purple, pink, or yellow, often
heterostylous, sometimes cleistogamous, solitary or in an umbel.
Sepals 5, equal, not joined. Petals 5, not joined or only at the base,
all equal, usually oblanceolate, twisted in bud. Stamens 10, short,
in 2 whorls of different lengths. Ovary superior, of 5 carpels with
5 styles. Pollination is by insects, usually by bees. The fruit is many-
seeded; the seeds have a smooth, turgid aril, which turns inside out,
bursting explosively through the thin wall of the capsule.

Key Recognition Features The regular flowers with all petals
similar and rounded, and the leaves with 3 or more deep divisions.

Ecology and Geography In woods, among damp or dry rocks,
and in sandy, open ground, often as weeds, or high into the
Andes; 1 or 2 species, such as *O. disticha* Jacq. in South Africa, are
aquatic, flowering on the water in vernal pools or *vleis*. Of the 20 or
so species found wild in Europe, only 2 are native, *O. acetosella* L., the
wood sorrel, and perhaps also the creeping, weedy *O. corniculata* L; all
the rest are weedy introductions from South Africa or the Americas.
The genus reaches its greatest diversity in the Andes and in the Cape
region of South Africa, where there are 129 species.

Comment The family Oxalidaceae was usually associated with the
Geraniaceae (see pp.112–15), but the similarities are now deemed to
have arisen independently. DNA evidence suggests that the
Oxalidales are rather isolated within the Eurosid group, and include
the Cephalotaceae, containing only the West Australian pitcher plant
Cephalotus follicularis Labill., the Cunoniaceae, a mainly southern-
hemisphere family that includes *Weinmannia* L. and *Eucryphia* (see
Volume 1), and *Crinodendron* (see Volume 1) in the Elaeocarpaceae.
Within Oxalidaceae, *Averrhoa carambola* L., the starfruit, is eaten in
the tropics. A few *Oxalis* species are grown as ornamentals, and 1,
O. tuberosa Molina, the oca, is cultivated in the Andes for its small,
potato-like tubers. Some weedy species, like the beautiful,
bright-yellow-flowered Bermuda buttercup, *O. pes-caprae* L.,
have become serious pests.

Polygala

Polygala L. (1787), in the family Polygalaceae, contains around 500 species throughout much of the world.

Description Dwarf perennials to 10cm, shrubs, or trees (in the tropics). The leaves are alternate or occasionally opposite, simple, evergreen or deciduous. The flowers are generally in loose spikes at the ends of the branches. Sepals 5, unequal, the inner 2 petal-like, the upper 2 sometimes fused. Petals 3, rarely 5, the upper 2 joined to the staminal tube, the lower boat-shaped, often with a 2-lobed crest. Stamens usually 8, the filaments joined into a split tube. Ovary superior, with 2 cells; style short. Pollination is by bees. The fruits are flattened and often notched capsules with 1 seed in each cell. The seeds have an appendage, an aril or caruncle, which is sometimes reduced to a tuft of hairs.

Key Recognition Features The pea-like flowers with a pair of petal-like sepals and a fringed lip.

Ecology and Geography Mostly in heath and rocky places, swamps, pine barrens, and woods; found throughout the world, apart from New Zealand.

Comment The flowers of *Polygala* show interesting parallelism with the pea-flowers of the Leguminosae (see pp.124–37), and DNA studies suggest that the 2 families are closely related, placing the Polygalaceae with the Leguminosae in the order Fabales. The low, herbaceous species are familiar on the moorlands, chalk hills, and mountains in Europe. There are dwarf, creeping, woodland shrubs in eastern North America (*P. pauciflora* Willd.), the mountains of Europe (*P. chamaebuxus* L.), and the Himalayas to western China (*P. arillata* D. Don). Another group of species are clover-like annuals, characteristic of the American prairies. The shrubby Polygala species, such as *P. virgata* Thunb. from South Africa, are very different in habit and often similar to broom or other shrubby Leguminosae.

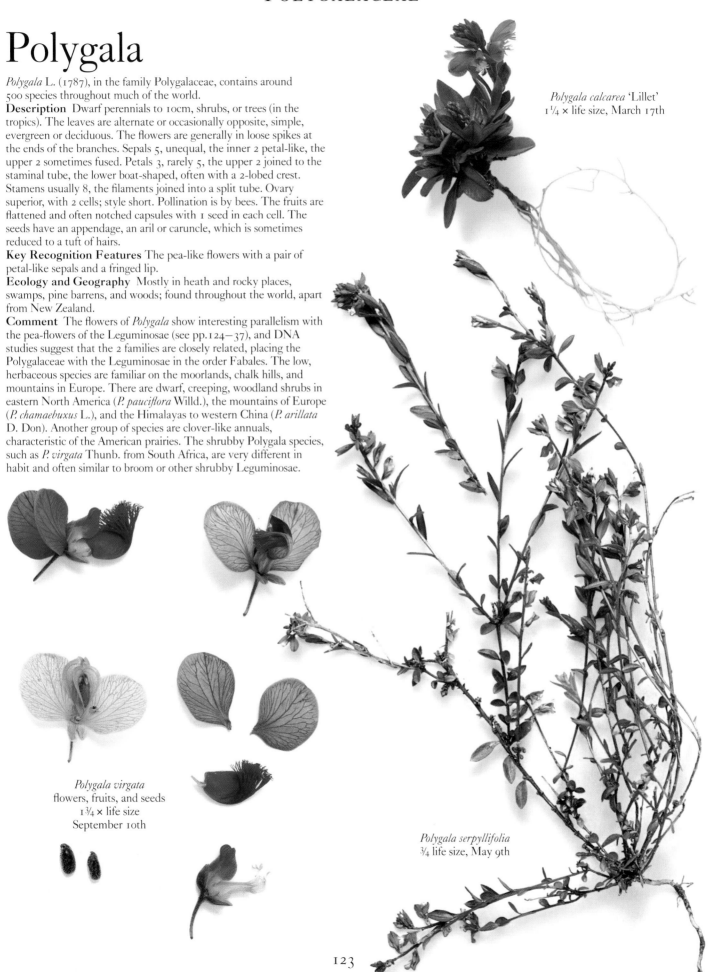

Polygala calcarea 'Lillet'
1¼ × life size, March 17th

Polygala virgata
flowers, fruits, and seeds
1¾ × life size
September 10th

Polygala serpyllifolia
¾ life size, May 9th

Lablab

Lablab Adans. (1763), in the Leguminosae subfamily Papilionoideae, contains 1 species, *L. purpureus* (L.) Sweet, syn. *Dolichos lablab* L., the lablab or hyacinth bean, common throughout the tropics.

Description Climbing annual or perennial to 10m. Leaves with 3 leaflets and very small stipules. The flowers are pea-like, in groups of 2–4, in loose spikes, red, purple, or white. Sepals 5, joined to form a wide calyx; petals 5, unequal, the uppermost a broad standard, flat or with the sides reflexed, the 2 outer forming rounded wings, joined to the keel, which covers the stamens, style, and ovary. Stamens 10, the uppermost free, the rest joined into a tube. Ovary superior, with 1 carpel containing several ovules; style 1, flattened and bearded. Pollination is by bees. The pods are flattened and curved, with several black or white and mottled seeds.

Key Recognition Features A tall climber with 3 large, triangular leaflets and whorled spikes of flowers. The whole plant is often purplish.

Ecology and Geography In gardens and hedges. Of uncertain origin, and long cultivated, but perhaps originally from Africa or possibly from India.

Comment The lablab bean is sometimes planted in temperate climates as a quick-growing ornamental. It is also cultivated in the tropics for fodder, to control erosion, and for its edible young pods and seeds.

The family Leguminosae is divided into 3 subfamilies, the Caesalpinoideae, Mimosoideae, and Papilionoideae. These are discussed in Volume 1; all the hardy herbaceous members of the family belong to the Papilionoidae, characterised by their distinctive pea-like flowers.

Lablab purpureus
½ life size, July 2nd

Lablab purpureus
flower parts and seed pods
1¼ × life size, July 7th

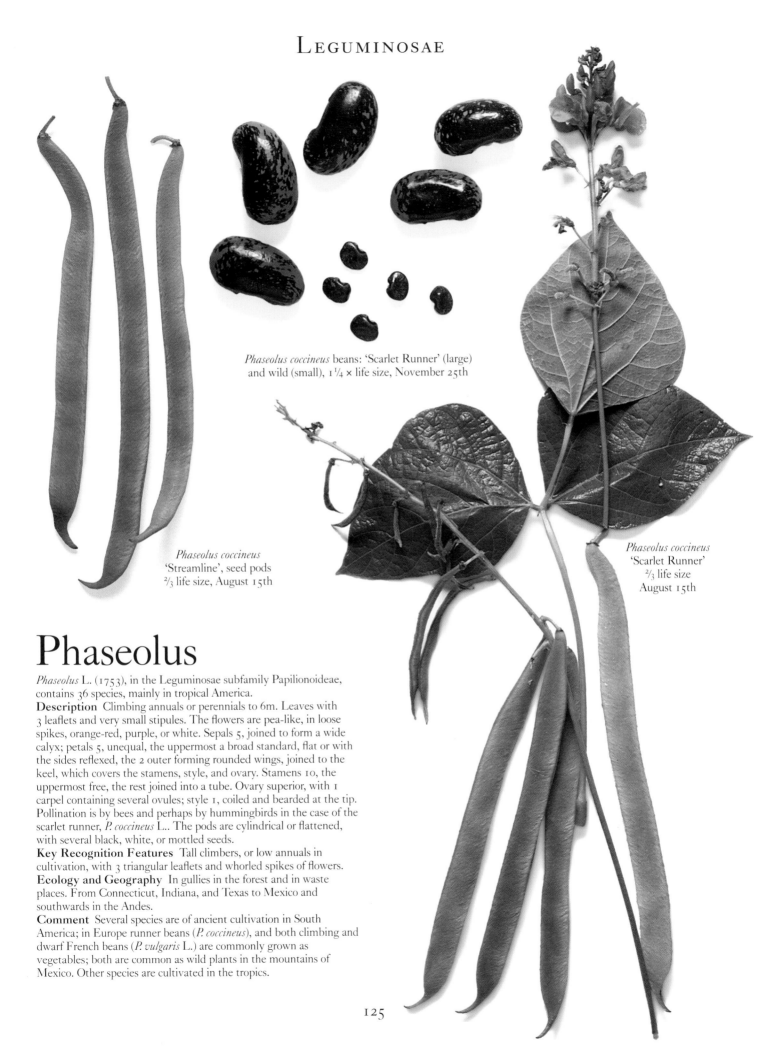

Phaseolus coccineus beans: 'Scarlet Runner' (large)
and wild (small), 1¼ × life size, November 25th

Phaseolus coccineus
'Streamline', seed pods
⅔ life size, August 15th

Phaseolus coccineus
'Scarlet Runner'
⅔ life size
August 15th

Phaseolus

Phaseolus L. (1753), in the Leguminosae subfamily Papilionoideae, contains 36 species, mainly in tropical America.

Description Climbing annuals or perennials to 6m. Leaves with 3 leaflets and very small stipules. The flowers are pea-like, in loose spikes, orange-red, purple, or white. Sepals 5, joined to form a wide calyx; petals 5, unequal, the uppermost a broad standard, flat or with the sides reflexed, the 2 outer forming rounded wings, joined to the keel, which covers the stamens, style, and ovary. Stamens 10, the uppermost free, the rest joined into a tube. Ovary superior, with 1 carpel containing several ovules; style 1, coiled and bearded at the tip. Pollination is by bees and perhaps by hummingbirds in the case of the scarlet runner, *P. coccineus* L.. The pods are cylindrical or flattened, with several black, white, or mottled seeds.

Key Recognition Features Tall climbers, or low annuals in cultivation, with 3 triangular leaflets and whorled spikes of flowers.

Ecology and Geography In gullies in the forest and in waste places. From Connecticut, Indiana, and Texas to Mexico and southwards in the Andes.

Comment Several species are of ancient cultivation in South America; in Europe runner beans (*P. coccineus*), and both climbing and dwarf French beans (*P. vulgaris* L.) are commonly grown as vegetables; both are common as wild plants in the mountains of Mexico. Other species are cultivated in the tropics.

Lupinus

Lupinus L. (1753), in the Leguminosae subfamily Papilionoideae, contains around 200 species, mainly in North America. For shrubby species see Volume 1.

Description Annuals, herbaceous perennials, and a few shrubs, to 2m. Leaves alternate, evergreen or deciduous, palmate, with 5–12 leaflets. The flowers are pea-like, in elongated spikes, reddish, blue, yellow, or white, usually scented. Sepals 5, unequal, joined to form a tubular, 2-lipped calyx; petals 5, unequal, the uppermost a broad standard with the sides folded back, the 2 outer wings, enclosing the keel, which covers the stamens, style, and ovary. Stamens 10, all joined into a tube at the base. Ovary superior, with 1 carpel containing several ovules; style 1. Pollination is by bees. The pods are usually silky, with numerous seeds.

Key Recognition Features The palmate leaves and the flower with the standard folded back and large, inflated wings.

Ecology and Geography In dry, sandy ground, on dunes, river gravel, stony deserts, and open grasslands, mainly in North America, extending south along the Andes, with a few mainly annual species in southern Europe and southwest Asia.

Comment *Lupinus* is related to *Laburnum* and *Robinia* (see Volume 1), rather than to other herbaceous genera. Many species are cultivated for fodder and for protein, although most wild species contain poisonous alkaloids. The perennial herbaceous species were bred from the North American *L. polyphyllus* Lindl., which usually has blue flowers.

Lupinus 'Noble Maiden'
½ life size, June 14th

Lupinus cultivar
⅔ life size, June 25th

Lupinus 'Noble Maiden'
flower parts, 1⅓ × life size, June 14th

Galega

Galega L. (1753), goat's rue, in the Leguminosae subfamily Papilionoideae, contains around 3 species, mainly in Europe and western Asia.

Description Herbaceous perennials to 2m, clump-forming or with creeping rhizomes. Leaves alternate, pinnate, with 4–8 pairs of pinnately-veined leaflets. The flowers are pea-like, in upright spikes, blue, white, or pinkish-lilac, usually scented. Sepals 5, subequal, joined to form a tubular calyx; petals 5, unequal, the uppermost a broad standard with the sides bent back, the 2 outer forming rounded wings, enclosing the keel, which covers the stamens, style, and ovary. Stamens 10, all equal, joined into a tube at the base. Ovary superior, with 1 carpel containing several ovules; style 1. Pollination is by bees. The pods are cylindrical and ridged, with numerous seeds.

Key Recognition Features The pinnate leaves with a terminal leaflet and the spikes of flowers in the leaf axils.

Ecology and Geography In open grassland and scrub, on riverbanks and roadsides, in southern Europe and southwestern Asia, naturalised further north; 1 species in the mountains of East Africa.

Comment Related to *Astragalus* (see p.128) and *Vicia* (see p.130), but with strong, upright stems and 10 equal stamens. The common species *G. officinalis* L. and *G. orientalis* Lam. are both grown in herbaceous gardens. Other named species are now considered synonyms of *G. officinalis*.

Securigera

Securigera DC (1805), in the Leguminosae subfamily Papilionoideae, contains around 12 species, mainly around the Mediterranean.

Description Herbaceous perennials to 1.2m, or annuals. Leaves alternate, pinnate with 5–20 pairs of narrow leaflets. The flowers are pea-like, in round heads of up to 40, yellow, white or pinkish-lilac. Sepals 5, subequal, joined to form a tubular calyx, the upper 2 teeth fused; petals 5, unequal, the uppermost a broad standard, with the sides bent back, the 2 outer form rounded wings, which enclose the pointed keel which covers the stamens, style and ovary. Stamens 10, the uppermost free, the rest joined into a tube. Ovary superior, with 1 carpel containing several ovules; style 1. Pollination is by bees. The pods are cylindrical with thick margins and a long beak.

Key Recognition Features The ridged stems, pinnate leaves with a terminal leaflet, and heads of flowers on stalks in the leaf axils.

Ecology and Geography In open grassland, scrub, open woods, and on cliffs, in southern Europe and southwestern Asia, naturalised further north. One species in the mountains of Somalia.

Comment Very close to *Coronilla* (see p.128): crown vetch, *Securigera varia* (L.) Lassen, is still often called *Coronilla varia* L; it is often found by roadsides and in other rough grassy places. *Securigera* was formerly confined to 1 species, *S. securidaca* (L.) Degen & Dörf., an annual with small, yellow flowers, but now encompasses species formerly in *Coronilla* with ridged stems.

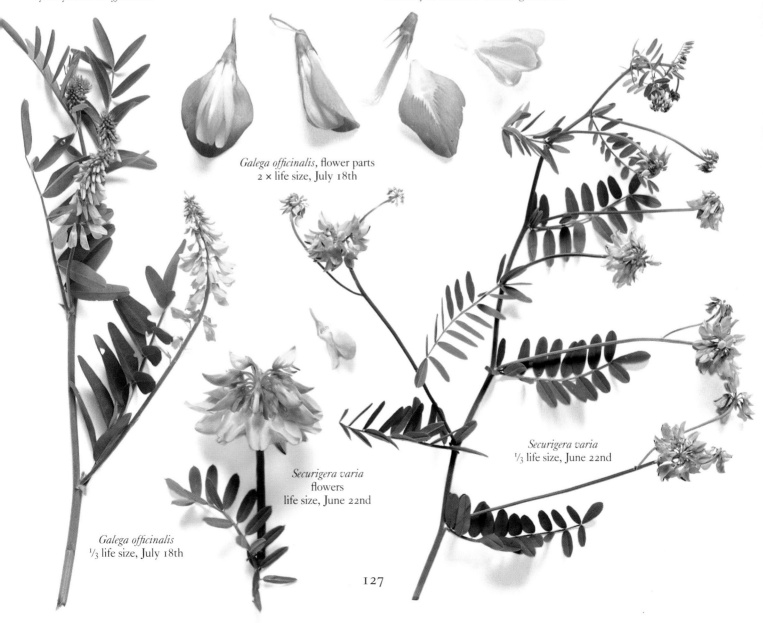

Galega officinalis, flower parts
2 × life size, July 18th

Securigera varia
flowers
life size, June 22nd

Securigera varia
¹/₃ life size, June 22nd

Galega officinalis
¹/₃ life size, July 18th

Coronilla minima
flowers and seed pods
1½ × life size, July 5th

Coronilla minima
just over life size
July 5th

Coronilla

Coronilla L. (1753), in the Leguminosae subfamily Papilionoideae, contains around 12 species, mainly in the Mediterranean area.
Description Shrubs, herbaceous perennials, and annuals to 1m. Leaves pinnate, with 1–6 pairs of wide leaflets. The flowers are pea-like, in round heads of up to 12, usually yellow. Sepals 5, subequal, joined to form a tubular calyx, the upper 2 teeth fused; petals 5, unequal, the uppermost a broad standard with the sides bent back, the 2 outer forming rounded wings, enclosing the pointed keel, which covers the stamens, style, and ovary. Stamens 10, the uppermost free, the rest joined into a tube. Ovary superior, with 1 carpel containing several ovules; style 1. Pollination is by bees. The pods are cylindrical and straight, with a long beak.
Key Recognition Features The rounded stems, rather pinnate leaves with a terminal leaflet, and heads of yellow flowers.
Ecology and Geography In scrub and dry, open woods, and on cliffs, in southern Europe and southwestern Asia.
Comment Very close to *Securigera* (see p.127), but with stems not ridged, and usually shrubby with yellow flowers.

Astragalus

Astragalus L. (1753), in the Leguminosae subfamily Papilionoideae, contains around 2000 species, mainly in central and western Asia.
Description Herbaceous perennials or subshrubs to 1m, occasionally annuals. Leaves pinnate, with few to many pairs of leaflets, sometimes ending in a spine. The flowers are pea-like, in tight heads, in the leaf axils or in elongated spikes, usually reddish, pink purplish, white, or yellow. Sepals 5, equal or unequal, joined to form a short or long tubular calyx; petals 5, unequal, the uppermost a broad standard with the sides folded back, the 2 outer forming rounded wings, enclosing the keel, which covers the stamens, style, and ovary. Stamens 10, the uppermost free, the rest joined into a tube. Ovary superior, with 1 or 2 carpels containing several ovules; style 1. Pollination is usually by bees. The pods are often swollen, curved, and leathery and have 1 to several seeds.
Key Recognition Features A genus with such a wide range of features that the best way to recognise its members is that they are not in any other genus. The flowers are mostly in smallish heads.
Ecology and Geography Steppes and prairies, scrub, dry, open woods, and mountain cliffs, mostly in Asia; over 370 species in Turkey, 133 in Europe, and 72 in Arizona, where it is the largest genus.
Comment Many species are low, spiny shrubs in the steppes of Asia. They contain the gum tragacanth, used in food products and cosmetics, and are sometimes separated in the genus *Astracantha* Podlech. Several species in North America, including the common and widespread *A. lentiginosus* Dougl., so-called locoweeds, concentrate selenium, and so are poisonous to cattle and horses. *Astragalus glycphyllos* L. is the wild liquorice, which can be used as a herbal tea; it grows in hedges and scrub, especially on chalk.

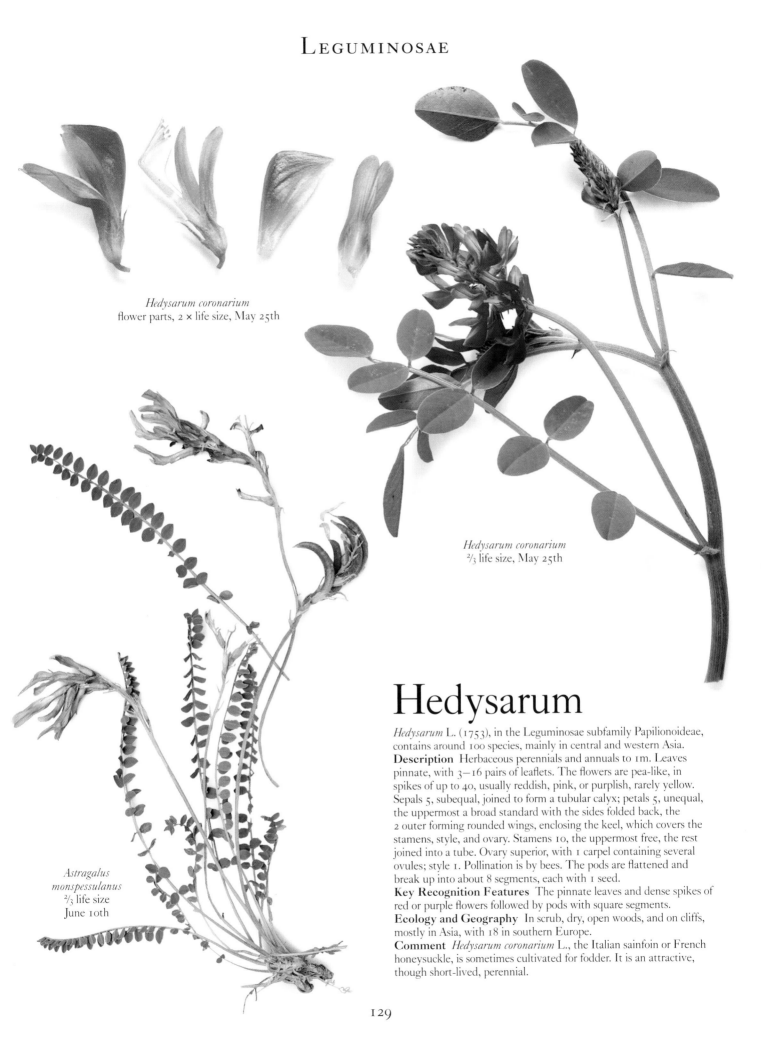

Hedysarum coronarium
flower parts, 2 × life size, May 25th

Hedysarum coronarium
²/₃ life size, May 25th

*Astragalus
monspessulanus*
²/₃ life size
June 10th

Hedysarum

Hedysarum L. (1753), in the Leguminosae subfamily Papilionoideae, contains around 100 species, mainly in central and western Asia.

Description Herbaceous perennials and annuals to 1m. Leaves pinnate, with 3–16 pairs of leaflets. The flowers are pea-like, in spikes of up to 40, usually reddish, pink, or purplish, rarely yellow. Sepals 5, subequal, joined to form a tubular calyx; petals 5, unequal, the uppermost a broad standard with the sides folded back, the 2 outer forming rounded wings, enclosing the keel, which covers the stamens, style, and ovary. Stamens 10, the uppermost free, the rest joined into a tube. Ovary superior, with 1 carpel containing several ovules; style 1. Pollination is by bees. The pods are flattened and break up into about 8 segments, each with 1 seed.

Key Recognition Features The pinnate leaves and dense spikes of red or purple flowers followed by pods with square segments.

Ecology and Geography In scrub, dry, open woods, and on cliffs, mostly in Asia, with 18 in southern Europe.

Comment *Hedysarum coronarium* L., the Italian sainfoin or French honeysuckle, is sometimes cultivated for fodder. It is an attractive, though short-lived, perennial.

Onobrychis

Onobrychis Mill. (1754), in the Leguminosae subfamily Papilionoideae, contains around 130 species, mainly in Asia.
Description Herbaceous perennials and annuals to 1m, rarely dwarf, prickly shrubs. Leaves pinnate, with 4–14 pairs of leaflets. The flowers are pea-like, in elongated spikes of up to 40 or more, usually reddish, pink, or purplish, rarely yellow, usually veined. Sepals 5, subequal, joined to form a tubular calyx; petals 5, unequal, the uppermost a broad standard with the sides folded back, the 2 outer forming rounded wings, enclosing the keel, which covers the stamens, style, and ovary. Stamens 10, the uppermost free, the rest joined into a tube. Ovary superior, with 1 carpel containing 1 ovule; style 1. Pollination is by bees. The pods are 1-seeded, usually strongly veined, with spines and often curved teeth.
Key Recognition Features The pinnate leaves and veined flowers followed by 1-seeded, usually spiny pods.
Ecology and Geography On steppes, in scrub and dry open woods, and on cliffs, mostly in Asia, with 46 species in Turkey, including *O. gracilis* Besser.
Comment Sainfoin, *O. viciifolia* Scop., is a common and valuable fodder crop in dry areas. *Onobrychis cornuta* (L.) Desv. is a dwarf, rounded shrub, common on dry steppes from Turkey to Afghanistan and Turkestan.

Vicia

Vicia L. (1753), vetch, in the Leguminosae subfamily Papilionoideae, contains around 140 species, mainly in the northern hemisphere.
Description Herbaceous perennials and annuals, often climbing to 2m or more; stems usually not winged. Leaves pinnate, with 2 to many leaflets, usually ending in a tendril. The flowers are pea-like, in heads of up to 40, yellow, purple, white, or pinkish. Sepals 5, equal or forming 2 lips, joined to form a calyx; petals 5, unequal, the uppermost a broad standard, flat or with the sides recurved, the 2 outer forming rounded wings, enclosing the keel, which covers the stamens, style, and ovary. Stamens 10, the uppermost free, the rest joined into a tube. Ovary superior, with 1 carpel containing many ovules; style 1. Pollination is by bees. The pods are many-seeded and usually cylindrical or flattened.
Key Recognition Features Climbing plants with many leaflets and smallish flowers followed by long, narrow pods.
Ecology and Geography In dry, grassy meadows, on sand-dunes and shingle, and in scrub; 59 species in Turkey, as many in Europe, and a few in the Americas, southwards along the Andes to Patagonia.
Comment The most important *Vicia* is the broad bean, *V. faba* L., cultivated throughout the world, but originally from the Middle East or perhaps North Africa; its beans have been found in pre-pottery neolithic deposits in Jericho. Other species, such as *V. sativa* L. are cultivated for fodder, and a few as ornamentals. *Vicia cracca* L. is an attractive climber, flowering in midsummer, a familiar sight on hedges and roadsides over much of Europe.

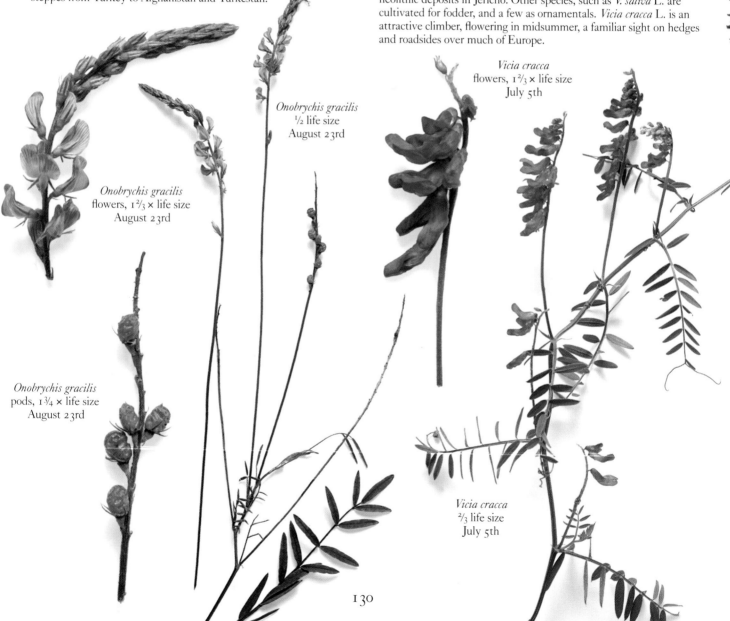

Onobrychis gracilis
½ life size
August 23rd

Onobrychis gracilis
flowers, 1⅔ × life size
August 23rd

Onobrychis gracilis
pods, 1¾ × life size
August 23rd

Vicia cracca
flowers, 1⅔ × life size
July 5th

Vicia cracca
⅔ life size
July 5th

Pisum

Pisum L. (1753), the garden pea, in the Leguminosae subfamily Papilionoideae, contains 2 species in southwestern Asia.

Description Climbing annuals, to 2m or more; stems usually not winged. Leaves pinnate, with 2–6 leaflets, usually ending in a tendril, and large, leafy stipules. The flowers are pea-like, solitary or up to 3, white, purple, pinkish, or yellow. Sepals 5, almost leafy, joined to form a calyx; petals 5, unequal, the uppermost a broad standard, flat or with the sides recurved, the 2 outer forming rounded wings, enclosing the keel, which covers the stamens, style, and ovary. Stamens 10, the uppermost free, the rest joined into a tube. Ovary superior, with 1 carpel containing many ovules; style 1. Pollination is by bees. The pods are many-seeded and usually cylindrical.

Key Recognition Features Climbing plants with few leaflets and leafy stipules; 1–3 flowers followed by long, narrow pods.

Ecology and Geography In rocky places, vineyards, and ruins, and on roadsides. Wild forms of the cultivated pea are found from western Turkey to northwestern Iran and northern Egypt.

Comment Seeds of primitive garden peas, *Pisum sativum* L. var. *pumilio* Meikle, have been found in neolithic deposits dating from 7000 BC. Large amounts were stored in Troy, and Schliemann famously boasted that he had "supped off Priam's peas". Some varieties of pea grown today are leafless, with very large tendrils and enlarged stipules. Mangetout peas and snowpeas are old varieties, without stiffening in the pod wall. In wild peas the pods open explosively, and the seeds are covered with fine papillae.

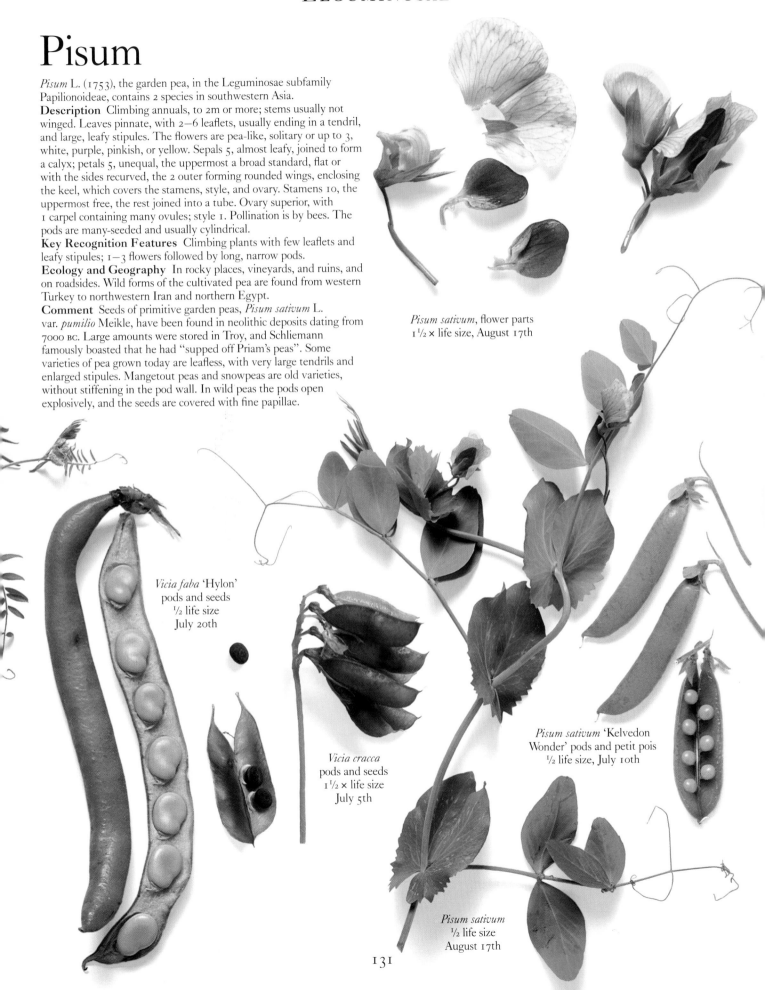

Pisum sativum, flower parts
1½ × life size, August 17th

Vicia faba 'Hylon'
pods and seeds
½ life size
July 20th

Vicia cracca
pods and seeds
1½ × life size
July 5th

Pisum sativum 'Kelvedon
Wonder' pods and petit pois
½ life size, July 10th

Pisum sativum
½ life size
August 17th

131

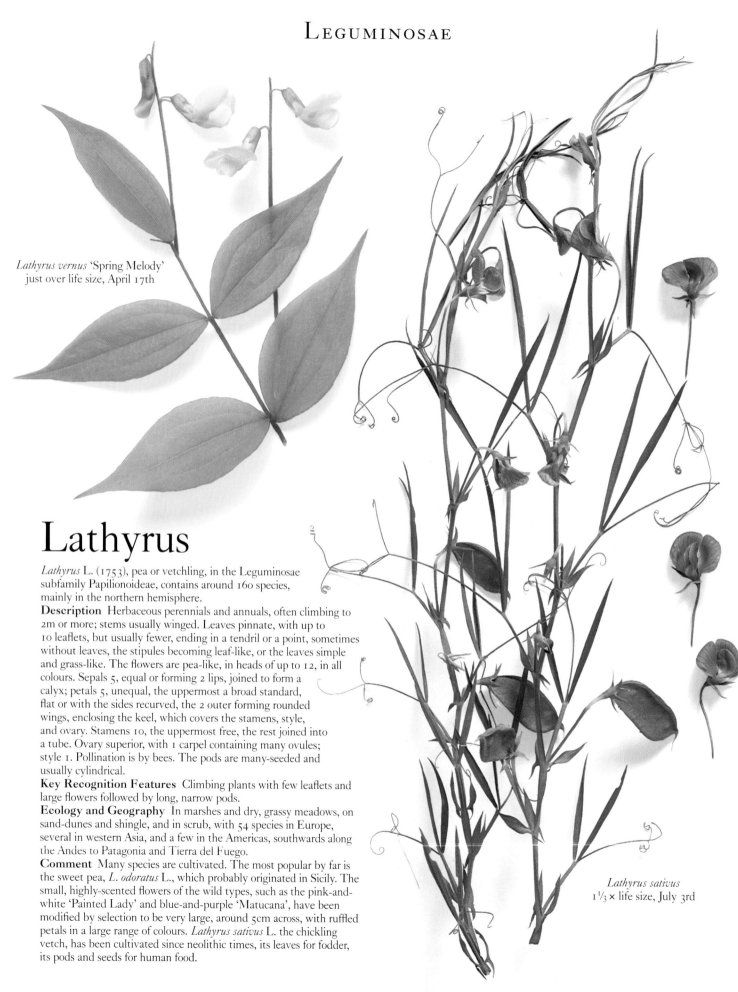

Lathyrus vernus 'Spring Melody'
just over life size, April 17th

Lathyrus

Lathyrus L. (1753), pea or vetchling, in the Leguminosae subfamily Papilionoideae, contains around 160 species, mainly in the northern hemisphere.

Description Herbaceous perennials and annuals, often climbing to 2m or more; stems usually winged. Leaves pinnate, with up to 10 leaflets, but usually fewer, ending in a tendril or a point, sometimes without leaves, the stipules becoming leaf-like, or the leaves simple and grass-like. The flowers are pea-like, in heads of up to 12, in all colours. Sepals 5, equal or forming 2 lips, joined to form a calyx; petals 5, unequal, the uppermost a broad standard, flat or with the sides recurved, the 2 outer forming rounded wings, enclosing the keel, which covers the stamens, style, and ovary. Stamens 10, the uppermost free, the rest joined into a tube. Ovary superior, with 1 carpel containing many ovules; style 1. Pollination is by bees. The pods are many-seeded and usually cylindrical.

Key Recognition Features Climbing plants with few leaflets and large flowers followed by long, narrow pods.

Ecology and Geography In marshes and dry, grassy meadows, on sand-dunes and shingle, and in scrub, with 54 species in Europe, several in western Asia, and a few in the Americas, southwards along the Andes to Patagonia and Tierra del Fuego.

Comment Many species are cultivated. The most popular by far is the sweet pea, *L. odoratus* L., which probably originated in Sicily. The small, highly-scented flowers of the wild types, such as the pink-and-white 'Painted Lady' and blue-and-purple 'Matucana', have been modified by selection to be very large, around 5cm across, with ruffled petals in a large range of colours. *Lathyrus sativus* L. the chickling vetch, has been cultivated since neolithic times, its leaves for fodder, its pods and seeds for human food.

Lathyrus sativus
$1\frac{1}{3}$ × life size, July 3rd

Lathyrus odoratus
'Painted Lady'
¾ life size
August 15th

Lathyrus magellanicus
flower parts, 1 ½ × life size
May 10th

Lathyrus magellanicus
⅔ life size
May 10th

Lathyrus magellanicus
ripe pods and seeds
¾ life size, December 1st

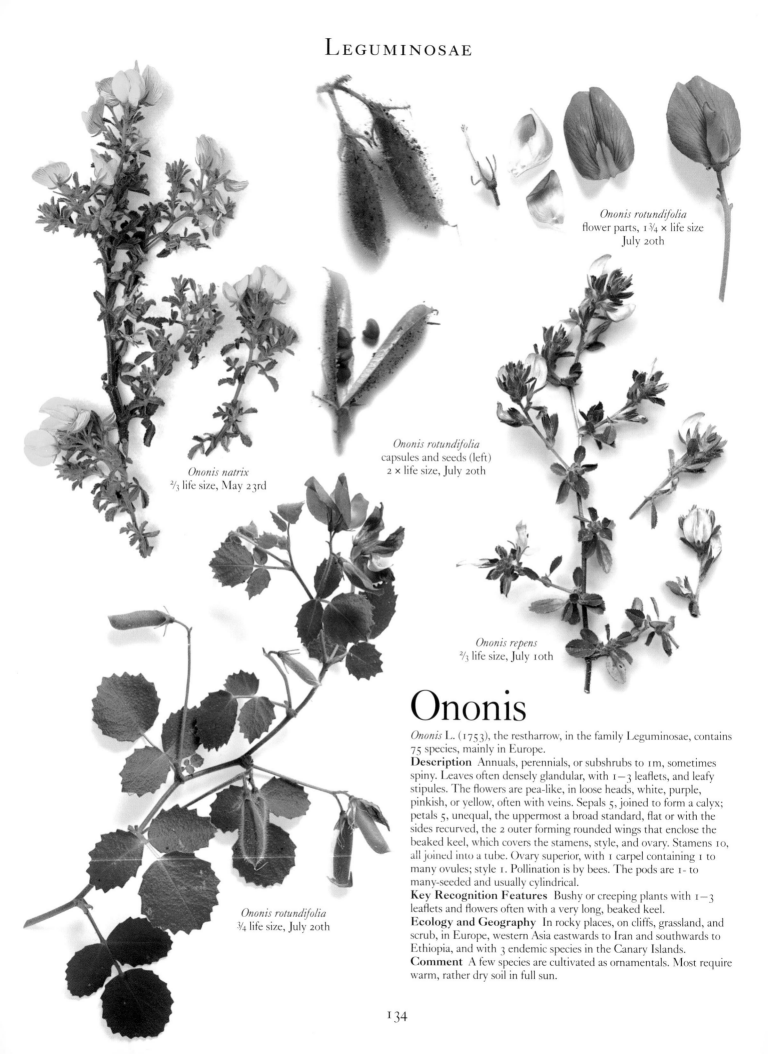

Ononis rotundifolia
flower parts, 1¾ × life size
July 20th

Ononis natrix
⅔ life size, May 23rd

Ononis rotundifolia
capsules and seeds (left)
2 × life size, July 20th

Ononis repens
⅔ life size, July 10th

Ononis rotundifolia
¾ life size, July 20th

Ononis

Ononis L. (1753), the restharrow, in the family Leguminosae, contains 75 species, mainly in Europe.

Description Annuals, perennials, or subshrubs to 1m, sometimes spiny. Leaves often densely glandular, with 1–3 leaflets, and leafy stipules. The flowers are pea-like, in loose heads, white, purple, pinkish, or yellow, often with veins. Sepals 5, joined to form a calyx; petals 5, unequal, the uppermost a broad standard, flat or with the sides recurved, the 2 outer forming rounded wings that enclose the beaked keel, which covers the stamens, style, and ovary. Stamens 10, all joined into a tube. Ovary superior, with 1 carpel containing 1 to many ovules; style 1. Pollination is by bees. The pods are 1- to many-seeded and usually cylindrical.

Key Recognition Features Bushy or creeping plants with 1–3 leaflets and flowers often with a very long, beaked keel.

Ecology and Geography In rocky places, on cliffs, grassland, and scrub, in Europe, western Asia eastwards to Iran and southwards to Ethiopia, and with 3 endemic species in the Canary Islands.

Comment A few species are cultivated as ornamentals. Most require warm, rather dry soil in full sun.

Trifolium

Trifolium L. (1753), the clover, in the family Leguminosae, contains around 238 species worldwide.

Description Annuals or perennials to 70cm. Leaves with 3 leaflets and small stipules. The flowers are small and pea-like, in dense heads, white, red, purple, pinkish, or yellow. Sepals 5, joined to form a calyx, often enlarging after flowering; petals 5, unequal, the uppermost a standard, the 2 outer forming wings, the 2 inner forming a keel, which covers the stamens, style, and ovary. Stamens 10, the uppermost free, the rest joined into a tube or with 5 having filaments dilated at the apex. Ovary superior, with 1 carpel containing 1 or more ovules; style 1. Pollination is by bees. The pods are 1- to 4-seeded and usually hidden in the persistent calyx.

Key Recognition Features Bushy or creeping plants with 3 leaflets and heads of small, narrow pea-flowers.

Ecology and Geography In rocky places, on cliffs, dunes, grassland, and steppe; 99 species in Europe, the rest worldwide, with the exception of Australia and New Zealand.

Comment Several species are grown for fodder, particularly white clover, *T. repens* L., and red clover, *T. pratense* L.. *Trifolium dubium* Sibth. is thought to be St Patrick's shamrock.

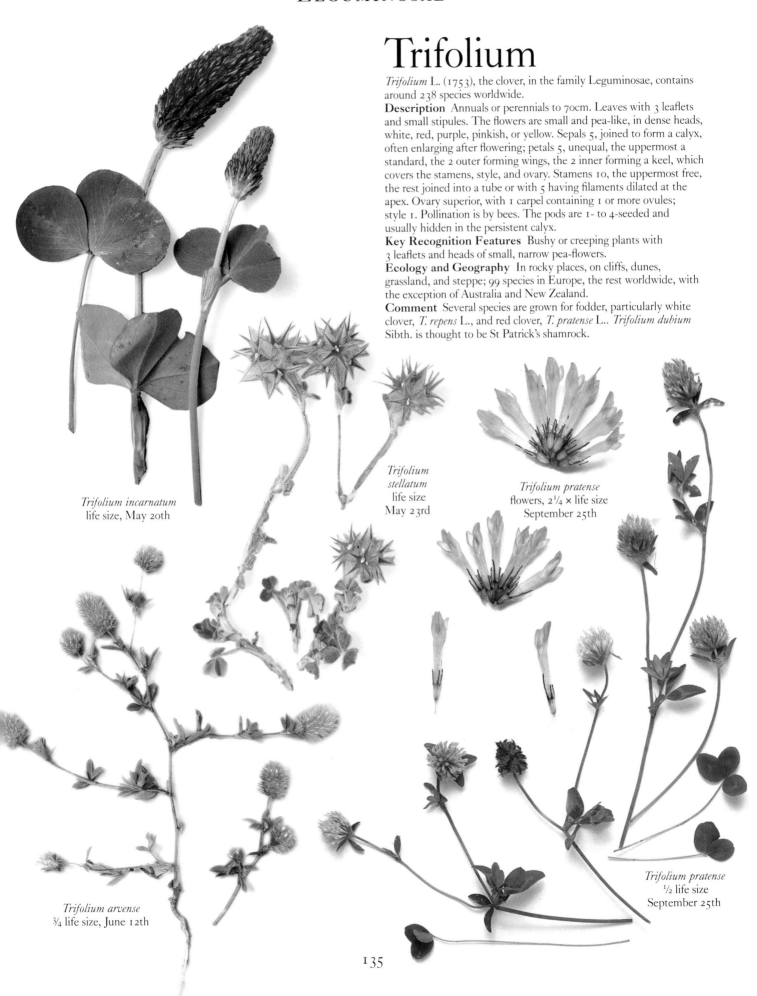

Trifolium incarnatum
life size, May 20th

Trifolium stellatum
life size
May 23rd

Trifolium pratense
flowers, 2¼ × life size
September 25th

Trifolium arvense
¾ life size, June 12th

Trifolium pratense
½ life size
September 25th

Lotus maritimus
flower parts, 1½ × life size
May 17th

Lotus maritimus
¾ life size, May 17th

Lotus

Lotus L. (1753), in the family Leguminosae, contains around
100 species, mainly in Europe and the Atlantic islands.

Description Herbaceous perennials and annuals to 1m, rarely
subshrubs. Leaves pinnate with 5 leaflets, the lowest pair stipule-like,
the stipules very small or absent. The flowers are usually pea-like, in
heads of up to 12, and usually yellowish, pink, or red, rarely dark
blackish-brown. Sepals 5, equal or the upper larger, joined to form a
calyx; petals 5, unequal, the uppermost a broad standard, flat or with
the sides recurved, the 2 outer forming wings that enclose the beaked
keel, which covers the stamens, style, and ovary. Stamens 10, the
upper free, the rest joined into a tube. Ovary superior, with 1 carpel
containing many ovules; style 1. Pollination is by bees. The pods are
many-seeded, smooth, and usually cylindrical.

Key Recognition Features The few leaflets, and usually yellow
flowers followed by long, narrow pods.

Ecology and Geography In marshes, dry meadows, and sandy
places and on cliffs, with 30 species in Europe and as many in the
Atlantic islands southwards to the Cape Verde islands.

Comment Most of the mainland species are quite ordinary-looking.
On Tenerife, however, there are 2 remarkable species, *L. berthelotii*
Masf. and *L. maculatus* Breitf, with large flowers in pairs or groups of
3, apparently adapted to pollination by birds; the standards curl back,
the keels have very long beaks, and the flowers are yellow or orange
with red tips. These are among several flowers in the Canaries that
are apparently adapted for pollination by sunbirds, which are no
longer found there (see also *Canarina* and *Kniphofia*). The genus
Tetragonolobus Scop., often united with *Lotus*, differs in having
3-foliate leaves with leafy stipules, and often winged pods, for
example in the edible asparagus pea, *T. purpureus* Moench.

Lotus uliginosus
⅔ life size, July 4th

Lotus berthelotii
life size, May 15th

Tetragonolobus purpureus
with flowers and fruit
²⁄₃ life size, June 20th

Lotus berthelotii
flower parts
1¾ × life size
May 15th

Lotus berthelotii
½ life size
May 15th

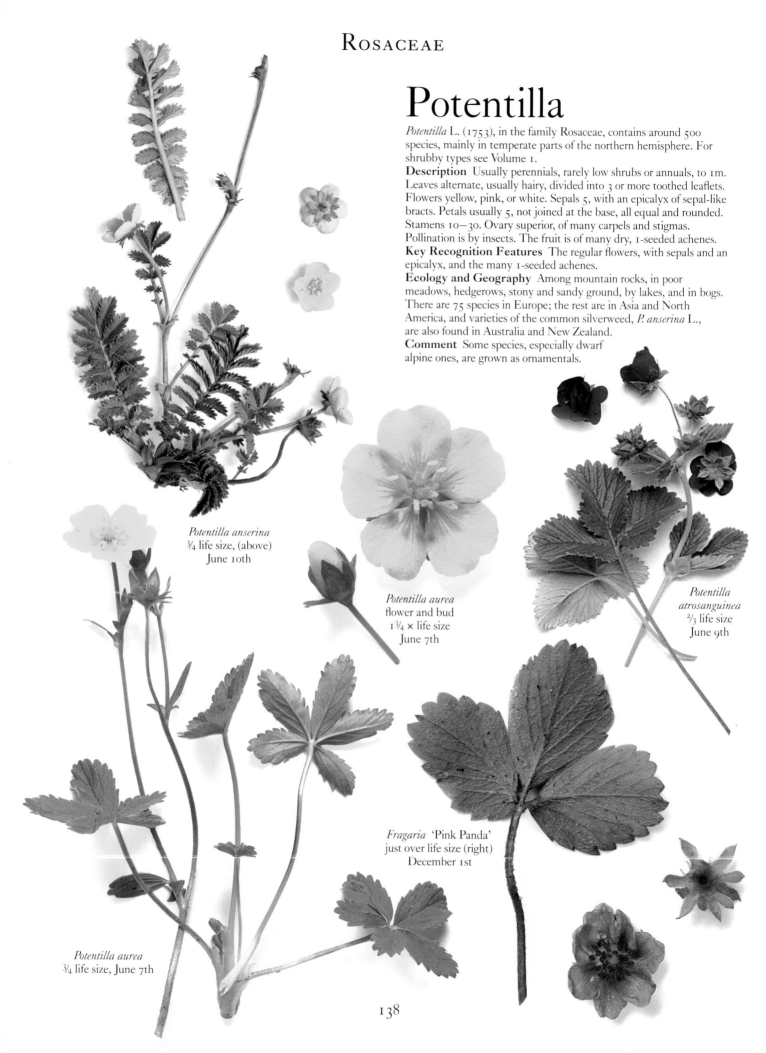

Potentilla

Potentilla L. (1753), in the family Rosaceae, contains around 500 species, mainly in temperate parts of the northern hemisphere. For shrubby types see Volume 1.

Description Usually perennials, rarely low shrubs or annuals, to 1m. Leaves alternate, usually hairy, divided into 3 or more toothed leaflets. Flowers yellow, pink, or white. Sepals 5, with an epicalyx of sepal-like bracts. Petals usually 5, not joined at the base, all equal and rounded. Stamens 10–30. Ovary superior, of many carpels and stigmas. Pollination is by insects. The fruit is of many dry, 1-seeded achenes.

Key Recognition Features The regular flowers, with sepals and an epicalyx, and the many 1-seeded achenes.

Ecology and Geography Among mountain rocks, in poor meadows, hedgerows, stony and sandy ground, by lakes, and in bogs. There are 75 species in Europe; the rest are in Asia and North America, and varieties of the common silverweed, *P. anserina* L., are also found in Australia and New Zealand.

Comment Some species, especially dwarf alpine ones, are grown as ornamentals.

Potentilla anserina
¾ life size, (above)
June 10th

Potentilla aurea
flower and bud
1¾ × life size
June 7th

Potentilla atrosanguinea
⅔ life size
June 9th

Fragaria 'Pink Panda'
just over life size (right)
December 1st

Potentilla aurea
¾ life size, June 7th

Waldsteinia

Waldsteinia Willd. (1799), in the family Rosaceae, contains 5 species in Europe, eastern Asia, and easternNorth America.

Description Perennials to 10cm, often creeping by stolons. Leaves 3-lobed or divided. Flowers yellow. Sepals 5, with the epicalyx very small or absent. Petals usually 5, not joined at the base, all equal and rounded. Stamens many. Ovary superior, of many carpels, and styles that fall after the flower fades. Pollination is by insects. The fruit is made up of 3–13 dry, 1-seeded achenes.

Key Recognition Features The regular flowers, with sepals but very small or no epicalyx, and many 1-seeded achenes, without persistent styles (see also *Geum*, p.140).

Ecology and Geography In woods in the mountains, with 3 species in eastern North America and 2 species in eastern Europe, 1 of which, *W. ternata* (Stefan) Fritsch, is also found in Japan and eastern Siberia, a remarkable example of discontinuous distribution and evolutionary stability over millions of years.

Comment The genus is named after Count Franz Adam Waldstein von Wartenburg (1759–1823), an Austrian botanist and, with P. Kitaibel, author of the 17-volume *Descriptiones et Icones Plantarum Rariorum Hungariae* in Vienna in 1799–1812. *Waldsteinia ternata* is commonly cultivated for ground cover in partial shade.

Waldsteinia ternata
½ life size, April 25th

Waldsteinia ternata, flowers
1¾ × life size, April 25th

Fragaria

Fragaria L. (1753), the strawberry, in the family Rosaceae, contains 12 species in Europe, Asia, North America, and Chile.

Description Perennials to 20cm, often creeping by stolons. Leaves divided into 3 toothed leaflets. Flowers white, rarely pinkish. Sepals 5, with the 5 epicalyx scales similar. Petals usually 5, not joined at the base, all equal and rounded. Stamens many. Ovary superior, of many carpels, and short styles, which fall as the fruit expands. Pollination is by insects. The fruit is a strawberry, made up of many achenes on the outside of a fleshy receptacle.

Key Recognition Features The regular flowers, with sepals and epicalyx, and the typical strawberry fruit.

Ecology and Geography On sunny banks and in open woods, with 3 wild species in Europe, the rest in the mountains of Asia, in western North America, and on the coast of Chile.

Comment The cultivated strawberry, *F.* × *ananassa* Duchesne, is derived from hybrids between the Pacific species *F. chiloensis* (L.) Duchesne, and the eastern American *F. virginiana* Duchesne. It was first grown in the 18th century. *Fragaria* 'Pink Panda' is a new pink-flowered ornamental strawberry with edible fruit, raised by crossing the purple-flowered *Potentilla palustris* with the strawberry, and backcrossing to a strawberry. The strawberry-like *Duchesnea* Sm. is named after A. N. Duchesne (1747–1827), who studied strawberries. It is now sometimes included in *Potentilla*, and has yellow flowers and fleshy but insipid fruit.

Fragaria vesca
flowers and fruit
1⅓ × life size
September 24th

Fragaria vesca
½ life size, September 24th

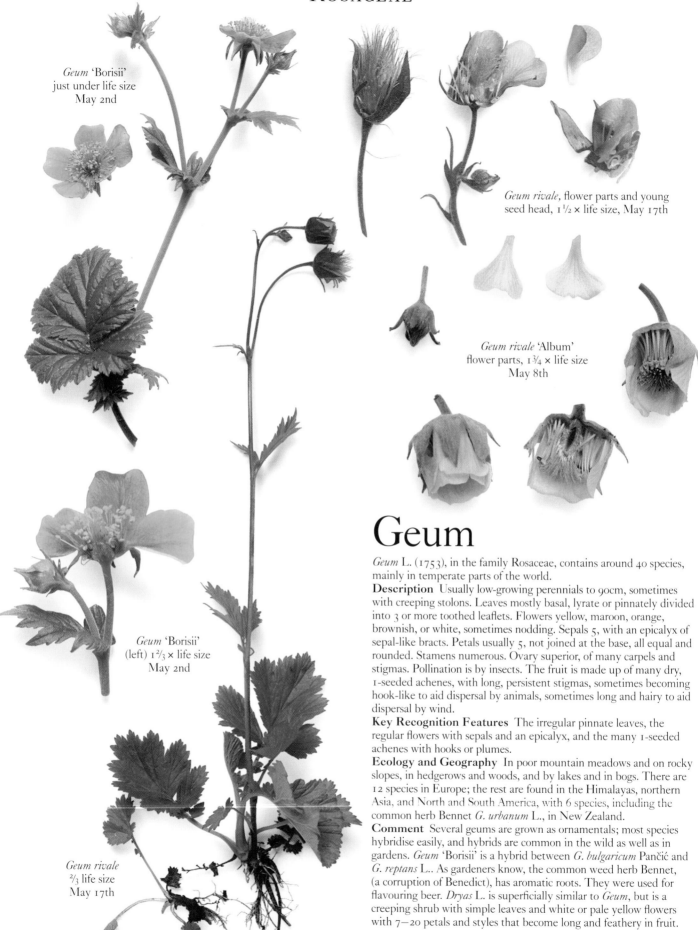

Geum 'Borisii'
just under life size
May 2nd

Geum rivale, flower parts and young
seed head, 1½ × life size, May 17th

Geum rivale 'Album'
flower parts, 1¾ × life size
May 8th

Geum 'Borisii'
(left) 1⅔ × life size
May 2nd

Geum rivale
⅔ life size
May 17th

Geum

Geum L. (1753), in the family Rosaceae, contains around 40 species, mainly in temperate parts of the world.

Description Usually low-growing perennials to 90cm, sometimes with creeping stolons. Leaves mostly basal, lyrate or pinnately divided into 3 or more toothed leaflets. Flowers yellow, maroon, orange, brownish, or white, sometimes nodding. Sepals 5, with an epicalyx of sepal-like bracts. Petals usually 5, not joined at the base, all equal and rounded. Stamens numerous. Ovary superior, of many carpels and stigmas. Pollination is by insects. The fruit is made up of many dry, 1-seeded achenes, with long, persistent stigmas, sometimes becoming hook-like to aid dispersal by animals, sometimes long and hairy to aid dispersal by wind.

Key Recognition Features The irregular pinnate leaves, the regular flowers with sepals and an epicalyx, and the many 1-seeded achenes with hooks or plumes.

Ecology and Geography In poor mountain meadows and on rocky slopes, in hedgerows and woods, and by lakes and in bogs. There are 12 species in Europe; the rest are found in the Himalayas, northern Asia, and North and South America, with 6 species, including the common herb Bennet *G. urbanum* L., in New Zealand.

Comment Several geums are grown as ornamentals; most species hybridise easily, and hybrids are common in the wild as well as in gardens. *Geum* 'Borisii' is a hybrid between *G. bulgaricum* Pančić and *G. reptans* L.. As gardeners know, the common weed herb Bennet, (a corruption of Benedict), has aromatic roots. They were used for flavouring beer. *Dryas* L. is superficially similar to *Geum*, but is a creeping shrub with simple leaves and white or pale yellow flowers with 7–20 petals and styles that become long and feathery in fruit.

Alchemilla

Alchemilla L. (1753), the lady's mantle, in the family Rosaceae, contains over 300 species worldwide.

Description Perennials to 30cm, often creeping by stolons. Leaves lobed or palmately or pinnately divided into toothed leaflets. Flowers very small, green. Sepals 4, rarely 5, with the 4 or 5 epicalyx segments smaller or of similar size. Petals absent. Stamens 4 or 5. Ovary of 1 carpel, with 1 short style. Pollination is by insects, but most species set seed apomictically, without fertilisation. The fruit is 1 achene, enclosed by the dry sepals.

Key Recognition Features The small, green flowers and distinct palmate leaves (pinnate leaves are found in the Andean species).

Ecology and Geography In meadows, among mountain rocks, and in scrub. Over 300 species have been described from Europe, nearly all apomictic. Others are found in the Caucasus, the mountains of Asia, North and South America, and mountains in the tropics and southern Africa. *Alchemilla xanthochlora* Rothm. is naturalised in Australia.

Comment Several species are grown as ornamentals, particularly the large and softly hairy *A. mollis* (Buser) Rothm. from Romania and western Russia.

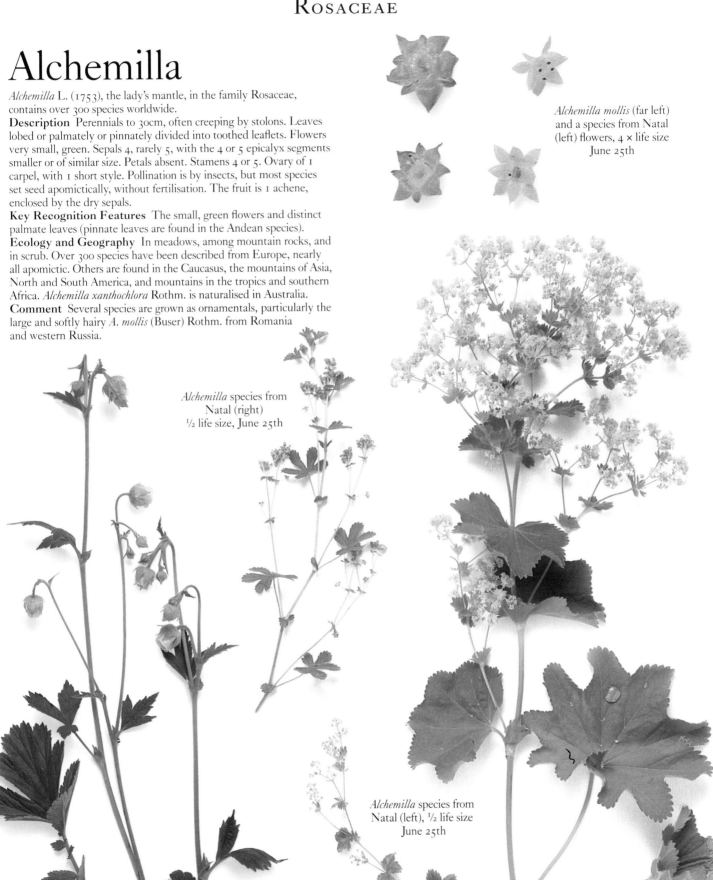

Alchemilla mollis (far left) and a species from Natal (left) flowers, 4 × life size June 25th

Alchemilla species from Natal (right) ½ life size, June 25th

Geum rivale 'Album' ½ life size May 8th

Alchemilla species from Natal (left), ½ life size June 25th

Alchemilla mollis ½ life size, June 25th

Agrimonia

Agrimonia L. (1753), in the family Rosaceae, contains around 15 species, mainly in Europe.

Description Usually upright, leafy perennials, 1−2m, sometimes with creeping rhizomes. Leaves mostly irregularly, pinnately divided into 3 to many toothed leaflets. Flowers yellow, small, sometimes nodding, in long spikes. Sepals 5, without an epicalyx. Petals 5, small. Stamens numerous. Ovary inferior, of 2 carpels and 1 style. Pollination is perhaps by insects. The fruit is 1 or 2-seeded, with a ring of hooked bristles to aid dispersal by animals.

Key Recognition Features The irregular, pinnate leaves, the spike of small, yellow flowers, and the burr-like fruit.

Ecology and Geography In meadows, and damp grassy places, with 3 species in Europe, 1 species in tropical and South Africa, and the rest in Asia and North America.

Comment One or two species were used in the past medicinally or as a yellow dye.

Sanguisorba

Sanguisorba L. (1753), in the family Rosaceae, contains around 10 species around the northern hemisphere.

Description Usually upright, leafy perennials, to 2m, sometimes forming dense mats. Leaves mostly regularly, pinnately divided into many toothed leaflets. Flowers green, dark red, pink, or white, small, in round heads or dense spikes, sometimes nodding; upper flowers sometimes male. Sepals 4, without an epicalyx. Petals absent. Stamens 4 or numerous, often long and conspicuous. Ovary inferior, of 1 or 2 carpels and 1 feathery style. Pollination is often by wind, possibly also by insects. The fruit is 1-seeded, sometimes angled or winged.

Key Recognition Features The regular, pinnate leaves and heads of small, yellow flowers, often with conspicuous stamens.

Ecology and Geography In dry or moist meadows, and rough, grassy places; 7 species in Europe, the rest mainly in eastern Asia.

Comment The green-flowered species such as salad burnet, *S. minor* Scop., are certainly wind-pollinated, but those with showy flowerheads, such as the pink-flowered *S. hakusanensis* Makino from Japan and Korea, probably attract insects such as butterflies. Many species are cultivated for their attractive foliage as well as their flowers. Some closely related shrubby species, such as *Sarcopoterium spinosum* (L.) Spach. in the Mediterranean area and *Marcetella* Svent. and *Dendriopoterium* Svent. in the Canary Islands, are sometimes put in distinct genera.

Agrimonia procera
young fruits
1¼ × life size
July 20th

Agrimonia procera
flowers, 1½ × life size
July 20th

Agrimonia procera
½ life size, July 20th

Sanguisorba minor
⅔ life size
September 8th

Sanguisorba minor
flowers
1½ × life size
September 8th

Acaena microphylla
fruit and seeds
1⅓ × life size, July 20th

Acaena microphylla
⅔ life size, July 20th

Acaena

Acaena L. (1771), in the family Rosaceae, contains around 100 species around the southern hemisphere.

Description Usually creeping, leafy perennials to 30cm, sometimes shrubs. Leaves mostly regularly, pinnately divided into many toothed leaflets, often bluish-grey or brown. Flowers green, dark red, pink, or white, small, usually bisexual, in round heads or short, dense spikes. Sepals 3 or 4, without an epicalyx. Petals absent. Stamens 1–10, often 2. Ovary inferior, of 1 or 2 carpels with feathery stigmas. Pollination is mostly (perhaps always) by wind. The fruit is made up of 1 or 2 achenes, sometimes winged, with 4 or more spines, sometimes barbed at the apex.

Key Recognition Features Dwarf, creeping plants with pinnate, often bluish-grey or brown leaves, and round heads of flowers with conspicuous fine spines.

Ecology and Geography In stony riverbeds and open grassland, mainly in Australia, New Zealand, and South America, including South Georgia, with a few species northwards to California and also in Hawaii, and 1 in South Africa.

Comment Many species are grown as ornamentals, and hybrids are common in gardens. A few, such as *A. anserinifolia* (J. R. & G. Forst.) Druce from southeastern Australia and New Zealand, are naturalised in the British Isles. Other species have appeared as weeds in wool shoddy used as fertiliser.

*Sanguisorba
hakusanensis*
½ life size
August 8th

143

Gillenia

Gillenia Moench. (1802), in the family Rosaceae, contains 2 species in eastern North America.

Description Usually tufted perennials to 1.3m. Leaves mostly divided into 3 toothed, lanceolate leaflets, with pairs of very small or large and conspicuous stipules. Flowers white or pinkish, small, usually bisexual, in long-stalked, loose sprays. Sepals 5, joined at the base. Petals 5, oblong-ovate. Stamens 10—20. Ovary inferior, of 5 carpels. Pollination is by insects. The fruit is made up of 5 leathery follicles, each with 1—4 seeds.

Key Recognition Features Elegant, wiry plants with jaggedly toothed leaves and loose sprays of small, white flowers.

Ecology and Geography In open woods in the mountains of eastern North America from New York to Alabama and Texas.

Comment The genus is named after Arnoldus Gillenius, a 17th-century German botanist. Both species are attractive plants for a partially shaded site. The roots are reported to be expectorant, and they were used medicinally by native Americans.

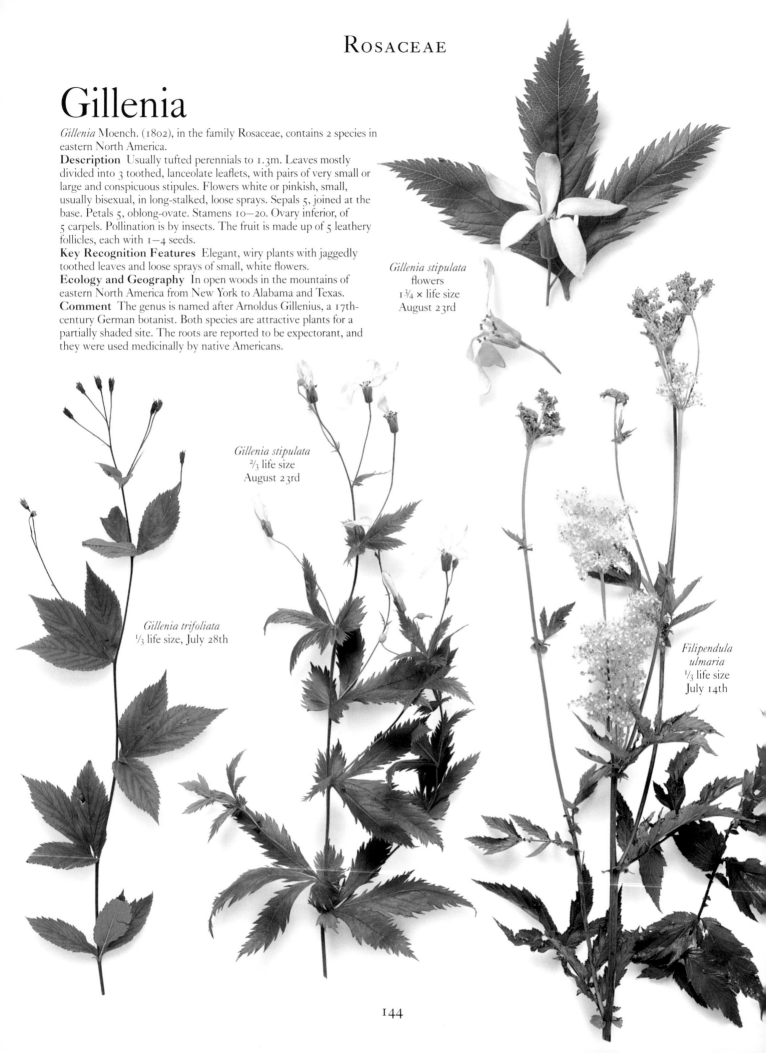

Gillenia stipulata
flowers
1 ¾ × life size
August 23rd

Gillenia stipulata
⅔ life size
August 23rd

Gillenia trifoliata
⅓ life size, July 28th

Filipendula ulmaria
⅓ life size
July 14th

144

Aruncus

Aruncus L. (1753), in the family Rosaceae, contains around 3 species in the northern hemisphere.

Description Usually tufted perennials to 2m. Leaves mostly divided into 3 parts, which are pinnately lobed into several toothed, lanceolate leaflets. Flowers white, small, unisexual, in branching spikes. Sepals 5, small. Petals 5, longer than the sepals. Stamens numerous. Ovary superior, of around 3 carpels. Pollination is by small insects. The hanging fruit is made up of 3 follicles, each containing 1 small seed.

Key Recognition Features Usually tall plants with spikes of small, fluffy, creamy-white flowers and divided, *Astilbe*-like leaves (see p.104).

Ecology and Geography In moist ground; *A dioicus* (Walt.) Fern. is found from France and Belgium to Korea, Japan, and North America, and there are 2 other smaller species in eastern Asia.

Comment All species are grown in gardens for their attractive foliage and flowers. *Astilbe rivularis* Buch.-Ham. ex D. Don is very similar to *Aruncus dioicus*, but has only 5 stamens and 2 carpels.

Aruncus dioicus
2 × life size, June 22nd

*Aruncus
sylvester*
1⅓ × life size
June 22nd

Filipendula ulmaria
¾ life size, July 14th

Filipendula ulmaria
fruit, 2 × life size
October 10th

Filipendula

Filipendula Mill. (1754), in the family Rosaceae, contains around 10 species in the northern hemisphere.

Description Usually tufted perennials to 3.5m. Leaves mostly pinnately divided into several toothed, lanceolate leaflets, with pairs of small or large stipules. Flowers white, pink, or purplish, small, usually bisexual, in branching heads. Sepals 5, joined at the base. Petals 5, usually rounded. Stamens numerous. Ovary superior, of around 10 carpels. Pollination is by insects. The fruit is of around 10 single-seeded segments, often twisted round each other.

Key Recognition Features Tall plants with branching heads of small, fluffy, creamy-white or pink flowers.

Ecology and Geography In moist ground and fens and by lakes; also on dry limestone slopes. There are 2 species native in Europe, the rest scattered around the northern hemisphere.

Comment The genus *Filipendula* includes the meadowsweet, *F. ulmaria* (L.) Maxim., a common plant in damp places, which smells like wintergreen and contains salicylic acid. It also includes dropwort, *F. vulgaris* Moench., a smaller plant that is common in chalk grassland; a double form is commonly cultivated. Queen of the prairie, *F. rubra* (Hill) Robinson, from eastern North America, has red or purple flowers, as have several species from eastern Siberia and Japan.

145

Aruncus sylvester
⅓ life size, June 22nd

Cannabis

Cannabis L. (1753), in the family Cannabaceae, contains 1 species, *C. sativa* L., originally from central Asia.

Description An annual with a tall, upright, and often branching stem to 3m, sometimes up to 6m, glandular and aromatic. Leaves alternate, usually hairy, and palmately divided into 3–9 toothed leaflets. Flowers small, green, the males and females on separate plants. Male flowers with 5 spreading sepals joined only at the base; female flowers with sepals reduced to a membranous sheath around the ovary. Petals absent. Stamens 5, with large, hanging anthers. Ovary superior, of 1 carpel and style with 2 long stigmas. Pollination is by wind. The fruit has 1 seed around 2mm long.

Key Recognition Features A tall, dark green plant with deeply divided and sharply toothed leaves.

Ecology and Geography On roadsides and in open ground. Now found worldwide in tropical and subtropical areas, and formerly common on old dumps from discarded birdseed.

Comment The families now thought to be most closely associated with Rosaceae include the woody Rhamnaceae, Ulmaceae, Celtidaceae (now considered a distinct family) and Moraceae (see Volume 1 for these), and the herbaceous Cannabaceae and Urticaceae. *Cannabis* itself, Indian hemp, is used both as a drug and as a fibre, and different varieties are grown for the two uses. Unpollinated female flowers are the most resinous, and held to have the most potent effects, and some Dutch companies are offering "guaranteed female seed". Recent research on rats in California suggests that cannabinol is a potent female aphrodisiac but at the same time a male antaphrodisiac. It has at last been licensed in the United Kingdom for research into disorders such as multiple sclerosis.

Cannabis sativa 'Durban Poison'
female shoot, ²⁄₃ life size,
September 25th

Cannabis sativa
'Durban Poison'
female plant, ¹⁄₃ life size
September 25th

Humulus lupulus
with hops
½ life size
October 17th

Humulus lupulus
hop and seeds (left)
1½ × life size
October 17th

Humulus lupulus
male flowers
just under life size
August 5th

Humulus

Humulus L. (1753), in the family Cannabaceae, contains 3 species, including *H. lupulus* L., the hop, found in Europe and Asia.

Description Perennials or annuals, with twining and climbing stems up to 4m. Leaves alternate, usually rough and palmately 3- to 7-lobed. Flowers small, green, the males and females on separate plants. Male flowers on a repeatedly branched inflorescence with 5 spreading sepals joined only at the base, and 5 stamens with large, hanging anthers. Female flowers in a dense head with 2 flowers in the axil of each bract, each with 1 style with 2 long stigmas. Petals absent. Pollination is by wind. The fruits are in a dense head, the hop, with a papery scale-like bract which encloses the seed at the base.

Key Recognition Features A tall, twining plant with rough, lobed leaves, and hops on the female plants.

Ecology and Geography In hedges and open scrub. The wild hop is a perennial found across Europe and Asia, *H. japonicus* Sieb. & Zucc. is an annual from China and Japan, and a third species is found in Yunnan.

Comment Hops are widely grown for brewing. In England the main areas of hop gardens were in Herefordshire and the Weald of Kent and Sussex, but most hops are now imported from eastern Europe, leaving the characteristic drying towers with conical roofs, called oast houses, to be converted to dwellings.

Begonia
'Coco Ducolor'
1 ¹/₃ × life size
August 15th

Begonia 'Coco Ducolor'
¹/₂ life size, August 15th

Begonia sutherlandii
¹/₃ life size, September 4th

Begonia

Begonia L. (1753), in the family Begoniaceae, contains around 1000 species throughout the tropics and subtropics.

Description Perennials or annuals, often tuberous and with stem bulbils, rarely climbing, sometimes with cane-like stems to 2m, sometimes stemless with creeping rhizomes. Leaves alternate, usually asymmetric at the base, and sometimes palmately lobed, often hairy or with colourful markings. Male and female flowers usually separate on the same plant, usually with rounded sepals, white, pink, yellow, orange, or red. Male flowers with 2 or 4 coloured sepals and numerous stamens with small anthers. Female flowers with 2–6 sepals and an inferior and usually 3-winged ovary with 2 or 3 fused carpels and 2 or 3 thick, curled styles. Petals absent. Pollination is by insects, rarely by birds. The fruits are fleshy or leathery, winged capsules, with minute, dust-like seeds, sometimes with air-filled "balloons" to help air dispersal.

Key Recognition Features Fleshy plants with asymmetric leaves and male flowers with 2 or 4 sepals.

Ecology and Geography In woods and rocky areas, on cliffs and tree trunks, usually in mossy places in partial shade but also on high mountain rocks in the Andes. Most species are from tropical regions of the Americas; there are none in Australia and New Zealand.

Comment The families Begoniaceae, Cucurbitaceae, and Datiscaceae are all now considered closely related. The genus *Begonia* is named after Admiral Michel Begon (1638–1710), governor of Canada and a patron of botany. Many species are grown as ornamentals. The hardiest species is probably *B. grandis* subsp. *evansiana* (Andr.) Irmsch. from China, which is dormant and leafless in winter. Two groups are especially popular and commonly grown; the Semperflorens type, grown as dwarf annuals with masses of small flowers, and the tuberous-rooted Tuberhybrida type, with large, double flowers. *Begonia sutherlandii* Hook. fil. is a small, tuberous woodland plant from southeastern Africa. Others, such as the Rex begonias, are tropical species, grown for their decorative leaves.

Begonia sutherlandii
flowers and winged capsules
1 ²/₃ × life size, September 4th

Thladiantha

Thladiantha Bunge (1833), in the family Cucurbitaceae, contains around 23 species, in Asia and Africa.

Description Climbing perennials, to 5m, with tuberous roots and tendrils. Leaves softly hairy, ovate, sometimes finely toothed, and with silver markings. Flowers yellow, males and females usually on separate plants, the males usually in clusters, the females solitary. Sepals 5, narrow, joined at the base. Petals forming a 5-lobed corolla. Stamens 5. Female flowers with 5 staminodes and 1 style with 3 stigmas. Pollination is by insects, especially bees. The fruits are ovoid-oblong, with shallow grooves and numerous seeds.

Key Recognition Features Tall climbers with tendrils, heart-shaped leaves, and yellow flowers.

Ecology and Geography In woods and scrub; mainly in the forests of eastern Asia and southern China, with 1 species, *T. dubia* Bunge, in northern China and naturalised in parts of Europe.

Comment *Thladiantha* and *Bryonia* L. are the only 2 genera of the Cucurbitaceae hardy in northern Europe. White bryony, *Bryonia cretica* L. subsp. *dioica* (Jacq.) Tutin is commonly found in hedges in scrub on the chalk in southern England; twining annual stems with deeply lobed leaves and small, green flowers followed by dull red fruit climb from a massive rootstock. Black bryony, *Tamus communis* L. with shining berries, is in the family Dioscoreaceae.

Ecballium

Ecballium A. Rich. (1824), in the family Cucurbitaceae, contains 1 species, *E. elaterium* (L.) A. Rich., the squirting cucumber, in the Mediterranean area.

Description A perennial with a tuberous root and trailing stems to 3m, without tendrils. Leaves bristly hairy, triangular, sometimes shallowly lobed. Flowers pale greenish, males and females usually separate on the same plant, the males in clusters, the females solitary. Sepals 5, joined at the base. Petals forming a 5-lobed corolla. Pollination is by insects. The fruits are bristly and fleshy, around 5cm long, ovoid, and burst explosively at the stalk, shooting out the seeds and juice.

Key Recognition Features Plants forming carpets of large, hairy leaves, with small, greenish flowers with explosive fruit.

Ecology and Geography On rocky and sandy shores and in waste places, around the Mediterranean and naturalised further north.

Comment The family Cucurbitaceae, which includes gourds, marrows, pumpkins, and melons, is mainly tropical. The large leaves, 5-lobed corolla, and large fruits with flattened seeds are typical of the family. *Ecballium* is a common weed in warm areas, sometimes grown as a curiosity, or as a medicine, the fruits being used as a purgative.

Thladiantha dubia
1/3 life size, June 22nd

Thladiantha dubia
flower parts
1 1/3 × life size
June 22nd

Ecballium elaterium
flower and fruit
1 1/4 × life size, July 20th

Ecballium elaterium
1/3 life size, July 20th

Lythrum

Lythrum L. (1753), in the family Lythraceae, contains around 36 species worldwide.

Description Perennials with stems to 2m, upright or creeping, sometimes angular or winged. Leaves simple and usually narrow, alternate, opposite, or whorled. Flowers pink or purplish. Sepals usually 6, narrow, joined to form a long calyx tube. Petals 6, narrow at the base, attached at the mouth of the calyx tube. Stamens 2–12; style 1, with a capitate stigma. Pollination is by insects, often bees or hoverflies. The fruits are capsules, splitting into 2, with numerous small seeds.

Key Recognition Features Usually tall perennials with pink or purple flowers and 6 narrow petals.

Ecology and Geography In marshes, bogs, and damp fields, or in shallow water, with 13 species in Europe, the rest mainly in Asia and North America.

Comment The family Lythraceae is associated with Myrtaceae (see Volume 1), Onagraceae (see pp.154–57), and Melastomataceae in the order Myrtales. Other important genera now included in Lythraceae include the crepe myrtle *Lagerstroemia* L., the pomegranate *Punica* L., and the water chestnut *Trapa* L.. *Lythrum salicaria* L., purple loosestrife, is common as an attractive wild flower in Europe, but has become a serious pest in meadows in western North America. This and several other species have flowers of 3 types, each on different plants, with 2 groups of stamens of different lengths and a style of another length (for example, flowers with medium styles have 6 long and 6 short stamens, and flowers with long styles have 6 short and 6 medium stamens); furthermore there are 3 sizes of pollen, and each pollen type fertilises best the stigma of the same length as the stamen that produced it: thus cross-pollination is encouraged, which leads to more viable offspring. The genus *Peplis* L., with creeping stems and small flowers, is now included in *Lythrum*.

Lythrum salicaria
'Feuerkerze'
½ life size, July 21st

Lythrum salicaria 'Feuerkerze'
parts of a short-styled flower
1⅔ × life size, July 21st

Lythrum salicaria 'Feuerkerze'
flowers, 1¼ × life size, July 21st

150

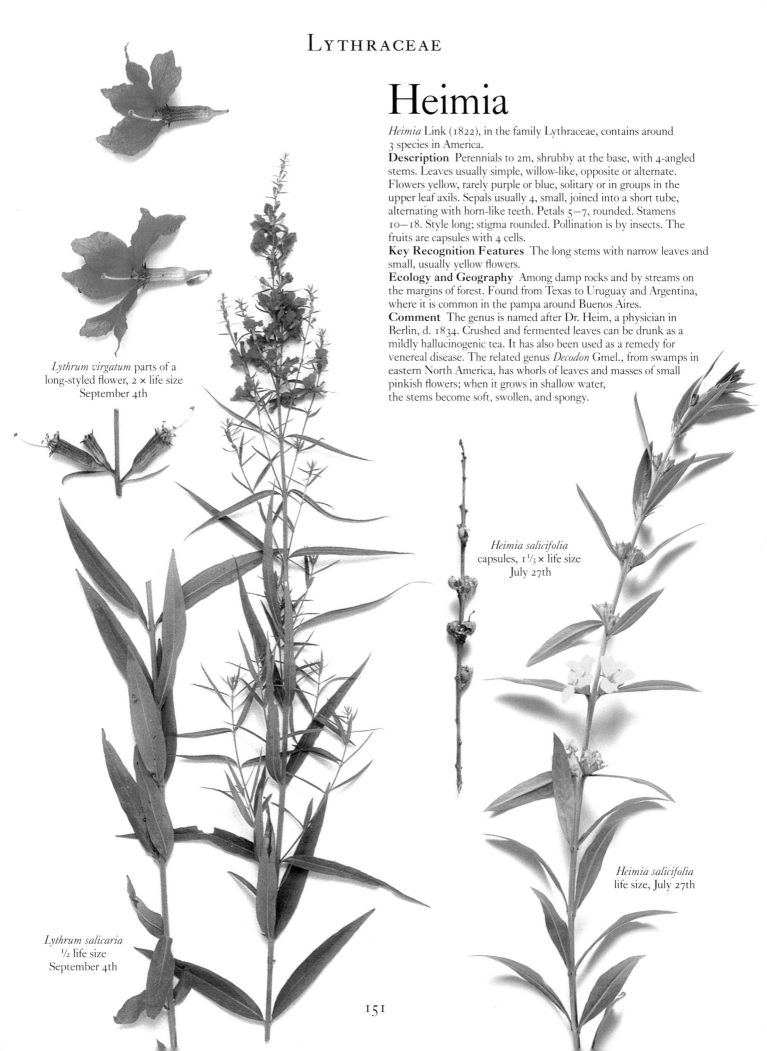

Heimia

Heimia Link (1822), in the family Lythraceae, contains around 3 species in America.

Description Perennials to 2m, shrubby at the base, with 4-angled stems. Leaves usually simple, willow-like, opposite or alternate. Flowers yellow, rarely purple or blue, solitary or in groups in the upper leaf axils. Sepals usually 4, small, joined into a short tube, alternating with horn-like teeth. Petals 5—7, rounded. Stamens 10—18. Style long; stigma rounded. Pollination is by insects. The fruits are capsules with 4 cells.

Key Recognition Features The long stems with narrow leaves and small, usually yellow flowers.

Ecology and Geography Among damp rocks and by streams on the margins of forest. Found from Texas to Uruguay and Argentina, where it is common in the pampa around Buenos Aires.

Comment The genus is named after Dr. Heim, a physician in Berlin, d. 1834. Crushed and fermented leaves can be drunk as a mildly hallucinogenic tea. It has also been used as a remedy for venereal disease. The related genus *Decodon* Gmel., from swamps in eastern North America, has whorls of leaves and masses of small pinkish flowers; when it grows in shallow water, the stems become soft, swollen, and spongy.

Lythrum virgatum parts of a long-styled flower, 2 × life size
September 4th

Heimia salicifolia capsules, 1⅓ × life size
July 27th

Heimia salicifolia life size, July 27th

Lythrum salicaria ½ life size
September 4th

Cuphea llavea
flower, 2 × life size,
August 10th

Cuphea silenoides
flowers, 1 1/2 × life size
July 20th

Cuphea hyssopifolia
life size, July 20th

Cuphea

Cuphea Browne (1756), in the family Lythraceae, contains around 275 species, mainly in tropical America.

Description Perennials, low shrubs, or annuals, to 2m. Leaves usually simple, opposite or whorled. Flowers red, yellow, pink, or purplish. Sepals usually 6, usually unequal, joined into a coloured tube, often with a short spur at the base. Petals 6, sometimes 2, or apparently absent, narrow at the base. Stamens 6, often hairy, usually equal or alternately long and short. Style long, often hairy; stigma capitate. Pollination is by insects and hummingbirds. The fruits are capsules, bursting through the calyx, with few, large seeds.

Key Recognition Features Usually branched perennials, rather woody at the base, with a long, tubular, coloured calyx and often minute petals of contrasting colour.

Ecology and Geography In damp fields and among rocks, with most species in Mexico and Central America southwards to Peru.

Comment *Cuphea* has flowers of 3 main types. The so-called cigar flowers, such as *C. ignea* DC, have a tubular and coloured calyx tube and minute petals. Species such as *C. lanceolata* Ait. have 2 large, ear-like petals, the other petals being small or absent. *Cuphea hyssopifolia* H. B. & K. is a small, branching shrub with masses of small, pink or white flowers in the leaf axils, with 6 equal petals.

Cuphea silenoides
3/4 life size, July 20th

Lopezia

Lopezia Cav. (1791), in the family Lythraceae, contains around 20 species, mainly in Mexico and Central America.

Description Perennials, or annuals to 60cm, sometimes shrubby at the base, sometimes tuberous. Leaves usually simple, opposite or alternate. Flowers white, red, pink, or purplish. Sepals usually 4, more or less equal, sometimes joined into a tube at the base. Petals 4, often unequal, the upper 2 sometimes joined to the upper sepals. Stamens 2, of which 1 is sterile and often petal-like; pollen blue. Style long; stigma rounded. Pollination is by insects or hummingbirds. The fruits are capsules, with few, large seeds.

Key Recognition Features The irregular flowers with 1 fertile stamen and spoon-shaped petals.

Ecology and Geography Among damp rocks and by streams, with most species in Mexico and Central America.

Comment The genus is named after Tomas Lopez (fl. 1540), a Spanish botanist who wrote on the flora of South America. The only commonly cultivated species is the very variable *L. racemosa* Cav., called mosquito flower because the flowers look like small mosquitoes.

Lopezia coronata
flower parts, 3 × life size
June 22nd

Lopezia racemosa
flower parts (above)
2½ × life size, July 20th

Lopezia racemosa
½ life size, July 20th

Lopezia coronata
¾ life size, June 22nd

Lopezia racemosa
fruits, 2 × life size
July 20th

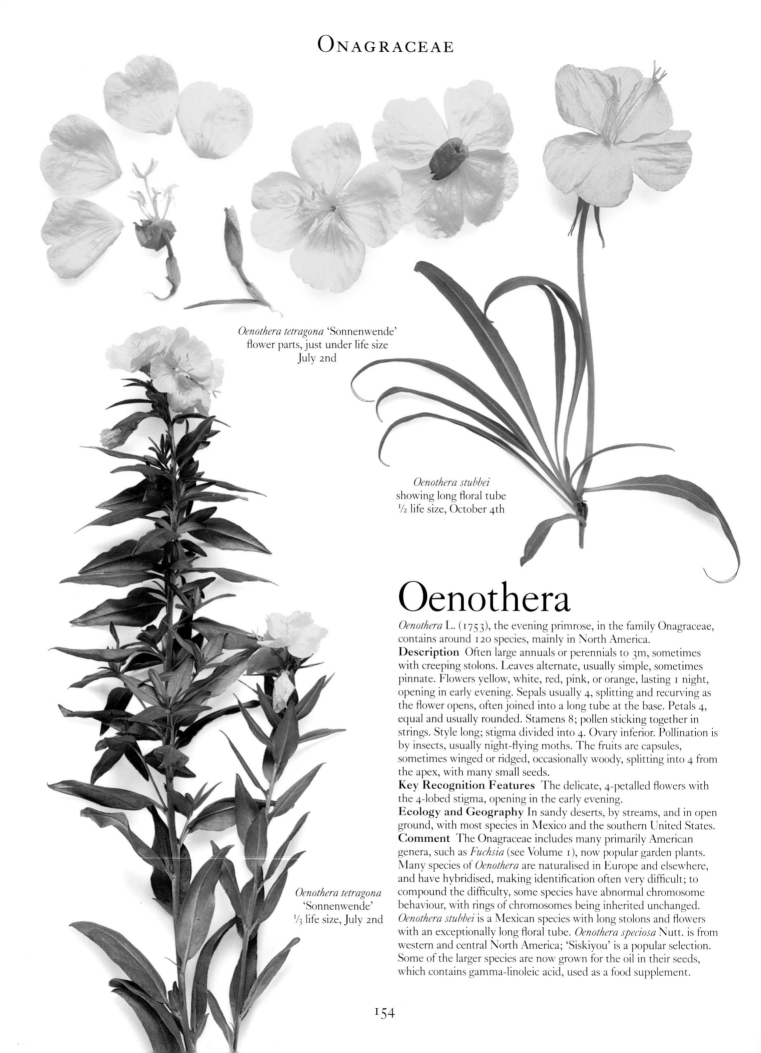

Oenothera tetragona 'Sonnenwende'
flower parts, just under life size
July 2nd

Oenothera stubbei
showing long floral tube
¹/₂ life size, October 4th

Oenothera tetragona
'Sonnenwende'
¹/₃ life size, July 2nd

Oenothera

Oenothera L. (1753), the evening primrose, in the family Onagraceae, contains around 120 species, mainly in North America.

Description Often large annuals or perennials to 3m, sometimes with creeping stolons. Leaves alternate, usually simple, sometimes pinnate. Flowers yellow, white, red, pink, or orange, lasting 1 night, opening in early evening. Sepals usually 4, splitting and recurving as the flower opens, often joined into a long tube at the base. Petals 4, equal and usually rounded. Stamens 8; pollen sticking together in strings. Style long; stigma divided into 4. Ovary inferior. Pollination is by insects, usually night-flying moths. The fruits are capsules, sometimes winged or ridged, occasionally woody, splitting into 4 from the apex, with many small seeds.

Key Recognition Features The delicate, 4-petalled flowers with the 4-lobed stigma, opening in the early evening.

Ecology and Geography In sandy deserts, by streams, and in open ground, with most species in Mexico and the southern United States.

Comment The Onagraceae includes many primarily American genera, such as *Fuchsia* (see Volume 1), now popular garden plants. Many species of *Oenothera* are naturalised in Europe and elsewhere, and have hybridised, making identification often very difficult; to compound the difficulty, some species have abnormal chromosome behaviour, with rings of chromosomes being inherited unchanged. *Oenothera stubbei* is a Mexican species with long stolons and flowers with an exceptionally long floral tube. *Oenothera speciosa* Nutt. is from western and central North America; 'Siskiyou' is a popular selection. Some of the larger species are now grown for the oil in their seeds, which contains gamma-linoleic acid, used as a food supplement.

Camissonia

Camissonia Link (1818), in the family Onagraceae, contains around 62 species, mainly in western America.

Description Usually dwarf annuals to 50cm. Leaves alternate, usually simple, sometimes pinnate. Flowers yellow, white, red, pink, or orange, lasting 1 day, opening in the morning. Sepals usually 4, splitting and recurving as the flower opens, joined into a short tube at the base. Petals 4, equal and usually rounded, often spotted at the base. Stamens 8; pollen sticking together in strings. Style long; stigma rounded and knob-like. Ovary inferior. Pollination is by insects, especially bees. The fruits are capsules, sometimes winged or ridged, occasionally woody, splitting into 4 from the apex, with many small seeds.

Key Recognition Features The small, delicate, 4-petalled flowers with a knob-like stigma, opening in the morning.

Ecology and Geography In sandy deserts and in open ground. Most species are found in California and adjacent states and in Chile.

Comment The genus *Camissonia* has in the past been included with *Oenothera*. Apart from the knob-like stigma, the flowers are usually smaller, and the petals have dark spots at the base.

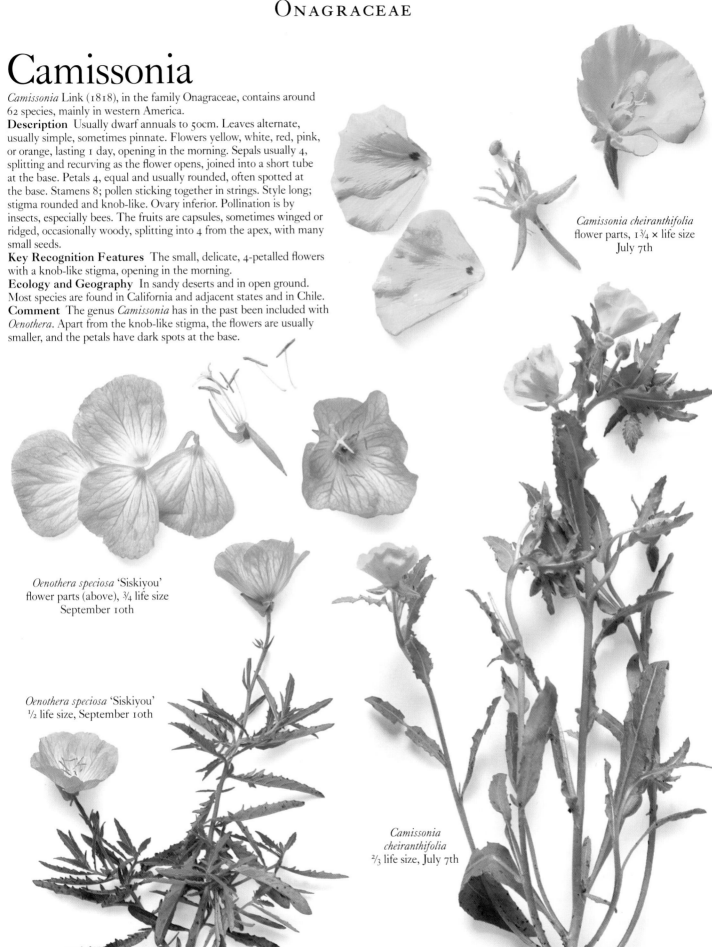

Camissonia cheiranthifolia
flower parts, 1¾ × life size
July 7th

Oenothera speciosa 'Siskiyou'
flower parts (above), ¾ life size
September 10th

Oenothera speciosa 'Siskiyou'
½ life size, September 10th

*Camissonia
cheiranthifolia*
⅔ life size, July 7th

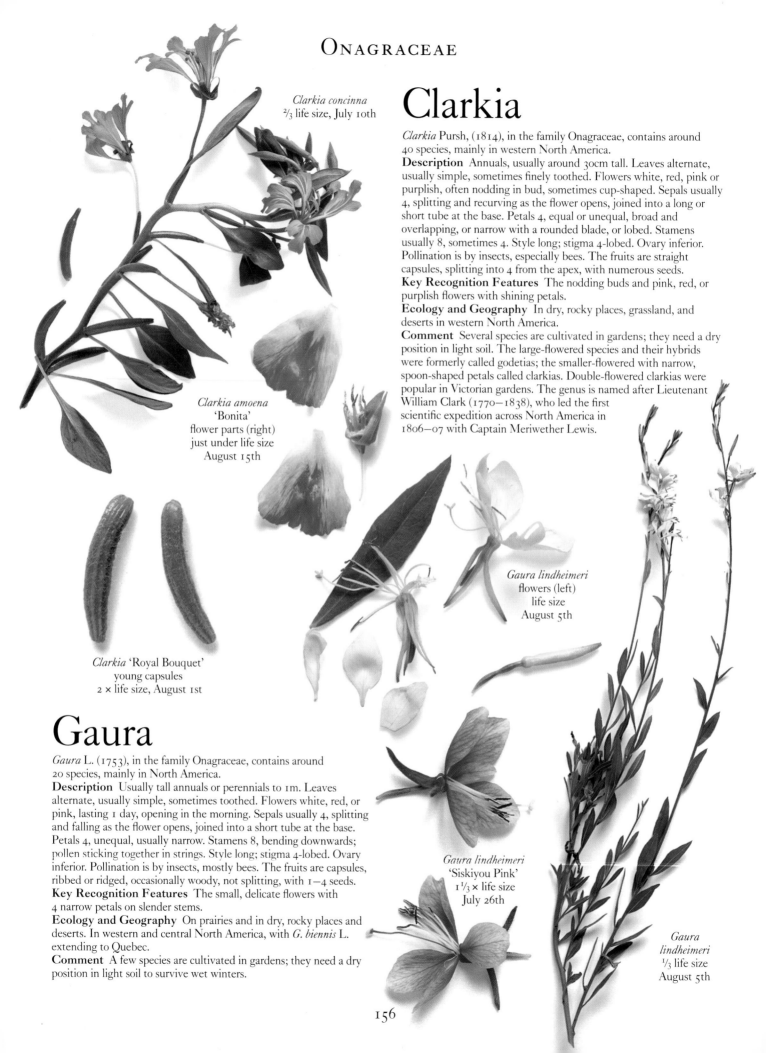

Clarkia concinna
⅔ life size, July 10th

Clarkia

Clarkia Pursh, (1814), in the family Onagraceae, contains around 40 species, mainly in western North America.

Description Annuals, usually around 30cm tall. Leaves alternate, usually simple, sometimes finely toothed. Flowers white, red, pink or purplish, often nodding in bud, sometimes cup-shaped. Sepals usually 4, splitting and recurving as the flower opens, joined into a long or short tube at the base. Petals 4, equal or unequal, broad and overlapping, or narrow with a rounded blade, or lobed. Stamens usually 8, sometimes 4. Style long; stigma 4-lobed. Ovary inferior. Pollination is by insects, especially bees. The fruits are straight capsules, splitting into 4 from the apex, with numerous seeds.

Key Recognition Features The nodding buds and pink, red, or purplish flowers with shining petals.

Ecology and Geography In dry, rocky places, grassland, and deserts in western North America.

Comment Several species are cultivated in gardens; they need a dry position in light soil. The large-flowered species and their hybrids were formerly called godetias; the smaller-flowered with narrow, spoon-shaped petals called clarkias. Double-flowered clarkias were popular in Victorian gardens. The genus is named after Lieutenant William Clark (1770–1838), who led the first scientific expedition across North America in 1806–07 with Captain Meriwether Lewis.

Clarkia amoena
'Bonita'
flower parts (right)
just under life size
August 15th

Gaura lindheimeri
flowers (left)
life size
August 5th

Clarkia 'Royal Bouquet'
young capsules
2 × life size, August 1st

Gaura

Gaura L. (1753), in the family Onagraceae, contains around 20 species, mainly in North America.

Description Usually tall annuals or perennials to 1m. Leaves alternate, usually simple, sometimes toothed. Flowers white, red, or pink, lasting 1 day, opening in the morning. Sepals usually 4, splitting and falling as the flower opens, joined into a short tube at the base. Petals 4, unequal, usually narrow. Stamens 8, bending downwards; pollen sticking together in strings. Style long; stigma 4-lobed. Ovary inferior. Pollination is by insects, mostly bees. The fruits are capsules, ribbed or ridged, occasionally woody, not splitting, with 1–4 seeds.

Key Recognition Features The small, delicate flowers with 4 narrow petals on slender stems.

Ecology and Geography On prairies and in dry, rocky places and deserts. In western and central North America, with *G. biennis* L. extending to Quebec.

Comment A few species are cultivated in gardens; they need a dry position in light soil to survive wet winters.

Gaura lindheimeri
'Siskiyou Pink'
1⅓ × life size
July 26th

Gaura lindheimeri
⅓ life size
August 5th

Epilobium

Epilobium L. (1753), the willow herb, in the family Onagraceae, contains around 165 species, mainly in New Zealand, Europe, and western North America.

Description Perennials, sometimes shrubby at the base, to around 2m tall, rarely annuals. Leaves alternate or opposite, usually simple. Flowers pink, magenta, white, red, or pale yellow. Sepals usually 4, splitting as the flower opens, joined into a short or long tube at the base. Petals 4, equal, sometimes forked or lobed at the tip. Stamens 8, often bent downwards or unequal. Style short; stigma club-shaped or 4-lobed. Ovary inferior. Pollination is by insects or hummingbirds. The fruits are narrow, straight capsules, splitting into 4 from the apex, with numerous small seeds, each with a tuft of long, silky hairs on the end to help dispersal by wind.

Key Recognition Features The 4 small petals on the tip of a long ovary and the silky hairs on the fruit.

Ecology and Geography In shallow water, swamps, and bogs, by mountain streams, and among dry rocks. Around 40 species are found in North America, and 50 in New Zealand. Species from both these areas are naturalised in Europe.

Comment A few species are cultivated in gardens. Two genera were sometimes separated, but are now usually found under *Epilobium*, at least in botanical textbooks. About 4 species are often put in *Zauschneria* Presl; found in western North America and called California fuchsia, these have often silvery leaves and bright scarlet flowers with a scarlet tube, adapted for pollination by hummingbirds, and they grow on dry, rocky slopes. A further 5 species were separated into *Chamaenerion* Séguier, the rosebay willow herbs, with showy flowers with a very short floral tube and rhizomes which creep to form large patches; they are found mostly in bare ground, either in places left bare by forest fires or clear felling, or on the moraines of retreating glaciers.

Epilobium hirsutum var. *album*
flowers and flower parts
1 ½ × life size, July 20th

Epilobium angustifolium var. *album*
flowers (left)
1 ⅓ × life size
July 14th

Epilobium caucasicum
flowers and capsules
½ life size
August 23rd

Epilobium angustifolium var. *album*
½ life size
July 14th

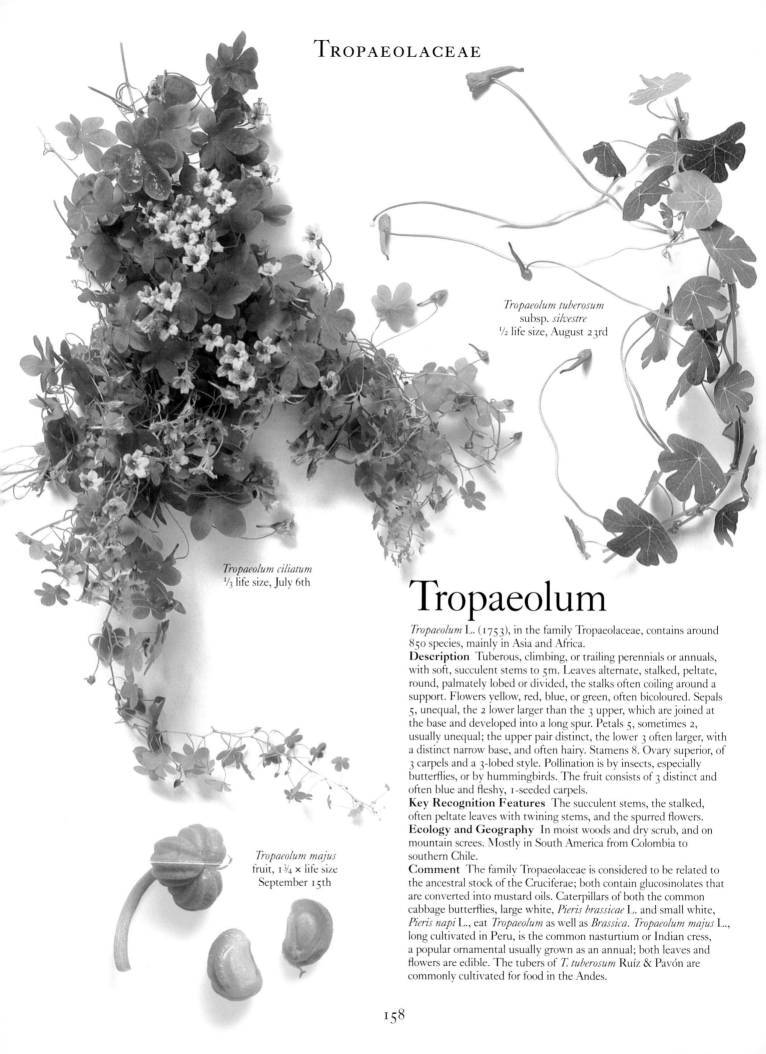

Tropaeolum tuberosum
subsp. *silvestre*
½ life size, August 23rd

Tropaeolum ciliatum
⅓ life size, July 6th

Tropaeolum majus
fruit, 1¾ × life size
September 15th

Tropaeolum

Tropaeolum L. (1753), in the family Tropaeolaceae, contains around 850 species, mainly in Asia and Africa.

Description Tuberous, climbing, or trailing perennials or annuals, with soft, succulent stems to 5m. Leaves alternate, stalked, peltate, round, palmately lobed or divided, the stalks often coiling around a support. Flowers yellow, red, blue, or green, often bicoloured. Sepals 5, unequal, the 2 lower larger than the 3 upper, which are joined at the base and developed into a long spur. Petals 5, sometimes 2, usually unequal; the upper pair distinct, the lower 3 often larger, with a distinct narrow base, and often hairy. Stamens 8. Ovary superior, of 3 carpels and a 3-lobed style. Pollination is by insects, especially butterflies, or by hummingbirds. The fruit consists of 3 distinct and often blue and fleshy, 1-seeded carpels.

Key Recognition Features The succulent stems, the stalked, often peltate leaves with twining stems, and the spurred flowers.

Ecology and Geography In moist woods and dry scrub, and on mountain screes. Mostly in South America from Colombia to southern Chile.

Comment The family Tropaeolaceae is considered to be related to the ancestral stock of the Cruciferae; both contain glucosinolates that are converted into mustard oils. Caterpillars of both the common cabbage butterflies, large white, *Pieris brassicae* L. and small white, *Pieris napi* L., eat *Tropaeolum* as well as *Brassica*. *Tropaeolum majus* L., long cultivated in Peru, is the common nasturtium or Indian cress, a popular ornamental usually grown as an annual; both leaves and flowers are edible. The tubers of *T. tuberosum* Ruíz & Pavón are commonly cultivated for food in the Andes.

TROPAEOLACEAE

*Tropaeolum
majus*
¾ life size
September 15th

*Tropaeolum
speciosum*
flower parts
just under life size
July 25th

Tropaeolum majus
flower parts, life size
October 4th

Tropaeolum tuberosum subsp. *silvestre*
flower and fruit (above)
1¾ × life size, August 23rd

*Tropaeolum
tuberosum*
'Ken Aslet'
tubers, ⅔ life size
October 10th

Tropaeolum speciosum
⅓ life size, July 25th

159

Limnanthes douglasii
⅔ life size, August 1st

Limnanthes

Limnanthes R. Br. (1833), in the family Limnanthaceae, contains around 8 species in western North America.

Description Trailing annuals to 50cm across with soft stems. Leaves alternate, pinnately divided, with dissected leaflets. Flowers yellow, half-yellow, half-white, white, or pinkish. Sepals 4–6, usually 5. Petals usually 5, equal, with a U-shaped band of hairs at the base. Stamens 6 or 10. Ovary superior, of 3–5 carpels and 5 stigmas. Pollination is by insects, often bees. Fruit of 5 single-seeded nutlets.

Key Recognition Features The pinnate and dissected leaves and the simple flowers, with a yellow centre and white edge in the frequently grown *L. douglasii* R. Br., hence the common name poached-egg plant.

Ecology and Geography In moist places by springs and vernal pools. Mostly in western North America, from Oregon southwards.

Comment The family Limnanthaceae contains *Limnanthes* and the monotypic *Floerkea proserpinacoides* Willd., which has 3 small petals and simply pinnate leaves and is found in eastern North America as well as along the Pacific coast.

Limnanthes douglasii, flowers
(below) life size, August 1st

Reseda lutea
flowers, 1⅔ × life size
July 5th

Reseda luteola
(right) ½ life size
August 3rd

Reseda

Reseda L. (1753), in the family Resedaceae, contains around 60 species, in Europe and Asia.

Description Annuals, biennials, or perennials, creeping or with tall, upright stems to 1.2m. Leaves alternate, simple to pinnatifid. Flowers small, greenish or whitish. Sepals 4–8. Petals 4–8, small, unequal, usually narrow at the base, variously lobed and divided, even in the same flower. Stamens 10–25, joined at the base, with often reddish anthers. Ovary superior, of 3 or 4 carpels and 3 or 4 stigmas. Pollination is by insects, especially butterflies. The fruit is a hollow capsule, open at the top, with numerous seeds.

Key Recognition Features The numerous small, greenish or whitish, often scented flowers with conspicuous stamens, and the capsules open at the end.

Ecology and Geography On roadsides and rocky mountainsides, and in dry, open ground, with most species in Mediterranean parts of Europe and western Asia.

Comment The family Resedaceae is close to Cruciferae. *Reseda odorata* L., sweet mignonette, originally from Libya, is grown for its scent. The tall, green-flowered *R. luteola* L., common in chalk grassland in southern England, is the dyer's weed or weld; it has a long history of use for yellow dye and was combined with woad to produce Lincoln green.

Reseda lutea
capsules, 2 × life size
July 5th

Reseda lutea
⅔ life size, July 5th

Cleome

Cleome L. (1753), in the family Capparidaceae, contains around 75 species, mainly in tropical America and Africa.

Description Annuals, biennials, or perennials, sometimes shrubby with tall, upright stems to 2m. Leaves simple to digitate with 3–7 leaflets, usually pungent. Flowers pink, purple, white, or yellow. Sepals 4, sometimes united at the base. Petals 4, often unequal, usually narrow at the base. Stamens 6, rarely 4, curved and much longer than the petals. Ovary superior, on a long gynophore, with 2 fused carpels a short style or sessile stigma. Pollination is by insects, especially bees and butterflies. The fruit is a narrow, many-seeded, 1-celled capsule, often nodding.

Key Recognition Features The leaves with several leaflets and the flowers with very long stamens, and with a long stalk between the base of the flower and the ovary, a so-called gynophore.

Ecology and Geography In prairies and meadows, on dry open ground, and among rocks. Around 4 species extend into California, the southern parts of the Rockies, and the Great Plains; the remainder are in Mexico southwards and in tropical Africa, with 2 species in southern Europe. The commonly cultivated *C. hassleriana* Chodat is from southern Brazil and northern Argentina.

Comment The family Capparidaceae, which includes *Capparis spinosa* L., the edible caper, is sometimes included in an expanded Cruciferae or Brassicaceae. The 2 families are closely related, and *Cleome* and its relatives are particularly close to Cruciferae, in which some genera such as *Stanleya* Nutt., the desert plume, also have a short gynophore and long stamens. *Cleome hassleriana* is a popular summer-flowering annual, available in shades of pink and purple as well as white.

Cleome hassleriana
flower parts, ¾ life size
September 9th

Cleome hassleriana
½ life size
September 9th

161

Isatis tinctoria
seeds, 1½ × life size
July 14th

Isatis tinctoria
½ life size, July 5th

Isatis tinctoria
flowers, 2 × life size
July 5th

Isatis

Isatis L. (1753), woad, in the family Cruciferae, contains around
30 species, mainly in southern Europe and Asia.
Description Annuals, biennials, or perennials, with usually bluish
and hairless stems to 1.2m. Leaves simple, usually surrounding the
stem at the base. Flowers yellow, numerous, in a flat-topped,
branching inflorescence. Sepals 4, not saccate at the base. Petals 4,
with a short, narrow base. Stamens 6. Ovary superior, with a sessile
stigma. Pollination is by insects, especially bees. The fruit is 1-seeded,
winged, hanging, usually blackish.
Key Recognition Features The small, yellow flowers and hanging,
1-seeded, winged fruits.
Ecology and Geography In dry, open ground, sandy places, and
among rocks, with around 10 species in Europe, 30 in Turkey, and the
others scattered across Asia.
Comment Common woad, the biennial *I. tinctoria* L., has been
cultivated as a dye plant since the Iron Age; the indigo produced by
its fermented leaves is mentioned by Herodotus, and was used in
England for uniforms for the police and the navy until superseded by
imported indigo (*Indigofera*, see Volume 1) after 1631. Woad is
particularly suitable for dyeing wool; a second species, *I. indigotica*
Fortune, with a higher dye content, was grown in China.

Erysimum cheiri
½ life size, April 29th

162

Erysimum

Erysimum L. (1753), in the family Cruciferae, contains around 200 species, mainly in southern Europe, Asia, and western North America.

Description Annuals, biennials, or perennials to 1.2m, sometimes subshrubby. Leaves simple, usually narrow at the base. Flowers yellow, orange, or purple, in an elongating inflorescence. Sepals 4, the inner sometimes saccate at the base. Petals 4, with a long, narrow base, usually with nectaries. Stamens 6. Ovary superior, with a distinct style. Pollination is by insects, especially bees. The fruit is a many-seeded, narrow capsule.

Key Recognition Features The 4-petalled flowers and narrow, greyish, rather fleshy leaves.

Ecology and Geography Rocks, cliffs, dry fields, and scrub, with around 38 species in Europe, 13 in California, the rest mainly in Asia.

Comment Some species are cultivated, and many of the cultivated varieties are hybrids of the garden wallflower, *Erysimum cheiri* (L.) Crantz syn. *Cheiranthus cheiri* L., which is a common feature of ancient walls throughout Europe, and is commonly grown as a biennial. It has scented flowers and petals without nectaries.

Hesperis

Hesperis L. (1753), dame's violet, in the family Cruciferae, contains 25 species, mainly in Europe.

Description Biennials or perennials to 90cm, variably hairy. Leaves simple, toothed, or pinnatifid, usually narrow at the base. Flowers pink, purple, white, or yellow, sweetly scented, in an elongating inflorescence. Sepals 4, the inner saccate at the base. Petals 4, with a long, narrow base. Stamens 6. Ovary superior, with a short style and 2-lobed stigma. Pollination is by insects, especially butterflies. The fruit is a many-seeded, narrow capsule.

Key Recognition Features The 4-petalled flowers, scented of violets, and the thin, toothed leaves.

Ecology and Geography In woods, by roadsides and ditches, and on cliffs and rocky areas, with 14 species mainly in eastern Europe, 1 widely naturalised as far north as Scotland.

Comment *Hesperis matronalis* L., the dame's violet, is commonly grown in gardens; there is a double-flowered form which has long been cultivated, but it is a weak grower.

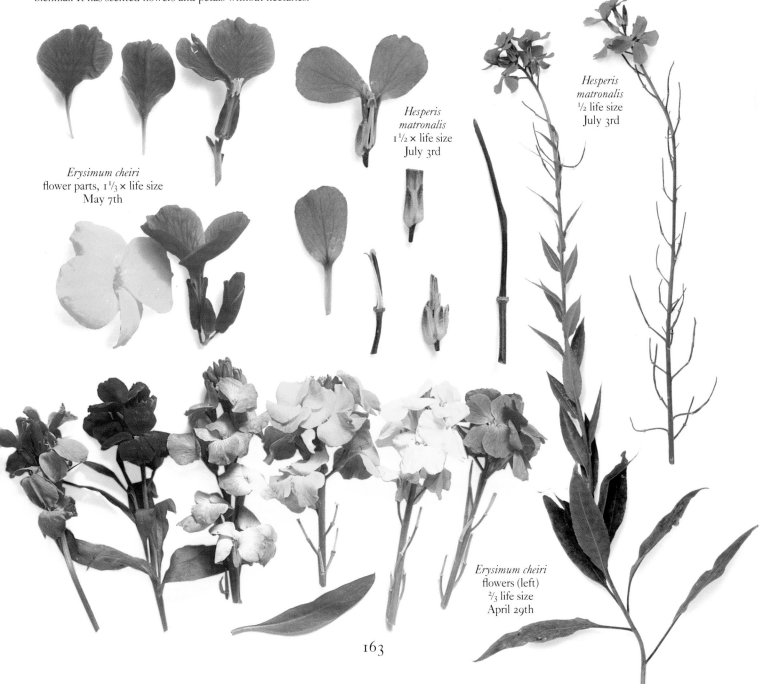

Erysimum cheiri
flower parts, 1 1/3 × life size
May 7th

Hesperis matronalis
1 1/2 × life size
July 3rd

Hesperis matronalis
1/2 life size
July 3rd

Erysimum cheiri
flowers (left)
2/3 life size
April 29th

Matthiola

Matthiola R. Br. (1812), the stock, in the family Cruciferae, contains around 55 species, mainly in Europe.

Description Annuals, biennials, or perennials to 90cm, often shrubby at the base. Leaves simple, toothed, or pinnatifid, often densely hairy with branched hairs. Flowers pink, purple, brown, white, or yellow, sweetly scented especially in the evening, in an elongating inflorescence. Sepals 4, the inner saccate at the base. Petals 4, with 2 lobes and a long, narrow base. Stamens 6. Ovary superior, with no style and a 2-lobed stigma. Pollination is by insects, especially butterflies and moths. The fruit is a many-seeded, narrow capsule, often with 2 or 3 horns at the apex.

Key Recognition Features The scented, 4-petalled flowers, grey, softly hairy leaves, and horned capsules.

Ecology and Geography On dunes and seaside cliffs and among mountain rocks, with 10 species in Europe, the rest scattered across Asia.

Comment Garden stocks are often either double-flowered and grown as annuals, so-called 10-week stocks, or biennials, so-called Brompton stocks, both developed from *M. incana* (L.) R. Br.. The night-scented stocks, with dull flowers that open in the evening, are selections of *M. longipetala* (Vent.) DC subsp. *bicornis* (Sm.) P. Ball.

Matthiola incana
½ life size, June 2nd

Matthiola incana
flower parts, fruit, and
section of fruit
(above) 1⅓ × life size
June 2nd

Matthiola longipetala
subsp. *bicornis*
¾ life size, July 2nd

Matthiola incana
(right) ½ life size
August 1st

Aubrieta

Aubrieta Adans. (1763), in the family Cruciferae, contains around 12 species, mainly in Europe and western Asia.

Description Mat-forming perennials to 10cm. Leaves short, simple, blunt-toothed, usually hairy with stellate hairs. Flowers reddish- or bluish-purple, occasionally white, in a short inflorescence. Sepals 4, the inner usually saccate at the base. Petals 4, with a long, narrow base. Stamens 6, the filaments of the outer stamens with a tooth. Ovary superior, with a short style and capitate stigma. Pollination is by insects, especially butterflies. The fruit is a many-seeded, ovate capsule, with 2 rows of seeds on each side.

Key Recognition Features The mat-forming plants, with 4-petalled, pink or purple flowers.

Ecology and Geography In mountain rocks, scree, and pine woods, with 6 species in Europe, the rest scattered across western Asia.

Comment Often called aubretia, these are commonly planted on walls and rocky banks, producing mats of colour in early spring. The genus is named after Claude Aubriet (1665–1742), flower painter for the French Royal Garden, who visited Crete, the Greek islands, and Turkey in 1700–1702.

Aubrieta deltoidea
⅔ life size, March 20th

Malcolmia maritima
flower parts, 2 × life size
June 27th

Malcolmia maritima
⅔ life size, June 27th

Malcolmia

Malcolmia R. Br. (1812), the Virginia stock, in the family Cruciferae, contains around 30 species, mainly in Europe.

Description Slender annuals, biennials, or perennials to 40cm. Leaves simple, toothed, or pinnatifid, often densely hairy with branched hairs. Flowers pink or purple, occasionally white, in an elongating inflorescence. Sepals 4, the inner usually saccate. Petals 4, 2-lobed, with a long, narrow base. Stamens 6. Ovary superior, with no style and a deeply 2-lobed stigma, the lobes erect and not spreading. Pollination is by insects, especially butterflies. The fruit is a many-seeded, narrow capsule.

Key Recognition Features The 4-petalled, pink or purple flowers, on a small, upright plant.

Ecology and Geography On dunes, seaside cliffs, and among mountain rocks; 15 species in Europe, the rest scattered across Asia.

Comment The Virginia stock, *M. maritima* (L.) R. Br., is a small, fast-growing annual, with pretty, bright pink, scentless flowers with a white eye. The genus is named after William Malcolm, a nurseryman in Kennington and Stockwell near London in the late 18th century.

Cardamine

Cardamine L. (1753), in the family Cruciferae, contains around 200 species, mainly in the northern hemisphere.

Description Annuals or perennials to 70cm, often with fleshy rhizomes, and in *C. bulbifera* (L.) Crantz with bulbils in the leaf axils. Leaves pinnate, digitate, 3-foliolate, or simple, usually without hairs. Flowers white, pink, purple, occasionally pale yellow. Sepals 4, the inner slightly saccate. Petals 4, with a narrow base. Stamens 6. Ovary superior, with a short style and slightly 2-lobed stigma. Pollination is by insects, or by selfing. The fruit is a many-seeded, narrow capsule.

Key Recognition Features The 4-petalled, pink or purple flowers, and usually pinnate leaves. Some species have relatively large flowers; others have very small flowers and are common garden weeds.

Ecology and Geography In woods and meadows and by streams, usually in wet places, with 36 species in Europe, the rest scattered across Asia and North America.

Comment Several species are grown in gardens, including double-flowered forms of the common lady's smock, *C. pratensis* L.. Around 15 species are often considered distinct from *Cardamine* in the genus *Dentaria* L., or are treated as a subgenus *Dentaria*. They have fleshy, subterranean rhizomes and petiolate cotyledons, while in subgenus *Cardamine* the rhizomes are on the surface.

*Cardamine
pratensis*
⅓ life size
May 3rd

*Cardamine
enneaphyllos*
flower parts, (left)
1¾ × life size
March 18th

Cardamine enneaphyllos
¾ life size, March 18th

*Cardamine
enneaphyllos*
fruit and seeds
just under life size
June 12th

*Cardamine
trifolia*
flower parts
2 × life size
May 15th

Arabis

Arabis L. (1753), in the family Cruciferae, contains around 180 species, mainly in the northern hemisphere.

Description Annuals, biennials, or perennials to 1.2m, but usually low and mat-forming. Leaves simple, toothed, usually hairy. Flowers white, pink, or purple. Sepals 4, the inner slightly saccate at the base. Petals 4, with a narrow base. Stamens 6. Ovary superior, with a short style and round or slightly indented stigma. Pollination is by insects. The fruit is a many-seeded, narrow capsule.

Key Recognition Features The 4-petalled white, pink, or purple flowers, simple leaves, and very narrow capsules.

Ecology and Geography On rocky areas, cliffs, sand dunes, and stony pastures, with 35 species in Europe, 75 in North America, the rest scattered across Asia and the mountains of Africa.

Comment Several species are grown on walls or rocky banks in gardens; *A. caucasica* Schlecht. with white flowers in early spring is commonly cultivated; there are double-flowered and variegated-leaved forms. The pink-flowered *A. blepharophylla* Hook. & Arn. is native in California, mainly around San Francisco.

*Arabis
blepharophylla*
2/3 life size
April 12th

Cardamine trifolia
3/4 life size
May 15th

Arabis caucasica
'Snowdrop'
2/3 life size
April 12th

Lunaria

Lunaria L. (1753), honesty, in the family Cruciferae, contains around 3 species, mainly in eastern Europe.

Description Biennials or perennials to 1.4m. Leaves simple, toothed, usually hairy. Flowers white, pink, or purple, sometimes scented. Sepals 4, the inner slightly saccate at the base. Petals 4, with a narrow base. Stamens 6. Ovary superior, with a short style and slightly indented stigma. Pollination is by insects. The fruit is a flat, few-seeded, oval or round capsule.

Key Recognition Features The 4-petalled white, pink, or purple flowers, simple leaves, and large, flat capsules with a persistent silvery septum, which remains into the winter after the seeds have fallen.

Ecology and Geography In woods, hedgrows, and scrub. Of the 3 species in Europe, *L. annua* L. is naturalised in North America.

Comment *L. rediviva* L. is an attractive herbaceous perennial with pale lilac, scented flowers and narrowly oval seed capsules. The common *L. annua* is a biennial, and forms with white flowers and variegated foliage are often cultivated.

Lunaria rediviva (left) and
Lunaria annua (right)
½ life size, September 29th

Lunaria annua, flower parts
1½ × life size, April 19th

Lunaria annua
seeds and septum of
capsule, 1⅓ × life size,
October 30th

Lunaria annua (left) and
Lunaria rediviva (right)
¾ life size, September 29th

Ionopsidium

Ionopsidium Rchb. (1829), in the family Cruciferae, contains around 4 species, mainly in southern Europe.

Description Small annuals to 40cm. Leaves simple, often rounded, the basal rosette leaves on long stalks, the stem leaves often clasping. Flowers purplish or white. Sepals 4, spreading, the inner not saccate. Petals 4, with a narrow base. Stamens 6. Ovary superior, with a short style and rounded stigma. Pollination is by insects. The fruit is a laterally compressed, 4- to 12-seeded, oval or round capsule.

Key Recognition Features Small annuals with 4-petalled, purplish or white flowers and round, stalked leaves.

Ecology and Geography On sand dunes and in sandy places that are wet in winter, in Portugal, Spain, Italy, and North Africa.

Comment Close to *Cochlearia* L. The commonly cultivated dwarf annual, *I. acaule* (Desf.) Rchb., is a native of Portugal, naturalised in Spain and southern France.

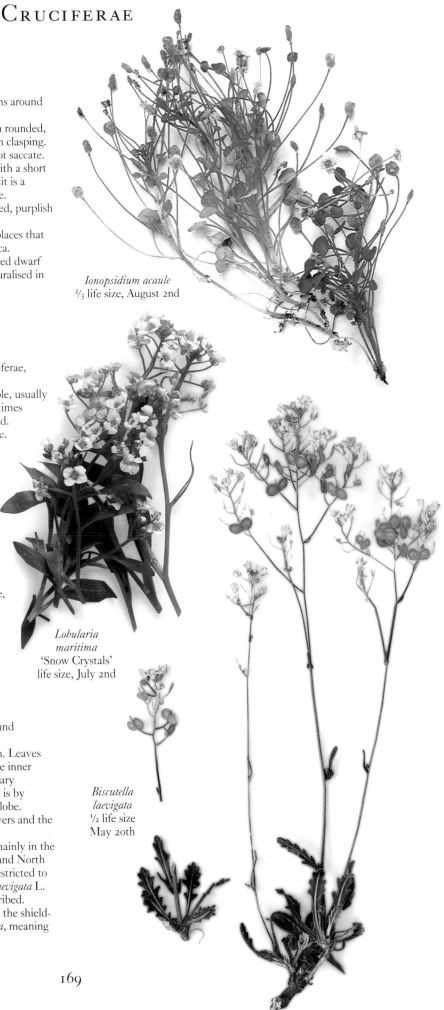

Ionopsidium acaule
²/₃ life size, August 2nd

Lobularia

Lobularia Desv. (1814), sweet alyssum, in the family Cruciferae, contains around 4 species, mainly in southern Europe.

Description Annuals or perennials to 40cm. Leaves simple, usually with hairs attached by their middles. Flowers white, sometimes purplish, cream, or pale orange in cultivated strains, scented. Sepals 4, the inner not saccate. Petals 4, with a narrow base. Stamens 6. Ovary superior, with a short style and rounded stigma. Pollination is by insects. The fruit is a 2- to 10-seeded, oval or round capsule.

Key Recognition Features The 4-petalled, white, purplish, or pale orange flowers, and the narrow, simple leaves.

Ecology and Geography On sand dunes and in dry, sunny places around the Mediterranean and southwards to the Cape Verde Islands; often naturalised further north.

Comment *Lobularia*, usually with white flowers, is sometimes confused with the yellow-flowered *Alyssum* L.. The genus *Aurinia* Desv. is sometimes considered separate, sometimes as a subgenus of *Alyssum*; it includes the commonly cultivated *Alyssum saxatile* L. syn. *Aurinia saxatilis* (L.) Desv., from central and eastern Europe and Turkey, and 9 other species, mostly perennials.

Lobularia maritima
'Snow Crystals'
life size, July 2nd

Biscutella

Biscutella L. (1753), in the family Cruciferae, contains around 40 species, mainly in southern Europe.

Description Perennials, often shrubby at the base, to 1m. Leaves simple, toothed, or pinnatifid. Flowers yellow. Sepals 4, the inner often saccate. Petals 4, with a narrow base. Stamens 6. Ovary superior, with a long style and rounded stigma. Pollination is by insects. The fruit is a 2-lobed capsule, with 1 seed in each lobe.

Key Recognition Features The 4-petalled, yellow flowers and the fruits with 2 rounded lobes.

Ecology and Geography In rocky areas and on cliffs, mainly in the mountains; from southeastern Belgium to France, Spain, and North Africa, and eastwards to western Iran. Many species are restricted to very small areas of mountain or cliff. The widespread *B. laevigata* L. is particularly variable; over 12 subspecies have been described.

Comment The common name buckler mustard refers to the shield-shaped lobes of the fruit, as does the Latin name *bi-scutella*, meaning 2 little shields.

Biscutella laevigata
¹/₂ life size
May 20th

Iberis

Iberis L. (1753), in the family Cruciferae, contains around 40 species, mainly in southern Europe.

Description Annuals, biennials, or perennials to 80cm, sometimes shrubby at the base. Leaves simple, sometimes rounded, or narrow and toothed. Flowers white or purplish, in flat heads. Sepals 4, the inner not saccate. Petals 4, narrowing gradually towards the base, the outer pair in the flower usually longer than the inner. Stamens 6. Ovary superior, with a long style and rounded stigma. Pollination is by insects, often butterflies. The fruit is a laterally compressed, 2-seeded, rounded capsule, winged and indented at the apex.

Key Recognition Features The flat heads of 4-petalled flowers, with the outer petals of the outer flowers elongated.

Ecology and Geography On cliffs, often by the sea, on screes, and in sandy places, usually on limestone. Around the Mediterranean, especially in Portugal, Spain, and North Africa.

Comment Many species are cultivated, both perennial and annual. Cultivars of the annual species *I. amara* L., with pink, red, and purplish flowers have been selected. The genus *Aethionema* R. Br., found mostly in Turkey, usually has pinkish flowers in rounded heads and rather similar fruits.

Lepidium

Lepidium L. (1753), in the family Cruciferae, contains around 140 species worldwide.

Description Annuals, biennials, or perennials to 1m, sometimes shrubby. Leaves simple, sometimes rounded, or narrow and toothed. Flowers small, white or purplish. Sepals 4, the inner not saccate. Petals 4, tapering abruptly towards the base, all equal. Stamens 6. Ovary superior, with a usually short style and small stigma. Pollination is by insects, and self-pollination is also common. The fruit is a laterally compressed, 2-seeded, rounded capsule, narrowly winged and with a small indentation at the apex.

Key Recognition Features The numerous small, dirty white, 4-petalled flowers, and the flattened, 2-seeded capsules.

Ecology and Geography On waste ground and sandy places, often near the sea, and in salt marshes, with 21 species in Europe, the rest scattered in temperate regions.

Comment The cress cultivated for salad is *L. sativum* L., probably native of western Asia and Egypt; the edible cotyledons are deeply 3-lobed. The perennial *L. latifolium* L., with large, flat leaves, was also grown for salad. Thanet cress, *L. draba* L. syn. *Cardaria draba* (L.) Desv. is a suckering perennial, common as a weed worldwide and especially in southern England; it is said to have been introduced to Kent with the bedding straw of fever-ridden troops disembarked at Ramsgate from the ill-fated Walcheren expedition against Napoleon in August 1805, and spread with manure to Thanet, where it was first noted as a weed in 1829. Its seeds were also ground and used as pepper.

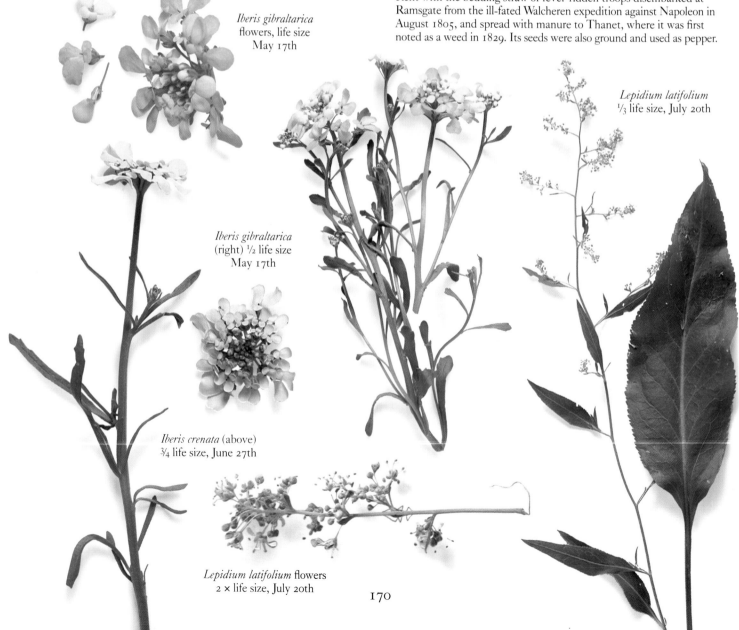

Iberis gibraltarica
flowers, life size
May 17th

Iberis gibraltarica
(right) ½ life size
May 17th

Iberis crenata (above)
¾ life size, June 27th

Lepidium latifolium
⅓ life size, July 20th

Lepidium latifolium flowers
2 × life size, July 20th

Brassica oleracea
flower parts
1¾ × life size
May 25th

Brassica juncea
⅓ life size, March 3rd

Brassica

Brassica L. (1753), in the family Cruciferae, contains around
35 species, mostly in Europe.
Description Annuals, biennials, or perennials to 2m, sometimes
shrubby at the base. Leaves pinnate or simple, fleshy. Flowers
yellow, white, or purplish. Sepals 4, slightly saccate. Petals 4, yellow
or white, tapering gradually into a long, narrow base, with green
nectaries. Stamens 6. Ovary superior, with a usually very short
style and rounded stigma. Pollination is by insects. The fruit is a
many-seeded, long, narrow, flattened capsule, with a beak at the end.
Key Recognition Features The yellow or white flowers, fleshy
leaves, and flattened capsules.
Ecology and Geography On sea cliffs and in waste ground and
sandy places, often near the sea, with 21 species in Europe, the rest
scattered across the northern hemisphere.
Comment *Brassica* includes some of the most useful cultivated
vegetables. The wild form of *B. oleracea* L. is close to purple-sprouting
broccoli; it has also been developed into cabbages, kales, Brussels
sprouts, cauliflower, broccoli, and kohlrabi. *Brassica rapa* L. is the
oil-seed rape and the turnip, as well as being the parent of many
forms of Chinese cabbage. *Brassica napus* L., the swede or rutabaga,
is a hybrid of these 2 species. *Brassica juncea* (L.) Czern. is often
grown for mustard seeds, and as a green vegetable in China, so-called
mustard greens or *kai tsoi*.

Brassica oleracea broccoli
'Early Purple Sprouting'
½ life size, May 25th

Raphanus sativus
young seedlings
(right) ¾ life size
April 12th

Raphanus sativus (below) left to right:
'Beacon', 'Sparkler' and 'Scarlet Globe'
⅓ life size, July 5th

Raphanus sativus
'Pfitzer's Maindreieek'
⅓ life size
November 1st

Raphanus

Raphanus L. (1753), the radish, in the family Cruciferae, contains around 3 species originating in Europe and western Asia.

Description Annuals, biennials, or perennials to 80cm, often with a swollen root. Leaves pinnate. Flowers pale yellow, white, or pinkish, often veined. Sepals 4, not saccate. Petals 4, tapering abruptly into a long, narrow base. Stamens 6. Ovary superior, with a short style and rounded stigma. Pollination is by insects. The fruit is a long, narrow, many-seeded capsule, constricted between the seeds, and with a beak at the end.

Key Recognition Features The pale yellow or white flowers, rough-textured leaves, and capsules constricted between the seeds.

Ecology and Geography On sand dunes and in waste ground and sandy places, often near the sea. Wild radishes are found on the coasts of Europe, but escapees from cultivation are common as weeds throughout the world.

Comment Cultivated radishes vary greatly, ranging from the small, red-and-white salad radishes favoured in Europe to the huge, long-rooted varieties grown for storage through the winter in Japan and China. The young fruits of some varieties are also edible.

CRUCIFERAE

Raphanus sativus
seeds, ¾ life size
April 12th

Raphanus sativus
'Pontvil', ½ life size
July 3rd

Raphanus raphanistrum
subsp. *maritimus*
½ life size, July 3rd

Raphanus sativus 'Black Spanish
Round' (right) and 'Black
Spanish Long' (far right)
⅓ life size, November 1st

173

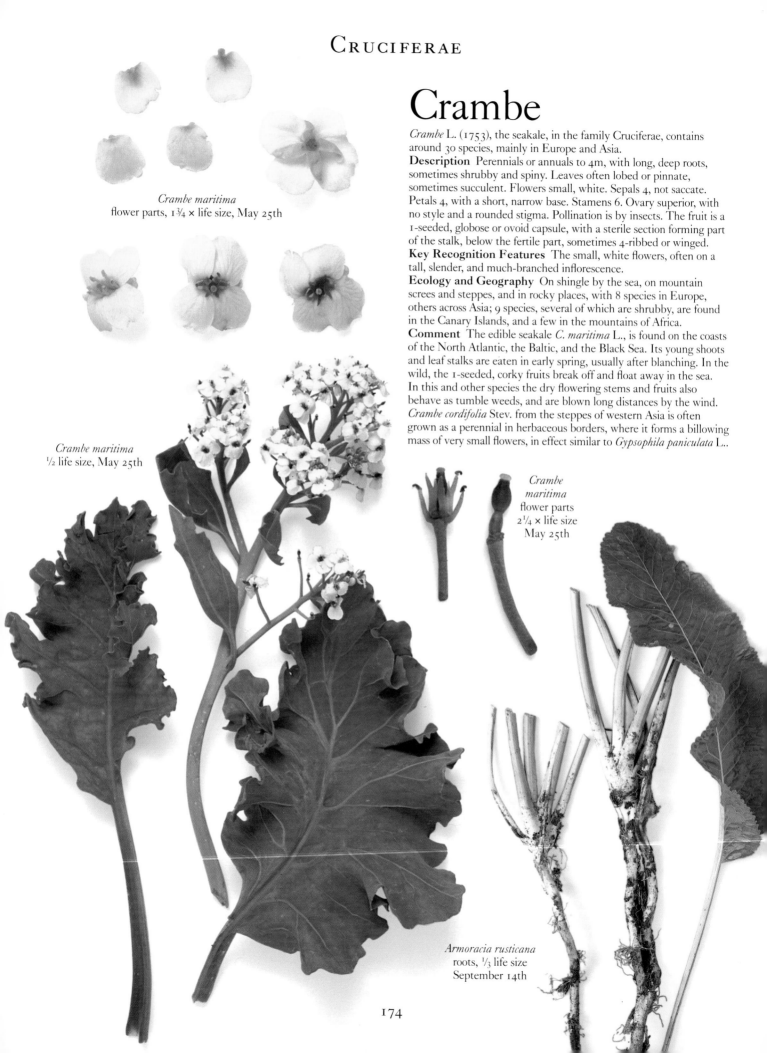

Crambe maritima
flower parts, 1¾ × life size, May 25th

Crambe maritima
½ life size, May 25th

Crambe

Crambe L. (1753), the seakale, in the family Cruciferae, contains around 30 species, mainly in Europe and Asia.

Description Perennials or annuals to 4m, with long, deep roots, sometimes shrubby and spiny. Leaves often lobed or pinnate, sometimes succulent. Flowers small, white. Sepals 4, not saccate. Petals 4, with a short, narrow base. Stamens 6. Ovary superior, with no style and a rounded stigma. Pollination is by insects. The fruit is a 1-seeded, globose or ovoid capsule, with a sterile section forming part of the stalk, below the fertile part, sometimes 4-ribbed or winged.

Key Recognition Features The small, white flowers, often on a tall, slender, and much-branched inflorescence.

Ecology and Geography On shingle by the sea, on mountain screes and steppes, and in rocky places, with 8 species in Europe, others across Asia; 9 species, several of which are shrubby, are found in the Canary Islands, and a few in the mountains of Africa.

Comment The edible seakale *C. maritima* L., is found on the coasts of the North Atlantic, the Baltic, and the Black Sea. Its young shoots and leaf stalks are eaten in early spring, usually after blanching. In the wild, the 1-seeded, corky fruits break off and float away in the sea. In this and other species the dry flowering stems and fruits also behave as tumble weeds, and are blown long distances by the wind. *Crambe cordifolia* Stev. from the steppes of western Asia is often grown as a perennial in herbaceous borders, where it forms a billowing mass of very small flowers, in effect similar to *Gypsophila paniculata* L..

*Crambe
maritima*
flower parts
2¼ × life size
May 25th

Armoracia rusticana
roots, ⅓ life size
September 14th

Armoracia

Armoracia L. (1753), the horseradish, in the family Cruciferae, contains around 4 species, originating in Europe and western Asia.
Description Perennials to 1m or more, with long, deep roots. Leaves often lobed and toothed. Flowers small, white. Sepals 4, not saccate. Petals 4, with a short, narrow base. Stamens 6. Ovary superior, with a short style and rounded stigma. Pollination is perhaps by insects or by selfing. The fruit is a many-seeded, globose or ovoid capsule, with seeds in 2 rows.
Key Recognition Features The broad, dark green leaves and masses of small, white flowers.
Ecology and Geography On waste ground, roadsides, and marshes, with 2 species in Europe, 1 in Asia, and 1 in eastern North America.
Comment Horseradish has been cultivated for over 2000 years by planting pieces of root, and does not normally set seed; it is possibly of hybrid origin. The ground-up root is used as a very hot flavouring. The sport with variegated leaves is sometimes cultivated, as it is more decorative than the plain green form. It is not related to the ordinary radish, but is closer to *Nasturtium officinale* L., the water cress, and *Cardamine* (see p.166).

Morisia

Morisia Gay (1829), in the family Cruciferae, contains 1 species, *M. monanthos* (Viv.) Ascherson, in Corsica and Sardinia.
Description Perennial to 2cm, with deep roots. Leaves in a rosette on the ground, pinnate, with jagged, triangular lobes, somewhat succulent. Flowers solitary, yellow. Sepals 4, not saccate. Petals 4, with a long, narrow base. Stamens 6. Ovary superior, with no style and a rounded stigma. Pollination is by insects. Fruit stalk elongating after flowering and curving over to bury the 2-lobed fruit. the fruit's basal segment is dehiscent, with 3–5 seeds; its apical segment is indehiscent, with 1 or 2 seeds.
Key Recognition Features The yellow flowers on a dwarf plant with jagged leaves.
Ecology and Geography In sandy and rocky places in Corsica and Sardinia.
Comment This is often grown as an interesting dwarf perennial, flowering in winter and spring. The fruit is unique in the family both in shape and in being pushed into the ground by its thickened stalk, which is reminiscent of the behaviour of the groundnut or peanut, *Arachis hypogea* L.. The genus commemorates Giuseppe Giacinto Moris, (1796–1869) professor of botany in Turin.

Armoracia rusticana
variegated form
½ life size July 5th

Morisia monanthos
'Fred Hemingway'
2 × life size, March 17th

Morisia monanthos
'Fred Hemingway'
just under life size, March 17th

Kitaibela vitifolia
flower parts, life size
July 5th

Kitaibela vitifolia
$^1/_3$ life size, July 5th

Lavatera trimestris
flower parts, $^2/_3$ life size, August 1st

Lavatera

Lavatera L. (1753), in the family Malvaceae, contains around
25 species, mainly in Europe and Asia.

Description Perennials, sometimes shrubby, or annuals, to 3m.
Leaves often 3–5 lobed, usually softly hairy. Flowers pink or purple,
solitary or clustered in the leaf axils. Epicalyx segments (sepal-like
bracts) 3, usually joined at the base. Sepals 5, joined at the base.
Petals 5, usually blunt or indented at the apex. Stamens many, joined
to form a column around the styles. Ovary superior, of numerous
carpels and styles joined into a column at the base. Pollination is by
insects. The fruit is many-seeded, the seeds packed in a circle inside
the persistent sepals.

Key Recognition Features The pink or purple flowers, and the
3 epicalyx segments joined at the base.

Ecology and Geography On shingle and cliffs by the sea, and in
rocky places and waste ground, with 11 species in Europe, the rest
across Asia, with 2 shrubby species in the Canary Islands.

Comment The annual *L. trimestris* L. is commonly cultivated, as is
the subshrubby *L. olbia* L. and its various hybrids, such as 'Rosea', a
rich pink, and 'Barnsley', white with a deep pink eye. *Malope* L.,
often cultivated as an annual, has petals very narrow at the base and
3 epicalyx segments wider than the petals.

Lavatera trimestris
$^1/_3$ life size, August 1st

Malva sylvestris
flower parts, life size
July 5th

Malva moschata
flower parts, life size
July 14th

Kitaibela

Kitaibela Willd. (1799), in the family Malvaceae, contains 2 species, 1 in eastern Europe, the other in western Turkey.

Description Perennials to 3m. Leaves triangular or 5- to 7-lobed, usually prickly-hairy. Flowers white or red, solitary or clustered in the leaf axils. Epicalyx segments (sepal-like bracts) 6–9, usually joined only at the base. Sepals 5, joined at the base. Petals 5, usually blunt or indented at the apex. Stamens many, joined to form a column around the styles. Ovary superior, of numerous carpels and styles joined into a column at the base. Pollination is by insects. The fruit is made up of around 5 whorls of 1-seeded carpels, dark brown and hairy.

Key Recognition Features Tall perennials with small, white or red flowers with 6–9 epicalyx segments.

Ecology and Geography In damp scrub and rough grassland, with *K. vitifolia* Willd. in Kosovo and Macedonia, and *K. balansae* Boiss. in western Turkey.

Comment *Kitaibela vitifolia* is sometimes cultivated, but it is too rank and leafy to be a first-rate garden plant; *K. balansae* is a rather mysterious plant, found first near the Cilician Gates in August 1855, and, as far as I can ascertain, never collected again.

Malva moschata
⅔ life size
July 14th

Malva

Malva L. (1753), in the family Malvaceae, contains around 40 species, mainly in Europe and Asia.

Description Perennials or annuals to 1.5m, but often sprawling. Leaves lobed or deeply divided. Flowers white, pink, or purple, solitary or clustered in the leaf axils. Epicalyx segments (sepal-like bracts) 3, not joined at the base. Sepals 5, joined at the base. Petals 5, usually blunt or indented at the apex. Stamens many, joined to form a column around the styles. Pollination is by insects. Ovary superior, of numerous carpels and styles joined into a column at the base. The fruit is many-seeded, the seeds packed in a circle inside the persistent sepals.

Key Recognition Features The small, white, pink, or purple flowers, and 3 epicalyx segments not joined at the base; in *Lavatera* the epicalyx segments are usually joined and the flowers are larger.

Ecology and Geography On waste ground, in fields, and on rocky hills, with 13 species in Europe, the rest across Asia, with a few in the mountains of tropical Africa.

Comment Many species are common weeds; the most commonly cultivated species are *M. sylvestris* L., especially the dark purple forms generally called subsp. *mauritanica*, and *M. moschata* L. with deeply divided leaves and pink or white flowers. Recent DNA studies suggest that the family Malvaceae should be extended to include the genera formerly grouped under Tiliaceae (lime trees, see Volume 1) and the mainly tropical Bombacaceae and Sterculiaceae (see Volume 1), which contain such fruit trees as the durian, *Durio zibethinus* Murray, and the cocoa plant, *Theobroma cacao* L.. Malvaceae is closely associated with the Cistaceae and Thymelaeaceae, and more distantly with Rutaceae, Sapindaceae, and Anacardiaceae, all of which are largely woody families (see Volume 1).

Alcea rosea
flower parts
just under life size
June 27th

Alcea rosea
½ life size, June 27th

Alcea rosea 'Nigra' (left) and 'Chater's Double White' (right)
²⁄₃ life size, August 1st

Alcea

Alcea L. (1753), the hollyhock, in the family Malvaceae, contains around 50 species, mainly in Asia.

Description Perennials to 7m, rarely stemless. Leaves lobed or deeply palmately divided. Flowers white, pink, purplish, or yellow, solitary or clustered in the axils of the upper leaves or of small bracts. Epicalyx segments (sepal-like bracts) usually 6, rarely 7–9, joined at the base. Sepals 5, joined at the base. Petals 5, usually blunt at the apex. Stamens many, joined to form a column around the styles; anthers yellow. Ovary superior, of numerous carpels and styles joined into a column at the base. Pollination is by insects. The fruit is many-seeded, the seeds packed in a circle inside the persistent sepals.

Key Recognition Features The large flowers on tall plants, and the 6 epicalyx segments joined at the base.

Ecology and Geography On dry, rocky hills, with 18 species in Turkey, and the rest scattered across Asia.

Comment The common hollyhock, *A. rosea* L., is frequently cultivated throughout the world. It is unknown in the wild, and probably arose in cultivation in southwestern Asia; it occurs in many colours, including black, and single or double forms. *Alcea rugosa* Alef. is a pale yellow species from the Caucasus and southern Russia.

Althaea

Althaea L. (1753), in the family Malvaceae, contains around 12 species, mainly in Europe and Asia.

Description Annuals or perennials to 1m or more. Leaves lobed or deeply palmately divided almost to the base. Flowers white, pink, bluish, or red, solitary or clustered in the axils of the upper leaves or of small bracts. Epicalyx segments (sepal-like bracts) usually 6–9, joined at the base. Sepals 5, joined at the base. Petals 5, usually blunt or indented at the apex. Stamens many, joined to form a column around the styles; anthers purplish or brownish. Ovary superior, of numerous carpels and styles joined into a column at the base. Pollination is by insects. The fruit is many-seeded, the seeds packed in a circle inside the persistent sepals.

Key Recognition Features The smallish flowers, with petals less than 15mm long, on small or tall plants, and the purplish or brownish anthers.

Ecology and Geography In marshy ground or open places, with 5 species in Europe, the rest scattered across Asia.

Comment The marsh mallow, *A. officinalis* L., which is found wild throughout Europe eastwards to Afghanistan, and naturalised on the east coast of North America, has roots which contain mucilage, the source of marshmallow.

Althaea officinalis
½ life size, October 1st

179

Sidalcea

Sidalcea A. Gray (1848), in the family Malvaceae, contains around 20 species, mainly in western North America.

Description Perennials to 1m, or annuals. Leaves lobed or deeply palmately divided almost to the base. Flowers white, pink, or purplish, in elongated spikes, sometimes female only. Epicalyx segments (sepal-like bracts) 1 or absent. Sepals 5, joined at the base. Petals 5, usually blunt or indented at the apex. Stamens many, joined to form a column around the styles. Ovary superior, of numerous carpels and styles joined into a column at the base. Pollination is by insects. The fruit is made up of 5–9 single-seeded capsules, packed in a circle inside the persistent sepals.

Key Recognition Features The spikes of flowers with petals less than 30mm long, on tall stems, usually from mats of shiny leaves.

Ecology and Geography In marshy ground or dry, open places, sometimes among sagebrush, with 18 species and many varieties in California, the rest elsewhere in western North America.

Comment There are many cultivars, such as 'Elsie Heugh' and hybrids of the variable species *S. malviflora* (DC) Gray ex Benth., which are cultivated in herbaceous borders. Even in the wild in California there are 10 subspecies. *Sidalcea candida* A. Gray from the Rockies is white-flowered and more delicate.

Sidalcea 'Elsie Heugh'
flower parts, life size
September 10th

Sphaeralcea fendleri
subsp. *venusta* (left) and
subsp. *fendleri* (right)
²⁄₃ life size, July 6th

Sidalcea 'Elsie Heugh'
¹⁄₂ life size
September 10th

Sphaeralcea

Sphaeralcea A. St Hil. (1825), in the family Malvaceae, contains around 60 species, mainly in western North America.

Description Perennials to 1.5m, sometimes creeping, often shrubby at the base. Leaves triangular, rounded, or lobed, usually softly hairy with dense, stellate hairs. Flowers orange or scarlet, less often white, pink, or purplish, in interrupted spikes. Epicalyx segments (sepal-like bracts) 2 or 3. Sepals 5, joined at the base. Petals 5, usually blunt or indented at the apex. Stamens many, joined to form a column around the styles. Ovary superior, of numerous carpels and styles joined into a column at the base. Pollination is by insects. The fruit is made up of 5 or more 1-, 2-, or 3-seeded capsules, the upper part of each opening when ripe, the lower part not opening.

Key Recognition Features The velvety-hairy leaves with dense, stellate hairs, and the interrupted spikes of flowers with petals less than 30mm long.

Ecology and Geography On rocky hills, in dry, open places, and on roadsides, sometimes among sagebrush and cactus. Around 16 species in Arizona, the rest elsewhere in the dry parts of North America.

Comment Several species are cultivated, and are useful as drought-resistant summer flowers. Extracts of *S. angustifolia* (Cav.) G. Don subsp. *cuspidata* (Gray) Kearn., the *yerba de negrita*, are used in hair conditioners; it grows wild from Kansas to Arizona and Mexico. Other species are used as eye remedies, and the mucilaginous stems are chewed. The South African genus *Anisodontea* C. Presl is somewhat similar, but usually has rough leaves and pinkish petals that are spotted near the base.

Sphaeralcea munroana
'Shell Pink' flower parts
1 ½ × life size, June 27th

Sphaeralcea fendleri subsp. *venusta*
life size, July 6th

Sphaeralcea munroana
¾ life size, August 23rd

Sphaeralcea munroana
flower parts, life size
August 23rd

Callirhoe involucrata
flower without petals
1⅓ × life size, August 23rd

Callirhoe involucrata
petals, life size
August 23rd

Callirhoe involucrata
(left) ½ life size
August 23rd

Callirhoe

Callirhoe Nutt. (1821), the poppy mallow, in the family Malvaceae, contains 9 species in North America.

Description Perennials to 50cm, upright or trailing. Leaves usually deeply, palmately lobed, not hairy, the lowest sometimes triangular or geranium-like (see pp.112–13). Flowers usually bright purplish-pink, sometimes white, pale pink, or deep purple, long-stemmed and solitary in the leaf axils. Epicalyx segments (sepal-like bracts) usually 3. Sepals 5, joined at the base. Petals 5, usually blunt or indented at the apex. Stamens many, joined to form a column around the styles. Ovary superior, of numerous carpels and styles joined into a column at the base. Pollination is by insects. The fruit is made up of many 1-seeded, often beaked capsules, which do not open.

Key Recognition Features The narrow leaflets and long-stalked flowers with petals less than 30mm long.

Ecology and Geography On rocky hills, in dry, open places and along roadsides, mainly in the prairie region from Illinois and Indiana to Texas and northern Mexico.

Comment *Callirhoe involucrata* (Torr. & Gray) Gray is the most commonly cultivated species. It is recognised by its geranium-like leaves and long-stalked flowers.

Helianthemum
'Henfield Brilliant'
just under life size, June 2nd

Helianthemum

Helianthemum Mill. (1768), the rock rose, in the family Cistaceae, contains around 110 species, mainly in the Mediterranean area.

Description Dwarf shrubs, perennials, or annuals to 1m, usually spreading. Leaves opposite, ovate to linear. Flowers yellow, white, pale pink, or sometimes red. Sepals 5, the 2 outer smaller than the 3 inner. Petals 5, usually rounded. Stamens many, very slender. Ovary superior, of 3 carpels and 1 usually short style. Pollination is by insects. The fruit is made up of 3 many-seeded cells, splitting when ripe.

Key Recognition Features The flowers with numerous slender stamens, and sepals of 2 sizes.

Ecology and Geography In dry, open places, with 31 species and many subspecies in Europe, and other species across the drier parts of Asia and in western North and South America.

Comment Many species of *Helianthemum* are grown in dry gardens for their attractive flowers, freely produced, but lasting only 1 day. The Cistaceae is a small, isolated family, most closely related to the tropical tree families Dipterocarpaceae and the Madagascan Sarcolaenaceae, all of which are associated with the Malvaceae.

Helianthemum
'Henfield Brilliant'
flower back
1¼ × life size
June 2nd

Dictamnus

Dictamnus L. (1753), the burning bush, in the family Rutaceae, contains 1 variable species, *D. albus* L., from southern Europe and western Asia.

Description Perennial to 80cm, with upright flowering stems, the whole plant covered with glandular hairs. Leaves pinnately divided, with 3–6 pairs of leaflets. Flowers pink or white. Sepals 5. Petals 5, usually with dark veins or spots. Stamens 10, with downward curving filaments. Ovary superior, of 5 carpels and 1 style. Pollination is by insects. The fruit is a capsule with 5 radiating lobes, splitting when ripe.

Key Recognition Features The flowers with curved stamens, and the pinnate leaves.

Ecology and Geography In dry, grassy places and scrub from Spain to the Caucasus and western Asia.

Comment An attractive perennial, called burning bush because the glands give off a volatile oil, which can be lit on still, warm evenings, and burns without harming the plant; a party trick at Glyndebourne during the open-air opera season.

Ruta

Ruta L. (1753), the rue, in the family Rutaceae, contains around 8 species, mainly in the Mediterranean area.

Description Perennials, sometimes shrubby at the base, to 75cm, usually bushy, with taller flowering stems. Leaves deeply and variously divided. Flowers yellow. Sepals 4. Petals 4, rarely 5, usually toothed or ringed with hairs. Stamens 8, rarely 10. Ovary superior, of 4 or 5 carpels. Pollination is by insects. The fruit is a 4- or 5-lobed capsule, splitting when ripe.

Key Recognition Features The divided and very pungent leaves, and yellow, 4-petalled flowers.

Ecology and Geography In dry, open places, with 5 species in Europe, North Africa, and the drier parts of Asia, and 3 shrubby species in the Canary Islands.

Comment Rue, *R. graveolens* L., was formerly much used as a flavouring and medicinal herb. It can cause serious skin lesions in some people. The family Rutaceae includes the important genus *Citrus* L., as well as the large tree *Phellodendron* Rupr.. It is associated with *Ailanthus* Desf. in the Simaroubaceae (for all see Volume 1), and the Meliaceae which includes *Swietenia* Jacq., the mahogany.

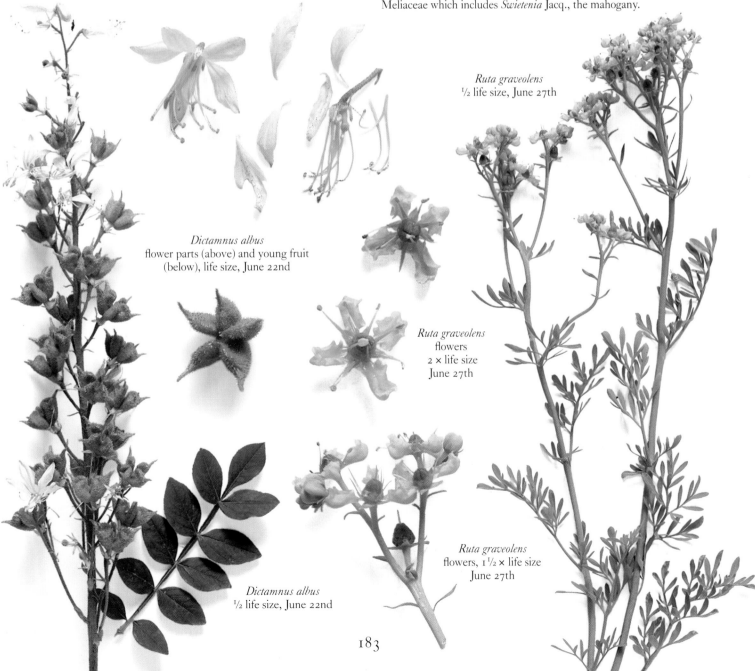

Ruta graveolens
½ life size, June 27th

Dictamnus albus
flower parts (above) and young fruit
(below), life size, June 22nd

Ruta graveolens
flowers
2 × life size
June 27th

Ruta graveolens
flowers, 1½ × life size
June 27th

Dictamnus albus
½ life size, June 22nd

Darlingtonia

Darlingtonia Torr. (1854), the Californian pitcher plant, in the family Sarraceniaceae, contains 1 species, *D. californica* Torr., in western North America.

Description Perennials to 1.2m. Leaves unequal in size, all basal, modified into pitchers, hooded at the apex, with 2 leaf-like flaps hanging down near the mouth, and transparent patches on the upper surface. Flowers nodding, on upright stems with scale-like leaves. Sepals 5, narrow, green, sometimes with purplish lines. Petals 5, usually dark maroon-purple, shorter than the sepals. Stamens numerous. Ovary superior, of 5 carpels and 1 style, with a 5-lobed stigma. Pollination is presumed to be by insects. The fruit is a capsule, with numerous small seeds.

Key Recognition Features The pitcher-shaped leaves with appendages at the mouth, and the narrow sepals and petals.

Ecology and Geography In bogs in pine and redwood forest in northern California and Oregon.

Comment The genus is named after William Darlington (1782–1863) an American botanist. The third genus in the family Sarraceniaceae is *Heliamphora* Benth., found in the mountains of Venezuela and Guyana.

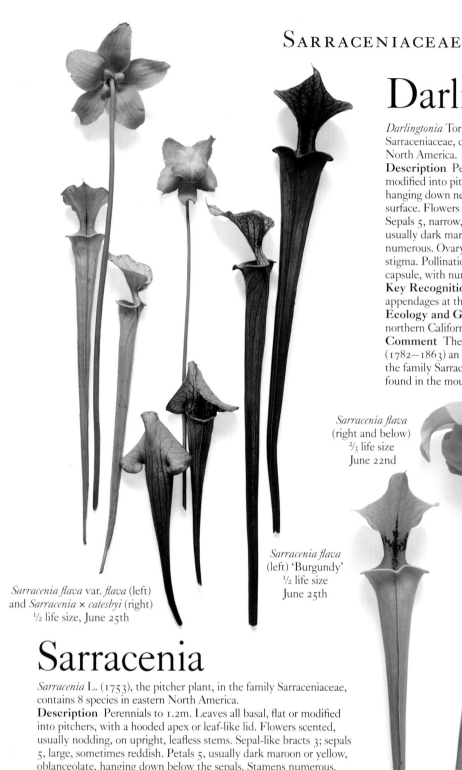

Sarracenia flava var. *flava* (left)
and *Sarracenia* × *catesbyi* (right)
½ life size, June 25th

Sarracenia flava
(left) 'Burgundy'
½ life size
June 25th

Sarracenia flava
(right and below)
⅔ life size
June 22nd

Sarracenia leucophylla
(right)
½ life size
June 25th

Sarracenia purpurea subsp. *venosa*
½ life size
June 25th

Sarracenia leucophylla
½ life size
June 25th

Sarracenia

Sarracenia L. (1753), the pitcher plant, in the family Sarraceniaceae, contains 8 species in eastern North America.

Description Perennials to 1.2m. Leaves all basal, flat or modified into pitchers, with a hooded apex or leaf-like lid. Flowers scented, usually nodding, on upright, leafless stems. Sepal-like bracts 3; sepals 5, large, sometimes reddish. Petals 5, usually dark maroon or yellow, oblanceolate, hanging down below the sepals. Stamens numerous. Ovary superior, of 5 carpels and 1 style, which is expanded at the tip, forming a 5-sided disc that fills the centre of the flower. Pollination is by insects. The fruit is a capsule with numerous small seeds.

Key Recognition Features The pitcher-shaped leaves and the large style.

Ecology and Geography In bogs and pine barrens from Newfoundland to Saskatchewan, southwards to Florida and Texas. Naturalised in a few places in Europe, such as near Tullamore in central Ireland and in western and northern Switzerland.

Comment Pitcher plants are easy to grow in wet, acidic soil. Several natural and artificial hybrids are cultivated. The genus is named after Dr M. Sarrazin de l'Etang (1659–1734), physician at the court of Quebec, who sent specimens to Tournfort in Paris. The Sarraceniaceae is associated with the Ericaceae (see pp.186–89), and most closely related to the woody Clethraceae (see Volume 1) and Cyrillaceae.

SARRACENIACEAE

Sarracenia × popei
²/₃ life size, June 25th

Sarracenia minor
²/₃ life size, June 25th

Sarracenia purpurea subsp.
purpurea f. *heterophylla*
(right) ²/₃ life size
June 25th

Darlingtonia
californica
²/₃ life size
June 25th

Sarracenia rubra
(left) ²/₃ life size
June 25th

Sarracenia psittacina
²/₃ life size, June 25th

Sarracenia purpurea
subsp. *purpurea*
²/₃ life size June 25th

Sarracenia alata
²/₃ life size
June 25th

Erica carnea
'Myretoun Ruby'
flower parts (left)
4 × life size, March 1st

Erica vagans
life size, July 3rd

Erica carnea
'Myretoun Ruby'
¾ life size, March 1st

Erica

Erica L. (1753), heather, in the family Ericaceae, contains around 735 species, mainly in South Africa and western Europe. It is the smaller, European species that are described here; for the tree species see Volume 1.

Description Subshrubs to 80cm. Leaves all small, short-stalked, in whorls of 3, 4, or 6. Flowers pink or purple, rarely white, in short spikes or umbels. Sepals 4, not petal-like. Petals 4, joined to form a tube or urn-shaped corolla, longer than the sepals. Stamens 8, anthers opening by pores, often with curved appendages. Ovary superior, of 4 carpels and 1 style. Pollination is mainly by bees, but by sunbirds in some of the large-flowered South African species. The fruit is a 4-celled capsule with many very small seeds.

Key Recognition Features The small leaves in whorls of 3, 4, or 6, and the tubular or urn-shaped corolla, with 4 lobes.

Ecology and Geography Common on moorland and in bogs, and found also in coniferous woods and on banks and stable dunes, usually but not always on acid soil. Found throughout northern Europe from Scotland, extending eastwards to western Turkey; also in the mountains of Africa, and reaching their greatest diversity in the Cape.

Comment European heathers (shown here) are a pale reflection of the wonderful diversity of species in the Cape, where some species have tubular flowers over 2cm long. The family Ericaceae is large and diverse, found throughout the world. DNA studies have indicated ways in which the genera may have evolved, and shown that the small families Empetraceae, Epacridaceae, and Pyrolaceae fall within the generally accepted limits of the family.

Erica cinerea
just under life size, July 3rd

Calluna

Calluna Salisb. (1802), ling, in the family Ericaceae, contains
1 species, *C. vulgaris* (L.) Hull, in Europe and western Asia.
Description Low subshrubs to 1m. Leaves all small, not stalked,
opposite. Flowers pinkish-purple, rarely white, in a branching spikes.
Sepals 4, petal-like. Petals 4, shorter than the sepals, joined at the
base. Stamens 8, anthers dark brown with curved, pale awns.
Pollination is mainly by bees and thrips, but possibly also by wind.
Ovary superior, of 4 carpels and 1 style. The fruit is a 4-celled capsule
with few seeds hidden in the dry calyx.
Key Recognition Features The small flowers with 4 petal-like
sepals and smaller petals.
Ecology and Geography Dominant on moorland, and found also
in acidic woods and on banks and stable dunes, throughout northern
Europe from Iceland, extending eastwards to eastern Turkey and
the Urals.
Comment This is the plant that colours the hills of Scotland purple.
It is the main food of the red grouse and also a source of nectar for
excellent honey.

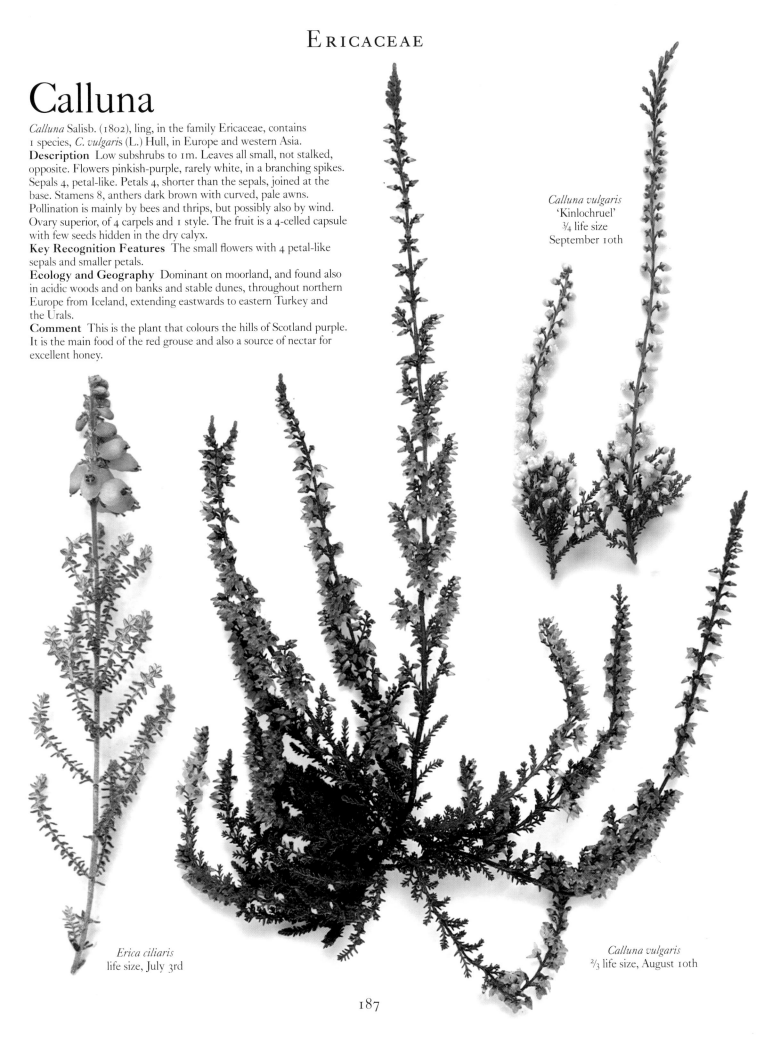

Calluna vulgaris
'Kinlochruel'
¾ life size
September 10th

Erica ciliaris
life size, July 3rd

Calluna vulgaris
⅔ life size, August 10th

Daboecia cantabrica 'Praegerae'
flower parts and leaves
2 × life size, August 10th

Daboecia cantabrica
⅔ life size, July 20th

Daboecia

Daboecia D. Don (1834), St Dabeoc's heath, in the family Ericaceae, contains 2 species in the Azores and southwestern Europe.

Description Subshrubs to 70cm. Leaves short-stalked, alternate, flat with recurved edges, silver beneath. Flowers purple, pink, or crimson, in loose spikes. Sepals 4, not petal-like. Petals 4, joined to form an urn-shaped corolla, longer than the sepals. Stamens 8, anthers without appendages. Ovary superior, hairy, of 4 carpels and 1 style. Pollination is mainly by bees. The fruit is a 4-celled capsule, with many small seeds.

Key Recognition Features The flat, oval, alternate leaves and large, urn-shaped flowers.

Ecology and Geography On rocky outcrops in bogs, and on the edges of woods in acid soil. *Daboecia cantabrica* (Hudson) C. Koch is found in western Ireland, France, northwestern Spain, and Portugal; *D. azorica* Tutin & E. F. Warburg in the Azores.

Comment The genus is named after St Dabeoc (the spelling has been corrupted over time), at one time abbot of Bangor, who worked in Ireland and founded a priory in Lough Derg in County Donegal in around 500 AD. *Daboecia cantabrica* is one of a small group of so-called Celtiberian plants found in Ireland and the Iberian peninsula and southwestern France, but not in mainland Britain.

Daboecia cantabrica
'Praegerae'
⅔ life size
August 10th

Cassiope

Cassiope 'Muirhead'
flowers, 1½ × life size
April 12th

Cassiope D. Don (1834), in the family Ericaceae, contains 11 species in the Arctic and the high Himalayas.

Description Dwarf subshrubs to 30cm. Leaves unstalked, densely overlapping, alternate or opposite. Flowers white, solitary on slender stalks in the leaf axils. Sepals 5, not petal-like. Petals 5, joined to form a bell-shaped or hemispherical corolla, longer than the sepals. Stamens 10, anthers with thread-like appendages. Ovary superior, hairy, of 5 carpels and 1 style. Pollination is mainly by bees. The fruit is a 5-celled capsule with many small seeds.

Key Recognition Features The minute, overlapping leaves producing conifer-like shoots and the white, bell-shaped flowers.

Ecology and Geography On sandy heaths, mountain and arctic tundra, and in damp, mossy places, sometimes on lime-rich soil. There are 2 species in northern Europe, Asia, and North America; the rest are in the high Himalayas and from Alaska to California.

Comment In Greek mythology Cassiope was the wife of Cepheus, king of Ethiopia, and mother of Andromeda. Several species are cultivated by alpine plant enthusiasts.

Pyrola media, flowers, 2¼ × life size
June 22nd

Pyrola

Pyrola L. (1753), wintergreen, in the family Ericaceae, contains 35 species around the northern hemisphere.

Description Perennials to 30cm, with creeping underground rhizomes and upright flowering stems. Leaves all basal, stalked, with a usually rounded blade. Flowers red, purplish, pink, or white, nodding, in a narrow spike. Sepals 5. Petals 5. Stamens 10. Ovary superior, of 5 carpels and 1 style, which is often conspicuous and downward-pointing. Pollination is by insects. The fruit is a 5-celled capsule with numerous very small seeds.

Key Recognition Features The rosette of stalked, basal leaves and the spike of nodding flowers.

Ecology and Geography In pine and open, deciduous woods, among heather, and in damp dune slacks. Found throughout the temperate northern hemisphere; also in Sumatra and in temperate South America.

Comment There are two other genera close to *Pyrola*, sometimes separated as Pyrolaceae: in *Moneses* Salisb. the plants are small, with 1 large flower; in *Chimaphila* Pursh the flowers are in an umbel-like corymb. Closely related are *Monotropa* L. and related genera, sometimes separated in the family Monotropaceae, which are saprophytes without chlorophyll, living on mycorrhizae that in turn grow on the roots of forest trees. They are fleshy, white, brownish, or bright red in the case of *Sarcodes sanguinea* Torr., the snow plant of California and Oregon. DNA studies show that all these have evolved within the large family Ericaceae. The genera *Galax* Sims, *Shortia* Torr. & Gray and *Diapensia* L. in the family Diapensiaceae are shown by their DNA to be close to the Styracaceae (see Volume 1) within the Ericales.

Pyrola media
1½ × life size, June 22nd

Collomia grandiflora
flowers, 1½ × life size
July 4th

Collomia

Collomia Nutt. (1818), in the family Polemoniaceae, contains around 15 species, mainly in western North America and southern South America.

Description Annuals, biennials, or rarely perennials to 1m. Leaves alternate, sometimes undivided, otherwise lobed or pinnately divided. Flowers red, blue, purplish, pink, orange-yellow, or white, often in tight heads. Sepals 5, joined at the base to form a lobed calyx, with membranes between the lobes forming a projecting fold. Petals 5, pointed at the apex, joined at the base into a tube. Stamens 5. Ovary superior, of 3 carpels and 1 style. Pollination is usually by insects. The fruit is a rounded capsule, with few seeds in each cell, enclosed by the papery remains of the calyx until it splits. Seeds oblong, and mucilaginous when wetted.

Key Recognition Features The common species have undivided leaves and rounded heads of crowded flowers with glandular sepals.

Ecology and Geography In dry, open woods, on rocky slopes, and along streams, with 8 species in California, and a few in Chile. Often naturalised elsewhere.

Comment Some species, such as *C. grandiflora* Dougl. ex Lindl. are occasionally grown as ornamentals, and can become weeds.

Polemonium

Polemonium L. (1753), Jacob's ladder or sky pilot, in the family Polemoniaceae, contains around 25 species around the northern hemisphere and in Chile.

Description Annuals, biennials, or usually perennials to 90cm, with upright and often glandular flowering stems. Leaves pinnately divided, with 12 or more pairs of leaflets. Flowers blue, yellowish, pinkish, or white. Sepals 5, joined at the base. Petals 5, usually rounded at the apex, joined at the base into a short or long tube. Stamens 5. Ovary superior, of 3 carpels and 1 style, 3-fid at the apex. Pollination is usually by bees, possibly by hummingbirds in the species with tubular flowers. The fruit is a rounded capsule with 4–14 seeds in each cell.

Key Recognition Features The flowers with 5 rounded petals, and the pinnate leaves.

Ecology and Geography In moist, grassy places and open woods, among rocks, and on mountain steppe. There are 3 species in Europe, others scattered across Asia in the mountains, 7 in California, mainly in the mountains, southwards to Mexico, several in the Rockies, and 2 in Chile.

Comment DNA studies show that the family Polemoniaceae is closest to Primulaceae (see pp.198–205) and Myrsinaceae, within the Ericales, not close to Solanaceae (see pp.222–31). It is particularly diverse in California (with 13 of the 20 genera) and the western Americas through the Andes to Chile. Many species and hybrids of *Polemonium* are cultivated in gardens; they need replanting every few years to remain healthy.

Collomia grandiflora
½ life size, July 4th

POLEMONIACEAE

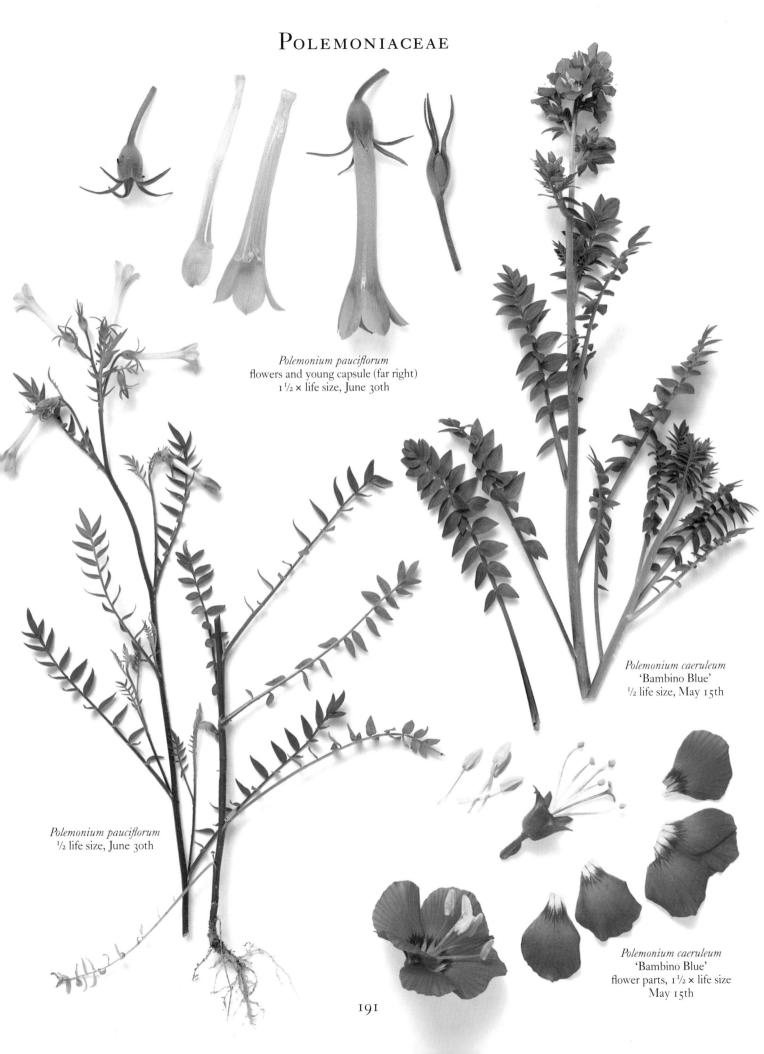

Polemonium pauciflorum
flowers and young capsule (far right)
$1\frac{1}{2}$ × life size, June 30th

Polemonium caeruleum
'Bambino Blue'
$\frac{1}{2}$ life size, May 15th

Polemonium pauciflorum
$\frac{1}{2}$ life size, June 30th

Polemonium caeruleum
'Bambino Blue'
flower parts, $1\frac{1}{2}$ × life size
May 15th

191

Gilia

Gilia Ruíz & Pavón (1794), in the family Polemoniaceae, contains around 25 species, mainly in western North America and southern South America.

Description Annuals to 80cm or, rarely, dwarf alpine perennials. Leaves alternate, usually undivided, sometimes lobed or pinnately divided. Flowers blue, purplish, pink, yellow, or white, often in tight heads. Sepals 5, joined at the base to form a lobed calyx, sometimes with membranes between the lobes. Petals 5, pointed or rounded at the apex, joined at the base into a short tube. Stamens 5. Ovary superior, of 3 carpels and 1 style, 3-fid at the apex. Pollination is usually by bees, flies, or hummingbirds. The fruit is a rounded capsule, with few to many seeds in each cell, enclosed until it splits by the papery remains of the calyx. Seeds small and rounded.

Key Recognition Features The often small, crowded flowers with 5 petals, and the variously divided leaves.

Ecology and Geography In dry, grassy or sandy places, with most species in California, and a few in Chile.

Comment The genus is named after the 18th-century Spanish botanist, Filipe Gil. A few species are cultivated in gardens. Species of some closely related genera are sometimes found under *Gilia*: *Ipomopsis* Michx. tend to have upright stems, rosettes of divided leaves, and red or yellow, long-tubed flowers with narrow lobes; *Linanthus* Benth. are mostly small desert annuals with very narrow leaves, long-tubed flowers and spreading round lobes.

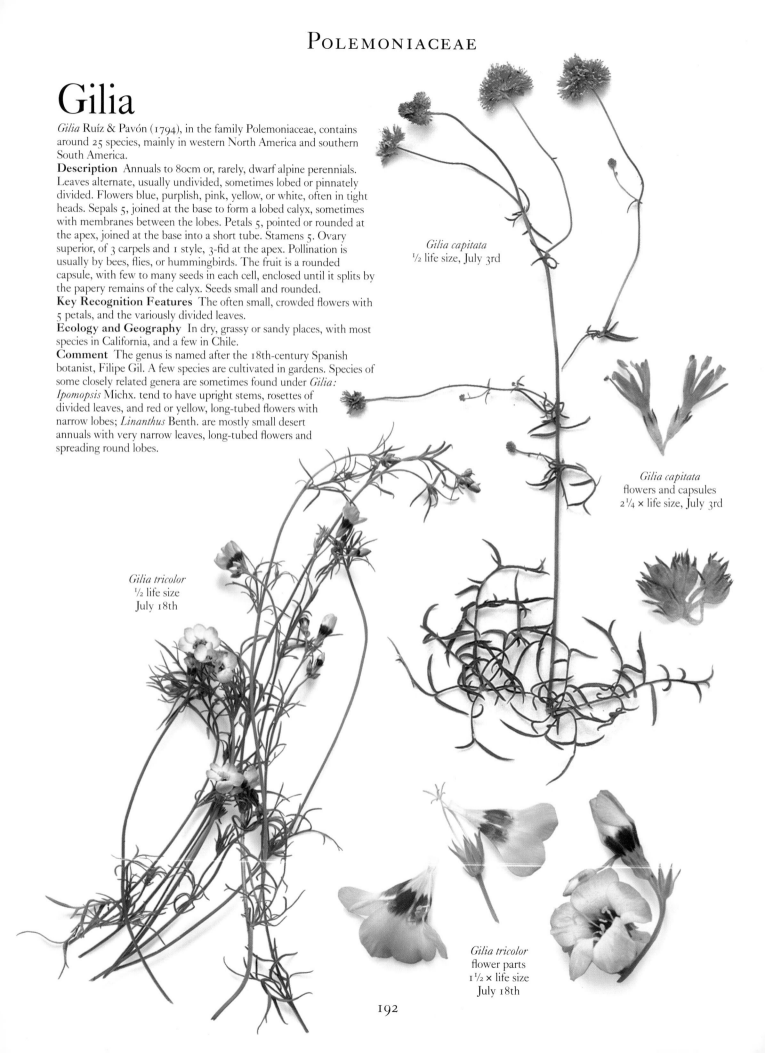

Gilia capitata
½ life size, July 3rd

Gilia capitata
flowers and capsules
2¼ × life size, July 3rd

Gilia tricolor
½ life size
July 18th

Gilia tricolor
flower parts
1½ × life size
July 18th

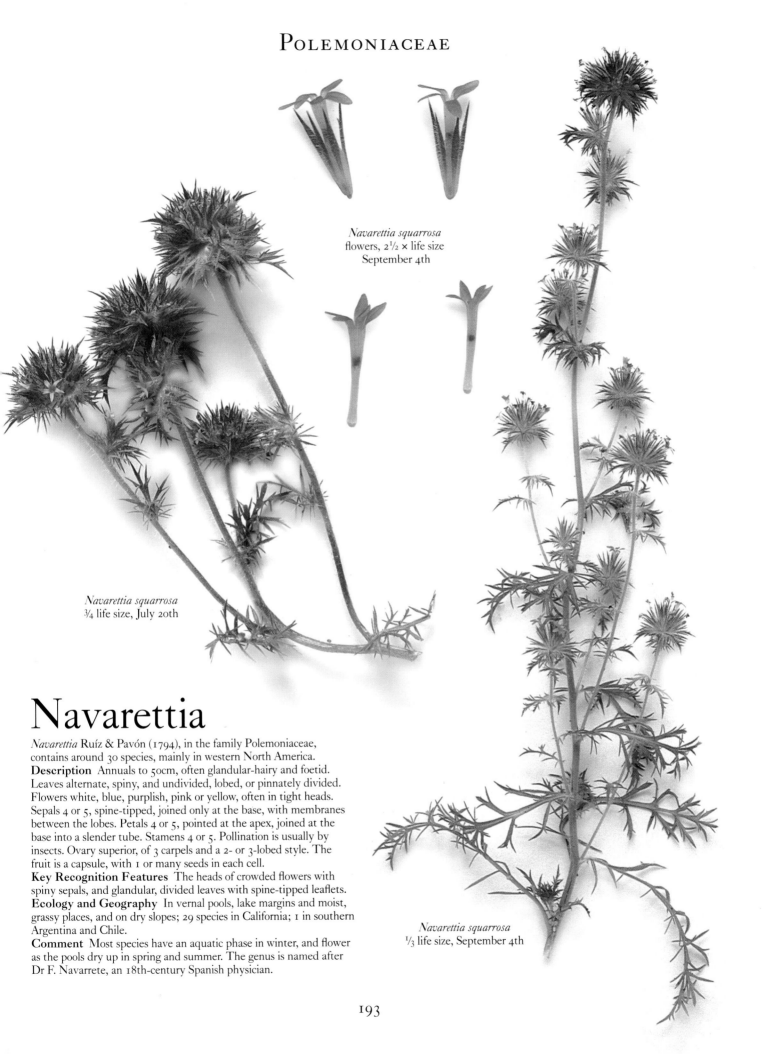

Navarettia squarrosa
flowers, 2½ × life size
September 4th

Navarettia squarrosa
¾ life size, July 20th

Navarettia

Navarettia Ruíz & Pavón (1794), in the family Polemoniaceae, contains around 30 species, mainly in western North America.

Description Annuals to 50cm, often glandular-hairy and foetid. Leaves alternate, spiny, and undivided, lobed, or pinnately divided. Flowers white, blue, purplish, pink or yellow, often in tight heads. Sepals 4 or 5, spine-tipped, joined only at the base, with membranes between the lobes. Petals 4 or 5, pointed at the apex, joined at the base into a slender tube. Stamens 4 or 5. Pollination is usually by insects. Ovary superior, of 3 carpels and a 2- or 3-lobed style. The fruit is a capsule, with 1 or many seeds in each cell.

Key Recognition Features The heads of crowded flowers with spiny sepals, and glandular, divided leaves with spine-tipped leaflets.

Ecology and Geography In vernal pools, lake margins and moist, grassy places, and on dry slopes; 29 species in California; 1 in southern Argentina and Chile.

Comment Most species have an aquatic phase in winter, and flower as the pools dry up in spring and summer. The genus is named after Dr F. Navarrete, an 18th-century Spanish physician.

Navarettia squarrosa
⅓ life size, September 4th

193

Phlox carolina 'Bill Baker'
flower parts, 1¼ × life size
June 1st

Phlox 'Kelly's Eye'
⅔ life size, May 15th

Phlox 'Kelly's Eye'
flowers (above)
1⅓ × life size
May 15th

Phlox carolina
'Bill Baker'
½ life size, June 1st

Phlox paniculata
'Alison Jane'
flower parts
1¼ × life size
August 2nd

Phlox

Phlox L. (1753), in the family Polemoniaceae, contains around
70 species, mainly in North America.

Description Annuals or usually perennials to 1m, with upright or
sprawling, leafy flowering stems. Leaves opposite, simple, round to
linear. Flowers blue, pink, purple, yellowish, red, or white. Sepals 5,
narrow, joined at the base. Petals 5, usually rounded or 2-lobed at the
apex, joined at the base into a long tube. Stamens 5, unequal, hidden
within the tube. Ovary superior, of 3 carpels and 1 style. Pollination is
usually by insects, particularly moths in many species, or butterflies.
The fruit is a rounded capsule, with 1 to few seeds in each cell.

Key Recognition Features The opposite, simple leaves and the
flowers with 5 petals joined into a narrow tube at the base.

Ecology and Geography In moist, grassy places, open woods, and
among rocks in the mountains. Throughout North America,
southwards to Mexico, with 1 species extending from Alaska
into Siberia.

Comment Phlox are one of the most attractive of all North
American genera, and many species are cultivated. The large,
perennial border phlox are derived from *P. paniculata* L., native in
damp, open woods, often on limestone, in eastern North America,
flowering in late summer. Very different are the creeping, rock-garden
species, forms of *P. subulata* L. from the eastern states and *P. douglasii*
Hook. from the west; both grow well on shallow soils overlying acid
rocks such as granite, and when happy can form lawn-like sheets
covered with flowers in spring. *Phlox stolonifera* Sims and *P. divaricata*
L. are woodland plants, covering the ground in semi-shade under
large trees; the flowers are often a lovely pale blue, as in 'Blue Ridge'
from the mountains of West Virginia. *Phlox carolina* L. is a variable
species from the southeastern states, growing on the edges of
woods and in grassy places. The annual phlox from Texas,
P. drummondii Hook., is now available in many different
forms and colours.

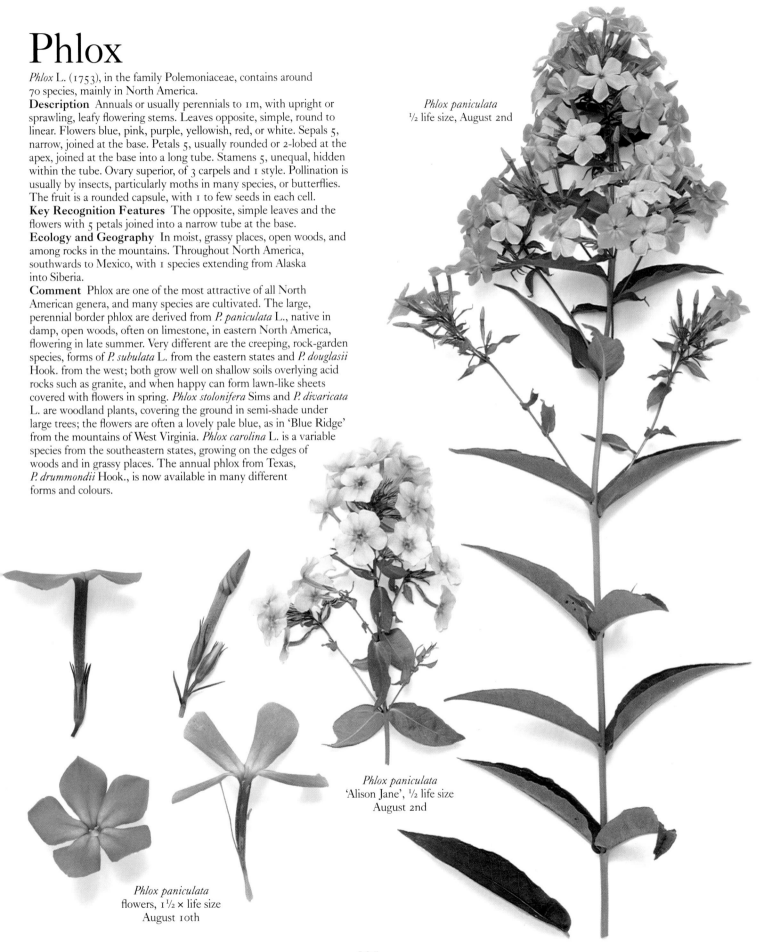

Phlox paniculata
½ life size, August 2nd

Phlox paniculata
'Alison Jane', ½ life size
August 2nd

Phlox paniculata
flowers, 1½ × life size
August 10th

Cobaea

Cobaea Cav. (1791), in the family Polemoniaceae, contains 10—20 species, mainly in Central and South America.

Description Perennial or annual climbers to 30m or more. Leaves alternate, pinnately divided, with 3 pairs of short-stalked leaflets, ending in finely branching tendrils. Flowers green, creamy-white, purplish, or clear, pale violet, solitary on long stalks. Sepals 5, not joined at the base, sometimes leafy. Petals 5, rounded at the apex and joined at the base into a corolla that is either long, narrow, and twisted or long or short, broad, and tubular. Stamens 5, usually as long or longer than the corolla. Ovary superior, of 3 carpels and 1 style, 3-fid at the apex. Pollination is discussed below. The fruit is an elliptic capsule, with several large, flat seeds in each cell.

Key Recognition Features Fast-growing climbers with 3 pairs of leaflets, long, branching tendrils ending in small hooks, and large flowers produced in the leaf axils.

Ecology and Geography In dry gorges, on grassy slopes, and in scrub from Mexico to Venezuela and northern Chile.

Comment *Cobaea* was sometimes placed in its own family, the Cobaeaceae, but DNA studies show that it should be included in Polemoniaceae. The genus is named after Fr Bernabé Cobo (1582—1657), a Jesuit missionary in Mexico and Peru. Three distinct flower shapes are found in the genus; in the familiar *C. scandens* Cav. and similar species, such as *C. pringlei* Standl., the greenish or purple flowers are broadly bell-shaped; these are said to be pollinated by bats in the wild, but in Europe the newly opened flowers, which have a foul smell, are visited by flies. Older flowers, which have turned purple and have a sweet smell, are visited by bees. The plants will continue to flower through the winter if there is no frost. In *C. minor* Mart. & Gal. from Costa Rica and southern Mexico, the pale violet flowers have spreading petals and a dark throat with a short tube at the base. In *C. hookeriana* Standl. and related species in section Rosenbergia from Venezuela, the flowers hang down and have long, narrow, twisted, green or yellow petals and even longer stamens and style; they open at night and are pollinated by hawkmoths.

Cobaea pringlei
flower parts, ¾ life size
November 15th

Cobaea pringlei
½ life size, November 15th

Polemoniaceae

Cobaea pringlei
flower parts, ¾ life size
November 29th

Cobaea scandens
capsules and seeds, life size
January 25th

Cobaea scandens
flowers (above and below)
¾ life size, January 25th

Cobaea pringlei
½ life size, November 15th

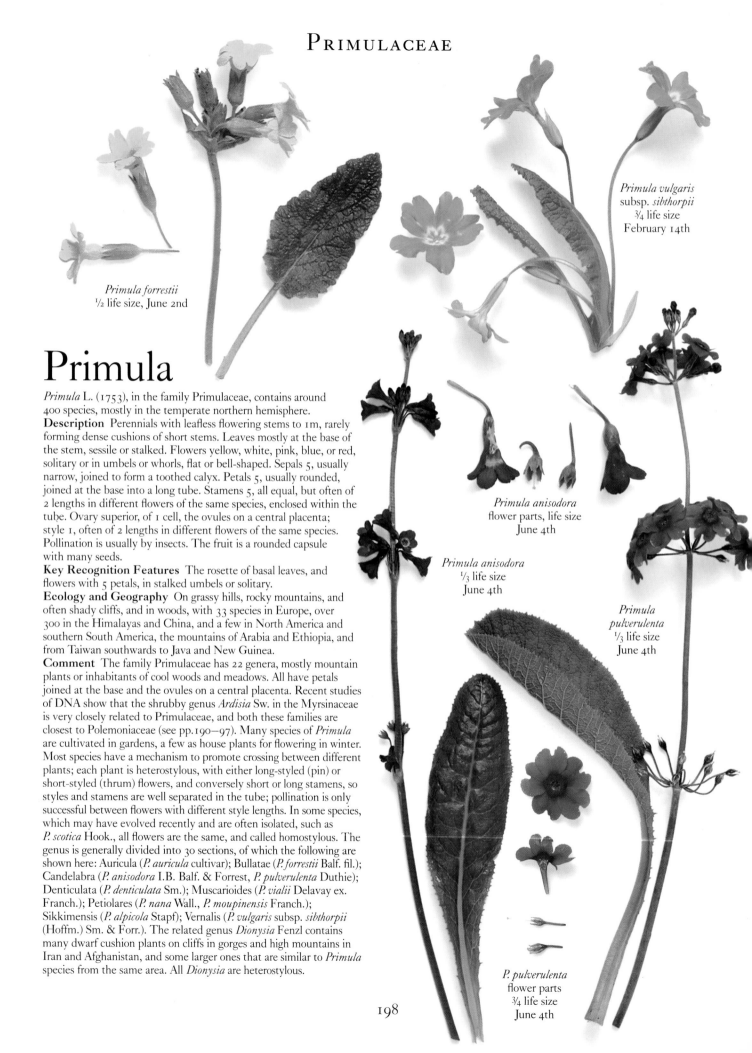

Primula forrestii
½ life size, June 2nd

Primula vulgaris
subsp. *sibthorpii*
¾ life size
February 14th

Primula

Primula L. (1753), in the family Primulaceae, contains around 400 species, mostly in the temperate northern hemisphere.

Description Perennials with leafless flowering stems to 1m, rarely forming dense cushions of short stems. Leaves mostly at the base of the stem, sessile or stalked. Flowers yellow, white, pink, blue, or red, solitary or in umbels or whorls, flat or bell-shaped. Sepals 5, usually narrow, joined to form a toothed calyx. Petals 5, usually rounded, joined at the base into a long tube. Stamens 5, all equal, but often of 2 lengths in different flowers of the same species, enclosed within the tube. Ovary superior, of 1 cell, the ovules on a central placenta; style 1, often of 2 lengths in different flowers of the same species. Pollination is usually by insects. The fruit is a rounded capsule with many seeds.

Key Recognition Features The rosette of basal leaves, and flowers with 5 petals, in stalked umbels or solitary.

Ecology and Geography On grassy hills, rocky mountains, and often shady cliffs, and in woods, with 33 species in Europe, over 300 in the Himalayas and China, and a few in North America and southern South America, the mountains of Arabia and Ethiopia, and from Taiwan southwards to Java and New Guinea.

Comment The family Primulaceae has 22 genera, mostly mountain plants or inhabitants of cool woods and meadows. All have petals joined at the base and the ovules on a central placenta. Recent studies of DNA show that the shrubby genus *Ardisia* Sw. in the Myrsinaceae is very closely related to Primulaceae, and both these families are closest to Polemoniaceae (see pp.190–97). Many species of *Primula* are cultivated in gardens, a few as house plants for flowering in winter. Most species have a mechanism to promote crossing between different plants; each plant is heterostylous, with either long-styled (pin) or short-styled (thrum) flowers, and conversely short or long stamens, so styles and stamens are well separated in the tube; pollination is only successful between flowers with different style lengths. In some species, which may have evolved recently and are often isolated, such as *P. scotica* Hook., all flowers are the same, and called homostylous. The genus is generally divided into 30 sections, of which the following are shown here: Auricula (*P. auricula* cultivar); Bullatae (*P. forrestii* Balf. fil.); Candelabra (*P. anisodora* I.B. Balf. & Forrest, *P. pulverulenta* Duthie); Denticulata (*P. denticulata* Sm.); Muscarioides (*P. vialii* Delavay ex. Franch.); Petiolares (*P. nana* Wall., *P. moupinensis* Franch.); Sikkimensis (*P. alpicola* Stapf); Vernalis (*P. vulgaris* subsp. *sibthorpii* (Hoffm.) Sm. & Forr.). The related genus *Dionysia* Fenzl contains many dwarf cushion plants on cliffs in gorges and high mountains in Iran and Afghanistan, and some larger ones that are similar to *Primula* species from the same area. All *Dionysia* are heterostylous.

Primula anisodora
flower parts, life size
June 4th

Primula anisodora
⅓ life size
June 4th

Primula pulverulenta
⅓ life size
June 4th

P. pulverulenta
flower parts
¾ life size
June 4th

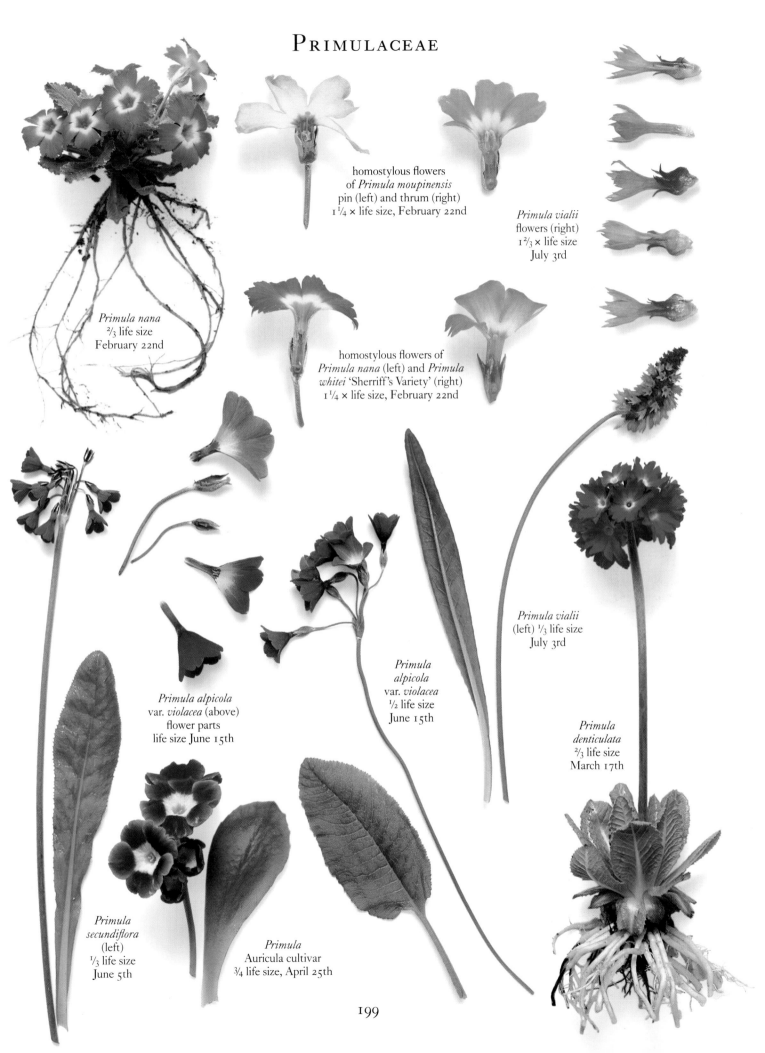

PRIMULACEAE

homostylous flowers
of *Primula moupinensis*
pin (left) and thrum (right)
1 1/4 × life size, February 22nd

Primula vialii
flowers (right)
1 2/3 × life size
July 3rd

Primula nana
2/3 life size
February 22nd

homostylous flowers of
Primula nana (left) and *Primula
whitei* 'Sherriff's Variety' (right)
1 1/4 × life size, February 22nd

Primula vialii
(left) 1/3 life size
July 3rd

Primula alpicola
var. *violacea* (above)
flower parts
life size June 15th

*Primula
alpicola*
var. *violacea*
1/2 life size
June 15th

*Primula
denticulata*
2/3 life size
March 17th

*Primula
secundiflora*
(left)
1/3 life size
June 5th

Primula
Auricula cultivar
3/4 life size, April 25th

Androsace rotundifolia
flower parts, 1⅔ × life size
May 4th

Androsace rotundifolia
½ life size, May 4th

Androsace

Androsace L. (1753), in the family Primulaceae, contains around 100 species, mostly in the northern hemisphere.

Description Annuals, biennials, or perennials to 10cm, often forming dense cushions of short stems. Leaves mostly at the base of the stem, sessile or stalked. Flowers white, pink, or red, solitary or in umbels, always with short styles (see *Primula*, pp.198–99). Sepals 5, narrow, joined to form a toothed calyx. Petals 5, usually rounded, joined at the base into a short tube, the mouth closed by a ring of scales. Stamens 5, all equal, enclosed within the tube. Ovary superior, of 1 cell, the ovules on a central placenta; style 1. Pollination is usually by insects. The fruit is a rounded capsule with 1 to many seeds.

Key Recognition Features The small flowers with 5 petals and scales in the throat, in stalked umbels or 1-flowered on cushion plants.

Ecology and Geography On dry hills, stony and rocky mountains, often in cold semi-desert, on high mountain cliffs, usually under overhangs, and also in open woods; 22 species in Europe, others in the Himalayas and China, and few in North America

Comment Many species are cultivated; the high-alpine species, which form dense cushions, are a challenge to grow successfully in lowland climates; the larger species, such as the Chinese woodlander *A. geraniifolia* Watt, illustrated here, are easier to grow and resemble small-flowered primulas. The related genus *Vitaliana* Sesler from Europe has yellow flowers with a longer tube. The American genus *Douglasia* Lindl. with pink or purplish flowers is now considered part of *Androsace*.

Dodecatheon

Dodecatheon L. (1753), in the family Primulaceae, contains around 14 species, mostly in western North America.

Description Perennials with leafless flowering stems to 80cm. Leaves at the base of the stem, sessile or stalked. Flowers white, pink, or red, solitary or in umbels, usually nodding, always homostylous. Sepals 5, narrow, joined to form a toothed calyx. Petals 5, usually pointed, joined at the base into a short tube, reflexed. Stamens 5, all equal, exserted from the tube, the anthers held tight against the style on short, broad, often fused filaments. Ovary superior, of 1 cell, the ovules on a central placenta; style 1, exserted. Pollination is usually by bees. The fruit is a rounded capsule, with 1 to many seeds.

Key Recognition Features The umbel of flowers with 5 reflexed petals.

Ecology and Geography In bogs and open woods and on stony mountainsides, with 9 species in California, a few further east.

Comment Dodecatheon, meaning 12 gods, was the name given by Pliny to the primrose. A few species are cultivated. The hanging flowers with reflexed petals and anthers held close to the style are found in many diverse genera in different parts of the world, notably *Solanum* (see p.223), *Trachystemon*, *Borago* (see pp.232–33 for both), *Cyclamen*, *Dianella* Lam. ex Juss., *Galanthus* L., and *Vaccinium* (see Volume 1) in Section Oxycoccus; pollination is usually by bees, which push their tongues between the anthers, disturbing the pollen. The European genus *Soldanella* L., with 10 species, has fringed, bell-shaped flowers and round, stalked leaves; the anthers are also held close around the style.

Dodecatheon clevelandii
subsp. *insulare*
flower parts, 1¾ × life size
February 25th

Dodecatheon clevelandii
subsp. *insulare*
½ life size, February 25th

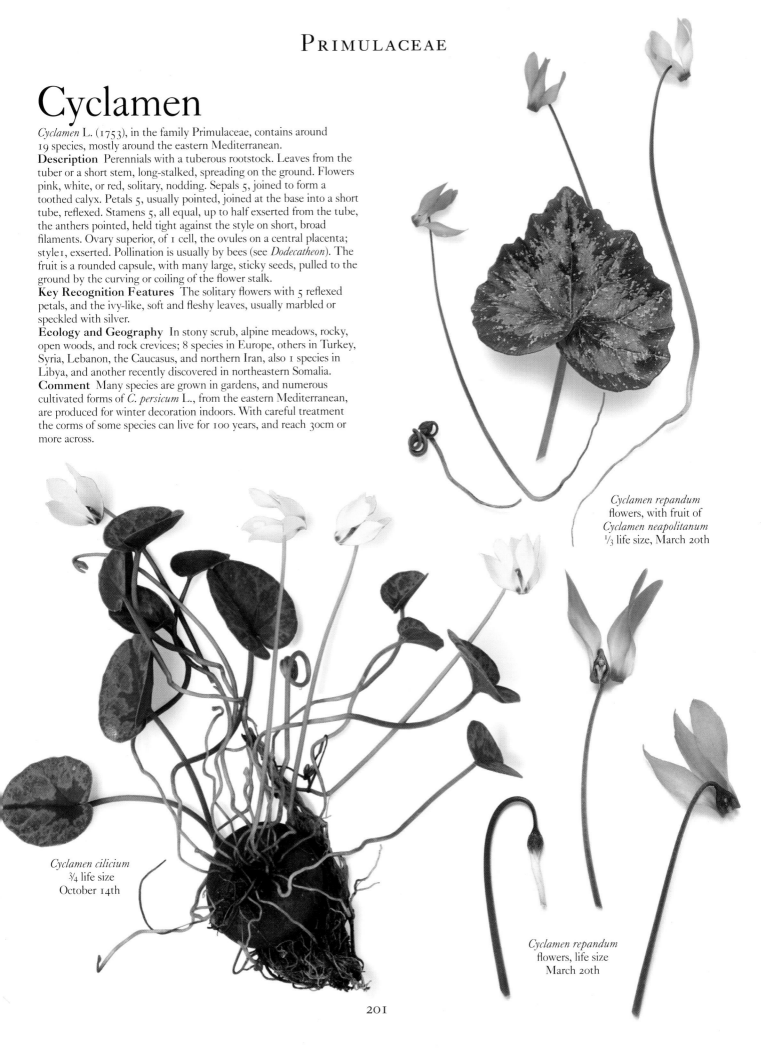

Cyclamen

Cyclamen L. (1753), in the family Primulaceae, contains around 19 species, mostly around the eastern Mediterranean.

Description Perennials with a tuberous rootstock. Leaves from the tuber or a short stem, long-stalked, spreading on the ground. Flowers pink, white, or red, solitary, nodding. Sepals 5, joined to form a toothed calyx. Petals 5, usually pointed, joined at the base into a short tube, reflexed. Stamens 5, all equal, up to half exserted from the tube, the anthers pointed, held tight against the style on short, broad filaments. Ovary superior, of 1 cell, the ovules on a central placenta; style 1, exserted. Pollination is usually by bees (see *Dodecatheon*). The fruit is a rounded capsule, with many large, sticky seeds, pulled to the ground by the curving or coiling of the flower stalk.

Key Recognition Features The solitary flowers with 5 reflexed petals, and the ivy-like, soft and fleshy leaves, usually marbled or speckled with silver.

Ecology and Geography In stony scrub, alpine meadows, rocky, open woods, and rock crevices; 8 species in Europe, others in Turkey, Syria, Lebanon, the Caucasus, and northern Iran, also 1 species in Libya, and another recently discovered in northeastern Somalia.

Comment Many species are grown in gardens, and numerous cultivated forms of *C. persicum* L., from the eastern Mediterranean, are produced for winter decoration indoors. With careful treatment the corms of some species can live for 100 years, and reach 30cm or more across.

Cyclamen repandum
flowers, with fruit of
Cyclamen neapolitanum
⅓ life size, March 20th

Cyclamen cilicium
¾ life size
October 14th

Cyclamen repandum
flowers, life size
March 20th

Anagallis

Anagallis L. (1753), in the family Primulaceae, contains around 28 species scattered around the world.

Description Annuals or perennials to 70cm, usually with sprawling or creeping stems. Leaves usually opposite, simple, round to linear-lanceolate. Flowers blue, pink, scarlet, or white. Sepals 5, narrow, joined at the base. Petals 5, usually rounded, joined at the base into a short tube. Stamens 5, equal, often with hairy filaments. Ovary superior, of 1 cell, the ovules on a central placenta; style 1. Pollination is usually by insects. The fruit is a rounded capsule, with 6 to many seeds.

Key Recognition Features The small, opposite, sessile leaves and the solitary flowers with 5 petals joined into a short tube at the base.

Ecology and Geography In moist places, on sand dunes and waste ground, and as weeds of cultivation; 6 species in Europe, others in the tropics, especially at high altitudes, and 2 species in South America.

Comment The scarlet and blue pimpernels, *A. arvensis* L. and subsp. *caerulea* Hartman, are familiar as weeds, the flowers opening only in the sun. The larger flowered *A. monelli* L. from Spain, Portugal, and North Africa, is often cultivated.

Anagallis monellii
young fruit (left) and flowers, 1¾ × life size, June 28th

Anagallis arvensis subsp. *caerulea*
fruits and flowers, 1⅓ × life size, July 20th

Anagallis monellii
½ life size, June 28th

Anagallis arvensis
life size, June 17th

Anagallis tenella
1²/₃ × life size, July 3rd

Glaux maritima
1¹/₃ × life size
June 28th

Hottonia palustris
¹/₂ life size, April 20th

Hottonia

Hottonia L. (1753), water violet, in the family Primulaceae, contains 2 species in Europe and North America.

Description Aquatic perennials with leafless flowering stems to 15cm, the flowering stems swollen in *H. inflata* Ell.. Submerged leaves in whorls, soft and deeply pinnate, with narrow segments; summer aerial leaves stiffer and smaller. Flowers lilac with a yellow eye, or white, in whorls. Sepals 5, narrow, joined only at the base. Petals 5, usually rounded, joined at the base into a tube. Stamens 5, all equal. Ovary superior, of 1 cell, the ovules on a central placenta; style 1. Pollination is presumed to be by insects. The fruit is a rounded capsule with many seeds.

Key Recognition Features The feathery, submerged leaves, and primula-like flowers or swollen stems.

Ecology and Geography In shallow ponds and ditches, with *H. palustris* L. throughout Europe and temperate Asia, and *H. inflata* in eastern North America from Maine to Florida.

Comment The genus is named after Peter Hotton, 1648−1709, professor of botany at Leyden. The flowers of the 2 species are very different; in *H. palustris* the flowers are usually heterostylous (see *Primula*, pp.198−99), up to 2.5cm across, like a candalabra primula, emerging from the water on a normal stem; in *H. inflata* the stems are grotesquely swollen and the flowers are very small, on short stalks, with petals shorter than the sepals, homostylous and self pollinated. *Glaux* L., with only 1 species, *G. maritima* L., the sea milkwort, is found in salt marshes around the northern hemisphere. The pink flowers have no petals, but 5 coloured sepals.

Lysimachia

Lysimachia L. (1753), in the family Primulaceae, contains around 150 species scattered around the northern hemisphere.

Description Perennials to 1.6m, usually upright but sometimes creeping or shrubby. Leaves usually opposite or whorled, simple, round to linear-lanceolate. Flowers yellow, white, pink, or dark reddish-purple. Sepals 5, narrow, joined at the base. Petals 5, rarely 7, joined at the base into a short tube, often pointed, sometimes toothed, often spotted. Stamens 5, equal. Ovary superior, of 1 cell, the ovules on a central placenta; style 1. Pollination is usually by insects. The fruit is a rounded capsule with many seeds.

Key Recognition Features The opposite leaves, the solitary flowers with 5 petals joined into a short tube at the base, and the rounded capsule.

Ecology and Geography In moist, grassy places, in shallow water, in woods, and among shady rocks; 11 species in Europe, over 130 in China, and 9 in eastern North America.

Comment Several species are cultivated. One European species, *L. minoricensis* Rodr., is thought to be extinct. Some species, such as *L. nummularia* L., moneywort or creeping Jenny, and *L. quadrifolia* L., the liberty tea, were used as tea substitutes. The closely related genus *Trientalis* has around 4 species: *T. europaea* L., the chickweed wintergreen, from acidic woods and heaths in northern Europe and Asia, and *T. americana* Pursh, in eastern North America, have starry pink or white flowers with 5–9 petals, held over whorls of leaves on short, wiry stems.

Lysimachia vulgaris
flower parts
1 1/3 × life size
July 14th

Trientalis europaea
2/3 life size, June 3rd

Lysimachia vulgaris
1/2 life size, July 14th

Lysimachia clethroides
3/4 life size, July 22nd

Primulaceae

Lysimachia nemorum
flowers, 2 × life size
May 31st

Lysimachia nemorum
²/₃ life size, May 31st

*Lysimachia
nummularia* 'Aurea'
²/₃ life size, July 16th

Lysimachia ciliata
½ life size, August 10th

Lysimachia ephemerum
½ life size, August 10th

205

BALSAMINACEAE

Impatiens

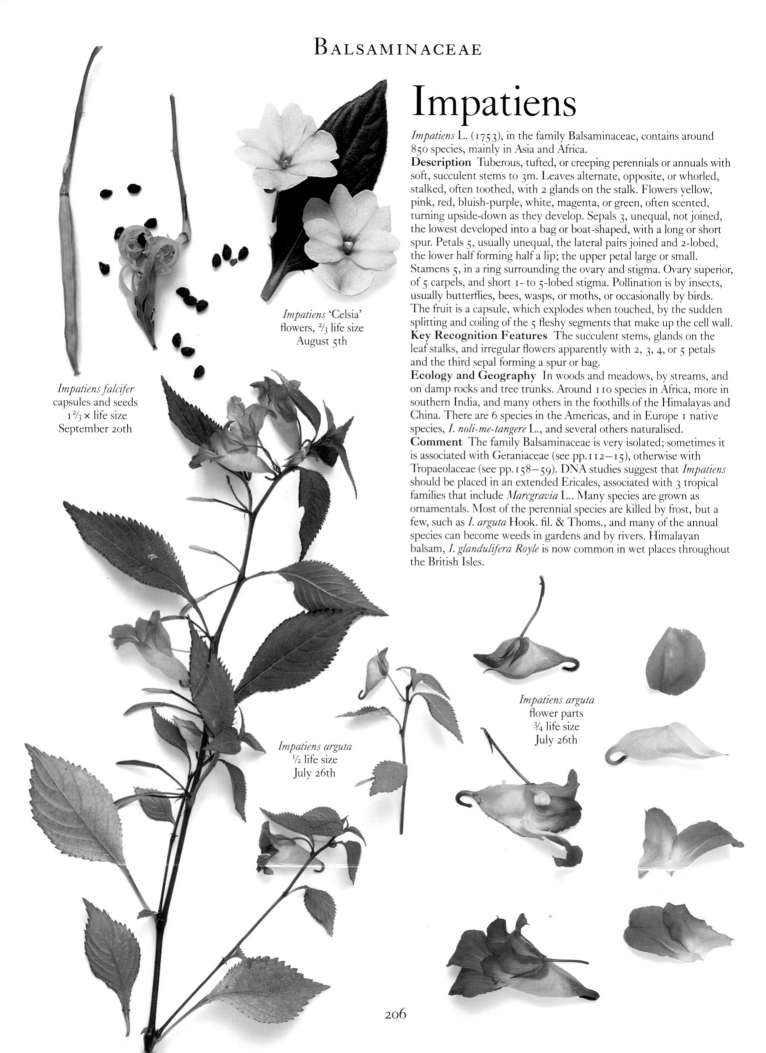

Impatiens L. (1753), in the family Balsaminaceae, contains around 850 species, mainly in Asia and Africa.

Description Tuberous, tufted, or creeping perennials or annuals with soft, succulent stems to 3m. Leaves alternate, opposite, or whorled, stalked, often toothed, with 2 glands on the stalk. Flowers yellow, pink, red, bluish-purple, white, magenta, or green, often scented, turning upside-down as they develop. Sepals 3, unequal, not joined, the lowest developed into a bag or boat-shaped, with a long or short spur. Petals 5, usually unequal, the lateral pairs joined and 2-lobed, the lower half forming half a lip; the upper petal large or small. Stamens 5, in a ring surrounding the ovary and stigma. Ovary superior, of 5 carpels, and short 1- to 5-lobed stigma. Pollination is by insects, usually butterflies, bees, wasps, or moths, or occasionally by birds. The fruit is a capsule, which explodes when touched, by the sudden splitting and coiling of the 5 fleshy segments that make up the cell wall.

Key Recognition Features The succulent stems, glands on the leaf stalks, and irregular flowers apparently with 2, 3, 4, or 5 petals and the third sepal forming a spur or bag.

Ecology and Geography In woods and meadows, by streams, and on damp rocks and tree trunks. Around 110 species in Africa, more in southern India, and many others in the foothills of the Himalayas and China. There are 6 species in the Americas, and in Europe 1 native species, *I. noli-me-tangere* L., and several others naturalised.

Comment The family Balsaminaceae is very isolated; sometimes it is associated with Geraniaceae (see pp.112–15), otherwise with Tropaeolaceae (see pp.158–59). DNA studies suggest that *Impatiens* should be placed in an extended Ericales, associated with 3 tropical families that include *Marcgravia* L.. Many species are grown as ornamentals. Most of the perennial species are killed by frost, but a few, such as *I. arguta* Hook. fil. & Thoms., and many of the annual species can become weeds in gardens and by rivers. Himalayan balsam, *I. glandulifera Royle* is now common in wet places throughout the British Isles.

Impatiens 'Celsia'
flowers, ²/₃ life size
August 5th

Impatiens falcifer
capsules and seeds
1²/₃ × life size
September 20th

Impatiens arguta
½ life size
July 26th

Impatiens arguta
flower parts
¾ life size
July 26th

206

BALSAMINACEAE

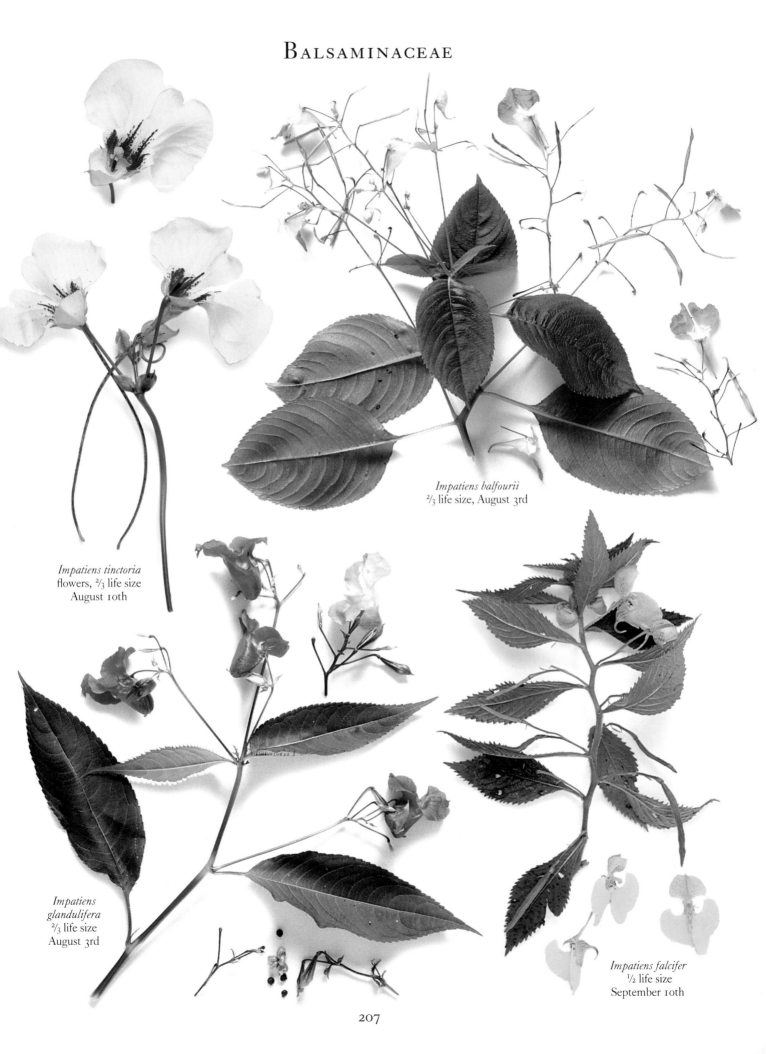

Impatiens balfourii
2/3 life size, August 3rd

Impatiens tinctoria
flowers, 2/3 life size
August 10th

*Impatiens
glandulifera*
2/3 life size
August 3rd

Impatiens falcifer
1/2 life size
September 10th

Gentiana

Gentiana L. (1753), gentian, in the family Gentianaceae, contains over 360 species in temperate areas worldwide.

Description Annuals, biennials, or perennials to 1.5m, but mostly dwarf alpine plants. Leaves opposite, simple, usually hairless. Flowers commonly blue, rarely purple, white, yellow, or red. Sepals usually 5, joined at the base to form a tubular calyx. Petals usually 5, twisted in bud, usually pointed, sometimes reflexed, joined at the base into a long or short tube, often striped or spotted, with translucent areas in the throat. Stamens 5, equal; anthers large; filaments very short. Ovary superior, of 2 cells; style 1, usually thick and forked, not falling as the flower fades. Pollination is generally by bees, especially bumblebees, also by butterflies. The fruit is a capsule, splitting into 2 valves; seeds small, often winged.

Key Recognition Features The opposite pairs of pointed, hairless, parallel-veined leaves and the usually large, bell-shaped or starry, blue flowers, which open in the sun.

Ecology and Geography Alpine meadows and rocky areas, marshes, and open woods, with 29 species in Europe and 312 in Asia, of which 190 are in the mountains of southwestern China. There are also several species in North America, some scarlet-flowered (sometimes put in *Gentianella* Moench.) in the Andes, and small, white-flowered, short-tubed species in South America and in New Zealand (24 species).

Comment The family Gentianaceae is closest to Loganiaceae, especially *Spigelia* L. and *Strychnos* L. famous for containing the poison strychnine, and the related genera; both of these families are close to Apocynaceae (see pp.212–15) and Rubiaceae (see pp.216–18). *Gentiana* itself is the largest genus in the family, famous for the wonderful, intense blue of the flowers of many of the alpine species. The tall, yellow-flowered *G. lutea* L. is an important medicinal plant, the root also used to flavour liqueurs. *Crawfurdia* Wall., with around 6 species in Asia, is very close to *Gentiana*, and now often included within it; the main distinction is that the stems twine into low shrubs and the flowers usually hang down; some species have fleshy capsules, which ripen reddish-purple, and have been put in the genus *Tripterospermum* Blume. *Gentiana trinervis* (Thunb.) Marquand syn. *Crawfurdia japonica* Sieb. & Zucc., *Tripterospermum japonicum* (Sieb. & Zucc.) Maxim. is found in China, Japan, and Korea. *Crawfurdia speciosa* Wall. is a more showy plant with deep purplish-blue flowers.

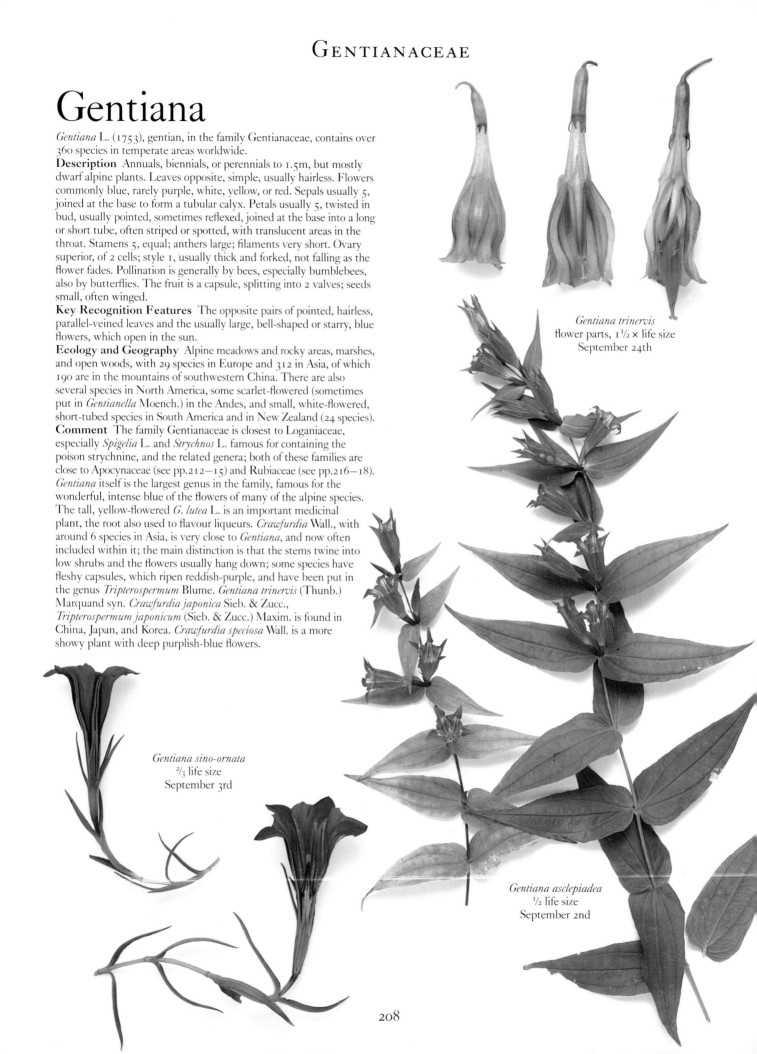

Gentiana trinervis
flower parts, 1½ × life size
September 24th

Gentiana sino-ornata
⅔ life size
September 3rd

Gentiana asclepiadea
½ life size
September 2nd

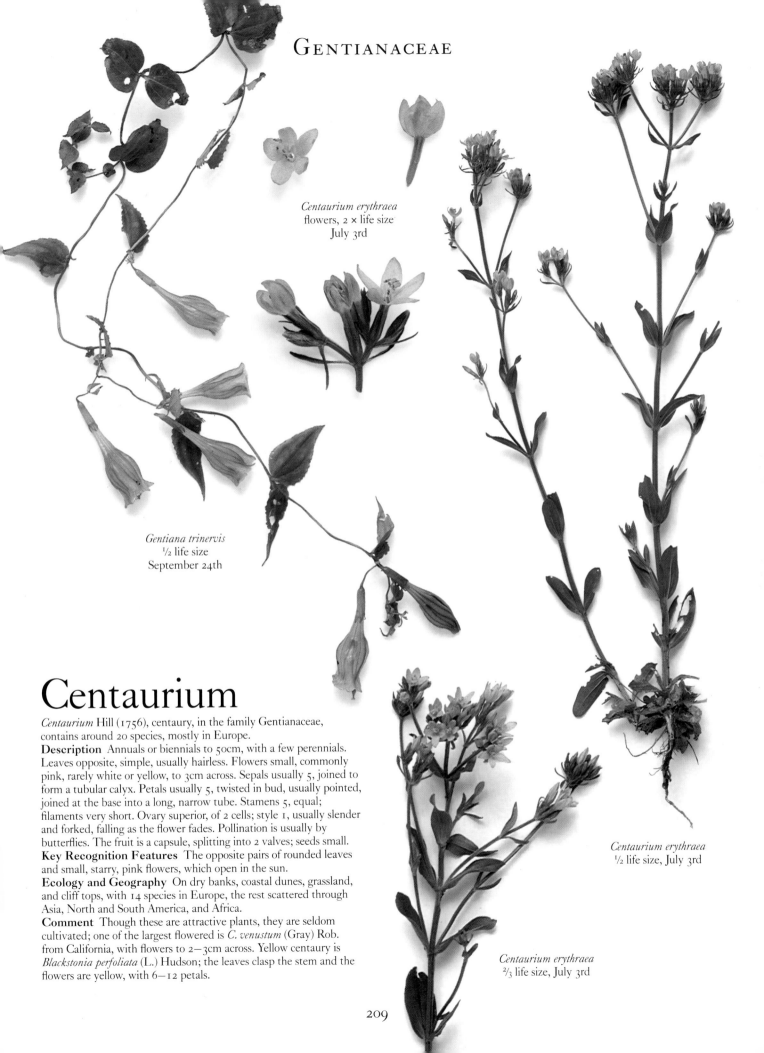

Centaurium erythraea
flowers, 2 × life size
July 3rd

Gentiana trinervis
¹⁄₂ life size
September 24th

Centaurium

Centaurium Hill (1756), centaury, in the family Gentianaceae,
contains around 20 species, mostly in Europe.

Description Annuals or biennials to 50cm, with a few perennials.
Leaves opposite, simple, usually hairless. Flowers small, commonly
pink, rarely white or yellow, to 3cm across. Sepals usually 5, joined to
form a tubular calyx. Petals usually 5, twisted in bud, usually pointed,
joined at the base into a long, narrow tube. Stamens 5, equal;
filaments very short. Ovary superior, of 2 cells; style 1, usually slender
and forked, falling as the flower fades. Pollination is usually by
butterflies. The fruit is a capsule, splitting into 2 valves; seeds small.

Key Recognition Features The opposite pairs of rounded leaves
and small, starry, pink flowers, which open in the sun.

Ecology and Geography On dry banks, coastal dunes, grassland,
and cliff tops, with 14 species in Europe, the rest scattered through
Asia, North and South America, and Africa.

Comment Though these are attractive plants, they are seldom
cultivated; one of the largest flowered is *C. venustum* (Gray) Rob.
from California, with flowers to 2–3cm across. Yellow centaury is
Blackstonia perfoliata (L.) Hudson; the leaves clasp the stem and the
flowers are yellow, with 6–12 petals.

Centaurium erythraea
¹⁄₂ life size, July 3rd

Centaurium erythraea
²⁄₃ life size, July 3rd

Eustoma

Eustoma Salisb. (1806), in the family Gentianaceae, contains around 3 species, mostly in North America.

Description Annuals or short-lived perennials to 70cm, with upright, branching stems. Leaves opposite, simple, hairless, grey-green. Flowers blue, purplish, yellow, pink, or white. Sepals 5 or 6, joined at the base. Petals 5 or 6, twisted in the bud, joined only at the base, sometimes with a fringe of irregular, fine teeth. Stamens 5 or 6, equal. Ovary superior, of 1 cell; style 1, slender, 2-lobed at the tip. Pollination is by insects. The fruit is a capsule, splitting into 2 valves; seeds small.

Key Recognition Features The simple, opposite, bluish-grey leaves and 5- or 6-petalled flowers, large and cup-shaped in the forms sold as cut flowers.

Ecology and Geography In prairies and along streams from Nebraska to Mexico and in California and the West Indies to northern South America.

Comment The annual *E. grandiflorum* (Raf.) Shinn., from the North American prairies southwards to Mexico, has been developed into a range of tall and long-lasting cut flowers, as well as dwarf varieties for growing in containers. It is sometimes known under the name *Lisianthus* P. Browne.

Eustoma grandiflorum cultivar
flower parts, just under life size
August 8th

Eustoma grandiflorum
cultivar
½ life size, August 8th

Halenia elliptica
flower and capsule
2 × life size, August 2nd

Halenia elliptica
capsules and seeds
2 × life size, December 1st

Halenia elliptica
2/3 life size
August 2nd

Halenia

Halenia Borkh. (1796), in the family Gentianaceae, contains
around 70 species, mostly in Asia and South America.
Description Annuals or biennials to 60cm, with upright, branching
stems, or short-stemmed or cushion-forming perennials. Leaves
opposite, simple, hairless. Flowers blue, purplish, greenish-yellow, or
white. Sepals 4, joined only at the base. Petals 4, joined at the base,
each with a long, backward-pointing spur. Stamens 4, equal. Ovary
superior, of 1 cell; style 1, thick, 2-lobed at the tip. Pollination is by
insects, probably by bumblebees. The fruit is a capsule, splitting into
2 valves; seeds small.
Key Recognition Features The simple, opposite leaves and
4-spurred flowers, superficially similar to those of some *Epimedium*
(see p.62). Most annual species flower in late summer and autumn.
Ecology and Geography In mountain meadows and on the edges
of woods, with 1 species in the Urals and the rest scattered through
Asia and North and South America, with several alpine species in the
high Andes.
Comment One or two annual species, such as *H. elliptica* D. Don,
are cultivated, the seed having been brought back from western
China. A few perennials from the Andes are also grown by specialists.

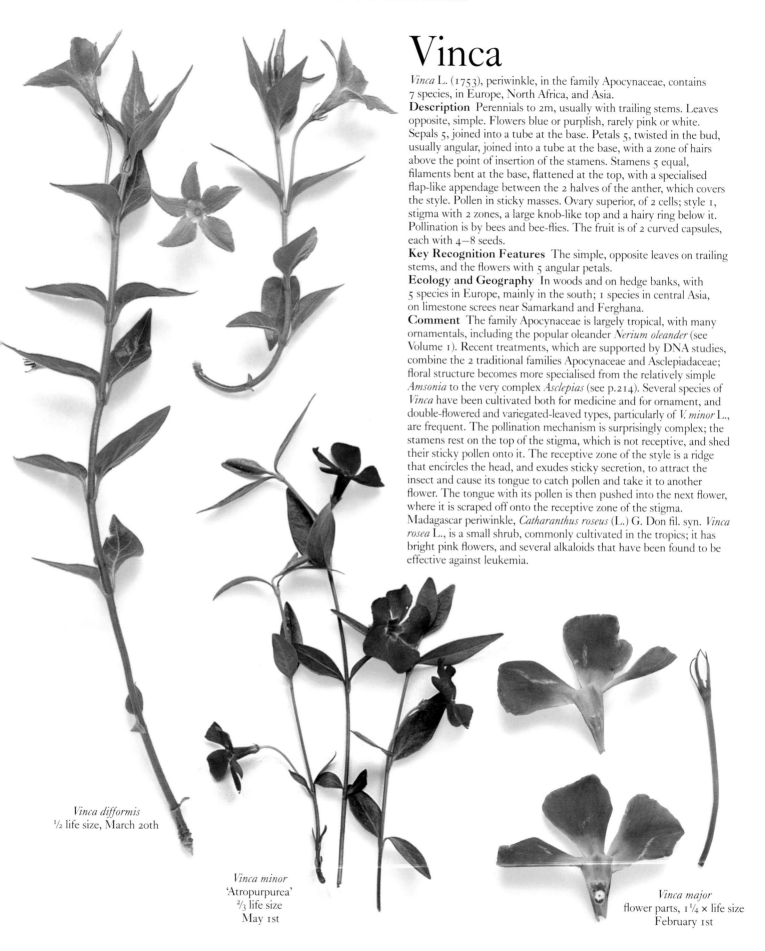

Vinca

Vinca L. (1753), periwinkle, in the family Apocynaceae, contains 7 species, in Europe, North Africa, and Asia.

Description Perennials to 2m, usually with trailing stems. Leaves opposite, simple. Flowers blue or purplish, rarely pink or white. Sepals 5, joined into a tube at the base. Petals 5, twisted in the bud, usually angular, joined into a tube at the base, with a zone of hairs above the point of insertion of the stamens. Stamens 5 equal, filaments bent at the base, flattened at the top, with a specialised flap-like appendage between the 2 halves of the anther, which covers the style. Pollen in sticky masses. Ovary superior, of 2 cells; style 1, stigma with 2 zones, a large knob-like top and a hairy ring below it. Pollination is by bees and bee-flies. The fruit is of 2 curved capsules, each with 4–8 seeds.

Key Recognition Features The simple, opposite leaves on trailing stems, and the flowers with 5 angular petals.

Ecology and Geography In woods and on hedge banks, with 5 species in Europe, mainly in the south; 1 species in central Asia, on limestone screes near Samarkand and Ferghana.

Comment The family Apocynaceae is largely tropical, with many ornamentals, including the popular oleander *Nerium oleander* (see Volume 1). Recent treatments, which are supported by DNA studies, combine the 2 traditional families Apocynaceae and Asclepiadaceae; floral structure becomes more specialised from the relatively simple *Amsonia* to the very complex *Asclepias* (see p.214). Several species of *Vinca* have been cultivated both for medicine and for ornament, and double-flowered and variegated-leaved types, particularly of *V. minor* L., are frequent. The pollination mechanism is surprisingly complex; the stamens rest on the top of the stigma, which is not receptive, and shed their sticky pollen onto it. The receptive zone of the style is a ridge that encircles the head, and exudes sticky secretion, to attract the insect and cause its tongue to catch pollen and take it to another flower. The tongue with its pollen is then pushed into the next flower, where it is scraped off onto the receptive zone of the stigma. Madagascar periwinkle, *Catharanthus roseus* (L.) G. Don fil. syn. *Vinca rosea* L., is a small shrub, commonly cultivated in the tropics; it has bright pink flowers, and several alkaloids that have been found to be effective against leukemia.

Vinca difformis
½ life size, March 20th

Vinca minor
'Atropurpurea'
⅔ life size
May 1st

Vinca major
flower parts, 1¼ × life size
February 1st

Amsonia

Amsonia Walter (1788), bluestar, in the Apocynaceae, contains around 20 species, in North America, Japan, and the eastern Mediterranean.

Description Perennials to 60cm, usually with upright stems. Leaves alternate, simple, sometimes white with hairs. Flowers pale blue. Sepals 5, narrow, joined into a tube at the base. Petals 5, twisted in the bud, narrow, joined into a tube at the base, hairy in the throat. Stamens 5, equal. Pollen in sticky masses. Ovary superior, of 2 cells; style 1, flat-topped. Pollination is presumed to be by insects. The fruit is made up of 2 curved capsules, each with 4–8 seeds.

Key Recognition Features The simple, alternate leaves and the flat-topped heads of pale blue flowers with narrow petals.

Ecology and Geography In woods, on hedge banks, and in places wet in winter; 1 species, *A. orientalis* Decne syn. *Rhazya orientalis* (Decne) A. DC, in Greece and western Turkey, 1 species in Japan, the rest scattered across North America, with 8 species in Arizona.

Comment The genus is named after Dr Charles Amson, a resident of Virginia in the 18th century. A few species are grown as ornamentals: *A. orientalis* Decne is now very rare in the wild; *A. ciliata* Walter is found from North Carolina to Texas.

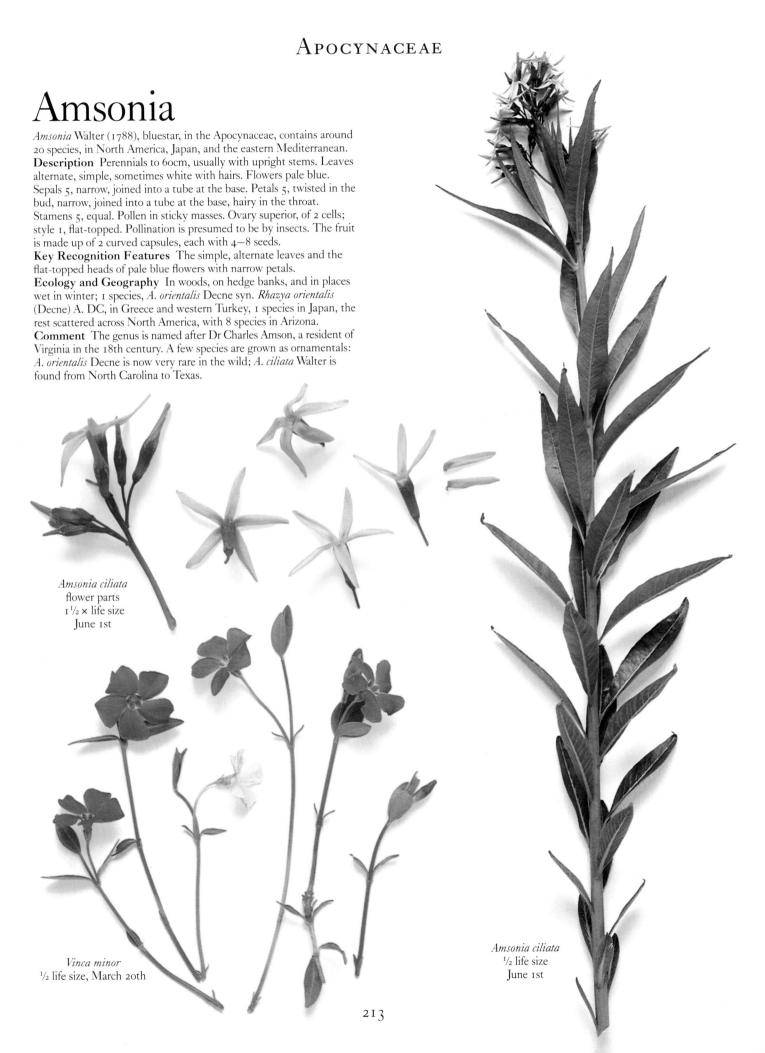

Amsonia ciliata
flower parts
1 ¹⁄₂ × life size
June 1st

Vinca minor
¹⁄₂ life size, March 20th

Amsonia ciliata
¹⁄₂ life size
June 1st

Asclepias

Asclepias L. (1753), milkweed, in the family Apocynaceae (including Asclepiadaceae), contains around 100 species in North and Central America.

Description Perennials to 1.5m, usually with upright stems with a milky latex, from a thick rootstock, or sometimes shrubby. Leaves alternate, opposite, or whorled, simple, sometimes white with hairs. Flowers yellow, red, purple, pink, or white. Sepals 5, small, joined only at the base. Petals 5, not twisted in the bud, reflexed. Stamens 5, equal. The ovary has 2 cells and 2 styles, which are joined at the apex, exuding nectar into 5 horned pouches. Pollination is by butterflies. The mechanism is complex: the filaments form a column and the anthers rest on ridges on the style. The pollen is held in pollinia, 2 in each anther, joined in pairs by translators, which rest in grooves between the ridges and trap a butterfly's leg. The fruit is a curved capsule with 2 rows of seeds, each with a silky parachute.

Key Recognition Features The narrow and whorled, or rounded pairs of leaves, and flat-topped heads of small flowers with anthers and nectaries on a central column.

Ecology and Geography In woods, on rocky banks and waste places, sometimes in swamps, with around 20 species in eastern North America, 14 in California, others in Mexico and Central America.

Comment The family Asclepiadaceae is now included in the Apocynaceae (see *Vinca* p.212). It includes many tender cultivated genera, such as the succulent *Stapelia* L. with stinking and carrion-like flowers, and the sweetly-scented climbers *Hoya* R. Br. and *Stephanotis* Thouars, now sometimes called *Marsdenia*. The genus *Asclepias* is named after the Greek god Asclepius or, in Latin, Aesculapius, originally a Thessalian prince and famous physician, later son of Apollo, god of medicine. Some species have oily latex, others usable fibre; the shoots of a few are edible when young; most have poisonous latex, utilised by the monarch butterfly (*Danaus plexippus*) to render both its larval and adult forms inedible to birds.

Asclepias incarnata
½ life size
August 8th

Asclepias syriaca
½ life size, July 7th

Asclepias syriaca
flowers and bud
1⅔ × life size
July 7th

Asclepias incarnata
flowers and stem
1 ⅓ × life size, August 8th

Vincetoxicum album
flowers, 2 × life size
July 5th

Vincetoxicum

Vincetoxicum N. M. Wolf (1776), in the family Apocynaceae, (including Asclepiadaceae), contains around 15 species, in eastern Europe and southwestern Asia.

Description Perennials to 1.5m, with many upright stems with a milky latex, sometimes climbing or shrubby. Leaves opposite, simple, the lower usually ovate, the upper narrower. Flowers white, yellow, reddish, dark purple, or greenish, in loose heads in the leaf axils. Sepals 5, small, spreading, joined only at the base. Petals 5, twisted in the bud, spreading. Stamens 5, equal; corona with 5 segments. Stigma thick, 5-sided. Pollination is not recorded. The fruit is a curved capsule with 2 rows of seeds, each with a silky parachute.

Key Recognition Features The opposite pairs of leaves, and the heads of small, dull-coloured flowers in the leaf axils.

Ecology and Geography In woods, on rocky banks, and in rough places. Around 11 of the species in Europe, 8 in Turkey, the rest scattered mainly in western Asia.

Comment These unusual plants are sometimes grown as curiosities; the genus *Cynanchum* L. is somewhat similar to *Vincetoxicum*, but has flowers with a double, 10-segmented corona, and many of its species are tropical climbers.

Vincetoxicum album
⅔ life size, July 5th

Asperula

Asperula L. (1753), in the family Rubiaceae, contains around 90 species, mainly in Europe and southwestern Asia.

Description Perennials to 80cm, a few annuals or low shrubs, with stems square in section. Leaves simple, in whorls of 5, 6, or more. Flowers white, pale blue, pink, yellowish, reddish, or greenish, in loose heads and in the upper leaf axils, often with narrow bracts. Sepals 4 or 5, very small. Petals 4 or 5, not twisted in the bud, spreading, joined into a usually long tube at the base. Stamens 4 or 5, equal, usually within the tube. Stigma often exserted, 2-lobed. Pollination is presumed to be by various insects. The fruit is a pair of dry, 1-seeded nutlets.

Key Recognition Features The whorls of leaves and the long-tubed flowers with very short stalks and narrow bracts; the closely related *Galium* has stalked flowers without bracts.

Ecology and Geography In woods, on rocky mountains, on cliffs and screes, and in open ground. Around 66 of the species in Europe, 40 in Turkey, the rest scattered across western Asia; also a small group of species in Australia.

Comment The family Rubiaceae is based on *Rubia* L., a climbing perennial with stiff leaves, small, green flowers and black, berry-like fruit; the root of *R. tinctorum* L. was the source of the dye madder. Rubiaceae is a huge family, with over 10,000 species, mainly in the tropics; it includes such important products as *Cinchona* L., the source of quinine, *Coffea* L., and ornamentals such as *Gardenia* Ellis, *Pentas* Benth. and *Mussaenda* L.. DNA studies show the Rubiaceae is closest to Apocynaceae and Gentianaceae (see pp.208–11). A few species of *Asperula* are grown as ornamentals: *A. orientalis* Boiss. & Hohen. syn. *A. azurea* Jaub. & Spach is an attractive annual, easily grown and quick to flower; *A. taurina* subsp. *caucasica* (Pobed.) Ehrend. is a creeping perennial for a shady area, spreading by orange rhizomes; *A. suberosa* Sibth. & Sm. from Greece and *A. hirta* Ramond from the Pyrenees are 2 of several dwarf, hairy, alpine species, sometimes grown in rock gardens; and *A. cynanchica* L. is a characteristic plant of chalk grassland throughout Europe.

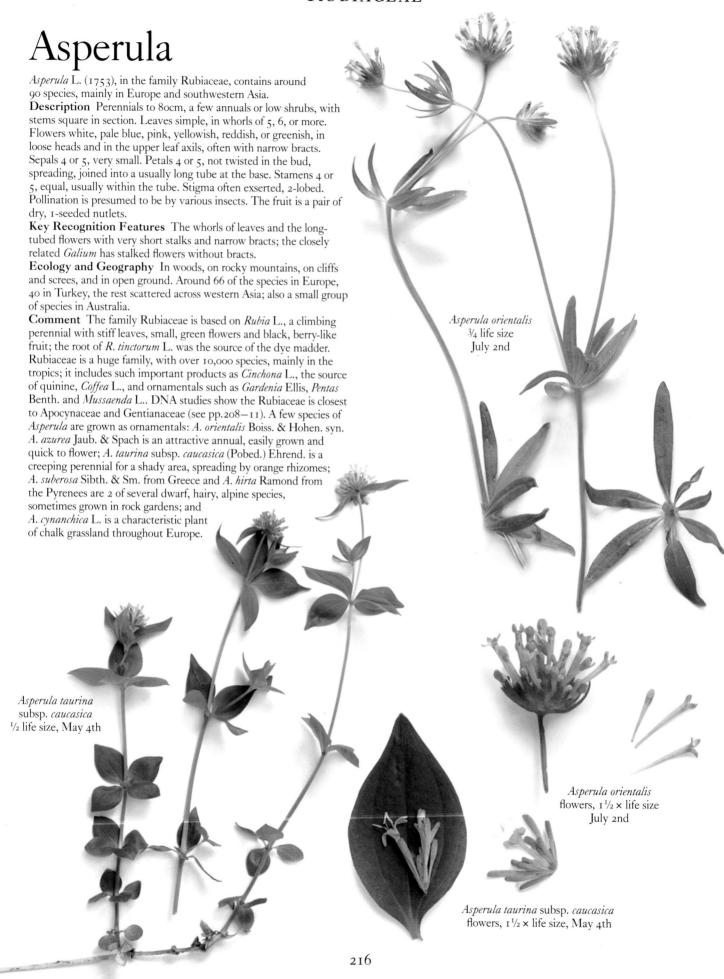

Asperula orientalis
¾ life size
July 2nd

Asperula taurina
subsp. *caucasica*
½ life size, May 4th

Asperula orientalis
flowers, 1½ × life size
July 2nd

Asperula taurina subsp. *caucasica*
flowers, 1½ × life size, May 4th

Galium odoratum
flowers, 2 × life size
May 3rd

Galium

Galium L. (1753), in the family Rubiaceae, contains around 300 species worldwide.

Description Perennials or annuals to 3m, a few low shrubs. Leaves simple, in whorls of 4 or more. Flowers white, yellow, reddish, or greenish, in loose heads and in the upper leaf axils, without bracts. Sepals 4, very small. Petals 4, not twisted in the bud, spreading, joined into a usually short tube at the base. Stamens 4, equal, usually exserted from the tube. Stigma exserted, 2-lobed. Pollination is by various small insects includig bee-flies. The fruit is a pair of dry, 1-seeded nutlets.

Key Recognition Features The whorls of leaves and the short-tubed flowers with long stalks and without bracts. *Galium odoratum* (L.) Scop. syn. *Asperula odorata* L. has long-tubed flowers, but stalked and without bracts.

Ecology and Geography In woods and hedges, on rocky mountains, in grassland and bogs, and in open ground. Around 145 species in Europe, 100 in Turkey, the rest scattered across the world as far as New Zealand.

Comment The sweet woodruff, *G. odoratum*, is a spreading perennial with white, long-tubed flowers, and 6–9 leaves per whorl; it was used for its sweetly scented dried stems, and is found in woods throughout Europe. *Galium verum* L., lady's bedstraw, has bright yellow flowers which smell of urine and attract flies; it is a tough perennial sometimes planted in meadow gardens, and its roots produce a red dye. *Galium aparine* L., goose grass or cleavers, is an annual weed of woodland and hedgerows; its stems are sticky with recurved teeth and the seeds form small, round burrs.

Galium aparine
with fruit and flowers
1⅓ × life size, June 12th

Galium odoratum
1¼ × life size, May 3rd

Galium verum
¾ life size
June 18th

Phuopsis

Phuopsis (Griseb.) Benth. & Hook. fil. (1873) in the family Rubiaceae, contains 1 species, *P. stylosa* (Trin.) B. D. Jackson, in western Asia.
Description A mat-forming perennial, close to *Asperula* (see p.216) but with 5 petals joined into a long tube at the base, and a club-shaped style that elongates while the flower is open.
Key Recognition Features The whorls of leaves and small, bright pink flowers with a long tube, 5 petals, and a distinctive foxy smell.
Ecology and Geography In woods, in the Caucasus and in northern Iran.
Comment *Phuopsis stylosa* is grown as an ornamental for its heads of bright pinkish flowers. Its strange name *Phuopsis* refers to its superficial similarity to *Valeriana phu* L.

Phuopsis stylosa
flowers, 1⅓ × life size
June 6th

Sherardia arvensis fruits and flowers
2 × life size, September 24th

Phuopsis stylosa
⅔ life size, June 6th

Sherardia

Sherardia L. (1753), field madder, in the family Rubiaceae, contains 1 species, *S. arvensis* L. in Europe and western Asia.
Description A creeping annual, close to *Asperula* (see p.216) but with a distinct 4- to 6-toothed calyx that enlarges as the fruit ripens.
Key Recognition Features The whorls of leaves, and the small, pink flowers and distinct sepals.
Ecology and Geography In waste ground and dry grassland throughout Europe, except Iceland and the Arctic, and in southwestern Asia; now widely naturalised elsewhere in the world.
Comment The genus is named after William Sherard (1659–1728), a pupil of Tournefort and consul at Smyrna (today Izmir) in 1703–16. He endowed the Sherardian Chair of Botany at Oxford, and brought J.J. Dillenius to England from Germany in 1721.

Sherardia arvensis
⅔ life size
September 24th

Calystegia

Calystegia R. Br. (1810), bindweed, in the family Convolvulaceae, contains around 25 species worldwide.

Description Perennials to 5m, usually with climbing and trailing stems, which burrow into the ground and root in late summer. Leaves alternate, simple. Flowers white, pink, or pale yellow, trumpet-shaped. Sepals 5, joined only at the base, almost covered by 2 large, sepal-like bracteoles. Petals 5, twisted in the bud, usually joined for the whole of their length, with 5 tubular nectaries. Stamens 5, equal, attached to the corolla tube; filaments pressed close to the style. Pollen smooth, spheroidal. Ovary superior, 1-celled, with 4 ovules; style 1, with 2 stigmas. Pollination is usually by bumblebees, hoverflies, or perhaps moths. The fruit is a capsule with up to 4 large seeds.

Key Recognition Features The large, trumpet-shaped flowers with 2 large bracteoles at the base, which distinguish it from *Convolvulus* (see p.220).

Ecology and Geography In hedges and scrub, and on sandy and pebbly seashores; 3 species and several hybrids in Europe, 13 in California, the rest scattered, particularly in eastern Asia, with a few species throughout the Americas, South Africa, Australia, and New Zealand (3 species). *Calystegia soldanella* (L.) R. Br. is found worldwide on temperate coasts and lake shores.

Comment Though beautiful, most species of *Calystegia* are too rampant to be welcome in the garden; *C. × howittiorum* Brummitt, a hybrid between *C. pulchra* Brumit & Heywood and *C. silvatica* (Kit.) Griseb. is a beautiful pest; it has stems and petioles with a few scattered hairs. A double-flowered form of *C. hederacea* Wall. from Japan is often grown, and is less invasive.

Calystegia × howittiorum
⅔ life size, August 10th

Calystegia soldanella
⅔ life size, June 13th

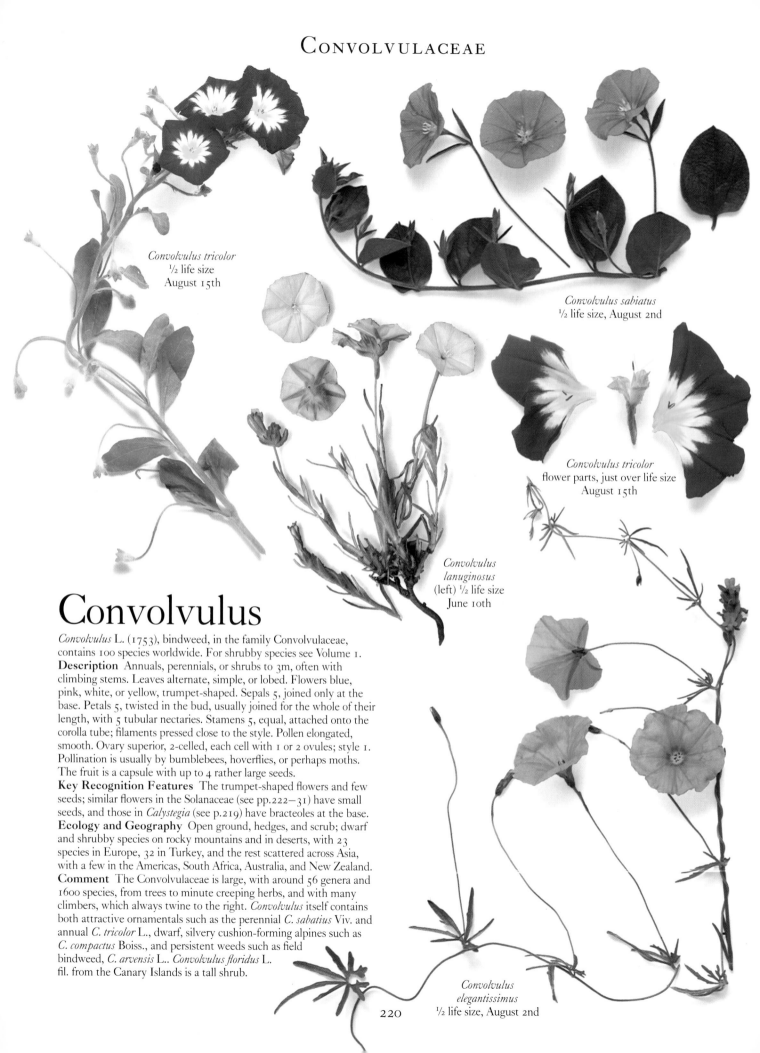

Convolvulus tricolor
½ life size
August 15th

Convolvulus sabiatus
½ life size, August 2nd

Convolvulus tricolor
flower parts, just over life size
August 15th

*Convolvulus
lanuginosus*
(left) ½ life size
June 10th

Convolvulus

Convolvulus L. (1753), bindweed, in the family Convolvulaceae, contains 100 species worldwide. For shrubby species see Volume 1.
Description Annuals, perennials, or shrubs to 3m, often with climbing stems. Leaves alternate, simple, or lobed. Flowers blue, pink, white, or yellow, trumpet-shaped. Sepals 5, joined only at the base. Petals 5, twisted in the bud, usually joined for the whole of their length, with 5 tubular nectaries. Stamens 5, equal, attached onto the corolla tube; filaments pressed close to the style. Pollen elongated, smooth. Ovary superior, 2-celled, each cell with 1 or 2 ovules; style 1. Pollination is usually by bumblebees, hoverflies, or perhaps moths. The fruit is a capsule with up to 4 rather large seeds.
Key Recognition Features The trumpet-shaped flowers and few seeds; similar flowers in the Solanaceae (see pp.222–31) have small seeds, and those in *Calystegia* (see p.219) have bracteoles at the base.
Ecology and Geography Open ground, hedges, and scrub; dwarf and shrubby species on rocky mountains and in deserts, with 23 species in Europe, 32 in Turkey, and the rest scattered across Asia, with a few in the Americas, South Africa, Australia, and New Zealand.
Comment The Convolvulaceae is large, with around 56 genera and 1600 species, from trees to minute creeping herbs, and with many climbers, which always twine to the right. *Convolvulus* itself contains both attractive ornamentals such as the perennial *C. sabatius* Viv. and annual *C. tricolor* L., dwarf, silvery cushion-forming alpines such as *C. compactus* Boiss., and persistent weeds such as field bindweed, *C. arvensis* L.. *Convolvulus floridus* L. fil. from the Canary Islands is a tall shrub.

*Convolvulus
elegantissimus*
½ life size, August 2nd

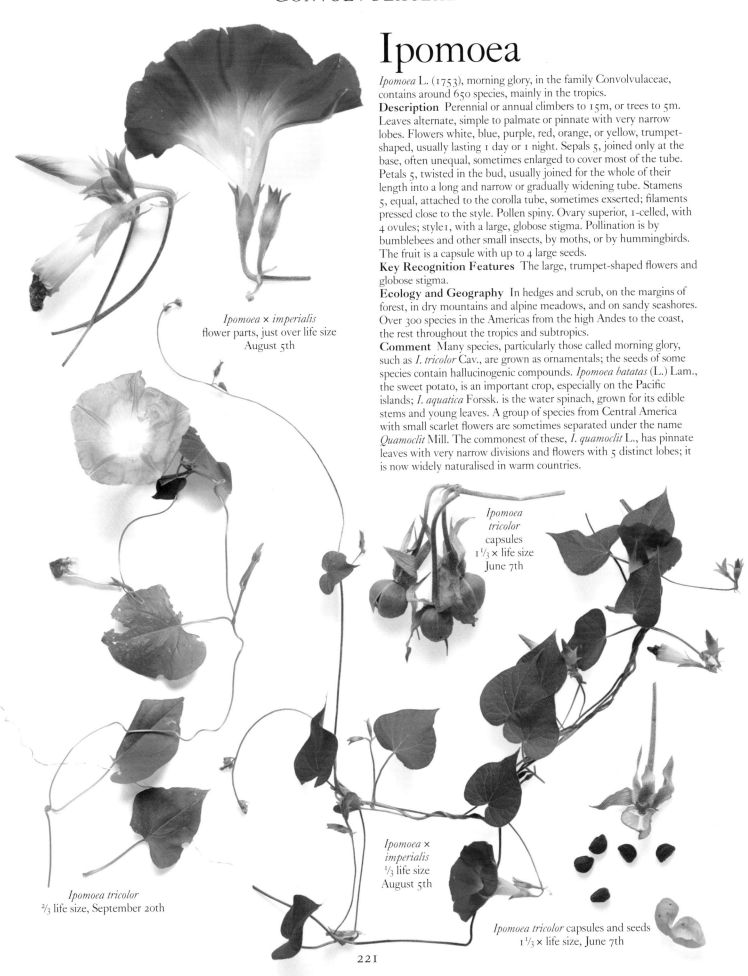

Ipomoea

Ipomoea L. (1753), morning glory, in the family Convolvulaceae, contains around 650 species, mainly in the tropics.

Description Perennial or annual climbers to 15m, or trees to 5m. Leaves alternate, simple to palmate or pinnate with very narrow lobes. Flowers white, blue, purple, red, orange, or yellow, trumpet-shaped, usually lasting 1 day or 1 night. Sepals 5, joined only at the base, often unequal, sometimes enlarged to cover most of the tube. Petals 5, twisted in the bud, usually joined for the whole of their length into a long and narrow or gradually widening tube. Stamens 5, equal, attached to the corolla tube, sometimes exserted; filaments pressed close to the style. Pollen spiny. Ovary superior, 1-celled, with 4 ovules; style 1, with a large, globose stigma. Pollination is by bumblebees and other small insects, by moths, or by hummingbirds. The fruit is a capsule with up to 4 large seeds.

Key Recognition Features The large, trumpet-shaped flowers and globose stigma.

Ecology and Geography In hedges and scrub, on the margins of forest, in dry mountains and alpine meadows, and on sandy seashores. Over 300 species in the Americas from the high Andes to the coast, the rest throughout the tropics and subtropics.

Comment Many species, particularly those called morning glory, such as *I. tricolor* Cav., are grown as ornamentals; the seeds of some species contain hallucinogenic compounds. *Ipomoea batatas* (L.) Lam., the sweet potato, is an important crop, especially on the Pacific islands; *I. aquatica* Forssk. is the water spinach, grown for its edible stems and young leaves. A group of species from Central America with small scarlet flowers are sometimes separated under the name *Quamoclit* Mill. The commonest of these, *I. quamoclit* L., has pinnate leaves with very narrow divisions and flowers with 5 distinct lobes; it is now widely naturalised in warm countries.

Ipomoea × imperialis
flower parts, just over life size
August 5th

Ipomoea tricolor
capsules
1 1/3 × life size
June 7th

Ipomoea × imperialis
1/3 life size
August 5th

Ipomoea tricolor
2/3 life size, September 20th

Ipomoea tricolor capsules and seeds
1 1/3 × life size, June 7th

SOLANACEAE

Lycopersicon esculentum
²/₃ life size, September 10th

Solanum tuberosum
'Salad Red'
½ life size, October 15th

Solanum nigrum var. *guineense*
⅓ life size, September 10th

Solanum tuberosum
'Pentland Beauty'
½ life size, October 15th

222

Solanum melongena
fruit, seeds and flower
²⁄₃ life size, August 10th

Solanum

Solanum L. (1753), nightshade and potato, in the family Solanaceae, contains around 1700 species, mainly in the tropics and subtropics.

Description Trees, shrubs, perennials, or annuals, often climbers to 5m. Leaves alternate, simple to pinnate. Flowers white, blue, purple, or yellow, usually star-shaped. Sepals 5, joined at the base, sometimes enlarging in fruit. Petals 5, usually joined for less than half their length into a short tube. Stamens 5, equal, attached to the base of the corolla tube, the anthers often pressed close to the style, dehiscing by pores. Ovary superior, 2- or rarely 4-celled, with numerous ovules; style 1, with a small stigma. Pollination is usually by bumblebees. The fruit is usually a berry, red, yellow, black, or green, with numerous small seeds.

Key Recognition Features The star-shaped flowers, the berries, and the usually acrid smell of the leaves.

Ecology and Geography In waste places, scrub, wet woods, rock crevices, and mountain meadows; 3 species in Europe, the rest throughout the tropics and subtropics, but mostly in Central and South America.

Comment The family Solanaceae is closest to the Convolvulaceae (see pp.219–21), but otherwise relatively isolated; it includes the genus *Nolana* L. ex L. fil., formerly separated in Nolanaceae. Many genera contain poisonous alkaloids, but many also have edible fruits or tubers; these are particularly important in Central America, where tomatoes, peppers, Cape gooseberries, and tomatillos were first domesticated. Many species of the genus *Solanum* are important as food crops: the most widely grown is the potato, and tuber-bearing species related to the cultivated potato are common over large parts of the mountains of America from Mexico to Argentina, growing in many different habitats from alpine meadows to screes, rocky slopes, and river gravels. Other common species are the American huckleberry, *S. melanocerasum* All., and the eggplant or aubergine, *S. melongena* L., which is one of the few economic species of *Solanum* to have originated in Asia. *Solanum muricatum* Ait. is the pepino from Peru, now widely cultivated for its edible fruit, eaten fresh. Closely related to *Solanum* is *Lycopersicon* Miller, the tomato, native of Central and South America; its flowers are always yellow, and the anthers dehisce by slits rather than by pores.

Solanum melongena
¹⁄₃ life size, August 10th

Mandragora

Mandragora L. (1753), mandrake, in the family Solanaceae, contains around 6 species in Europe and Asia.

Description Perennials to 20cm, with deep, thick, and forking roots. Leaves simple, all in a basal rosette. Flowers violet-purple or greenish, low among the leaves, upright or nodding. Sepals 5, joined at the base, enlarging in fruit. Petals 5, usually joined for around half their length into a wide tube, around 25mm long. Stamens 5, equal, attached to the base of the corolla tube. Ovary superior, 2-celled, with numerous ovules; style 1, with a large, round stigma. Pollination is by insects. The fruit is a large, round or egg-shaped berry, 2–3cm across, yellow or orange, with numerous small, brown seeds.

Key Recognition Features The purple or green flowers among the rosette of leaves, and groups of large berries lying on the ground in summer.

Ecology and Geography In scrub and on open, dry hills, with 2 species in Europe, the rest in Asia.

Comment Of the 2 European species, *M. autumnalis* Bertol. has purple flowers in winter and spring and egg-shaped fruits, whereas *M. officinarum* L. has pale green flowers in spring and spherical fruits. The Himalayan *M. caulescens* C.B. Clarke has green, bell-shaped, nodding flowers on stems longer than the leaves. The mandrake was famous in ancient medicine, used as a narcotic and as an anaesthetic for operations, and it came to be surrounded by all sorts of myths. The thick, forked root was likened to a human torso, and to dig it up was said to drive men mad; therefore a dog was tied to the root, and made to pull it up. A famous illustration in the *Codex Vindobonensis* of Dioscorides, which dates from around 512 AD, shows the humunculus-like mandrake being handed to Dioscorides, and the expiring dog.

Atropa

Atropa L. (1753), deadly nightshade, in the family Solanaceae, contains around 4 species in Europe and Asia.

Description Perennials to 2m. Leaves alternate, simple. Flowers dull purple or dirty yellow, bell-shaped, solitary in the leaf axils. Sepals 5, joined at the base, enlarging and becoming leafy in fruit. Petals 5, usually joined for most of their length into a wide tube, 25–30mm long. Stamens 5, equal, attached to the base of the corolla tube. Ovary superior, 2-celled, with numerous ovules; style 1, with a large, round stigma. Pollination is usually by bumblebees. The fruit is a black berry, with numerous small, black seeds.

Key Recognition Features The solitary, bell-shaped flowers produced in summer, and shining black berries with a leafy calyx.

Ecology and Geography In scrub and open woods and on rocky mountainsides, with 2 species in Europe, the others in Asia.

Comment *Atropa belladonna* L. is common throughout Europe; it was used by ladies to make their eyes more lovely, as the atropine causes the pupils to dilate. It is also used medicinally: the berries are very deadly; the leaves can be used as a poultice with less danger. *Physochlaina* G. Don fil. is similar in leaf and flower shape, but has loose heads of flowers in spring. *Scopolia* Jacq. has brown or greenish, solitary, bell-shaped flowers, but the sepals are not leafy and the fruit is a capsule; the flowers appear with the leaves in early spring.

Atropa belladonna
fruits and seeds (left)
just over life size
September 8th

Atropa belladonna
flower (above)
1⅓ × life size, July 13th

Mandragora officinarum
fruit (below and right)
½ life size, July 20th

Atropa belladonna (right)
⅓ life size, July 13th

*Mandragora
officinarum*
leaf and
flower parts
1¼ × life size
February 28th

Hyoscyamus

Hyoscyamus L. (1753), henbane, in the family Solanaceae, contains around 15 species in Europe, Africa, and Asia.

Description Annuals, biennials, or perennials to 1m. Leaves simple or toothed, often soft and sticky with glandular hairs. Flowers purple, greenish, white, or yellow, nodding in bud, opening in succession along the stems. Sepals 5, joined into a tubular calyx, enlarging in fruit. Petals 5, often veined and netted, rounded, usually joined for around half their length into a wide tube. Stamens 5, equal, attached to the base of the corolla tube. Ovary superior, 2-celled, with numerous ovules; style 1, with a round stigma. Pollination is by insects. The fruit is a dry capsule, held within the calyx, with numerous small, brown seeds.

Key Recognition Features The purple or yellow, often net-veined flowers with a dark throat, opening in succession along the stems, and the capsules within the enlarged calyx.

Ecology and Geography In rough places, often near rabbit warrens, in scrub and deserts, also in rock crevices and old walls; 5 species in Europe, the rest in Asia and northern Africa.

Comment Like most of the family Solanaceae, the henbanes are very poisonous; they were used in ancient medicine as narcotics, and in small doses caused beneficial sleep; larger doses produced hallucinations and, it is said, the sensation of being covered with long hair, like a werewolf. Hyoscine, one of the poisons in henbane, was used by the infamous Dr Crippen to poison his wife Cora in 1910.

Hyoscyamus aureus
flower parts and
section of ovary
1 1/2 × life size
June 2nd

Hyoscyamus aureus
1/2 life size, June 2nd

Hyoscyamus niger flower parts and enlarged calyx
just over life size, July 20th

Hyoscyamus aureus
1/2 life size
June 2nd

Nolana

Nolana L. ex L. fil. (1762), in the family Solanaceae, contains around 18 species in South America.

Description Annuals, perennials, or subshrubs to 25cm, and usually more across. Leaves often succulent, simple, often stickily hairy, sometimes heather-like. Flowers blue or purplish, with a white or yellow throat, solitary or clustered in the leaf axils. Sepals 5, joined to form a tubular calyx. Petals 5, usually joined at the base to form a bell-shaped corolla around 2–4cm across. Stamens 5, unequal, 3 longer than the rest. Ovary superior, cells in groups of 5, with 1 or numerous ovules; style 1, with a round stigma, inserted at the base of the ovary. Pollination is presumed to be by bees. The fruit is a head of nutlets with 1 to several seeds.

Key Recognition Features The blue or purplish flowers with a white centre and tubular, toothed calyx, and the fruits of several nutlets. Superficially similar to *Nicandra* (see p.229), but without the large, overlapping sepals.

Ecology and Geography On rocky hills and coastal sands on the Pacific coast of Chile and Peru and on the Galapagos.

Comment *Nolana* was formerly placed in its own family, the Nolanaceae, on account of its unusual style and ovary arrangement, but DNA studies have shown that it falls within the Solanaceae. Two species are grown as annuals, often planted in baskets because of their trailing stems. *Nolana paradoxa* Lindl. is the more beautiful and showy of these commonly grown species.

Datura

Datura L. (1753), thorn apple, in the family Solanaceae, contains around 10 species in America.

Description Annuals to 2m. Leaves simple or wavy-edged, sometimes soft and sticky with glandular hairs. Flowers white or purplish. Sepals 5, joined into a tubular and often 5-angled calyx. Petals 5, usually joined for most of their length into a large, trumpet-shaped corolla, with 5 or 10 shallow lobes or teeth. Stamens 5, equal. Ovary superior, 2-celled, with numerous ovules; style 1, with a 2-lobed stigma. Pollination is presumed to be by moths. The fruit is a dry and usually spiny capsule with 4 openings and numerous seeds.

Key Recognition Features The trumpet-shaped flowers with 5 or 10 teeth, and the large, round, often spiny fruit, giving it the name thorn apple.

Ecology and Geography In semi-deserts, on dry, rocky slopes, and in waste places, often as a garden weed. In southern North America and much of South America, with 1 species, *D. ferox* L., possibly native in eastern Asia.

Comment One species, *D. stramonium* L., the thorn apple or Jimson or Jamestown weed, a native of North America, is common in old gardens; its seeds can remain dormant in the soil for many years, so the plant can appear unexpectedly. All species of Datura are very poisonous, and were used by the Aztecs to induce hallucinations; more recently, they have been used in treatments for asthma.

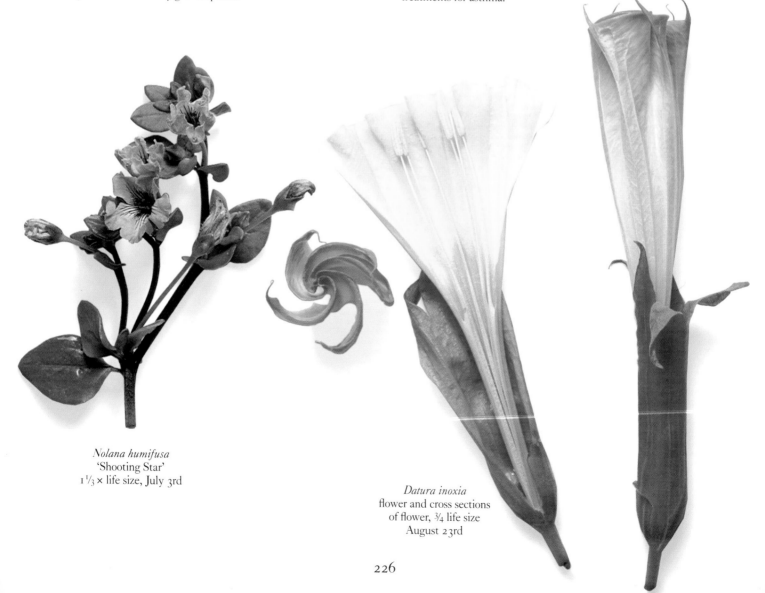

Nolana humifusa
'Shooting Star'
1 1/3 × life size, July 3rd

Datura inoxia
flower and cross sections
of flower, ¾ life size
August 23rd

SOLANACEAE

Datura stramonium
½ life size, September 30th

Datura stramonium
fruit and seeds, 1 ⅓ × life size
September 30th

Datura inoxia flower
⅔ life size, August 23rd

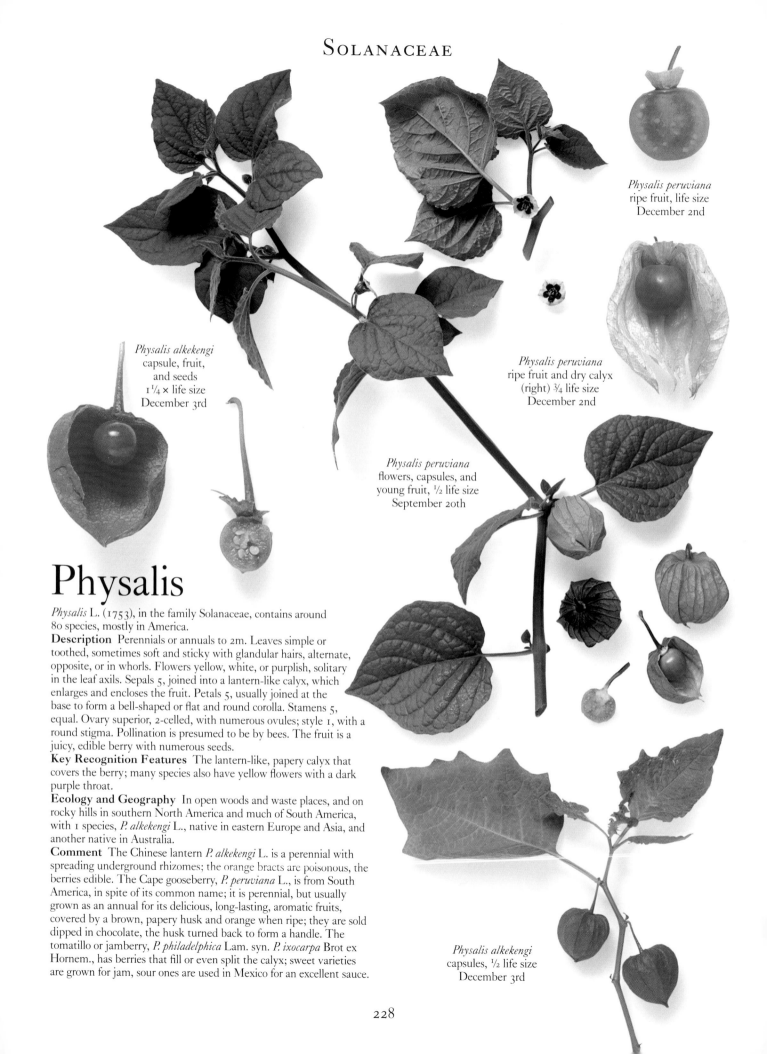

Physalis peruviana
ripe fruit, life size
December 2nd

Physalis peruviana
ripe fruit and dry calyx
(right) ¾ life size
December 2nd

Physalis alkekengi
capsule, fruit,
and seeds
1¼ × life size
December 3rd

Physalis peruviana
flowers, capsules, and
young fruit, ½ life size
September 20th

Physalis alkekengi
capsules, ½ life size
December 3rd

Physalis

Physalis L. (1753), in the family Solanaceae, contains around 80 species, mostly in America.

Description Perennials or annuals to 2m. Leaves simple or toothed, sometimes soft and sticky with glandular hairs, alternate, opposite, or in whorls. Flowers yellow, white, or purplish, solitary in the leaf axils. Sepals 5, joined into a lantern-like calyx, which enlarges and encloses the fruit. Petals 5, usually joined at the base to form a bell-shaped or flat and round corolla. Stamens 5, equal. Ovary superior, 2-celled, with numerous ovules; style 1, with a round stigma. Pollination is presumed to be by bees. The fruit is a juicy, edible berry with numerous seeds.

Key Recognition Features The lantern-like, papery calyx that covers the berry; many species also have yellow flowers with a dark purple throat.

Ecology and Geography In open woods and waste places, and on rocky hills in southern North America and much of South America, with 1 species, *P. alkekengi* L., native in eastern Europe and Asia, and another native in Australia.

Comment The Chinese lantern *P. alkekengi* L. is a perennial with spreading underground rhizomes; the orange bracts are poisonous, the berries edible. The Cape gooseberry, *P. peruviana* L., is from South America, in spite of its common name; it is perennial, but usually grown as an annual for its delicious, long-lasting, aromatic fruits, covered by a brown, papery husk and orange when ripe; they are sold dipped in chocolate, the husk turned back to form a handle. The tomatillo or jamberry, *P. philadelphica* Lam. syn. *P. ixocarpa* Brot ex Hornem., has berries that fill or even split the calyx; sweet varieties are grown for jam, sour ones are used in Mexico for an excellent sauce.

Nicandra

Nicandra Adans. (1763), in the family Solanaceae, contains 1 species, *N. physalodes* (L.) Scop., from South America.

Description Annual to 1.5m, and usually more across. Leaves simple or toothed, usually smooth. Flowers purplish with a white centre, solitary in the leaf axils. Sepals 5, heart-shaped, not joined but overlapping to form a strongly 5-ridged, lantern-like calyx, which enlarges and encloses the fruit. Petals 5, usually joined at the base to form a bell-shaped corolla around 4cm across. Stamens 5, equal. Ovary superior, 3- to 5-celled, with numerous ovules; style 1, with a round stigma. Pollination is presumed to be by bees. The fruit is a purplish berry, which becomes dry and dehiscent on ripening, with numerous seeds.

Key Recognition Features The purple flowers with a white centre and separate sepals forming a strongly 5-ridged, papery calyx that covers the berry.

Ecology and Geography In waste places and on rocky hills. Said to be native of Peru, but now found commonly throughout Central America and in the tropics worldwide.

Comment This is commonly called the shoo-fly plant, as it is supposed to keep flies away; it certainly contains poisonous alkaloids.

Nicandra physalodes
flowers, life size
August 23rd

Nicandra physalodes
flowers, 1¼ × life size
August 23rd

Nicandra physalodes
½ life size, August 23rd

Nicandra physalodes
capsules, fruit, and seeds
just under life size
September 30th

229

Nicotiana

Nicotiana L. (1753), tobacco, in the family Solanaceae, contains around 70 species, mainly in America.

Description Annuals, biennials, and perennials to large shrubs around 5m. Leaves simple, often soft and sticky with glandular hairs. Flowers white, pink, purple, yellow, or greenish, opening in succession, in loose heads. Sepals 5, joined into a tubular calyx. Petals 5, usually joined for more than half their length into a narrow tube. Stamens 5, subequal, or with 1 shorter. Ovary superior, 2-celled, with numerous ovules; style 1, with a round stigma. Pollination is by bees, moths, or hummingbirds. The fruit is a dry capsule, splitting into 2 or 4, with numerous small, brown seeds.

Key Recognition Features The short and green, pink, or yellow, or long and narrow, white or purple flowers, and the flat, simple leaves.

Ecology and Geography In rough places, on cliffs, in scrub, and by streams in deserts. Mostly in America, with a few species in Australia and 1 in southern Africa.

Comment Many species are grown as ornamentals, a few for tobacco. The fleshy and shrubby *N. glauca* R.C. Graham, with yellow flowers and small, bluish-green leaves, is common in the Andes of northern Argentina, and commonly naturalised in Africa, southern Europe, Asia, and Australia; it is often pollinated by birds. The main species grown for tobacco are the pinkish-flowered *N. tabacum* L. from South America and the green-flowered *N. rustica* L. from North America, now used mainly for the production of nicotine. The ornamental annual species are mostly forms of the South American *N. alata* Link & Otto and the hybrid *N.* × *sanderae* hort..

Nicotiana glauca
½ life size
August 4th

Nicotiana glauca **flower parts** (right)
1 ½ × life size
August 4th

Nicotiana rustica
½ life size, July 14th

Nicotiana species from Cordoba
½ life size
September 25th

Petunia

Petunia Juss. (1803), petunia, in the family Solanaceae, contains around 35 species in South America.

Description Annuals, biennials, or short-lived perennials to 1m. Leaves simple, soft, and sticky with glandular hairs. Flowers white, pink, or purple, rarely pale yellow or red, opening in succession, scented at night. Sepals 5, joined into a tubular calyx. Petals 5, usually joined for their entire length into a trumpet-shaped corolla. Stamens 4, equal, with 1 staminode. Ovary superior, 2-celled, with numerous ovules; style 1, with a round stigma. Pollination is often by hawkmoths. The fruit is a dry capsule, splitting into 2, with numerous small, brown seeds.

Key Recognition Features The trumpet-shaped flowers with a round, unlobed margin, and the 4 stamens and 1 staminode.

Ecology and Geography By streams in deserts, in open, sandy ground in the mountains, and on dunes by the sea, in South America.

Comment The name is derived from the Brazilian *petun*, meaning tobacco, to which petunias are very closely related; Mabberley records that in Ecuador at least 1 species is used to induce a feeling of flying. Many are grown as ornamentals, and a large range of flower sizes and colours has been developed. They are all forms of *P. × hybrida* hort., a cross between the tall, white-flowered *P. axillaris* (Lam.) Britton, Sterns & Pogg. and the shorter, purple-flowered *P. integrifolia* (Hook.) Schinz & Thell.. The genus *Calibrachoa* Llave & Lex., usually included in *Petunia*, is the source of the very small-flowered cultivars such as 'Million Bells'.

Petunia 'Million Bells'
⅔ life size, July 10th

Petunia Surfinia
'Pink Vein' (below)
⅔ life size, August 20th

Salpiglossis 'Bolero'
½ life size
August 30th

Petunia hybrids (left to right):
'Violet Blue', 'Purple', and 'Pastel Pink'
⅔ life size, August 20th

Salpiglossis

Salpiglossis Ruíz & Pavón (1794), in the family Solanaceae, contains 2 species in South America.

Description Annuals or perennials to 60cm. Leaves simple, wavy-edged, or pinnate, soft, and sticky with glandular hairs. Flowers dark purple, yellow, or red, usually heavily veined, in loose sprays on long stalks. Sepals 5, joined into a tubular calyx. Petals 5, usually joined for most of their length into a spreading, trumpet-shaped corolla with 4 lower lobes and 1 wide, indented upper lobe. Stamens 4, with 1 staminode. Ovary superior, 2-celled, with numerous ovules; style 1, with a round stigma. Pollination is not recorded. The fruit is a dry capsule, splitting into 2, with numerous very small seeds.

Key Recognition Features The trumpet-shaped flowers with 5 lobes, the upper largest, with beautiful veins, and the 4 stamens and 1 staminode.

Ecology and Geography In deserts and on dry, rocky slopes in the southern Andes of Chile, Argentina, and southern Peru.

Comment One species, *S. sinuata* Ruíz & Pavón, with many varieties, is grown as an ornamental.

Salpiglossis 'Bolero'
life size, August 30th

231

Trachystemon

Trachystemon D. Don (1837), in the family Boraginaceae, contains 1 species, *T. orientalis* (L.) D. Don, in the Black Sea area.

Description Perennials with flowering stems to 60cm. Leaves mostly basal, large, to 20cm wide, with scattered, bristly hairs. Flowers purplish-blue, with reflexed and coiled petals. Sepals 5, joined at the base. Petals 5, usually pointed, joined at the base into a short tube, with white scales between the stamens. Stamens 5, equal, nearly as long as the petals, without a claw-like appendage; filaments long. Ovary superior, of 4 cells; style 1. Pollination is usually by bees. The fruit is made up of 4 separate, keeled nutlets.

Key Recognition Features The large basal leaves and the flowers with reflexed petals and long stamens.

Ecology and Geography Beech woods and moist, rocky, and shady places in Bulgaria, northern Turkey, and the western Caucasian region.

Comment An unusual, early-flowering perennial, sometimes cultivated in a shady position. The large leaves develop after the flowers have faded.

Borago

Borago L. (1753), borage, in the family Boraginaceae, contains 3 species in the Mediterranean area.

Description Annuals to 70cm or perennials with sprawling stems. Leaves alternate, simple, with bristly hairs. Flowers blue, rarely white, with spreading petals or bell-shaped. Sepals 5, joined only at the base. Petals 5, usually pointed, joined at the base into a short tube, with scales between the stamens. Stamens 5, equal, anthers large, pointed, and exserted, with a claw-like appendage; filaments very short. Ovary superior, of 4 cells; style 1. Pollination is usually by bees. The fruit is made up of 4 separate, rugose nutlets with a thickened ring at the base.

Key Recognition Features The bristly-hairy leaves and starry or bell-shaped, blue flowers with long, pointed stamens around the style.

Ecology and Geography *Borago officinalis* L., the common borage, in waste places throughout the Mediterranean region; *B. pygmaea* (DC) Chater & W. Greuter among shady rocks and in woods, especially after fires, in Corsica, Sardinia, and Capri; *B. longifolia* Poir. in Libya.

Comment The family Boraginaceae is large, with around 150 genera and over 3000 species, mainly herbaceous, but including some trees and shrubs (see Volume 1). The inflorescence is usually a cyme, coiled in the bud. The fruit is generally made up of 4 nutlets, which develop around the base of the style and are often strangely ornamented or hooked to act as burrs. Recent studies of DNA suggest that the Hydrophyllaceae, a mainly American family close to traditional Boraginaceae, should be included in a wider Boraginaceae; it has many-seeded capsules, but a similar inflorescence. The Boraginaceae is an isolated family, distantly related to both the Solanaceae (see pp.222−31) and the Labiatae (see pp.278−99) and their attendant families. The blue, starry flowers of *B. officinalis* are an ingredient of a Pimm's cocktail. This species is now cultivated on a field scale for the oil in its seeds, which is rich in gamma-linoleic acid, similar to evening primrose oil (see *Oenothera*, p.154). *Borago pygmaea* is also sometimes cultivated. This species was formerly known under the more descriptive name of *B. laxiflora* Poir.; unfortunately de Candolle had mistakenly called the plant *Campanula pygmaea* before Poiret named it *B. laxiflora*.

Trachystemon orientalis
½ life size
March 18th

Trachystemon orientalis
flower parts, 2 × life size
March 18th

BORAGINACEAE

Borago pygmaea
flowers and fruit
2 × life size
June 12th

Borago pygmaea
½ life size
June 12th

Borago officinalis
¾ life size, July 23rd

Borago officinalis
flower parts and fruit
1¼ × life size, July 23rd

Borago officinalis
½ life size, July 23rd

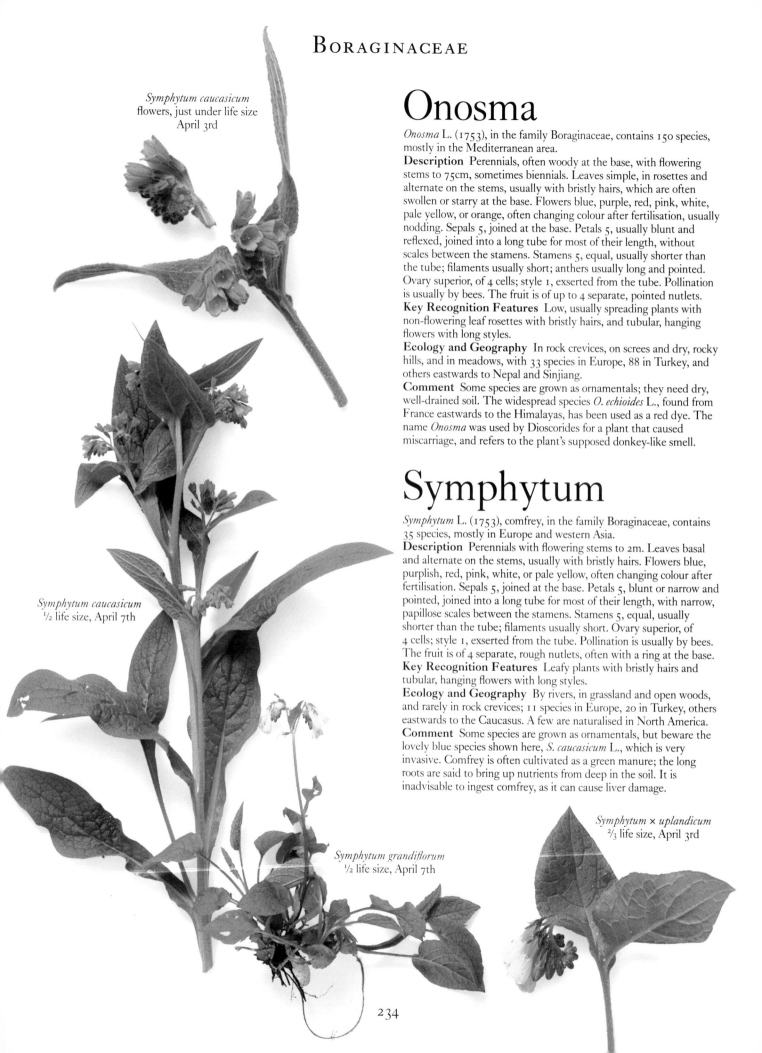

Symphytum caucasicum
flowers, just under life size
April 3rd

Symphytum caucasicum
½ life size, April 7th

Symphytum grandiflorum
½ life size, April 7th

Symphytum × uplandicum
⅔ life size, April 3rd

Onosma

Onosma L. (1753), in the family Boraginaceae, contains 150 species, mostly in the Mediterranean area.

Description Perennials, often woody at the base, with flowering stems to 75cm, sometimes biennials. Leaves simple, in rosettes and alternate on the stems, usually with bristly hairs, which are often swollen or starry at the base. Flowers blue, purple, red, pink, white, pale yellow, or orange, often changing colour after fertilisation, usually nodding. Sepals 5, joined at the base. Petals 5, usually blunt and reflexed, joined into a long tube for most of their length, without scales between the stamens. Stamens 5, equal, usually shorter than the tube; filaments usually short; anthers usually long and pointed. Ovary superior, of 4 cells; style 1, exserted from the tube. Pollination is usually by bees. The fruit is of up to 4 separate, pointed nutlets.

Key Recognition Features Low, usually spreading plants with non-flowering leaf rosettes with bristly hairs, and tubular, hanging flowers with long styles.

Ecology and Geography In rock crevices, on screes and dry, rocky hills, and in meadows, with 33 species in Europe, 88 in Turkey, and others eastwards to Nepal and Sinjiang.

Comment Some species are grown as ornamentals; they need dry, well-drained soil. The widespread species *O. echioides* L., found from France eastwards to the Himalayas, has been used as a red dye. The name *Onosma* was used by Dioscorides for a plant that caused miscarriage, and refers to the plant's supposed donkey-like smell.

Symphytum

Symphytum L. (1753), comfrey, in the family Boraginaceae, contains 35 species, mostly in Europe and western Asia.

Description Perennials with flowering stems to 2m. Leaves basal and alternate on the stems, usually with bristly hairs. Flowers blue, purplish, red, pink, white, or pale yellow, often changing colour after fertilisation. Sepals 5, joined at the base. Petals 5, blunt or narrow and pointed, joined into a long tube for most of their length, with narrow, papillose scales between the stamens. Stamens 5, equal, usually shorter than the tube; filaments usually short. Ovary superior, of 4 cells; style 1, exserted from the tube. Pollination is usually by bees. The fruit is of 4 separate, rough nutlets, often with a ring at the base.

Key Recognition Features Leafy plants with bristly hairs and tubular, hanging flowers with long styles.

Ecology and Geography By rivers, in grassland and open woods, and rarely in rock crevices; 11 species in Europe, 20 in Turkey, others eastwards to the Caucasus. A few are naturalised in North America.

Comment Some species are grown as ornamentals, but beware the lovely blue species shown here, *S. caucasicum* L., which is very invasive. Comfrey is often cultivated as a green manure; the long roots are said to bring up nutrients from deep in the soil. It is inadvisable to ingest comfrey, as it can cause liver damage.

Onosma alborosea
flower parts, 1½ × life size
May 12th

Onosma alborosea
⅔ life size
May 12th

Cerinthe major
½ life size
August 17th

Cerinthe major
flower parts, 1½ × life size
August 17th

Cerinthe major
'Purpurascens'
½ life size
June 2nd

Cerinthe major
'Purpurascens', flower parts
2 × life size, June 2nd

Cerinthe

Cerinthe L. (1753), in the family Boraginaceae, contains 10 species, mostly in the Mediterranean area.

Description Annuals, biennials, or occasionally perennials to 75cm. Leaves simple, alternate on the stems, usually hairless, often spotted with silver. Bracts broad, leafy, and conspicuous, often deep blue. Flowers deep blue, purple, dark red, yellow, or white, usually 2-coloured and nodding. Sepals 5, joined only at the base. Petals 5, usually blunt and reflexed, joined into a long tube for most of their length, without scales between the stamens. Stamens 5, equal, usually shorter than the tube; filaments usually short; anthers usually long and pointed, joined at the base. Ovary superior, of 4 cells; style 1, exserted from the tube. Pollination is usually by bees. The fruit is of up to 4 separate, black or brown, smooth and shining nutlets.

Key Recognition Features Usually leafy plants without hairs and with tubular, hanging flowers, yellow below, purple above; the dark greeny-blue bracts of *C. major* L. can be very striking.

Ecology and Geography In dry, grassy places and meadows, or in damp woods, with 4 species in Europe and others around the Mediterranean area.

Comment Some species are cultivated: *C. major*, from all around the Mediterranean, is a popular ornamental annual; *C. glabra* Mill. is a perennial with green leaves and yellow flowers; in *C. minor* L. the petals are long and pointed.

Echium

Echium L. (1753), in the family Boraginaceae, contains 60 species, mostly in the Canary Islands and the Mediterranean area.

Description Annuals, biennials, perennials, or shrubs, to 4m. Leaves simple, numerous on the stems, usually bristly-hairy. Bracts narrow. Flowers deep blue, purple, red, or white, usually horizontal. Sepals 5, joined only at the base. Petals 5, usually rounded, joined into a spreading tube for most of their length, without scales between the stamens, but sometimes with tufts of hairs or 10 minute scales at the base. Stamens 5, unequal, usually longer than the tube; filaments usually long; anthers short, exserted. Ovary superior, of 4 cells; style 1, exserted from the tube. Pollination is usually by bees or hummingbird hawkmoths. The fruit is of up to 4 separate, rugose nutlets.

Key Recognition Features Usually narrow-leaved plants with bristly hairs and trumpet-shaped flowers with long, slender stamens.

Ecology and Geography In dry, grassy places and meadows, with 18 species in Europe and around 28 species, often shrubby, in the Canary Islands and Madeira.

Comment Some species are cultivated, and the large, shrubby species make good garden plants in frost-free areas; *E. vulgare* L., a hardy blue-flowered biennial or perennial, is common in southern England near the sea and a bad weed in parts of North America. *Echium plantagineum* L., from all around the Mediterranean, is a popular annual, and *E. pininana* Webb & Berth. from La Palma, a biennial with stems to 4m, will survive a few degrees of frost.

Echium vulgare
flowers, life size
June 22nd

Echium plantagineum
'Blue Bedder' flowers
life size, August 30th

Echium plantagineum
'Blue Bedder'
¹/₂ life size, August 30th

Echium vulgare
¹/₂ life size, June 22nd

Mertensia

Mertensia Roth. (1797), Virginia cowslip, in the family Boraginaceae, contains 45 species around the northern hemisphere.

Description Perennials to 1m. Leaves simple, smooth, often bluish-grey. Flowers blue, usually nodding. Sepals 5, joined at the base. Petals 5, usually rounded, joined into a tube for most of their length, the tube often narrow in the basal half, wider towards the apex; without scales between the stamens, but sometimes with tufts of hairs at the base or folds in the throat. Stamens 5, equal, usually shorter than the tube; filaments usually long; anthers short. Ovary superior, of 4 cells; style 1, exserted from the tube. Pollination is usually by bees. The fruit is of up to 4 separate, smooth or rugose nutlets, sometimes with a winged margin.

Key Recognition Features Usually soft, greyish, fleshy-leaved plants without hairs and with trumpet-shaped, pale blue flowers.

Ecology and Geography In woods and damp meadows and on mountains; on seashores in the north, with 1 species in northern Europe and 24 in North America.

Comment Virginia cowslip, *M. pulmonarioides* Roth (previously *M. virginica* (L.) DC), is an attractive perennial; *M. ciliata* (James) G. Don is smaller flowered but easier to grow. *Mertensia maritima* S.F. Gray and its east Asian equivalent subsp. *asiatica* Takeda syn. *M. simplicissima* G. Don have a rosette of blue-grey basal leaves and trailing flowering stems, and grow on shingly or sandy beaches. The genus is named after German botanist F.K. Mertens (1764–1831).

Mertensia ciliata
just under life size
June 6th

Mertensia maritima
subsp. *asiatica*
²/₃ life size, July 25th

Mertensia maritima subsp. *asiatica*, fruits
and flower parts 2 × life size, July 25th

237

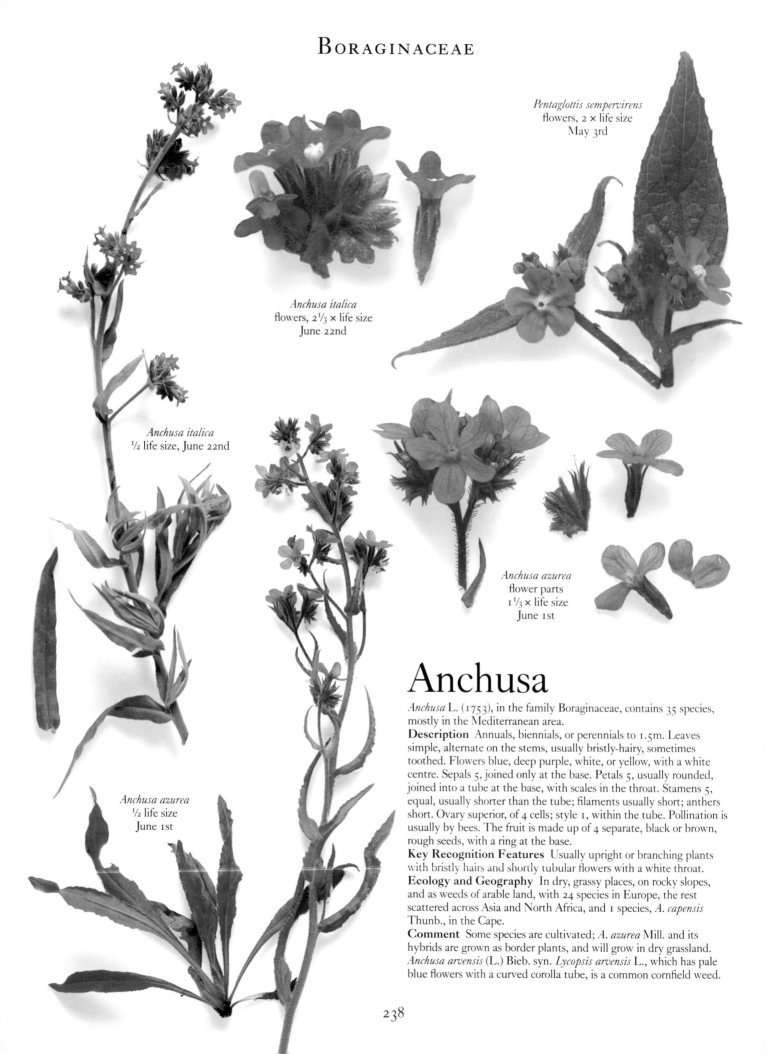

Pentaglottis sempervirens
flowers, 2 × life size
May 3rd

Anchusa italica
flowers, 2⅓ × life size
June 22nd

Anchusa italica
½ life size, June 22nd

Anchusa azurea
flower parts
1⅓ × life size
June 1st

Anchusa azurea
½ life size
June 1st

Anchusa

Anchusa L. (1753), in the family Boraginaceae, contains 35 species, mostly in the Mediterranean area.

Description Annuals, biennials, or perennials to 1.5m. Leaves simple, alternate on the stems, usually bristly-hairy, sometimes toothed. Flowers blue, deep purple, white, or yellow, with a white centre. Sepals 5, joined only at the base. Petals 5, usually rounded, joined into a tube at the base, with scales in the throat. Stamens 5, equal, usually shorter than the tube; filaments usually short; anthers short. Ovary superior, of 4 cells; style 1, within the tube. Pollination is usually by bees. The fruit is made up of 4 separate, black or brown, rough seeds, with a ring at the base.

Key Recognition Features Usually upright or branching plants with bristly hairs and shortly tubular flowers with a white throat.

Ecology and Geography In dry, grassy places, on rocky slopes, and as weeds of arable land, with 24 species in Europe, the rest scattered across Asia and North Africa, and 1 species, *A. capensis* Thunb., in the Cape.

Comment Some species are cultivated; *A. azurea* Mill. and its hybrids are grown as border plants, and will grow in dry grassland. *Anchusa arvensis* (L.) Bieb. syn. *Lycopsis arvensis* L., which has pale blue flowers with a curved corolla tube, is a common cornfield weed.

Pentaglottis

Pentaglottis Tausch (1829), in the family Boraginaceae, contains 1 species, *P. sempervirens* (L.) Tausch ex L.H. Bailey syn. *Anchusa sempervirens* L., in southwestern Europe.

Description A deep-rooted perennial with leafy stems to 1m. Leaves simple, alternate on the stems, bristly-hairy. Flowers blue with a white centre, 8–10mm across. Sepals 5, joined only at the base. Petals 5, rounded, joined into a tube at the base, with hairy scales in the throat. Stamens 5, equal, shorter than the tube; filaments short; anthers short. Ovary superior, of 4 cells; style 1, within the tube. Pollination is usually by bees. The fruit is made up of 4 separate, blackish, rough seeds with a ring and a stalked attachment at the base.

Key Recognition Features A coarse, bristly plant like a large, dark blue forget-me-not (*Myosotis*, see p.243).

Ecology and Geography On hedge banks and in rocky woods: wild in southwestern France, Spain, and Portugal; naturalised in the west of England, Ireland, Belgium, Italy, and California near San Francisco.

Comment Sometimes cultivated, but often naturalised on hedge banks. The name *Pentaglottis* refers to the 5 scales or tongues in the mouth of the corolla tube.

Brunnera

Brunnera Steven (1851), in the family Boraginaceae, contains 3 species in southwestern Asia.

Description A perennial with blackish rhizomes and short, leafy stems to 40cm. Leaves simple, heart-shaped, to 14cm long, sometimes marked or edged with white. Flowers blue with a white centre, 3–7mm across. Sepals 5, joined only at the base. Petals 5, rounded, joined into a tube at the base, with 2-lobed, papillose scales in the throat. Stamens 5, equal, shorter than the tube; filaments short; anthers short. Ovary superior, of 4 cells; style 1, within the tube. Pollination is usually by bees. The fruit is made up of 4 separate, blackish, rough seeds to 4mm long, with a ring at the base.

Key Recognition Features Like a tall forget-me-not (*Myosotis*, see p.243) with stalked, heart-shaped basal leaves and small, dark flowers.

Ecology and Geography In rocky coniferous woods and oakwoods, and on shady banks, from northern Turkey to the Caucasus and southwards to western Iran and Palestine.

Comment *Brunnera macrophylla* (Adam) Johnston is commonly cultivated, especially the forms with silver-blotched or white-margined leaves.

Brunnera macrophylla
flowers, $2\frac{1}{4} \times$ life size
April 10th

Pentaglottis sempervirens
½ life size, May 3rd

Brunnera macrophylla (right)
½ × life size, April 10th

Alkanna

Alkanna Tausch (1824), in the family Boraginaceae, contains around 50 species, mostly in the Mediterranean area.

Description Perennials to 40cm. Leaves simple, alternate on the stems, often bristly-hairy. Flowers blue, white, or yellow. Sepals 5, joined only at the base. Petals 5, usually rounded, joined into a usually dark tube at the base, with hairs in the throat. Stamens 5, equal, shorter than the tube; filaments very short; anthers short. Ovary superior, of 4 cells; style 1, within the tube. Pollination is presumed to be by bees. The fruit is made up of 4 separate, black or brown, rugose, wrinkled, or tuberculate, arched nutlets, with a smooth ring at the base.

Key Recognition Features Usually low, branching plants with bristly hairs and blue or yellow flowers with a dark tube.

Ecology and Geography In dry, grassy places, on rocky slopes, and as weeds of abandoned arable land, with 31 species in Turkey and the rest scattered across Europe, Asia, and North Africa.

Comment Roots of *A. tinctoria* (L.) Tausch were formerly used for a crimson dye. The yellow-flowered *A. orientalis* (L.) Boiss. is sometimes grown as an ornamental, as is the cushion-forming *A. aucheriana* A. DC.

Alkanna tinctoria
just under life size
May 28th

Pulmonaria longifolia hybrid
¹⁄₂ life size, March 20th

left to right: *Pulmonaria officinalis* 'Coral', *Pulmonaria rubra*
'Bowles' Red', and *Pulmonaria rubra* 'Redstart'
²⁄₃ life size, April 10th

Pulmonaria officinalis and
Pulmonaria officinalis 'Alba'
¾ life size, March 8th

Pulmonaria, short styled flower (above): calyx and
style (left), section of corolla (centre)
Long styled flower (below): calyx and style (left)
section of corolla (centre), 1⅔ × life size, March 1st

Pulmonaria mollis
⅔ life size, April 10th

Pulmonaria

Pulmonaria L. (1753), lungwort, in the family Boraginaceae, contains
around 18 species, mostly in the eastern Europe.

Description Perennials with spreading rhizomes and flowering
stems to 40cm. Leaves simple, lanceolate to heart-shaped, often
bristly-hairy, and marked, often heavily, with silver patches. Flowers
blue, purple, red, pink, or white, often opening reddish and becoming
blue, often of 2 kinds, long- or short-styled, in the same species.
Sepals 5, joined for the lower two-thirds. Petals 5, usually rounded,
joined into a narrow tube at the base, with 5 tufts of hairs forming a
ring in the throat. Stamens 5, equal, shorter than the tube; filaments
very short; anthers short. Ovary superior, of 4 cells; style 1, longer or
shorter than the stamens. Pollination is usually by bees. The fruit is
made up of 4 separate, not ridged but hairy nutlets, with a smooth
ring at the base.

Key Recognition Features Usually low, spreading plants with
silver-marked leaves and blue, purple, pink, red, or white flowers.

Ecology and Geography In moist, grassy places and open woods;
14 species in Europe, the rest scattered across western Asia.

Comment Many species and hybrids are cultivated in gardens for
their attractive spring flowers and the handsome, often beautifully
marked leaves, which are formed in summer. The old name lungwort
refers to *Pulmonaria*, so called because the spotted leaves reminded
early herbalists of a diseased lung. The genus *Nonea* Medicus is
similar, but the leaves are always unmarked and the flowers usually
brownish or yellowish, with 5 hairy scales near the mouth of the tube.

Pulmonaria hybrid
½ life size, March 20th

Pulmonaria hybrid
½ life size, March 20th

241

Buglossoides purpurocaerulea
flower parts, 1¾ × life size
June 12th

Buglossoides

Buglossoides Moench. (1794), in the family Boraginaceae, contains around 7 species, mostly in eastern Europe.

Description Annuals or perennials, sometimes shrubby at the base, to 60cm. Leaves simple, often bristly-hairy, alternate. Flowers blue, purplish, or white, often opening purplish and becoming blue. Sepals 5, joined only at the base. Petals 5, usually rounded, joined into a tube at the base, without scales, but sometimes with 5 longitudinal bands of hairs in the throat. Stamens 5, equal, usually shorter than the tube; filaments very short; anthers short. Ovary superior, of 4 cells; style 1, shorter than the stamens. Pollination is usually by bees. The fruit is of usually 4 shining, whitish nutlets, with a smooth ring at the base.

Key Recognition Features The blue or white flowers with bands of hairs in the throat and the 4 shining white nutlets.

Ecology and Geography In dry, grassy places, scrub, rocks, and open pine woods, and as weeds in arable fields in Europe, mainly in the south, and in western Asia.

Comment *Buglossoides purpurocaerulea* (L.) I.M. Johnston is the only species commonly cultivated. It was first described in *Lithospermum* L., but that genus differs in having whitish flowers with scale-like flaps in the throat. Some authorities keep *B. purpurocaerulea* and other perennials in *Lithospermum*, and restrict *Buglossoides* to the weedy annual species.

Buglossoides purpurocaerulea
½ life size, June 12th

Lithodora diffusa
'Heavenly Blue' (right)
just under life size
April 10th

Lithodora diffusa 'Heavenly Blue'
1¼ × life size, April 10th

Myosotis scorpioides
²⁄₃ life size, June 10th

Myosotis

Myosotis L. (1753), forget-me-not, in the family Boraginaceae, contains around 100 species, mostly in temperate regions and on mountains in the tropics.

Description Annuals, biennials, or perennials to 100cm. Leaves simple, often hairy, alternate. Flowers blue, yellow, or white, often opening yellow and becoming blue, sometimes turning pink if the plant is stressed. Sepals 5, joined at the base. Petals 5, usually rounded, joined into a tube at the base, with 5 white or yellow scales in the throat. Stamens 5, equal, shorter than the tube, with an appendage; filaments very short; anthers short. Ovary superior, of 4 cells; style 1, shorter than the stamens. Pollination is usually by bees. The fruit is made up of usually 4 small, shining, ovate, black nutlets.

Key Recognition Features The small, blue or white flowers with scales in the throat, and 4 small, shining black nutlets.

Ecology and Geography In dry, grassy places, scrub, mountain rocks, sand dunes, marshes, and shallow water; 41 species in Europe, 23 in Turkey, 33 in New Zealand, and the rest scattered around the world, with few in Africa and America.

Comment The most commonly cultivated species, *M. sylvatica* Hoffm., is a biennial or short-lived perennial, flowering in spring, and much used for bedding; several more compact cultivars have been developed. Water forget-me-not, *M. scorpioides* L., is a creeping perennial that flowers throughout the summer and can spread to form large patches in damp ground. The New Zealand species are unusual in that most have white or yellow flowers, and half the species have exserted stamens.

Myosotis sylvatica
2¼ × life size
April 3rd

Myosotis sylvatica
²⁄₃ life size, April 3rd

Lithodora

Lithodora Griseb. (1846), in the family Boraginaceae, contains around 7 species, mostly in eastern Europe.

Description Perennials, sometimes shrubby at the base, to 40cm or more if supported by shrubs. Leaves small, simple, often bristly-hairy, alternate. Flowers blue, purplish, or white, often opening pinkish and becoming blue. Sepals 5, joined only at the base. Petals 5, usually rounded, joined into a tube at the base, without scales, but sometimes with scattered hairs. Stamens 5, equal, usually shorter than the tube; filaments very short; anthers short. Ovary superior, of 4 cells; style 1, shorter than the stamens. Pollination is usually by bees. The fruit is of usually 1 smooth, whitish nutlet, with a smooth ring at the base.

Key Recognition Features Usually low, spreading, small-leaved, and shrubby perennials with bright or pale blue flowers and smooth, white, solitary seeds.

Ecology and Geography In grassy places, among rocks, and in open pine woods, with 7 species in Europe, mainly in the west, from northwestern France southwards.

Comment A few species are cultivated for their attractive flowers, notably *L. diffusa* 'Heavenly Blue' and the striped-flowered 'Star'. All were first described in the genus *Lithospermum* L., but that genus differs in having whitish flowers with scale-like flaps in the throat and 4 shining white nutlets.

Trigonotis

Trigonotis Steven (1851), in the family Boraginaceae, contains around 50 species, mostly in temperate Asia

Description Annuals or perennials to 1m. Leaves simple, often hairy, alternate or opposite. Flowers blue. Sepals 5, joined at the base. Petals 5, usually rounded, joined into a tube at the base, with 5 white, papillose or hairy scales in the throat. Stamens 5, equal, usually shorter than the tube; filaments very short; anthers short. Ovary superior, of 4 cells; style 1, shorter than the stamens. Pollination is presumed to be by bees. The fruit is made up of usually 4 very small, shining black, sharply 3-angled nutlets.

Key Recognition Features The small, blue or white flowers with scales in the throat, and 4 very small, 3-angled, shining black nutlets.

Ecology and Geography In open, sandy ground, among mountain rocks, by streams, and in woods, with 1 species in Europe, 1 in New Guinea, and the rest mostly in the Himalayas and eastwards to Japan.

Comment These small, *Myosotis*-like plants (see p.243) are seldom cultivated; some, such as *T. rotundifolia* (Wall. ex Benth.) Benth. ex C.B. Clarke, are cushion-forming alpines. *Trigonotis omeiensis* Matsuda from western China has attractive, silvery leaves, like a small, rounded *Pulmonaria* (see pp.240–41).

Omphalodes

Omphalodes Miller (1768), in the family Boraginaceae, contains around 30 species, mostly in Europe and Asia.

Description Annuals, biennials, or perennials to 40cm. Leaves simple, often hairy, the basal leaves heart-shaped to lanceolate or spathulate, alternate. Flowers blue or white, to 1cm across. Sepals 5, joined only at the base. Petals 5, usually rounded, joined into a short tube at the base, with 5 swollen or V-shaped flaps almost blocking the throat. Stamens 5, equal, shorter than the tube; filaments very short; anthers short. Ovary superior, of 4 cells; style 1, shorter than the stamens. Pollination is presumed to be by bees. The fruit is made up of usually 4 nutlets, flattened, smooth or hairy, winged, the wing erect or curved in towards the middle.

Key Recognition Features The usually heart-shaped basal leaves, flat, blue or white flowers with flaps in the throat, and 4 large, incurved nutlets.

Ecology and Geography In open, sandy ground, among rocks in woods, and on shady, moist cliffs and the roofs of caves, with 8 species in Europe, the rest scattered across Asia to the Himalayas, China, and Japan.

Comment A few species are commonly cultivated, notably the large-flowered *O. cappadocica* (Willd.) DC, from woods in northern Turkey, and its cultivar 'Starry Eyes', and the grey-leaved, white-flowered annual *O. linifolia* (L.) Moench, from dry hills in southwestern Europe. The name *Omphalodes* refers to the navel-like nutlets.

Trigonotis omeiensis
just under life size, May 4th

Trigonotis omeiensis
leaves, ²⁄₃ life size
March 28th

Trigonotis omeiensis
flowers, 3 × life size
May 4th

Omphalodes verna
flower parts, 1 ½ × life size
March 20th

Omphalodes verna
½ life size
March 20th

Cynoglossum

Cynoglossum L. (1753), hound's tongue, in the family Boraginaceae, contains around 75 species, mostly in Europe and Asia.

Description Annuals, biennials, or usually perennials to 60cm. Leaves simple, often hairy, the basal leaves broadly lanceolate, alternate. Flowers blue, purple, reddish, or crimson, to 8mm across. Sepals 5, joined only at the base. Petals 5, usually rounded, joined into a short tube at the base, with 5 scales blocking the throat. Stamens 5, equal, shorter than the tube; filaments very short; anthers short. Ovary superior, of 4 cells; style 1, shorter than the stamens. Pollination is by bees, usually bumblebees in *C. officinale* L.. The fruit is made up of 4 flattened nutlets covered with hooked spines to form very sticky burrs.

Key Recognition Features The strongly veined stem leaves, usually without stalks, the flat, blue or reddish flowers with flaps in the throat, and the 4 large nutlets, which form very effective burrs.

Ecology and Geography In open, chalky ground, on rocky hills, in open woods, and in waste places, with 11 species in Europe, the rest scattered across Asia to the Himalayas, China, and Japan; a few in the mountains of East Africa, 2 in the Cape.

Comment The most commonly cultivated species have blue, forget-me-not like flowers (*Myosotis,* see p.243). The common hound's tongue, *C. officinale,* is usually found in chalky places, often in areas disturbed by rabbits.

Cynoglossum amabile
flowers and fruits, 2¼ × life size
September 24th

Cynoglossum amabile
½ life size, August 1st

*Omphalodes
cappadocica*
'Starry Eyes'
(above)
1⅓ × life size
April 7th

*Omphalodes
linifolia*
nutlets
¾ life size
July 23rd

*Cynoglossum
cheirifolium*
nutlets (left)
1½ × life size
June 22nd

Myosotidium

Myosotidium Hook. (1859), the Chatham Island forget-me-not, in the family Boraginaceae, consists of 1 species, *M. hortensia* (Decne) Baill., in New Zealand.

Description Large perennial to 1m, with thick, blackish rhizomes. Basal leaves simple, with parallel veins. Flowers bright blue or white, to 8mm across. Sepals 5, joined only at the base. Petals 5, usually rounded, joined into a short tube at the base, with 5 swellings in the throat. Stamens 5, equal, shorter than the tube; filaments very short; anthers short. Ovary superior, of 4 cells; style 1, shorter than the stamens. Pollination is presumed to be by bees. The fruit is made up of 4 corky, flattened nutlets with a toothed wing.

Key Recognition Features The strongly parallel-veined and shining basal leaves, and large heads of blue or rarely white flowers.

Ecology and Geography On rocky and sandy sea shores and banks of cockle shells on Chatham Island, east of New Zealand.

Comment This unusual plant is easily cultivated in cool places in sandy, peaty soil with ample fertiliser, and does well in coastal gardens; it needs protection from frost and snails. It is closely related to *Cynoglossum* (see p.245). These giant herbaceous perennials are a feature of the New Zealand offshore islands, particularly the Aukland and Campbell Islands. They are vulnerable to grazing by introduced sheep and goats.

Hackelia

Hackelia Opiz (1838), stickseed, in the family Boraginaceae, contains around 45 species, mostly in Asia and North America.

Description Perennials or biennials to 80cm, with leafy flowering stems. Leaves simple, often hairy. Flowers blue, pink, or white, to 2cm across. Sepals 5, joined only at the base, spreading or reflexed in fruit. Petals 5, usually rounded, joined into a short tube at the base, with 5 white or yellow swellings the throat. Stamens 5, equal, shorter than the tube; filaments very short; anthers short. Ovary superior, of 4 cells; style 1, shorter than the stamens. Pollination is by bees. The fruit is of 4 nutlets, flattened, covered with hooked spines to form very sticky burrs.

Key Recognition Features Very similar to *Cynoglossum* (see p.245), but with a more leafy inflorescence and with the nutlets attached by their middle, not all along their length.

Ecology and Geography Open woods, grassy places, and sometimes rock crevices; 13 species in California, the rest scattered across Central and South America, and Asia from the Himalayas to China and Japan.

Comment The species commonly cultivated are leafy perennials with forget-me-not like flowers (*Myosotis*, see p.243); *H. uncinata* (Royle ex Benth.) C. Fisher is native of the Himalayas from Pakistan to southwestern China.

Myosotidium hortensia
flower parts (below)
1¾ × life size, May 10th

Myosotidium hortensia
½ life size, May 10th

Hackelia uncinata
2 × life size, May 17th

Hackelia uncinata
²/₃ life size, May 17th

Lindelofia

Lindelofia Lehm. (1850), in the family Boraginaceae, contains around 11 species, mostly in Asia.

Description Perennials to 90cm. Leaves simple, often hairy, the basal broadly lanceolate, alternate. Flowers blue, purple, or crimson, to 15mm across. Sepals 5, joined only at the base. Petals 5, usually rounded, joined into a long tube at the base, with the 5 throat scales forming a cone. Stamens 5, equal, shorter than the tube; filaments very short; anthers short. Ovary superior, of 4 cells; style 1, often exserted from the flower. Pollination is by bees. The fruit is made up of 4 nutlets, flattened, covered with hooked spines to form very sticky burrs.

Key Recognition Features Very similar to *Cynoglossum* (see p.245), but with a long-tubed flower and the throat scales forming a cone.

Ecology and Geography On open, stony and rocky hills. Mostly in the Himalayas, central Asia, and China.

Comment One species, *L. longiflora* (Benth.) Baillon, native of the Himalayas from Pakistan to western Nepal, is sometimes cultivated.

*Lindelofia
longiflora*
flower parts
2¼ × life size
June 6th

Lindelofia longiflora
²/₃ life size, June 6th

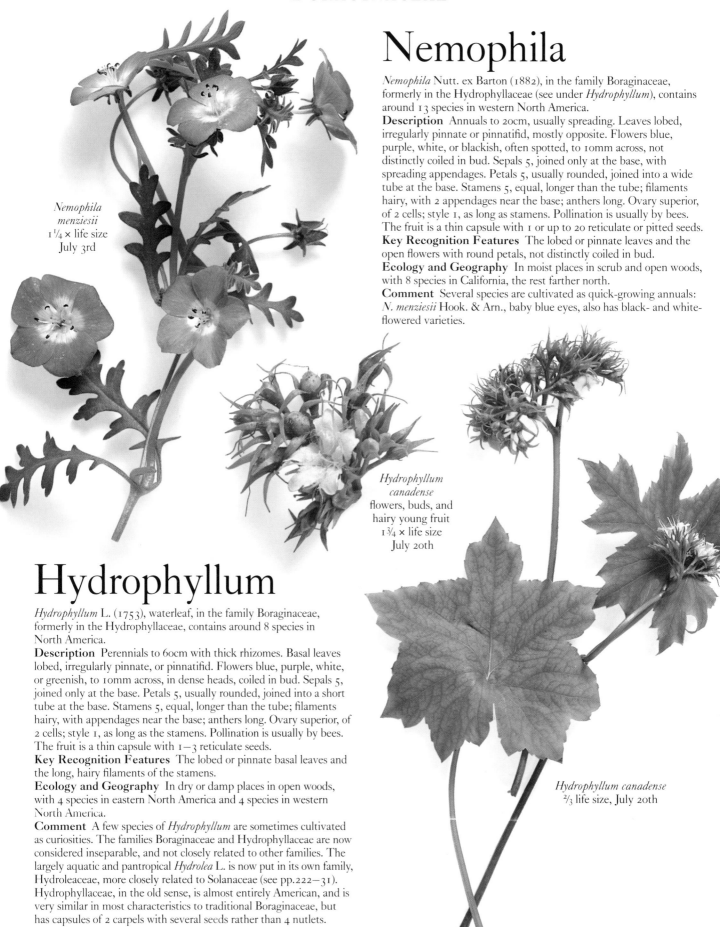

Nemophila

Nemophila Nutt. ex Barton (1882), in the family Boraginaceae, formerly in the Hydrophyllaceae (see under *Hydrophyllum*), contains around 13 species in western North America.

Description Annuals to 20cm, usually spreading. Leaves lobed, irregularly pinnate or pinnatifid, mostly opposite. Flowers blue, purple, white, or blackish, often spotted, to 10mm across, not distinctly coiled in bud. Sepals 5, joined only at the base, with spreading appendages. Petals 5, usually rounded, joined into a wide tube at the base. Stamens 5, equal, longer than the tube; filaments hairy, with 2 appendages near the base; anthers long. Ovary superior, of 2 cells; style 1, as long as stamens. Pollination is usually by bees. The fruit is a thin capsule with 1 or up to 20 reticulate or pitted seeds.

Key Recognition Features The lobed or pinnate leaves and the open flowers with round petals, not distinctly coiled in bud.

Ecology and Geography In moist places in scrub and open woods, with 8 species in California, the rest farther north.

Comment Several species are cultivated as quick-growing annuals: *N. menziesii* Hook. & Arn., baby blue eyes, also has black- and white-flowered varieties.

Nemophila menziesii
1¼ × life size
July 3rd

Hydrophyllum canadense
flowers, buds, and hairy young fruit
1¾ × life size
July 20th

Hydrophyllum

Hydrophyllum L. (1753), waterleaf, in the family Boraginaceae, formerly in the Hydrophyllaceae, contains around 8 species in North America.

Description Perennials to 60cm with thick rhizomes. Basal leaves lobed, irregularly pinnate, or pinnatifid. Flowers blue, purple, white, or greenish, to 10mm across, in dense heads, coiled in bud. Sepals 5, joined only at the base. Petals 5, usually rounded, joined into a short tube at the base. Stamens 5, equal, longer than the tube; filaments hairy, with appendages near the base; anthers long. Ovary superior, of 2 cells; style 1, as long as the stamens. Pollination is usually by bees. The fruit is a thin capsule with 1−3 reticulate seeds.

Key Recognition Features The lobed or pinnate basal leaves and the long, hairy filaments of the stamens.

Ecology and Geography In dry or damp places in open woods, with 4 species in eastern North America and 4 species in western North America.

Comment A few species of *Hydrophyllum* are sometimes cultivated as curiosities. The families Boraginaceae and Hydrophyllaceae are now considered inseparable, and not closely related to other families. The largely aquatic and pantropical *Hydrolea* L. is now put in its own family, Hydroleaceae, more closely related to Solanaceae (see pp.222−31). Hydrophyllaceae, in the old sense, is almost entirely American, and is very similar in most characteristics to traditional Boraginaceae, but has capsules of 2 carpels with several seeds rather than 4 nutlets.

Hydrophyllum canadense
⅔ life size, July 20th

Nemophila menziesii
'Penny Black', flowers
2 × life size, June 28th

Nemophila menziesii
'Penny Black', life size
June 28th

Phacelia campanularia
just over life size
July 9th

Phacelia 'Lavender Lass'
life size, July 9th

Phacelia

Phacelia Juss. (1789), in the family Boraginaceae, formerly in the Hydrophyllaceae (see under Hydrophyllum), contains around 200 species in North and South America.

Description Annuals, biennials, or perennials to 80cm, often low and spreading. Leaves simple, lobed, irregularly pinnate, or pinnatifid, mostly alternate. Flowers blue, purple to white, or yellow, to 10mm across, distinctly coiled in bud. Sepals 5, joined only at the base, with spreading appendages. Petals 5, usually rounded, joined into a narrow tube or almost flat. Stamens 5, equal, longer than the tube; filaments with 2 appendages near the base, longer or shorter than the tube. Ovary superior, of 2 cells; style 1, as long as the stamens. Pollination is by bees or flies. The fruit is a thin capsule with many small seeds.

Key Recognition Features The usually hairy and lobed or pinnate leaves and the flowers distinctly coiled in bud, usually with long stamens. The flowers vary from small and tubular to almost flat, with a wide speckled zone in the middle.

Ecology and Geography In deserts, dry or moist places in scrub, and open woods, with around 90 species in California, and the rest scattered throughout North and South America.

Comment Several species are grown as ornamental annuals; others, especially *P. tanacetifolia* Benth., are grown as bee fodder or as a fast-growing green manure, and have become naturalised in Europe.

Plantago

Plantago L. (1753), plantain, in the family Plantaginaceae, contains around 270 species worldwide.

Description Small shrubs, perennials, or annuals to 50cm. Leaves in a basal rosette or opposite, simple to pinnate. Flowers greenish, very small, usually in spikes, each flower subtended by a thin, transparent bract. Sepals 4, joined at the base. Petals 4, thin and transparent, joined at the base. Stamens 4, the anthers on long filaments. Ovary superior, 2- or 4-celled, with few ovules; style 1, long and slender, papillose. Pollination is usually by wind, sometimes by bees. The fruit is a capsule, opening by splitting all round to leave a cap; the seeds are relatively large, mucilaginous when wetted.

Key Recognition Features The spikes of very small flowers with thin, transparent petals and long, conspicuous stamens.

Ecology and Geography In waste places, salt marshes, sand dunes, and meadows; 35 species in Europe, the rest throughout the world, but with another concentration of 24 species in Australia and 9 native species in New Zealand.

Comment The Plantaginaceae traditionally contained 3 genera: *Plantago*, *Bougueria* Decne, with 1 species in the Andes, and *Litorella* Bergius, with 1 semi-aquatic species, *L. uniflora* (L.) Aschs. However, DNA studies show that the Plantaginaceae is very close to *Digitalis* and many other genera traditionally included in the Scrophulariaceae, as well as to the isolated aquatic genera *Callitriche* L., water starwort, and *Hippuris* L., mare's tail. Traditional Scrophulariaceae has been shown to be very diverse, with some genera more closely allied to Bignoniaceae or Labiatae. Here we have arranged the genera as indicated by DNA studies, but retained the traditional family names until more detailed studies have been completed and a fuller account of this group is available. *Plantago* is a common genus in open habitats, and adapted for wind pollination; large proportions of *Plantago* pollen in ancient peat deposits indicate a treeless environment. Seeds of some species, which have a bulky, mucilaginous coating when wet, are used medicinally as a laxative.

Plantago coronopus
just under life size, May 20th

Plantago major
'Rubrifolia'
flower spike
¾ life size
August 9th

Plantago major
'Rubrifolia'
½ life size
May 25th

Digitalis parviflora
flower parts, 2 × life size, July 2nd

Digitalis

Digitalis L. (1753), foxglove, in the family Scrophulariaceae, contains around 19 species, mainly in southern Europe and western Asia.

Description Perennials or biennials to 2m. Leaves alternate, simple. Flowers pinkish, white, brown, reddish-orange, or yellow, usually tubular, in long spikes. Sepals 5, joined only at the base. Petals 5, usually joined for most of their length into a tube, the lowest forming a lip. Stamens 4, in 2 pairs, attached to the base of the corolla tube. Ovary superior, 2-celled, with numerous ovules; style 1, with a forked stigma. Pollination is usually by bumblebees. The fruit is a capsule, splitting into 2, with numerous small seeds.

Key Recognition Features The tubular flowers in a long spike.

Ecology and Geography In open woods, scrub, and rock crevices, with 12 species in Europe, particularly in Spain and Portugal, and another concentration in eastern Europe and northern Turkey.

Comment Most species are very poisonous, containing digitalis, a powerful heart stimulant used medicinally since the late 18th century, but its mechanism only understood since the 1930s. The brown-and-white-flowered *D. lanata* L. is usually grown for the drug.

Digitalis obscura
flower parts
1 ½ × life size
June 18th

Digitalis purpurea
unripe capsule (top)
and flower parts
life size, July 3rd

Digitalis parviflora
½ life size
July 2nd

Digitalis purpurea
½ life size
July 3rd

Digitalis obscura
½ life size, June 18th

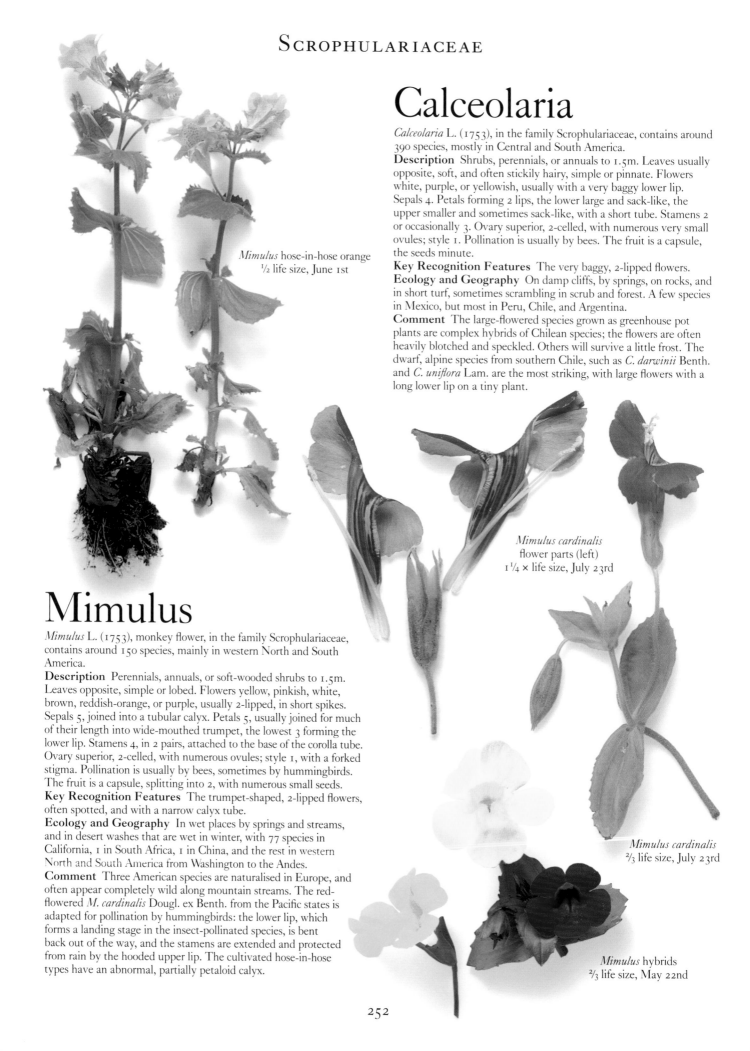

Calceolaria

Calceolaria L. (1753), in the family Scrophulariaceae, contains around 390 species, mostly in Central and South America.

Description Shrubs, perennials, or annuals to 1.5m. Leaves usually opposite, soft, and often stickily hairy, simple or pinnate. Flowers white, purple, or yellowish, usually with a very baggy lower lip. Sepals 4. Petals forming 2 lips, the lower large and sack-like, the upper smaller and sometimes sack-like, with a short tube. Stamens 2 or occasionally 3. Ovary superior, 2-celled, with numerous very small ovules; style 1. Pollination is usually by bees. The fruit is a capsule, the seeds minute.

Key Recognition Features The very baggy, 2-lipped flowers.

Ecology and Geography On damp cliffs, by springs, on rocks, and in short turf, sometimes scrambling in scrub and forest. A few species in Mexico, but most in Peru, Chile, and Argentina.

Comment The large-flowered species grown as greenhouse pot plants are complex hybrids of Chilean species; the flowers are often heavily blotched and speckled. Others will survive a little frost. The dwarf, alpine species from southern Chile, such as *C. darwinii* Benth. and *C. uniflora* Lam. are the most striking, with large flowers with a long lower lip on a tiny plant.

Mimulus hose-in-hose orange
½ life size, June 1st

Mimulus cardinalis
flower parts (left)
1¼ × life size, July 23rd

Mimulus

Mimulus L. (1753), monkey flower, in the family Scrophulariaceae, contains around 150 species, mainly in western North and South America.

Description Perennials, annuals, or soft-wooded shrubs to 1.5m. Leaves opposite, simple or lobed. Flowers yellow, pinkish, white, brown, reddish-orange, or purple, usually 2-lipped, in short spikes. Sepals 5, joined into a tubular calyx. Petals 5, usually joined for much of their length into wide-mouthed trumpet, the lowest 3 forming the lower lip. Stamens 4, in 2 pairs, attached to the base of the corolla tube. Ovary superior, 2-celled, with numerous ovules; style 1, with a forked stigma. Pollination is usually by bees, sometimes by hummingbirds. The fruit is a capsule, splitting into 2, with numerous small seeds.

Key Recognition Features The trumpet-shaped, 2-lipped flowers, often spotted, and with a narrow calyx tube.

Ecology and Geography In wet places by springs and streams, and in desert washes that are wet in winter, with 77 species in California, 1 in South Africa, 1 in China, and the rest in western North and South America from Washington to the Andes.

Comment Three American species are naturalised in Europe, and often appear completely wild along mountain streams. The red-flowered *M. cardinalis* Dougl. ex Benth. from the Pacific states is adapted for pollination by hummingbirds: the lower lip, which forms a landing stage in the insect-pollinated species, is bent back out of the way, and the stamens are extended and protected from rain by the hooded upper lip. The cultivated hose-in-hose types have an abnormal, partially petaloid calyx.

Mimulus cardinalis
⅔ life size, July 23rd

Mimulus hybrids
⅔ life size, May 22nd

Calceolaria crenata, flower parts
1 ⅓ × life size, July 20th

Calceolaria crenata
½ life size, July 20th

Antirrhinum majus
ripe capsules and seeds
2 × life size, March 2nd

Antirrhinum cultivars
½ life size, June 27th

Antirrhinum cultivar
flower parts, 1 ⅔ × life size
June 27th

Antirrhinum

Antirrhinum L. (1753), snapdragon, in the family Scrophulariaceae, contains around 20 species, mostly in the Mediterranean area.

Description Perennials or annuals to 50cm, sometimes trailing and occasionally shrubby at the base. Leaves simple, usually opposite below, alternate above. Flowers red, white, purple, or yellowish, usually with 2 lips. Sepals 5, joined only at the base. Petals forming a wide tube, the lower lip large, with hairy swellings in the throat and a short pouch below, the upper slightly smaller and folded back. Stamens 4, in 2 pairs. Ovary superior, 2-celled, with numerous very small ovules; style 1. Pollination is mainly by bumblebees. The fruit is a capsule with 2 unequal parts, the longer with 1 pore, the shorter, wider part with 2 pores. Seeds many, very small.

Key Recognition Features The 2-lipped flowers, with large swellings blocking the throat.

Ecology and Geography On dry cliffs, in rocky areas, and on old walls, with 17 species and several subspecies in Europe, nearly all in Spain and Portugal, others in North Africa.

Comment Antirrhinums, or snapdragons, are very popular biennials for bedding. The natural shape of the flowers is often lost in modern cultivars, such as 'Madame Butterfly', which are generally shorter-lived than older varieties. The creeping *Asarina procumbens* Mill. with yellow flowers is very close to *Antirrhinum,* but has toothed or lobed, heart-shaped leaves, and a capsule with 2 equal parts, each with 1 pore.

Collinsia

Collinsia Nutt. (1817), in the family Scrophulariaceae, contains around 20 species, mostly in western North America.

Description Annuals to 50cm. Leaves opposite, simple or with blunt teeth. Flowers white and purple, purplish-blue, or yellowish, usually 2-lipped, in whorls or solitary in the upper leaf axils. Sepals 5. Petals 5, usually joined for much of their length into wide-mouthed trumpet, the lowest 3 forming the lower lip, with a short, baggy spur on the upper side. Stamens 4, in 2 pairs, attached to the inside of the corolla tube, the filaments hairy, the anthers enclosed in the keeled middle lobe of the lower lip. Ovary superior, 2-celled, with rather few ovules; style 1, with a forked stigma. Pollination is usually by bees. The fruit is a capsule; seeds flattened and winged.

Key Recognition Features The bicoloured, 2-lipped flowers, often in whorls, the baggy, short spur and the stamens enfolded in a keel.

Ecology and Geography In dry, often shady places, with 16 of the species in California and 2 in the eastern states.

Comment The most commonly cultivated species, *C. heterophylla* Buist ex Graham, is often called Chinese houses because of its tiered whorls of flowers. The arrangement of the stamens and style held within the keel-like lower petal imitates the pea-flowers (Leguminosae, see pp.124–37). The genus is named after Zacchaeus Collins (1764–1831), a botanist in Philadelphia.

Linaria

Linaria L. (1753), toadflax, in the family Scrophulariaceae, contains around 150 species, mostly in Europe and Asia.

Description Perennials or annuals to 1.3m, sometimes trailing. Leaves simple, usually whorled below, alternate above. Flowers red, white, purple, brown, black, or yellow, usually with a long, slender spur and 2 lips. Sepals 5, usually unequal, joined only at the base. Petals forming a short tube with 2 lips, the lower large, with hairy swellings in the throat, the upper slightly smaller and upright. Stamens 4, in 2 pairs. Ovary superior, 2-celled, with numerous very small ovules; style 1. Pollination is mainly by bees. The fruit is a capsule, with 2 parts, opening by several pores; seeds several, often flat and winged.

Key Recognition Features The 2-lipped flowers, with large swellings blocking the throat, and a slender spur. The flowers are always smaller than *Antirrhinum* (see p.253).

Ecology and Geography On cliffs and stony slopes, in rocky areas, and in grassland and open woods: 70 species and several subspecies in Europe, mostly around the Mediterranean, and particularly in Spain and Portugal; 1 species, *L. canadensis* (L.) Dum.-Cours., with bluish-purple flowers, is widespread in North America.

Comment Several species and hybrids are cultivated. So-called peloric forms, with regular flowers and 5 spurs, are occasionally found in the wild.

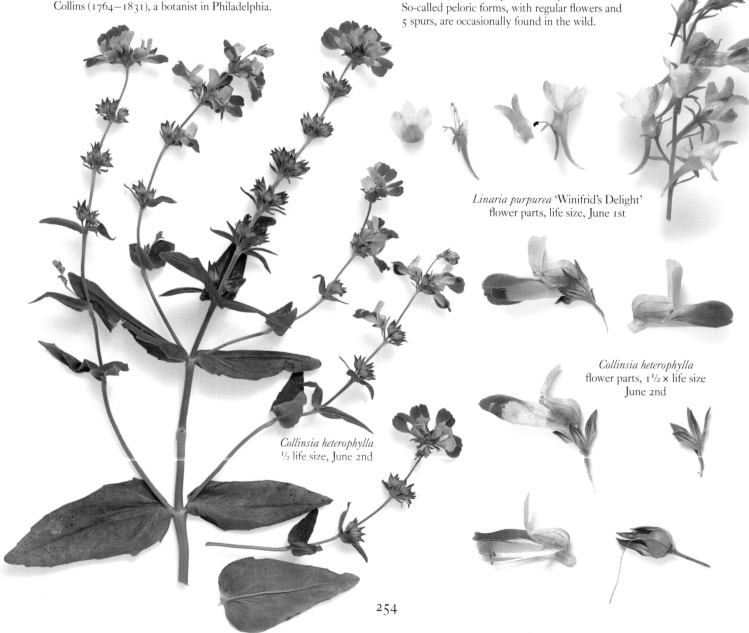

Linaria purpurea 'Winifrid's Delight'
flower parts, life size, June 1st

Collinsia heterophylla
flower parts, 1½ × life size
June 2nd

Collinsia heterophylla
½ life size, June 2nd

Maurandya

Maurandya Ortega (1797), in the family Scrophulariaceae, contains 2 or 3 species in western North America and Central America.

Description Perennials with climbing stems to 3m, sometimes shrubby at the base, with twining leaf stalks. Leaves toothed or lobed, often triangular or hastate. Flowers red, white, purple, or yellowish, with 2 lips. Sepals 5, joined to form a glandular calyx. Petals forming a wide tube, the lower lip large, with ridges in the throat, the upper slightly smaller and upright. Stamens 4, in 2 pairs. Ovary superior, 2-celled, with numerous small ovules; style 1. Pollination is presumed to be by bumblebees. The fruit is a capsule, splitting irregularly near the apex.

Key Recognition Features The climbing stems, triangular leaves, and 2-lipped flowers, often with a prickly, glandular calyx.

Ecology and Geography On dry cliffs and in rocky scrub from southern California to Mexico.

Comment The genus is named after Mme Catharina Pancratia Maurandy, a student of botany at Carthagena, c.1797. Some, such as the Mexican *M. barclayana* Lindl., are grown as ornamentals and will survive a few degrees of frost if kept dry in winter. *Lophospermum* D. Don is similar, but generally has thicker stems and flowers with a leafy calyx. In *Rhodochiton* Zucc. ex Otto & Dietr. the flowers hang down; the calyx is enlarged and bell-shaped, the corolla blackish-purple with a long, straight tube.

Maurandya barclayana
½ life size
September 24th

Linaria triornithophora
½ life size, August 10th

Linaria × *dominii*
'Yuppie Surprise'
flower parts, 1½ × life size
June 7th

Maurandya barclayana
flower parts, 1⅓ × life size
September 24th

Penstemon

Penstemon Schmid. (1762), beardtongue, in the Scrophulariaceae, contains around 250 species, mainly in western North America.

Description Perennials or shrubs to 1.5m. Leaves opposite, rarely whorled or the upper alternate, simple. Flowers pinkish, white, blue, purple, or red, usually tubular, in short or long spikes or branching heads. Sepals 5, joined only at the base. Petals 5, usually joined for most of their length into a tube, the lowest 3 forming a lip. Stamens 4 fertile, in 2 pairs, attached to the base of the corolla tube, a fifth reduced to a long sterile filament, often hairy. Ovary superior, 2-celled, with numerous ovules; style 1, with a simple stigma. Pollination is by bumblebees or hummingbirds. The fruit is a capsule, splitting into 2, with numerous small seeds.

Key Recognition Features The tubular flowers, hairy sterile filament, and mostly opposite leaves.

Ecology and Geography In open woods, scrub, and rocky places, often in semi-desert; also in dry or damp grassy places. There are 58 species in California; the rest are scattered throughout North America, with 1 species, *P. frutescens* Lamb, in eastern Asia.

Comment Many species are cultivated for their flowers, often produced for a long time into late summer. Most are intolerant of frost combined with wet. *Chelone* L., the turtle-head, is close to *Penstemon*, but has flowers in tight heads at the top of the stem and the sterile stamen shorter than the rest; there are around 5 species, all tall, herbaceous perennials from eastern North America.

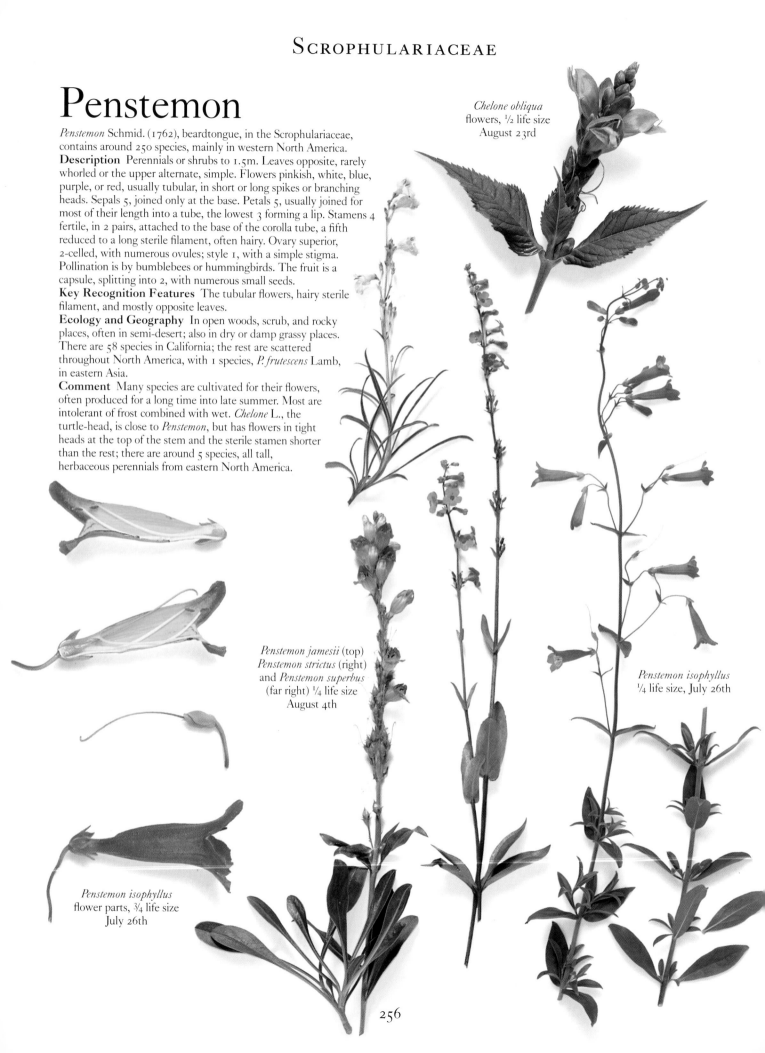

Chelone obliqua
flowers, ½ life size
August 23rd

Penstemon jamesii (top)
Penstemon strictus (right)
and *Penstemon superbus*
(far right) ¼ life size
August 4th

Penstemon isophyllus
¼ life size, July 26th

Penstemon isophyllus
flower parts, ¾ life size
July 26th

256

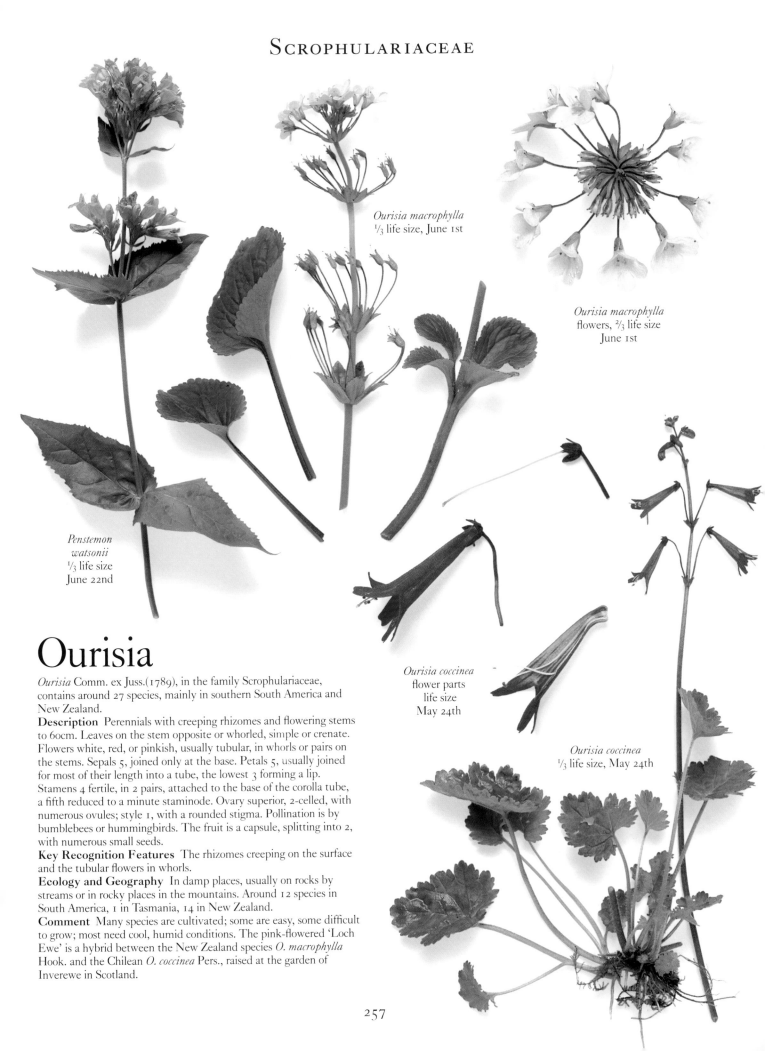

Ourisia macrophylla
$^{1}/_{3}$ life size, June 1st

Ourisia macrophylla
flowers, $^{2}/_{3}$ life size
June 1st

*Penstemon
watsonii*
$^{1}/_{3}$ life size
June 22nd

Ourisia coccinea
flower parts
life size
May 24th

Ourisia coccinea
$^{1}/_{3}$ life size, May 24th

Ourisia

Ourisia Comm. ex Juss.(1789), in the family Scrophulariaceae, contains around 27 species, mainly in southern South America and New Zealand.

Description Perennials with creeping rhizomes and flowering stems to 60cm. Leaves on the stem opposite or whorled, simple or crenate. Flowers white, red, or pinkish, usually tubular, in whorls or pairs on the stems. Sepals 5, joined only at the base. Petals 5, usually joined for most of their length into a tube, the lowest 3 forming a lip. Stamens 4 fertile, in 2 pairs, attached to the base of the corolla tube, a fifth reduced to a minute staminode. Ovary superior, 2-celled, with numerous ovules; style 1, with a rounded stigma. Pollination is by bumblebees or hummingbirds. The fruit is a capsule, splitting into 2, with numerous small seeds.

Key Recognition Features The rhizomes creeping on the surface and the tubular flowers in whorls.

Ecology and Geography In damp places, usually on rocks by streams or in rocky places in the mountains. Around 12 species in South America, 1 in Tasmania, 14 in New Zealand.

Comment Many species are cultivated; some are easy, some difficult to grow; most need cool, humid conditions. The pink-flowered 'Loch Ewe' is a hybrid between the New Zealand species *O. macrophylla* Hook. and the Chilean *O. coccinea* Pers., raised at the garden of Inverewe in Scotland.

Diascia

Diascia Link & Otto (1820), in the family Scrophulariaceae, contains around 57 species in South Africa.

Description Perennials or annuals to 30cm. Leaves opposite, simple or toothed. Flowers pink, pinkish-orange, red, or purple, rarely white, in slender spikes. Sepals 5, joined only at the base. Petals 5, joined at the base into a short tube, the lowest 3 forming the lower lip, with 2 dark spurs on the lateral petals; the upper 2 petals with a yellow translucent "window" between them. Stamens 4, in 2 pairs, 1 pair sometimes sterile; pollen often green. Ovary superior, 2-celled, with 2 to many ovules; style 1, with a short stigma. Pollination is usually by small bees. The fruit is a capsule, splitting into 2, with seeds often curved, winged, or ribbed.

Key Recognition Features The opposite leaves and flat, usually pinkish flowers with 2 dark spurs.

Ecology and Geography In wet places, by springs and streams, and in dry, sandy places that are wet in winter. Around 20 mainly perennial species in the summer-rainfall area of northeastern South Africa, the rest, mainly annual species, in winter-rainfall areas of the Cape and northwards to Namibia.

Comment Several perennial species and many hybrids are cultivated for their long summer flowering season. The pollination of *Diascia* is unusual; the species are pollinated by oil-collecting bees, which feed on the black glands that are concentrated within the spurs and in patches on the flower; pollination has seldom been observed in South Africa, and was first described from South America, in various species of *Angelonia* and *Calceolaria* (see p.252). The fertile pollen is green and inconspicuous, and some species produce a little yellow pollen in addition as an attractant. It is noticeable that seed is seldom set in cultivation, and the garden hybrids are produced by careful hand-pollination.

Angelonia

Angelonia Humb. & Bonpl. (1809), in the family Scrophulariaceae, contains around 25 species in Central and South America.

Description Perennials or subshrubs to 1m. Leaves opposite or the upper alternate, simple or toothed. Flowers blue to purplish-pink, often spotted, in slender spikes. Sepals 5, joined only at the base. Petals 5, joined at the base into a very short tube, the lowest 3 forming the lower lip, with a short sac behind. Stamens 4, in 2 pairs. Ovary superior, 2-celled, with 2 to many ovules; style 1. Pollination is usually by small bees (see comments under *Diascia*). The fruit is a capsule.

Key Recognition Features The opposite leaves and flat, usually pinkish flowers without spurs.

Ecology and Geography In wet places, by springs and streams, often by the sea.

Comment Several perennial species, such as *A. gardneri* Hook. from Brazil, are grown as summer bedding. 'Mandiana' is also sold as 'Imperial Star'.

Diascia integerrima
flowers: front (right) and back (below right), showing spurs with dark oil glands
1⅓ × life size, June 30th

Diascia integerrima
½ life size, June 30th

Angelonia 'Mandiana'
½ life size July 20th

Angelonia 'Mandiana' flowers: sections (above), back (right), and front (far right), 1⅓ × life size, July 20th

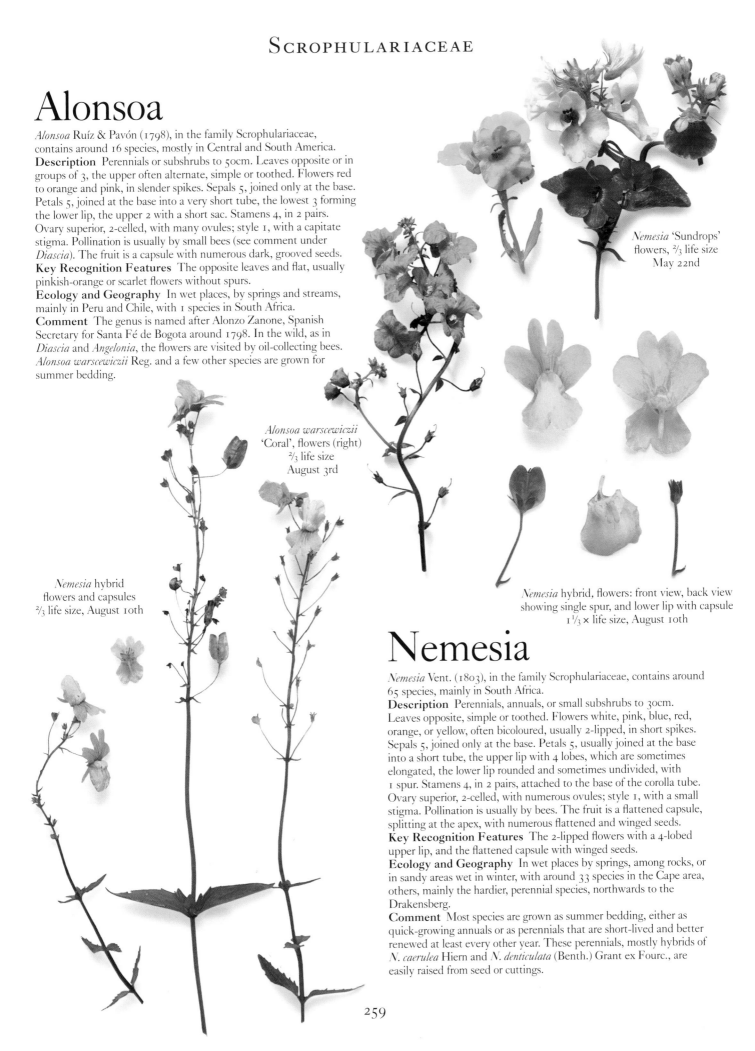

Alonsoa

Alonsoa Ruíz & Pavón (1798), in the family Scrophulariaceae, contains around 16 species, mostly in Central and South America.

Description Perennials or subshrubs to 50cm. Leaves opposite or in groups of 3, the upper often alternate, simple or toothed. Flowers red to orange and pink, in slender spikes. Sepals 5, joined only at the base. Petals 5, joined at the base into a very short tube, the lowest 3 forming the lower lip, the upper 2 with a short sac. Stamens 4, in 2 pairs. Ovary superior, 2-celled, with many ovules; style 1, with a capitate stigma. Pollination is usually by small bees (see comment under *Diascia*). The fruit is a capsule with numerous dark, grooved seeds.

Key Recognition Features The opposite leaves and flat, usually pinkish-orange or scarlet flowers without spurs.

Ecology and Geography In wet places, by springs and streams, mainly in Peru and Chile, with 1 species in South Africa.

Comment The genus is named after Alonzo Zanone, Spanish Secretary for Santa Fé de Bogota around 1798. In the wild, as in *Diascia* and *Angelonia*, the flowers are visited by oil-collecting bees. *Alonsoa warscewiczii* Reg. and a few other species are grown for summer bedding.

Nemesia 'Sundrops'
flowers, ²⁄₃ life size
May 22nd

Alonsoa warscewiczii
'Coral', flowers (right)
²⁄₃ life size
August 3rd

Nemesia hybrid
flowers and capsules
²⁄₃ life size, August 10th

Nemesia hybrid, flowers: front view, back view
showing single spur, and lower lip with capsule
1¹⁄₃ × life size, August 10th

Nemesia

Nemesia Vent. (1803), in the family Scrophulariaceae, contains around 65 species, mainly in South Africa.

Description Perennials, annuals, or small subshrubs to 30cm. Leaves opposite, simple or toothed. Flowers white, pink, blue, red, orange, or yellow, often bicoloured, usually 2-lipped, in short spikes. Sepals 5, joined only at the base. Petals 5, usually joined at the base into a short tube, the upper lip with 4 lobes, which are sometimes elongated, the lower lip rounded and sometimes undivided, with 1 spur. Stamens 4, in 2 pairs, attached to the base of the corolla tube. Ovary superior, 2-celled, with numerous ovules; style 1, with a small stigma. Pollination is usually by bees. The fruit is a flattened capsule, splitting at the apex, with numerous flattened and winged seeds.

Key Recognition Features The 2-lipped flowers with a 4-lobed upper lip, and the flattened capsule with winged seeds.

Ecology and Geography In wet places by springs, among rocks, or in sandy areas wet in winter, with around 33 species in the Cape area, others, mainly the hardier, perennial species, northwards to the Drakensberg.

Comment Most species are grown as summer bedding, either as quick-growing annuals or as perennials that are short-lived and better renewed at least every other year. These perennials, mostly hybrids of *N. caerulea* Hiern and *N. denticulata* (Benth.) Grant ex Fourc., are easily raised from seed or cuttings.

Verbascum sinuatum, flower
parts showing hairy stamens
1⅓ × life size, July 5th

Verbascum
'Raspberry Ripple'
⅓ life size
September 8th

Verbascum sinuatum
(left) ½ life size
July 5th

Verbascum

Verbascum L. (1753), mullein, in the family Scrophulariaceae, contains around 360 species in Europe, western Asia, and North Africa; some of the species were formerly separated in *Celsia* L..

Description Annuals, biennials, and perennials to 3m, or small shrubs. Leaves alternate, often woolly, entire or wavy-edged. Flowers yellow, white, brown, or purple, not 2-lipped, in long spikes. Sepals 5, joined at the base. Petals 5, more or less equal, joined at the base into a short tube. Stamens usually 5, sometimes 4, and then often with 1 sterile staminode, often with hairy filaments; anthers often of 2 types. Ovary superior, 2-celled, with numerous ovules; style 1, with a club-shaped stigma. Pollination is usually by bees. The fruit is a capsule, splitting into 2, with numerous small seeds.

Key Recognition Features The flat, 5-petalled flowers in tall spikes, and the hairy filaments.

Ecology and Geography In dry, waste places, on dunes and cliffs, with 87 species in Europe and around 230 in Turkey.

Comment *Celsia* L., formerly distinguished by having 4 stamens, is now included in *Verbascum*. Many species are cultivated for their handsome spikes of flowers, and may seed themselves in gardens; they are conspicuous features of roadsides on limestone soils in late summer. They are often attacked by the larvae of the mullein moth, *Cucullia verbasci* L., which are spotted with grey, yellow, and black. The seeds of some species are very long-lived, and have been found to germinate after 100 years.

Gratiola

Gratiola L. (1753), in the family Scrophulariaceae, contains 20 species in Europe, North America, and on mountains in the tropics.

Description Perennials to 80cm. Leaves opposite, linear to lanceolate. Flowers white to pinkish, yellow in the throat, tubular, somewhat 2-lipped, in the upper leaf axils. Sepals 5, unequal, joined at the base. Petals 5, more or less equal, joined into a wide tube. Stamens usually 2, with 3 staminodes. Ovary superior, 4-celled, with numerous ovules; style 1, with a 2-lobed stigma. Pollination is presumed to be by bees. The fruit is a capsule with numerous small seeds.

Key Recognition Features The tubular flowers in the upper leaf axils.

Ecology and Geography On the banks of ditches and rivers, and in marshes; 2 of the species in Europe, 12 or more in North America.

Comment *Gratiola officinalis* L., the hedge hyssop, is poisonous to cattle and was formerly used medicinally as a purgative and emetic, and as part of a remedy for gout.

Gratiola officinalis, flower parts
1¾ × life size, July 2nd

Phygelius

Phygelius E. Mey. ex Benth. (1836), Cape figwort, in the family Scrophulariaceae, contains 2 species in South Africa.

Description Perennials or spreading shrubs to 2m, with square stems. Leaves opposite, heart-shaped, stalked. Flowers red to pinkish, rarely yellow, tubular, 2-lipped, hanging down, in loose, branching heads. Sepals 5, joined at the base. Petals 5, more or less equal, joined into a long tube, swollen at the base. Stamens usually 4, sometimes 5; anthers exserted from the tube. Ovary superior, 2-celled, with numerous ovules; style 1, long and persistent, with a small stigma. Pollination is usually by sunbirds. The fruit is a capsule, splitting into 2, with numerous small seeds.

Key Recognition Features The hanging, tubular flowers in tall, branching heads, and the stalked leaves.

Ecology and Geography On the banks of mountain streams and in wet, rocky areas, with both species in the Drakensberg mountains of Natal and the northern Cape.

Comment Both species and many named hybrids between them are cultivated, particularly 'Yellow Trumpet', the yellow-flowered form of *P. aequalis* Harv. ex Hiern. The plant is sometimes called Cape fuchsia, but is unrelated to the true *Fuchsia* (see Volume 1). It is, however, closely related to European figwort, *Scrophularia* L., and is often damaged by the small speckled figwort weevil, *Cionus scrophulariae*, which is camouflaged by resembling a minute bird dropping, and whose pupae are very like the capsules of a *Scrophularia*.

Phygelius 'Moonraker'
flower parts, ¾ life size, June 15th

Phygelius 'Moonraker'
capsules and seeds
life size, November 24th

Gratiola officinalis
⅔ life size, July 2nd

Phygelius 'Moonraker'
½ life size, June 15th

261

Sutera

Sutera Roth. (1807), in the family Scrophulariaceae, contains around 130 species in South Africa, with 1 reported from the Canary Islands.
Description Annuals, perennials, or dwarf shrubs to 1m. Leaves opposite, often toothed or deeply divided and sticky with glandular hairs, sometimes small and heath-like, often acrid-scented. Flowers white to pinkish, red, magenta, or mauve, tubular, usually 2-lipped. Sepals 5, small, joined into a tube at the base. Petals 5, joined into a short, broad or long, narrow tube, the 2 upper forming the upper lip, the 3 lower pointing downwards. Stamens usually 4, in 2 pairs. Ovary superior, 2-celled, with numerous ovules; style 1, with a small stigma. Pollination is presumed to be by insects. The fruit is a capsule with numerous small seeds.
Key Recognition Features The often acrid, sticky leaves and 5-petalled flowers. The common South African annual *S. tristis* (L.fil.) Hiern, which has long-tubed, green, white, or yellow flowers, is now put in the genus *Lyperia* Benth.
Ecology and Geography On sand dunes, in dry scrub, and on rocky hillsides and moist cliff ledges, with 39 species in the Cape area, others further north.
Comment The genus is named after Johann Rudolf Suter (1766–1827), a Swiss botanist, professor at Bern and author of *Flora Helvetica* (1802). The small, white-flowered *S. cordata* (Thunb.) Kuntze, is commonly sold for hanging baskets with the name *Bacopa* 'Snowflake'.

Sutera cordata
1¾ × life size
June 20th

Ellisiophyllum pinnatum
flower parts
1¾ × life size
June 12th

Ellisiophyllum pinnatum
¾ life size, June 12th

Ellisiophyllum

Ellisiophyllum Maxim. (1871), in the family Scrophulariaceae, contains 1 species, *E. pinnatum* (Benth.) Makino, in eastern Asia.
Description Dwarf, creeping perennial to 7.5cm, with creeping and rooting stolons. Leaves thin, softly hairy, pinnate, with rounded lobes. Flowers white, not 2-lipped. Sepals 5, small, joined into a tube at the base. Petals 5, joined into a short, broad tube. Stamens 4, equal. Ovary superior, 2-celled, with few ovules; style 1, with a 2-lobed stigma. Pollination is presumed to be by small insects. The fruit is a capsule with rounded seeds, which become sticky when wet.
Key Recognition Features The pinnate leaves with rounded lobes, creeping stems and small, white flowers.
Ecology and Geography In woods in the mountains from India to Japan and New Guinea.
Comment The genus is superficially like some of the Boraginaceae, especially those genera from North America formerly placed in Hydrophyllaceae (see *Hydrophyllum*, p.248), and notably *Ellisia* L., which has similar leaves. *Ellisiophyllum* is sometimes cultivated as a curiosity, and forms attractive dwarf groundcover.

Zaluzianskya capensis
½ life size
November 2nd

Zaluzianskya capensis
flower parts, 1⅔ × life size
November 2nd

Zaluzianskya ovata
flower parts, 1⅓ × life size
May 26th

Zaluzianskya

Zaluzianskya F.W. Schmidt (1793), in the family Scrophulariaceae, contains around 55 species in southern Africa.

Description Annuals or perennials to 50cm, occasionally subshrubby. Leaves opposite, often toothed. Flowers white with a red back, pinkish, red, or yellow, often with a contrasting eye, not 2-lipped. Sepals 5, small, joined into a narrow tube. Petals 5, all equal, often forked, spreading, often curled up in the day, joined into a long, narrow tube at the base. Stamens 2 or 4, rarely 5. Ovary superior, 2-celled, with numerous ovules; style 1, long, with a club-shaped stigma. Pollination is presumed to be by insects, including night-flying moths. The fruit is a capsule with numerous small seeds.

Key Recognition Features The long-tubed flowers with forked or rounded petals, often red on the back; the leaves are usually acrid and often sticky with glandular hairs.

Ecology and Geography On sand dunes, in dry scrub, and on rocky hillsides and moist cliff ledges, wet rocks, and damp, gravelly places in the mountains. Around 15 species in the Cape area, others further north.

Comment The genus is named after Adam Zaluziansky von Zaluzian (1558–1613), physician and author of *Methodus herbariae* (1592). The flowers of several species, notably *Z. capensis* (L.) Walp., are interesting in their similarity to night-flowering Caryophyllaceae (see pp.74–81) such as *Silene noctiflora* L. The petals uncurl and the flowers become sweetly-scented at dusk or in dull weather, and coil up again in sunlight.

Zaluzianskya ovata
life size, May 26th

263

Rehmannia elata, flowers, stamens
and style, and inside of corolla
¾ life size, May 25th

Rehmannia glutinosa
calyx and style, and
sections of corolla
life size, May 8th

Rehmannia elata
½ life size, May 25th

Rehmannia

Rehmannia Libosch. ex Fischer & C. Meyer (1835), in the family
Gesneriaceae, contains around 9 species in eastern Asia.

Description Perennials to 2m, usually softly hairy. Leaves alternate,
often deeply toothed. Flowers reddish-pink, red-brown, or yellow,
often spotted inside, stickily hairy outside, 2-lipped. Sepals 5, small,
joined into a wide tube. Petals 5, the lower 3 sometimes larger than
the upper 2. Stamens 4. Ovary superior, 2-celled, with numerous
ovules; style 1, long, with a 2-lobed or flat and swollen stigma.
Pollination is presumed to be by bees. The fruit is a 1-celled capsule
with numerous small seeds.

Key Recognition Features The soft, stickily hairy leaves and the
Mimulus-like flowers (see p.252).

Ecology and Geography On dry cliffs, old walls, and rocky
roadsides, and in woods, mostly in central and eastern China.

Comment The genus is named after Joseph Rehmann (1799–1831),
a physician in St Petersberg. The brown-flowered *R. glutinosa* Libosch.
ex Fischer & C. Meyer is common in cracks in old walls in Beijing
and the neighbouring hills. *Rehmannia elata* N.E. Br. is a fine plant for
a frost-free climate. The family Gesneriaceae is mainly tropical,
though it includes a few hardy alpine genera, such as *Ramonda* Rich.
ex Pers. and *Haberlea* Friv. from the mountains of Europe, as well as
familiar tropical genera like *Saintpaulia* H. Wendl. and *Streptocarpus*
Lindl.. DNA studies indicate that the Gesneriaceae should be
included within a wider Scrophulariaceae (see pp.250–77), being
closely related to *Verbascum* (see p.260) and *Scrophularia* in the
Scrophulariaceae, as well as to the insectivorous genera *Pinguicula* and
Utricularia L., traditionally put in the Lentibulariaceae. The capsule
of *Rehmannia* has characteristics of both Scrophulariaceae and
traditional Gesneriaceae; when young it is 2-celled, resembling the
former, but when mature becomes 1-celled, like the latter.

Pinguicula

Pinguicula L.(1753), butterwort, in the family Lentibulariaceae, contains around 46 species, mainly in America and southern Europe.
Description Perennials with leafless flowering stems to 15cm. Leaves in a rosette on the ground, stickily hairy and trapping insects. Flowers purple, reddish-pink, pale lilac, white, and yellow, often hairy inside, usually 2-lipped. Sepals 5, small, joined to form a short, 2-lipped calyx. Petals 5, the lower 3 larger than the upper 2, the lower with a long spur. Stamens 2. Ovary superior, 1-celled, with numerous ovules; style 1, short, with a 2-lobed stigma. Pollination is mainly by flies or bees, but self-pollination is common in the smaller-flowered species. The fruit is a 1-celled capsule with numerous small seeds.
Key Recognition Features The fleshy, sticky rosette of leaves and the solitary, often long-spurred flowers.
Ecology and Geography In bogs and wet, rocky areas, and on cliffs, with 12 species in Europe, the rest mainly in Central America.
Comment Some of the larger-flowered species of *Pinguicula* are cultivated by specialists. The genus is carnivorous, digesting small animals that are trapped by the sticky glands on the leaves. The related aquatic badderwort, *Utricularia* L., catches its prey in bladders, which are triggered by sensitive hairs and suck in water and the minute crustacean that is swimming past. DNA studies show the Lentibulariaceae is most closely related to Gesneriaceae, and should be included in a wider Scrophulariaceae.

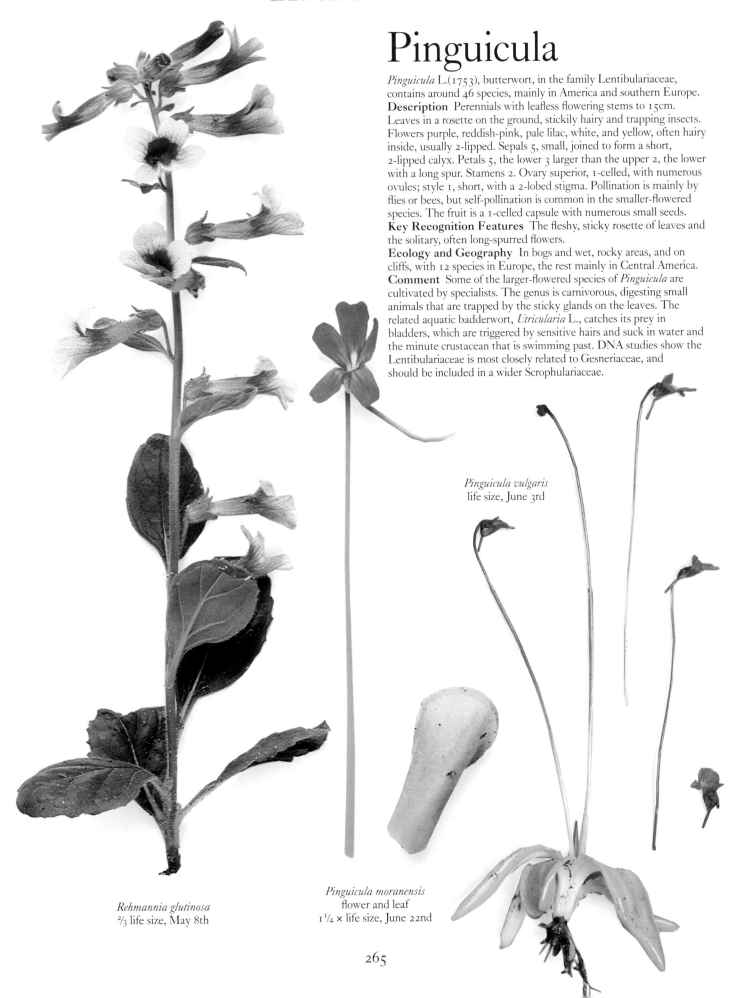

Pinguicula vulgaris
life size, June 3rd

Rehmannia glutinosa
⅔ life size, May 8th

Pinguicula moranensis
flower and leaf
1¼ × life size, June 22nd

265

VERBENACEAE

Verbena bonariensis
flowers, 1 ¹/₂ × life size
July 22nd

Verbena bonariensis
¹/₂ life size, July 22nd

Verbena officinalis
life size, July 20th

266

Verbena

Verbena L. (1753), in the family Verbenaceae, contains around 200 species, mainly in tropical South and Central America.

Description Annuals, perennials, or subshrubs to 1.5m, with rough hairs. Leaves usually opposite, pinnate or deeply toothed. Flowers white, purple, pale lilac, or red, in flat heads or elongated spikes, on the tips of the branches. Sepals 5, often covered in glands, joined to form a short calyx. Petals 4 or 5, more or less equal, with a long or short tube. Stamens 4, in 2 pairs, or rarely 2, attached to the inside of the tube. Ovary superior, 4-celled, with 1 ovule per cell; style 1, long, with an unequally 2-lobed stigma. Pollination is mainly by butterflies or moths. The fruit is dry and made up of 4 narrow nutlets.

Key Recognition Features The heads or spikes of tubular flowers with blunt or 2-lobed petals, and the 4 nutlets.

Ecology and Geography In open, grassy places, particularly by roadsides, with 2 species in Europe and the rest in America, but many species naturalised in other parts of the world.

Comment Many species and hybrids are cultivated in gardens. The majority of the American species, which include the garden hybrids of the scarlet *V. peruviana* L. and the white *V. platensis* Spreng., are sometimes separated in the genus *Glandularia* J. Gmelin. The vervain, *V. officinalis* L., common in grassy places in Europe, was used medicinally for eye problems. The family Verbenaceae formerly included several genera now placed in Labiatae (see pp.278–99), such as *Callicarpa, Caryopteris, Clerodendrum,* and *Vitex* (for all see Volume 1). *Lantana* L., including the common tropical weed *L. camara* L,. and *Lippia* L. remain in Verbenaceae. DNA studies indicate that Verbenaceae should be included in a wider Scrophulariaceae.

Verbena 'Sissinghurst'
½ life size, July 20th

Verbena 'Royal Purple'
flower parts, 2 × life size
June 14th

Verbena
'Royal Purple'
⅔ life size
June 14th

Verbena platensis
flowers, 1⅓ × life size
August 23rd

Verbena platensis
⅔ life size
August 23rd

267

Veronica gentianoides
flowers (right)
1¼ × life size, May 17th

Veronica peduncularis
'Georgia Blue'
flowers, showing the
2 stamens, 1½ × life size
April 5th

*Veronica
gentianoides*
⅔ life size
May 17th

Veronica

Veronica L.(1753), speedwell, in the family Scrophulariaceae, contains around 180 species, mainly in temperate parts of the northern hemisphere.

Description Annuals and perennials to 1.2m. Leaves opposite, toothed or divided. Flowers blue, pink, white, or pale lilac, solitary or in elongated spikes in the leaf axils. Sepals 4, joined only at the base. Petals 4, unequal, the lowest usually narrower than the other 3, all joined at the base into a short tube. Stamens 2, longer than the tube. Ovary superior, 2-celled, with 1 ovule per cell; style 1, with a rounded stigma. Pollination is by insects, especially hoverflies and small wasps, but many species are self-pollinated. The fruit is a 2-lobed capsule with 2 seeds.

Key Recognition Features The blue flowers with the lower petal narrower than the others, and with 2 stamens.

Ecology and Geography In dry or damp, grassy places, on rocky mountains, or as a weed of open ground, with 62 species and many subspecies in Europe, the rest mainly in western Asia and North America. Many weedy species are now common worldwide.

Comment Many dwarf species and a few of the taller ones are popular as garden plants. Among the more remarkable weedy species are *V. filiformis* Sm. from the Caucasus and northern Turkey, a delicate, creeping perennial, which was introduced as an ornamental but since 1927 has become widespread as a weed in lawns and on grassy river banks in both Europe and North America. Buxbaum's speedwell, *V. persica* Poir. syn. V. *buxbaumii* Ten., was first recorded in Britain in 1825 and is now a common weed in vegetable gardens; it has been found to be of hybrid origin, an allopolyploid, between 2 western Asiatic species, associated with Neolithic agriculture. Around 20 species are sometimes separated in the genus *Pseudolysimachium* (Koch) Opiz; the most familiar of these are *V. spicata* L. the spiked speedwell, and *V. longifolia* L., several forms of which are cultivated; the flowers are small, in terminal spikes. The genus *Veronicastrum* Heister ex Fabr. differs from *Veronica* in having alternate or whorled leaves and flowers with the tube longer than the lobes, long, exserted stamens, and a pointed capsule. A few species are found in eastern Asia, and 1, *V. virginicum* (L.) Farw., Culver's root, in eastern North America; it is very poisonous, but sometimes grown as an ornamental for its tall spikes of flowers.

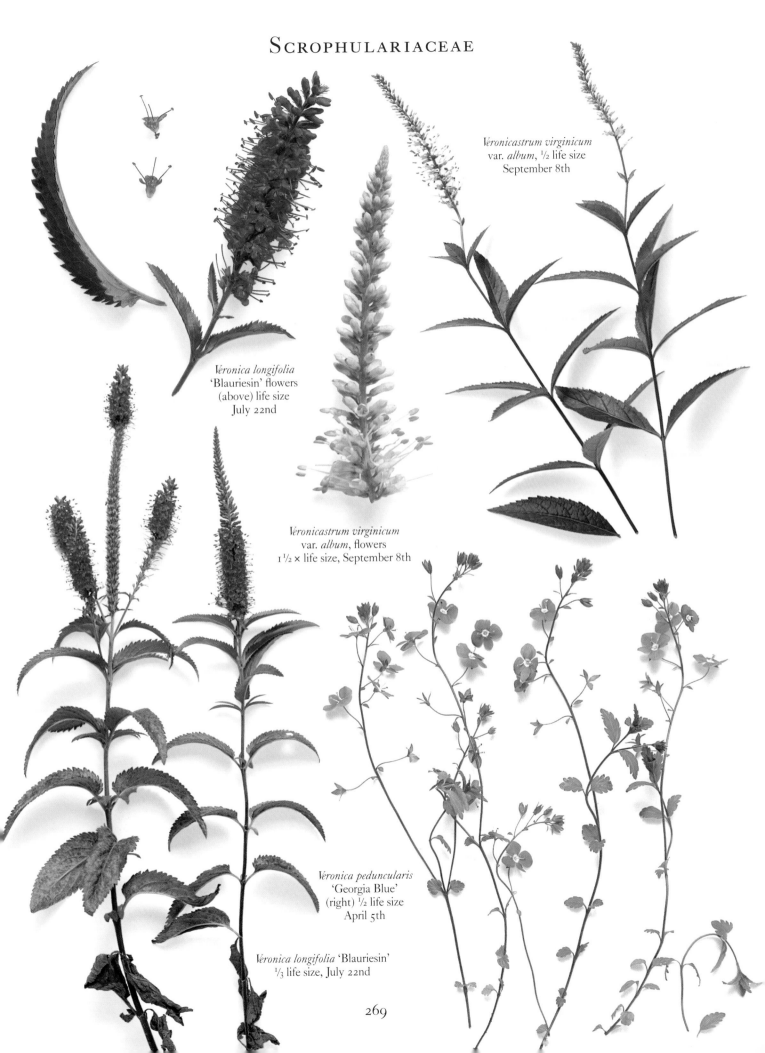

Veronicastrum virginicum
var. *album*, ½ life size
September 8th

Veronica longifolia
'Blauriesin' flowers
(above) life size
July 22nd

Veronicastrum virginicum
var. *album*, flowers
1½ × life size, September 8th

Veronica peduncularis
'Georgia Blue'
(right) ½ life size
April 5th

Veronica longifolia 'Blauriesin'
⅓ life size, July 22nd

Incarvillea

Incarvillea Juss. (1789), in the family Bignoniaceae, contains around 15 species, mainly in eastern Asia.

Description Perennials or subshrubs to 1m, rarely annuals. Leaves in rosettes or alternate, usually pinnately divided, often with the terminal leaflet the largest. Flowers red, pink, or pale yellow, rarely white, in elongated spikes or solitary. Sepals joined to form a 5-toothed calyx. Petals 5, more or less equal, with a long tube, widening towards the mouth. Stamens 4, anthers 2-lobed, each lobe with a bristle. Ovary superior, 2-celled, with numerous ovules per cell; style 1, with an flattened stigma. Pollination is presumed to be by bees. The fruit is a dry, elongated, and pointed capsule, with numerous flattened seeds.

Key Recognition Features The large, trumpet-shaped flowers and the elongated capsules.

Ecology and Geography In dry, grassy places and on cliffs, usually on limestone, from central Asia through the Himalayas eastwards to the mountains of western China, particularly in Yunnan.

Comment The genus is named after Père Pierre Nicholas le Chéron d'Incarville (1706–57), French Jesuit and botanist who lived in Beijing from 1740 until his death. The flowers are large and almost incongruous on a hardy perennial; indeed, this is one of the few hardy members of the largely tropical and woody Bignoniaceae. DNA studies suggest that Bignoniaceae is closely allied to *Buddleja* (see Volume 1) and to *Veronica* (see pp.268–69), traditionally placed in the Scrophulariaceae.

Incarvillea mairei
stamens and style
$2^{1}/_{2}$ × life size
June 6th

Incarvillea delavayii
$^{3}/_{4}$ life size, June 1st

270

BIGNONIACEAE

Incarvillea delavayii flower sections
showing stamens and style
life size, June 1st

Incarvillea mairei
flower sections
1 ¼ life size, June 6th

Incarvillea mairei
²/₃ life size
whole plant, showing
tuberous root
June 6th

271

Acanthus

Acanthus L. (1753), in the family Acanthaceae, contains around 30 species, mainly in southern Europe, Africa, and Asia.

Description Perennials or shrubs to 3m, rarely annuals. Leaves in rosettes or opposite, often spiny and deeply divided. Flowers white, green, pink, or red, in elongated spikes, with large, spiny bracts. Sepals 4, joined to form a 2-lipped calyx, the upper large and green, arched over the flower, the lateral short and narrow, and the lower notched at the apex. Petals joined, with a short tube, and a single, 3-lobed lower lip. Stamens 4, anthers 1-celled, joined in pairs, with a fringe of hairs. Ovary superior, 2-celled, with 2 ovules per cell; style 1, with a 2-lobed stigma. Pollination is by bees, or sometimes by birds. The fruit is a capsule with usually 1 or 2 large seeds which are ejected explosively.

Key Recognition Features The spiny bracts and the spikes of 1-lipped flowers.

Ecology and Geography Subtropical species in mangrove swamps and desert areas; others in dry woods and on hillsides from Spain and Portugal around the Mediterranean to Turkey; the shrubby *A. ilicifolius* L. extends to northern Australia.

Comment Many species are cultivated, including *A. mollis* L., the leaves of which are supposed to be the model for the leaf motif on Corinthian capitals. The family Acanthaceae is mainly tropical; DNA studies indicate that it is most closely related to the Pedaliaceae, which includes *Sesamum indicum* L., the source of sesame oil and seed, and the Martyniaceae, which includes *Proboscoidea louisiana* (Mill.) Thell., with strange fruits with a curved and hooked beak.

Acanthus mollis
½ life size, July 27th

272

ACANTHACEAE

Acanthus mollis, flower parts, showing spiny bracts
and notched purple sepals, ¾ life size, July 27th

Acanthus dioscoridis, whole flower
(above right), spiny bract and bristle-like
lateral sepals (centre), and upper and lower
sepals (below), life size, July 28th

Acanthus dioscoridis
corolla (left), style and
stamens separated
(centre) and together
(below), life size
July 28th

Acanthus dioscoridis
½ life size, July 28th

Justicia

Justicia L. (1753), in the family Acanthaceae, contains around 600 species, mainly in the tropics.

Description Perennials or subshrubs to 2m. Leaves opposite, often silvery, or absent. Flowers red or white, in short spikes, often with coloured, overlapping bracts. Sepals 5, joined to form a 2-lipped calyx. Petals joined to form a 2-lipped corolla, the upper lip 2-lobed, the lower lip 3-lobed. Stamens 4 or 2. Ovary superior, 2-celled, with 2 ovules per cell; style 1, with a rounded stigma. Pollination is by bees or hummingbirds. The fruit is a capsule with 2 or 4 seeds.

Key Recognition Features The narrow-lipped, often red flowers, usually in dense spikes.

Ecology and Geography By streams in deserts, on rocky mountainsides, in forest, and in swamps. Worldwide in the tropics, but particularly in Central and South America.

Comment As described here, *Justicia* includes *Jacobinia*, *Adhatoda*, and *Beloperone*. The common shrimp plant, formerly called *Beloperone guttata*, is now *Justicia brandegeeana* Wassh. & L.B. Smith. *Justicia suberecta* André, with silvery leaves and scarlet flowers, is sometimes put in the genus *Dicliptera* Juss.. The genus *Justicia* is named after James Justice (1698–1763), a Scottish lawyer and gentleman gardener with a particular interest in tulips, hyacinths, and pineapples; the extravagance of his garden bankrupted him.

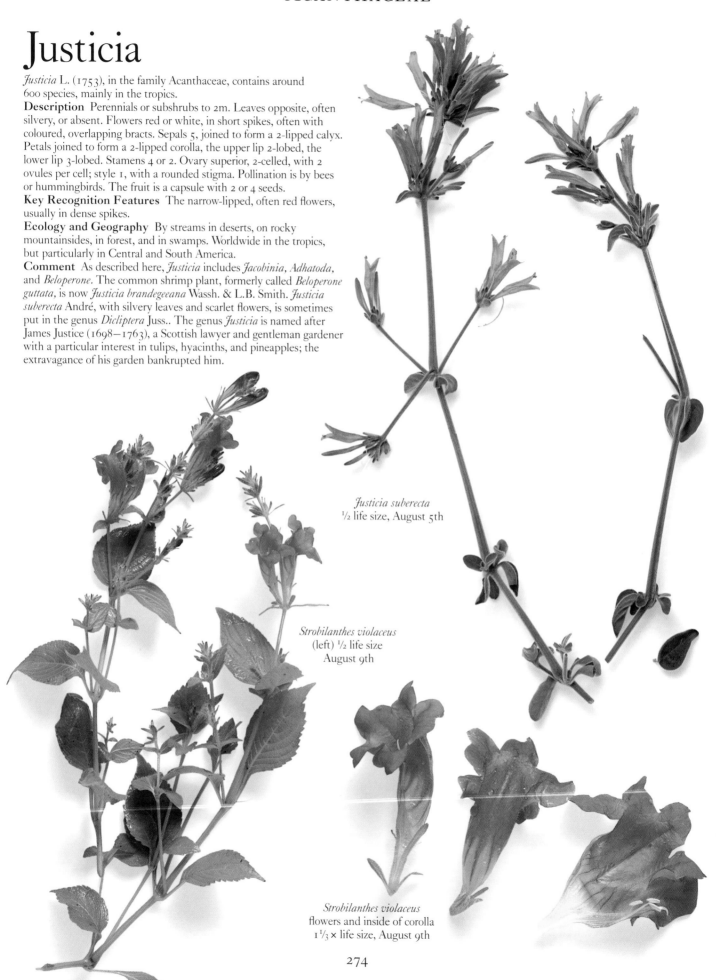

Justicia suberecta
½ life size, August 5th

Strobilanthes violaceus
(left) ½ life size
August 9th

Strobilanthes violaceus
flowers and inside of corolla
1⅓ × life size, August 9th

Strobilanthes

Strobilanthes Blume (1826), in the family Acanthaceae, contains around 250 species, mainly in the tropics.

Description Perennials or subshrubs to 2m. Leaves opposite, usually toothed, often marked with silver. Flowers blue, purple, yellow, or white, in short spikes, with narrow bracts. Sepals 4 or 5, narrow, joined only at the base. Petals joined into a long, curving tube, and 5 more or less equal lobes. Stamens usually 4, sometimes 2, with 2 staminodes. Ovary superior, 2-celled, with 2 ovules per cell; style 1, with a 2-lobed stigma, one lobe very small. Pollination is usually by bees, or sometimes by moths. The fruit is a capsule, with usually 4 seeds.

Key Recognition Features The flowers, produced in autumn, with a usually curved tube and small bracts.

Ecology and Geography In woods, where they often carpet the woodland floor, and in scrub and grassland, mainly in eastern Asia from the Himalayas to Japan and Java, with around 60 species in southern India.

Comment A few species are cultivated as ornamentals, valuable for their late flowering. *Strobilanthes cusia* (Nees) Kuntze, syn. *S. flaccidifolia* Nees, Chinese or Assam indigo, is cultivated for use as an indigo substitute, mainly in China. Colonel R.H. Beddome, (1830–1911), who wrote on ferns, trees of southern India, and Acanthaceae, reported that in southern India these plants grow for several years, then all flower, seed, and die, leaving acres of dead stems before the seeds germinate in the next rains. Some species are also put into the genus *Goldfussia* Nees.

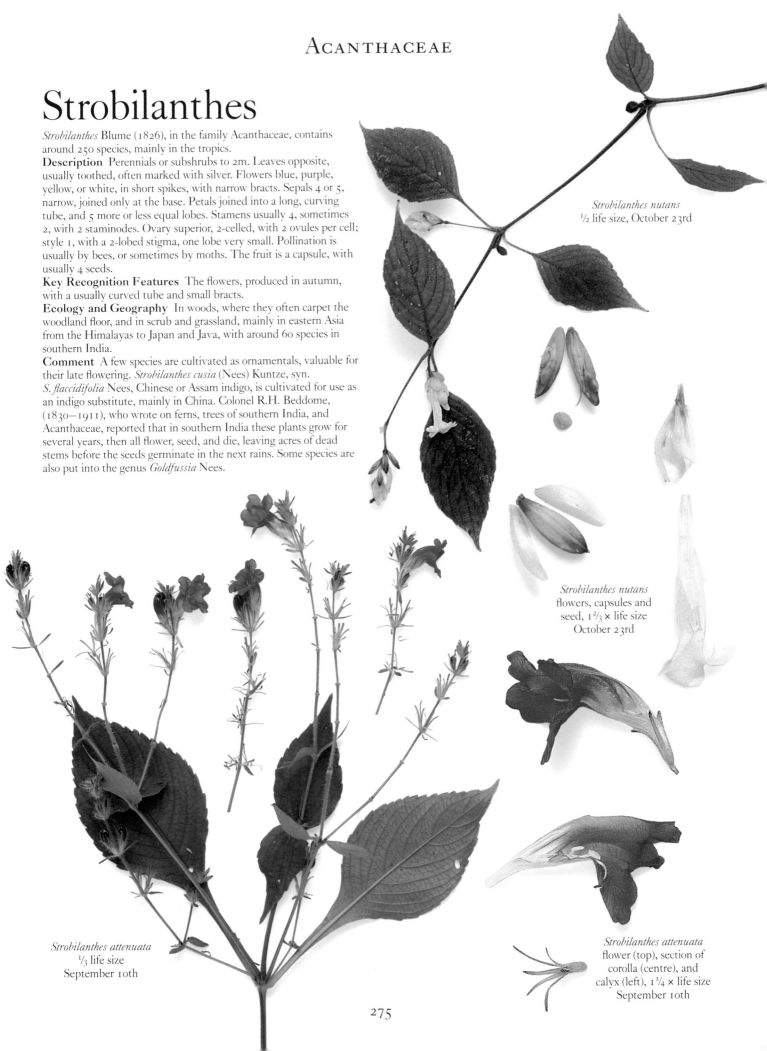

Strobilanthes nutans
½ life size, October 23rd

Strobilanthes nutans
flowers, capsules and
seed, 1⅔ × life size
October 23rd

Strobilanthes attenuata
⅓ life size
September 10th

Strobilanthes attenuata
flower (top), section of
corolla (centre), and
calyx (left), 1¼ × life size
September 10th

Orobanche

Orobanche L.(1753), broomrape, in the family Orobanchaceae, contains around 150 species, mainly in southern Europe and Asia.
Description Perennials or annuals, without chlorophyll, with fleshy stems to 80cm. Flowers brown, bluish, reddish, white, or yellow, often hairy inside, usually 2-lipped. Sepals 4, small, joined to form a short tube, or sometimes deeply divided into 2. Petals 5, the lower 3 forming a lip, the upper 2 often hooded. Stamens 4, in 2 pairs. Ovary superior, 1-celled, with numerous ovules; style 1, curved, with a 2-lobed stigma. Pollination is mainly by bees, but self-pollination is probably also common. The fruit is a 1-celled capsule with numerous small seeds.
Key Recognition Features The brownish, usually stickily hairy plant without green leaves.
Ecology and Geography Usually in rather dry, open places, parasitic on herbaceous plants and small shrubs such as *Cistus*, *Berberis*, and brooms (for all see Volume 1); 45 species in Europe, more in Turkey and farther east, and 9 species in California.
Comment The species are often difficult to identify; some, such as *O. hederae* Duby, shown here, are restricted to ivy; others are found on many genera and families. Related genera include *Phelypaea* L. from eastern Europe and western Asia, a dwarf with solitary, red, pansy-like flowers, and the yellow, waxy *Cistanche* Hoffmans. & Link, which can reach 1m above ground and more below, growing out of sand dunes in deserts, parasitic on the roots of various Amaranthaceae (see pp.83–85).

Lathraea

Lathraea L. (1753), toothwort, in the family Scrophulariaceae, contains around 7 species, mainly in Europe and western Asia.
Description Fleshy perennials with flowering stems to 30cm, without chlorophyll, from a tuberous base. Leaves scale-like. Flowers purple, white, or pale pink, usually 2-lipped. Sepals 4, small, joined to form a short calyx. Petals 4, the lower 3 forming a lip, shorter than the upper 1. Stamens 4. Ovary superior, 1-celled, with numerous small ovules; style 1, short, curved. Pollination is mainly by flies or bees, but self-pollination is common. The fruit is a 1-celled capsule with numerous seeds, sometimes dehiscing explosively.
Key Recognition Features The short, fleshy stems without chlorophyll, produced in spring on forest trees.
Ecology and Geography Parasitic on the roots of various trees, usually in moist woods and by rivers. The pinkish-flowered *L. squamaria* L., wild toothwort, is found from western Europe to the Himalayas. The bright purple flowered *L. clandestina* L. from the Pyrenees is often cultivated and grows particularly easily on willows and poplars. Other species are found as far east as Japan.
Comment *Lathraea* is traditionally put in the family Scrophulariaceae, and considered close to the partially parasitic *Rhinanthus* and related genera, whereas *Orobanche* and a few other totally parasitic genera were considered distinct, in the family Orobanchaceae. DNA studies, however, suggest that the differences between the 2 groups are trivial, and that *Orobanche*, *Lathraea*, *Rhinanthus*, and related genera should all be separated from Scrophulariaceae into a much larger Orobanchaceae.

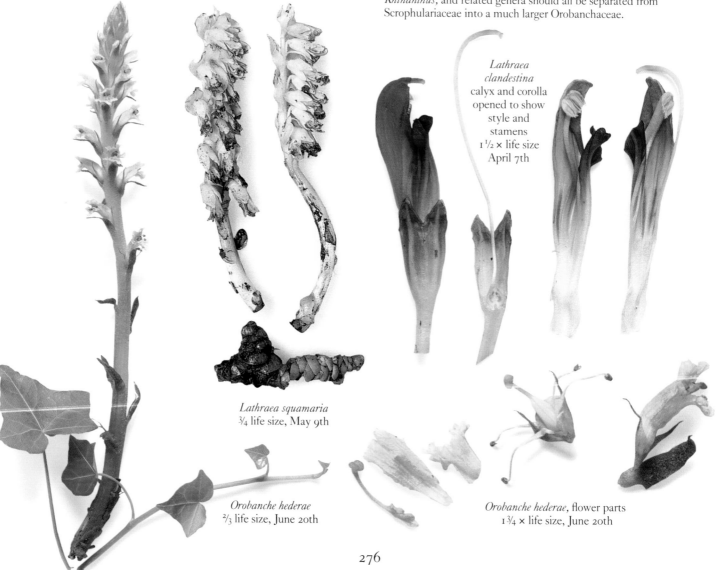

Lathraea clandestina calyx and corolla opened to show style and stamens 1 ½ × life size April 7th

Lathraea squamaria ¾ life size, May 9th

Orobanche hederae ⅔ life size, June 20th

Orobanche hederae, flower parts 1¾ × life size, June 20th

Rhinanthus

Rhinanthus L.(1753), yellow rattle, in the family Scrophulariaceae, contains around 45 species, mainly in Europe.

Description Annuals to 50cm, with wiry stems. Leaves opposite, toothed. Flowers yellowish, 2-lipped. Sepals 4, small, joined into an inflated calyx, in which the seeds rustle when ripe. Petals 5, the upper 2 forming a hooded lip, all joined at the base into a tubular corolla. Stamens 4, in 2 pairs, concealed in the upper lip; anthers hairy. Ovary superior, 2-celled, with numerous ovules; style 1, with a 2-lobed or flat and swollen stigma. Pollination is by bumblebees. The fruit is a capsule with several winged seeds within a swollen, persistent calyx.

Key Recognition Features The wiry stems, opposite leaves, and hooded, yellow flowers, with an inflated calyx and winged seeds.

Ecology and Geography In hay meadows or open grassland, partially parasitic on grasses. Around 25 species and many variations in Europe, others in Asia and eastern North America

Comment *Rhinanthus* is a good and easily grown plant for a meadow garden, as it suppresses the growth of grass, allowing orchids and other wild flowers to thrive. Its taxonomy is confusing, because of its so-called pseudoseasonal polymorphism: the same species can look very different if it flowers in spring, summer, or autumn, or if it is growing in montane or alpine habitats. Similar polymorphism is found in the related genus *Melampyrum* L. the cow-wheat. Other partially parasitic genera in this group are familiar wild flowers: eyebright, *Euphrasia* L.; red bartsia, *Odontites* Ludwig; and the lousewort, *Pedicularis* L. Both *Pedicularis* (in China) and *Euphrasia* (in New Zealand) have showy perennial species, but they are seldom cultivated.

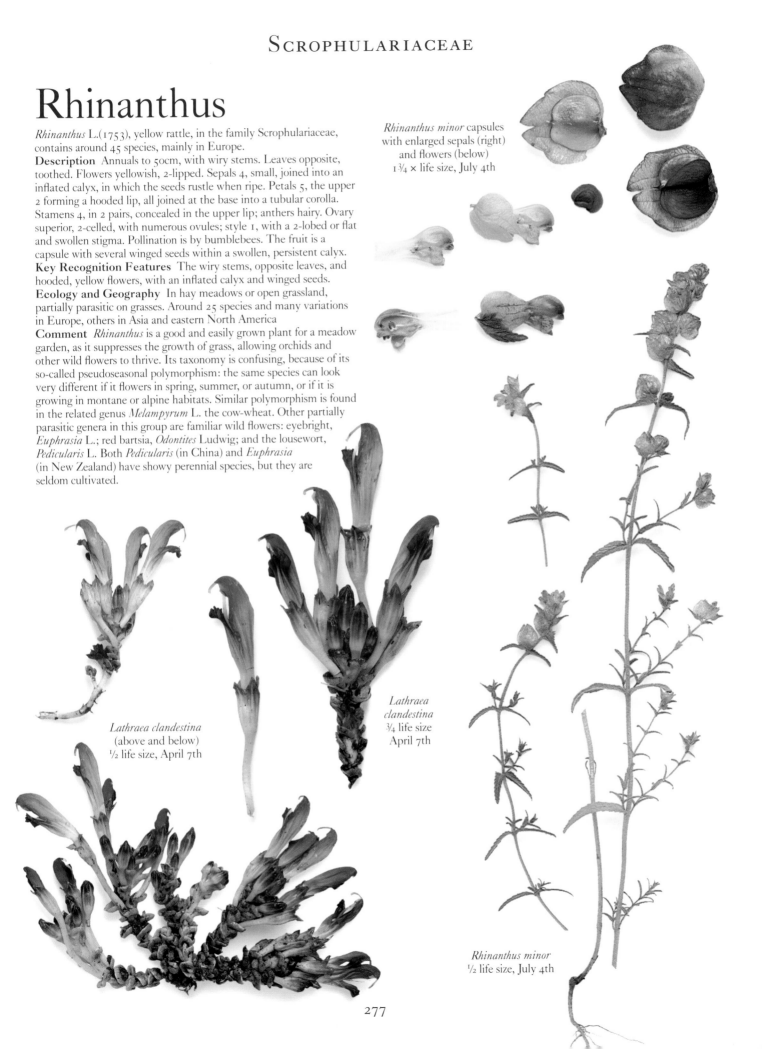

Rhinanthus minor capsules
with enlarged sepals (right)
and flowers (below)
1 ¾ × life size, July 4th

Lathraea clandestina
(above and below)
½ life size, April 7th

*Lathraea
clandestina*
¾ life size
April 7th

Rhinanthus minor
½ life size, July 4th

277

Scutellaria

Scutellaria L. (1753), in the family Labiatae (sometimes called Lamiaceae), contains around 350 species worldwide, mainly in Asia.

Description Herbaceous perennials, rarely shrubs, with flowering stems to 1m, sometimes with stolons. Leaves not aromatic, opposite, often toothed. Flowers blue, yellow, purple, pink, or white, in pairs in the upper leaf axils. Sepals joined to form a 2-lipped calyx, with an upright dorsal scale. Petals joined at the base, forming a curved tube, the upper lip hooded, the lower lip with a wide central lobe. Stamens 4, usually not exserted from the flower. Ovary superior, with 2 cells and 2 ovules per cell; style 1, slender. Pollination is mainly by various bees. The fruit is made up of 4 nutlets.

Key Recognition Features The pairs of flowers with the shield-like scale on the top of the calyx, and the curved corolla tube.

Ecology and Geography In shallow water, bogs, open woodland, and semi-desert, with 13 species in Europe, others across Asia and in North America.

Comment Some species are used in herbal medicine; 1 or 2 are cultivated in gardens.

Scutellaria albida
flower parts (above), showing the
upright scale on the calyx
2 × life size, July 23rd

Scutellaria albida
close up of calyx (above)
2 × life size, July 23rd

Teucrium scorodonia
flowers, 1¼ × life size
August 1st

Scutellaria albida
½ life size, July 23rd

Teucrium

Teucrium L. (1753), in the family Labiatae (sometimes called Lamiaceae), contains around 100 species worldwide, mainly in the Mediterranean area. For woody species see Volume 1.

Description Herbaceous perennials, rarely annuals, sometimes shrubs scrambling to 2m. Leaves aromatic, opposite, usually undivided, sometimes toothed. Flowers white or yellowish, pinkish, or blue, solitary or in groups in the upper leaf axils. Sepals 5, joined to form a toothed calyx. Petals joined at the base, forming a tube, the upper lip very small or absent, the lower lip with a rounded central lobe and 2 teeth on each side. Stamens 4, exserted from the flower, curving downwards. Ovary superior, with 2 cells and 2 ovules per cell; style 1, forked, slender. Pollination is mainly by various bees. The fruits are made up of 4 nutlets.

Key Recognition Features The flowers with the upper lip apparently absent.

Ecology and Geography In dry, open scrub, or seasonally wet places from Europe (49 species), across Asia to Japan and southwards to Australia and New Zealand.

Comment Recent studies suggest that *Teucrium* is related to *Caryopteris* and *Clerodendrum* (see Volume 1), traditionally in the Verbenaceae (see pp.266–67), rather than to the superficially similar *Ajuga*. The herbaceous species include the wood sage *T. scorodonia* L., formerly used medicinally; it smells like hops (*Humulus*, see p.147).

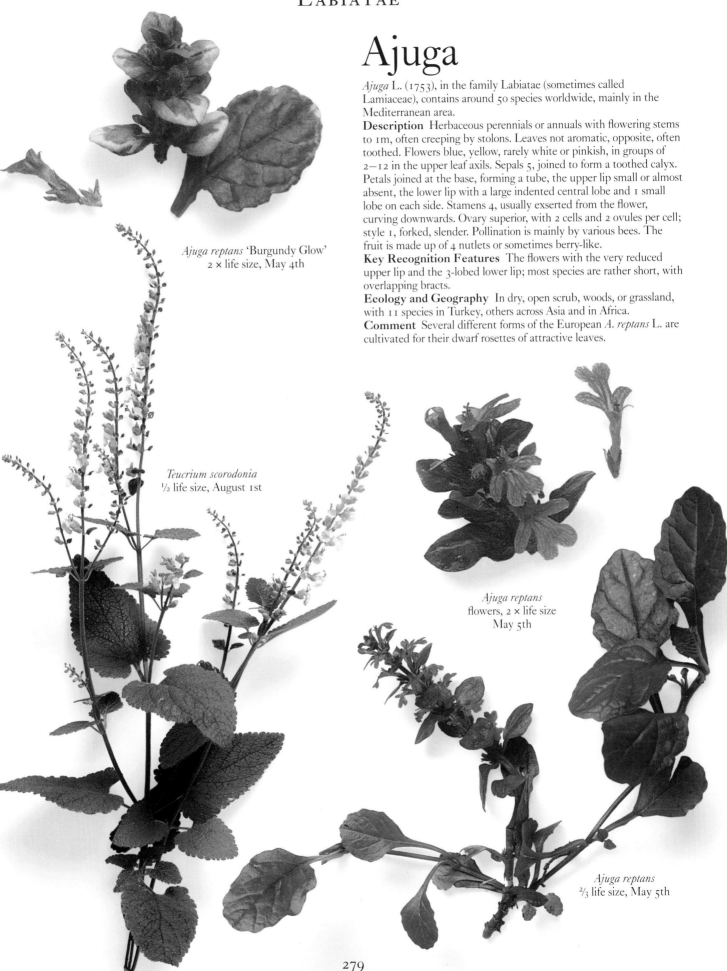

Ajuga

Ajuga L. (1753), in the family Labiatae (sometimes called Lamiaceae), contains around 50 species worldwide, mainly in the Mediterranean area.

Description Herbaceous perennials or annuals with flowering stems to 1m, often creeping by stolons. Leaves not aromatic, opposite, often toothed. Flowers blue, yellow, rarely white or pinkish, in groups of 2—12 in the upper leaf axils. Sepals 5, joined to form a toothed calyx. Petals joined at the base, forming a tube, the upper lip small or almost absent, the lower lip with a large indented central lobe and 1 small lobe on each side. Stamens 4, usually exserted from the flower, curving downwards. Ovary superior, with 2 cells and 2 ovules per cell; style 1, forked, slender. Pollination is mainly by various bees. The fruit is made up of 4 nutlets or sometimes berry-like.

Key Recognition Features The flowers with the very reduced upper lip and the 3-lobed lower lip; most species are rather short, with overlapping bracts.

Ecology and Geography In dry, open scrub, woods, or grassland, with 11 species in Turkey, others across Asia and in Africa.

Comment Several different forms of the European *A. reptans* L. are cultivated for their dwarf rosettes of attractive leaves.

Ajuga reptans 'Burgundy Glow'
2 × life size, May 4th

Teucrium scorodonia
½ life size, August 1st

Ajuga reptans
flowers, 2 × life size
May 5th

Ajuga reptans
⅔ life size, May 5th

Nepeta

Nepeta L. (1753), in the family Labiatae (sometimes called Lamiaceae), contains around 250 species, mostly in Europe and Asia.
Description Perennials, rarely annuals, to 1.2m. Leaves usually aromatic, opposite, often toothed. Flowers blue or white, rarely yellow, in clusters at the stem tips, often forming spikes. Sepals 5, joined to form a toothed calyx with 15 veins. Petals 5, joined to form a 2-lipped, funnel- or bell-shaped tube, the upper lip 2-lobed, the lower lip 3-lobed with a large central lobe. Stamens 4, the upper pair longest, not exserted from the flower. Ovary superior, with 2 cells and 2 ovules per cell; style 1, with unequal branches. Pollination is by bees. The fruit is made up of 4 nutlets.
Key Recognition Features Aromatic plants with spikes or clusters of blue, white, or yellow flowers in summer.
Ecology and Geography In dry places, usually on rocky ground and sometimes on mountains; 24 species in Europe, the others in Asia, North Africa, and the mountains of tropical Africa.
Comment Several species are cultivated for their attractive flower spikes. The leaves of some are very attractive, even narcotic, to cats, which may destroy the plants in their ecstasy. *Glechoma* L. the ground ivy, is closely related to *Nepeta*. It has long, trailing stems and short, upright flowering stems in early spring; variegated forms are commonly grown in hanging baskets.

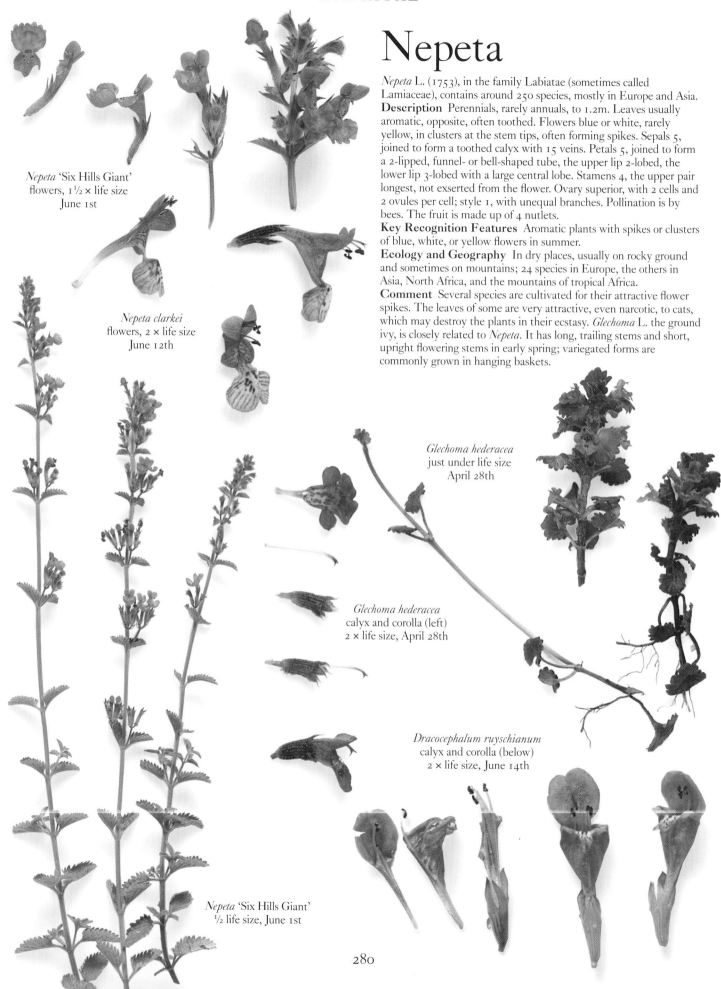

Nepeta 'Six Hills Giant'
flowers, 1½ × life size
June 1st

Nepeta clarkei
flowers, 2 × life size
June 12th

Glechoma hederacea
just under life size
April 28th

Glechoma hederacea
calyx and corolla (left)
2 × life size, April 28th

Dracocephalum ruyschianum
calyx and corolla (below)
2 × life size, June 14th

Nepeta 'Six Hills Giant'
½ life size, June 1st

Dracocephalum

Dracocephalum L. (1753), in the family Labiatae (sometimes called Lamiaceae), contains around 45 species, mostly in Europe and Asia.

Description Annuals, perennials, and dwarf shrubs to 90cm. Leaves usually aromatic, opposite, and entire, toothed, or lobed. Flowers violet-blue, white, or pinkish, in whorls forming terminal spikes. Sepals joined to form a 2-lipped calyx, the upper lip with 3 teeth, the lower with 2 teeth. Petals 5, joined to form a tube widening towards the mouth, the upper lip 2-lobed, the lower 3-lobed with a large central lobe. Stamens 4, in 2 pairs, the upper pair longest, exserted from the tube but curved under the upper lip. Ovary superior, with 2 cells and 2 ovules per cell; style 1, with equal branches. Pollination is mainly by bees. The fruit is made up of 4 nutlets.

Key Recognition Features Mostly low-growing perennials with rich violet-blue flowers.

Ecology and Geography In dry, open places, sometimes in low mountains, with 3 species in Europe, 1 in North America, the others in Asia eastwards to Japan.

Comment *Dracocephalum* differs from the closely related to *Nepeta* mainly in the 2-lipped calyx; 1 or 2 species are grown in gardens for their showy, deep blue flowers.

Melissa

Melissa L. (1753), in the family Labiatae (sometimes called Lamiaceae), contains 3 species in Europe and central Asia.

Description Herbaceous perennials to 1.5m. Leaves aromatic, opposite, short-stalked, ovate, with rounded teeth. Flowers pale yellow to white or pale pink, in whorls in the upper leaf axils. Sepals 5, joined to form a 2-lipped calyx with 13 veins, the upper lip with 3 teeth, the lower with 2 teeth. Petals 5, joined to form a curved tube widening towards the mouth, the upper lip erect and notched, the lower 3-lobed. Stamens 4, in 2 pairs, not exserted from the flower. Ovary superior, with 2 cells and 2 ovules per cell; style 1, with almost equal branches. Pollination is mainly by bees. The fruit is made up of 4 nutlets.

Key Recognition Features Leafy plants with strongly aromatic leaves and small, whitish flowers.

Ecology and Geography In open scrub; 1 species in Europe, the others in central Asia.

Comment *Melissa officinalis* L., lemon balm, is common in gardens: its leaves are used for potpourri, and to make a lemon-scented tisane. Like many Labiatae, it is attractive to bees.

Dracocephalum ruyschianum
¾ life size, June 14th

Melissa officinalis
flowers and calyces
(right) 1¾ × life size
August 15th

Melissa officinalis
¾ life size
August 15th

Hyssopus

Hyssopus L. (1753), in the family Labiatae (sometimes called Lamiaceae), contains about 10 species, mostly in the Mediterranean area.

Description Perennials and dwarf shrubs to 60cm. Leaves aromatic, opposite, linear-lanceolate, entire. Flowers violet-blue, white, or pink, in whorls forming 1-sided terminal spikes. Sepals 5, joined to form a toothed calyx. Petals 5, joined to form a funnel-shaped tube, the upper lip erect, notched, the lower 3-lobed with a larger central lobe. Stamens 4, exserted from the flower. Ovary superior, with 2 cells and 2 ovules per cell; style 1, with equal branches. Pollination is mainly by bees. The fruit is made up of 4 nutlets.

Key Recognition Features Plants with narrow, aromatic leaves and flowers in a 1-sided spike.

Ecology and Geography On dry, rocky hills; 1 species in Europe, the others in the Mediterranean area and western and central Asia.

Comment *Hyssopus officinalis* L. is an attractive perennial, and is often grown in herb collections or as a dwarf hedge. It has also been used medicinally, the essential oil having antiseptic properties, and in perfumery.

Mentha

Mentha L. (1753), mint, in the family Labiatae (sometimes called Lamiaceae), contains 25 species in Europe, northern Asia, and Africa.

Description Herbaceous perennials with creeping rhizomes, rarely annuals, to 1.5m. Leaves aromatic, opposite, entire or toothed. Flowers light purple, pink, or white, in whorls forming terminal spikes or in upper leaf axils. Sepals 5 or 4, joined to form a toothed, 10- to 13-veined calyx. Petals joined to form a short, slightly 2-lipped tube with 4 lobes, the upper lobe usually broadest. Stamens 4, exserted from the flower. Ovary superior, with 2 cells and 2 ovules per cell; style 1, with almost equal branches. Pollination is mainly by bees. The fruit is made up of 4 nutlets.

Key Recognition Features Rhizomatous plants with strongly mint-scented foliage and fluffy flower-heads.

Ecology and Geography In open, damp or even wet places, rarely in dry steppes, with 10 species in Europe, the others throughout temperate Asia and Africa. Several species are naturalised in North America and other parts of the worls

Comment Several mints are grown in gardens, primarily for use in the kitchen. The tiny *Mentha requienii* Benth. is sometimes grown in shady places on rock gardens.

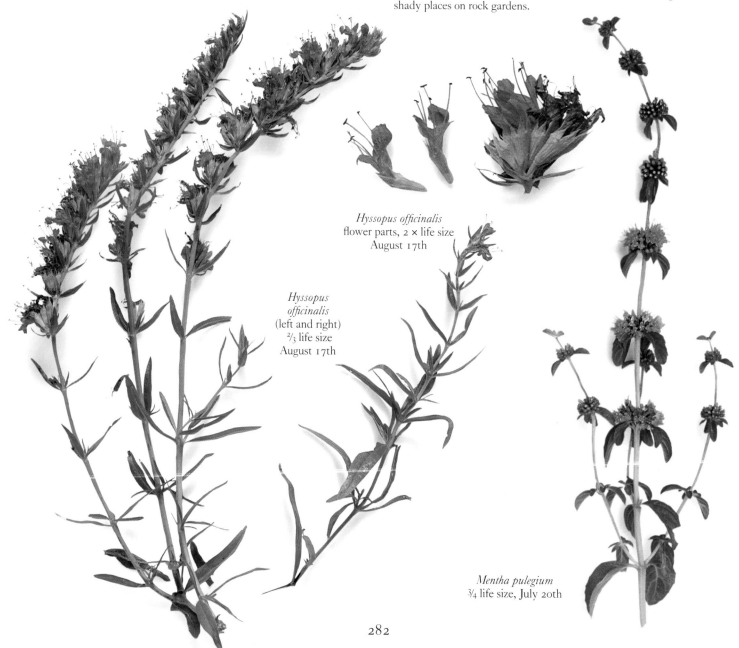

Hyssopus officinalis
flower parts, 2 × life size
August 17th

Hyssopus officinalis
(left and right)
⅔ life size
August 17th

Mentha pulegium
¾ life size, July 20th

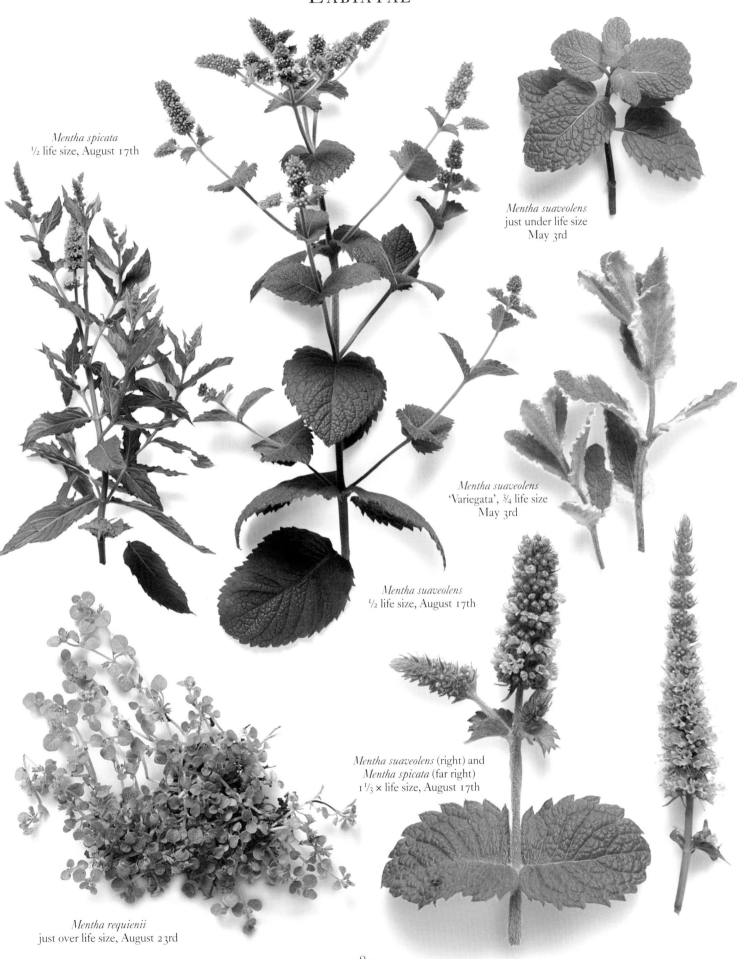

Mentha spicata
½ life size, August 17th

Mentha suaveolens
just under life size
May 3rd

Mentha suaveolens
'Variegata', ¾ life size
May 3rd

Mentha suaveolens
½ life size, August 17th

Mentha suaveolens (right) and
Mentha spicata (far right)
1⅓ × life size, August 17th

Mentha requienii
just over life size, August 23rd

283

Monarda

Monarda L. (1753), in the family Labiatae (sometimes called Lamiaceae), contains about 12 species in North America.
Description Annuals and rhizomatous herbaceous perennials to 1.2m. Leaves aromatic, opposite, usually toothed. Flowers white, yellow, pink, crimson, or purple, in dense terminal whorls or interrupted spikes, subtended by leaf-like, often brightly coloured bracts. Sepals 5, joined to form a toothed calyx with 13 to 15 veins. Petals 5, joined to form a tube widening towards the mouth, the upper lip erect and linear or hooded, the lower 3-lobed with a large central lobe. Stamens 2, exserted or not exserted from the flower. Ovary superior, with 2 cells and 2 ovules per cell; style 1, with unequal branches. Pollination is mainly by bees. The fruit is made up of 4 nutlets.
Key Recognition Features Aromatic plants with dense whorls of flowers and showy bracts.
Ecology and Geography In woods, dry fields, and prairies in North America from Canada to Mexico.
Comment Oswego tea or bergamot, *M. didyma* L., is a popular border plant with numerous varieties in a range of flower colours. A couple of leaves added to a pot of tea make a refreshing summer drink.

Agastache foeniculum
flowers, just over life size
September 25th

Agastache

Agastache Clayton ex Gronov. (1762), in the family Labiatae (sometimes called Lamiaceae), contains 30 species in Asia and North America.
Description Herbaceous perennials to 2m. Leaves aromatic, opposite, toothed or entire. Flowers orange, red, blue, pink, or white, in dense whorls forming terminal spikes. Sepals 5, joined to form a toothed calyx, the upper 3 teeth sometimes partly united. Petals 5, joined to form a tube widening towards the mouth, 2-lipped. Stamens 4, in 2 pairs, the upper pair longest, exserted from the tube or the lower ones curved up under the upper lip. Ovary superior, with 2 cells and 2 ovules per cell; style 1, forked at the tip. Pollination is mainly by bees. The fruit is made up of 4 nutlets.
Key Recognition Features Aromatic plants with dense spikes of flowers in various colours.
Ecology and Geography In woods, on prairies, and in grassy places in low mountains, with about 12 species in North America southwards to Mexico, the others in central and eastern Asia.
Comment A couple of species are cultivated in gardens and recently several selections in various colours have been introduced; *Agastache foeniculum* (Pursh) Kuntze been used for flavouring.

Agastache foeniculum
½ life size
September 25th

Monarda 'Adam'
flowers, ⅔ life size
July 14th

Agastache cana
flowers and section of corolla
2 × life size, August 2nd

Monarda 'Adam'
⅓ life size, July 14th

Agastache cana
⅓ life size, August 2nd

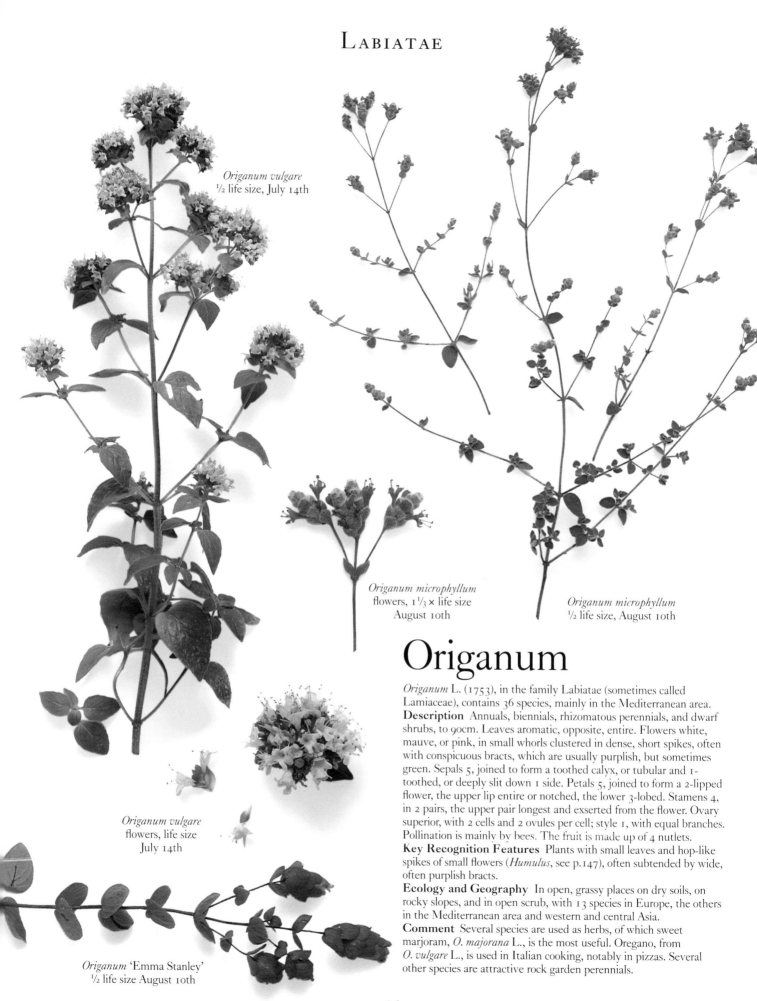

Origanum vulgare
½ life size, July 14th

Origanum microphyllum
flowers, 1⅓ × life size
August 10th

Origanum microphyllum
½ life size, August 10th

Origanum vulgare
flowers, life size
July 14th

Origanum 'Emma Stanley'
½ life size August 10th

Origanum

Origanum L. (1753), in the family Labiatae (sometimes called Lamiaceae), contains 36 species, mainly in the Mediterranean area.
Description Annuals, biennials, rhizomatous perennials, and dwarf shrubs, to 90cm. Leaves aromatic, opposite, entire. Flowers white, mauve, or pink, in small whorls clustered in dense, short spikes, often with conspicuous bracts, which are usually purplish, but sometimes green. Sepals 5, joined to form a toothed calyx, or tubular and 1-toothed, or deeply slit down 1 side. Petals 5, joined to form a 2-lipped flower, the upper lip entire or notched, the lower 3-lobed. Stamens 4, in 2 pairs, the upper pair longest and exserted from the flower. Ovary superior, with 2 cells and 2 ovules per cell; style 1, with equal branches. Pollination is mainly by bees. The fruit is made up of 4 nutlets.
Key Recognition Features Plants with small leaves and hop-like spikes of small flowers (*Humulus*, see p.147), often subtended by wide, often purplish bracts.
Ecology and Geography In open, grassy places on dry soils, on rocky slopes, and in open scrub, with 13 species in Europe, the others in the Mediterranean area and western and central Asia.
Comment Several species are used as herbs, of which sweet marjoram, *O. majorana* L., is the most useful. Oregano, from *O. vulgare* L., is used in Italian cooking, notably in pizzas. Several other species are attractive rock garden perennials.

286

Prunella

Prunella L. (1753), in the family Labiatae (sometimes called Lamiaceae), contains 4 species in Europe and North Africa.

Description Spreading perennials to 60cm, with decumbent rooting stems. Leaves not aromatic, opposite, entire or pinnately lobed. Flowers violet-blue, white, or pink, in 6-flowered whorls forming dense terminal spikes. Sepals 5, joined to form a 2-lipped calyx with 10 veins, the upper lip with 3 short teeth, the lower with 2 slender teeth. Petals 5, joined to form a tube widening towards the mouth, the upper lip hooded, the lower 3-lobed with a large central lobe. Stamens 4, in 2 pairs, the lower pair longest, exserted from the tube but curved under the upper lip. Ovary superior, with 2 cells and 2 ovules per cell; style 1, forked, with equal branches. Pollination is mainly by bees. The fruit is made up of 4 nutlets.

Key Recognition Features Mat-forming plants with short, erect spikes of flowers.

Ecology and Geography In open grassland and more shady places, with 4 species in Europe, Asia, and North Africa.

Comment Selfheal, *P. vulgaris* L., was once used to treat sore throats. *Prunella grandiflora* (L.) Scholler and its cultivars are colourful ground-cover perennials, with pink-, white-, and reddish-flowered cultivars.

Thymus

Thymus L. (1753), thyme, in the family Labiatae (sometimes called Lamiaceae), contains around 350 species in Europe and Asia.

Description Dwarf shrubs and woody-based perennials to 50cm, often creeping. Leaves aromatic, opposite, entire, small. Flowers female or bisexual, white, pink, or purplish, in whorls often forming dense terminal heads. Sepals 5, joined to form a usually 2-lipped calyx, the upper lip with 3 teeth, the lower with 2 teeth. Petals 5, joined to form a short, straight tube, the upper lip entire or notched, the lower with 3 equal lobes. Stamens 4, straight, diverging and usually exserted from the flower. Ovary superior, with 2 cells and 2 ovules per cell; style 1, forked. Pollination is mainly by bees. The fruit is made up of 4 nutlets.

Key Recognition Features Subshrubs with small, highly aromatic leaves and tight heads of flowers.

Ecology and Geography In open, dry grassland and sandy heaths, often in mountains, with 66 species in Europe, the others mostly in western and central Asia but extending to Japan.

Comment *Thymus vulgaris* L. is an important culinary herb; several others species are cultivated for ornament, including some with variegated foliage.

Thymus (left to right): *Thymus serpyllum* var. *albus*, *Thymus serpyllum* 'Russetings', and *Thymus vulgaris*, ½ life size, July 3rd

Thymus serpyllum var. *albus* life size, July 3rd

Prunella grandiflora ⅔ life size, July 20th

Prunella grandiflora flowers, 1⅓ × life size July 20th

Salvia involucrata, flower and section of corolla
1 1/3 × life size, December 1st

Salvia viridis 'Claryssa'
flowers and bracts
1 1/2 × life size, August 1st

Salvia hians
2/3 life size, July 10th

Salvia viridis 'Claryssa'
1/3 life size, August 1st

Salvia glutinosa
2/3 life size, August 5th

Salvia

Salvia L. (1753), in the family Labiatae (sometimes
called Lamiaceae), contains around 900 species worldwide, mainly in
central Asia. For shrubby species see Volume 1.
Description Annuals, biennials, perennials, and shrubs to 5m.
Leaves aromatic, opposite, and entire, toothed, or pinnately lobed.
Flowers blue, purple, pink, red, yellow, or white, in whorls forming
terminal spikes, racemes, or panicles. Sepals 5, joined to form a
2-lipped calyx, the upper lip entire or with 3 unequal teeth, the lower
with 2 teeth. Petals 5, joined to form a tube widening towards the
mouth, the upper lip hooded, entire or 2-lobed, the lower 3-lobed
with a large central lobe. Stamens 2, exserted or not exserted from the
flower, staminodes present or absent. Ovary superior, with 2 cells and
2 ovules per cell; style 1, forked. Pollination is mainly by bees. The
fruit is made up of 4 nutlets.
Key Recognition Features Plants with spike-like inflorescences,
the 2-lipped calyx, and flowers with a hooded upper lip.
Ecology and Geography In dry grassland, open, stony places,
occasionally in woodland, with 36 species in Europe, the others in
Asia, Africa, and North and South America.
Comment Sage, *S. officinalis* L., is an important culinary herb.
Many other species are grown as ornamentals.

Perovskia

Perovskia Karelin (1841), in the family Labiatae, contains around 7 species in central Asia.

Description Subshrubs to 1.5m, woody only at the base, stems silvery. Leaves powerfully aromatic, with a hint of disinfectant, opposite, usually deeply and jaggedly toothed and pinnate, deciduous. The flowers are blue, in loose whorls on branching and leafless spikes. Sepals 5, joined to form a toothed calyx, covered with golden glands. Petals 5, forming a 2-lipped corolla, the upper lip furry outside, sometimes 3-toothed, the lower lip 2-toothed. Stamens 4, 2 fertile and 2 small sterile ones hidden in the upper lip. Ovary superior, with 2 cells and 2 ovules per cell; style 1, forked, slender. Pollination is mainly by bees. The fruit is made up of 4 nutlets.

Key Recognition Features The soft, very pungent, often dissected leaves, and the tall, slender spikes of furry blue flowers in late summer.

Evolution and Relationships *Perovskia* is allied to *Salvia* and *Nepeta* (see p.280) and adapted to climates with a wet spring and dry summer.

Ecology and Geography On dry steppe from central Asia to Afghanistan and Pakistan.

Comment A few species and hybrids are grown for ornament; they are especially valuable for late flowering and tolerating dry summers. Some are more shrubby (see Volume 1).

Salvia forsskaolii, flower parts
1⅓ × life size, July 5th

Perovskia 'Blue Spire'
½ life size, July 20th

Salvia forsskaolii
½ life size, July 5th

Perovskia 'Blue Spire'
flowers, 2 × life size
July 20th

Plectranthus

Plectranthus L'Herit. (1785), in the family Labiatae (sometimes called Lamiaceae), contains around 150 species worldwide, mostly in Africa.

Description Annuals, perennials, and dwarf shrubs to 2m. Leaves usually aromatic, opposite, crenately toothed, often somewhat succulent. Flowers white, mauve-blue, or purple, in loose whorls forming terminal panicles or spikes. Sepals 5, joined to form a 2-lipped calyx, the upper lip with 1 tooth, the lower with 4 equal teeth. Petals 5, joined to form a tube spurred or saccate at the base, the upper lip more-or-less 4-lobed, the lower longer and unlobed. Stamens 4, sometimes only 2 fertile, lying within the lower lip of the corolla. Ovary superior, with 2 cells and 2 ovules per cell; style 1, with equal branches. Pollination is mainly by bees. The fruit is made up of 4 nutlets.

Key Recognition Features Often trailing plants with slightly succulent leaves and spurred or saccate flowers.

Ecology and Geography In woodland and scrub in tropical and warm temperate parts of Africa and Asia, with a few species in Australia.

Comment A few species, including *P. argentatus* S.T. Blake from Queensland, Australia, and the blue-flowered *P. thyrsoideus* (Baker) B. Matthew, are grown in conservatories or as summer bedding. *Plectranthus oertendahlii* T.C.E. Fries and variegated form of *P. forsteri* Benth. are much grown in hanging baskets. Many *Coleus* species are now included in *Plectranthus*, although the commonly grown coleus, with its beautifully coloured leaves, is now called *Solenostemon scutellarioides* (L.) Codd.

Plectranthus argentatus
flowers, 2 × life size
September 13th

"Coleus" *Solenostemon scutellarioides*, 'White Pheasant' (above) and 'Mission Gem' (right) young leaves, ½ life size
July 4th

Plectranthus argentatus
⅔ life size, September 13th

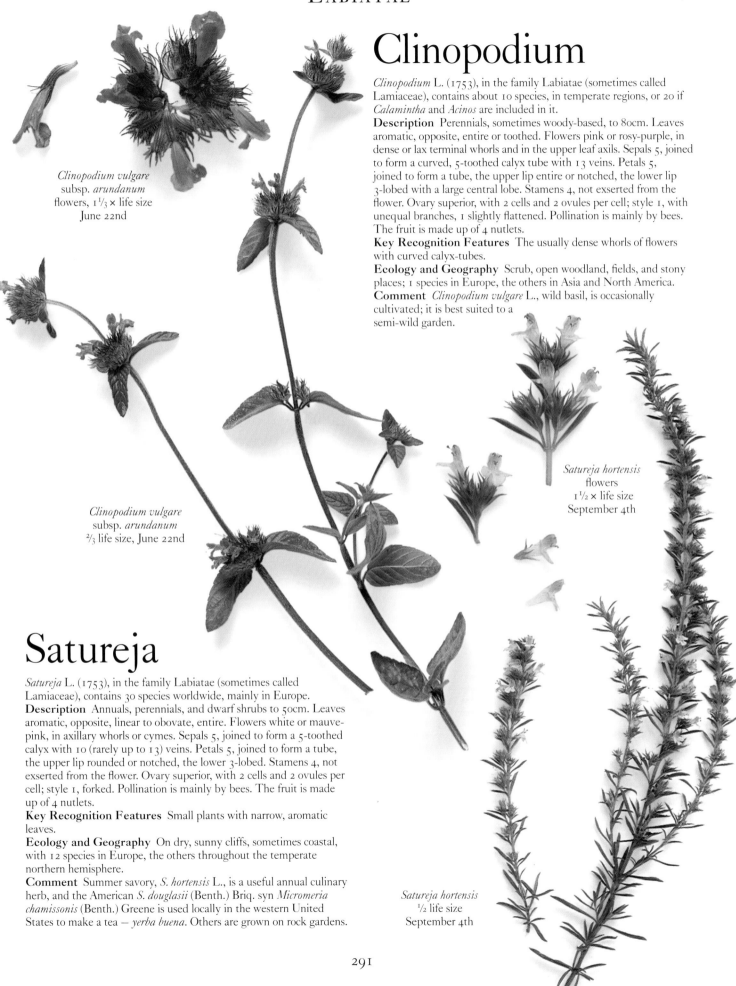

Clinopodium

Clinopodium L. (1753), in the family Labiatae (sometimes called Lamiaceae), contains about 10 species, in temperate regions, or 20 if *Calamintha* and *Acinos* are included in it.

Description Perennials, sometimes woody-based, to 80cm. Leaves aromatic, opposite, entire or toothed. Flowers pink or rosy-purple, in dense or lax terminal whorls and in the upper leaf axils. Sepals 5, joined to form a curved, 5-toothed calyx tube with 13 veins. Petals 5, joined to form a tube, the upper lip entire or notched, the lower lip 3-lobed with a large central lobe. Stamens 4, not exserted from the flower. Ovary superior, with 2 cells and 2 ovules per cell; style 1, with unequal branches, 1 slightly flattened. Pollination is mainly by bees. The fruit is made up of 4 nutlets.

Key Recognition Features The usually dense whorls of flowers with curved calyx-tubes.

Ecology and Geography Scrub, open woodland, fields, and stony places; 1 species in Europe, the others in Asia and North America.

Comment *Clinopodium vulgare* L., wild basil, is occasionally cultivated; it is best suited to a semi-wild garden.

Clinopodium vulgare
subsp. *arundanum*
flowers, 1⅓ × life size
June 22nd

Clinopodium vulgare
subsp. *arundanum*
⅔ life size, June 22nd

Satureja hortensis
flowers
1½ × life size
September 4th

Satureja

Satureja L. (1753), in the family Labiatae (sometimes called Lamiaceae), contains 30 species worldwide, mainly in Europe.

Description Annuals, perennials, and dwarf shrubs to 50cm. Leaves aromatic, opposite, linear to obovate, entire. Flowers white or mauve-pink, in axillary whorls or cymes. Sepals 5, joined to form a 5-toothed calyx with 10 (rarely up to 13) veins. Petals 5, joined to form a tube, the upper lip rounded or notched, the lower 3-lobed. Stamens 4, not exserted from the flower. Ovary superior, with 2 cells and 2 ovules per cell; style 1, forked. Pollination is mainly by bees. The fruit is made up of 4 nutlets.

Key Recognition Features Small plants with narrow, aromatic leaves.

Ecology and Geography On dry, sunny cliffs, sometimes coastal, with 12 species in Europe, the others throughout the temperate northern hemisphere.

Comment Summer savory, *S. hortensis* L., is a useful annual culinary herb, and the American *S. douglasii* (Benth.) Briq. syn *Micromeria chamissonis* (Benth.) Greene is used locally in the western United States to make a tea — *yerba buena*. Others are grown on rock gardens.

Satureja hortensis
½ life size
September 4th

Molucella laevis
flowers and inflated calyx
1²⁄₃ × life size, September 12th

Molucella laevis
flowers, 2¹⁄₄ × life size,
September 12th

Molucella laevis
¹⁄₂ life size
September 12th

Molucella

Molucella L. (1753), in the family Labiatae (sometimes called Lamiaceae), contains around 4 species, mainly in western Asia.

Description Usually annuals, or sometimes short-lived perennials, with flowering stems to 1m. Leaves not aromatic, opposite, often toothed or crenate. Flowers with a large, cup-shaped calyx and small corolla, in whorls of 6–8. Sepals joined to form a large, membranous or stiff and spiny calyx. Petals 5, purplish-pink to white, or white with reddish veins, joined at the base, forming a tube, with upper lip hooded, hairy outside, the lower lip 3-lobed, the large middle lobe sometimes forked. Stamens 4, the anthers held beneath the upper lip. Ovary superior, with 2 cells and 2 ovules per cell; style 1, slender. Pollination is presumed to be by bees. The fruit is made up of four 3-sided nutlets.

Key Recognition Features The small flowers with a very large, green calyces, crowding the stems.

Ecology and Geography In dry fields and steppes from the southern Mediterranean to northwestern India; 2 species in Turkey.

Comment *Molucella laevis* L., sometimes called bells of Ireland, is often grown as an annual for its green, papery, bell-like calyces, which may be dried.

Ballota

Ballota L. (1753), in the family Labiatae, (sometimes called Lamiaceae), contains around 35 species, mainly in southern Europe and western Asia.

Description Perennials with flowering stems to 1m. Leaves not aromatic, opposite, often woolly. Flowers with calyx sometimes enlarged, spreading from a narrow base, and with small corolla, in dense whorls. Sepals often stiff and spiny, usually divided, forming a 10-toothed calyx. Petals 5, purplish, pink or white, often with purple markings, joined at the base, forming a tube, with upper lip straight and often forked, the lower lip 3-lobed. Stamens 4, the anthers held beneath the upper lip. Ovary superior, with 2 cells and 2 ovules per cell; style 1, slender. Pollination is presumed to be by bees. The fruit is made up of 4 smooth nutlets.

Key Recognition Features The calyx tube dilated, with 10 teeth, or 5 in *B. nigra* L., and the small flowers.

Ecology and Geography In dry fields and on rocky slopes, screes, cliffs, and ruins. From southern Europe eastwards to Syria, the Caucasus, and Iran.

Comment *Ballota acetabulosa* (L.) Benth. from Greece, Crete, and western Turkey, is a woolly plant with an enlarged calyx like a *Molucella*. In *B. pseudodictamnus* (L.) Benth., the calyx is smaller. The common *B. nigra*, black horehound, is very close to *Stachys* L. (see p.294) with its 5 calyx teeth.

Ballota acetabulosa
½ life size, August 5th

Ballota acetabulosa
flowers and calyces
1½ × life size, August 5th

Ballota nigra
½ life size, July 10th

Stachys

Stachys L. (1753), woundwort, in the family Labiatae, (sometimes called Lamiaceae), contains around 300 species worldwide, mainly in temperate areas.

Description Perennials or annuals, with flowering stems to 70cm, sometimes tuberous. Leaves opposite, usually densely hairy. Flowers with a small calyx, in many-flowered whorls. Sepals joined to form a 10-ribbed and 5-, 10-, or 30-toothed calyx. Petals 5, purple to white, cream, red, orange, or yellowish, joined at the base to form a tube, with upper lip straight, forked, the lower lip 3-lobed. Stamens 4, in 2 pairs within the tube. Ovary superior, with 2 cells and 2 ovules per cell; style 1, slender. Pollination is by bumblebees, or possibly by hummingbirds in the red-flowered American species. The fruit is made up of 4 smooth nutlets.

Key Recognition Features Usually hairy plants with smallish flowers and the calyx tube not dilated.

Ecology and Geography In rocky places and dry hedgerows, with 72 species in Turkey, 58 in Europe, 9 in California, and others worldwide except Australasia.

Comment A large and diverse genus. Wood betony, *S. officinalis* (L.) Trevisan, often called *Betonica officinalis* L., is common across Europe on acidic soils; the pink form 'Rosea' is often cultivated, as is the larger-flowered *S. macrantha* (C. Koch) Stearn. *Stachys byzantina* C. Koch is widely grown for its white, woolly leaves; *S. thirkei* C. Koch is similar, but usually smaller. *Stachys coccinea* Jacq. from Mexico has red and orange flowers. *Stachys affinis* Bunge, the Chinese artichoke, has whitish, edible tubers.

Stachys affinis
tubers, ¾ life size
April 6th

Stachys byzantina (2 forms)
½ life size, July 11th

Stachys officinalis
⅓ life size, July 5th

Stachys byzantina
'Primrose Heron'
½ life size
July 11th

Leonurus cardiaca
flowers, ¾ life size, July 20th

Leonurus

Leonurus L. (1753), in the family Labiatae, (sometimes called Lamiaceae), contains 3 or 4 species, mainly in Europe and western Asia.

Description Many-stemmed perennials, with flowering stems to 1m. Leaves not aromatic, opposite, usually deeply 3- or 5-lobed. Flowers small, many in a whorl. Sepals joined to form a 5-veined and spiny calyx. Petals 5, pale purplish, joined at the base to form a tube, the upper lip hooded, hairy on the back, the lower lip 3-lobed. Stamens 4. Ovary superior, with 2 cells and 2 ovules per cell; style 1, slender. Pollination is presumed to be by bees. The fruit is made up of 4 nutlets, 3-cornered, with a tuft of hair at the apex.

Key Recognition Features The stalked leaves divided into narrow segments, and nutlets with a tuft of hair at the apex.

Ecology and Geography In rocky places, especially where sheep or cattle have been kept, from the Mediterranean area to central Asia.

Comment *Leonurus cardiaca* L., motherwort, was used medically as a sedative and yields a green dye.

Marrubium

Marrubium L. (1753), in the family Labiatae, (sometimes called Lamiaceae), contains around 30 species, mainly in Europe and western Asia.

Description Perennials or annuals, with flowering stems to 70cm. Leaves opposite, usually densely hairy. Flowers with a small calyx and small corolla, in many-flowered whorls. Sepals joined to form a 10-ribbed and 5-, 10-, or 30-toothed calyx. Petals 5, purple to white, cream or yellowish, joined at the base, forming a tube, with the upper lip straight, forked, the lower lip 3-lobed. Stamens 4, in 2 pairs, within the tube. Ovary superior, with 2 cells and 2 ovules per cell; style 1, slender. Pollination is presumed to be by bees. The fruit is made up of 4 smooth nutlets.

Key Recognition Features Hairy plants with small flowers and the calyx tube not dilated.

Ecology and Geography In rocky places and dry hedgerows from the Mediterranean area to central Asia, with 18 species in Turkey.

Comment *Marrubium vulgare* L., white horehound, was used medicinally in the past, especially for coughs and breathing problems; it is naturalised in North America.

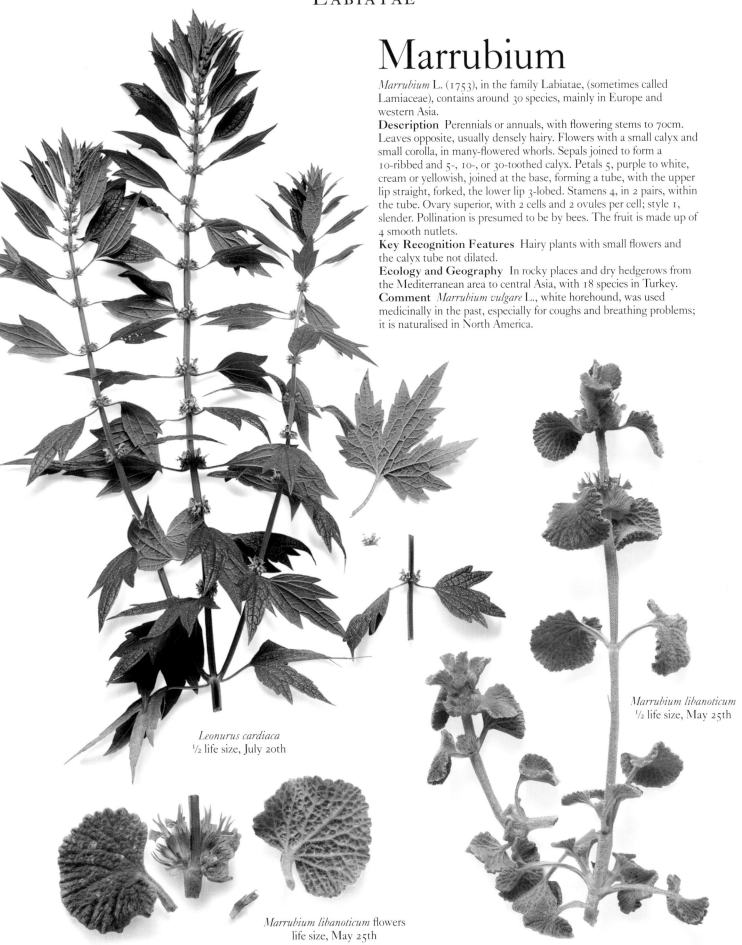

Leonurus cardiaca
¹/₂ life size, July 20th

Marrubium libanoticum
¹/₂ life size, May 25th

Marrubium libanoticum flowers
life size, May 25th

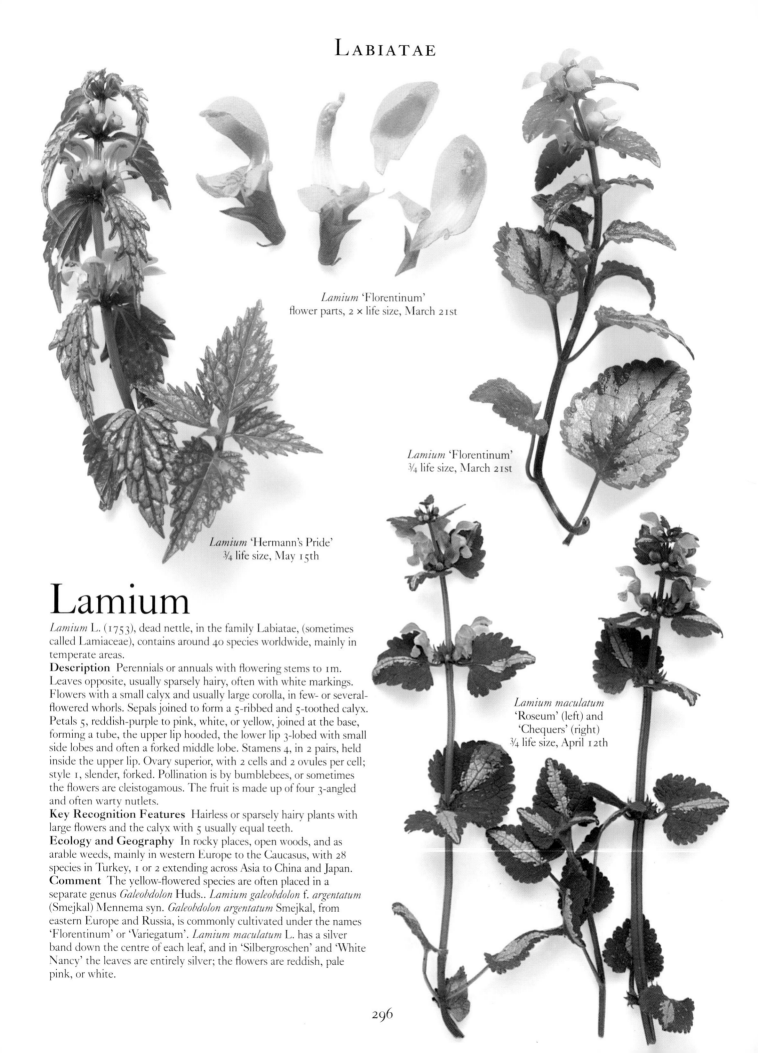

Lamium 'Florentinum'
flower parts, 2 × life size, March 21st

Lamium 'Florentinum'
¾ life size, March 21st

Lamium 'Hermann's Pride'
¾ life size, May 15th

Lamium maculatum
'Roseum' (left) and
'Chequers' (right)
¾ life size, April 12th

Lamium

Lamium L. (1753), dead nettle, in the family Labiatae, (sometimes called Lamiaceae), contains around 40 species worldwide, mainly in temperate areas.

Description Perennials or annuals with flowering stems to 1m. Leaves opposite, usually sparsely hairy, often with white markings. Flowers with a small calyx and usually large corolla, in few- or several-flowered whorls. Sepals joined to form a 5-ribbed and 5-toothed calyx. Petals 5, reddish-purple to pink, white, or yellow, joined at the base, forming a tube, the upper lip hooded, the lower lip 3-lobed with small side lobes and often a forked middle lobe. Stamens 4, in 2 pairs, held inside the upper lip. Ovary superior, with 2 cells and 2 ovules per cell; style 1, slender, forked. Pollination is by bumblebees, or sometimes the flowers are cleistogamous. The fruit is made up of four 3-angled and often warty nutlets.

Key Recognition Features Hairless or sparsely hairy plants with large flowers and the calyx with 5 usually equal teeth.

Ecology and Geography In rocky places, open woods, and as arable weeds, mainly in western Europe to the Caucasus, with 28 species in Turkey, 1 or 2 extending across Asia to China and Japan.

Comment The yellow-flowered species are often placed in a separate genus *Galeobdolon* Huds.. *Lamium galeobdolon* f. *argentatum* (Smejkal) Mennema syn. *Galeobdolon argentatum* Smejkal, from eastern Europe and Russia, is commonly cultivated under the names 'Florentinum' or 'Variegatum'. *Lamium maculatum* L. has a silver band down the centre of each leaf, and in 'Silbergroschen' and 'White Nancy' the leaves are entirely silver; the flowers are reddish, pale pink, or white.

Melittis

Melittis L. (1753), bastard balm, in the family Labiatae, (sometimes called Lamiaceae), contains 1 species, *M. melissophyllum* L., in Europe and western Asia.

Description Perennial with flowering stems to 70cm. Leaves opposite, short-stalked, sparsely hairy and sometimes glandular. Flowers with a small calyx and usually large corolla, in few-flowered whorls. Sepals joined to form a 10-veined and unequally 5-toothed calyx. Petals 5, reddish-purple to pink and white, joined at the base, forming a tube, with the upper lip slightly hooded, the lower lip large, 3-lobed. Stamens 4. Ovary superior, with 2 cells and 2 ovules per cell; style 1, slender, forked. Pollination is by bumblebees. The fruit is made up of four 3-angled nutlets.

Key Recognition Features Sparsely hairy plants with large flowers and the calyx with 5 unequal teeth.

Ecology and Geography In rocky places, open woods, and hedgerows in Europe from southwestern England to the Ukraine and northern Turkey.

Comment An attractive perennial with scentless leaves and large flowers that vary in colour from purplish-pink to pink and white or white with purplish markings; 3 subspecies are recognised, differing in leaf size and the presence or absence of glandular hairs.

Meehania

Meehania Britt. (1893), in the family Labiatae, (sometimes called Lamiaceae), contains 6 or 7 species in eastern Asia and eastern North America.

Description Perennials, often with creeping stolons, with flowering stems to 30cm, or annuals. Leaves opposite, usually not hairy, stalked and heart-shaped to lanceolate. Flowers with a scented calyx and usually large corolla, in few- or several-flowered whorls. Sepals joined to form a 15-veined and 5-toothed calyx. Petals 5, purplish-blue, joined at the base, forming a long tube with the upper lip 2-lobed or notched, the lower lip 3-lobed. Stamens 4, in 2 pairs, held inside the tube. Ovary superior, with 2 cells and 2 ovules per cell; style 1, slender, forked. Pollination is presumed to be by bees. The fruit is made up of 4 ovate, smooth or shortly hairy nutlets.

Key Recognition Features Hairless or sparsely hairy plants with relatively large flowers and the calyx 2-lipped, with 5 unequal teeth.

Ecology and Geography In damp, rocky woods in the mountains, with *M. cordata* (Nutt.) Britt. in eastern North America from Illinois to Pennsylvania, Tennessee, and North Carolina, *M. fargesii* (Léveillé) Wu in Sichuan in western China, and 2 species in Japan.

Comment The genus is named after Thomas Meehan (1826–1901), a botanist and horticulturist of Philadelphia. Species are sometimes grown in woodland gardens, and are unusual in that the scent comes from the glandular calyx.

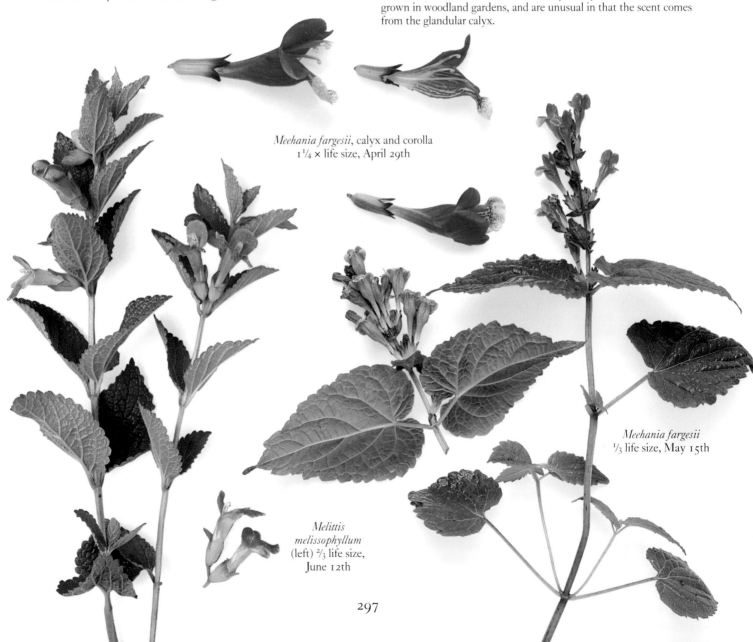

Meehania fargesii, calyx and corolla
1¼ × life size, April 29th

Meehania fargesii
⅓ life size, May 15th

*Melittis
melissophyllum*
(left) ⅔ life size,
June 12th

Phlomis

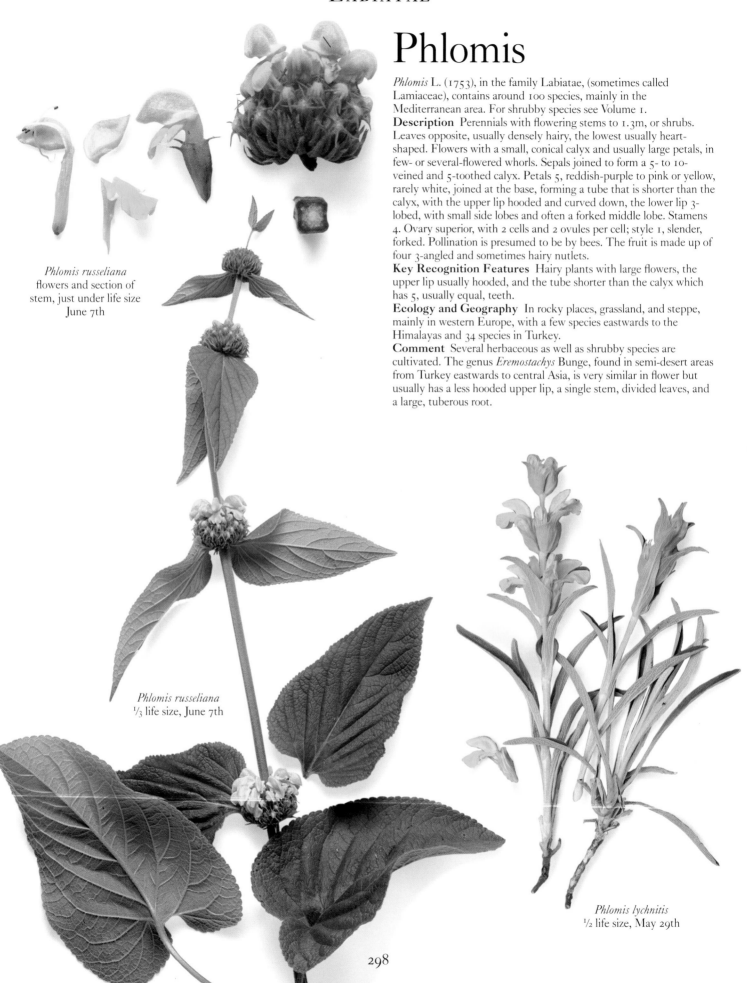

Phlomis L. (1753), in the family Labiatae, (sometimes called Lamiaceae), contains around 100 species, mainly in the Mediterranean area. For shrubby species see Volume 1.

Description Perennials with flowering stems to 1.3m, or shrubs. Leaves opposite, usually densely hairy, the lowest usually heart-shaped. Flowers with a small, conical calyx and usually large petals, in few- or several-flowered whorls. Sepals joined to form a 5- to 10-veined and 5-toothed calyx. Petals 5, reddish-purple to pink or yellow, rarely white, joined at the base, forming a tube that is shorter than the calyx, with the upper lip hooded and curved down, the lower lip 3-lobed, with small side lobes and often a forked middle lobe. Stamens 4. Ovary superior, with 2 cells and 2 ovules per cell; style 1, slender, forked. Pollination is presumed to be by bees. The fruit is made up of four 3-angled and sometimes hairy nutlets.

Key Recognition Features Hairy plants with large flowers, the upper lip usually hooded, and the tube shorter than the calyx which has 5, usually equal, teeth.

Ecology and Geography In rocky places, grassland, and steppe, mainly in western Europe, with a few species eastwards to the Himalayas and 34 species in Turkey.

Comment Several herbaceous as well as shrubby species are cultivated. The genus *Eremostachys* Bunge, found in semi-desert areas from Turkey eastwards to central Asia, is very similar in flower but usually has a less hooded upper lip, a single stem, divided leaves, and a large, tuberous root.

Phlomis russeliana
flowers and section of
stem, just under life size
June 7th

Phlomis russeliana
⅓ life size, June 7th

Phlomis lychnitis
½ life size, May 29th

298

Physostegia

Physostegia Benth. (1834), in the family Labiatae, (sometimes called Lamiaceae), contains around 12 species in North America.

Description Perennials with flowering stems to 1m. Leaves opposite, usually glabrous, the lowest usually lanceolate. Flowers with a small, cup-shaped or inflated, 5-toothed calyx and large petals, in pairs on dense spikes. Petals 5, reddish-purple to pink, or rarely white, joined at the base, forming an expanding tube that is longer than the calyx, with the upper lip hooded, the lower lip 3-lobed. Stamens 4, with hairy filaments. Ovary superior, with 2 cells and 2 ovules per cell; style 1, slender, forked. Pollination is presumed to be by bees. The fruit is made up of 4 smooth nutlets.

Key Recognition Features Upright perennials with narrow leaves and spikes of flowers in pairs.

Ecology and Geography In moist grassland, prairies, and open woods throughout most of North America, with the exception of the southwest.

Comment *Physostegia virginiana* (L.) Benth. is commonly cultivated in gardens in North America and Europe. It is closely allied to *Dracocephalum* (see p.281).

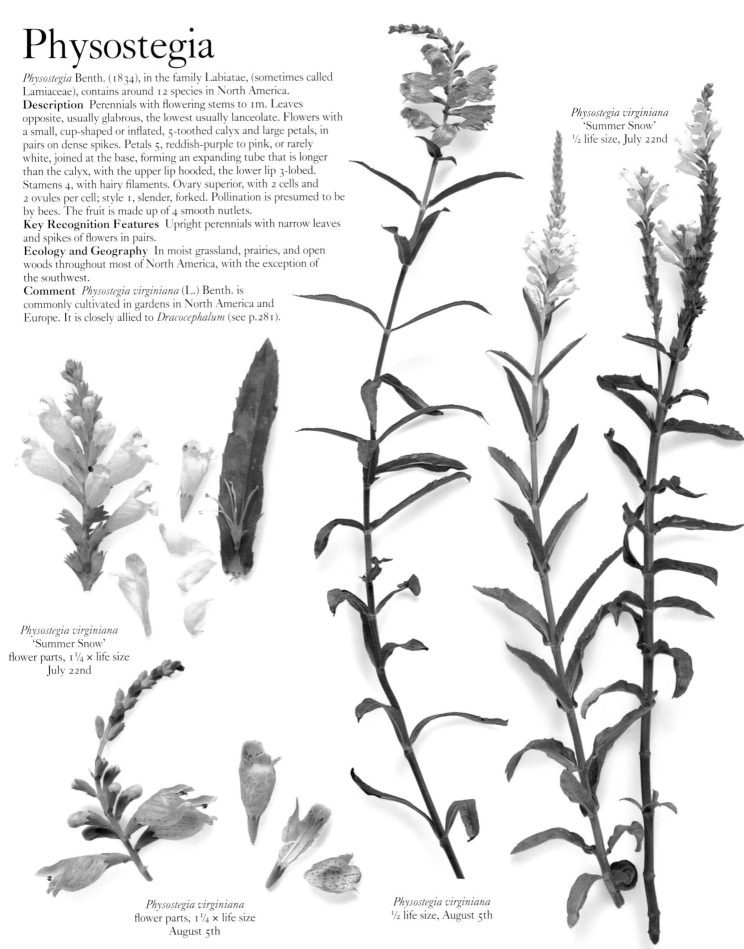

Physostegia virginiana
'Summer Snow'
½ life size, July 22nd

Physostegia virginiana
'Summer Snow'
flower parts, 1¼ × life size
July 22nd

Physostegia virginiana
flower parts, 1¼ × life size
August 5th

Physostegia virginiana
½ life size, August 5th

Trachymene

Trachymene Rudge (1811), syn. *Didiscus* DC, in the family Umbelliferae (sometimes called Apiaceae), contains around 45 species, mainly in South East Asia and Australia.

Description Annuals, biennials, or perennials with upright stems to 30cm. Leaves variously divided into narrow segments. Flowers in rounded, simple umbels, pink, white, or blue, with numerous bracts. Sepals minute. Petals 5, separate, the outer longer than the inner. Stamens 5. Ovary inferior, with 2 cells and 1 ovule per cell; styles 2. Pollination is not recorded. The fruit is made up of 2 mericarps, flattened, ovate to orbicular, with 5 narrow ridges.

Key Recognition Features Upright plants with dense, simple umbels of flowers.

Ecology and Geography In dry, open places, especially after fires, with 35 species in Australia, and the rest in South East Asia, eastwards to Fiji.

Comment *Trachymeme caerulea* Graham from Western Australia is an attractive annual, often cultivated as an ornamental; the flowers are usually pale blue in the wild, pink and white also in cultivation.

Trachymene caerulea
flowerhead, 2 × life size
September 11th

Trachymene caerulea
just under life size
September 11th

Azorella

Azorella Lam. (1783), in the family Umbelliferae (sometimes called Apiaceae), contains 130 species, mainly in South America.

Description Mat-forming perennials to 60cm tall and often over 1m across. Leaves sometimes undivided, variously forked or lobed. Flowers in small umbels. Sepals minute. Petals 5, small, separate, yellow to green or brownish. Stamens 5. Ovary inferior, with 2 cells and 1 ovule per cell; styles 2. Pollination is presumed to be by various small insects. The fruit is made up of 2 mericarps.

Key Recognition Features Mat-forming plants with shining, leathery leaves and small, insignificant, greenish-yellow flowers.

Ecology and Geography In rocky, gravelly, and peaty places and open grassland in the Antarctic islands and South America.

Comment Some species, such as *A. trifurcata* (Gaertn.) Hook. fil. from southern Chile and Argentina, are grown on rock gardens for their interesting mats of shiny rosettes.

Azorella trifurcata
life size, July 20th

Hydrocotyle vulgaris
¾ life size, August 23rd

Hydrocotyle

Hydrocotyle L. (1753), in the family Umbelliferae (sometimes called Apiaceae), contains 130 species worldwide.

Description Perennials with creeping stems to 20cm tall. Leaves all basal, usually rounded, and often peltate. Flowers in umbels or loose spikes, small and green. Sepals minute. Petals 5, small, separate, greenish. Stamens 5. Ovary inferior, with 2 cells and 1 ovule per cell; styles 2. Self-pollination is presumed to be normal. The fruit is made up of 2 mericarps, flattened, ovate to orbicular, with 5 narrow ridges.

Key Recognition Features Creeping plants with peltate or rounded leaves and small, insignificant, green flowers.

Ecology and Geography In marshy places or shallow water, with 1 species, *H. vulgaris* L., the marsh pennywort, widespread in Europe, 3 species in California, 55 species in Australia, and the rest scattered around the world.

Comment Some species are grown for their interesting leaves.

Astrantia

Astrantia L. (1753), masterwort, in the family Umbelliferae (sometimes called Apiaceae), contains around 8 species, mainly in eastern Europe.

Description Perennials to 1m. Leaves palmately lobed or divided, or sometimes with only 3 lobes. Flowers in simple umbels surrounded by a ring of green or coloured, pointed, petal-like bracts. Sepals conspicuous. Petals 5, small, separate, whitish. Stamens 5. Ovary inferior, with 2 cells and 1 ovule per cell; styles 2. Pollination is by various bees and flies. The fruit is made up of 2 mericarps, with inflated ridges.

Key Recognition Features Clump-forming plants with lobed leaves and small, insignificant, whitish flowers, surrounded by a ring of petal-like bracts.

Ecology and Geography In rocky meadows and open woods, with 5 species in Europe, the rest from Turkey and the Caucasus.

Comment Several species, and particularly richly claret-coloured forms of *A. major* L., are popular in gardens. With its crowded, small flowers surrounded by petal-like bracts, the flowerhead is superficially similar to that of a daisy (Compositae, see pp. 336–81).

Astrantia major
½ life size, June 7th

Astrantia major 'Rubra'
flowerheads, 1¼ × life size
June 7th

Astrantia major
flowers and bracts
1¼ × life size
June 7th

Sanicula

Sanicula L. (1753), in the family Umbelliferae (sometimes called Apiaceae), contains around 40 species worldwide.

Description Perennials with flowering stems to 80cm. Leaves mostly basal, 3- or 5-lobed or divided, the segments lobed, toothed, or unlobed. Flowers in irregularly compound umbels surrounded by small bracts, the central few bisexual, those around the edge of the umbel male. Sepals pointed. Petals 5, small, separate, green, yellow, pink, purplish, or blue. Stamens 5. Ovary inferior, with 2 cells and 1 ovule per cell; styles 2. Pollination is by small flies and beetles, and probably also by self-pollination. The fruit is made up of 2 mericarps, covered with tubercles or hooked bristles.

Key Recognition Features Small woodland plants with lobed leaves and irregular, stalked umbels of small flowers.

Ecology and Geography In woods and scrub and on grassy slopes, from Europe to China, in South Africa and South America, and with the greatest concentration of species in California, where there are 13.

Comment Some species are modest but attractive woodland plants.

Sanicula europaea
2/3 life size, May 10th

Sanicula europaea
fruit, 1 1/2 × life size
June 22nd

Hacquetia

Hacquetia DC (1830), in the family Umbelliferae (sometimes called Apiaceae), contains 1 species, *H. epipactis* (Scop.) DC, in central and eastern Europe.

Description Perennial to 25cm, with a creeping rhizome. Leaves 3-lobed or divided, the segments lobed or toothed. Flowers in simple umbels surrounded by a ring of rounded, toothed, green bracts. Sepals conspicuous. Petals 5, small, separate, yellowish. Stamens 5. Ovary inferior, with 2 cells and 1 ovule per cell; styles 2. Pollination is presumed to be by various bees and flies. The fruit is made up of 2 mericarps, with conspicuous ridges.

Key Recognition Features Small plants with 3-lobed leaves and small, yellow flowers, surrounded by a ring of rounded, green bracts.

Ecology and Geography In mountain woods from northern Italy and Austria to Yugoslavia and Poland.

Comment An attractive plant, often cultivated in woodland gardens.

Hacquetia epipactis
1 1/3 × life size
September 12th

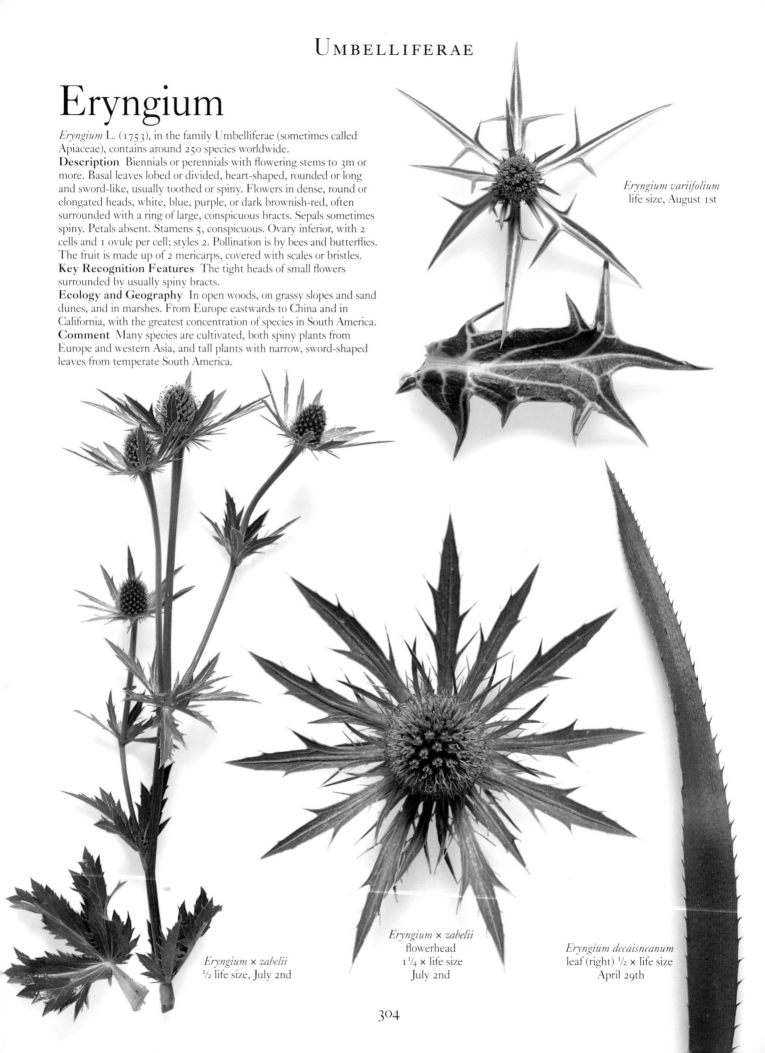

Eryngium

Eryngium L. (1753), in the family Umbelliferae (sometimes called Apiaceae), contains around 250 species worldwide.

Description Biennials or perennials with flowering stems to 3m or more. Basal leaves lobed or divided, heart-shaped, rounded or long and sword-like, usually toothed or spiny. Flowers in dense, round or elongated heads, white, blue, purple, or dark brownish-red, often surrounded with a ring of large, conspicuous bracts. Sepals sometimes spiny. Petals absent. Stamens 5, conspicuous. Ovary inferior, with 2 cells and 1 ovule per cell; styles 2. Pollination is by bees and butterflies. The fruit is made up of 2 mericarps, covered with scales or bristles.

Key Recognition Features The tight heads of small flowers surrounded by usually spiny bracts.

Ecology and Geography In open woods, on grassy slopes and sand dunes, and in marshes. From Europe eastwards to China and in California, with the greatest concentration of species in South America.

Comment Many species are cultivated, both spiny plants from Europe and western Asia, and tall plants with narrow, sword-shaped leaves from temperate South America.

Eryngium variifolium
life size, August 1st

Eryngium × zabelii
½ life size, July 2nd

Eryngium × zabelii
flowerhead
1¼ × life size
July 2nd

Eryngium decaisneanum
leaf (right) ½ × life size
April 29th

Eryngium giganteum 'Silver Ghost', flowers, showing
5 stamens (above) and 2 styles (below)
3 × life size, September 4th

Eryngium giganteum 'Silver Ghost' with detail of stem leaf (left)
and basal leaf (above right), ½ life size, September 4th

Eryngium giganteum 'Silver Ghost'
flowerhead, just over life size
September 4th

Anthriscus

Anthriscus Pers. (1805), in the family Umbelliferae (sometimes called Apiaceae), contains around 12 species, mainly in Europe.

Description Annuals, biennials, or perennials with flowering stems to 1m or more. Basal leaves 2- or 3-pinnate. Flowers in compound umbels, usually without bracts. Sepals minute or absent. Petals 5, white, the outer petals of the outer flowers larger than the inner. Stamens 5, conspicuous. Ovary inferior, with 2 cells and 1 ovule per cell; styles 2. Pollination is mainly by flies. The fruit is made up of 2 mericarps, ovoid or oblong, beaked, the ridges confined to the beak.

Key Recognition Features The flat, loose heads of white flowers in compound umbels with no bracts, and flat, parsley-like leaves.

Ecology and Geography In open woods, and on grassy slopes and roadsides from Europe eastwards to Asia, with 1 species, *A. sylvestris* (L.) Hoffm. extending southwards into Ethiopia and to the Drakensberg mountains in Natal, where it is apparently native.

Comment Chervil, *A. cereifolium* (L.) Hoffm., has been cultivated for its aniseed-flavoured leaves since Roman times. *Anthriscus sylvestris* is the hedge or cow parsley or Queen Anne's lace, a common roadside flower in England in the spring; it has a dark-leaved cultivar, 'Ravenswing'.

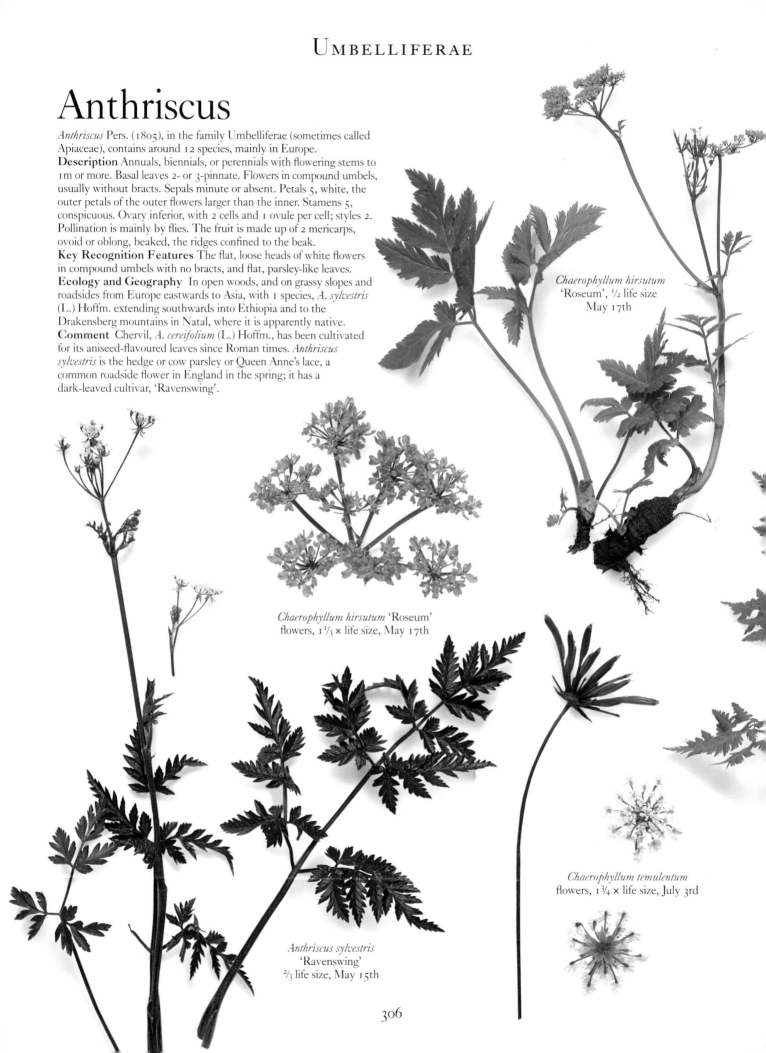

Chaerophyllum hirsutum 'Roseum', ½ life size May 17th

Chaerophyllum hirsutum 'Roseum' flowers, 1⅓ × life size, May 17th

Anthriscus sylvestris 'Ravenswing' ⅔ life size, May 15th

Chaerophyllum temulentum flowers, 1¾ × life size, July 3rd

Chaerophyllum

Chaerophyllum L. (1753), in the family Umbelliferae (sometimes called Apiaceae), contains around 35 species, mainly in Europe and Asia.

Description Biennials or perennials with flowering stems to 1m or more. Basal leaves 2- or 3-pinnate. Flowers in compound umbels, usually without bracts. Sepals minute or absent. Petals 5, white, pinkish, or yellow, those of the outer flowers slightly larger. Stamens 5. Ovary inferior, with 2 cells and 1 ovule per cell; styles 2. Pollination is mainly by flies. The fruit is made up of 2 mericarps, ovoid or oblong, and scarcely beaked.

Key Recognition Features Roughly hairy, often purple-spotted stems, flat, loose heads of white, pink, or yellow flowers in compound umbels with no bracts, and flat, parsley-like leaves.

Ecology and Geography In open woods and on roadsides from Europe eastwards to Asia and into North Africa.

Comment *Chaerophyllum hirsutum* is often cultivated, especially the pink form 'Roseum'. *Chaerophyllum temulentum* L., the rough chervil, is very similar to *Anthriscus sylvestris*, but flowers later and is distinguished by the tougher, purple-spotted stems.

*Chaerophyllum
temulentum*
$^1/_3$ life size
July 4th

Myrrhis odorata showing a female
umbel with developing fruits and
3 umbels with male flowers only
$^1/_2$ life size, May 15th

Myrrhis

Myrrhis Mill. (1768), sweet cicely, in the family Umbelliferae, (sometimes called Apiaceae), contains 1 species, *M. odorata* (L.) Scop. in Europe and western Asia.

Description Perennial with flowering stems to 2m. Basal leaves 2- or 3-pinnate, softly hairy, and scented of aniseed. Flowers in compound umbels, usually without bracts, the later flowers often male only. Sepals minute or absent. Petals 5, white. Stamens 5. Ovary inferior, with 2 cells and 1 ovule per cell; styles 2. Pollination is mainly by flies. The fruit is made up of 2 mericarps, linear-oblong, short-beaked, dark brown, and shiny, with the ridges almost winged.

Key Recognition Features Softly hairy leaves, often with silvery markings, scented of aniseed, and long, dark brown, shiny fruit.

Ecology and Geography In mountain woods, and in meadows in the mountains of southern Europe; widely naturalised elsewhere in cool, moist areas, for example in Chile.

Comment Sweet cicely was widely cultivated in the past for cooking, for strewing on floors, and for fodder. It is particularly characteristic of northern England and Scotland.

Myrrhis odorata
young fruit
$1^3/_4$ × life size
May 15th

307

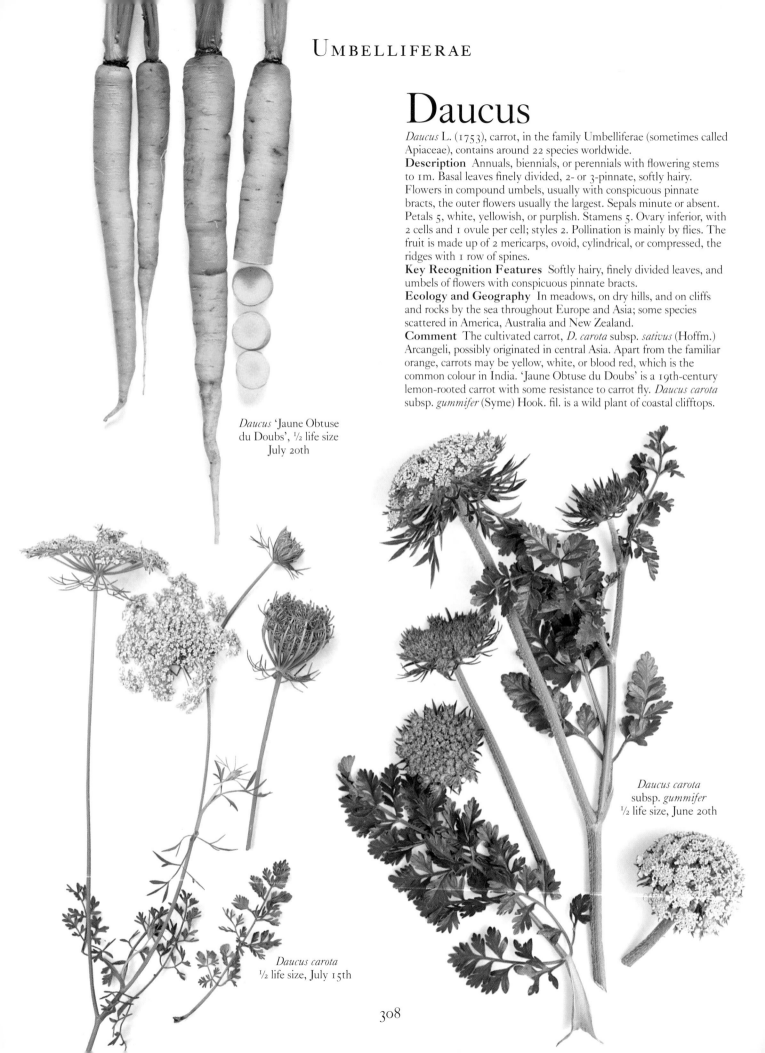

Daucus

Daucus L. (1753), carrot, in the family Umbelliferae (sometimes called Apiaceae), contains around 22 species worldwide.

Description Annuals, biennials, or perennials with flowering stems to 1m. Basal leaves finely divided, 2- or 3-pinnate, softly hairy. Flowers in compound umbels, usually with conspicuous pinnate bracts, the outer flowers usually the largest. Sepals minute or absent. Petals 5, white, yellowish, or purplish. Stamens 5. Ovary inferior, with 2 cells and 1 ovule per cell; styles 2. Pollination is mainly by flies. The fruit is made up of 2 mericarps, ovoid, cylindrical, or compressed, the ridges with 1 row of spines.

Key Recognition Features Softly hairy, finely divided leaves, and umbels of flowers with conspicuous pinnate bracts.

Ecology and Geography In meadows, on dry hills, and on cliffs and rocks by the sea throughout Europe and Asia; some species scattered in America, Australia and New Zealand.

Comment The cultivated carrot, *D. carota* subsp. *sativus* (Hoffm.) Arcangeli, possibly originated in central Asia. Apart from the familiar orange, carrots may be yellow, white, or blood red, which is the common colour in India. 'Jaune Obtuse du Doubs' is a 19th-century lemon-rooted carrot with some resistance to carrot fly. *Daucus carota* subsp. *gummifer* (Syme) Hook. fil. is a wild plant of coastal clifftops.

Daucus 'Jaune Obtuse du Doubs', ½ life size July 20th

Daucus carota subsp. *gummifer* ½ life size, June 20th

Daucus carota ½ life size, July 15th

Pastinaca

Pastinaca L. (1753), parsnip, in the family Umbelliferae (sometimes called Apiaceae), contains around 14 species in Europe and Asia.

Description Biennials or perennials with flowering stems to 2m. Basal leaves coarsely divided, simple or pinnate, roughly hairy. Flowers in compound umbels, usually without bracts. Sepals absent. Petals 5, yellow, incurved. Stamens 5. Ovary inferior, with 2 cells and 1 ovule per cell; styles 2. Pollination is mainly by flies and small wasps. The fruit is made up of 2 mericarps, elliptical, compressed, with the ridges winged.

Key Recognition Features Coarse, pinnate leaves, and umbels of yellow flowers without bracts.

Ecology and Geography On roadsides, dry, grassy hills, and riverbanks throughout Europe and Asia. Naturalised in North and South America, Australia, and New Zealand.

Comment The cultivated parsnip, *P. sativa* L. subsp. *sativus*, is close to the wild type, but develops a thickened root at the end of the first year.

Pastinaca sativa
'Tender and True'
$\frac{1}{3}$ life size
September 27th

Pastinaca sativa
$\frac{2}{3}$ life size, August 3rd

Bupleurum

Bupleurum L. (1753), in the family Umbelliferae (sometimes called Apiaceae), contains around 180 species, mostly in southern Europe and southwestern Asia.

Description Annuals or perennials with flowering stems to 1m or more; rarely shrubs. Basal leaves simple, often lanceolate with parallel veins, smooth. Flowers in compound umbels, sometimes without bracts, but usually with conspicuous bracteoles. Sepals absent. Petals 5, yellow. Stamens 5. Ovary inferior, with 2 cells and 1 ovule per cell; styles 2. Pollination is mainly by flies. The fruit is made up of 2 mericarps, with 5 ridges, sometimes winged.

Key Recognition Features The smooth leaves, the upper ones yellow or brown, often encircling the stem, and the flowers with conspicuous bracteoles.

Ecology and Geography In grassy places and arable fields, on dry hills, and in scrub throughout southern Europe, North Africa, and Asia eastwards to Japan. There are 46 species in Turkey, 1 in arctic North America, and 1 in South Africa.

Comment *Bupleurum rotundifolium* L., thorow wax, was formerly a cornfield weed in England; it is sometimes grown as an annual and used by florists. Other species are sometimes cultivated.

Smyrnium

Smyrnium L. (1753), alexanders, in the family Umbelliferae (sometimes called Apiaceae), contains around 7 species in southern Europe and southwestern Asia.

Description Biennials with flowering stems to 2m. Basal leaves coarsely divided, 2- to 4-pinnate or ternate, smooth. Flowers in compound umbels, usually without bracts. Sepals absent. Petals 5, yellow. Stamens 5. Ovary inferior, with 2 cells and 1 ovule per cell; styles 2. Pollination is mainly by flies, commonly species of *Bibio*. The fruit is made up of 2 mericarps, curved, not flattened, usually black when ripe.

Key Recognition Features The smooth leaves and yellowish flowers followed by black seeds.

Ecology and Geography On roadsides, especially near the sea, on rocky hills, and in scrub and open woods throughout southern Europe, North Africa, and Asia.

Comment Alexanders, *S. olusatrum* L., called the parsley of Alexandria, was cultivated as a winter vegetable until superseded by celery in the 15th century; it is said to have been brought to Britain by the Romans and is still common around the ruins at Portus Lemanis in Kent. Certainly it was used as lenten fare in the Middle Ages and is still associated with old monastic settlements. *Smyrnium perfoliatum* L., in which the stems appear to go through the rounded leaves, is often grown as an ornamental for its bright yellow-green upper leaves in spring.

Bupleurum rotundifolium
flowers and bracteoles (above)
and upper leaves (below)
2 × life size, September 4th

Bupleurum rotundifolium
½ life size
September 4th

Smyrnium perfoliatum
1 1/3 × life size, May 2nd

Smyrnium perfoliatum
seeds, 1 1/3 × life size
July 9th

Smyrnium perfoliatum
1/2 life size, May 2nd

Smyrnium olusatrum
seeds, 2 × life size
July 20th

Smyrnium olusatrum
fruiting head, 3/4 life size
July 20th

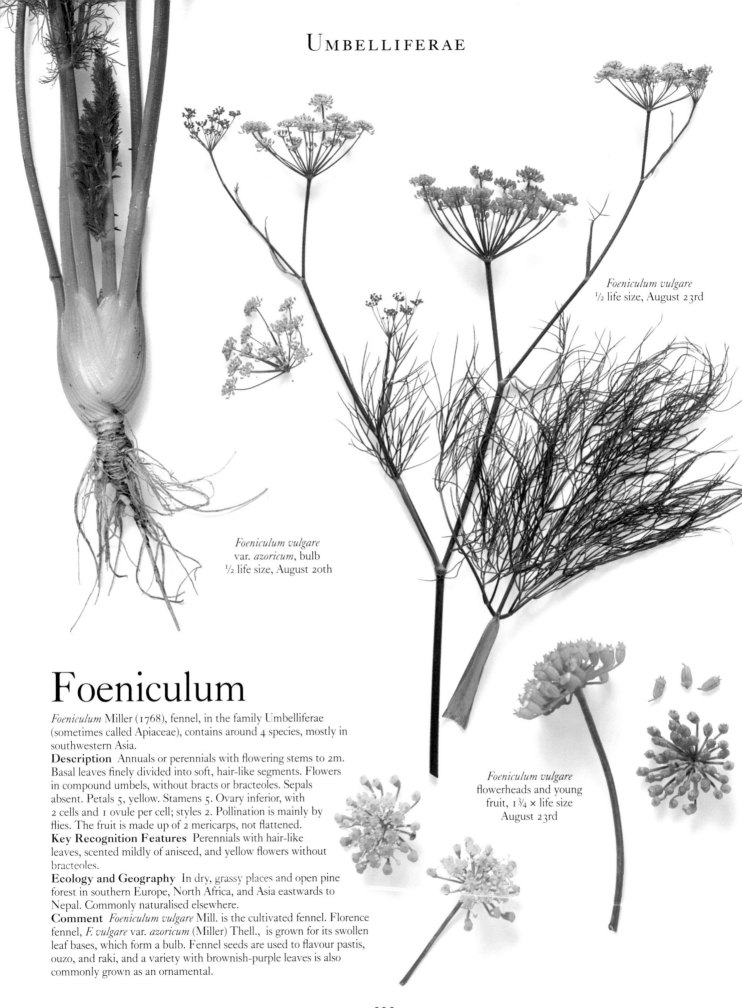

Foeniculum vulgare
½ life size, August 23rd

Foeniculum vulgare
var. *azoricum*, bulb
½ life size, August 20th

Foeniculum

Foeniculum Miller (1768), fennel, in the family Umbelliferae (sometimes called Apiaceae), contains around 4 species, mostly in southwestern Asia.

Description Annuals or perennials with flowering stems to 2m. Basal leaves finely divided into soft, hair-like segments. Flowers in compound umbels, without bracts or bracteoles. Sepals absent. Petals 5, yellow. Stamens 5. Ovary inferior, with 2 cells and 1 ovule per cell; styles 2. Pollination is mainly by flies. The fruit is made up of 2 mericarps, not flattened.

Key Recognition Features Perennials with hair-like leaves, scented mildly of aniseed, and yellow flowers without bracteoles.

Ecology and Geography In dry, grassy places and open pine forest in southern Europe, North Africa, and Asia eastwards to Nepal. Commonly naturalised elsewhere.

Comment *Foeniculum vulgare* Mill. is the cultivated fennel. Florence fennel, *F. vulgare* var. *azoricum* (Miller) Thell., is grown for its swollen leaf bases, which form a bulb. Fennel seeds are used to flavour pastis, ouzo, and raki, and a variety with brownish-purple leaves is also commonly grown as an ornamental.

Foeniculum vulgare
flowerheads and young
fruit, 1¾ × life size
August 23rd

Ferula

Ferula L. (1753), in the family Umbelliferae (sometimes called Apiaceae), contains around 170 species, mainly in southwestern Asia.

Description Perennials with flowering stems to 5m. Basal leaves finely divided into soft and hair-like or flat and fern-like segments. Flowers in compound umbels, without bracts or bracteoles, the lateral umbels usually male only. Sepals minute or absent. Petals 5, usually yellow. Stamens 5. Ovary inferior, with 2 cells and 1 ovule per cell; styles 2. Pollination is mainly by flies. The fruit is made up of 2 mericarps, large and strongly flattened, often winged.

Key Recognition Features Often huge perennials with hair-like leaves and yellow flowers without bracteoles, followed by large, flattened seeds.

Ecology and Geography In dry, open ground, on steppes and rocky hillsides, with 17 species in Turkey, the rest scattered across southern Europe, North Africa, and Asia.

Comment Ferulas are particulaly rich in gums and resins, which have been used widely since ancient times as flavourings, medicines, and incense. They are conspicuous plants, valuable in dry gardens for their statuesque flowering stems. The genus *Ferulago* W. Koch is similar, but has persistent bracts and bracteoles.

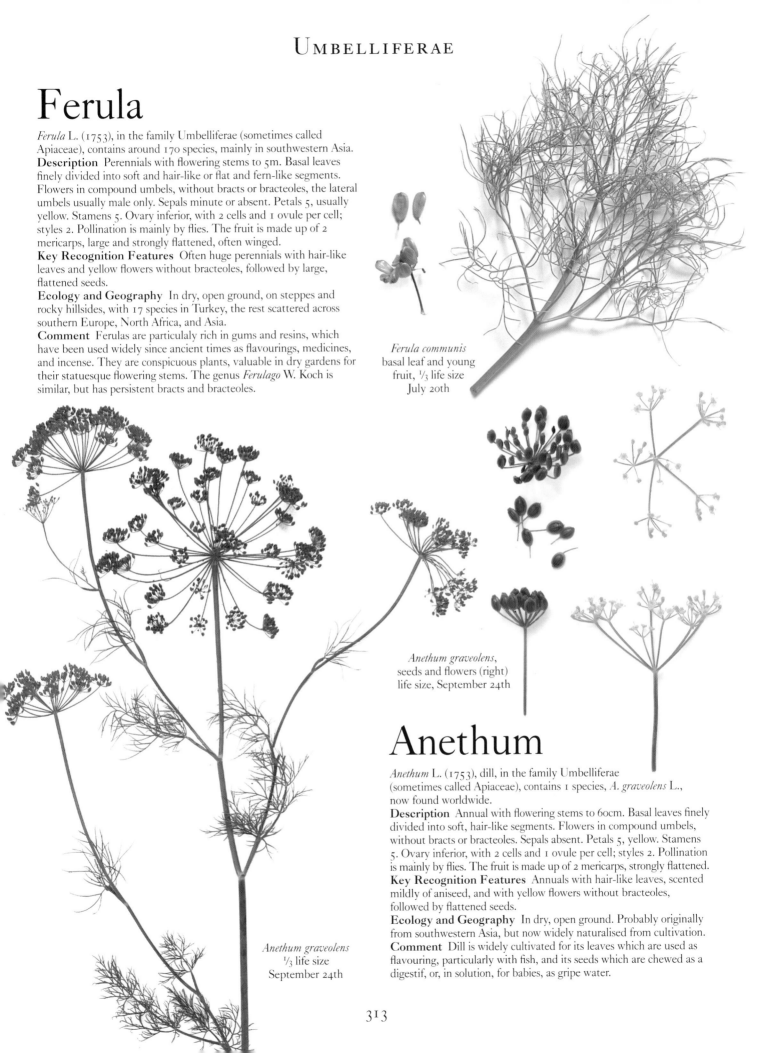

Ferula communis
basal leaf and young
fruit, ⅓ life size
July 20th

Anethum graveolens,
seeds and flowers (right)
life size, September 24th

Anethum

Anethum L. (1753), dill, in the family Umbelliferae (sometimes called Apiaceae), contains 1 species, *A. graveolens* L., now found worldwide.

Description Annual with flowering stems to 60cm. Basal leaves finely divided into soft, hair-like segments. Flowers in compound umbels, without bracts or bracteoles. Sepals absent. Petals 5, yellow. Stamens 5. Ovary inferior, with 2 cells and 1 ovule per cell; styles 2. Pollination is mainly by flies. The fruit is made up of 2 mericarps, strongly flattened.

Key Recognition Features Annuals with hair-like leaves, scented mildly of aniseed, and with yellow flowers without bracteoles, followed by flattened seeds.

Ecology and Geography In dry, open ground. Probably originally from southwestern Asia, but now widely naturalised from cultivation.

Comment Dill is widely cultivated for its leaves which are used as flavouring, particularly with fish, and its seeds which are chewed as a digestif, or, in solution, for babies, as gripe water.

Anethum graveolens
⅓ life size
September 24th

313

Meum

Meum Mill. (1768), in the family Umbelliferae (sometimes called Apiaceae), contains 1, perhaps 3, species in Europe and North Africa.
Description Perennials with flowering stems to 60cm. Basal leaves divided into numerous hair-like segments. Flowers in compound umbels, with few, narrow bracts and bracteoles. Sepals absent. Petals 5, white. Stamens 5. Ovary inferior, with 2 cells and 1 ovule per cell; styles 2. Pollination is mainly by flies. The fruit is made up of 2 mericarps, ovoid-oblong, scarcely flattened.
Key Recognition Features The feathery leaves and white flowers.
Ecology and Geography In moist, grassy mountain meadows throughout Europe and southwards to the Sierra Nevada and in North Africa.
Comment *Meum athamanticum* Jacq. is the baldmoney, spignel, or meu, formerly cultivated for its edible roots, and found mainly in cool, mountain meadows; it is a mystery why this rare, though attractive plant should have so many names. Geoffrey Grigson records that Highlanders chewed the roots. *Meum nevadense* Boiss. is doubtfully distinct: it or another closely related species is found in North Africa.

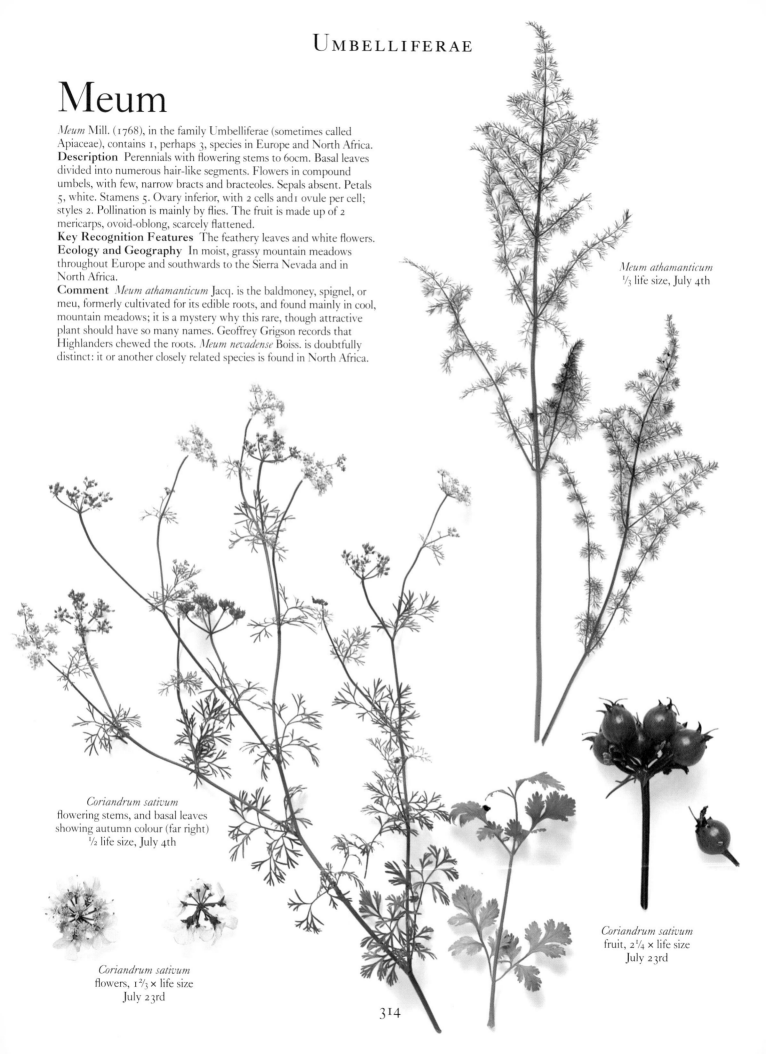

Meum athamanticum
⅓ life size, July 4th

Coriandrum sativum
flowering stems, and basal leaves
showing autumn colour (far right)
½ life size, July 4th

Coriandrum sativum
flowers, 1⅔ × life size
July 23rd

Coriandrum sativum
fruit, 2¼ × life size
July 23rd

314

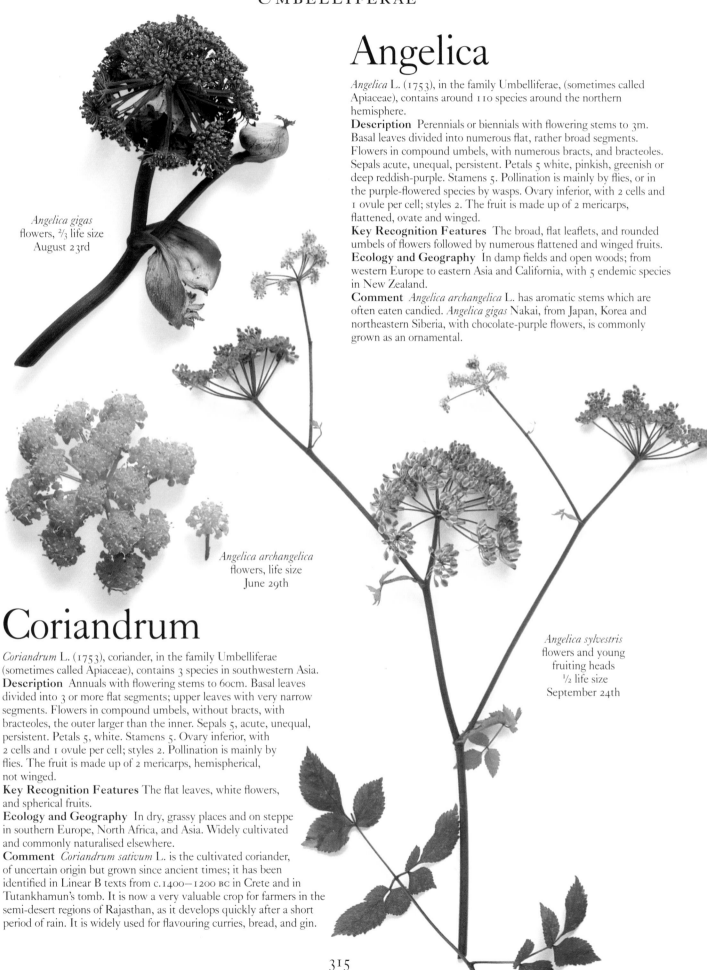

Angelica

Angelica L. (1753), in the family Umbelliferae, (sometimes called Apiaceae), contains around 110 species around the northern hemisphere.

Description Perennials or biennials with flowering stems to 3m. Basal leaves divided into numerous flat, rather broad segments. Flowers in compound umbels, with numerous bracts, and bracteoles. Sepals acute, unequal, persistent. Petals 5 white, pinkish, greenish or deep reddish-purple. Stamens 5. Pollination is mainly by flies, or in the purple-flowered species by wasps. Ovary inferior, with 2 cells and 1 ovule per cell; styles 2. The fruit is made up of 2 mericarps, flattened, ovate and winged.

Key Recognition Features The broad, flat leaflets, and rounded umbels of flowers followed by numerous flattened and winged fruits.

Ecology and Geography In damp fields and open woods; from western Europe to eastern Asia and California, with 5 endemic species in New Zealand.

Comment *Angelica archangelica* L. has aromatic stems which are often eaten candied. *Angelica gigas* Nakai, from Japan, Korea and northeastern Siberia, with chocolate-purple flowers, is commonly grown as an ornamental.

Angelica gigas
flowers, ⅔ life size
August 23rd

Angelica archangelica
flowers, life size
June 29th

Angelica sylvestris
flowers and young
fruiting heads
½ life size
September 24th

Coriandrum

Coriandrum L. (1753), coriander, in the family Umbelliferae (sometimes called Apiaceae), contains 3 species in southwestern Asia.

Description Annuals with flowering stems to 60cm. Basal leaves divided into 3 or more flat segments; upper leaves with very narrow segments. Flowers in compound umbels, without bracts, with bracteoles, the outer larger than the inner. Sepals 5, acute, unequal, persistent. Petals 5, white. Stamens 5. Ovary inferior, with 2 cells and 1 ovule per cell; styles 2. Pollination is mainly by flies. The fruit is made up of 2 mericarps, hemispherical, not winged.

Key Recognition Features The flat leaves, white flowers, and spherical fruits.

Ecology and Geography In dry, grassy places and on steppe in southern Europe, North Africa, and Asia. Widely cultivated and commonly naturalised elsewhere.

Comment *Coriandrum sativum* L. is the cultivated coriander, of uncertain origin but grown since ancient times; it has been identified in Linear B texts from c.1400–1200 BC in Crete and in Tutankhamun's tomb. It is now a very valuable crop for farmers in the semi-desert regions of Rajasthan, as it develops quickly after a short period of rain. It is widely used for flavouring curries, bread, and gin.

315

Adoxa

Adoxa L. (1753), moschatel, in the family Adoxaceae, contains 5 species, of which 1, *A. moschatellina* L., is widespread in Europe, Asia, and North America.

Description Perennial with flowering stems to 10cm from a fleshy rhizome. Leaves opposite, hairless, divided into 3, the divisions further lobed. Flowers small and green, usually 5 in a tight head, 1 facing upwards and 4 facing outwards; the upward-facing flower with a 2-lobed calyx, 4 petals, and 4 stamens, and the outward-facing flowers with a 3-lobed calyx, 5 petals, and 5 stamens. Ovary inferior, with 3 cells, 2 sterile, 1 with 1 ovule. Styles 4 or 5. Pollination is by small wasps. The fruit is seldom seen, but is greenish and slightly fleshy, with 1 seed.

Key Recognition Features Small, soft, and fleshy plants with small, green flowers facing in different directions.

Ecology and Geography In woods and moist, shady places from western Europe to Japan, and in eastern North America.

Comment This is a modest plant which lives up to its name: *a-doxa*, unremarkable. Apart from *A. moschatellina*, the other 4 species are little known and recently described from western China and northeastern Asia. DNA studies have suggested a division of the traditional Caprifoliaceae between Lonicera and Symphoricarpos, which remain as Caprifoliaceae, and *Viburnum* and *Sambucus*, which are close to Adoxa and are placed in Adoxaceae (for all see Volume 1). Valerianaceae (see pp. 318–19), Dipsacaceae (see pp. 320–23), and Linnaeaceae are also sometimes included in Caprifoliaceae.

Adoxa moschatellina, flowerheads
2¼ × life size, April 10th

Adoxa moschatellina
just over life size
April 10th

Morina

Morina L. (1753), in the family Morinaceae, contains around 10 species in eastern Europe and Asia.

Description Often spiny perennials or rarely annuals with flowering stems to 80cm. Leaves opposite, usually toothed and spiny, narrowly lanceolate. Flowers white, white changing to pink, red, or yellow, in dense whorls on the stem or aggregated into a head. Sepals joined to form a 2-lobed calyx, which is enclosed in a bristle-tipped cup. Petals 5, joined to form a curved tube and a 2-lipped corolla. Stamens 2. Ovary inferior, with 1 cell, with 1 ovule; style 1. Pollination is by bees. The fruit is a hard, wrinkled seed, enclosed in the dry remains of the sepals and bristly cup.

Key Recognition Features Often spiny plants with whorls of flowers with a long, curved tube.

Ecology and Geography On rocky or grassy, dry or wet mountainsides and in open woods, from southeastern Europe to central Asia, the Himalayas, and western China.

Comment The family Morinaceae is very close to the Dipsacaceae (see pp. 320–23) and the Valerianaceae, and is often combined with one or the other, but differs in a number of small characters, such as the 2 stamens, the pollen, and the chromosome number. Several species make attractive garden plants, but are not easy to grow, apart from *M. longifolia* DC, from damp places in the Himalayas. Mabberley records that the seeds can be eaten like rice.

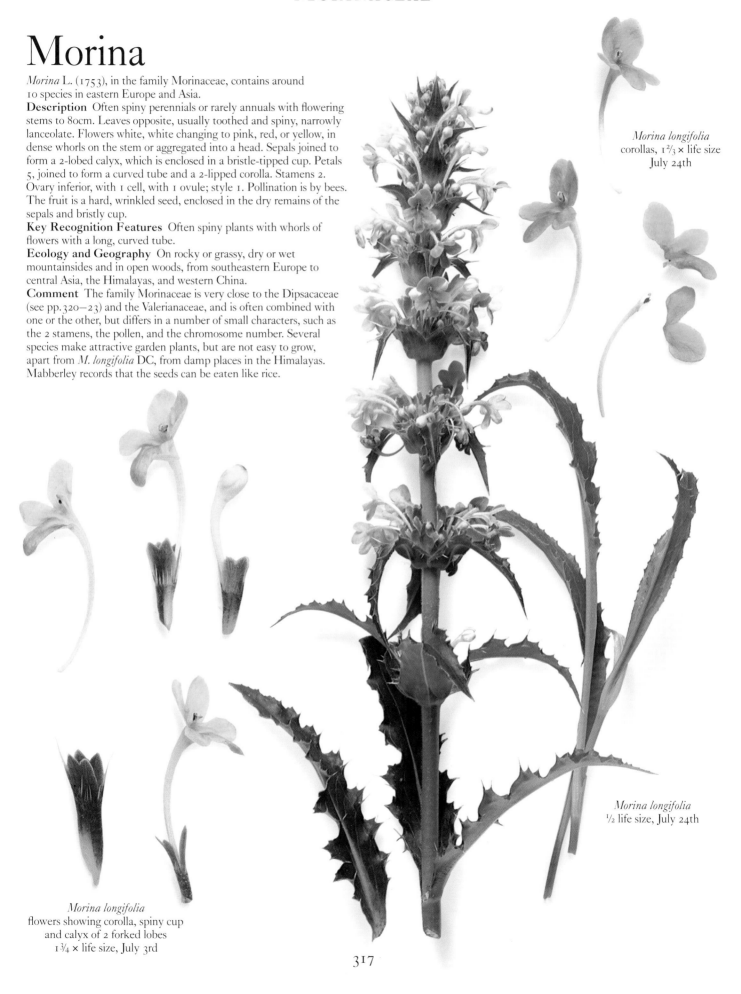

Morina longifolia
corollas, 1²/₃ × life size
July 24th

Morina longifolia
½ life size, July 24th

Morina longifolia
flowers showing corolla, spiny cup
and calyx of 2 forked lobes
1¾ × life size, July 3rd

Valeriana

Valeriana L. (1753), in the family Valerianaceae, contains around 200 species in the northern hemisphere and South Africa and South America.

Description Perennials with flowering stems to 1.1m, often tuberous. Basal leaves often undivided, stem leaves opposite, usually lobed or pinnate. Flowers white or pink, sometimes unisexual, in branched, usually flat-topped heads. Sepals 5–15, forming a pappus in fruit. Petals 5, joined to form a short corolla with a slightly swollen base. Stamens 3. Ovary inferior, with 3 cells, 2 sterile, 1 with 1 ovule. Style 1, with 3 lobes. Pollination is usually by butterflies, craneflies, caddis flies, and small wasps. The fruit is a seed with a feathery pappus.

Key Recognition Features Upright plants with masses of small flowers in a flat-topped head, followed by fruit with a hairy pappus like a small parachute.

Ecology and Geography On rocky or grassy, dry or wet mountainsides and in marshes and open woods. Found throughout temperate parts of the northern hemisphere, with a few species in the Andes and the mountains of tropical and southern Africa.

Comment The family Valerianaceae is close to Dipsacaceae (see pp. 320–23), Caprifoliaceae (see Volume 1), and Linnaeaceae. *Patrinia* Juss., from eastern Asia, is close to *Valeriana*, but has yellow flowers with 4 stamens and a calyx that does not become feathery.

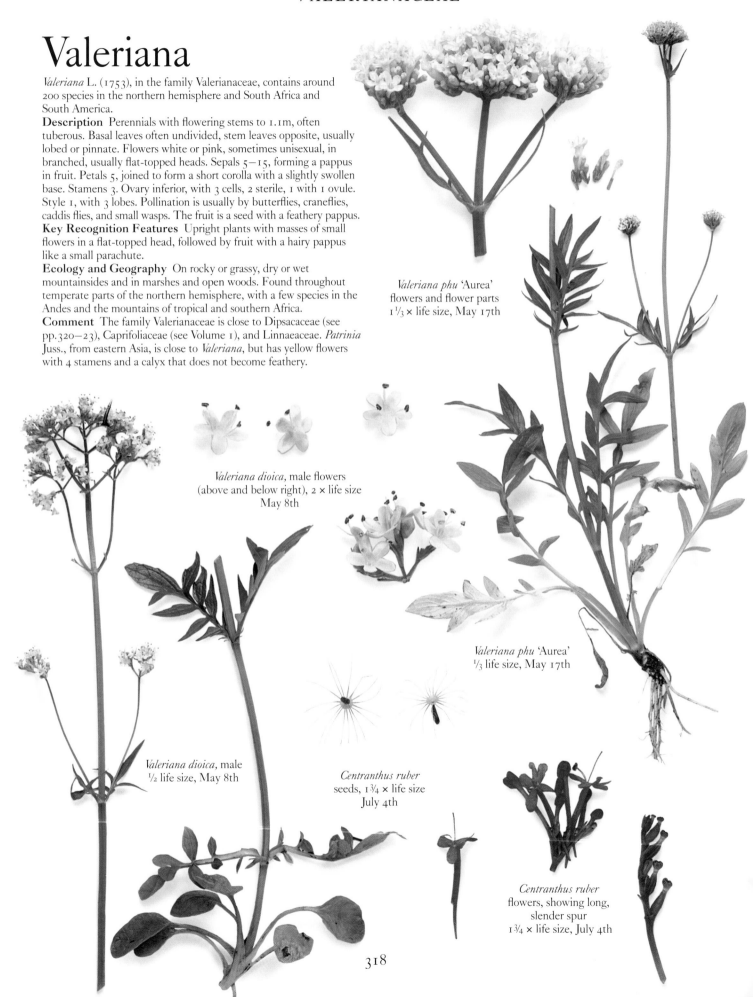

Valeriana phu 'Aurea'
flowers and flower parts
1⅓ × life size, May 17th

Valeriana dioica, male flowers
(above and below right), 2 × life size
May 8th

Valeriana phu 'Aurea'
⅓ life size, May 17th

Valeriana dioica, male
½ life size, May 8th

Centranthus ruber
seeds, 1¾ × life size
July 4th

Centranthus ruber
flowers, showing long,
slender spur
1¾ × life size, July 4th

Valerianella

Valerianella L. (1753), in the family Valerianaceae, contains around 50 species in Europe and western Asia.

Description Annuals with flowering stems to 40cm. Lower leaves rounded, upper sometimes lobed or pinnate. Flowers very small, pale blue or pink, in branched, usually flat-topped, heads. Sepals various, reduced to a toothed rim, or absent. Petals 5, joined to form a short corolla without a swollen base. Stamens 3. Ovary inferior, with 3 cells, 2 sterile, 1 with 1 ovule. Style 1, with 3 lobes. Pollination is by selfing. The fruit is a seed, topped sometimes with the persistent remains of the calyx, sometimes with only the corky remains of the sterile cells.

Key Recognition Features Much-branched plants from a rosette of winter leaves, with masses of minute flowers in flat-topped heads.

Ecology and Geography On rocky slopes or in arable fields or old walls, from the British Isles and Portugal to Afghanistan, with 31 species in Turkey.

Comment Lamb's lettuce, *V. locusta* (L.) Laterr., is sometimes grown as a winter salad, popular in Switzerland where it is called *nüsslisalad*, because of its mild, nutty flavour. The species are distinguished mainly by their fruits, which have an amazing range of appendages in the form of horns, hooks, hairs, or spikes, sometimes with papery wings or bladders.

Valerianella locusta
1/3 life size, May 31st

Valerianella locusta
flowers and seeds (above)
1 3/4 × life size, May 31st

Centranthus ruber
3 colour forms
1/2 life size, July 4th

Centranthus

Centranthus Necker ex DC. (1805), red spur valerian, in the family Valerianaceae, contains around 9 species in the Mediterranean region and eastwards to the Caucasus. It is sometimes spelled *Kentranthus*.

Description Annuals or perennials with flowering stems to 2m. Leaves opposite, usually fleshy, the upper sometimes pinnate. Flowers white, pink, or red, in branched, usually flat-topped, heads. Sepals 10–25, inrolled in bud, forming a parachute in fruit. Petals 5, narrow and unequal, joined to form a long, narrow corolla with a long spur near the base, or a short corolla with a swollen middle. Stamen 1. Ovary inferior, with 3 cells, 2 sterile, 1 with 1 ovule. Style 1. Pollination is usually by butterflies, hawk moths, or noctuids. The fruit is a seed with a ring of bristles, each with many white hairs.

Key Recognition Features Spreading plants with masses of small red, pink, or white flowers with long spurs or a swollen middle in a flat-topped head, followed by fruit with a hairy pappus like a small parachute.

Ecology and Geography On cliffs, rocky places, road cuttings, screes, or shingle, in the Mediterranean area eastwards to the Caucasus, and now naturalised as for north as the British Isles.

Comment *Centranthus ruber* (L.) DC, the red or red-spur valerian, is now a conspicuous feature of new road verges in Europe. The flowers are generally red, but the white-flowered form is commonly cultivated, and the pink appears as a cross between these two. The flowers are very attractive to migratory moths, particularly hummingbird hawk moths in late summer.

Succisa

Succisa Haller (1768), in the family Dipsacaceae, contains 3 species in Europe, western Asia, and West Africa.

Description Perennials with flowering stems to 35cm. Leaves opposite, simple or the lowest toothed, stem leaves sometimes lobed. Flowers bisexual or female, purplish-blue or rarely pink, in tight, rounded heads, surrounded by a ring of short, soft bracts, and with non-spiny bracteoles between the flowers, the outer ring of flowers not larger than the rest. Sepals with 5 bristles; petals 4, rounded, joined to form a short corolla. Stamens 4. Ovary inferior, with 1 cell, with 1 ovule; style 1. Pollination is usually by bees, flies, or butterflies. The fruit is a seed with the 4 bristles of the calyx.

Key Recognition Features Scabious-like plants (*Scabiosa*, see p.323) with small, round heads of purplish-blue, 4-petalled flowers.

Ecology and Geography In marshy places and heathland, with 1 widespread species, *S. pratensis* Moench, devil's bit scabious, from northwestern Europe to Siberia and the Caucasus, 1 in northwestern Spain and Portugal, and 1 in the Cameroon.

Comment The European species are characteristic of acid soils, flowering in late summer and autumn. The larger flowerheads are bisexual, the smaller are all female.

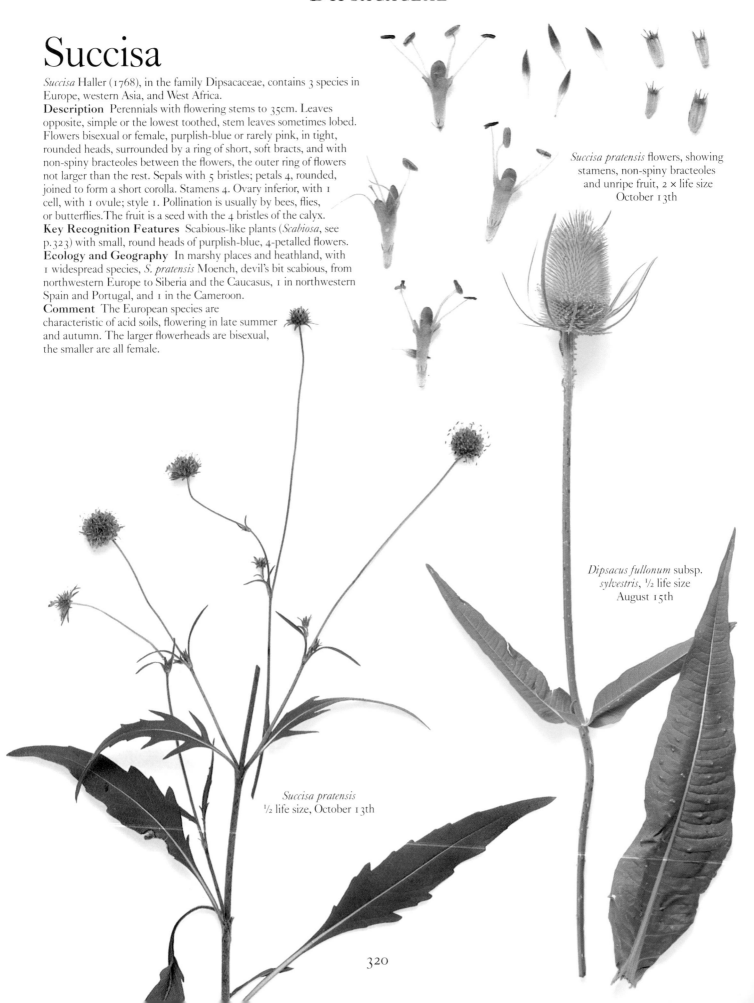

Succisa pratensis flowers, showing stamens, non-spiny bracteoles and unripe fruit, 2 × life size
October 13th

Dipsacus fullonum subsp. *sylvestris*, ½ life size
August 15th

Succisa pratensis
½ life size, October 13th

Dipsacus fullonum subsp.
sylvestris flowers
1¾ × life size, August 15th

Dipsacus fullonum subsp.
sylvestris, section of flowerhead
life size, August 15th

Cephalaria

Cephalaria Schrad. ex Roem. & Schult. (1818), in the family Dipsacaceae, contains around 65 species in the Mediterranean area and western Asia.

Description Annuals, biennials, perennials with flowering stems to 3.5m, or low shrubs. Leaves opposite, simple or pinnate. Flowers white to yellowish or rarely pale lilac, in tight, rounded heads, surrounded by a ring of short, tough bracts, and with non-spiny bracteoles between the flowers, the outer ring of flowers sometimes larger than the rest. Sepals cup-like; petals 4, rounded, joined to form a short corolla. Stamens 4. Ovary inferior, with 1 cell and 1 ovule; style 1. Pollination is usually by bees, flies or butterflies. The fruit is a seed with the toothed remains of the calyx.

Key Recognition Features Scabious-like plants (*Scabiosa*, see p.323) with round or flattish heads of white, yellowish, or pale lilac, 4-petalled flowers.

Ecology and Geography On screes and in fields, marshy places, and clearings in woods, from southern France to Iran and the Caucasus, with 29 species in Turkey.

Comment *Cephalaria gigantea* (Ledeb.) Bobrov, with stems to 3.5m and large pale yellow flowers, is commonly grown in herbaceous borders.

Cephalaria gigantea
½ life size, August 17th

Dipsacus

Dipsacus L. (1753), teasel, in the family Dipsacaceae, contains around 15 species from Europe eastwards to the mountains of Asia.

Description Annuals or biennials with flowering stems to 2m or more. Leaves opposite, often joined and holding rain at the base, the upper sometimes pinnate. Flowers white, yellowish, or pale lilac, in tight, rounded or cylindrical heads, surrounded by a ring of often long, spiny bracts, and with stiff, sometimes hooked bracteoles between the flowers. Sepals cup-like, with a ring of hairs. Petals 4, rounded, joined to form a short corolla. Stamens 4. Ovary inferior, with 1 cell and 1 ovule; style 1. Pollination is usually by bees, flies, or butterflies. The fruit is a seed with the bristly remains of the calyx.

Key Recognition Features Upright, spiny plants with round or cylindrical heads of small, pale lilac, white, or yellowish flowers and spiny bracteoles between the flowers.

Ecology and Geography In dry, grassy places, on the banks of streams, and in clearings in woods. Found from western Europe through western and central Asia to the mountains of Sri Lanka.

Comment The water held in the lower leaves is said to prevent ants and other such crawling animals from reaching the flowers. The hooked bracteoles of fuller's teasel, *D. sativus* (L.) Honckeny, syn. *D. fullonum* subsp. *sativus* (L.) Thell., have been used since Roman times for fulling or teasing, that is, raising the nap of woollen cloth. The wild teasel, *D. fullonum* subsp. *sylvestris* (L.) Thell. has bracteoles without hooks.

Knautia macedonica
flowerhead and flower
parts, 1¼ × life size
June 22nd

Scabiosa minoana
young fruiting head
and flowerhead
life size, July 20th

Scabiosa minoana
⅓ life size, July 20th

Knautia macedonica
flower buds
1½ × life size, June 22nd

Knautia

Knautia L. (1753), in the family Dipsacaceae, contains 60 species in Europe and western Asia.

Description Annuals, biennials, or perennials with flowering stems to 2m. Leaves opposite, simple or the lowest toothed, the stem leaves sometimes pinnate. Flowers purplish-blue, pink, white, or yellow, in flattish heads, surrounded by a ring of short, soft bracts, the flowers becoming progressively larger towards the margin of the flowerhead; some of the flowerheads are all female. Sepals with 8 or more bristles. Petals 4, rounded, joined to form a short corolla. Stamens 4. Ovary inferior, with 1 cell and 1 ovule; style 1. Pollination is usually by bees, flies or butterflies. The fruit is a seed with up to 16 bristles.

Key Recognition Features Scabious-like plants (*Scabiosa*) with small, flattish heads of 4-petalled flowers, whereas the flowers of *Scabiosa* have 5 petals and only 5 bristles.

Ecology and Geography Grassy hills and arable fields, meadows, and open woods; from western Europe to the Caucasus and Syria.

Comment Most species are similar to small species of *Scabiosa*.

Knautia macedonica
⅓ life size, June 22nd

Scabiosa caucasica
'Clive Greaves'
flowers, life size
July 22nd

Scabiosa atropurpurea
seeds and fruiting heads
1 ¹/₂ × life size, October 17th

Scabiosa caucasica, section of flower head
1 ¹/₂ × life size, July 27th

Scabiosa

Scabiosa L. (1753), in the family Dipsacaceae, contains 80 species in Europe and western Asia.

Description Annuals, biennials, or perennials with flowering stems to 1m, or occasionally low shrubs. Leaves opposite, simple or the lowest pinnatisect, the stem leaves often pinnate. Flowers purplish-blue, pink, white, or yellow, in flat or rounded heads, surrounded by short, soft bracts, the flowers becoming progressively larger towards the margin of the flowerhead. Sepals with 5 bristles. Epicalyx enclosing the ovary and corolla, with 8 ridges or pits, often becoming enlarged and papery in fruit. Petals 5, rounded, ridged, joined to form a short corolla. Stamens 4. Ovary inferior, with 1 cell and 1 ovule; style 1. Pollination is usually by bees, flies, or butterflies. The fruit is a seed with 5 bristles.

Key Recognition Features Typical scabious flowerheads of flowers with 5 petals and 5 bristles, the outer flowers and petals often distinctly larger than the inner, the epicalyx often papery in fruit.

Ecology and Geography In arable fields and meadows, on grassy hills and rocky slopes, and in open woods, from western Europe to the Caucasus and Siberia, and in the mountains of east and South Africa.

Comment Some annual species of *Scabiosa*, such as *S. stellata* L., are grown for their beautiful, papery seed heads. Some species, including the common garden perennial *S. caucasica* M. Bieb., are sometimes separated into the genus *Lomelosia* Raf., and the annual *S. atropurpurea* L. is occasionally put in *Sixalix* Raf.

Scabiosa caucasica
'Clive Greaves'
¹/₂ life size, July 22nd

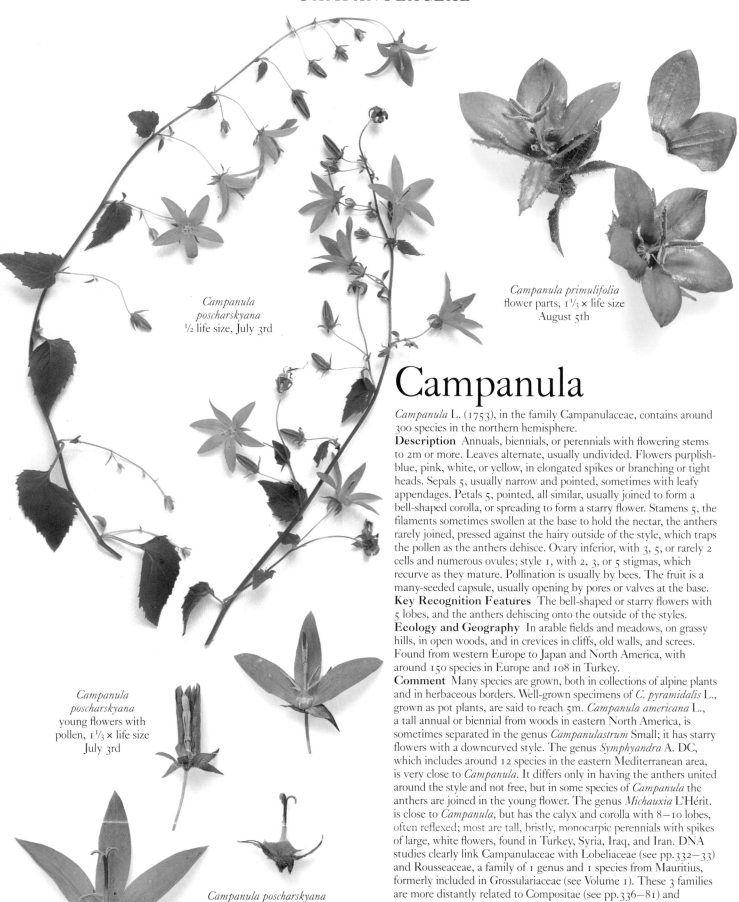

Campanula poscharskyana
½ life size, July 3rd

Campanula primulifolia
flower parts, 1⅓ × life size
August 5th

Campanula poscharskyana
young flowers with
pollen, 1⅓ × life size
July 3rd

Campanula poscharskyana
old flowers with receptive
stigmas, 1½ × life size, July 3rd

Campanula

Campanula L. (1753), in the family Campanulaceae, contains around 300 species in the northern hemisphere.

Description Annuals, biennials, or perennials with flowering stems to 2m or more. Leaves alternate, usually undivided. Flowers purplish-blue, pink, white, or yellow, in elongated spikes or branching or tight heads. Sepals 5, usually narrow and pointed, sometimes with leafy appendages. Petals 5, pointed, all similar, usually joined to form a bell-shaped corolla, or spreading to form a starry flower. Stamens 5, the filaments sometimes swollen at the base to hold the nectar, the anthers rarely joined, pressed against the hairy outside of the style, which traps the pollen as the anthers dehisce. Ovary inferior, with 3, 5, or rarely 2 cells and numerous ovules; style 1, with 2, 3, or 5 stigmas, which recurve as they mature. Pollination is usually by bees. The fruit is a many-seeded capsule, usually opening by pores or valves at the base.

Key Recognition Features The bell-shaped or starry flowers with 5 lobes, and the anthers dehiscing onto the outside of the styles.

Ecology and Geography In arable fields and meadows, on grassy hills, in open woods, and in crevices in cliffs, old walls, and screes. Found from western Europe to Japan and North America, with around 150 species in Europe and 108 in Turkey.

Comment Many species are grown, both in collections of alpine plants and in herbaceous borders. Well-grown specimens of *C. pyramidalis* L., grown as pot plants, are said to reach 5m. *Campanula americana* L., a tall annual or biennial from woods in eastern North America, is sometimes separated in the genus *Campanulastrum* Small; it has starry flowers with a downcurved style. The genus *Symphyandra* A. DC, which includes around 12 species in the eastern Mediterranean area, is very close to *Campanula*. It differs only in having the anthers united around the style and not free, but in some species of *Campanula* the anthers are joined in the young flower. The genus *Michauxia* L'Hérit. is close to *Campanula*, but has the calyx and corolla with 8–10 lobes, often reflexed; most are tall, bristly, monocarpic perennials with spikes of large, white flowers, found in Turkey, Syria, Iraq, and Iran. DNA studies clearly link Campanulaceae with Lobeliaceae (see pp.332–33) and Rousseaceae, a family of 1 genus and 1 species from Mauritius, formerly included in Grossulariaceae (see Volume 1). These 3 families are more distantly related to Compositae (see pp.336–81) and Goodeniaceae (see p.334), and the more isolated Menyanthaceae (see p.335) and *Corokia* (see Volume 1).

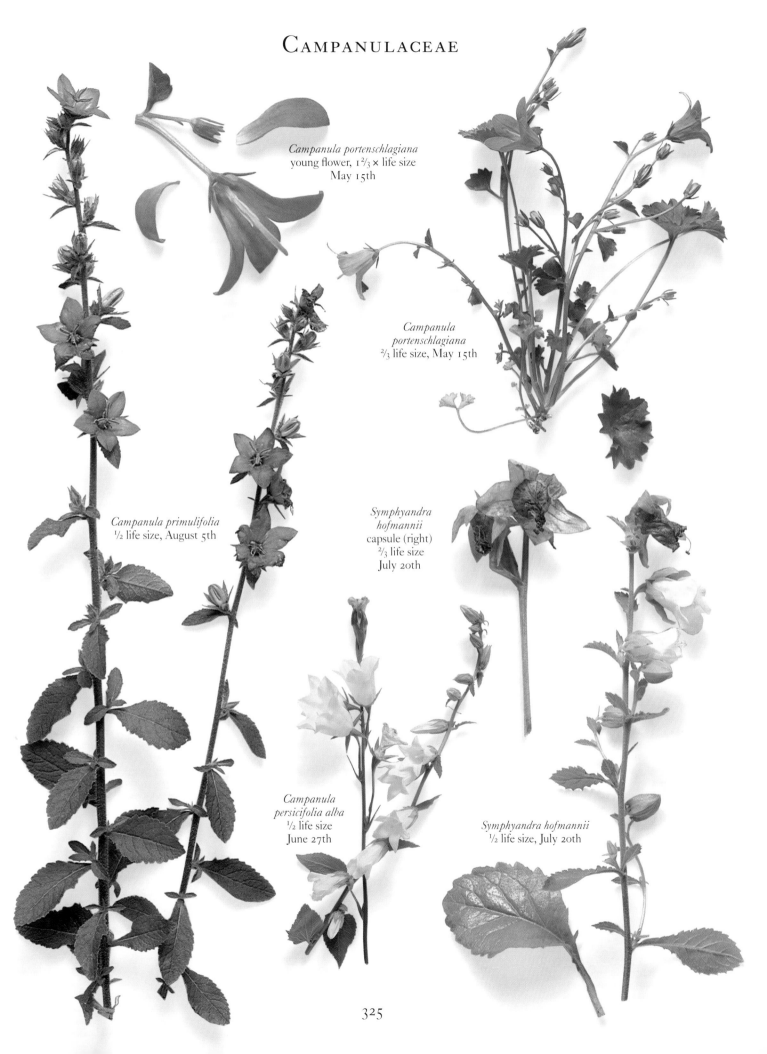

Campanulaceae

Campanula portenschlagiana
young flower, 1²⁄₃ × life size
May 15th

Campanula portenschlagiana
²⁄₃ life size, May 15th

Campanula primulifolia
½ life size, August 5th

Symphyandra hofmannii
capsule (right)
²⁄₃ life size
July 20th

Campanula persicifolia alba
½ life size
June 27th

Symphyandra hofmannii
½ life size, July 20th

325

Adenophora

Adenophora Fisch. (1823), in the family Campanulaceae, contains around 40 species in northern Europe and Asia.

Description Perennials with usually upright flowering stems to 1.5m. Leaves often whorled, alternate, or opposite, usually undivided. Flowers purplish-blue, rarely white, on elongated spikes or branching stems. Sepals 5, without appendages. Petals 5, pointed, all similar, joined to form a tubular or bell-shaped corolla. Stamens 5, the filaments hairy and swollen at the base to hold the nectar, the anthers not joined, pressed against the hairy outside of the style, which traps the pollen as the anthers dehisce. Ovary inferior, with 3 cells and numerous ovules; style 1, with 3 stigmas, which recurve as they mature; a fleshy disc surrounds and covers the base of the style. Pollination is usually by bees. The fruit is a many-seeded capsule, opening by pores near the base.

Key Recognition Features Like a delicate *Campanula* (see pp.324–25) with bell-shaped flowers with 5 lobes, and a whitish, fleshy, cylindrical or ring-like disc at the base of the style.

Ecology and Geography In open woods and grassy places from eastern Europe to China, eastern Siberia, and Japan.

Comment A few species are grown as ornamentals; many have upright stems with whorls of narrower, more tubular flowers than those of *A. confusa* Nannf., shown here. The genus *Hanabusaya* Nakai, from Korea, is related to *Adenophora*, but has few, large flowers with the anthers joined.

Adenophora confusa
flower and flower section
just under life size
August 23rd

Adenophora confusa
½ life size, August 23rd

Platycodon grandiflorus
flowers, 1¼ × life size
August 5th

Platycodon grandiflorus
½ life size
August 5th

Platycodon

Platycodon A. DC (1830), in the family Campanulaceae, contains 1 species, *P. grandiflorus* (Jacq.) A. DC., in northeastern Asia.

Description Perennials with upright flowering stems to 70cm. Leaves bluish-green, hairless, alternate or whorled, usually shallowly toothed. Flowers purplish-blue, rarely pink or white, upright, solitary or up to 6 on each stem, 4–5cm across. Sepals 5, without appendages. Petals usually 5, pointed, all similar, joined to form an open, bell-shaped corolla. Stamens 5, the filaments hairy and swollen at the base to hold the nectar, the anthers not joined, pressed against the hairy outside of the style, which traps the pollen as the anthers dehisce. Ovary inferior, with 5 cells, with numerous ovules; style 1, with 5 stigmas, which recurve as they mature. Pollination is presumed to be by large bees. The fruit is a many-seeded capsule, opening by valves opposite the sepals.

Key Recognition Features Like a robust *Campanula* (see pp.324–25) with open, upright, bell-shaped flowers with 4 or 5 lobes.

Ecology and Geography In meadows and open woods in eastern Siberia and Japan.

Comment This plant is commonly cultivated in Europe and North America as well as in Japan; it is a robust and long-lived perennial, with thick, fleshy roots. 'Apoyama' is a low-growing form from Mount Apoi, a serpentine mountain in southeastern Hokkaido in Japan, the home of several endemic plants.

Wahlenbergia

Wahlenbergia Schrad. ex Roth (1813), in the family Campanulaceae, contains around 200 species, mainly in the southern hemisphere.

Description Annuals or perennials with flowering stems to 50cm. Leaves opposite or alternate, simple, lobed, or wavy edged. Flowers blue to white, usually upright, to 3cm across. Sepals 5, without appendages. Petals 3−5, pointed, all similar, joined to form an often shallow, bell-shaped corolla. Stamens 3−5, the anthers not joined, pressed against the hairy outside of the style, which traps the pollen as the anthers dehisce. Ovary inferior, with 2−5 cells and numerous ovules; style 1, with 2−5 stigmas, recurving as they mature. Pollination is by various insects. The fruit is a many-seeded capsule, opening by valves near the apex.

Key Recognition Features Like a small *Campanula* (see pp. 324−25) with upright flowers and uusually narrow capsules, opening by valves near the apex.

Ecology and Geography Wet, grassy places, rocky hillsides, and semi-desert; 1 perennial, *W. hederacea* (L.) Rchb. in western Europe, 1 annual *W. nutabunda* (Guss.) A. DC. from the Mediterranean area; most of the rest in South Africa, with 40 species in the Cape area, Australia, and New Zealand, which has 10 species.

Comment One or two of the larger-flowered species are cultivated. The miniature *W. hederacea* is typical of cool, damp, sheep-grazed grass by streams.

Legousia

Legousia Durand (1782), Venus' looking glass, in the family Campanulaceae, contains around 15 species in Europe and Asia.

Description Annuals with upright flowering stems to 50cm. Leaves simple or with wavy edges. Flowers blue to reddish-purplish, rarely white, upright, to 2.5cm across. Sepals 5, without appendages. Petals 5, pointed, all similar, joined to form a starry or shallow bell-shaped corolla. Stamens 5, the anthers not joined, pressed against the hairy outside of the style, which traps the pollen as the anthers dehisce. Ovary inferior, with 3 cells and numerous ovules; style 1, with 3 stigmas, which recurve as they mature. Pollination is by various insects. The fruit is a narrow, many-seeded capsule, opening by 3 valves near the apex.

Key Recognition Features Like a small *Campanula* (see pp. 324−25) with upright, flat, starry flowers and long, narrow capsules.

Ecology and Geography In arable fields, steppe, meadows, and open woods in Europe and the Mediterranean region.

Comment One or two of the larger-flowered species are cultivated. The genus was often called *Specularia* A. DC. The 7 American species of *Legousia*, which often have broad, conspicuous bracts, are now separated into the genus *Triodanis* Raf.; the Mediterranean *L. falcata* (Ten.) Fritsch. is sometimes included in *Triodanis* too.

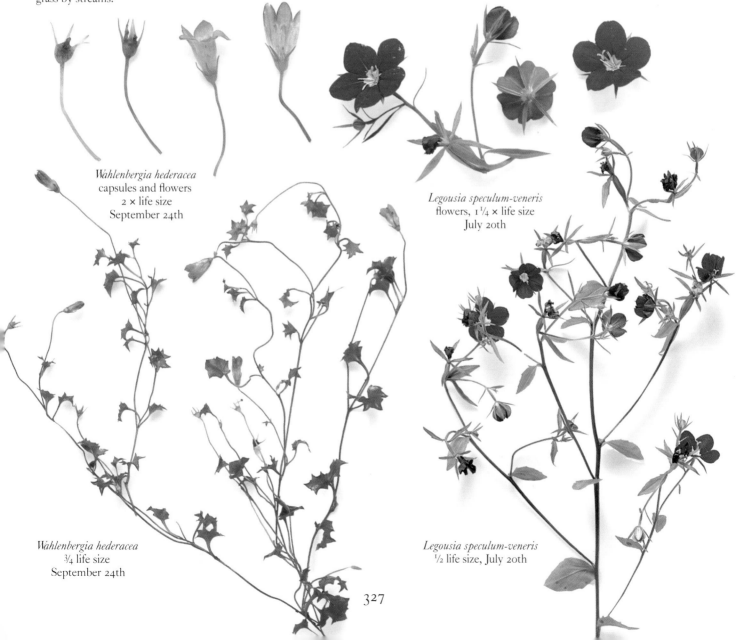

Wahlenbergia hederacea
capsules and flowers
2 × life size
September 24th

Legousia speculum-veneris
flowers, 1¼ × life size
July 20th

Wahlenbergia hederacea
¾ life size
September 24th

Legousia speculum-veneris
½ life size, July 20th

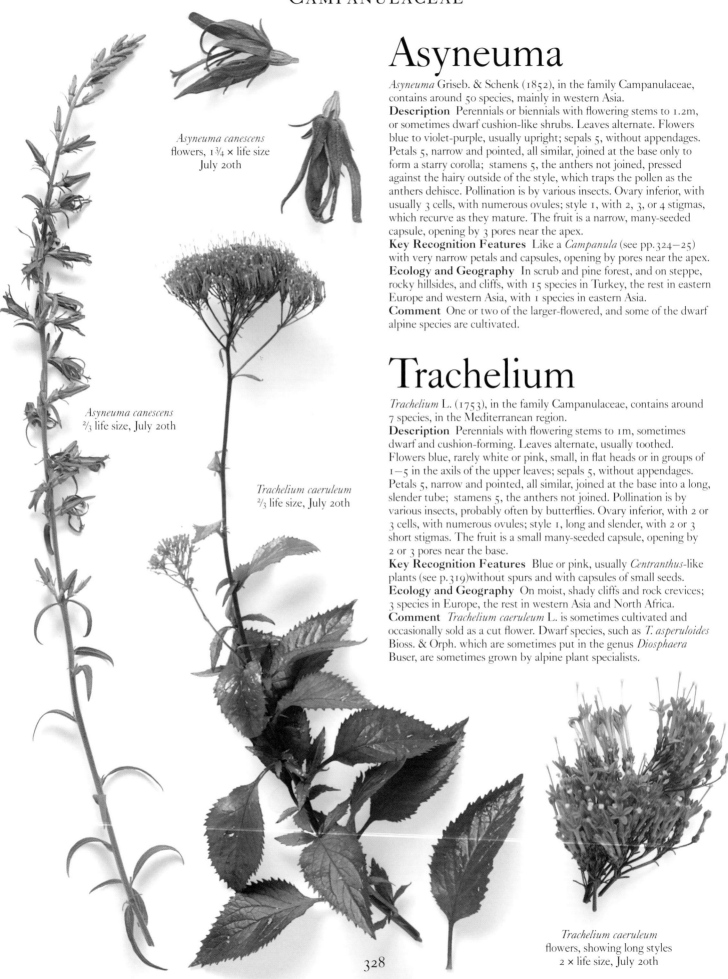

Asyneuma

Asyneuma Griseb. & Schenk (1852), in the family Campanulaceae, contains around 50 species, mainly in western Asia.

Description Perennials or biennials with flowering stems to 1.2m, or sometimes dwarf cushion-like shrubs. Leaves alternate. Flowers blue to violet-purple, usually upright; sepals 5, without appendages. Petals 5, narrow and pointed, all similar, joined at the base only to form a starry corolla; stamens 5, the anthers not joined, pressed against the hairy outside of the style, which traps the pollen as the anthers dehisce. Pollination is by various insects. Ovary inferior, with usually 3 cells, with numerous ovules; style 1, with 2, 3, or 4 stigmas, which recurve as they mature. The fruit is a narrow, many-seeded capsule, opening by 3 pores near the apex.

Key Recognition Features Like a *Campanula* (see pp. 324–25) with very narrow petals and capsules, opening by pores near the apex.

Ecology and Geography In scrub and pine forest, and on steppe, rocky hillsides, and cliffs, with 15 species in Turkey, the rest in eastern Europe and western Asia, with 1 species in eastern Asia.

Comment One or two of the larger-flowered, and some of the dwarf alpine species are cultivated.

Trachelium

Trachelium L. (1753), in the family Campanulaceae, contains around 7 species, in the Mediterranean region.

Description Perennials with flowering stems to 1m, sometimes dwarf and cushion-forming. Leaves alternate, usually toothed. Flowers blue, rarely white or pink, small, in flat heads or in groups of 1–5 in the axils of the upper leaves; sepals 5, without appendages. Petals 5, narrow and pointed, all similar, joined at the base into a long, slender tube; stamens 5, the anthers not joined. Pollination is by various insects, probably often by butterflies. Ovary inferior, with 2 or 3 cells, with numerous ovules; style 1, long and slender, with 2 or 3 short stigmas. The fruit is a small many-seeded capsule, opening by 2 or 3 pores near the base.

Key Recognition Features Blue or pink, usually *Centranthus*-like plants (see p. 319)without spurs and with capsules of small seeds.

Ecology and Geography On moist, shady cliffs and rock crevices; 3 species in Europe, the rest in western Asia and North Africa.

Comment *Trachelium caeruleum* L. is sometimes cultivated and occasionally sold as a cut flower. Dwarf species, such as *T. asperuloides* Bioss. & Orph. which are sometimes put in the genus *Diosphaera* Buser, are sometimes grown by alpine plant specialists.

Asyneuma canescens
flowers, 1¾ × life size
July 20th

Asyneuma canescens
⅔ life size, July 20th

Trachelium caeruleum
⅔ life size, July 20th

Trachelium caeruleum
flowers, showing long styles
2 × life size, July 20th

Jasione

Jasione L. (1753), the sheepsbit, in the family Campanulaceae, contains around 20 species, mainly around the Mediterranean and in western Asia.

Description Annuals, biennials or perennials with flowering stems to 80cm. Leaves alternate. Flowers blue, rarely white or reddish, small, in tight heads; sepals 5, without appendages. Petals 5, narrow and pointed, all similar, joined at the base only; stamens 5, the anthers joined into a tube at the base. Pollination is by various insects, but especially by wasps. Ovary inferior, with usually 2 cells, with numerous ovules; style 1, with usually 2 short stigmas. The fruit is a small, many-seeded capsule, opening by 2 valves near the apex.

Key Recognition Features Like a small scabious (*Scabiosa*, see p.323), but with short-stalked flowers, narrow petals, and capsules of small seeds.

Ecology and Geography In short turf on banks, dunes, steppe, and rocky hillsides; 9 species and numerous subspecies in Europe, the rest in western Asia and North Africa.

Comment One or two species are grown in rock gardens. *Jasione montana* L. is annual or biennial and found throughout Europe, mostly on acid soils; *J. laevis* Lam. is usually perennial.

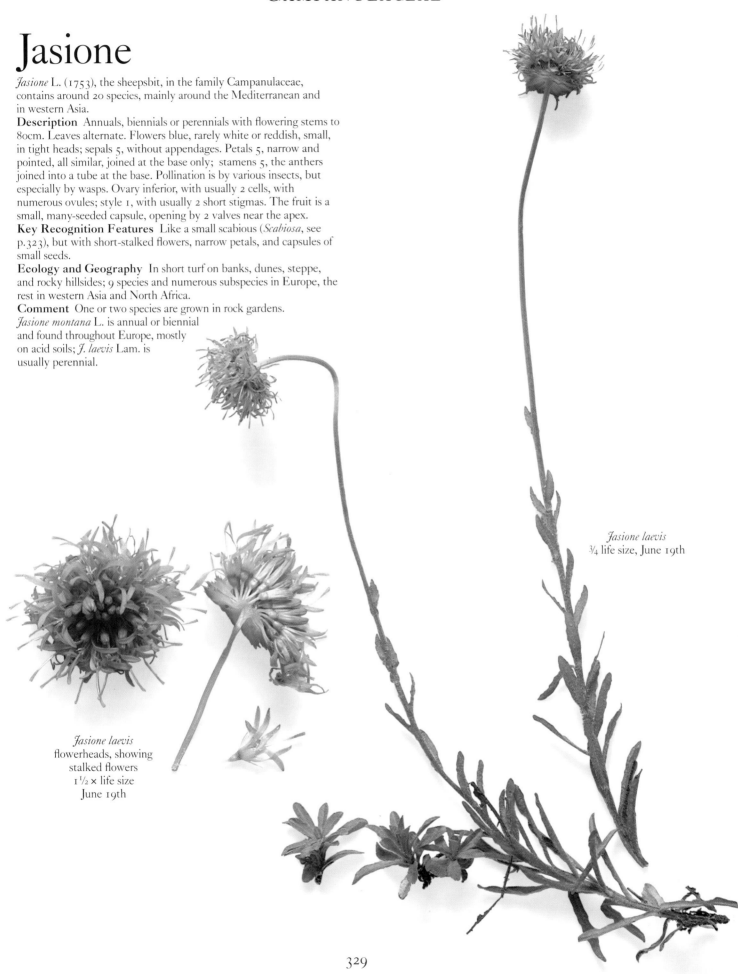

Jasione laevis
¾ life size, June 19th

Jasione laevis
flowerheads, showing
stalked flowers
1 ½ × life size
June 19th

Codonopsis

Codonopsis Wallich (1824), in the family Campanulaceae, contains around 40 species in central and eastern Asia.

Description Perennials, often tuberous, with upright or twining flowering stems to 3.5m. Leaves alternate or whorled, usually shallowly toothed. Flowers greenish, purplish-blue, pale blue, white, or yellow, often veined or tessellated, sometimes marked with orange at the base inside, solitary or many on a stem. Sepals usually 5, without appendages. Petals usually 5, pointed, all similar, joined to form a bell-shaped corolla or joined only at the base, forming a flat star. Stamens 5, the filaments hairy and swollen at the base to hold the nectar, the anthers not joined, pressed against the hairy outside of the style, which traps the pollen as the anthers dehisce. Ovary inferior or semi-inferior, with 3–6 cells and numerous ovules; style 1, with 3–5 stigmas, recurving as they mature. Pollination is by bees, or by wasps in the green-flowered species. The fruit is a many-seeded capsule, opening by valves on the top opposite the sepals; seeds sometimes flat and winged.

Key Recognition Features Often evil-smelling, *Campanula*-like (see pp.324–25) perennials with bell-shaped flowers marked with orange inside; other species are twiners with starry blue or green and brown flowers.

Ecology and Geography In meadows, on rocky hillsides, and in scrub, hedges, and open woods from central Asia along the Himalayas to Japan and southwards to Java.

Comment Many species are cultivated for their beautiful flowers, in spite of the unpleasant smell of the leaves.

Codonopsis tubulosa
flower parts (above and below)
1 1/4 × life size, October 3rd

Codonopsis viridis section of flower and ovary (above) and capsule (below)
1 1/4 × life size, October 3rd

Codonopsis lanceolata
(right), 1/2 life size
October 3rd

Codonopsis tubulosa
(left), 1/2 life size
October 3rd

Codonopsis viridis
(above left), 1/2 life size
October 3rd

Canarina canariensis
sections through flower and
ovary, just under life size
December 9th

Canarina

Canarina L. (1753), in the family Campanulaceae, contains 3 species in the Canary Islands and the mountains of Africa.

Description Perennials with a thick, tuberous rootstock and climbing or hanging stems to 2m. Leaves bluish-green, hairless, opposite or in groups of 3, usually shallowly toothed. Flowers orange or red, with dark veins, thick and fleshy, pendulous, terminal on the branches. Sepals 6, without appendages. Petals 6, pointed, all similar, joined to form a bell-shaped corolla. Stamens 6, the filaments hairy and swollen at the base to hold the copious watery nectar, the anthers not joined, pressed against the hairy outside of the style, which traps the pollen as the anthers dehisce. Ovary inferior, with 6 cells and numerous ovules; style 1, with 6 stigmas, which recurve as they mature. Pollination is by large bees and birds. The fruit is a many-seeded, fig-like fruit, turning orange when ripe.

Key Recognition Features Like a robust *Campanula* (see pp.324–25) with orange or red, bell-shaped flowers with 6 lobes.

Ecology and Geography In moist woods and heather scrub, often among brambles or bracken, or epiphytic on forest trees; 1 species, *C. canariensis* (L.) Kuntze in the Canary Islands; the others in East Africa from Ethiopia to Tanzania. This is a good example of the antiquity of the Canary Islands' flora, with many related species now found in the mountains of East Africa, the intervening Sahel region having become too dry.

Comment *Canarina canariensis* is often cultivated in mild climates for its winter flowering. Its flowers bear a remarkable similarity to those of *Fritillaria imperialis* (see pp.416–17) from Turkey and Iran; both also have copious watery nectar and are typical bird-pollinated flowers, but both now grow in areas where specialised nectar-feeding birds are absent; tits and bumblebees are now regular visitors to the flowers. In the mountains of eastern Africa, the flowers are probably visited by sunbirds. *Azorina vidalii* (Watson) Feer, from the Azores, is a fleshy shrub with pink or white flowers in a spike, closer to *Campanula*, in which it is sometimes included.

Canarina canariensis
½ life size, December 9th

Lobelia 'Kompliment Scharlach'
½ life size, August 5th

Lobelia laxiflora
var. *angustifolia*
⅔ life size, July 20th

Lobelia tupa
½ life size, August 2nd

Lobelia tupa
flower parts and section of ovary
1¾ × life size, August 2nd

Lobelia

Lobelia L. (1753), in the family Lobeliaceae, also sometimes placed within the Campanulaceae (see pp.324−31), contains around 350 species worldwide.

Description Perennials with stems to 2m, biennials, or annuals, or shrubs to 4m in the tropics. Leaves usually alternate. Flowers blue, purple, red, white, or yellow, usually 2-lipped, occasionally unisexual. Sepals usually 5, without appendages. Petals usually 5, usually pointed, joined in the lower half to form a narrow tube, which is split to the base on the upper side, the lower 3 forming the lower lip, the upper 2 forming the upper lip. Stamens 5, the anthers joined into a tube around the curved style; 2 smaller anthers each with a tuft of bristles. Ovary inferior or semi-inferior, with 2 cells and numerous ovules; style 1, with 2 stigmas, which recurve as they mature. Pollination is by bees, or by hummingbirds in the red-flowered American species. The fruit is a many-seeded capsule, opening by slits on the top.

Key Recognition Features The 2-lipped flowers with narrow upper petals, the tube split to the base on the top.

Ecology and Geography In lakes, meadows, scrub, and open woods, and on rocky coasts, with a few species in Europe, but most in tropical America and southern Africa and Australia. Some tall, shrubby, and thick-stemmed species are found on the high mountains of Africa, where they are pollinated by sunbirds.

Comment Many species are cultivated for their flowers, including the common *L. erinus* L. from South Africa, grown as a dwarf or creeping annual. The American *L. cardinalis* L. is commonly grown in wet borders for its red flowers. Other orange-flowered species from Central and South America, such as *L. tupa* L. from Argentina and Chile, are perennial in mild gardens; this and some other species can be hallucinogenic if smoked or even if roughly handled. The European *L. dortmanna* L. is an aquatic, found in cold, shallow, acid lakes from Russia to Scotland, Ireland, and North America; the leaves form a rosette on the bottom, and the flowers emerge on the surface. The family Lobeliaceae is close to and often included in the Campanulaceae, distinguished as subfamily Lobelioideae. In this subfamily the flowers turn upside down as they develop; the anthers dihisce inwards and the style pushes the pollen out as it elongates, with the stigmas becoming receptive after the pollen is dispersed. In the bird-pollinated species such as *L. tupa,* the style and stamens are held clear of the petals.

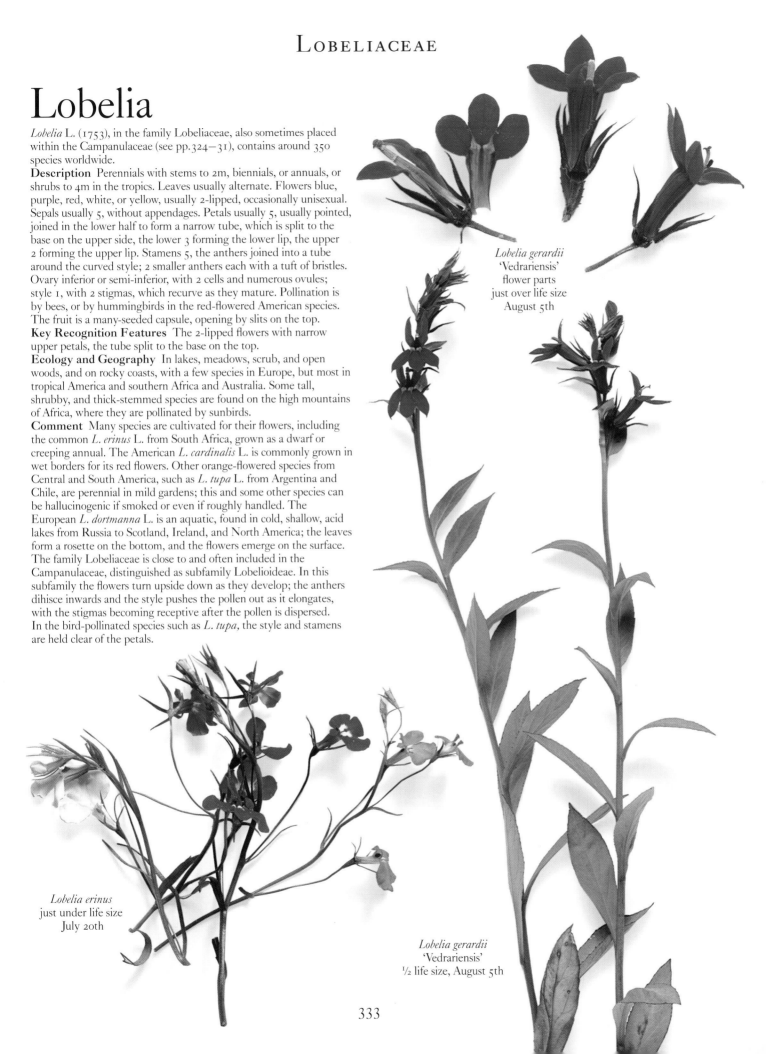

Lobelia gerardii
'Vedrariensis'
flower parts
just over life size
August 5th

Lobelia erinus
just under life size
July 20th

Lobelia gerardii
'Vedrariensis'
¹/₂ life size, August 5th

Scaevola

Scaevola L. (1753), in the family Goodeniaceae, contains around 96 species, mainly in Australia.

Description Perennials with stems to 70cm, shrubs or small trees to 4m. Leaves usually alternate. Flowers blue, purple, white or yellow, usually 2-lipped, occasionally unisexual; sepals usually 5, joined to form a tube. Petals usually 5, equal, forming a fan, joined in the lower half to form a narrow tube, which is split to the base on the lower side; stamens 5, the anthers not joined into a tube. Pollination is presumed to be by insects. Ovary inferior, with 1–4 cells, each with 1 ovule; style 1, unbranched, bent at the apex. The fruit is fleshy.

Key Recognition Features The fan-shaped flowers with the tube split to the base, and the few-seeded, fleshy fruit.

Ecology and Geography On sandy and rocky coasts and scrub; around 70 species in Australia. Several others in the Pacific islands, and a few elsewhere on tropical and subtropical coasts.

Comment *Scaevola aemula* R. Br. is commonly cultivated as a hanging basket plant, with names such as 'Blue Wonder', 'Mauve Clusters' and 'Saphira'. Two species, *S. plumieri* (L.) Vahl and *S. taccada* (Geartn.) Roxb., are widespread on coasts in the tropics, often forming the first line of defence against salt-laden gales. Their fruits remain viable for long periods in seawater, but only germinate when washed up on the beach. The genus *Lechenaultia* R. Br., also in the Goodeniaceae, contains around 26 species of small shrubs, many with strange and very beautiful flowers, of which 20 are endemic to Western Australia. Although superficially similar to Lobeliaceae (see pp. 332–33), DNA studies indicate that the family Goodeniaceae is closer to Compositae (see pp. 336–81) and to Menyanthaceae.

Scaevola aemula 'Saphira'
flower sections
2 × life size, May 15th

Scaevola aemula 'Saphira'
just over life size, May 15th

Menyanthes

Menyanthes L. (1753), bogbean or buckbean, in the family Menyanthaceae, contains 1 species, *M. trifoliata* L., around the northern hemisphere.

Description Perennial with flowering stems to 50cm from a creeping rhizome. Leaves alternate, with 3 leaflets. Flowers heterostylous, white or pinkish, in a loose, pyramidal head. Sepals 5. Petals 5, equal, with a fringe of long, white threads, joined at the base. Stamens 5, either longer than the short style or shorter than the long style. Ovary superior, with 1 cell and numerous ovules; style 1, with a 2-lobed stigma. Pollination is by various flies. The fruit is a many-seeded capsule.

Key Recognition Features The leaves with 3 leaflets and the flowers with fringed petals.

Ecology and Geography In shallow water on the margins of lakes, marshes, and bogs throughout Europe and in Morocco, northern Asia, and North America southwards to Tulare County in California.

Comment The family Menyanthaceae contains 5 genera, of which the largest, *Nymphoides* Hill., is exclusively aquatic, with small, waterlily-like plants with white or yellow, fringed flowers. *Nephrophyllidium* Gilg., syn. *Fauria* Franch., contains 1 species, *N. crista-gallii* (Hook.) Gilg., from mountain slopes on the Olympic peninsula, the Kurile Islands, and northern Japan; it is close to *Menyanthes*, but has kidney-shaped leaves and heads of smaller flowers without fringed petals. *Liparophyllum* Hook. fil., with 1 species, *L. gunnii* Hook. fil., in Tasmania and New Zealand, has narrow leaves and small, white, slightly hairy flowers and fleshy fruit. The family Menyanthaceae was traditionally associated with or even included in the Gentianaceae (see pp.208–211). DNA studies now suggest that it is an isolated family closest to the Goodeniaceae and the Compositae (see pp.336–81).

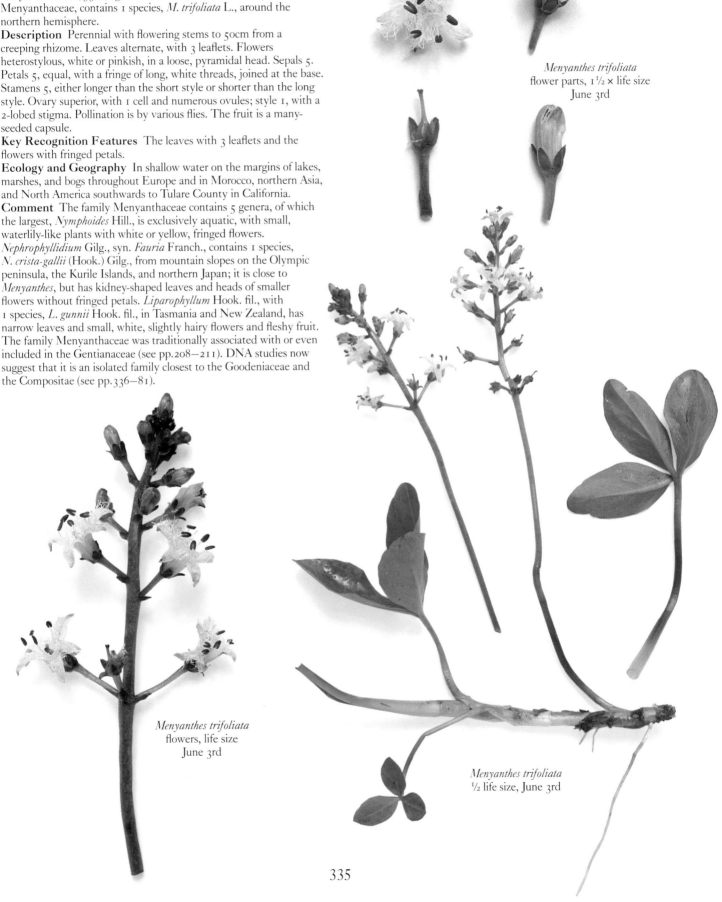

Menyanthes trifoliata
flower parts, 1 1/2 × life size
June 3rd

Menyanthes trifoliata
flowers, life size
June 3rd

Menyanthes trifoliata
1/2 life size, June 3rd

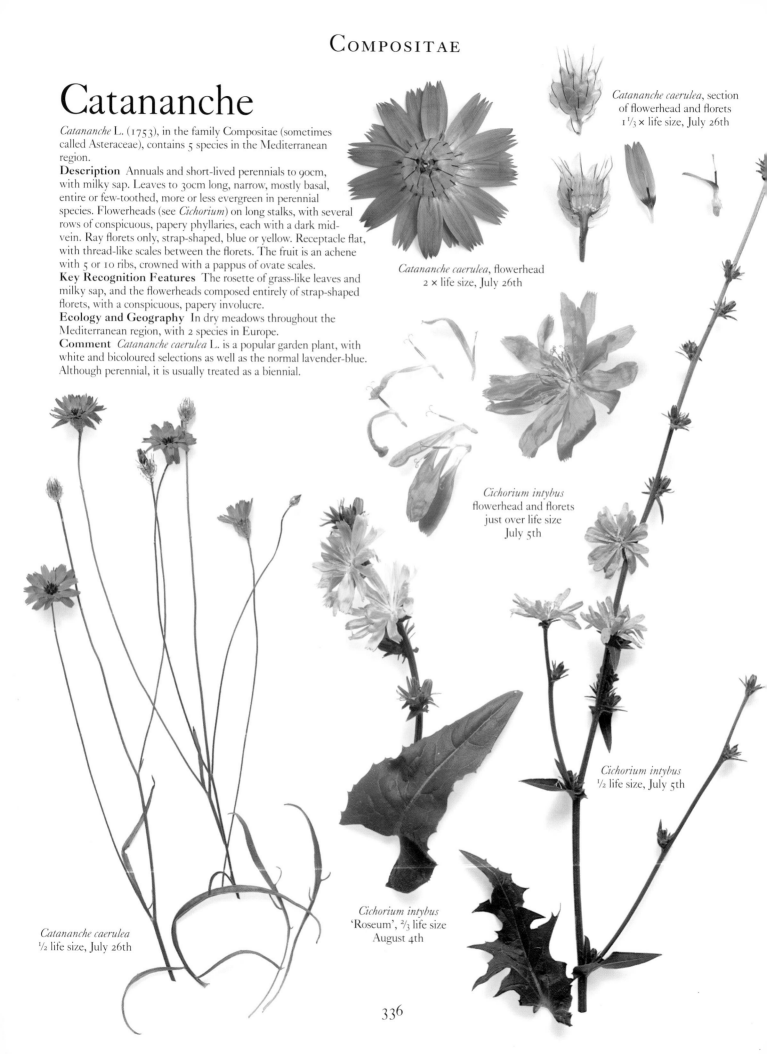

Catananche

Catananche L. (1753), in the family Compositae (sometimes called Asteraceae), contains 5 species in the Mediterranean region.

Description Annuals and short-lived perennials to 90cm, with milky sap. Leaves to 30cm long, narrow, mostly basal, entire or few-toothed, more or less evergreen in perennial species. Flowerheads (see *Cichorium*) on long stalks, with several rows of conspicuous, papery phyllaries, each with a dark mid-vein. Ray florets only, strap-shaped, blue or yellow. Receptacle flat, with thread-like scales between the florets. The fruit is an achene with 5 or 10 ribs, crowned with a pappus of ovate scales.

Key Recognition Features The rosette of grass-like leaves and milky sap, and the flowerheads composed entirely of strap-shaped florets, with a conspicuous, papery involucre.

Ecology and Geography In dry meadows throughout the Mediterranean region, with 2 species in Europe.

Comment *Catananche caerulea* L. is a popular garden plant, with white and bicoloured selections as well as the normal lavender-blue. Although perennial, it is usually treated as a biennial.

Catananche caerulea, section of flowerhead and florets
1⅓ × life size, July 26th

Catananche caerulea, flowerhead
2 × life size, July 26th

Cichorium intybus
flowerhead and florets
just over life size
July 5th

Cichorium intybus
½ life size, July 5th

Catananche caerulea
½ life size, July 26th

Cichorium intybus
'Roseum', ⅔ life size
August 4th

Cichorium

Cichorium L. (1753), in the family Compositae (sometimes called Asteraceae), contains 8 species in Europe and North Africa.

Description Annuals and perennials to 1.2m. Leaves pinnately lobed or toothed, with milky sap. The flowers are typical of the family Compositae (see Comment). Flowerheads stalkless, mostly in the leaf axils. Ray florets only, blue. Phyllaries in 2 rows, the outer short. Receptacle flat, without scales. The fruit is a club-shaped, ribbed achene, with a pappus of 1 or 2 rows of short scales.

Key Recognition Features Mostly erect, tap-rooted plants with lobed leaves, milky sap, and stalkless, blue flowerheads.

Ecology and Geography Roadsides and waste places in full sun; often naturalised. Found in the Mediterranean region, with 3 species in Europe, and Ethiopia.

Comment *Cichorium* includes the salad plants endive, *C. endivia* L., and chicory (*C. intybus* L.). The tap roots of *C. intybus* have been used as a coffee substitute, and a pink form, 'Roseum', is sometimes grown for ornament; the flowers close in the afternoon. The spiny, woody-based perennial *C. spinosum* L. is sometimes grown on rock gardens.

The Compositae is one of the largest plant families, containing over 1500 genera and 22,000 species; it is sometimes called Asteraceae. The characteristic, often daisy-like flowerheads of Compositae are called "capitula". Each has a calyx-like involucre of 1 or more rows of bracts, also called phyllaries, and is made up of numerous minute flowers (florets). In most genera, the central and outer florets are different, the central or disc florets being tubular, with 4 or 5 teeth, and usually either male or bisexual. The outer florets are usually extended into strap-like rays or ligules, and are generally either female or sterile. In some genera all the florets are ligulate and hermaphrodite. (As elsewhere, if no gender is given in the description the florets are bisexual.) Stamens are 4 or 5; style 1, the ovary inferior with 1 cell and 1 ovule. Pollination is by insects. The seed is an achene, often topped by a pappus composed of simple or feathery hairs to aid wind dispersal, or of teeth, which may be barbed to stick to the coats of animals.

Stokesia laevis, flowerheads and florets, ½ life size, July 28th

Stokesia laevis ½ life size, August 17th

Stokesia laevis ⅓ life size, July 28th

Stokesia

Stokesia L'Herit. (1788), Stokes' aster, in the family Compositae (sometimes called Asteraceae), contains 1 species in the southeastern United States.

Description Erect perennial to 60cm. Leaves alternate, elliptic, with entire margins, sometimes spiny at the base. Flowerheads (see *Cichorium*) to 10cm across. Florets all tubular and fringed, the outer much larger than the inner. Phyllaries in several overlapping rows, the outer with a bristly tip. The fruit is an angled achene with a pappus of a few narrow scales.

Key Recognition Features Plants with large, cornflower-like flowers (*Centaurea*, see p.343).

Ecology and Geography In moist, open habitats and pine barrens in the southeastern United States, from North Carolina to Florida.

Comment *Stokesia laevis* (Hill) Greene is an attractive border perennial; it also has some potential as an oilseed plant. As well as light and deep blue forms, there are selections with purple, pink, or white flowers. The genus is named after Jonathon Stokes (1755–1831), an English doctor and botanist.

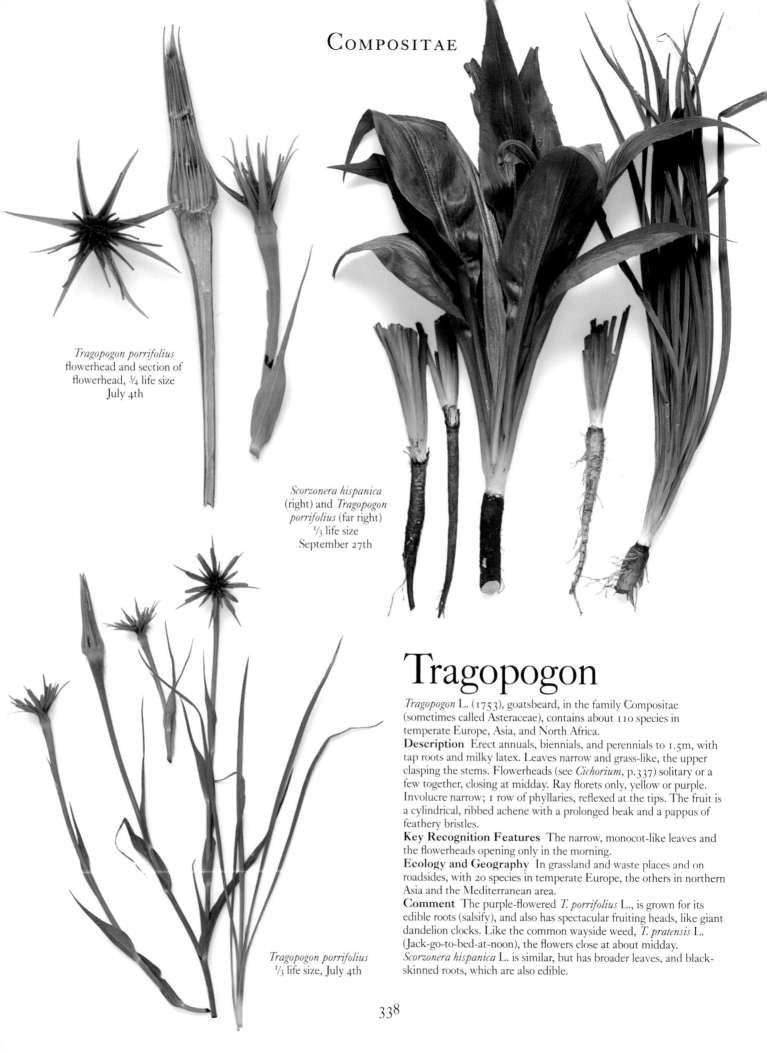

Tragopogon porrifolius
flowerhead and section of
flowerhead, ¾ life size
July 4th

Scorzonera hispanica
(right) and *Tragopogon
porrifolius* (far right)
⅓ life size
September 27th

Tragopogon

Tragopogon L. (1753), goatsbeard, in the family Compositae
(sometimes called Asteraceae), contains about 110 species in
temperate Europe, Asia, and North Africa.

Description Erect annuals, biennials, and perennials to 1.5m, with
tap roots and milky latex. Leaves narrow and grass-like, the upper
clasping the stems. Flowerheads (see *Cichorium*, p.337) solitary or a
few together, closing at midday. Ray florets only, yellow or purple.
Involucre narrow; 1 row of phyllaries, reflexed at the tips. The fruit is
a cylindrical, ribbed achene with a prolonged beak and a pappus of
feathery bristles.

Key Recognition Features The narrow, monocot-like leaves and
the flowerheads opening only in the morning.

Ecology and Geography In grassland and waste places and on
roadsides, with 20 species in temperate Europe, the others in northern
Asia and the Mediterranean area.

Comment The purple-flowered *T. porrifolius* L., is grown for its
edible roots (salsify), and also has spectacular fruiting heads, like giant
dandelion clocks. Like the common wayside weed, *T. pratensis* L.
(Jack-go-to-bed-at-noon), the flowers close at about midday.
Scorzonera hispanica L. is similar, but has broader leaves, and black-
skinned roots, which are also edible.

Tragopogon porrifolius
⅓ life size, July 4th

338

Prenanthes

Prenanthes L. (1753), in the family Compositae (sometimes called Asteraceae), contains 25 species in the temperate northern hemisphere and the mountains of North Africa.

Description Erect perennials to 1.5m, with milky sap. Leaves entire, toothed, or pinnately or palmately lobed, the lower stalked, the upper stalkless. Flowerheads (see *Cichorium*, p.337) small, nodding. Ray florets only, few, yellow, white, or purple. Involucre cylindrical; 2 or 3 rows of phyllaries. The fruit is a flattened achene with a fine, bristly pappus.

Key Recognition Features Upright plants with small, nodding heads of strap-shaped, yellow, white, or purple flowers.

Ecology and Geography Upland meadows and woodland margins in Europe (1 species), North Africa, northern Asia, and North America.

Comment The name comes from *pranes* and *anthos*, the Greek for drooping flower. *Prenanthes purpurea* L. from Europe and some Asiatic species are quietly attractive, rarely cultivated.

Cicerbita

Cicerbita Wallr. (1822), in the family Compositae (sometimes called Asteraceae), contains about 18 species in the temperate northern hemisphere.

Description Robust, clump-forming perennials to 3m tall. Leaves deciduous, deeply lobed, clasping the stem, to 25cm long. Sap milky. Flowerheads (see *Cichorium*, p.337) small, borne in large panicles. Ray florets only, blue, lilac, or violet; pappus of 2 rows of hairs, the outer very short. Phyllaries narrow, green, in several rows. The fruit is a flattened achene.

Key Recognition Features Very large plants with clasping leaves, milky sap, and large panicles of small, blue or violet flowerheads.

Ecology and Geography In woods and damp, shady places in mountains across the northern temperate region; 4 species in Europe.

Comment Striking perennials for a shady wild garden, the best suited being *C. plumieri* (L.) Kirschl. and *C. alpina* (L.) Wallr.; *C. bourgiaei* (Boiss.) Beauv. is cultivated, but is very invasive.

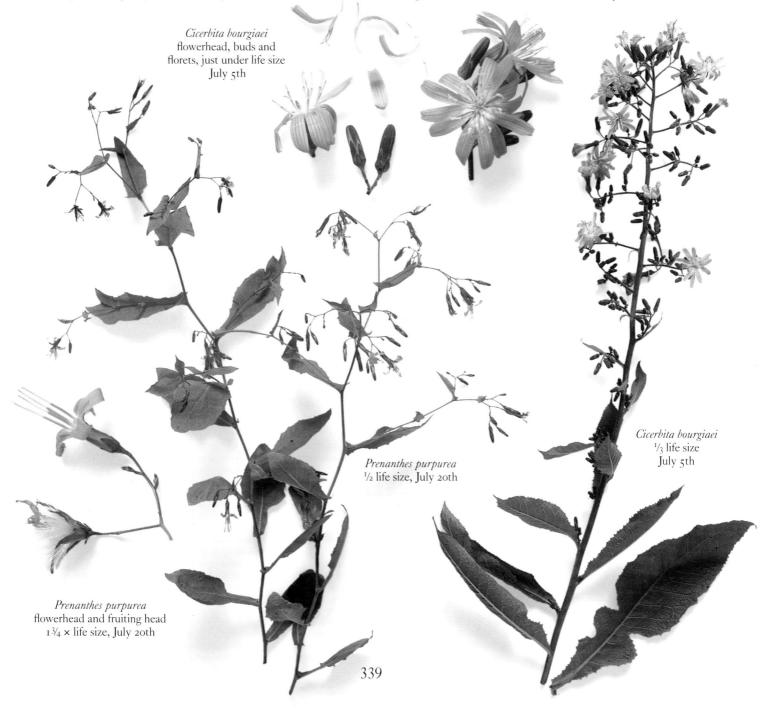

Cicerbita bourgiaei
flowerhead, buds and
florets, just under life size
July 5th

Prenanthes purpurea
½ life size, July 20th

Cicerbita bourgiaei
⅓ life size
July 5th

Prenanthes purpurea
flowerhead and fruiting head
1¾ × life size, July 20th

Hieracium

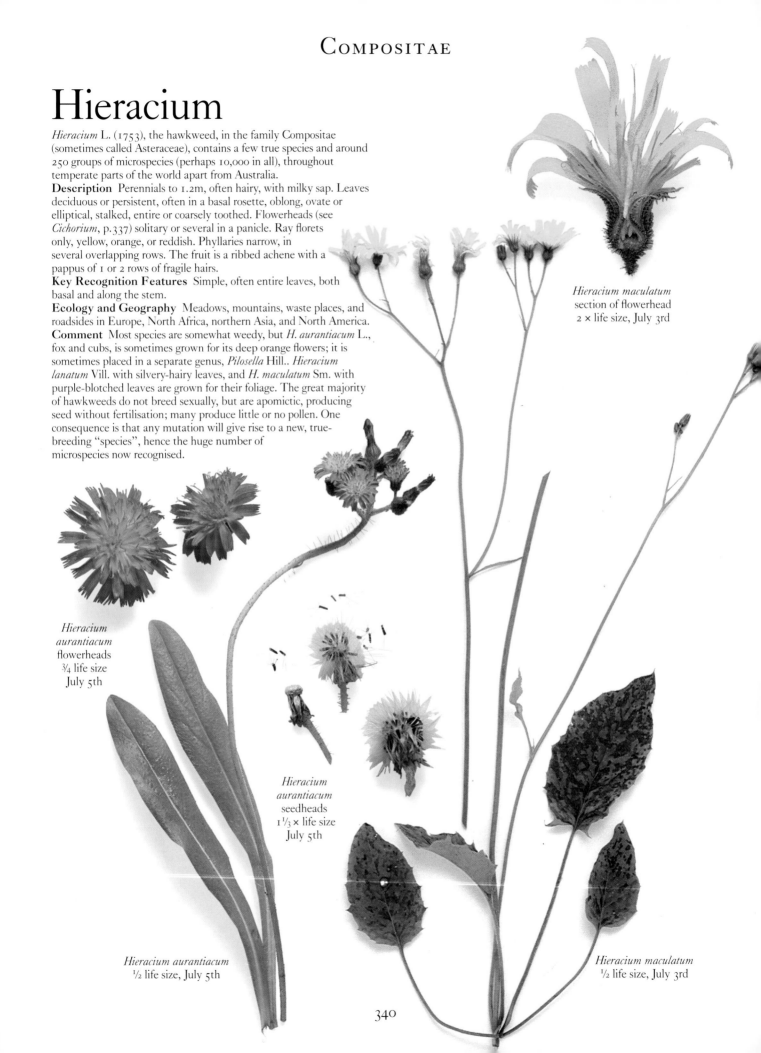

Hieracium L. (1753), the hawkweed, in the family Compositae (sometimes called Asteraceae), contains a few true species and around 250 groups of microspecies (perhaps 10,000 in all), throughout temperate parts of the world apart from Australia.

Description Perennials to 1.2m, often hairy, with milky sap. Leaves deciduous or persistent, often in a basal rosette, oblong, ovate or elliptical, stalked, entire or coarsely toothed. Flowerheads (see *Cichorium*, p.337) solitary or several in a panicle. Ray florets only, yellow, orange, or reddish. Phyllaries narrow, in several overlapping rows. The fruit is a ribbed achene with a pappus of 1 or 2 rows of fragile hairs.

Key Recognition Features Simple, often entire leaves, both basal and along the stem.

Ecology and Geography Meadows, mountains, waste places, and roadsides in Europe, North Africa, northern Asia, and North America.

Comment Most species are somewhat weedy, but *H. aurantiacum* L., fox and cubs, is sometimes grown for its deep orange flowers; it is sometimes placed in a separate genus, *Pilosella* Hill.. *Hieracium lanatum* Vill. with silvery-hairy leaves, and *H. maculatum* Sm. with purple-blotched leaves are grown for their foliage. The great majority of hawkweeds do not breed sexually, but are apomictic, producing seed without fertilisation; many produce little or no pollen. One consequence is that any mutation will give rise to a new, true-breeding "species", hence the huge number of microspecies now recognised.

Hieracium maculatum
section of flowerhead
2 × life size, July 3rd

Hieracium aurantiacum
flowerheads
¾ life size
July 5th

Hieracium aurantiacum
seedheads
1⅓ × life size
July 5th

Hieracium aurantiacum
½ life size, July 5th

Hieracium maculatum
½ life size, July 3rd

Xeranthemum

Xeranthemum L. (1753), in the family Compositae (sometimes called Asteraceae), contains about 5 species in the Mediterranean area.

Description Annuals to 75cm. Leaves entire, narrowly oblong or linear, woolly at least beneath. Flowerheads (see *Cichorium*, p.337) solitary, composed of white or pink, tubular florets, the outer row sterile. Inner phyllaries large, resembling ray-florets, papery, white, pink or lilac. Outer phyllaries small and scale-like. The fruit is a silky achene with a few small pappus scales.

Key Recognition Features Small annuals with white or pink, papery flowers.

Ecology and Geography In dry, stony places in the Mediterranean area, with 3 species in Europe, the others in North Africa and western Asia.

Comment The name comes from the Greek words *xeros* and *anthos*, meaning dry flower; the papery bracts keep their colour when dried, and *X. annuum* L. is a popular "everlasting", grown for use in dried flower arrangements.

Xeranthemum annuum
flowers, ¾ life size
September 11th

Leontodon

Leontodon L. (1753), the hawkbit, in the family Compositae (sometimes called Asteraceae), contains about 50 species in temperate Europe and Asia.

Description Perennials to 80cm, with short rhizomes and milky sap. Leaves in rosettes, entire, toothed, or pinnately cut. Flowerheads (see *Cichorium*, p.337) in panicles or solitary. Ray florets only, yellow, often grey or reddish on the underside. Phyllaries in several overlapping rows. The fruit is a ribbed, slightly flattened achene; pappus usually of 2 rows of feathery or roughened hairs, rarely of scales or absent.

Key Recognition Features Plants with a rosette of leaves and panicles of yellow flowers in summer or early autumn.

Ecology and Geography In meadows and alpine pastures, with 27 species in Europe, the others in western Asia.

Comment *Leontodon rigens* (Ait.) Paiva & Ormonde, from the Azores, is commonly sold as *Microseris ringens*, and is the only species widely grown in gardens. 'Girandole' is a selection with slightly larger flowers.

Xeranthemum annuum
½ life size
September 11th

Leontodon rigens
flowerheads and florets (below)
just over life size, July 21st

Leontodon rigens
½ life size, July 21st

341

Echinops

Echinops L. (1753), the globe thistle, in the family Compositae (sometimes called Asteraceae), contains about 120 species from Europe to Central Asia, and a few in the mountains of tropical Africa.
Description Erect annuals, biennials, or perennials to 2m. Leaves mostly pinnately toothed or lobed, often white-hairy beneath. Flowerheads (see *Cichorium*, p.337) formed of many 1-flowered heads, each of which has several rows of phyllaries, united into a tight, globose cluster. Florets tubular, blue, greyish, or white. The fruit is a densely hairy, oblong achene with a pappus of short bristles.
Key Recognition Features Tall perennials with leaves that are white beneath, and globose blue or white flowerheads.
Ecology and Geography In open, dry, rocky places, with 12 species in Europe, the others mostly in the Mediterranean area and from central Asia to the western Himalayas and Siberia, with a few in the mountains of tropical Africa.
Comment The name, derived from the Greek *echinos*, meaning hedgehog, alludes to the spiky flower clusters. Globe thistles are statuesque plants for a sunny border, and have handsome foliage.

Echinops sphaerocephalus
single flowerheads
1 ½ × life size
August 1st

Echinops sphaerocephalus
compound flowerhead
and section, ⅔ life size
August 1st

Echinops sphaerocephalus
⅓ life size, August 1st

Centaurea cariensis, ⅓ life size
September 25th

342

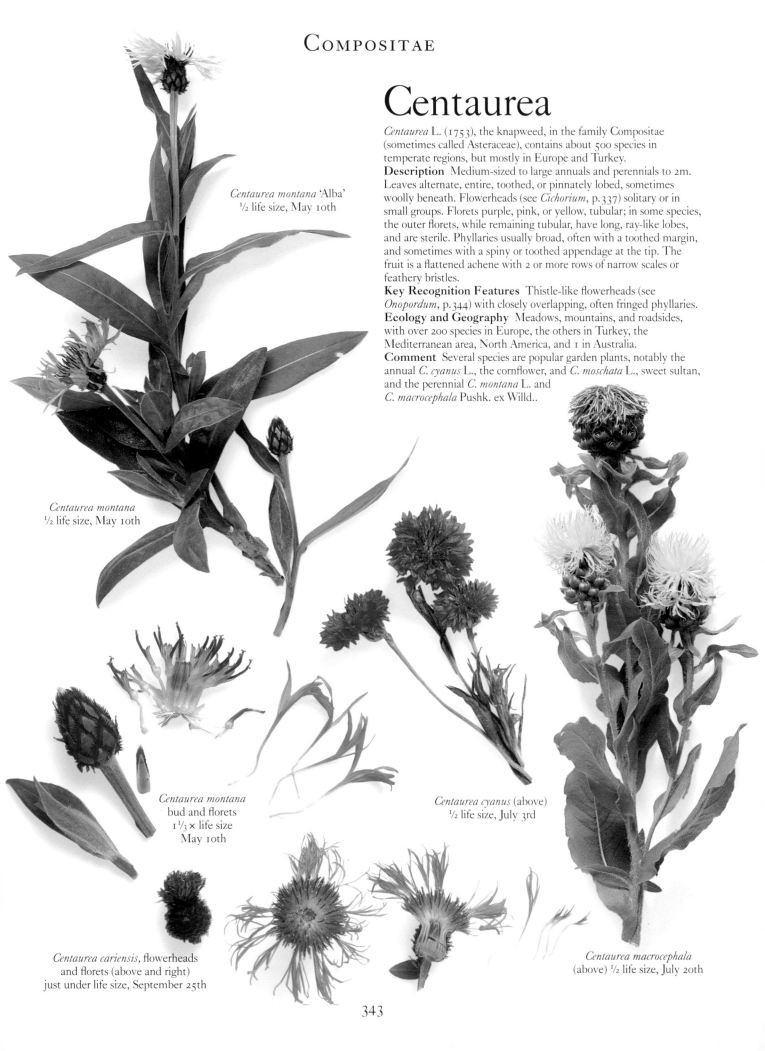

Centaurea

Centaurea L. (1753), the knapweed, in the family Compositae (sometimes called Asteraceae), contains about 500 species in temperate regions, but mostly in Europe and Turkey.

Description Medium-sized to large annuals and perennials to 2m. Leaves alternate, entire, toothed, or pinnately lobed, sometimes woolly beneath. Flowerheads (see *Cichorium*, p.337) solitary or in small groups. Florets purple, pink, or yellow, tubular; in some species, the outer florets, while remaining tubular, have long, ray-like lobes, and are sterile. Phyllaries usually broad, often with a toothed margin, and sometimes with a spiny or toothed appendage at the tip. The fruit is a flattened achene with 2 or more rows of narrow scales or feathery bristles.

Key Recognition Features Thistle-like flowerheads (see *Onopordum*, p.344) with closely overlapping, often fringed phyllaries.

Ecology and Geography Meadows, mountains, and roadsides, with over 200 species in Europe, the others in Turkey, the Mediterranean area, North America, and 1 in Australia.

Comment Several species are popular garden plants, notably the annual *C. cyanus* L., the cornflower, and *C. moschata* L., sweet sultan, and the perennial *C. montana* L. and *C. macrocephala* Pushk. ex Willd..

Centaurea montana 'Alba'
½ life size, May 10th

Centaurea montana
½ life size, May 10th

Centaurea montana
bud and florets
1⅓ × life size
May 10th

Centaurea cyanus (above)
½ life size, July 3rd

Centaurea cariensis, flowerheads
and florets (above and right)
just under life size, September 25th

Centaurea macrocephala
(above) ½ life size, July 20th

Saussurea

Saussurea DC (1810), in the family Compositae (sometimes called Asteraceae), contains about 300 species in temperate Europe, Asia, and North America.

Description Perennials to 3m, although many are smaller. Leaves simple or pinnately divided and thistle-like. Flowerheads (see *Cichorium*, p.337) solitary or in panicles. Florets small, tubular, pink, purple, or violet, interspersed with scales. Involucre bell-shaped or cylindrical, with many rows of overlapping phyllaries. The fruit is a ribbed, cylindrical achene with a pappus of roughened, feathery bristles.

Key Recognition Features Plants often resembling *Centaurea* (see p.343), but the phyllaries are without an appendage at the tip.

Ecology and Geography Lowland and alpine meadows, alpine bogs and screes; 9 species in Europe, the others in Asia from the Caucasus to the Himalayas, China, and Japan, and a few in North America.

Comment Several alpine species are worthy of cultivation, although often difficult, especially the highly adapted dwarf species from the Himalayas, such as *S. gossypiphora* D. Don. Most lowland species are rather weedy. The name commemorates two Swiss botanists, Horace Benedict de Saussure (1740–99) and his son Theodor (1767–1845).

Onopordum

Onopordum L. (1753), the cotton thistle, in the family Compositae (sometimes called Asteraceae), contains about 60 species in Europe, the Mediterranean area, and western Asia.

Description Mostly biennials to 3m, often with spiny-winged stems. Leaves pinnately lobed and spiny, usually woolly at least beneath. Flowerheads (see *Cichorium*, p.337) solitary or in corymbs. Florets tubular, purple or white. Involucre globose, with several rows of overlapping, spiny-tipped phyllaries with recurved tips. The fruit is a 4-angled achene with a pappus of soft hairs.

Key Recognition Features Very large thistles with white-hairy leaves and purple flowerheads.

Ecology and Geography Dry, open roadsides and waste places, sometimes in mountains, with 13 species in Europe, the others in the Mediterranean area and western Asia.

Comment *Onopordum acanthium* L. is a popular, statuesque plant that sometimes becomes naturalised. The splendid, but very spiny foliage of these large thistles is highly ornamental. The name is from the Greek *onos* and *pordos*, meaning donkey and flatulence, and presumed to refer to the effect on donkeys of eating thistles.

Saussurea tinctoria
½ life size, August 2nd

Onopordum acanthium
½ life size, July 5th

Onopordum acanthium
section of flowerhead
just under life size, July 5th

Silybum marianum
section of flowerhead
⅔ life size, August 1st

Silybum marianum, seedhead
and achenes with pappus
¾ life size, September 11th

Silybum

Silybum Adans. (1763), the milk thistle, in the family
Compositae (sometimes called Asteraceae), contains 2
species in southern Europe, North Africa, and western Asia.
Description Annuals or biennials to 1.5m, with erect,
simple stems. Leaves both basal and stem, pinnately lobed or
sinuate, spiny, the main veins white. Flowerheads (see
Cichorium, p.337) solitary. Florets tubular, purple. Phyllaries
overlapping, the outer and middle ending in a toothed appendage
and long, recurved spine. The fruit is a slightly flattened, oblong,
black achene with a rough white pappus of hairs joined together at
the base.
Key Recognition Features Large thistles with broad, white-
veined leaves and purple flowerheads.
Ecology and Geography On roadsides and field margins in
southern Europe and the Mediterranean region eastwards to
Afghanistan, including western North Africa.
Comment The milk thistle, *S. marianum* (L.) Gaertn., is sometimes
grown in gardens, mainly for the large, handsomely marked, rich green
leaves. *Silybum* is an old Greek name, used by Dioscorides.

Silybum marianum
⅓ life size, August 1st

Ageratum

Ageratum L. (1753), in the family Compositae (sometimes called Asteraceae), contains about 43 species in the tropical Americas.

Description Annuals, perennials, and shrubs to 1m or more. Leaves linear to rounded, entire or toothed. Flowerheads (see *Cichorium*, p.337) solitary or several in a panicle. Florets all blue, white, or mauve, tubular, fluffy. Involucre bell-shaped, with several rows of narrow, overlapping phyllaries. The fruit is an angled oblong achene with a pappus of 5 or 6 scales.

Key Recognition Features The fluffy heads of blue, pink, or white flowers and the achenes with a pappus of scales.

Ecology and Geography In dry, sunny places in from Florida to Mexico, South America, and the West Indies.

Comment Selections of *A. houstonianum* Mill. are very popular bedding plants in Europe; many cultivars are available. An oil extracted from the plant has given some control against certain fungal diseases of the pigeon pea, *Cajanus cajan* (L.) Millsp., an important leguminous crop plant in Africa.

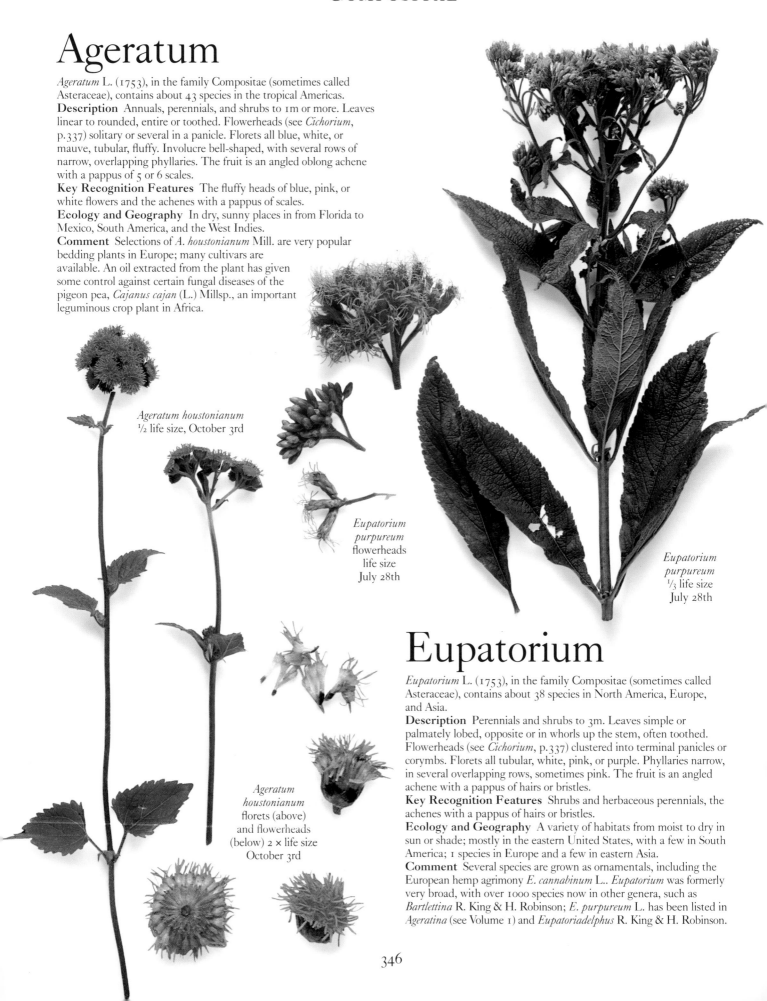

Ageratum houstonianum
½ life size, October 3rd

Eupatorium purpureum
flowerheads
life size
July 28th

Eupatorium purpureum
⅓ life size
July 28th

Ageratum houstonianum
florets (above)
and flowerheads
(below) 2 × life size
October 3rd

Eupatorium

Eupatorium L. (1753), in the family Compositae (sometimes called Asteraceae), contains about 38 species in North America, Europe, and Asia.

Description Perennials and shrubs to 3m. Leaves simple or palmately lobed, opposite or in whorls up the stem, often toothed. Flowerheads (see *Cichorium*, p.337) clustered into terminal panicles or corymbs. Florets all tubular, white, pink, or purple. Phyllaries narrow, in several overlapping rows, sometimes pink. The fruit is an angled achene with a pappus of hairs or bristles.

Key Recognition Features Shrubs and herbaceous perennials, the achenes with a pappus of hairs or bristles.

Ecology and Geography A variety of habitats from moist to dry in sun or shade; mostly in the eastern United States, with a few in South America; 1 species in Europe and a few in eastern Asia.

Comment Several species are grown as ornamentals, including the European hemp agrimony *E. cannabinum* L.. *Eupatorium* was formerly very broad, with over 1000 species now in other genera, such as *Bartlettina* R. King & H. Robinson; *E. purpureum* L. has been listed in *Ageratina* (see Volume 1) and *Eupatoriadelphus* R. King & H. Robinson.

COMPOSITAE

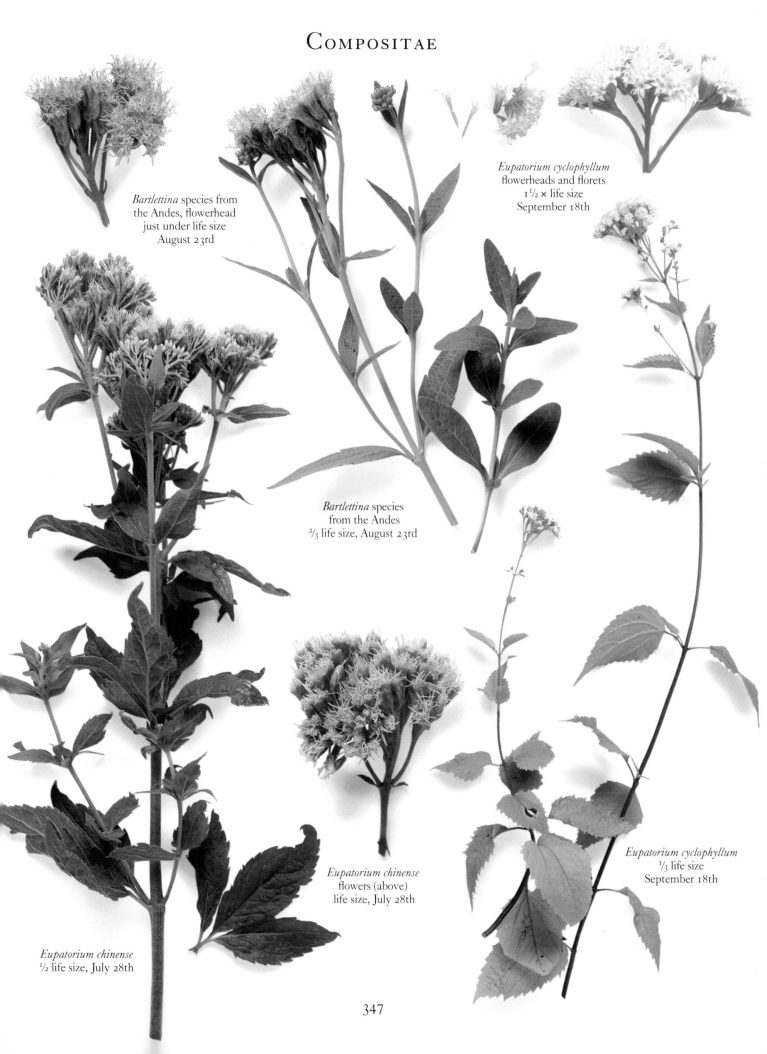

Bartlettina species from
the Andes, flowerhead
just under life size
August 23rd

Eupatorium cyclophyllum
flowerheads and florets
1 ½ × life size
September 18th

Bartlettina species
from the Andes
⅔ life size, August 23rd

Eupatorium chinense
flowers (above)
life size, July 28th

Eupatorium cyclophyllum
⅓ life size
September 18th

Eupatorium chinense
½ life size, July 28th

Liatris

Liatris Schreb. (1791), the gayfeather, in the family Compositae (sometimes called Asteraceae), contains about 43 species in eastern North America.

Description Erect perennials to 1.5m, with tuberous roots. Leaves linear to narrowly lance-shaped, both basal and stem. Flowerheads (see *Cichorium*, p.337) small, in a terminal spike or raceme. Florets all tubular, rosy-purple. Phyllaries in several overlapping rows. The fruit is a 10-ribbed, cylindrical achene with a pappus of feathery bristles.

Key Recognition Features Erect perennials with fluffy, deep pink flowerheads arranged in narrow spikes; unusually, these open from the top of the spike downwards.

Ecology and Geography Mostly in dry open places, or on the banks of streams, in eastern North America from Manitoba and Ontario to Texas and New Mexico.

Comment *Liatris spicata* (L.) Willd. is a popular garden perennial; there are many selections, with flowers from white to violet.

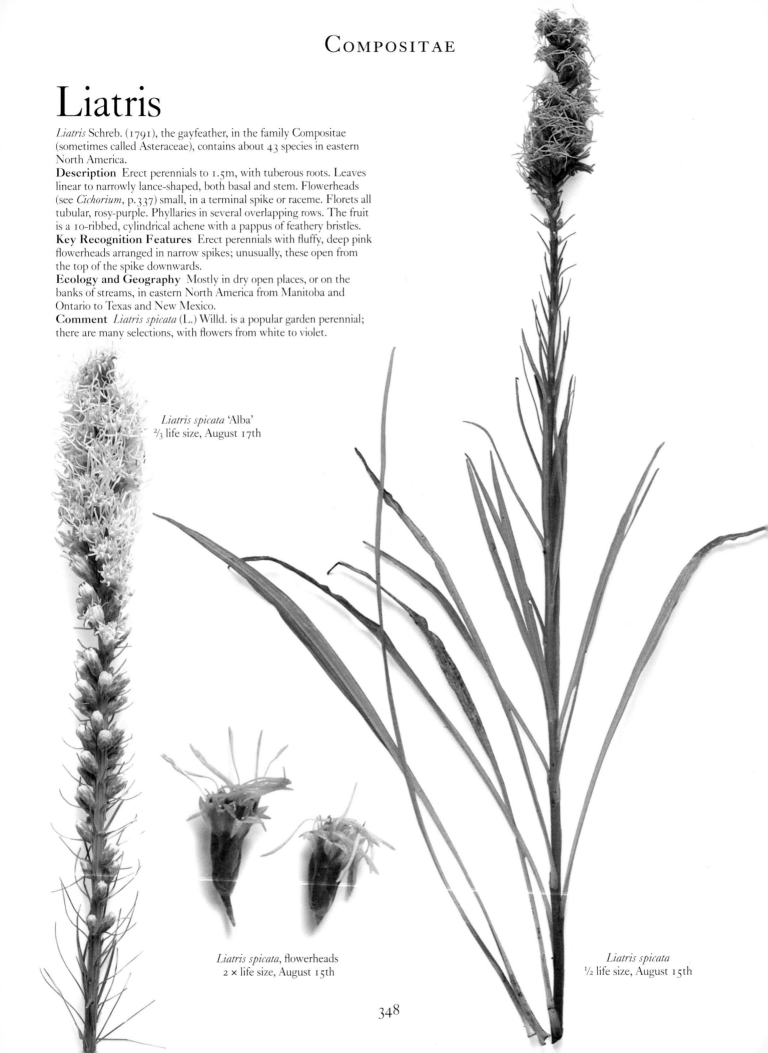

Liatris spicata 'Alba'
⅔ life size, August 17th

Liatris spicata, flowerheads
2 × life size, August 15th

Liatris spicata
½ life size, August 15th

Petasites

Petasites Mill. (1754), the butterbur, in the family Compositae (sometimes called Asteraceae), contains about 19 species in northern temperate areas.

Description Dioecious perennials to 1m, with far-spreading rhizomes. Basal leaves long-stalked, rounded or kidney-shaped, and often lobed; stem leaves small and scale-like. Flowerheads (see *Cichorium*, p.337) white, pink, or yellowish, borne in short, spike-like panicles appearing before the leaves, and elongating dramatically after flowering. Male flowerheads have tubular male florets with an outer ring of either sterile ray florets or tubular female ones; female flowerheads have tubular or raylike florets, sometimes a few sterile. Phyllaries in 1 or 2 rows. The fruit is a hairless, cylindrical achene with a pappus of simple hairs.

Key Recognition Features Robust plants forming extensive colonies of large leaves, flowering in early spring.

Ecology and Geography In damp, shady places and on stream banks, with 10 species in Europe, the others in temperate regions from western Asia to China and Japan.

Comment Although the flowers of the butterburs are not showy, the large leaves are striking in a wild garden setting, and the vanilla-scented flowers of *P. fragrans* (Vill.) Presl are welcome in late winter. Most species are much too invasive for a border. The leaf-stalks of *P. japonicus* (Sieb. & Zucc.) Maxim. are eaten as a vegetable in Japan.

Petasites fragrans, florets and flowerheads (above) 2 × life size January 14th

Stevia species from Mexico just under life size August 23rd

Stevia

Stevia Cav. (1797), in the family Compositae (sometimes called Asteraceae), contains about 235 species in tropical and warm parts of the Americas.

Description Annuals, perennials, and shrubs to 1m. Leaves mostly opposite, entire or toothed, simple or formed of 3 leaflets. Flowerheads (see *Cichorium*, p.337) small, in panicles or corymbs. Florets few, tubular, purplish or white. Involucre cylindrical, with 1 row of narrow phyllaries. The fruit is a slender, ribbed achene with a pappus of scales or bristles.

Key Recognition Features Plants with small, purple flowerheads with cylindrical involucres.

Ecology and Geography In sunny, dry habitats from Arizona and New Mexico to Paraguay.

Comment *Stevia rebaudiana* Bertoni is occasionally grown; it carries flat heads of small, white flowers over a long period. The genus is named for P.J. Esteve (d.1566), a doctor and professor of botany at the university at Valencia, Spain.

Petasites fragrans ½ life size, January 14th

Doronicum plantagineum
section of flowerhead
and florets, 1⅓ × life size
April 3rd

Doronicum

Doronicum L. (1753), the leopard's bane, in the family Compositae (sometimes called Asteraceae), contains about 35 species in temperate Europe, the Mediterranean area, and Asia.

Description Perennials to 1m, with tuberous or stoloniferous roots. Leaves ovate, often heart-shaped, entire or toothed. Daisy-like flowerheads (see *Cichorium*, p.337) bright yellow. Disk florets bisexual; ray florets spreading, female. Phyllaries green, in 2 or 3 overlapping rows. The fruit is a ribbed achene with 1 or 2 rows of simple pappus hairs.

Key Recognition Features Medium-sized perennials with heart-shaped leaves, and yellow daisies in spring.

Ecology and Geography In woods, mountain pastures, and screes; 12 species in Europe, the others in southwestern Asia and Siberia.

Comment Several species are popular in gardens, providing reliable bright colour in early spring. *Doronicum orientale* Hoffm., from southeastern Europe and the Caucasus, is showy and compact; others, such as *D. pardalianches* L. and *D. plantagineum* L., are taller.

Doronicum plantagineum
⅔ life size, April 3rd

Asteriscus

Asteriscus Mill. (1768), in the family Compositae (sometimes called Asteraceae), contains 3 species in the Mediterranean area.

Description Branching annuals or perennials with flowering stems to 50cm, without milky sap. Leaves simple. Flowers (see *Cichorium*, p.337) yellow, usually with leaf-like outer bracts. Ray florets in 2 rows, narrow, female, disc florets with a terete tube. Pollination is by various insects. Outer fruits triangular or compressed, inner terete, with a very short pappus of numerous small scales.

Key Recognition Features Yellow-flowered, daisy-like plants with spreading branches.

Ecology and Geography Damp, sandy, or rocky coastal areas.

Comment *Asteriscus aquaticus* (L.) Less is an annual, found in sandy places that are damp in winter; *A. maritimus* (L.) Less. is almost shrubby and grows in rocks areas by the sea. The very common *Pallenis spinosa* (L.) Cass. is sometimes placed in Asteriscus; it is similar, with leafy outer bracts, but the tubular florets are compressed.

Farfugium

Farfugium Lindl. (1857), in the family Compositae (sometimes called Asteraceae), contains 2 species in northeastern Asia.

Description Perennials to 80cm, with a short, erect stock. Leaves evergreen, rounded or ovate, entire or toothed. Daisy-like flowerheads (see *Cichorium*, p.337) in open corymbs. Ray florets bright yellow, female; disc florets dull yellow. Involucre tubular, with 1 row of bracts. The fruit is a smooth, slender achene with a pappus of bristles.

Key Recognition Features Evergreen perennials with oval or rounded leaves and bright yellow daisies in summer.

Ecology and Geography Woodland, damp meadows, and by streams in Japan and Korea.

Comment Cultivars of *Farfugium japonicum* (L.) Kitam. syn. *Ligularia tussilaginea* (Burm. f.) Mak. with spotted or variegated leaves are sometimes grown; they are especially popular in Japan. The habitat of *F. hiberniflorum* (Mak.) Kitam., endemic to Yakushima and Tanegashima in southern Japan, is theatened by logging.

Doronicum orientale
½ life size, April 10th

Asteriscus maritimus (above) just over life size, May 10th

Farfugium japonicum 'Aureomaculatum' ½ life size September 12th

Senecio

Senecio L. (1753), in the family Compositae (sometimes called Asteraceae), contains about 1250 species almost throughout the world. See Volume 1 for woody species.

Description Small, medium, or large annuals, perennials, shrubs, or climbers to 5m. Leaves alternate, entire or lobed. Usually daisy-like flowerheads (see *Cichorium*, p.337) in corymbs or solitary, yellow, white, or purple. Ray florets female or absent; disc florets bisexual. Phyllaries narrow, in 1 row, or sometimes 2, the outer being much shorter. The fruit is a cylindrical achene with a pappus of simple hairs.

Key Recognition Features A huge, diverse genus. Small flowers, often yellow, have 1 or 2 rows of phyllaries, and may lack ray florets.

Ecology and Geography In almost every habitat, from woodland to alpine, desert, and tropical; 60 species in Europe, the others throughout the world.

Comment Many species have been placed in other genera: the shrubby *S. compactus* T. Kirk and its hybrid 'Sunshine' are now in *Brachyglottis* (see Volume 1). The name comes from the Latin *senex*, an old man, alluding to the conspicuous grey or white pappus hairs. Among the remaining species are many common garden weeds including ragwort (*S. jacobaea* L.) which is poisonous to livestock, and groundsel (*S. vulgaris* L.). *Senecio squalidus* L. from southern Europe, is famous for escaping onto the walls of Oxford Botanic Garden around 1890, and following the railways across Britain; it is still common along railway tracks.

Ligularia

Ligularia Cass. (1816), in the family Compositae (sometimes called Asteraceae), contains about 125 species in temperate Europe and Asia.

Description Perennials to 2m, with short rhizomes. Basal leaves large, ovate to kidney-shaped, toothed or somewhat lobed, on long stalks with bases that sheathe the stem. Stem leaves smaller, often bract-like. Daisy-like flowerheads (see *Cichorium*, p.337) in corymbs or racemes. Ray florets yellow to orange, female; disc florets dull yellow, bisexual. Phyllaries in 1 row, partially joined. The fruit is a smooth, cylindrical achene with a pappus of hairs.

Key Recognition Features Large perennials with yellow or orange daisies and handsome leaves.

Ecology and Geography In wet woodland and by streams, with 2 species in Europe, the others from central Asia to China, which has most species, and Japan.

Comment Several species of *Ligularia* are valued in gardens for their large, handsome leaves and yellow or orange flowerheads. Several smaller Himalayan alpine species formerly in *Cremanthodium* Benth. are now put in *Ligularia*.

Ligularia wilsoniana
½ life size, July 26th

Senecio squalidus
life size, April 10th

Compositae

Ligularia stenocephala
flowerheads and florets
just under life size, July 14th

Ligularia wilsoniana
section of flowerhead
with florets (above left)
and flowerhead (left)
⅔ life size, July 26th

Ligularia stenocephala
½ life size, July 14th

353

Rudbeckia fulgida var. *deamii*
flowerheads and florets
¾ life size, August 5th

Rudbeckia

Rudbeckia L. (1753), the coneflower or black-eyed Susan, in the family Compositae (sometimes called Asteraceae), contains 15 species in North America.

Description Annuals, biennials, and perennials to 2.5m. Leaves alternate, simple or pinnately lobed. Daisy-like flowerheads (see *Cichorium*, p.337) usually solitary, long-stalked. Ray florets yellow to orange, often drooping, sterile; disc florets yellow to deep red, in a prominent cone. Phyllaries green, in several rows. The fruit is an angled achene with no pappus or a few scales.

Key Recognition Features Plants with large flowers with conical centres and usually drooping rays.

Ecology and Geography Meadows, prairies, woodlands, and the banks of streams from Ontario to Florida, Texas, and Mexico.

Comment Reliable and easily grown plants for any sunny situation, coneflowers are popular in gardens, with bright yellow flowers in late summer. *Rudbeckia fulgida* Ait. var. *deamii* Blake, black-eyed Susan, is relatively compact. The genus is named after the Swedish botanist Olof Rudbeck (1660–1740), who was Linnaeus's predecessor at Uppsala University.

Rudbeckia fulgida var. *deamii*
½ life size, August 5th

Echinacea

Echinacea Moench (1794), in the family Compositae (sometimes called Asteraceae), contains about 9 species in North America.
Description Perennials to 2m, with rhizomes. Leaves simple, alternate, both basal and up the stem. Daisy-like flowerheads (see *Cichorium*, p.337) usually solitary, long-stalked. Ray florets drooping, pink or purple, sterile; disc florets orange-brown, forming a cone. Phyllaries in 2–4 overlapping rows. The fruit is an achene with a pappus of 4 short teeth.
Key Recognition Features Large flowerheads with somewhat drooping ray florets and a prominent central boss of orange-brown disc florets.
Ecology and Geography In both dry and moist prairie habitats in North America, from Saskatchewan to Texas and Alabama.
Comment The name *Echinacea*, from the Greek *echinos,* meaning hedgehog, refers to the spiky phyllaries, which remain prominent after the flowers have faded. *Echinacea purpurea* Moench has given rise to cultivars with rays varying from rich crimson-purple to light mauve and white. Extracts have been found to stimulate the production of white blood cells and show antiviral effects.

Echinacea purpurea
'Abendsonne'
section of flowerhead
and florets, life size
August 23rd

Echinacea purpurea
'Alba', ²⁄₃ life size
August 23rd

Echinacea purpurea
'Abendsonne', ²⁄₃ life size
August 23rd

Echinacea purpurea
¹⁄₃ life size, August 20th

355

Lindheimera

Lindheimera A. Gray & Engelm. (1847), in the family Compositae (sometimes called Asteraceae), contains 1 or 2 species in southern North America.

Description Annuals to 65cm. Lower leaves alternate, upper ones opposite, narrowly lance-shaped, untoothed. Flowerheads (see *Cichorium*, p.337) in corymbs. Ray florets 4 or 5, broad, yellow, female, surrounding a few yellow disc florets. Phyllaries green, in 2 rows. The fruit is a flattened, green achene with a pappus of 2 bristles.

Key Recognition Features Plants with 5-rayed, yellow flowers and bract-like leaves persisting below the flowers and seedheads.

Ecology and Geography In moist, sunny sites, often on limestone, in western Texas and Mexico.

Comment Although rather leafy, *L. texana* A. Gray is occasionally grown as a half-hardy annual, mainly for use as a cut flower. The genus is named after German botanist Ferdinand Jacob Lindheim (1801–79).

Helenium

Helenium L. (1753), the sneezeweed, in the family Compositae (sometimes called Asteraceae), contains about 40 species in the Americas.

Description Annuals, biennials, and perennials to 1.5m, with erect, sometimes winged stems. Leaves alternate, narrow, entire, toothed, or pinnately lobed, dotted with minute glands. Daisy-like flowerheads (see *Cichorium*, p.337) long-stalked, solitary or in loose clusters. Ray florets sometimes absent, yellow, red to brown near the base, female or sterile; disk florets yellow. Phyllaries narrow, in 2 rows, the outer longer and reflexed. The fruit is a hairy, top-shaped achene with a pappus of up to 10 membranous, often spine-tipped scales.

Key Recognition Features Large plants with yellow daisies tinged red at the base of the rays.

Ecology and Geography In wet meadows and swamps in North, Central, and South America.

Comment The easily grown sneezeweeds are an important element in the late summer border. Most plants in gardens are of hybrid origin, derived from North American species, with flowers ranging from light to deep yellow and mahogany red. The plants contain substances that are toxic to herbivores in their native habitat.

Helenium 'Butterpat'
½ life size, August 5th

Helenium 'Butterpat'
flowerheads and florets
just over life size
August 5th

Gaillardia

Gaillardia Foug. (1786), the blanket flower, in the family Compositae (sometimes called Asteraceae), contains about 28 species in North and temperate South America.

Description Annuals, biennials, and perennials to 1m. Leaves basal or alternate, usually toothed or pinnately lobed. Daisy-like flowerheads (see *Cichorium*, p.337) solitary. Ray florets yellow or red, tipped with red or yellow, sterile; disk florets purple. Phyllaries in 2 or 3 rows hairy, oval, becoming reflexed after flowering. The fruit is a top-shaped, hairy achene with a pappus of up to 12 spine-tipped scales.

Key Recognition Features Plants with large, bicoloured daisies and mostly basal leaves.

Ecology and Geography Dry woods and prairies in the central United States and Mexico, with 1 species in South America.

Comment Cultivated blanket flowers, *G.* × *grandiflora* Van Houtte, are derived from various North American species, and range from yellow to orange and deep red. The flowers last well when cut.

Lindheimera texana
½ life size
July 20th

Gaillardia 'Dazzler', flowerhead
section of flowerhead and florets
⅔ life size, July 22nd

Layia platyglossa
section of flowerhead
and florets
1¼ × life size
July 18th

Layia platyglossa
(left) ½ life size
July 18th

Layia

Layia Hook. & Arn. ex. DC (1838), tidytips, in the family Compositae (sometimes called Asteraceae), contains about 15 species in western North America.

Description Annuals to 40cm. Leaves narrow, alternate, toothed or pinnately lobed. Daisy-like flowerheads (see *Cichorium*, p.337) solitary. Ray florets broad, 3-toothed at the tips, white, yellow, or yellow tipped with white, female; disc florets interspersed with scales. Phyllaries narrow, green, in 1 row enfolding the achenes. The fruit is a flattened achene with a pappus of numerous bristles.

Key Recognition Features Plants with broad, lobed, usually bicoloured ray florets.

Ecology and Geography In dry, open places with sandy soils from British Columbia to California and New Mexico.

Comment The attractive white-edged yellow flowers of *L. platyglossa* (Fischer & C. Meyer) A. Gray, syn. *L. elegans* Hook. & Arn., are slightly fragrant, making it an attractive summer-flowering annual for a sunny, well-drained site. *Layia* is named after George Tradescant Lay (died *c*.1845), a naturalist on Captain Beechey's exploration of the Pacific in 1823–28.

Gaillardia
'Dazzler' (right)
⅓ life size
July 22nd

357

Bidens

Bidens L. (1753), in the family Compositae (sometimes called Asteraceae), contains about 240 species throughout the world, mostly in Central and South America.

Description Erect or spreading annuals, perennials, and shrubs to 1.5m. Leaves opposite, simple or pinnately divided. Flowerheads (see *Cichorium*, p.337) solitary or clustered. Ray florets sometimes absent, yellow, white, or purple, sterile, surrounding yellow florets. Phyllaries in 2 rows, the inner membranous, the outer green. The fruit is a slightly flattened achene with a pappus of usually 2 barbed teeth.

Key Recognition Features Plants with small, yellow flowers and hooked teeth on the fruits.

Ecology and Geography In wet places, even in streams, or in dry habitats throughout the world, but mainly in Central and South America; 3 species in Europe.

Comment Although many species are rather weedy, some of the tender ones such as *B. ferulifolia* (Jacq.) DC. and *B. aurea* (Ait.) Sherff have recently become very popular for summer bedding, producing bright yellow flowers over a long season. The name refers to the 2 awns or teeth of the pappus.

Dahlia

Dahlia Cav. (1791), in the family Compositae (sometimes called Asteraceae), contains about 28 species in Central America, mostly in Mexico.

Description Perennials, sometimes woody at the base, to 9m (garden types to 1.5m), with tuberous roots. Leaves opposite, toothed or pinnately lobed. Daisy-like flowerheads (see *Cichorium*, p.337). Ray florets showy, white, pink, purple, or orange, female or sterile; disc florets tubular. Phyllaries spreading or reflexed, in 2 rows, the inner membranous, the outer fleshy. The fruit is a slender achene with a pappus of 2 bristles.

Key Recognition Features Plants with divided, opposite leaves and large flowers.

Ecology and Geography In woodland and more open habitats from Mexico to Colombia.

Comment Dahlias have long been grown in Central America for the edible tubers. The thousands of cultivated hybrids, derived primarily from *D. coccinea* Cav. and *D. pinnata* Cav., are among the most popular garden flowers. Many are strikingly different from the wild species, all the florets being ray-like and showy.

Bidens humilis
1½ × life size, August 23rd

Bidens humilis
⅔ life size
August 23rd

Dahlia 'David Howard'
⅓ life size, September 9th

Dahlia 'Red Rigoletto'
²/₃ life size, August 9th

Dahlia 'Ella Britton'
florets, bud and sections of
flowerheads, just under life
size, September 10th

Dahlia 'Bishop of
Llandaff' (right)
²/₃ life size
September 18th

Dahlia 'Ella Britton'
(above left) ²/₃ life size
September 10th

Dahlia Cactus-flowered
variety, ½ life size
August 17th

Dahlia 'Bishop of Llandaff'
½ life size, September 18th

Arnica montana, flowerheads
1 ½ × life size, July 20th

Arnica

Arnica L. (1753), in the family Compositae (sometimes called Asteraceae), contains about 32 species in northern temperate areas and the Arctic.

Description Perennials to 1m, with shortly creeping rhizomes. Leaves opposite, sometimes clustered near the base, entire or toothed. Daisy-like flowerheads (see *Cichorium*, p.337) solitary or clustered in a cyme, yellow. Ray florets female. Phyllaries in 2 rows, overlapping. The fruit is a cylindrical achene with a pappus of roughened hairs.

Key Recognition Features Clump-forming plants with mostly basal leaves and erect stems with yellow daisies.

Ecology and Geography In meadows, moist woods, on mountain screes, sometimes at high elevations; 2 species in Europe, the others in North America, the Arctic, and Asia eastwards to Japan and Sakhalin Island.

Comment The roots of *A. montana* L. have long been used medicinally, and are still utilised in various healing ointments. It is also a popular ornamental species.

Helianthus

Helianthus L. (1753), the sunflower, in the family Compositae (sometimes called Asteraceae), contains about 50 species in North America.

Description Annuals and perennials to 5m, the perennials often with rhizomes or tuberous roots. Leaves simple, alternate, sometimes opposite towards the base, the main veins usually diverging from the base of the midrib. Daisy-like flowerheads (see *Cichorium*, p.337) large or very large. Ray florets yellow or red, sterile, surrounding a large disc of tubular, yellow or red florets interspersed with small scales. Phyllaries green, in several rows, overlapping. The fruit is a flattened achene with a pappus of 2 scales or bristles.

Key Recognition Features Large plants with yellow daisies.

Ecology and Geography In dry prairies, meadows, and dry or moist woodland from Nova Scotia and British Columbia to Florida and New Mexico.

Comment The annual sunflower, *H. annuus* L., is cultivated for sunflower oil and for the edible seeds, and also as a statuesque ornamental. The perennial species are smaller, with showy daisies in late summer and autumn, and grow well in most soils given full sun. *Helianthus tuberosus* L. is the Jerusalem artichoke, grown for its edible tubers.

Arnica montana
½ life size, July 20th

Arnica montana
seedhead, 1 ½ × life size
July 20th

Helianthus annus
seeds and phyllaries
just over life size
October 20th

Helianthus annus
'Velvet Queen'
⅓ life size, August 15th

Helianthus annus
seeds, 1⅓ × life size
October 20th

Helianthus annus 'Elite Sun'
⅓ life size, August 15th

Helianthus annus 'Elite Sun'
section of flowerhead and florets,
¾ life size, August 15th

Helianthus annus 'Elite Sun'
section of flowerhead
⅔ life size, August 15th

Helianthus tuberosus
tubers, ½ life size
October 15th

361

Coreopsis

Coreopsis L. (1753), the tickseed, in the family Compositae (sometimes called Asteraceae), contains about 50 species in the Americas.

Description Annuals and perennials to 1.5m. Leaves opposite, simple, ternate, or pinnate, margins entire or toothed. Daisy-like flowerheads (see *Cichorium*, p.337) solitary or in loose clusters. Ray florets yellow, red, or bicoloured, female or sterile; disc florets yellow or red-tipped, tubular. Phyllaries membranous or green, in 2 to 4 rows. The fruit is an oblong or circular, flattened achene, sometimes with 2 wings, and a pappus of 2 teeth.

Key Recognition Features Plants with opposite leaves and showy, yellow flowers.

Ecology and Geography In dry, sunny places and on moist riverbanks in Mexico and the southern United States, with some species in South America.

Comment *Coreopsis grandiflora* Nutt. and *C. verticillata* L. are reliable and popular hardy perennials; like other species, the flowers last well when cut. The name is derived from *koris*, the Greek for bug, referring to the shape of the achenes.

Coreopsis verticillata 'Moonbeam' flowerheads and florets 1¼ × life size July 14th

Coreopsis grandiflora ⅓ life size, July 2nd

Coreopsis verticillata 'Moonbeam' (right) ½ life size, July 14th

Coreopsis grandiflora, flowerheads front and back, ⅔ life size, July 2nd

362

Cosmos

Cosmos Cav. (1791), in the family Compositae (sometimes called Asteraceae), contains about 26 species in tropical and warm parts of the Americas, mostly in Mexico.

Description Annuals and perennials to 2m or more. Leaves opposite, simple or pinnately divided. Daisy-like flowerheads (see *Cichorium*, p.337) solitary or several in a loose panicle, long-stalked. Ray florets showy, white, orange, pink, or red, sterile. Disk florets tubular. Phyllaries in 2 rows, broad, membranous, sometimes reflexed. The fruit is a spindle-shaped achene narrowed into a slender 'beak', with a pappus of up to 8 bristles or teeth.

Key Recognition Features Plants with finely dissected, opposite leaves and showy flowers.

Ecology and Geography In open habitats or woodland and by roadsides in Central and northern South America, especially in Mexico.

Comment The tender *C. atrosanguineus* (Hook.) Stapf has beautiful deep maroon flowers scented of rich chocolate; *C. bipinnatus* Cav. is a very popular annual with long-stalked flowers in shades of red, pink, and white, excellent for cutting.

Cosmos bipinnatus
flowerheads, ⅔ life size
August 5th

Cosmos atrosanguineus
section of flowerhead
and outer florets (right)
just under life size
September 16th

Cosmos atrosanguineus
½ life size
September 16th

Cosmos bipinnatus
½ life size, August 5th

COMPOSITAE

Zinnia

Zinnia L. (1759), in the family Compositae (sometimes called Asteraceae), contains about 11 species in North and South America.

Description Annuals, perennials, and shrubs to 1m, but usually less. Leaves opposite, entire, the bases joined across the stem. Daisy-like flowerheads (see *Cichorium*, p.337). Ray-florets broad, often lobed at the tip, white, yellow, orange, red, or purple, female. Disc florets yellow, interspersed with scales. Phyllaries in several rows, overlapping. The fruit is a flattened achene with a pappus of bristles or teeth, sometimes absent.

Key Recognition Features Plants with showy daisies in a wide range of colours.

Ecology and Geography In dry, open habitats from the southern central United States and Mexico southwards to Argentina.

Comment These showy and popular annuals are available in a wide range of colours and also in double and bicoloured forms. The name commemorates Johann Gottfried Zinn (1727–59), professor of medicine at Göttingen.

Zinnia elegans, flowerheads and
section of flowerhead
just over life size, August 1st

Zinnia elegans
½ life size, August 1st

Zinnia haageana
'Persian Carpet'
life size, August 1st

Madia elegans, flowerheads and section of
flowerhead, just over life size, August 15th

364

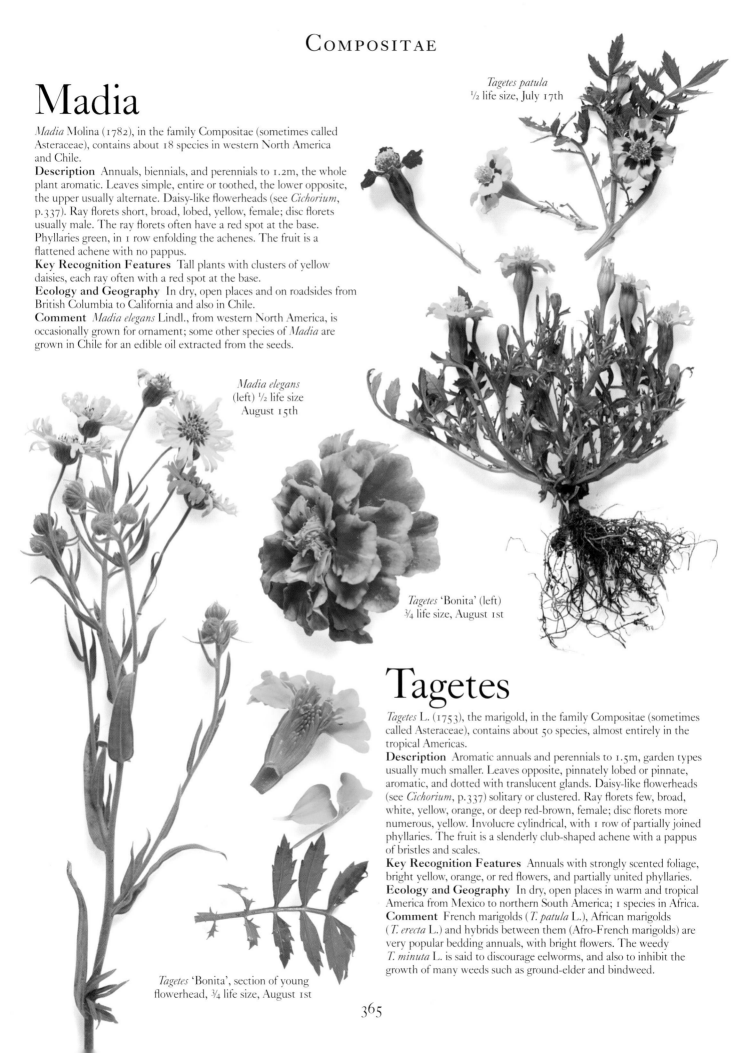

Madia

Madia Molina (1782), in the family Compositae (sometimes called Asteraceae), contains about 18 species in western North America and Chile.

Description Annuals, biennials, and perennials to 1.2m, the whole plant aromatic. Leaves simple, entire or toothed, the lower opposite, the upper usually alternate. Daisy-like flowerheads (see *Cichorium*, p.337). Ray florets short, broad, lobed, yellow, female; disc florets usually male. The ray florets often have a red spot at the base. Phyllaries green, in 1 row enfolding the achenes. The fruit is a flattened achene with no pappus.

Key Recognition Features Tall plants with clusters of yellow daisies, each ray often with a red spot at the base.

Ecology and Geography In dry, open places and on roadsides from British Columbia to California and also in Chile.

Comment *Madia elegans* Lindl., from western North America, is occasionally grown for ornament; some other species of *Madia* are grown in Chile for an edible oil extracted from the seeds.

Tagetes patula
½ life size, July 17th

Madia elegans
(left) ½ life size
August 15th

Tagetes 'Bonita' (left)
¾ life size, August 1st

Tagetes

Tagetes L. (1753), the marigold, in the family Compositae (sometimes called Asteraceae), contains about 50 species, almost entirely in the tropical Americas.

Description Aromatic annuals and perennials to 1.5m, garden types usually much smaller. Leaves opposite, pinnately lobed or pinnate, aromatic, and dotted with translucent glands. Daisy-like flowerheads (see *Cichorium*, p.337) solitary or clustered. Ray florets few, broad, white, yellow, orange, or deep red-brown, female; disc florets more numerous, yellow. Involucre cylindrical, with 1 row of partially joined phyllaries. The fruit is a slenderly club-shaped achene with a pappus of bristles and scales.

Key Recognition Features Annuals with strongly scented foliage, bright yellow, orange, or red flowers, and partially united phyllaries.

Ecology and Geography In dry, open places in warm and tropical America from Mexico to northern South America; 1 species in Africa.

Comment French marigolds (*T. patula* L.), African marigolds (*T. erecta* L.) and hybrids between them (Afro-French marigolds) are very popular bedding annuals, with bright flowers. The weedy *T. minuta* L. is said to discourage eelworms, and also to inhibit the growth of many weeds such as ground-elder and bindweed.

Tagetes 'Bonita', section of young
flowerhead, ¾ life size, August 1st

Anaphalis

Anaphalis DC (1837), in the family Compositae (sometimes called Asteraceae), contains about 100 species, mostly in the temperate northern hemisphere.

Description Perennials to 1m, with white, felt-like hairs on the stems. Leaves narrow, alternate, entire, often white-hairy. Flowerheads (see *Cichorium*, p.337) small, in corymbs; male and female flowerheads usually on separate plants. Ray florets absent; disc florets predominantly male or female. Phyllaries papery white, in several rows, overlapping. The fruit is a small achene with a pappus of soft bristles.

Key Recognition Features Plants with flattish clusters of small, white "everlasting" flowers.

Ecology and Geography On streambanks, by roadsides and other open places, in Asia, North America, a few in the mountains of the tropics, and 1 species naturalised in Europe.

Comment *Anaphalis margaritacea* (L.) Benth. & Hook., the pearly everlasting, a very variable species with a wide distribution, is popular in gardens, but the flowers are unsatisfactory as everlastings, tending to go to seed rapidly.

Helichrysum

Helichrysum Mill. (1754), in the family Compositae (sometimes called Asteraceae), contains about 500 species in warm parts of the Europe, Africa, Asia, and Australia.

Description Annuals, biennials, perennials, subshrubs, and shrubs to 2m. Leaves alternate, opposite, or all basal, entire, often covered with grey or white woolly hairs. Daisy-like flowerheads (see *Cichorium*, p.337) solitary or clustered. Outer florets may be tubular or ray florets, female. Phyllaries in several rows overlapping, membranous, papery white or coloured, sometimes large and showy. The fruit is a small achene with a pappus of fine, often feathery hairs that soon drop.

Key Recognition Features Plants often with grey, woolly foliage and papery, frequently brightly coloured phyllaries.

Ecology and Geography Dry, sunny places and mountains; around 15 species in Europe, others mostly in southern Africa and Australia.

Comment The annual *H. bracteatum* (Vent.) Andrews, from Australia, often separated as *Bracteantha bracteata* (Vent.) Anderberg & Haegi, on the basis of differently shaped achenes, is much grown for drying for winter decoration; 'Schwefellicht' is a perennial hybrid with grey leaves and sulphur-yellow flowerheads. Other perennials, such as *H. sibthorpii* Rouy and the curry plant *H. italicum* (Roth) G. Don, are grown mainly for their silvery or grey foliage.

Helichrysum bracteatum
²/₃ life size, August 27th

Helichrysum bracteatum
¹/₃ life size, August 30th

Anaphalis triplinervis
'Sommerschnee'
flowerheads, just over life size
August 13th

Anaphalis triplinervis
'Sommerschnee'
¹/₃ life size
August 13th

Inula orientalis
sections of flowerhead
life size, June 14th

Inula

Inula L. (1753), in the family Compositae (sometimes called Asteraceae), contains about 90 species in temperate and warmer areas of Europe, North Africa, and Asia.

Description Erect annuals, biennials, and perennials to 2m. Leaves alternate, simple and entire or toothed, the base sometimes clasping the stem. Daisy-like flowerheads (see *Cichorium*, p.337) solitary or in panicles. Ray florets usually present, slender, yellow, female; disc florets yellow. Phyllaries green or membranous, in several rows, overlapping. The fruit is a ribbed, cylindrical achene with a pappus of roughened hairs.

Key Recognition Features Erect plants with very narrow, yellow ray-florets.

Ecology and Geography In woodland, by streams, and in dry, open places, with 18 species in Europe, the others in North Africa and in Asia from the Caucasus to China and Japan.

Comment *Inula orientalis* Lam. and several other species are popular and reliable border perennials. Some, like *I. magnifica* Lipsky, are very large; others, such as *I. ensifolia* L., small and suitable for rock gardens.

Buphthalmum salicifolium
flower and bud
1¼ × life size
June 22nd

Buphthalmum

Buphthalmum L. (1753), in the family Compositae (sometimes called Asteraceae), contains 2 or 3 species in Europe and western Asia.

Description Erect perennials to 1.5m, with vigorous rhizomes. Leaves alternate, entire or toothed, the lower stalked, the upper stalkless. Daisy-like flowerheads (see *Cichorium*, p.337) solitary, long-stalked. Ray florets many, slender, strong yellow, female; disc florets dull yellow. Phyllaries in several overlapping rows. The fruit is a flattened achene with a pappus of papery scales or teeth.

Key Recognition Features Tall plants with numerous very narrow ray florets.

Ecology and Geography In open woodland and stony places, often on limestone, in central Europe and western Asia.

Comment *Buphthalmum salicifolium* L. is sometimes grown. The rampant *B. speciosum* L. is sometimes listed as *Telekia speciosa* (Schreber) Baumg..

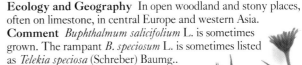

Buphthalmum salicifolium
½ life size, June 22nd

Inula orientalis
½ life size, June 14th

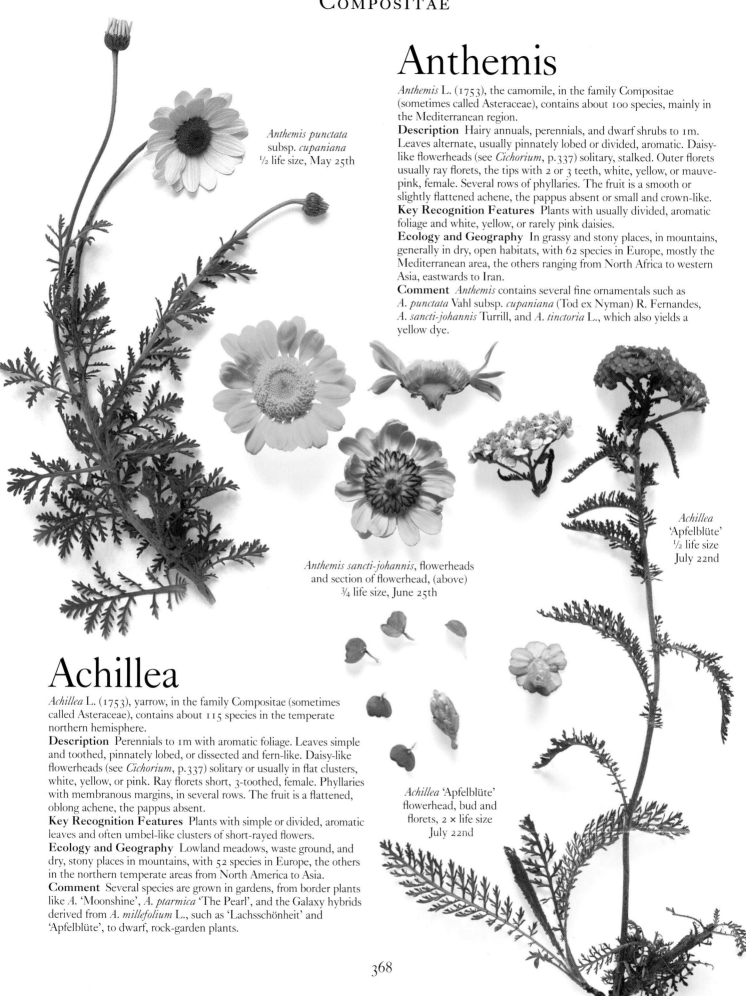

Anthemis

Anthemis L. (1753), the camomile, in the family Compositae (sometimes called Asteraceae), contains about 100 species, mainly in the Mediterranean region.

Description Hairy annuals, perennials, and dwarf shrubs to 1m. Leaves alternate, usually pinnately lobed or divided, aromatic. Daisy-like flowerheads (see *Cichorium*, p.337) solitary, stalked. Outer florets usually ray florets, the tips with 2 or 3 teeth, white, yellow, or mauve-pink, female. Several rows of phyllaries. The fruit is a smooth or slightly flattened achene, the pappus absent or small and crown-like.

Key Recognition Features Plants with usually divided, aromatic foliage and white, yellow, or rarely pink daisies.

Ecology and Geography In grassy and stony places, in mountains, generally in dry, open habitats, with 62 species in Europe, mostly the Mediterranean area, the others ranging from North Africa to western Asia, eastwards to Iran.

Comment *Anthemis* contains several fine ornamentals such as *A. punctata* Vahl subsp. *cupaniana* (Tod ex Nyman) R. Fernandes, *A. sancti-johannis* Turrill, and *A. tinctoria* L., which also yields a yellow dye.

Anthemis punctata subsp. *cupaniana* ½ life size, May 25th

Anthemis sancti-johannis, flowerheads and section of flowerhead, (above) ¾ life size, June 25th

Achillea 'Apfelblüte' ½ life size July 22nd

Achillea 'Apfelblüte' flowerhead, bud and florets, 2 × life size July 22nd

Achillea

Achillea L. (1753), yarrow, in the family Compositae (sometimes called Asteraceae), contains about 115 species in the temperate northern hemisphere.

Description Perennials to 1m with aromatic foliage. Leaves simple and toothed, pinnately lobed, or dissected and fern-like. Daisy-like flowerheads (see *Cichorium*, p.337) solitary or usually in flat clusters, white, yellow, or pink. Ray florets short, 3-toothed, female. Phyllaries with membranous margins, in several rows. The fruit is a flattened, oblong achene, the pappus absent.

Key Recognition Features Plants with simple or divided, aromatic leaves and often umbel-like clusters of short-rayed flowers.

Ecology and Geography Lowland meadows, waste ground, and dry, stony places in mountains, with 52 species in Europe, the others in the northern temperate areas from North America to Asia.

Comment Several species are grown in gardens, from border plants like *A.* 'Moonshine', *A. ptarmica* 'The Pearl', and the Galaxy hybrids derived from *A. millefolium* L., such as 'Lachsschönheit' and 'Apfelblüte', to dwarf, rock-garden plants.

Matricaria

Matricaria L. (1753), in the family Compositae (sometimes called Asteraceae), contains about 30 species in the temperate northern hemisphere.

Description Annuals and perennials to 1.5m, often with aromatic foliage. Leaves alternate, 2- or 3-pinnatisect, with linear segments. Daisy-like flowerheads (see *Cichorium*, p.337). Ray florets usually white or pink, female; disc florets yellow. Phyllaries with membranous margins, in several rows, overlapping. Fruit a slightly flattened, ribbed, obovoid achene with the pappus reduced to a small crown or absent.

Key Recognition Features Plants with finely-dissected leaves and white, rarely pink, daisies.

Ecology and Geography Fields and waste places, alpine meadows, and stony mountain slopes, with 8 species in Europe, the others in Asia and western North America.

Comment Most of the perennial species are sometimes placed in the genus *Tripleurospermum* Schultz-Bip on the basis of minute details of the fruit and other technicalities. Most species of *Matricaria* are arable weeds, but a few, such as *M. perforata* Merat. syn. *Tripleurospermum inodorum* (L.) Schultz-Bip., are suitable for cottage or meadow gardens.

Achillea 'Moonshine'
½ life size
September 10th

Achillea millefolium
flowerheads (above)
1½ × life size
December 1st

Achillea ptarmica
'The Pearl'
flowerheads and
florets (above)
life size, July 22nd

Matricaria perforata
½ life size, August 2nd

Achillea ptarmica
'The Pearl'
(left) ½ life size
July 22nd

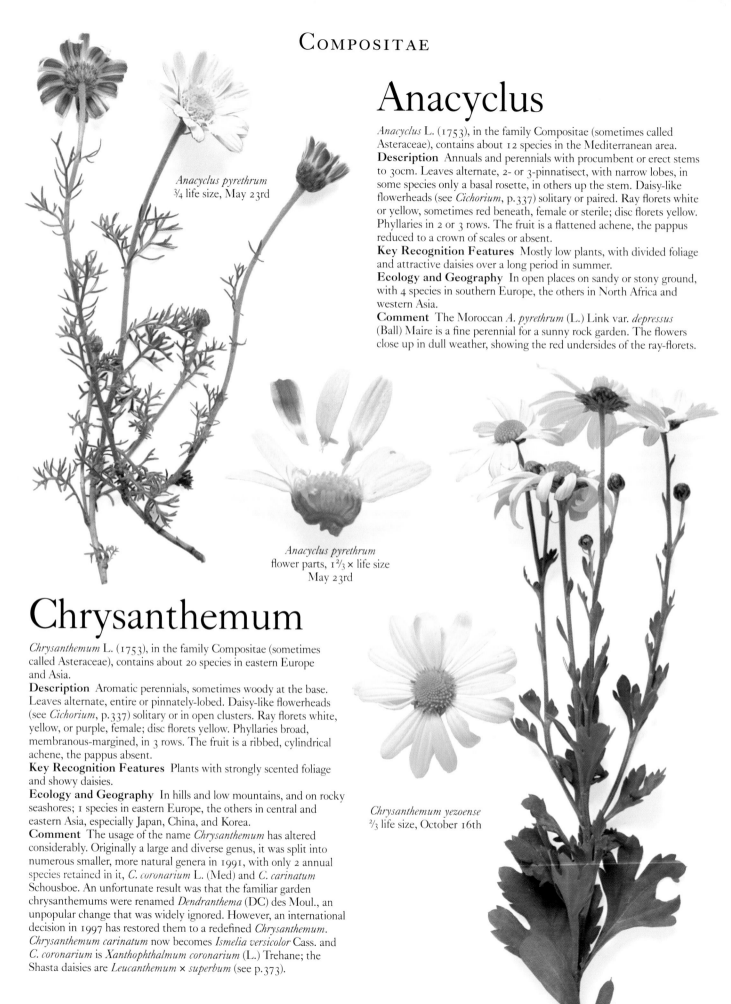

Anacyclus

Anacyclus L. (1753), in the family Compositae (sometimes called Asteraceae), contains about 12 species in the Mediterranean area.

Description Annuals and perennials with procumbent or erect stems to 30cm. Leaves alternate, 2- or 3-pinnatisect, with narrow lobes, in some species only a basal rosette, in others up the stem. Daisy-like flowerheads (see *Cichorium*, p.337) solitary or paired. Ray florets white or yellow, sometimes red beneath, female or sterile; disc florets yellow. Phyllaries in 2 or 3 rows. The fruit is a flattened achene, the pappus reduced to a crown of scales or absent.

Key Recognition Features Mostly low plants, with divided foliage and attractive daisies over a long period in summer.

Ecology and Geography In open places on sandy or stony ground, with 4 species in southern Europe, the others in North Africa and western Asia.

Comment The Moroccan *A. pyrethrum* (L.) Link var. *depressus* (Ball) Maire is a fine perennial for a sunny rock garden. The flowers close up in dull weather, showing the red undersides of the ray-florets.

Anacyclus pyrethrum
¾ life size, May 23rd

Anacyclus pyrethrum
flower parts, 1²⁄₃ × life size
May 23rd

Chrysanthemum

Chrysanthemum L. (1753), in the family Compositae (sometimes called Asteraceae), contains about 20 species in eastern Europe and Asia.

Description Aromatic perennials, sometimes woody at the base. Leaves alternate, entire or pinnately-lobed. Daisy-like flowerheads (see *Cichorium*, p.337) solitary or in open clusters. Ray florets white, yellow, or purple, female; disc florets yellow. Phyllaries broad, membranous-margined, in 3 rows. The fruit is a ribbed, cylindrical achene, the pappus absent.

Key Recognition Features Plants with strongly scented foliage and showy daisies.

Ecology and Geography In hills and low mountains, and on rocky seashores; 1 species in eastern Europe, the others in central and eastern Asia, especially Japan, China, and Korea.

Comment The usage of the name *Chrysanthemum* has altered considerably. Originally a large and diverse genus, it was split into numerous smaller, more natural genera in 1991, with only 2 annual species retained in it, *C. coronarium* L. (Med) and *C. carinatum* Schousboe. An unfortunate result was that the familiar garden chrysanthemums were renamed *Dendranthema* (DC) des Moul., an unpopular change that was widely ignored. However, an international decision in 1997 has restored them to a redefined *Chrysanthemum*. *Chrysanthemum carinatum* now becomes *Ismelia versicolor* Cass. and *C. coronarium* is *Xanthophthalmum coronarium* (L.) Trehane; the Shasta daisies are *Leucanthemum × superbum* (see p.373).

Chrysanthemum yezoense
²⁄₃ life size, October 16th

370

Ismelia

Ismelia Cass. (1826), in the family Compositae (sometimes called Asteraceae), contains 1 species (sometimes split) in Morocco. *Ismelia* is the name now used for *Chrysanthemum carinatum* Schousboe.
Description Erect annual to 1m, often little-branched. Leaves alternate, pinnately dissected, slightly fleshy. Daisy-like flowerheads (see *Cichorium*, p.337) solitary or in a loose corymb. Ray florets yellow, red, or white in the lower part, female; disc florets purplish or red. Phyllaries broad, keeled on the back, in several rows. The fruit is an achene, those of the ray florets triangular in section and winged on each angle, the others flattened; pappus absent.
Key Recognition Features Showy annuals with large flowerheads, the rays often bicoloured.
Ecology and Geography Sunny places on stony ground in Morocco.
Comment There are many cultivars of the colourful *Ismelia versicolor* Cass., notably 'Court Jesters' with flowers in white, yellow, orange, pink, and red shades, some with a contrasting zone at the base of the rays.

Xanthophthalmum

Xanthophthalmum Schultz-Bip. (1844), in the family Compositae (sometimes called Asteraceae), contains 2 species in Europe and the Mediterranean area. *Xanthophthalmum* is the name now used for *Chrysanthemum coronarium* L. and *C. segetum* L.
Description Annuals to 70cm. Leaves alternate, pinnately divided, or the upper simple. Daisy-like flowerheads (see *Cichorium*, p.337) usually solitary at the ends of branches. Ray florets white or yellow, female or sterile; disc florets yellow. Phyllaries in several rows, with broad, membranous margins. The fruit is an achene, those of the ray florets triangular in section, the others cylindrical; pappus absent.
Key Recognition Features Bushy annuals with showy yellow and white flowerheads, the rays sometimes bicoloured.
Ecology and Geography Fields and waste places in southern Europe, North Africa, and southwestern Asia: sometimes naturalised elsewhere in Europe.
Comment The leaves of corn marigold, *X. segetum* (L.) Schultz-Bip., are cultivated and eaten as *shinguku* in Japan. Several cultivars of *X. coronarium* (L.) Trehane are available, often having flowers in white and yellow or 2 shades of yellow.

Ismelia versicolor 'German Flag'
1⅓ × life size, August 15th

Ismelia versicolor
'German Flag' (right)
½ life size, August 15th

Xanthophthalmum coronarium (right)
¾ life size, May 29th

Ismelia versicolor 'German Flag'
section of flowerhead and florets
1⅓ × life size, August 15th

Tanacetum

Tanacetum L. (1753), in the family Compositae (sometimes called Asteraceae), contains about 150 species in the northern temperate regions, mostly in Europe, Asia, and Africa.

Description Annuals and perennials to 1m, usually strongly aromatic. Leaves alternate, simple or pinnately dissected. Flowerheads (see *Cichorium*, p.337) in corymbs, rarely solitary. Ray florets absent in most species; when present, small, white or yellow, female. Disc florets yellow. Phyllaries often with membranous margins, in 3 rows. The fruit is a ribbed achene with the pappus reduced to a small crown.

Key Recognition Features Strongly aromatic plants, mostly with pinnately divided leaves and often ray-less flowers.

Ecology and Geography Waste places, river gravels, open woodland, and meadows; 14 species in Europe, the others in northern temperate regions from North America to eastern Asia.

Comment Several species of tansy are cultivated. *Tanacetum densum* subsp. *amani* is an excellent rock-garden perennial. Feverfew, *T. parthenium* L., is grown as a bedding plant, especially in forms with double flowerheads or yellow leaves; it has also been shown to be effective in preventing migraines. Some species, especially *T. cinerariifolium* (Trev.) Schultz-Bip. were the original source of pyrethrum insecticide, now synthesised.

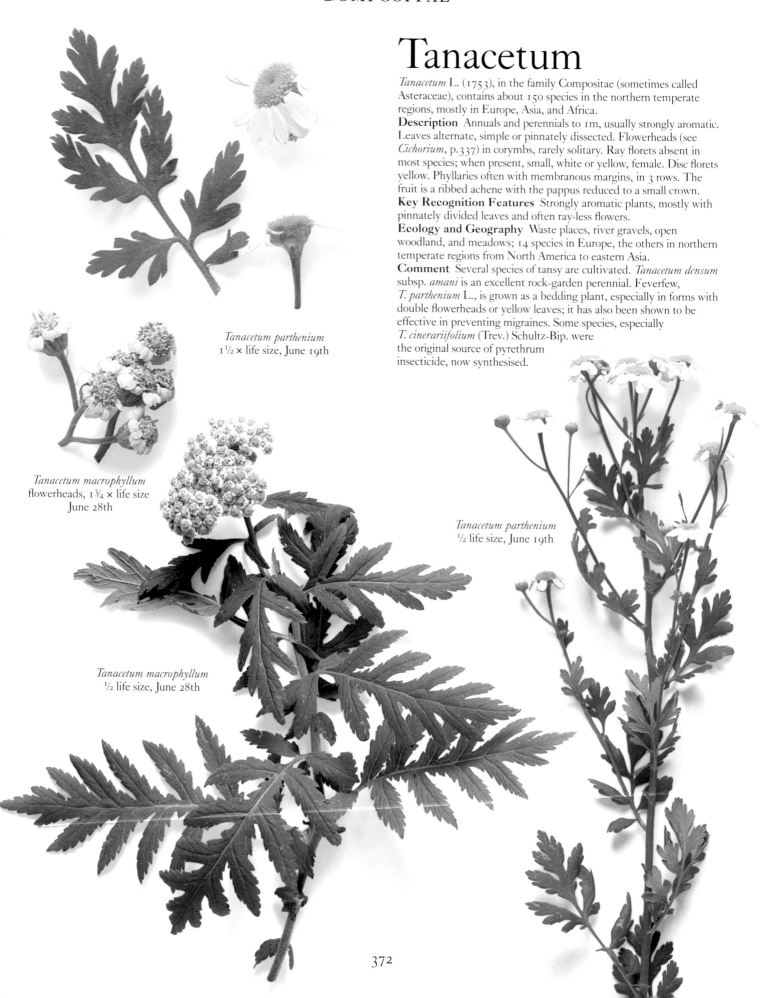

Tanacetum parthenium
1½ × life size, June 19th

Tanacetum macrophyllum
flowerheads, 1¾ × life size
June 28th

Tanacetum macrophyllum
½ life size, June 28th

Tanacetum parthenium
½ life size, June 19th

COMPOSITAE

Leucanthemum

Leucanthemum Mill. (1754), in the family Compositae (sometimes called Asteraceae), contains about 25 species in Europe and northern Asia.

Description Annuals and perennials to 1m. Leaves alternate, simple, lobed or pinnately divided. Daisy-like flowerheads (see *Cichorium*, p.337) usually solitary, long-stalked. Ray florets white, female; disc florets tubular, yellow. Phyllaries in 2 or 3 rows. The fruit is a ribbed, oblong achene with a small, crown-like pappus.

Key Recognition Features Plants with dark foliage and showy, white daisies.

Ecology and Geography Meadows, mountain pastures, stony slopes, and roadsides; 12 species in Europe, others in northern Asia.

Comment The moon daisy or oxeye daisy, *L. vulgare* Lam., and Shasta daisy, *L. × superbum* (J. Ingram) Bergmans ex Kent, are both popular garden plants, the latter having given rise to several cultivars with double flowerheads.

Tanacetum densum
subsp. *amani*
flowerheads (above)
1 ¹/₂ × life size, July 4th

Tanacetum densum
subsp. *amani* (above)
¹/₂ life size, July 4th

Leucanthemum vulgare
²/₃ life size, June 25th

Leucanthemum × superbum
(left) ²/₃ life size, July 23rd

373

Calendula

Calendula L. (1753), the marigold, in the family Compositae (sometimes called Asteraceae), contains about 20 species in the Mediterranean area and Azores.

Description Annuals and perennials to 50cm, sometimes woody at the base. Leaves alternate, simple, entire or toothed, usually aromatic. Daisy-like flowerheads (see *Cichorium*, p.337) solitary. Ray florets yellow or orange, female; disc florets yellow, orange, brown, or purple. Phyllaries in 1 or 2 rows, uniformly sized, linear. The fruit is an achene: those from the outer florets sometimes 3-winged, the inner achenes smaller, strongly curved and roughened on the back; pappus absent.

Key Recognition Features Aromatic plants with showy orange, yellow, or reddish flowers.

Ecology and Geography In rocky places, often by the sea, and in cultivated ground; 4 species in Europe, others in the Mediterranean area and the Azores.

Comment The common marigold, *C. officinalis* L., is a popular and showy annual with many selections, varying from yellow to reddish-orange. The ray florets can be used for food colouring, and some species have been used medicinally to treat chilblains.

Arctotis

Arctotis L. (1753), in the family Compositae (sometimes called Asteraceae), contains 50 species in southern Africa.

Description Annuals, perennials, and shrubs to 1m, but mostly smaller. Leaves often evergreen, entire or pinnately lobed, usually in a basal rosette, often white-felted beneath. Daisy-like flowerheads (see *Cichorium*, p.337). Ray florets yellow, orange, red, or purplish, often with with a dark marking at the base, female; disc florets often a contrasting colour. Phyllaries in several overlapping rows, the inner membranous, the outer sometimes leaf-like. The fruit is a ridged or winged achene, the pappus formed of 2 rows of scales.

Key Recognition Features The showy flowers with several rows of phyllaries, and the distinctive, membranous pappus scales.

Ecology and Geography In open, sunny places and sandy coastal areas from South Africa northwards to Angola.

Comment The name *Arctotis* comes from the Greek *arktos* and *ous*, bear and ear, alluding to the scales of the pappus. Several species, and especially hybrids derived from them, are popular summer bedding plants, available in a wide range of brilliant colours. Current opinion includes the species previously placed in *Venidium* Less. in *Arctotis*.

Arctotis × hybrida
just over life size
September 11th

Calendula vulgaris
⅔ life size, July 18th

Calendula vulgaris, section of flowerhead
and florets, 2 × life size, July 18th

Osteospermum jucundum
section of flowerhead and florets
1 ¾ × life size, December 1st

Arctotis × *hybrida*
¹/₃ life size
September 11th

Osteospermum

Osteospermum L. (1753), in the family Compositae (sometimes called Asteraceae), contains about 70 species, mostly in southern Africa.

Description Annuals, perennials, and shrubs to 1m, somewhat aromatic. Leaves alternate, entire, coarsely toothed, or pinnately cut. Daisy-like flowerheads (see *Cichorium*, p.337) solitary or loosely clustered. Ray florets white, yellow, orange, pink, or purple, sometimes grey or purple on the reverse, sometimes curiously crimped, female; disc florets yellow, violet, or white, male. Phyllaries in up to 5 rows, the outer shortest, with membranous margins. The fruit is a cylindrical, winged achene, the pappus absent.

Key Recognition Features Plants with large daisies, often with contrasting backs to the rays.

Ecology and Geography In grassland and open woodland, mostly in southern Africa, with some in tropical Africa and the Arabian peninsula, and 1 species on St Helena.

Comment The many hybrid cultivars of *Osteospermum* have become very popular, in spite of their tendency to close in cloudy weather. They range from bushy to prostrate or sprawling, with flowers from white to deep purple, usually with a contrasting colour on the reverse. The name, from the Greek for bone and Latin for seed, refers to the hard achenes.

Osteospermum jucundum
¹/₂ life size
December 1st

375

Bellis

Bellis L. (1753), the daisy, in the family Compositae (sometimes called Asteraceae), contains about 7 species in Europe and the Mediterranean area.

Description Annuals and perennials to 45cm, most species much smaller. Leaves mostly or all basal, in a rosette, entire or slightly toothed. Typical daisy flowerheads (see *Cichorium*, p.337) solitary, long-stalked. Ray florets white or pale blue, often reddish beneath, female; disc florets yellow. Phyllaries green, in 2 rows. The fruit is a flattened achene, the pappus absent or of short bristles.

Key Recognition Features Mostly small plants with basal rosettes of leaves and small, pink-tinged or white daisies.

Ecology and Geography In pastures and other grassy places, rocky mountain areas, and damp woodlands in Europe and North Africa.

Comment *Bellis perennis* L., a very common lawn weed in northern Europe, has given rise to numerous selections with much larger flowers in various shades of red, white, and pink; in the "double" forms the florets are all strap-shaped or all tubular.

Bellis perennis cultivated form
²⁄₃ life size, February 25th

Bellis perennis
cultivated form
section of flowerhead
and florets, 1¾ × life size
February 25th

Bellis perennis
'Rusher White'
²⁄₃ life size
March 19th

Solidago

Solidago L. (1753), golden rod, in the family Compositae (sometimes called Asteraceae), contains about 80 species, mostly in North America, with a few in South America, the Atlantic islands, Europe, and Asia.

Description Perennials to 2m, with short rhizomes and the upper stems branched. Leaves alternate, sometimes in basal rosettes, usually toothed. Flowerheads (see *Cichorium*, p.337) numerous, in narrow or broad panicles, small, yellow. Ray florets female. Phyllaries in several overlapping rows. The fruit is a small, angled achene with 1 or 2 rows of ciliate pappus hairs.

Key Recognition Features Sprays of small, yellow flowerheads.

Ecology and Geography Rocky woods, dry or moist soils, riverbanks, and mountains; 1 species in Europe, most others in North America, and a few in South America, the Azores, and Asia.

Comment Several species and hybrids are popular in gardens, the latter mostly derived from the European *S. virgaurea* L., formerly used as a diuretic, and the North American *S. canadensis* L.. A good yellow dye is obtained from the flowerheads of some species.

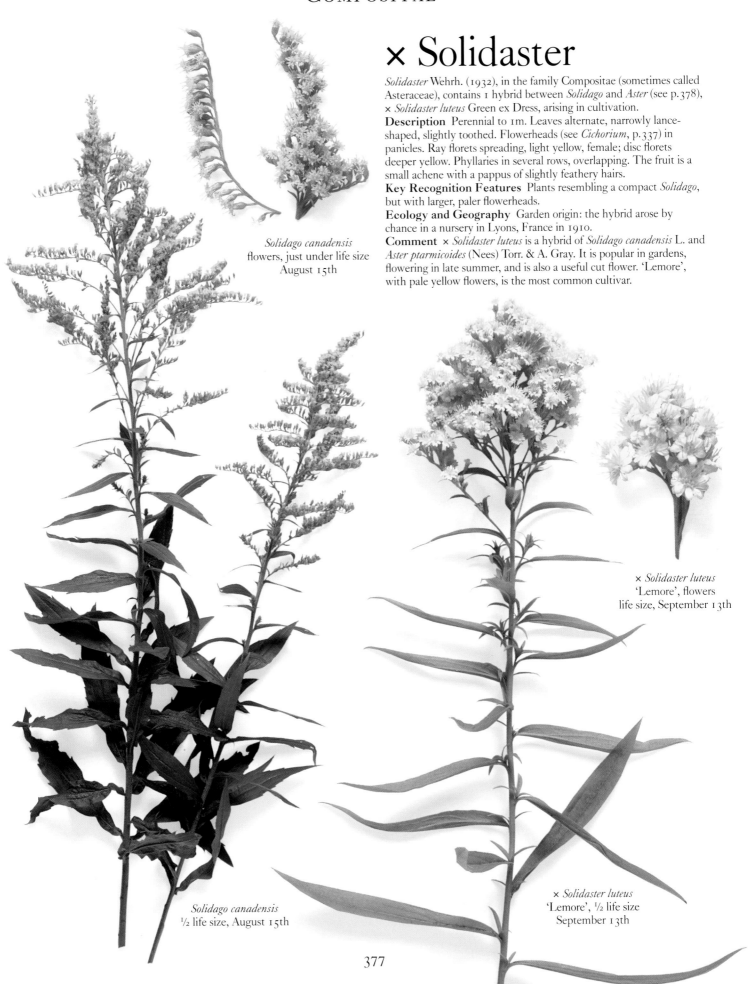

× Solidaster

Solidaster Wehrh. (1932), in the family Compositae (sometimes called Asteraceae), contains 1 hybrid between *Solidago* and *Aster* (see p.378), × *Solidaster luteus* Green ex Dress, arising in cultivation.

Description Perennial to 1m. Leaves alternate, narrowly lance-shaped, slightly toothed. Flowerheads (see *Cichorium*, p.337) in panicles. Ray florets spreading, light yellow, female; disc florets deeper yellow. Phyllaries in several rows, overlapping. The fruit is a small achene with a pappus of slightly feathery hairs.

Key Recognition Features Plants resembling a compact *Solidago*, but with larger, paler flowerheads.

Ecology and Geography Garden origin: the hybrid arose by chance in a nursery in Lyons, France in 1910.

Comment × *Solidaster luteus* is a hybrid of *Solidago canadensis* L. and *Aster ptarmicoides* (Nees) Torr. & A. Gray. It is popular in gardens, flowering in late summer, and is also a useful cut flower. 'Lemore', with pale yellow flowers, is the most common cultivar.

Solidago canadensis
flowers, just under life size
August 15th

× *Solidaster luteus*
'Lemore', flowers
life size, September 13th

Solidago canadensis
½ life size, August 15th

× *Solidaster luteus*
'Lemore', ½ life size
September 13th

Aster

Aster L. (1753), in the family Compositae (sometimes called Asteraceae), contains about 250 species in North America, Europe, Asia, and Africa.

Description Annuals, biennials, and perennials to 2m, sometimes woody at the base, with rhizomes or fibrous roots. Leaves usually alternate, simple, entire or toothed. Daisy-like flowerheads (see *Cichorium*, p.337) solitary or clustered. Ray florets sometimes absent; where present, white, pink, or pale or deep violet-blue, female or sterile; disc florets yellow or purple. Phyllaries in several rows, similar-sized, narrow, green. The fruit is a flattened, oblong achene, with a persistent pappus of roughened hairs.

Key Recognition Features Plants often with narrow leaves and white or mauve daisies in summer or autumn.

Ecology and Geography On riverbanks, railway embankments, and waste ground, in damp woods and grassland, in urban areas, by the sea, and in the mountains, with most species in North America, 15 in Europe, and others in Asia and Africa.

Comment The asters include the familiar, large Michaelmas daisies (so-called for their autumn flowering), a name used for *A. novi-belgii* L. alone or also to include *A. novae-angliae* L., *A.* × *frikartii* hort., and the European *A. amellus* L., all in a wide range of colours. *Aster thomsonii* C.B. Clarke 'Nanus' is an excellent dwarf plant, and cultivars of the tiny-flowered *A. ericoides* L. are also popular. Some Asian species are sometimes placed in *Boltonia*.

Aster novi-belgii
just over life size
October 17th

Aster novi-belgii
seedheads
just over life size
November 24th

Aster novi-belgii
½ life size, October 17th

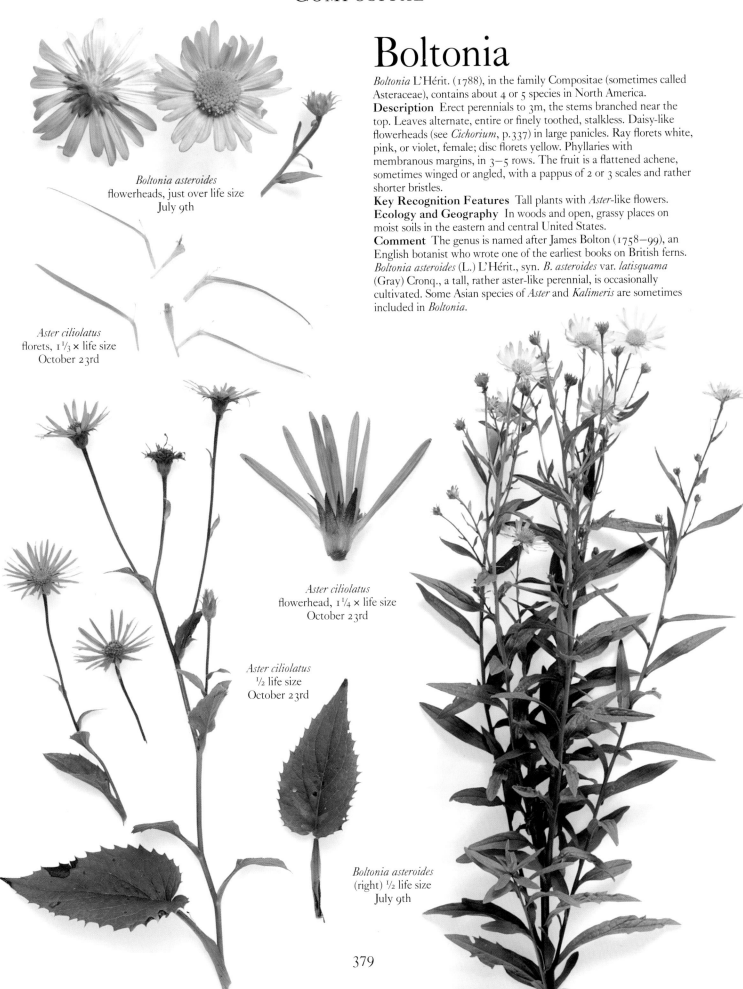

Boltonia

Boltonia L'Hérit. (1788), in the family Compositae (sometimes called Asteraceae), contains about 4 or 5 species in North America.

Description Erect perennials to 3m, the stems branched near the top. Leaves alternate, entire or finely toothed, stalkless. Daisy-like flowerheads (see *Cichorium*, p.337) in large panicles. Ray florets white, pink, or violet, female; disc florets yellow. Phyllaries with membranous margins, in 3–5 rows. The fruit is a flattened achene, sometimes winged or angled, with a pappus of 2 or 3 scales and rather shorter bristles.

Key Recognition Features Tall plants with *Aster*-like flowers.

Ecology and Geography In woods and open, grassy places on moist soils in the eastern and central United States.

Comment The genus is named after James Bolton (1758–99), an English botanist who wrote one of the earliest books on British ferns. *Boltonia asteroides* (L.) L'Hérit., syn. *B. asteroides* var. *latisquama* (Gray) Cronq., a tall, rather aster-like perennial, is occasionally cultivated. Some Asian species of *Aster* and *Kalimeris* are sometimes included in *Boltonia*.

Boltonia asteroides
flowerheads, just over life size
July 9th

Aster ciliolatus
florets, 1⅓ × life size
October 23rd

Aster ciliolatus
flowerhead, 1¼ × life size
October 23rd

Aster ciliolatus
½ life size
October 23rd

Boltonia asteroides
(right) ½ life size
July 9th

379

Felicia

Felicia Cass. (1818), in the family Compositae (sometimes called Asteraceae), contains about 83 species, mostly in southern Africa.
Description Annuals, perennials, and dwarf shrubs to 1m. Leaves alternate or opposite, entire or toothed. Daisy-like flowerheads (see *Cichorium*, p.337) solitary on long stalks. Ray florets blue, violet-pink, or white, female; disc florets yellow. Phyllaries narrow, with membranous margins, in 1 or more rows. The fruit is a flattened, often hairy achene with a pappus of bristles that may fall early.
Key Recognition Features Plants with long-stalked, *Aster*-like flowerheads (see p.378).
Ecology and Geography In dry, sunny places, mostly in South Africa, a few in tropical Africa and the Arabian peninsula.
Comment Several species are popular garden plants, mainly used for summer bedding in northern Europe, especially the violet-blue *F. amelloides* (L.) Voss and the kingfisher daisy, *F. bergeriana* (Spreng.) O. Hoffm., with vivid blue ray florets.

Erigeron

Erigeron L. (1753), in the family Compositae (sometimes called Asteraceae), contains about 150 species throughout the world, but mostly in North America.
Description Annuals and perennials to 1m, many evergreen. Leaves usually stalkless, basal or alternate on the stems, entire or toothed. Daisy-like flowerheads (see *Cichorium*, p.337). Ray florets many, slender, white, yellow, pink, or mauve, female; disc florets numerous, yellow. Phyllaries green, in 2 overlapping rows. The fruit is a flattened, oval achene with an outer row of short bristles surrounding an inner set of long, fine bristles.
Key Recognition Features Plants with *Aster*-like flowerheads (see p.378) in summer, often mauve or pink, with very narrow rays.
Ecology and Geography In dry, stony places, marshes, woodland, seashores, and mountain grassland; 15 species in Europe, others found throughout the world, but mostly in North America.
Comment Several species are cultivated, including the creeping Mexican *E. karvinskianus* DC, which forms billowing colonies in old walls, the mat-forming *E. glaucus* Ker-Gawl., and numerous more erect cultivars of hybrid origin, such as 'Gaiety' and 'Foersters Liebling'.

Erigeron 'Prosperity'
½ life size, July 2nd

Erigeron 'Prosperity'
just under life size, July 2nd

Erigeron 'Dignity'
½ life size, June 24th

Felicia amelloides
½ life size, July 4th

Felicia amelloides
flowerhead and florets
(left) 1 ⅓ × life size
May 3rd

Erigeron karvinskianus
1 ½ × life size, May 17th

Erigeron
karvinskianus
just under life size
May 17th

Erigeron 'Quakeress'
½ life size, June 24th

Nymphaea

Nymphaea L. (1753), the waterlily, in the family Nymphaeaceae, contains around 50 species worldwide.

Description Aquatic perennials or sometimes annuals, with flower stems to 80cm above water level in some tropical species, often with tuberous roots. Leaves long-stalked, floating, with rounded blades and a deep sinus. Flowers white, pale yellow, pale blue, or pink, sometimes red or purple in cultivars. Sepals usually 4, greenish. Petals many, becoming spirally arranged and merging into the numerous stamens. Ovary semi-inferior; styles short with capitate stigmas. Pollination is usually by insects, mainly beetles, wasps, and flies. The fruit is usually many-seeded. Seeds with a bell-shaped aril, which causes them to float at first, eventually sinking when the aril has decayed.

Key Recognition Features The simple flowers with many spirally arranged petals, and the round, floating leaf blades with a deep sinus.

Ecology and Geography In many habitats from Arctic lakes to slow-flowing rivers and seasonal ponds in the tropics.

Comment Many species are cultivated for their beautiful, often scented flowers. In the temperate species the flowers rest on the water surface; in many of the tropical species the flowers emerge on stiff stalks, and some open only at night. Other genera in the Nymphaeaceae include the giant-leaved *Victoria* Lindl., *Barclaya* Wall., with mainly submerged leaves and petals joined into a tube, and *Cabomba* Aublet, which has submerged feathery leaves like an aquatic *Ranunculus* (see p.47), as well as small waterlily-like floating leaves. *Cabomba* has 7 species mainly in tropical and temperate America.

The family Nymphaeaceae is thought to be the most basic of all the Angiosperms, apart from the rare and even more primitive Amborellaceae: this contains only 1 species, *Amborella trichopoda* Baill., a shrub from New Caledonia that was formerly thought close to the families Magnoliaceae or Illiciaceae (see Volume 1). A minute fossil flower of the *Nymphaea* type has been found in early Cretaceous deposits in Portugal, which dates the early waterlilies to at least 115–125 million years ago. DNA studies indicate that the Nymphaeaceae separated from the rest of the angiosperm family tree soon after the Amborellaceae and shortly before the Illiciaceae, Schisandraceae (see Volume 1) and Austrobaileyaceae, and before the separation of the monocots and dicots. All these families, rather than those related to the magnolias, are now thought to be the most primitive flowering plants.

Nuphar

Nuphar Smith (1809), a waterlily in the family Nymphaeaceae, contains around 10 species, in north temperate regions.

Description Aquatic perennials with leaves often to 60cm above the surface of the water, with stout, creeping rhizomes. Leaves long-stalked, submerged, floating, or emergent, with rounded or arrow-shaped blades and a deep sinus. Flowers yellow or orange. Sepals around 6, the outer greenish, the inner yellow or orange. Petals many, linear and scale-like, with a small nectary, merging into the numerous stamens. Ovary superior, of 5–20 carpels; stigmas radiating on a concave disc. Pollination is usually by beetles. The fruit is bottle-shaped and many seeded, the seeds without an aril.

Key Recognition Features The simple, yellowish flowers with few, petal-like sepals, and the round, floating leaf blades with a deep sinus, as well as thin and wavy submerged leaves.

Ecology and Geography In ponds and slow-flowing rivers in North America, Europe, and Asia.

Comment Many species have been named, which are doubtfully distinct. The fruits are shaped like an ancient squat bottle, which has given rise to the alternative name brandy-bottle. In America some species are called spatter dock or beaver-lily.

Nuphar advena
½ life size, July 20th

Cabomba piauhyensis
¾ life size, May 25th

Nymphaeaceae

Nymphaea alba, stamens and perianth segments
¾ life size, July 23rd

Nuphar advena
flower, just under life size
July 20th

Nymphaea alba
section through flower
¾ life size, July 23rd

Nymphaea alba
ovary and stigmas
just under life size
July 23rd

Nymphaea alba
⅔ life size, July 23rd

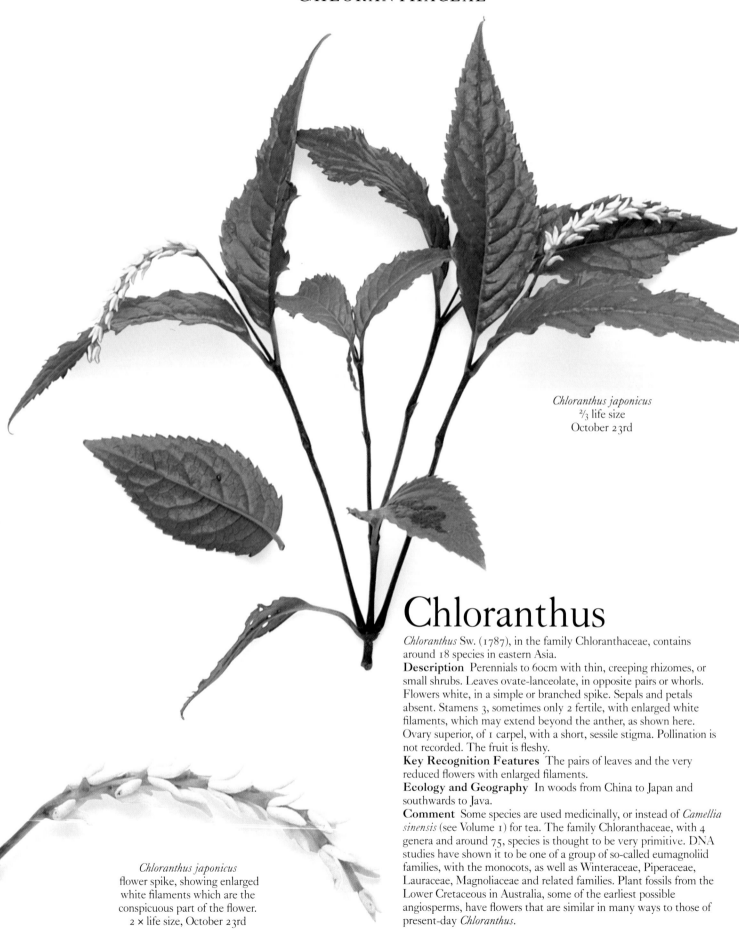

Chloranthus japonicus
⅔ life size
October 23rd

Chloranthus

Chloranthus Sw. (1787), in the family Chloranthaceae, contains around 18 species in eastern Asia.

Description Perennials to 60cm with thin, creeping rhizomes, or small shrubs. Leaves ovate-lanceolate, in opposite pairs or whorls. Flowers white, in a simple or branched spike. Sepals and petals absent. Stamens 3, sometimes only 2 fertile, with enlarged white filaments, which may extend beyond the anther, as shown here. Ovary superior, of 1 carpel, with a short, sessile stigma. Pollination is not recorded. The fruit is fleshy.

Key Recognition Features The pairs of leaves and the very reduced flowers with enlarged filaments.

Ecology and Geography In woods from China to Japan and southwards to Java.

Comment Some species are used medicinally, or instead of *Camellia sinensis* (see Volume 1) for tea. The family Chloranthaceae, with 4 genera and around 75, species is thought to be very primitive. DNA studies have shown it to be one of a group of so-called eumagnoliid families, with the monocots, as well as Winteraceae, Piperaceae, Lauraceae, Magnoliaceae and related families. Plant fossils from the Lower Cretaceous in Australia, some of the earliest possible angiosperms, have flowers that are similar in many ways to those of present-day *Chloranthus*.

Chloranthus japonicus
flower spike, showing enlarged
white filaments which are the
conspicuous part of the flower.
2 × life size, October 23rd

Ceratophyllum submersum
just under life size, July 20th

Chloranthus oldhamii
young plant, ½ life size
May 8th

Ceratophyllum

Ceratophyllum L. (1753), hornwort, in the family Ceratophyllaceae, contains around 3 or possibly more species worldwide.

Description Aquatic perennials to 80cm, without roots, forming resting buds in winter. Leaves in whorls of 6–8 at each node, forked and toothed 1–4 times over. Flowers small, stalkless, in the leaf axils, unisexual, with males and females on alternate nodes. Sepals 8–12, narrow and joined at the base. Petals absent. Stamens 10–20, spirally arranged, with enlarged filaments. Ovary superior, of 1 carpel, with a short, sessile stigma. Pollination is by water. The fruit has spines, a spiny style, and 1 seed with 2 cotyledons.

Key Recognition Features The whorls of forking leaves, often rather stiff, and the sessile, reduced flowers on the outsides of the whorls of leaves.

Ecology and Geography In ponds, lakes, and rivers worldwide except the Arctic.

Comment In some areas this has become a pest and choked rivers and lakes, expanding to plague densities soon after its introduction to a new body of water before settling down to be part of a mixed aquatic flora. *Ceratophyllum* has long been regarded as one of the most primitive of all flowering plants, but its exact position has been the subject of considerable discussion. Some DNA studies suggest that it is an early offshoot of the main branch of the dicots, rather than an offshoot of the common ancestor of both dicots and monocots (see *Acorus*, p.390). Other studies suggest that it is more closely associated with the monocots.

Saururus

Saururus L. (1753), lizard's tail, in the family Saururaceae, contains 2 species in eastern Asia and eastern North America.

Description Perennials to 1m with a creeping rootstock, rooting at the nodes. Leaves aromatic, heart-shaped, stalked, alternate on the stem. Flowers small, on short stalks, in the axil of a small bract, densely set on an elongated spike, the lowest bracts little larger than the rest. Sepals and petals absent. Stamens 6 or sometimes 4, with narrow filaments. Ovary superior, of 3 or 4 carpels, each with a curved stigma and 2–4 ovules. Pollination is by insects and perhaps also by wind. The fruit is globose and indehiscent.

Key Recognition Features The alternate, heart-shaped leaves, and the reduced flowers on a nodding spike.

Ecology and Geography In shallow water in swamps, ponds, and lakes; sometimes as a weed in rice fields. *Saururus cernuus* L. in eastern North America; *S. chinensis* (Lour.) Baill. in South East Asia, and now a weed in North America.

Comment Sometimes grown as a curiosity. The family Saururaceae is related to Aristolochiaceae (see p. 388) and to Piperaceae, which includes *Piper* L., the pepper, and *Peperomia* Ruíz & Pavón, a large tropical genus of over 1000 species, which includes several popular houseplants such as *P. obtusifolia* (L.) Dietr.. Their flowers are very small, in dense spikes.. The other genera in the Saururaceae are *Houttuynia*, *Gymnotheca* Decne with 2 species in western China, and *Anemopsis* Hook. & Arn. with 1 species, *A. californica* (Nutt.) Hook. & Arn. in alkaline swamps in California and Mexico.

Saururus cernuus
flower spike, 1½ × life size
July 20th

Saururus cernuus
½ life size, July 20th

Houttuynia

Houttuynia Thunb (1784), in the family Saururaceae, contains
1 species, *H. cordata* Thunb. in eastern Asia.

Description Perennials to 40cm with a creeping rootstock, rooting
at the nodes. Leaves aromatic, heart-shaped, stalked, alternate on the
stem. Flowers small, stalkless, densely set on a short spike, with 4
petal-like bracts at the base, bisexual but functionally female through
degeneration of the pollen. Sepals and petals absent. Stamens 3, with
narrow filaments. Ovary superior, of 3 carpels, each with a recurved
stigma and 2–4 ovules. Seeds generally develop without pollination
(parthenogenesis). The fruit is globose and indehiscent.

Key Recognition Features The alternate, heart-shaped leaves,
and the reduced flowers on short spike with 4 petal-like bracts, or
more in the cultivated form 'Plena'.

Ecology and Geography In woods and damp places, often on
the margins of rice fields. From Nepal to western China, Japan,
and southwards to Java.

Comment The genus is named after Martinus Houttuyn
(c.1720–98), a Dutch physician and author of books on
wood and on natural history, an early follower of Linnaeus.
The highly aromatic leaves of *Houttuynia* are eaten as a
salad in China, and considered a protection against cancer.
Varieties with beautifully coloured leaves are cultivated,
such as 'Chameleon', 'Pied Piper', and 'Variegata'.

Houttuynia cordata 'Chameleon'
just under life size, June 19th

Peperomia obtusifolia
just under life size
May 11th

Houttuynia cordata
'Chameleon'
1½ × life size, June 19th

387

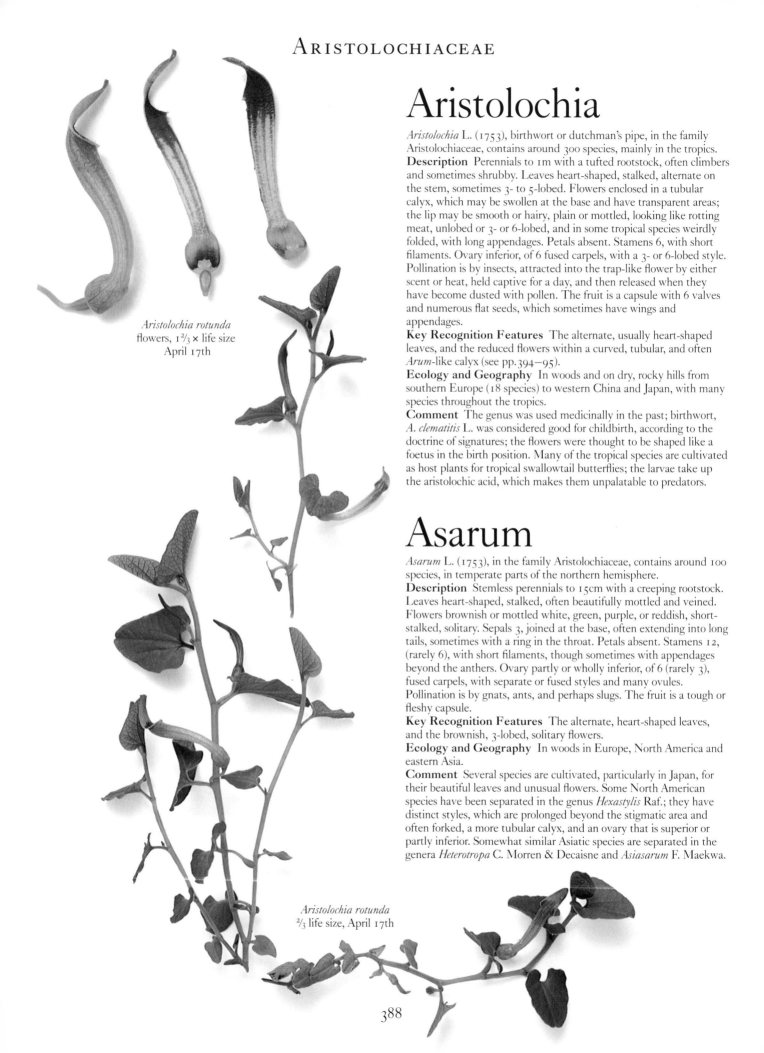

Aristolochia rotunda
flowers, 1²/₃ × life size
April 17th

Aristolochia

Aristolochia L. (1753), birthwort or dutchman's pipe, in the family Aristolochiaceae, contains around 300 species, mainly in the tropics.

Description Perennials to 1m with a tufted rootstock, often climbers and sometimes shrubby. Leaves heart-shaped, stalked, alternate on the stem, sometimes 3- to 5-lobed. Flowers enclosed in a tubular calyx, which may be swollen at the base and have transparent areas; the lip may be smooth or hairy, plain or mottled, looking like rotting meat, unlobed or 3- or 6-lobed, and in some tropical species weirdly folded, with long appendages. Petals absent. Stamens 6, with short filaments. Ovary inferior, of 6 fused carpels, with a 3- or 6-lobed style. Pollination is by insects, attracted into the trap-like flower by either scent or heat, held captive for a day, and then released when they have become dusted with pollen. The fruit is a capsule with 6 valves and numerous flat seeds, which sometimes have wings and appendages.

Key Recognition Features The alternate, usually heart-shaped leaves, and the reduced flowers within a curved, tubular, and often *Arum*-like calyx (see pp. 394–95).

Ecology and Geography In woods and on dry, rocky hills from southern Europe (18 species) to western China and Japan, with many species throughout the tropics.

Comment The genus was used medicinally in the past; birthwort, *A. clematitis* L. was considered good for childbirth, according to the doctrine of signatures; the flowers were thought to be shaped like a foetus in the birth position. Many of the tropical species are cultivated as host plants for tropical swallowtail butterflies; the larvae take up the aristolochic acid, which makes them unpalatable to predators.

Asarum

Asarum L. (1753), in the family Aristolochiaceae, contains around 100 species, in temperate parts of the northern hemisphere.

Description Stemless perennials to 15cm with a creeping rootstock. Leaves heart-shaped, stalked, often beautifully mottled and veined. Flowers brownish or mottled white, green, purple, or reddish, short-stalked, solitary. Sepals 3, joined at the base, often extending into long tails, sometimes with a ring in the throat. Petals absent. Stamens 12, (rarely 6), with short filaments, though sometimes with appendages beyond the anthers. Ovary partly or wholly inferior, of 6 (rarely 3), fused carpels, with separate or fused styles and many ovules. Pollination is by gnats, ants, and perhaps slugs. The fruit is a tough or fleshy capsule.

Key Recognition Features The alternate, heart-shaped leaves, and the brownish, 3-lobed, solitary flowers.

Ecology and Geography In woods in Europe, North America and eastern Asia.

Comment Several species are cultivated, particularly in Japan, for their beautiful leaves and unusual flowers. Some North American species have been separated in the genus *Hexastylis* Raf.; they have distinct styles, which are prolonged beyond the stigmatic area and often forked, a more tubular calyx, and an ovary that is superior or partly inferior. Somewhat similar Asiatic species are separated in the genera *Heterotropa* C. Morren & Decaisne and *Asiasarum* F. Maekwa.

Aristolochia rotunda
²/₃ life size, April 17th

Saruma

Saruma Oliver (1895), in the family Aristolochiaceae, contains
1 species, *S. henryi* Oliver in western China.

Description Perennial to 60cm with a tufted rootstock and upright,
leafy stems. Leaves heart-shaped, stalked, alternate, hairy. Flowers
yellow, stalked, solitary. Sepals 3. Petals 3. Stamens 12, with very
short filaments. Ovary superior, of 6 nearly separate carpels, each
with a short stigma and many ovules. Pollination is by insects.
The fruit is starry, with each follicle dehiscent along the top edge.

Key Recognition Features The alternate, heart-shaped leaves,
and the yellow, 3-petalled, solitary flowers.

Ecology and Geography In woods in western China.

Comment This interesting, unspecialised member of the family
Aristolochiaceae is easily cultivated in woodland conditions. The
name is an anagram of the related genus *Asarum* L.

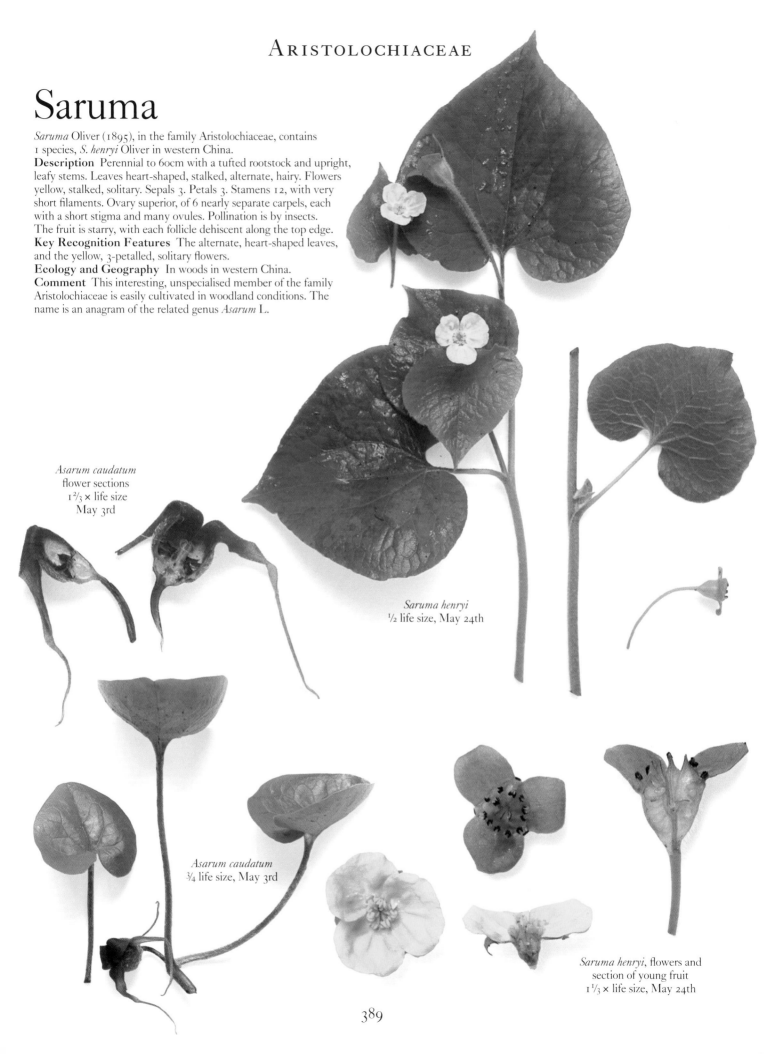

Asarum caudatum
flower sections
1⅔ × life size
May 3rd

Saruma henryi
½ life size, May 24th

Asarum caudatum
¾ life size, May 3rd

Saruma henryi, flowers and
section of young fruit
1⅓ × life size, May 24th

Acorus calamus
rhizome, 1½ × life size
July 20th

Acorus

Acorus L. (1753), sweet flag, in the family Acoraceae,
contains 2 species in North America and eastern Asia.
Description Perennials to 2m with a creeping rootstock.
Leaves iris-like (see pp.438–41), aromatic, linear, flat, with a
characteristic wavy edge. Flowers small, stalkless, densely set on
a 4–10cm long spike, which appears to grow out of the side of a
leaf. Perianth segments 6, small, thick, incurved, in 2 whorls.
Stamens 6, with narrow filaments. Ovary superior, with 2 or 3 carpels,
each with a small stigma and numerous ovules. Pollination is not
recorded. The fruit is a red, fleshy berry, with few seeds.
Key Recognition Features The linear, aromatic leaves and lateral
spike of minute flowers.
Ecology and Geography In swamps and shallow water and in wet
places along streams. *Acorus calamus* L. is found in North America
and in eastern Asia and Siberia; both diploid and tetraploid plants are
recorded. In Europe, where the plant was introduced in the middle
ages, the plant is triploid, as it is in temperate India. The second
species, *A. gramineus* Soland, is found only in central and eastern Asia.
Comment *Acorus calamus* was grown for its scented rhizomes and
leaves, and is still used in Chinese herbal medicine. Its leaves were
used for strewing on floors, and contain an insecticide. It was also
used in ancient Egypt, and is mentioned in the works of Hippocrates
and in *Exodus*, as sweet calamus, an ingredient in the sacred oil for
anointing the altar. *Acorus gramineus* is often cultivated for its dark
green, shining leaves, particularly the form 'Variegatus' with white-
striped leaves. DNA studies have confirmed the isolated position of
Acorus, and its distinctness from Araceae (see pp.394–401), in which
it was often included. *Acorus* is perhaps the most primitive genus in
the monocots, the smaller of the 2 main divisions of flowering plants.
The first leaf of a monocot seedling is single and grassy, in contrast to
the pair of leaves of the dicot seedling. Other main differences are that
monocots usually have narrow leaves with parallel veins, and have
floral parts in groups of 3, with little or no differentiation between
sepals and petals, which are collectively called perianth segments.
Traditional treatments of the flowering plants held that monocots and
dicots were the 2 basic divisions, and that the major groups
Magnoliales, Winterales, Chloranthales, Piperales and Laurales, were
the primitive dicots. Nowadays, DNA studies suggest that monocots
evolved later than previously thought, within the dicots, and are
equivalent to the major dicot groups Magnoliales, Winterales,
Chloranthales, Piperales, and Laurales.

Acorus gramineus 'Variegatus'
½ life size, April 28th

*Acorus
gramineus*
flower spike
3 × life size
April 28th

Aponogeton

Aponogeton L. fil. (1781), water hawthorn, in the family Aponogetonaceae, contains around 45 species, mainly in tropical parts of Africa and Asia.

Description Aquatic perennials to 3cm with a rhizome or tuberous rootstock. Leaves submerged or floating, flat, oval to linear. Flowers small, stalkless, on a forking or simple spike. Perianth segments up to 6 or absent, usually 2, thick, incurved, and petal-like or bract-like. Stamens 6 or more; anthers often black. Ovary superior, with 2−9, but usually 3 or 4 separate carpels, each with a narrow stigmatic ridge and 1−8 ovules. Pollination is presumed to be by insects. Fruit is dry.

Key Recognition Features Water plants with stalked leaves and often branched flower spikes; flowers with bract-like perianth segments and separate carpels.

Ecology and Geography In ponds and shallow water, with most species in Africa and Madagascar, a few in the warmer parts of Asia, southwards to Australia.

Comment *Aponogeton distachyos* L. fil. from South Africa is commonly naturalised in Europe, Australia, and South America; its scented flowers and young fruiting heads are eaten in a traditional mutton stew called *waterblommetjiebredie*. Other species have edible tubers. The family Aponogetonaceae, with only 1 genus, is most closely related to the aquatic families Alismataceae, Hydrocharitaceae (see p. 392), and the marine grass-like Zosteraceae.

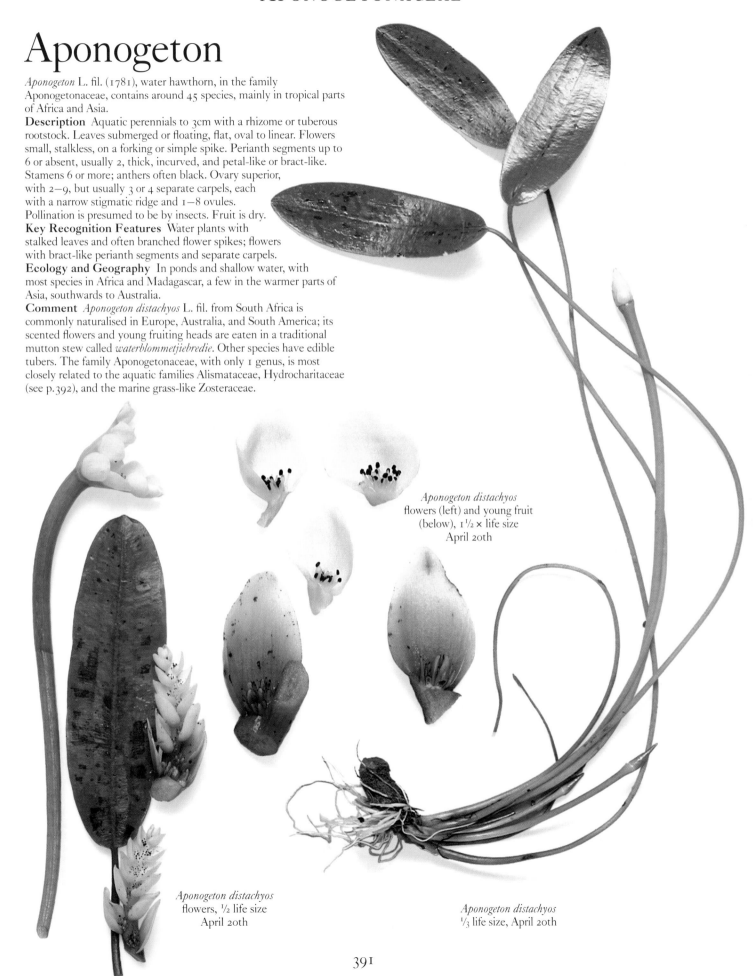

Aponogeton distachyos
flowers (left) and young fruit
(below), 1 1/2 × life size
April 20th

Aponogeton distachyos
flowers, 1/2 life size
April 20th

Aponogeton distachyos
1/3 life size, April 20th

Hydrocharis

Hydrocharis L. (1753), frog-bit, in the family Hydrocharitaceae, contains around 5 species, mainly in Europe and eastern Asia.

Description Aquatic perennials to 7.5cm with long, thin stolons and rosettes of rounded or kidney-shaped, floating leaves. Flowers unisexual, the males short-stalked, the females long-stalked from a thin spathe. Sepals 3. Petals 3, white, sometimes with a yellow base, thin and rounded. Stamens 9–12. Ovary superior, with 6 fused carpels, and 6 flat, forked styles. Pollination is by insects. The fruit is a berry, with 6 ribs and numerous seeds.

Key Recognition Features The round floating leaves and white, 3-petalled flowers.

Ecology and Geography In ponds, lakes and shallow water. *Hydrocharis morsus-ranae* L. is frequent throughout Europe and Asia and introduced in North America.

Comment *Hydrocharis morsus-ranae* is sometimes cultivated in ornamental ponds. The family Hydrocharitaceae has 15 specialised aquatic genera, including the common and often weedy Canadian pondweed *Elodea canadensis* Michaux and the related genera *Egeria* Planch., *Hydrilla* L.C. Rich., and *Lagarosiphon* Harvey. In *Lagarosiphon* and *Hydrilla* the female flowers lie on the surface, while the male flowers are free-floating on reflexed perianth segments, with 3 fertile stamens, and 3 sterile that act as sails.

Hydrocharis morsus-ranae
½ life size, July 4th

Sagittaria latifolia
½ life size, July 9th

Sagittaria latifolia
flowers, 1⅓ × life size
July 9th

Butomus

Butomus L. (1753), flowering rush, in the family Butomaceae, contains 1 species, *B. umbellatus* L. in Europe and temperate Asia.
Description Aquatic perennial to 1m with a tufted rootstock. Leaves usually emergent, triangular in cross-section. Flowers pink, in a simple umbel. Sepals 3, petal-like. Petals 3, longer than the sepals. Stamens 6–9. Ovary superior, with 6–9 carpels joined at the base. Pollination is by insects. The fruit has a ring of persistent styles, with numerous seeds scattered over the inner surface of the carpels.
Key Recognition Features The usually pink, 3-petalled flowers in an umbel, and the leaves triangular in cross-section.
Ecology and Geography In marshes, ponds, lakes, and slow-flowing water throughout Europe to eastern Turkey and central Asia, but not reaching Japan.
Comment This beautiful plant is commonly cultivated. The starchy rhizomes were used to make bread in northern Europe. *Butomus* is usually put in its own family, but is sometimes included in the Limnocharitaceae, an aquatic family related to Alismataceae.

Sagittaria

Sagittaria L. (1753), arrowhead, in the family Alismataceae, contains around 20 species worldwide.
Description Aquatic perennials or occasionally annuals to 1.2m, often with stolons or tubers. Leaves submerged, emergent, or floating, linear or often with the blade shaped like an arrowhead. Flowers usually unisexual, in 1 to several whorls on an upright or floating stem. Sepals 3. Petals 3, white or yellowish, sometimes with a purple spot near the base, thin and rounded. Stamens 7 or more. Ovary superior, with numerous separate carpels. Pollination is by insects. The fruit is made up of numerous 1-seeded nutlets.
Key Recognition Features The usually white, 3-petalled flowers in whorls on an upright stalk, and the numerous small seeds; arrowhead-shaped leaves are characteristic of many species.
Ecology and Geography In ponds, lakes, and running water, with most species in North America.
Comment A few species are cultivated as ornamentals: hardy species with emergent leaves in gardens, and tropical species with narrow, ribbon-like, submerged leaves in fish tanks. The Chinese *S. sinensis* Sims is cultivated in flooded fields in China and the tubers eaten as water chestnut. Tubers of *S. latifolia* L., the *wapato*, were commonly eaten in North America.

Butomus umbellatus, flowers and flower parts
1 ½ × life size, August 10th

*Butomus
umbellatus*
½ life size
August 10th

Sagittaria sinensis
tubers, ⅔ life size, March 8th

Arum dioscroidis
⅓ life size, April 28th

Arisarum

Arisarum Targioni-Tozzetti. (1810), in the family Araceae, contains 2 or 3 species mainly in the Mediterranean area.

Description Perennials to 20cm with a tuberous and creeping rootstock. Leaves all basal, with a heart-shaped or arrowhead-shaped blade. Flowers unisexual, small, stalkless, few on a spike, the whole wrapped round with a purplish or brownish spathe, which in *A. proboscideum* (L.) Savi has a long, thread-like tip, and transparent areas at the base. Spadix short, green or whitish. Perianth segments absent. Male flowers several, each with 1 stamen. Female flowers few, of 1 carpel, a stigmatic tip, and around 6 ovules. Pollination of *A. proboscideum* is by fungus gnats. The fruit is a green, fleshy berry with around 6 seeds.

Key Recognition Features The spathe wrapped round the spadix and the simple male and female flowers.

Ecology and Geography In woods and on rocky hills, mainly in the Mediterranean area, also in the Canaries and the Azores.

Comment *Arisarum proboscideum* is the mouse plant, grown as a curiosity. The flowers are hidden beneath the leaves, only the "tail of the mouse" being visible from above.

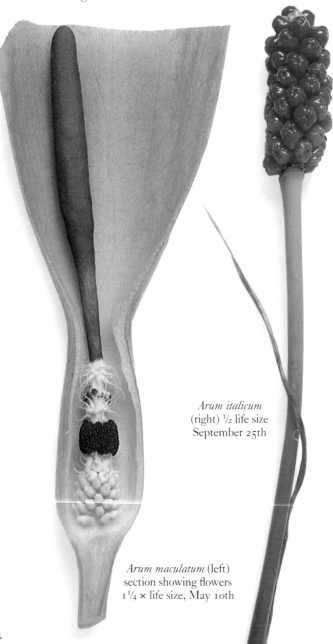

Arum italicum
(right) ½ life size
September 25th

Arum maculatum (left)
section showing flowers
1¼ × life size, May 10th

Arum

Arum L. (1753), in the family Araceae, contains around 26 species in Europe, the Mediterranean area and Asia.

Description Perennials to 60cm with a tuberous rootstock. Leaves all basal, with a heart-shaped or arrowhead-shaped blade. Flowers unisexual, small, stalkless, densely set on a spike, the whole wrapped round with a green, yellow, or purple spathe. Hair-like sterile flowers above and between the fertile ones. Perianth segments absent. Stamens 3 or 4, fused, the anthers reddish before they dehisce. Ovary with 1 carpel, a stigmatic tip, and 1–6 ovules. Pollination is detailed below. The fruit is a red, fleshy berry with few seeds.

Key Recognition Features The spathe wrapped round the spadix and flowers with males and females separated by hairs.

Ecology and Geography In woods and on rocky hills, with 2 species in northern Europe, but mainly in the Mediterranean area, eastwards to central Asia around Tashkent.

Comment Several species are cultivated as curiosities, and forms of *A. italicum* L. for their beautifully white-veined leaves and heads of shining red berries. Pollination of *Arum* is complex and interesting; the whole inflorescence forms a trap to catch the pollinating insects. The spike consists of a smooth, sterile, purple or yellow spadix, then a ring of hairs, below which are the male flowers; below the male flowers is a further ring of hairs, then the female flowers at the base of the spike. The female flowers mature first; when ready, the spadix emits a smell and heats up, attracting small flies. These fall down the smooth surface of the spathe and past the downward-pointing hairs, to the base of the trap, where any pollen carried on the flies fertilises the female flowers. The flies remain trapped until the male flowers are ready to shed their pollen. Once the pollen has fallen onto the trapped flies, the hairs wither and the surface of the spathe becomes wrinkled, allowing the flies to escape and visit the next flower.

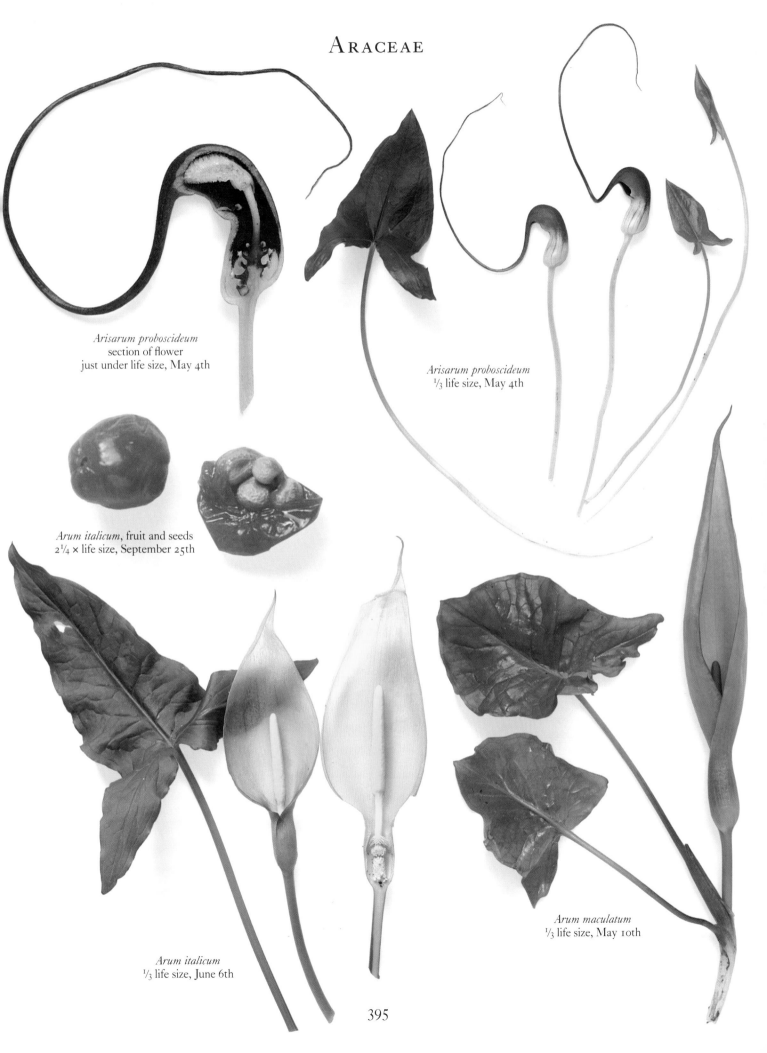

ARACEAE

Arisarum proboscideum
section of flower
just under life size, May 4th

Arisarum proboscideum
⅓ life size, May 4th

Arum italicum, fruit and seeds
2¼ × life size, September 25th

Arum italicum
⅓ life size, June 6th

Arum maculatum
⅓ life size, May 10th

395

Arisaema serratum
fruit and seeds, 2 × life size
September 29th

Arisaema serratum
¹/₂ life size
September 29th

Arisaema triphyllum
¹/₃ life size, May 12th

Arisaema

Arisaema C. Martius (1831), in the family Araceae, contains around 150 species, mainly in eastern Asia.

Description Perennials to 1.5m with a tuberous rootstock (strictly a corm, a swollen stem base). Leaves all basal, sheathing to form a false stem, with the blade divided into 3 or more leaflets. Flowers unisexual, often with males and females on different plants, small, stalkless, many on a spike, the whole wrapped round with a green, white, pink, purplish, or brownish spathe, which is often bent forward, sometimes with a long, thread-like tip. Spadix long, purplish, green, or white, often with a long, thread-like tip. Perianth segments absent. Male flowers several, each with 1−5 fused stamens. Female flowers of 1 carpel, a stigmatic tip, and few ovules. Pollination is by various flies and fungus gnats, and in some species perhaps by snails. The fruit is a crowded, usually nodding head of red, fleshy berries with few seeds.

Key Recognition Features The spathe wrapped round the spadix and the extended or swollen spadix.

Ecology and Geography In woods, mainly in the Himalayas and China, with a few species in North America and East Africa.

Comment Many species are grown as ornamentals; in some, the corms are edible. In some species, such as the American *A. triphyllum* (L.) Schott, Jack-in-the-pulpit, the smallest inflorescences are sterile, the intermediate ones are male, and the largest female.

Pinellia

Pinellia Tenore (1830), in the family Araceae, contains around 6 species, mainly in eastern Asia.

Description Perennials to 60cm with a tuberous rootstock producing numerous bulbils. Leaves all basal, with the blade undivided or split into 3 or more leaflets. Inflorescence on a separate stem from the leaves. Flowers unisexual, often with males and females on different plants, small, stalkless, many on a spike, the whole wrapped round with a narrow, green spathe, which clasps the long tip of the spadix. Perianth segments absent. Male flowers several, each with 1 or 2 fused stamens. Female flowers of 1 carpel, a stigmatic tip, and 1 ovule, the zone of the female flowers joined to the spathe. Pollination is not recorded, but self-pollination is suspected. The fruit is a head of green, fleshy berries, each with 1 seed.

Key Recognition Features The inflorescence on a separate stem from the leaves, and the short spathe with a long, thin spadix.

Ecology and Geography In woods, cultivated fields, and by roadsides, mainly in China, Korea, and Japan.

Comment A few species, including *P. ternata* (Thunb.) Breitenbach, are sometimes cultivated as curiosities.

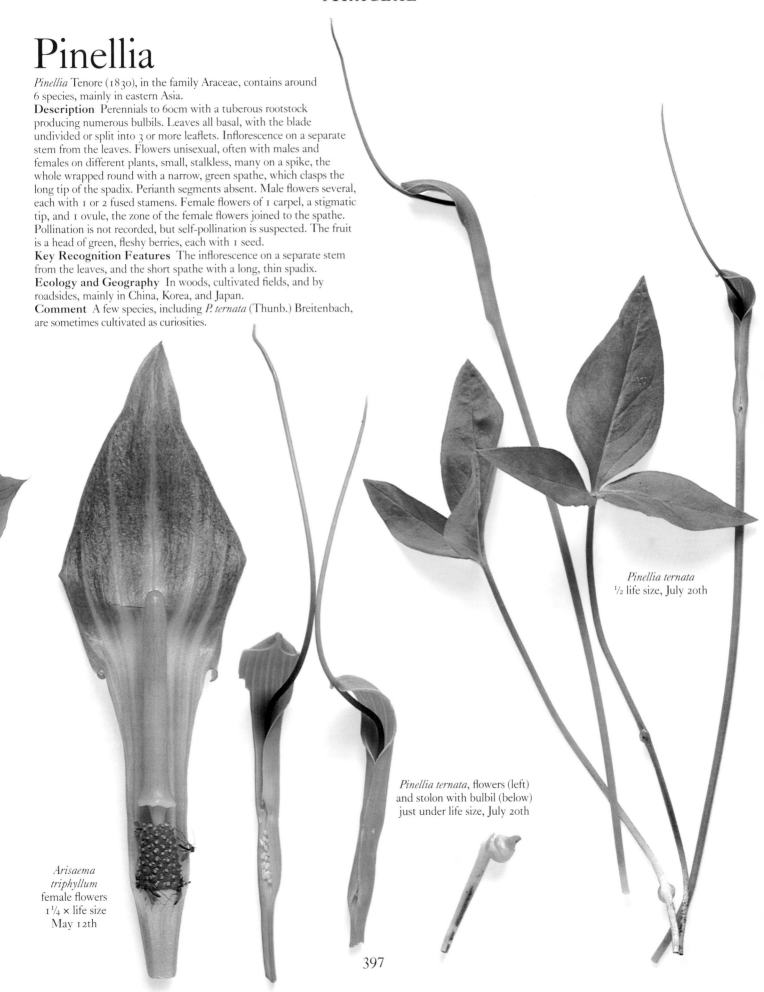

Pinellia ternata
½ life size, July 20th

Pinellia ternata, flowers (left)
and stolon with bulbil (below)
just under life size, July 20th

*Arisaema
triphyllum*
female flowers
1 ¼ × life size
May 12th

Dracunculus

Dracunculus Miller (1754), in the family Araceae, contains around 3 species in the Mediterranean area.

Description Perennials with a large tuber. Leaves all basal, sheathing to form a false soft stem to 1m, with the blade divided into several narrow, pointed leaflets. Flowers unisexual, with the males above the females, small, stalkless, many on a spike, the whole wrapped round with a reddish-black, greenish-white, pale yellow, or rarely orange, sometimes hairy spathe. Spadix long, blackish, or white, often with a large appendix. Sterile flowers few, at base of appendix. Perianth segments absent. Male flowers several, each with 2 or 3 fused stamens. Female flowers of 1 carpel, a stigmatic tip, and few ovules. Pollination is by blow flies and other carrion eaters, attracted by the smell of rotting meat that is emitted from the hole. The fruit is a crowded, upright head of orange-red fleshy berries, with few seeds.

Key Recognition Features The compound sheathing leaves, large, usually black spadix, and foul smell of rotting meat.

Ecology and Geography In rocky places near the sea, among old ruins, such as those of Troy, and in open woods. *Dracunculus vulgaris* Schott is mainly in the eastern Mediterranean from Sardinia and Sicily to Bulgaria, Turkey, and Israel, *D. muscivorus* (L. fil.) Parl. on the balearic islands, Corsica and Sardinia, and *D. canariensis* Kunth in the Canaries and Madeira.

Comment *Dracunculus vulgaris* and *D. canariensis* are similar tall plants with a smooth upright spathe and spadix; in some parts of Crete, they have a whitish spathe, and a green, yellow, or white spadix. The common black form of *D. vulgaris* smells strongly of bad meat. In *D. muscivorus,* often called *Helicodiceros muscivorus* (L. fil.) Engl., the likeness to a dead animal is taken to extremes, the black, hairy hole which emits the smell having been likened to the anus. The foul smell is produced only when the flower first opens; by the time the stamens ripen the smell has gone, and those flies which are still alive can escape to visit another flower; many lay their eggs in the flower and then die. The flower shown here was full of dead flies and small but live maggots, and had lost its foul smell. The habitat of *D. muscivorus* is usually on cliffs close to the sea, and it has been suggested that the hairy flower mimics a dead, rotting seagull chick.

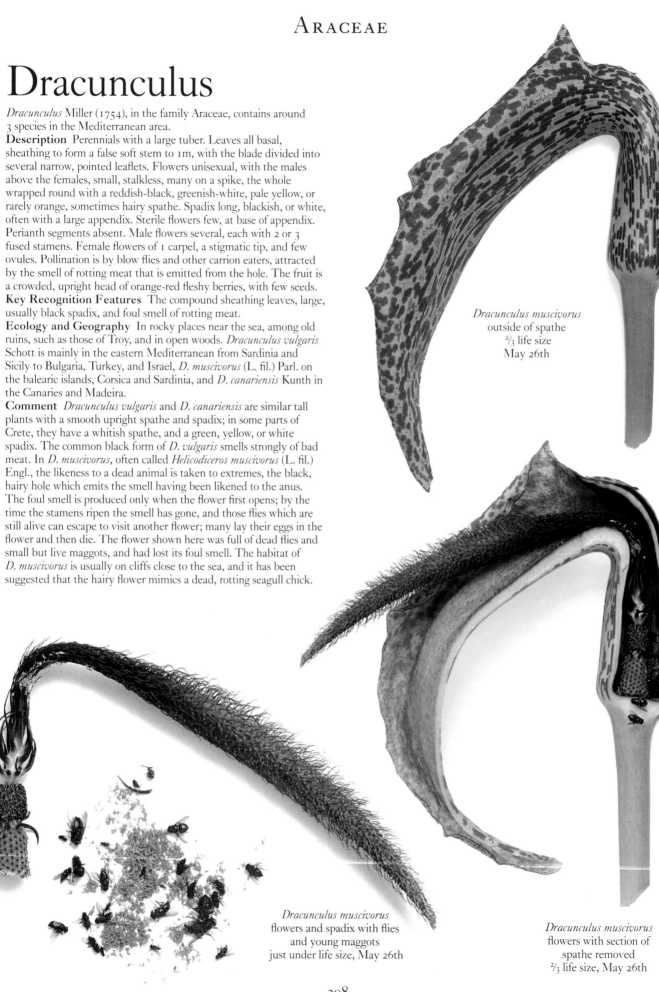

Dracunculus muscivorus
outside of spathe
²/₃ life size
May 26th

Dracunculus muscivorus
flowers and spadix with flies
and young maggots
just under life size, May 26th

Dracunculus muscivorus
flowers with section of
spathe removed
²/₃ life size, May 26th

Dracunculus muscivorus
piece of spathe showing
animal-like skin and hair
1 ½ × life size, May 26th

Dracunculus muscivorus
½ life size, May 26th

Lysichiton

Lysichiton Schott (1857), in the family Araceae, contains 2 species in eastern Asia and western North America.

Description Perennials with a short rootstock. Leaves all basal, with an ovate-oblong, undivided blade to 1.5m tall. Inflorescence on a separate stem from among the outer leaves, foetid or pleasantly scented. Flowers small, stalkless, many on a rather stout spike, before opening protected by a white or yellow spathe, which arises from below ground and folds back by the time the flowers open. Perianth segments 4. Stamens 4. Female flowers of 2 carpels, a stigmatic tip, and 2 ovules. Pollination is by insects. The fruit is a green, fleshy berry, becoming soft and putrid; seeds woody, floating.

Key Recognition Features The yellow or white spathe appearing with or before the leaves, and the large, ovate leaf blades.

Ecology and Geography In swamps and wet woods, and on the edges of ponds, with *L. americanus* Hulten & St John from Alaska to central California, and *L. camtschatcensis* (L.) Schott from northeastern Siberia and southern Kamchatka to central Honshu.

Comment Both the yellow-flowered, foetid *L. americanus* and the white-flowered, sweetly-scented *L. camtschatcensis* are commonly cultivated; they often hybridise in gardens, producing very robust hybrids with a creamy-white spathe. *Symplocarpus foetidus* (L.) Nutt., skunk cabbage, from eastern North America and eastern Asia, has similar leaves with a heart-shaped blade, but very different flowers, brown, green or spotted, shaped like a large snail shell, at ground level.

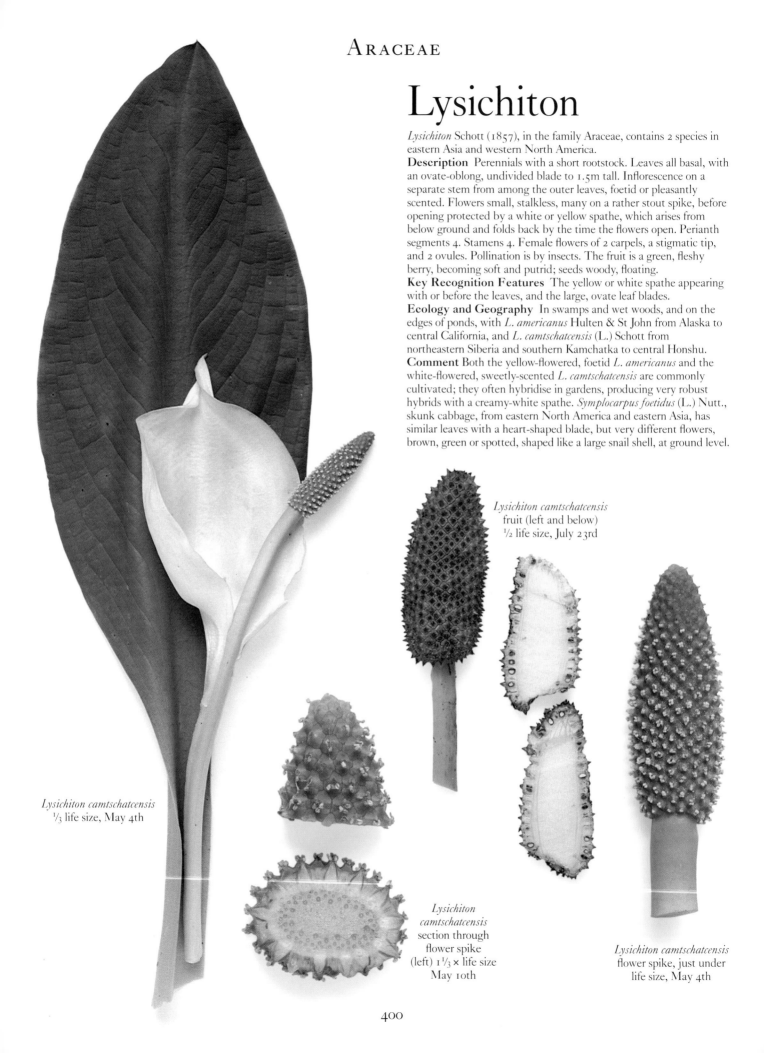

Lysichiton camtschatcensis
fruit (left and below)
½ life size, July 23rd

Lysichiton camtschatcensis
⅓ life size, May 4th

Lysichiton camtschatcensis
section through flower spike
(left) 1⅓ × life size
May 10th

Lysichiton camtschatcensis
flower spike, just under life size, May 4th

Zantedeschia aethiopica
cross-section showing
flower spike with male
flowers above and
female flowers below
$^2/_3$ life size, May 24th

Zantedeschia

Zantedeschia Sprengel (1826), in the family Araceae, contains
6 species in southern Africa.

Description Perennials to 1.5m with a tuberous rootstock. Leaves
all basal, with a heart-shaped or lanceolate blade. Inflorescence on a
separate stem, from among the leaves, often sweetly scented. Flowers
unisexual, small, stalkless, many on a spike, the females protected by
a white, yellow, or reddish spathe, the males above. Perianth
segments absent. Stamens 1. Staminodes sometimes present among
the female flowers. Female flowers of 3 carpels, each with 1–8 ovules.
Pollination is by insects. The fruit is a green, fleshy berry.

Key Recognition Features The white or coloured spathe
appearing on a tall, soft, and fleshy stem with the leaves.

Ecology and Geography In swamps and on rock ledges, from the
Cape northwards to the Traansvaal and tropical Africa. The common
white arum or calla lily, *Z. aethiopica* (L.) Sprengel, often occurs in
vast numbers in marshy valleys in the Cape area.

Comment Many species and hybrids are commonly cultivated and
may become naturalised in areas where the ground does not freeze.
The hybrids are popular as long-lasting cut flowers.

Zantedeschia aethiopica
$^1/_2$ life size, August 8th

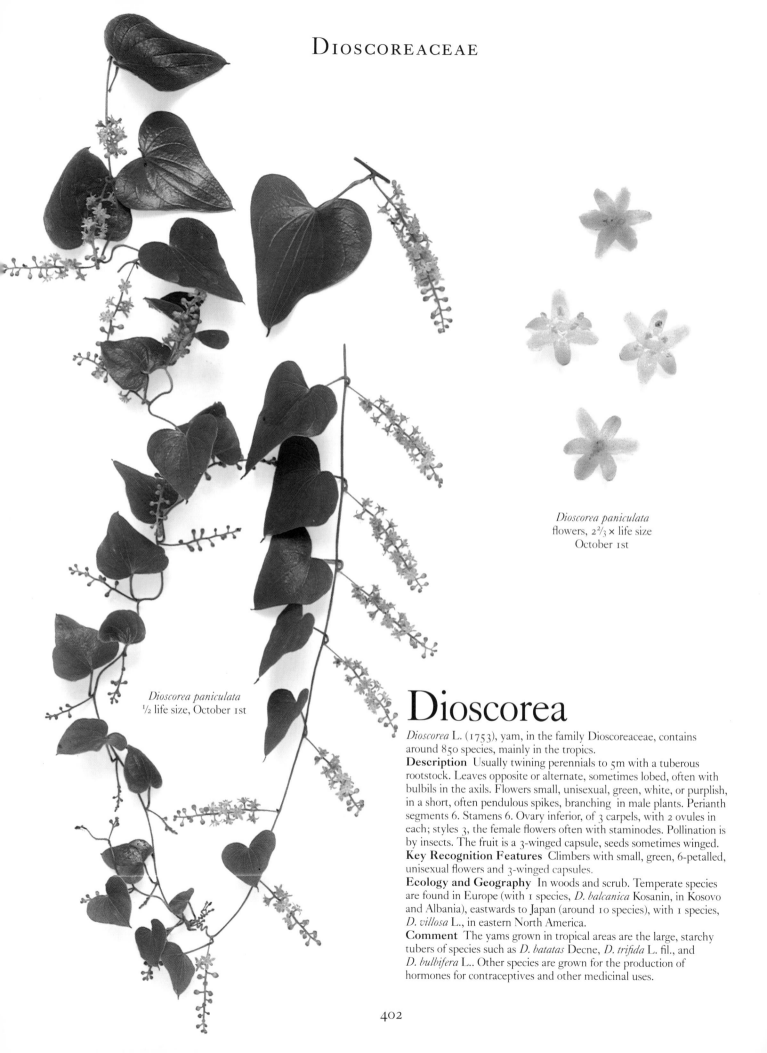

Dioscorea paniculata
flowers, 2²/₃ × life size
October 1st

Dioscorea paniculata
¹/₂ life size, October 1st

Dioscorea

Dioscorea L. (1753), yam, in the family Dioscoreaceae, contains around 850 species, mainly in the tropics.

Description Usually twining perennials to 5m with a tuberous rootstock. Leaves opposite or alternate, sometimes lobed, often with bulbils in the axils. Flowers small, unisexual, green, white, or purplish, in a short, often pendulous spikes, branching in male plants. Perianth segments 6. Stamens 6. Ovary inferior, of 3 carpels, with 2 ovules in each; styles 3, the female flowers often with staminodes. Pollination is by insects. The fruit is a 3-winged capsule, seeds sometimes winged.

Key Recognition Features Climbers with small, green, 6-petalled, unisexual flowers and 3-winged capsules.

Ecology and Geography In woods and scrub. Temperate species are found in Europe (with 1 species, *D. balcanica* Kosanin, in Kosovo and Albania), eastwards to Japan (around 10 species), with 1 species, *D. villosa* L., in eastern North America.

Comment The yams grown in tropical areas are the large, starchy tubers of species such as *D. batatas* Decne, *D. trifida* L. fil., and *D. bulbifera* L.. Other species are grown for the production of hormones for contraceptives and other medicinal uses.

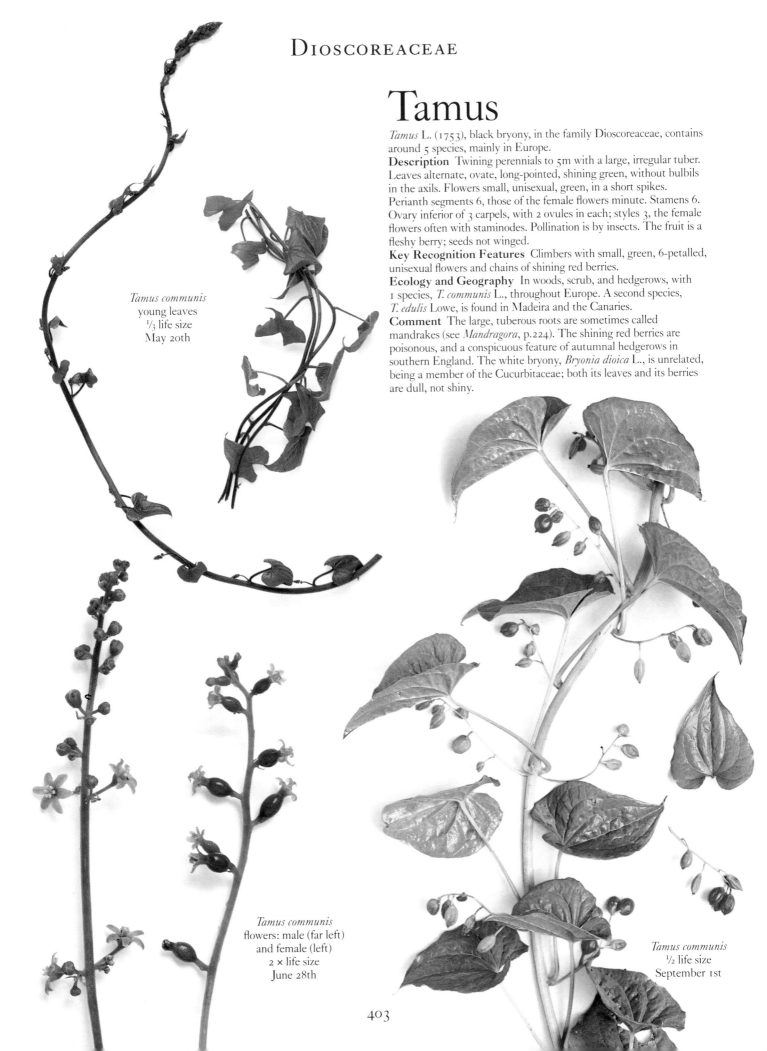

Tamus

Tamus L. (1753), black bryony, in the family Dioscoreaceae, contains around 5 species, mainly in Europe.

Description Twining perennials to 5m with a large, irregular tuber. Leaves alternate, ovate, long-pointed, shining green, without bulbils in the axils. Flowers small, unisexual, green, in a short spikes. Perianth segments 6, those of the female flowers minute. Stamens 6. Ovary inferior of 3 carpels, with 2 ovules in each; styles 3, the female flowers often with staminodes. Pollination is by insects. The fruit is a fleshy berry; seeds not winged.

Key Recognition Features Climbers with small, green, 6-petalled, unisexual flowers and chains of shining red berries.

Ecology and Geography In woods, scrub, and hedgerows, with 1 species, *T. communis* L., throughout Europe. A second species, *T. edulis* Lowe, is found in Madeira and the Canaries.

Comment The large, tuberous roots are sometimes called mandrakes (see *Mandragora*, p.224). The shining red berries are poisonous, and a conspicuous feature of autumnal hedgerows in southern England. The white bryony, *Bryonia dioica* L., is unrelated, being a member of the Cucurbitaceae; both its leaves and its berries are dull, not shiny.

Tamus communis
young leaves
⅓ life size
May 20th

Tamus communis
flowers: male (far left)
and female (left)
2 × life size
June 28th

Tamus communis
½ life size
September 1st

403

Veratrum

Veratrum L. (1753), in the family Melanthiaceae, contains around 20 species, mainly in Asia.

Description Perennials to 2m, with tufted rhizomes. Leaves pleated, mostly basal, deciduous. Flowers on an upright, often branching inflorescence, bisexual or unisexual, bisexual flowers mostly at the base of the inflorescence, male only towards the top, white, green, or purplish-black. Perianth segments 6, all similar, sometimes fringed. Stamens 6. Ovary superior, with 3 carpels, each with several ovules; styles usually 3. Pollination is by insects, often flies or wasps, attracted by the smell of rotten fruit of some species. The fruit is surrounded by the persistent perianth, of 3 almost separate cells, with several narrowly winged seeds.

Key Recognition Features The pleated leaves around an upright stem with numerous small flowers.

Ecology and Geography In mountain meadows and open woods in North America, Europe, and temperate Asia, with a few in the Himalayas and northeastern Asia.

Comment A few species are grown as ornamentals, mainly for their handsome leaves. The whole plant is very poisonous, and sheep that have fed on the plants are said to give birth to lambs with 1 eye in the middle of the forehead, a phenomenon that gave rise to the legend of Polyphemus, the Cyclops in the *Odyssey*. The family Melanthiaceae is a subdivision of the greater Liliaceae, and contains *Veratrum* and *Zigadenus* and several other rather similar genera from America including *Melanthium virginicum* L. and the very tall *Stenanthium robustum* S. Wats.. Most Melanthiaceae have pleated or grassy leaves and numerous small, starry, green, white, or purplish flowers.

Veratrum album
1⅔ × life size, July 28th

Veratrum album (left) and
Veratrum nigrum (right)
½ life size, July 28th

Veratrum viride
flower parts (left)
and fruit (right)
1½ × life size
July 14th

Veratrum nigrum
flowers (above)
1¾ × life size
July 28th

Veratrum nigrum
capsules and seeds
just over life size
December 1st

Veratrum viride
½ life size, July 14th

Narthecium

Narthecium Huds. (1762), bog asphodel, in the family Melanthiaceae, contains around 7 species in northern temperate regions.

Description Perennials to 25cm, with tufted rhizomes. Leaves narrow, flat, upright, mostly basal, evergreen. Flowers on an upright inflorescence, yellow to orange. Perianth segments 6, all similar, narrow and pointed. Stamens 6, with white, woolly filaments. Ovary superior, with 3 carpels, each with several ovules; style 1, with 3 short branches. Pollination is by raindrops. The fruit is a reddish, 3-celled, slender, pointed capsule, surrounded by the persistent perianth, with several very narrow seeds.

Key Recognition Features The narrow, flat leaves and the starry flowers with white, woolly filaments.

Ecology and Geography In acid bogs and on wet rocks, with 2 species in North America, 3 in Europe, others in temperate Asia.

Comment *Narthecium ossifragum* (L.) with its bright yellow flowers and red fruit in late summer is familiar to hill walkers in northern and western Europe. DNA studies suggest that its relationships are with *Dioscorea* and *Tamus* (see pp.402–403), and the tropical *Tacca* Forster & Forster, rather than the superficially similar Melanthiaceae.

Zigadenus

Zigadenus Michx. (1803), in the family Melanthiaceae, contains around 18 species, mainly in north America.

Description Perennials to 90cm, with bulbs. Leaves narrow, flat, upright, mostly basal. Flowers on an upright inflorescence with narrow bracts, usually bisexual, greenish- or yellowish-white. Perianth segments 6, all similar, short, rounded, forming a starry flower. Stamens 6. Ovary superior or semi-inferior, with 3 carpels, each with several ovules; styles 3. Pollination is by insects. The fruit is a 3-lobed capsule with many angular seeds.

Key Recognition Features The narrow, flat leaves and starry, greenish-white flowers with narrow bracts.

Ecology and Geography In moist, grassy places and open woods, with 7 species in California, others across North America, 1 in eastern Europe, and 1 in northern Asia.

Comment Several species are poisonous to sheep and cattle, and the bulbs of *Z. venenosus* Wats., the death camash, should not be mistaken for the edible *Camassia* (see p.491).

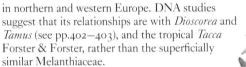

Narthecium ossifragum flowers, 2⅓ × life size August 1st

Narthecium ossifragum ½ life size, August 1st

Zigadenus fremontii ⅔ life size, April 28th

Ypsilandra

Ypsilandra Franch. (1888), in the family Melanthiaceae, contains perhaps 2 species in the Himalayas and western China.

Description Perennials to 20cm, with tufted rhizomes. Leaves narrowly lanceolate, in a rosette, spreading, evergreen, and with short leaves sheathing the stem. Flowers many, on an arching inflorescence, white or pale blue, becoming pinkish-brown. Perianth segments 6, all similar, narrow and blunt. Stamens 6, with filaments about equalling the perianth. Ovary superior, with 3 carpels, each with several ovules; style 1, with a capitate stigma or 3 recurved lobes. Pollination is by insects. The fruit is a 3-celled, almost winged capsule, surrounded by the persistent perianth, and with numerous seeds with thread-like tails on each end.

Key Recognition Features The rosette of narrowly lanceolate leaves and the white or pale blue, sweetly or unpleasantly scented flowers with long stamens.

Ecology and Geography In woods and on wet cliffs in western Sichuan, Yunnan, and westwards to Bhutan.

Comment *Ypsilandra thibetica* Franch. is sometimes cultivated, and is valuable for its early flowering. The genera *Ypsilandra* Franch., *Helonias* L., and *Heloniopsis* Gray are often combined under *Helonias*. *Heloniopsis* is found mostly in Japan, Taiwan, and northeastern Siberia; the species are vegetatively similar to *Ypsilandra*, but have pink or green flowers and fewer flowers in the inflorescence, which is not covered with leaves.

Helonias

Helonias L. (1753), in the family Melanthiaceae, contains 1 species, *H. bullata* L. in eastern North America.

Description Perennials to 30cm, with stout, slightly swollen rootstock. Leaves narrowly oblanceolate, in a rosette, spreading, evergreen, and with few reduced leaves on the stem. Flowers many, in a short, dense spike, pinkish-purple. Perianth segments 6, all similar, blunt. Stamens 6, with filaments longer than the perianth. Ovary superior, with 3 carpels, each with several ovules; styles 3, short and spreading. Pollination is by insects. The fruit is a 3-celled, lobed capsule, surrounded by the persistent perianth, with seeds with a thread-like appendage at each end.

Key Recognition Features The rosette of oblanceolate leaves and the short spike of numerous small, pinkish-purple flowers.

Ecology and Geography In bogs in eastern North America, from New Jersey to North Carolina.

Comment *Helonias* is often cultivated as an ornamental. The genera *Ypsilandra* and *Heloniopsis* Gray are often also placed within it.

Ypsilandra thibetica
fruits and seeds
1⅓ × life size, June 25th

Ypsilandra thibetica
in fruit, ¾ life size
June 25th

Helonias bullata
1¼ × life size, May 3rd

Helonias bullata, flower parts
2½ × life size, May 3rd

MELANTHIACEAE

Ypsilandra thibetica
late flower, 2 × life size
March 20th

Ypsilandra thibetica
late flower spike
life size, March 20th

Ypsilandra thibetica
½ life size, March 6th

Ypsilandra thibetica
just under life size
March 6th

Ypsilandra thibetica, flower parts
2 × life size, March 6th

Paris

Paris L. (1753), herb paris, in the family Melanthiaceae, contains around 20 species, mainly in Europe.

Description Perennials to 50cm, with tuberous creeping rhizomes. Leaves in whorls of 3 or more. Flowers green, solitary. Outer perianth segments 4–6, green. Inner perianth segments 4–6, usually yellowish, very narrow. Stamens 4–10, with short filaments. Ovary superior, with 4 carpels, each with several ovules; styles usually 4. Pollination is by insects, especially flies. The fruit is a fleshy, often purplish capsule, opening to show the seeds, which sometimes have a red, juicy covering.

Key Recognition Features Simple stems with 4 or more leaves in a whorl, and flowers with long, narrow inner segments.

Ecology and Geography In woods and scrub, with 1 species, *P. quadrifolia* L., throughout Europe, and the others mainly in the Himalayas and China.

Comment Some species are cultivated as curiosities. Many of the Himalayan ones are sometimes placed in the genus *Daiswa* Raf., mainly distinguished by the scarlet, fleshy coating on their seeds. The Japanese *P. japonica* (Franch. & Sav.) Franch. is unusual in having 8–10 often broad, white outer perianth segments, the inner ones being minute or absent.

Paris lancifolia
flower, 1⅔ × life size
May 28th

Paris lancifolia
½ life size, May 28th

Trillium

Trillium L. (1753), wake robin, in the family Melanthiaceae, contains around 30 species, mainly in North America.

Description Perennials to 30cm with tuberous, shortly creeping rhizomes. Leaves in whorls of 3, sometimes stalked. Flowers white, yellow, pink, purple, or green, solitary. Outer perianth segments 3, green sometimes suffused with purple. Inner perianth segments 3. Stamens 6, with short filaments. Ovary superior, with 3 carpels, each with several ovules; styles usually 3. Pollination is by insects. The fruit is a fleshy, often purplish capsule, with seeds with a white aril.

Key Recognition Features Simple stems with 3 leaves in a whorl, and flowers with broad, coloured inner perianth segments.

Ecology and Geography In woods and scrub. Most species in North America, with a few in northeastern Asia and the Himalayas.

Comment Many species are cultivated as ornamentals in woodland gardens, where they are valuable for their decorative leaves and unusual, long-lasting flowers. DNA studies suggest that *Trillium* and *Paris*, formerly separated in Trilliaceae, should be included within Melanthiaceae.

Trillium luteum
⅔ life size
April 22nd

Melanthiaceae

Trillium cernuum
flower (below)
¾ life size, May 12th

Trillium erectum
flower, ¾ life size
May 12th

Trillium cernuum (left)
and *Trillium erectum*
(right) ½ life size
May 12th

Trillium chloropetalum var. *giganteum*
flower parts, ⅔ life size, April 15th

Trillium chloropetalum var.
giganteum, ½ life size, April 15th

Trillium chloropetalum var.
giganteum, seeds showing
fleshy aril, 2¼ × life size
August 10th

Trillium chloropetalum var.
giganteum, seed capsule
½ life size, August 10th

Disporum

Disporum Salisb. (1812), in the family Uvulariaceae, contains around 15 species, mainly in western China.

Description Perennials to 2m, with creeping rhizomes. Leaves narrowly lanceolate to ovate, alternate on the deciduous stems. Flowers usually few, on a nodding and branching inflorescence, white, green, purple, or yellow. Perianth segments 6, all similar, narrow and blunt. Stamens 6, with filaments about equalling the perianth. Ovary superior, with 3 carpels, each with 2 ovules; styles 3, slender and curved. Pollination is by insects. The fruit is a 3-celled, black or blue berry with globose seeds.

Key Recognition Features The alternate leaves on a branching stem, and the nodding, narrow flowers, sweetly scented in *D. megalanthum* F.T. Wang & T. Tang.

Ecology and Geography In moist woods and hedges in the Himalayas, China, and Japan.

Comment Several species are cultivated in woodland gardens. The affinities of *Disporum* and *Uvularia* are still uncertain. Formerly they were often put with the Convallariaceae (see pp.498–503), because of similarities with *Polygonatum* (see pp.500–501), but they have characters in common with the Colchicaceae (see p.412–13), as well as with both *Streptopus* Michx. and *Prosartes* (see p.421) in the Liliaceae; some species formerly included in *Disporum* are now put in *Prosartes*, which is a close relative of *Tricyrtis* (see p.426–27).

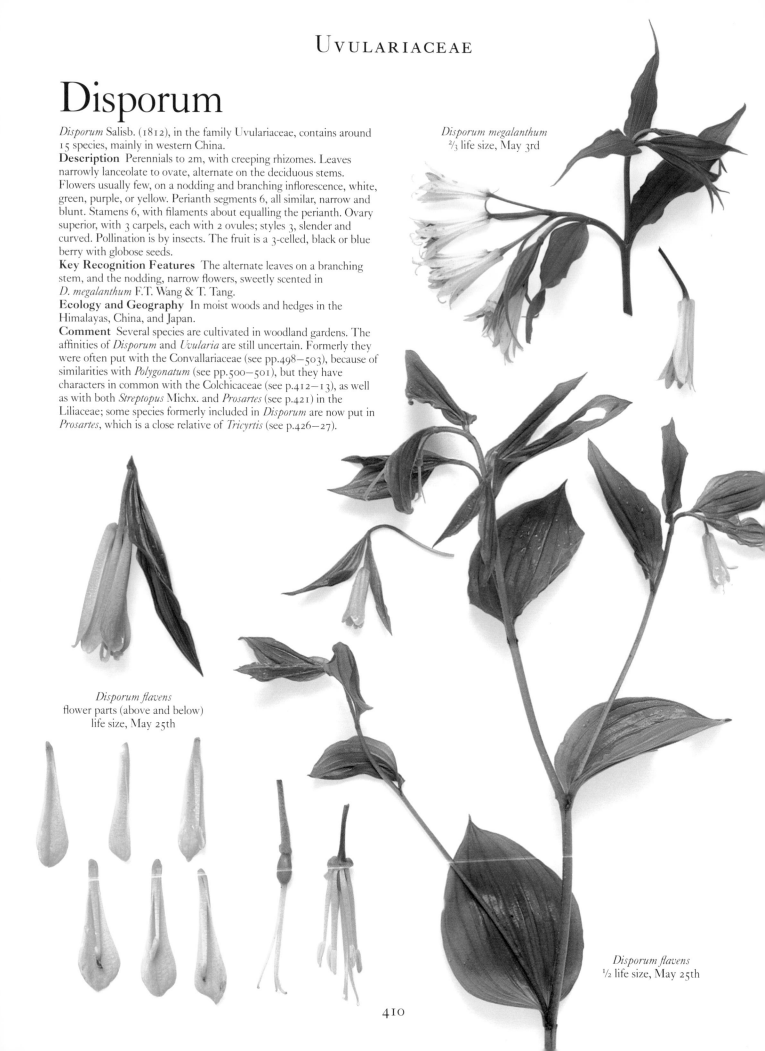

Disporum megalanthum
²/₃ life size, May 3rd

Disporum flavens
flower parts (above and below)
life size, May 25th

Disporum flavens
¹/₂ life size, May 25th

Uvularia

Uvularia Salisb. (1812), in the family Uvulariaceae, contains 5 species in eastern North America.

Description Perennials to 40cm, with shortly creeping rhizomes. Leaves narrowly lanceolate to ovate, alternate and often surrounding the stems. Flowers usually few, on a nodding and branching inflorescence, yellow or whitish. Perianth segments 6, all similar, narrow and often twisted. Stamens 6, with filaments shorter than the anthers. Pollination is by insects. Ovary superior, with 3 carpels, each with 1−3 ovules; styles 3, joined in the lower part, slender and curved. The fruit is a 3-celled, often winged capsule with globose seeds.

Key Recognition Features The alternate, often perfoliate leaves on a branching stem, and the hanging, narrow flowers with twisted perianth segments.

Ecology and Geography In moist woods in eastern North America from Quebec to Florida, westwards to Minnesota and Kansas.

Comment Several species are cultivated in woodland gardens for their unusual hanging flowers.

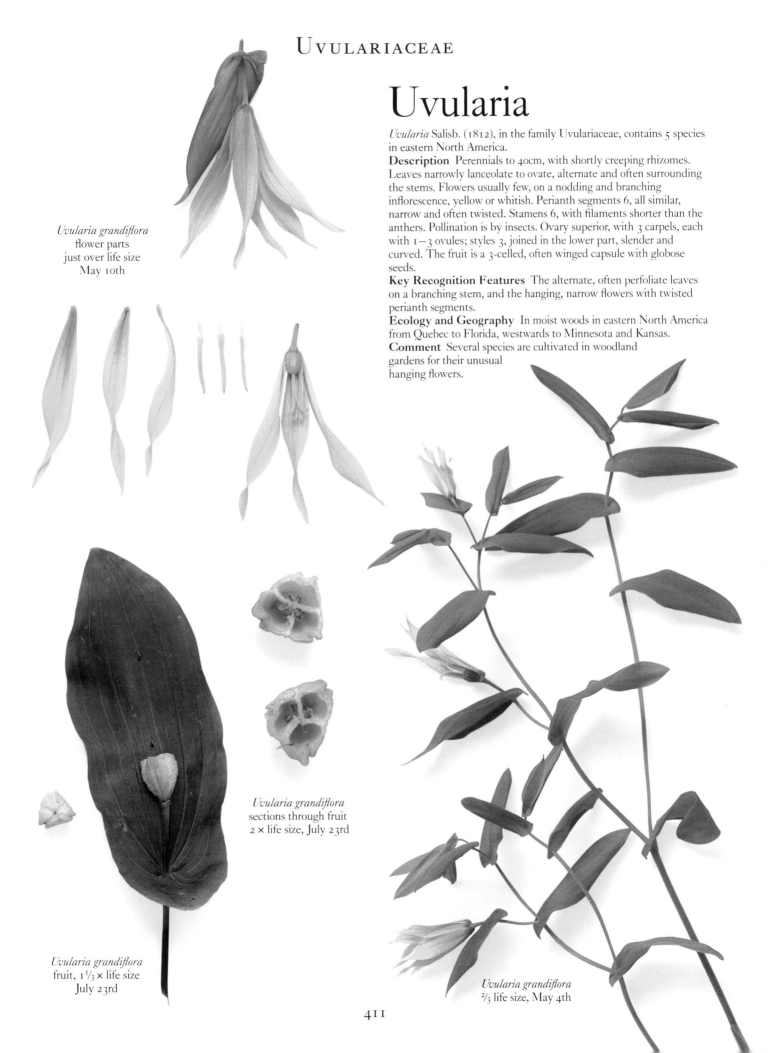

Uvularia grandiflora
flower parts
just over life size
May 10th

Uvularia grandiflora
sections through fruit
2 × life size, July 23rd

Uvularia grandiflora
fruit, 1 1/3 × life size
July 23rd

Uvularia grandiflora
2/3 life size, May 4th

Colchicum

Colchicum L. (1753), in the family Colchicaceae, contains around 50 species, mainly in the eastern Mediterranean area.

Description Perennials with leaves to 30cm, flowering stems to 15cm, with corms, which are often stoloniferous. Leaves all basal, sometimes pleated. Flowers pink, purplish, white, or rarely yellow, sometimes tessellated, produced from a short underground stem. Perianth segments all similar. Stamens 6, with long filaments; anthers versatile. Pollination is by insects. Ovary subterranean, superior, with 3 carpels, each with several ovules; styles 3, long and slender, arising from the ovary. The fruit is a papery, often inflated capsule, surrounded by the leaves at the soil surface; seeds round, pale brown.

Key Recognition Features The *Crocus*-like flowers (see pp.448—49), usually before the leaves in autumn, or with the leaves in spring.

Ecology and Geography In meadows, on rocky hillsides, and in scrub and open woods, from southwestern England to central Asia and the Himalayas in western China, and in North Africa.

Comment Many species are cultivated as ornamentals. The leaves are very poisonous and avoided by cattle, so the plants may occur in large numbers where grazing is heavy. The yellow-flowered *C. luteum* L. grows in central Asia, often with the purple-and-white-flowered *Crocus alatavicus* Regel & Semenow. In other areas the purple-and-white-flowered *Colchicum kesselringii* Regel grows with the yellow-flowered *Crocus korolkovii* Regel & Maw. Only occasionally do similar-coloured *Crocus* and *Colchicum* flower together. *Crocus* is easily recognised by its 3 stamens. The underground ovary, which only comes up above ground as the capsules ripen, is found in several genera in different families in the Mediterranean area, South Africa, and the Andes. *Colchicum* plants contain the alkaloid colchicine, which can be used medicinally for gout, in chromosome studies as a treatment to halt cell division, and in plant breeding to obtain artificial polyploids. *Merendera* Ramond, with about 10 species in Europe, western Asia and southwards to Ethiopia, is close to *Colchicum*, and sometimes placed in it, but has the perianth segments not joined below and falling apart when the flower is fully open. *Bulbocodium* L. with 2 species in Europe and western Asia, is very similar to *Merendera*, but has a single style that is 3-fid only at the apex. Like *Colchicum* it grows especially well in areas of heavy grazing. Other genera placed in the family Colchicaceae are mainly African, and include *Androcymbium* Willd. with white flowers among the leaves, *Wurmbea* Thunb. with a spike of starry flowers, and the tropical climbers *Gloriosa* L., *Littonia* Hook., and *Sandersonia* Hook. *Gloriosa*, the familiar greenhouse "glory-lily" plant, climbs by its coiling leaf tips and also contains colchicine and other poisons.

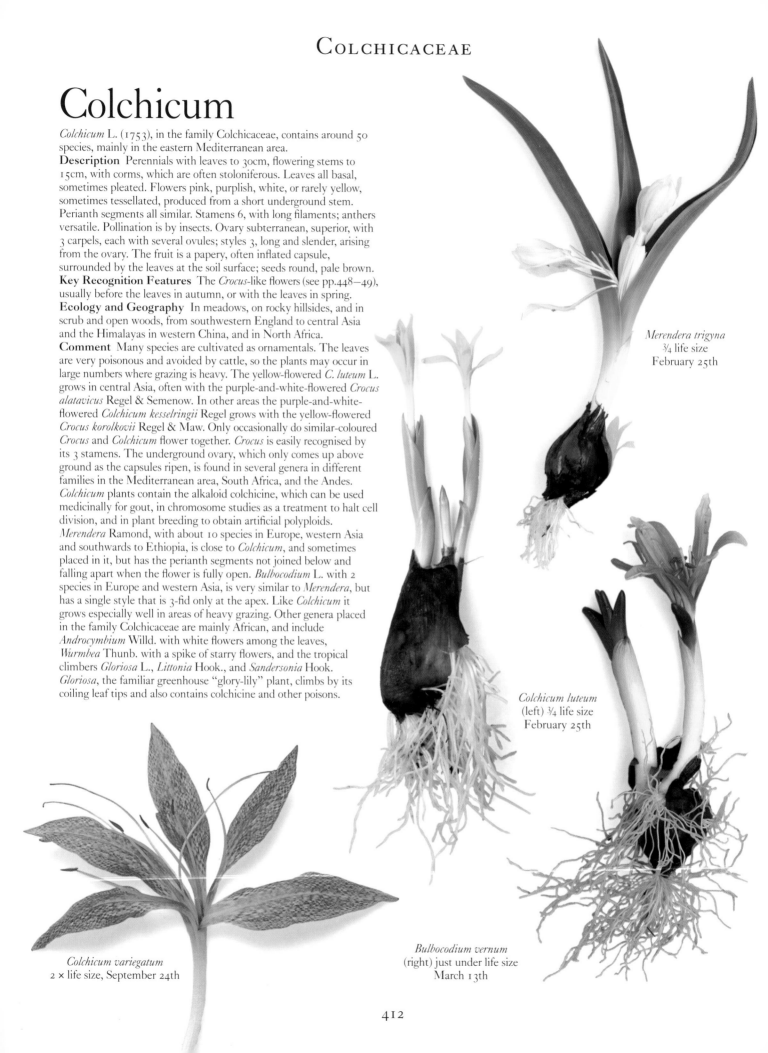

Merendera trigyna
¾ life size
February 25th

Colchicum luteum
(left) ¾ life size
February 25th

Colchicum variegatum
2 × life size, September 24th

Bulbocodium vernum
(right) just under life size
March 13th

Colchicaceae

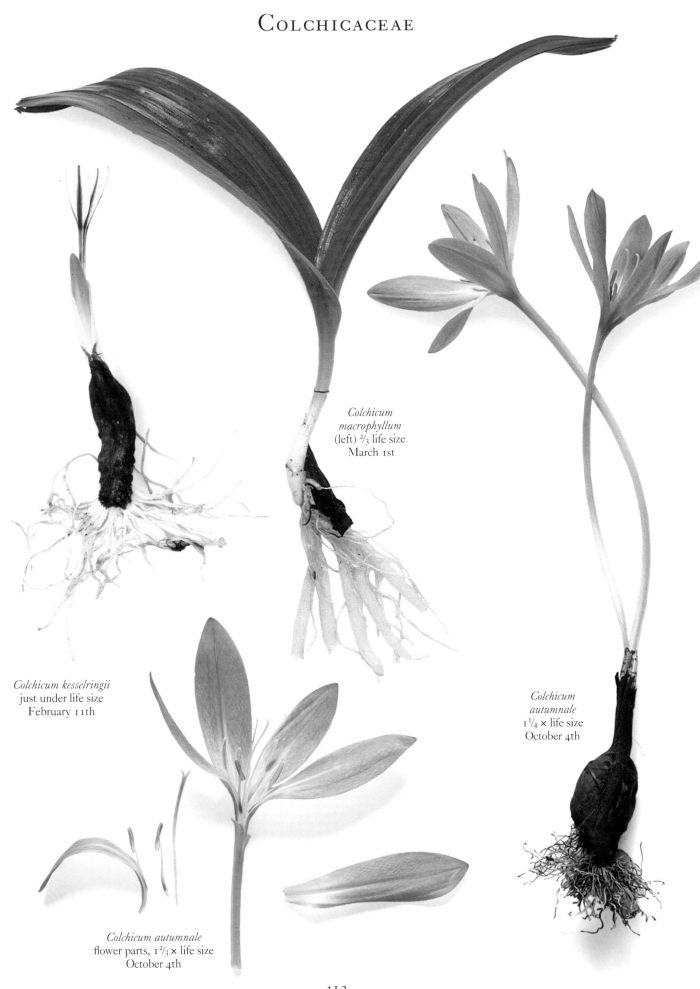

Colchicum
macrophyllum
(left) ⅔ life size
March 1st

Colchicum kesselringii
just under life size
February 11th

Colchicum
autumnale
1¼ × life size
October 4th

Colchicum autumnale
flower parts, 1⅔ × life size
October 4th

Alstroemeria

Alstroemeria L. (1753), in the family Alstroemeriaceae, contains around 50 species in South America.

Description Perennials to 1m, with fleshy roots, often with tubers or creeping rhizomes. Leaves ovate to narrowly lanceolate, scattered up the stem, their stalks twisted through 180°. Flowers on a branching inflorescence, red, yellow, orange, white, or pale blue. Perianth segments 6, unequal, the outer 3 usually wider than the inner, the uppermost pair of which are often recurved and beautifully marked. Stamens 6, sometimes longer than the perianth, the filaments usually curved. Ovary inferior, with 3 carpels, each with several ovules; style 1, with 3 recurved branches. Pollination is by insects or hummingbirds. The fruit is a conic, 3-celled capsule with numerous round seeds.

Key Recognition Features The scattered, twisted stem leaves and the flowers with the upper perianth segments marked.

Ecology and Geography On screes and rocky hills from Peru to southern Chile, mainly in the Andes.

Comment Many are cultivated, and others have been bred especially for the cut-flower trade. These large-flowered cultivars are usually triploid and sterile. Most will grow happily outdoors in mild areas, if the roots are protected from freezing. The family Alstroemeriaceae contains 5 genera, all in Central and South America, of which only *Alstroemeria* and *Bomarea* are cultivated; the family seems to be closest to Colchicaceae (see pp.412–13).

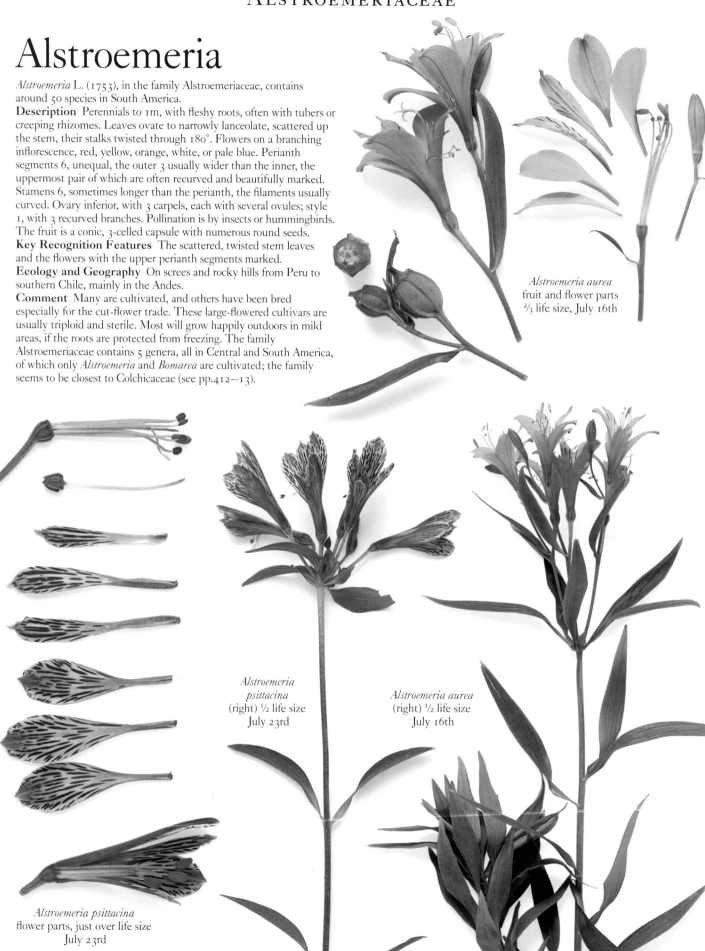

Alstroemeria aurea
fruit and flower parts
²⁄₃ life size, July 16th

*Alstroemeria
psittacina*
(right) ½ life size
July 23rd

Alstroemeria aurea
(right) ½ life size
July 16th

Alstroemeria psittacina
flower parts, just over life size
July 23rd

414

Bomarea species
½ life size, May 8th

Bomarea

Bomarea Mirbel. (1804), in the family Alstroemeriaceae, contains around 120 species from Mexico to South America.

Description Perennials to 4m, with fleshy roots, often with tubers or creeping rhizomes. Stems often twining to several metres. Leaves ovate to lanceolate, scattered up the stem, the stalks twisted through 180°. Flowers in an umbel or on a branching inflorescence, red, yellow, orange, or green, often green and red. Perianth segments 6, unequal, the outer 3 usually shorter and narrower than the inner 3, which are often beautifully marked, and modified into a nectar-filled tube at the base. Stamens 6, sometimes longer than the perianth, the filaments usually slightly curved to 1 side. Ovary inferior, with 3 carpels, each with several ovules; style 1, with 3 recurved branches. Pollination is usually by hummingbirds. The fruit is a short, conic 3-celled capsule with numerous round seeds, sometimes dry, but often covered with a sticky, red seed coat.

Key Recognition Features The scattered, twisted stem leaves and the flowers with the upper perianth segments marked.

Ecology and Geography In forests, scrambling over hedges, and on rock ledges, from Mexico to Chile and Argentina, but most species in Colombia.

Comment Several species are cultivated. They grow well outdoors in frost-free areas and some species will flower outdoors provided that the roots do not freeze.

Bomarea multiflora
½ life size, June 2nd

Bomarea multiflora
flower parts, 1⅓ × life size
June 2nd

415

Lilium

Lilium L. (1753), lily, in the family Liliaceae, contains around 100 species in Europe, Asia, and North America.

Description Perennials to 2.5m, with scaly bulbs, often with stolons or creeping rhizomes. Stems often producing roots above the bulb. Leaves ovate to narrowly lanceolate or linear, in whorls or scattered up the stem. Flowers solitary or up to 50 on a simple or branching inflorescence, red, yellow, orange, white, green, or purplish. Perianth segments 6, more or less equal, the inner 3 usually wider than the outer. Stamens 6, sometimes longer than the perianth, the filaments often curved, with versatile anthers. Ovary superior, with 3 carpels, each with many ovules; style 1, stigma knob-like with 3 lobes. Pollination is by insects, often hawkmoths, or by hummingbirds. The fruit is a cylindrical, 3-celled capsule with numerous flat seeds, often with a narrow wing.

Key Recognition Features The large flowers with 6 stamens and 6 perianth segments, which may be fully recurved (turk's cap), spreading and nodding (trumpet), flat and upright-facing, or occasionally bell-shaped; combinations of these shapes are rare, except in hybrids.

Ecology and Geography On screes and rocky hills, in wet or dry woods and scrub, and in mountain meadows and bogs; from western Europe to Siberia, eastern Asia southwards to the Philippines and southern India, and throughout North America north of Mexico.

Comment Many species are cultivated, and others have been bred especially for cut flowers. The Madonna lily, *L. candidum* L. has been cultivated mainly for its scent since 1500 BC, and in China and Japan some species are grown as vegetables. The family Liliaceae has been the subject of much study and several different treatments. In its widest sense, the family contains around 300 genera and 5000 species, all with 6 stamens and a superior ovary. Aided by DNA data, however, Fay and Chase, writing in the *Botanical Magazine*, restrict Liliaceae to only 16 genera: those shown on pp.416–29, together with *Notholirion* Wall. ex Boiss., *Streptopus* Rich., *Clintonia* Raf., *Medeola* L., and *Lloydia* Salisb. ex Rchb..

Nomocharis

Nomocharis Franch. (1889), in the family Liliaceae, contains around 7 species, mainly in western China.

Description Perennials to 1m, with scaly bulbs. Leaves ovate to narrowly lanceolate, in whorls or scattered up the stem. Flowers solitary or up to 20 on a simple or branching inflorescence, usually pink, red, or white, often beautifully spotted, usually opening flat. Perianth segments 6, more or less equal, the inner 3 usually wider than the outer, and often fringed, with a fan-like nectary. Stamens 6, shorter than the perianth, the filaments usually straight, swollen. Ovary superior, with 3 carpels, each with many ovules; style 1, stigma knob-like with 3 lobes. Pollination is by insects. The fruit is a cylindrical, 3-celled capsule with numerous flat seeds, with a narrow wing.

Key Recognition Features Very close to *Lilium* but with flat flowers with the segments usually spotted, and with short, swollen filaments.

Ecology and Geography On rock ledges and in scrub at high altitudes in western China, northern Burma and northern Assam, with most species in western Yunnan.

Comment Most of the species are cultivated by specialists, but they are not easy to grow well, requiring cold, dry winters and cool, moist summers, the same conditions as are preferred by *Meconopsis* (see p.67). Gardeners in Scotland and the northwestern United States have grown them most successfully.

Lilium monadelphum
½ life size, July 3rd

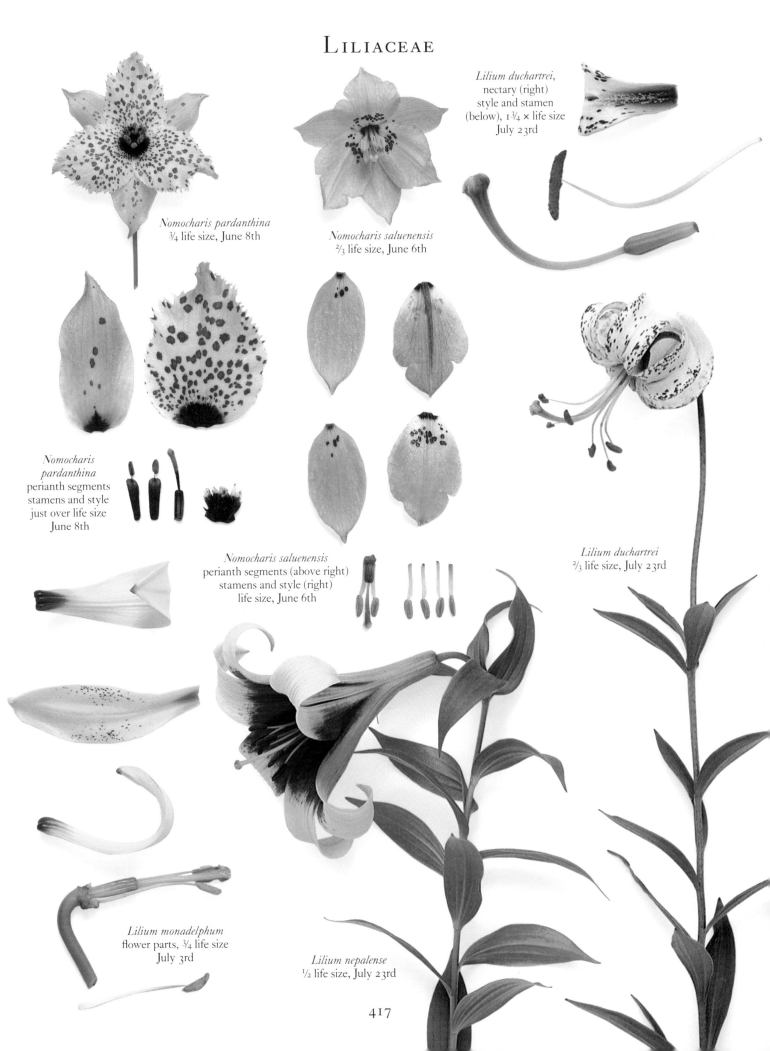

LILIACEAE

Nomocharis pardanthina
¾ life size, June 8th

Nomocharis saluenensis
⅔ life size, June 6th

Lilium duchartrei,
nectary (right)
style and stamen
(below), 1¾ × life size
July 23rd

Nomocharis pardanthina
perianth segments
stamens and style
just over life size
June 8th

Nomocharis saluenensis
perianth segments (above right)
stamens and style (right)
life size, June 6th

Lilium duchartrei
⅔ life size, July 23rd

Lilium monadelphum
flower parts, ¾ life size
July 3rd

Lilium nepalense
½ life size, July 23rd

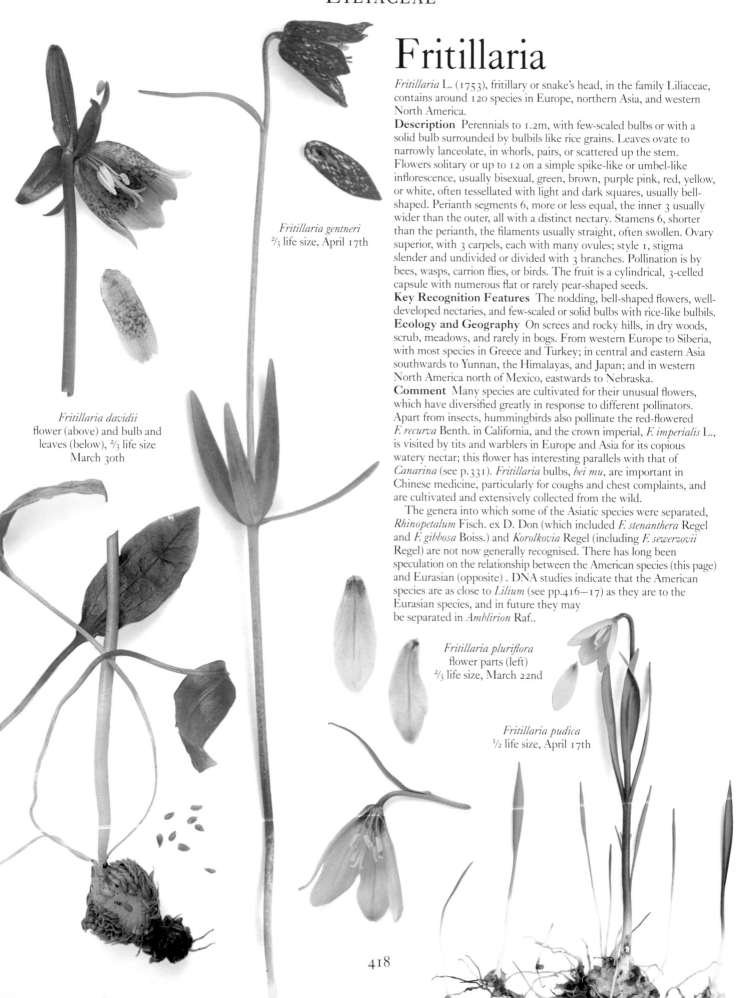

Fritillaria

Fritillaria L. (1753), fritillary or snake's head, in the family Liliaceae, contains around 120 species in Europe, northern Asia, and western North America.

Description Perennials to 1.2m, with few-scaled bulbs or with a solid bulb surrounded by bulbils like rice grains. Leaves ovate to narrowly lanceolate, in whorls, pairs, or scattered up the stem. Flowers solitary or up to 12 on a simple spike-like or umbel-like inflorescence, usually bisexual, green, brown, purple pink, red, yellow, or white, often tessellated with light and dark squares, usually bell-shaped. Perianth segments 6, more or less equal, the inner 3 usually wider than the outer, all with a distinct nectary. Stamens 6, shorter than the perianth, the filaments usually straight, often swollen. Ovary superior, with 3 carpels, each with many ovules; style 1, stigma slender and undivided or divided with 3 branches. Pollination is by bees, wasps, carrion flies, or birds. The fruit is a cylindrical, 3-celled capsule with numerous flat or rarely pear-shaped seeds.

Key Recognition Features The nodding, bell-shaped flowers, well-developed nectaries, and few-scaled or solid bulbs with rice-like bulbils.

Ecology and Geography On screes and rocky hills, in dry woods, scrub, meadows, and rarely in bogs. From western Europe to Siberia, with most species in Greece and Turkey; in central and eastern Asia southwards to Yunnan, the Himalayas, and Japan; and in western North America north of Mexico, eastwards to Nebraska.

Comment Many species are cultivated for their unusual flowers, which have diversified greatly in response to different pollinators. Apart from insects, hummingbirds also pollinate the red-flowered *F. recurva* Benth. in California, and the crown imperial, *F. imperialis* L., is visited by tits and warblers in Europe and Asia for its copious watery nectar; this flower has interesting parallels with that of *Canarina* (see p.331). *Fritillaria* bulbs, *bei mu*, are important in Chinese medicine, particularly for coughs and chest complaints, and are cultivated and extensively collected from the wild.

The genera into which some of the Asiatic species were separated, *Rhinopetalum* Fisch. ex D. Don (which included *F. stenanthera* Regel and *F. gibbosa* Boiss.) and *Korolkovia* Regel (including *F. sewerzovii* Regel) are not now generally recognised. There has long been speculation on the relationship between the American species (this page) and Eurasian (opposite) . DNA studies indicate that the American species are as close to *Lilium* (see pp.416–17) as they are to the Eurasian species, and in future they may be separated in *Amblirion* Raf..

Fritillaria gentneri
²⁄₃ life size, April 17th

Fritillaria davidii
flower (above) and bulb and leaves (below), ²⁄₃ life size
March 30th

Fritillaria pluriflora
flower parts (left)
²⁄₃ life size, March 22nd

Fritillaria pudica
¹⁄₂ life size, April 17th

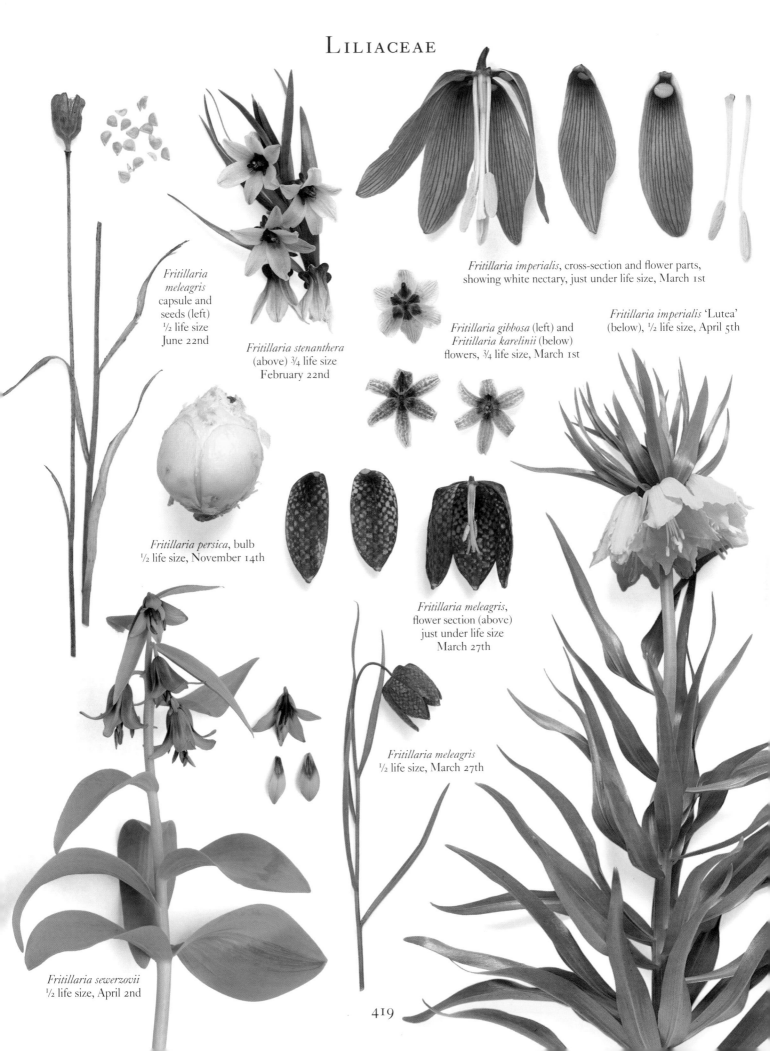

LILIACEAE

Fritillaria meleagris capsule and seeds (left) ½ life size June 22nd

Fritillaria stenanthera (above) ¾ life size February 22nd

Fritillaria imperialis, cross-section and flower parts, showing white nectary, just under life size, March 1st

Fritillaria gibbosa (left) and *Fritillaria karelinii* (below) flowers, ¾ life size, March 1st

Fritillaria imperialis 'Lutea' (below), ½ life size, April 5th

Fritillaria persica, bulb ½ life size, November 14th

Fritillaria meleagris, flower section (above) just under life size March 27th

Fritillaria meleagris ½ life size, March 27th

Fritillaria sewerzovii ½ life size, April 2nd

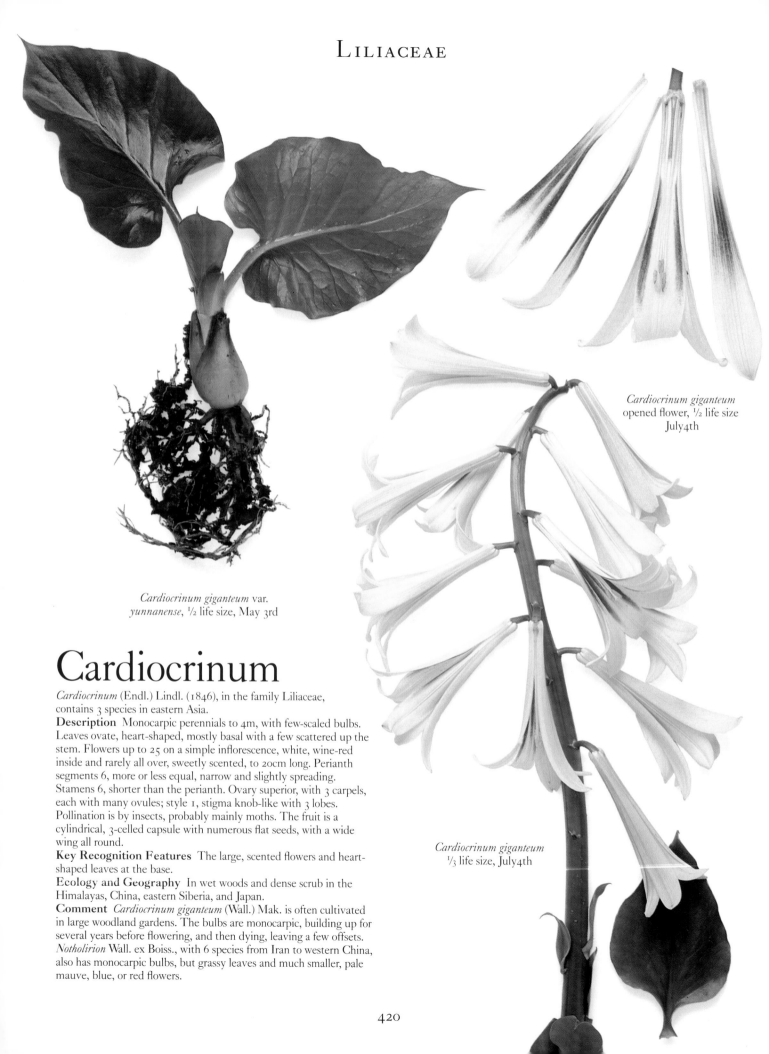

Cardiocrinum giganteum
opened flower, ¹/₂ life size
July 4th

Cardiocrinum giganteum var.
yunnanense, ¹/₂ life size, May 3rd

Cardiocrinum

Cardiocrinum (Endl.) Lindl. (1846), in the family Liliaceae,
contains 3 species in eastern Asia.

Description Monocarpic perennials to 4m, with few-scaled bulbs.
Leaves ovate, heart-shaped, mostly basal with a few scattered up the
stem. Flowers up to 25 on a simple inflorescence, white, wine-red
inside and rarely all over, sweetly scented, to 20cm long. Perianth
segments 6, more or less equal, narrow and slightly spreading.
Stamens 6, shorter than the perianth. Ovary superior, with 3 carpels,
each with many ovules; style 1, stigma knob-like with 3 lobes.
Pollination is by insects, probably mainly moths. The fruit is a
cylindrical, 3-celled capsule with numerous flat seeds, with a wide
wing all round.

Key Recognition Features The large, scented flowers and heart-
shaped leaves at the base.

Ecology and Geography In wet woods and dense scrub in the
Himalayas, China, eastern Siberia, and Japan.

Comment *Cardiocrinum giganteum* (Wall.) Mak. is often cultivated
in large woodland gardens. The bulbs are monocarpic, building up for
several years before flowering, and then dying, leaving a few offsets.
Notholirion Wall. ex Boiss., with 6 species from Iran to western China,
also has monocarpic bulbs, but grassy leaves and much smaller, pale
mauve, blue, or red flowers.

Cardiocrinum giganteum
¹/₃ life size, July 4th

Prosartes

Prosartes D. Don (1832), in the family Liliaceae, contains
2 or 3 species in North America.

Description Perennials to 50cm, with short rhizomes. Leaves
obovate to oblanceolate, alternate. Flowers in pairs or up to 5 in a
cluster, white or greenish-yellow, 2cm long. Perianth segments 6,
more or less equal. Stamens 6. Ovary superior, of 3 carpels, with few
ovules in each; style 1, stigma with 3 lobes. Pollination is by insects.
The fruit is a 3-celled, orange or red berry with few seeds.

Key Recognition Features The alternate, veined leaves and
hanging, cylindrical or swollen flowers.

Ecology and Geography In moist, shady woods. In western North
America from British Columbia to California.

Comment These are modest and attractive plants for the woodland
garden, formerly included in *Disporum* (see p.410). *Prosartes smithii*
(Hook.) Torr. is sometimes cultivated. *Clintonia* Raf., with 4 species in
North America and 1 in eastern Asia, is closely related, but has broad
basal leaves in a rosette and heads of small, starry, white, green, or red
flowers. *Medeola virginica* L., the Indian cucumber-root, from woods
in eastern North America, is related to *Clintonia,* but has whorls of
leaves on the stem and an umbel of small, greenish-yellow flowers
with long styles, as well as a long, white cucumber-like edible root.
Medeola was formerly considered a relative of *Trillium* (see pp.408–409),
while *Clintonia* was considered close to *Convallaria* L., but both are
now placed near *Gagea*. DNA studies show that *Prosartes* is closest to
Streptopus Rich., *Scoliopus* (see p.426), and *Tricyrtis* (see pp.426–27).

Gagea

Gagea Salisb. (1806), yellow star of Bethlehem, in the family
Liliaceae, contains around 50 species in Europe and Asia.

Description Perennials to 15cm, with bulbs sometimes surrounded by
thickened roots, often with a hard, dark tunic. Stems sometimes with
bulbils in the leaf axils. Leaves linear to narrowly lanceolate, basal and
often in pairs on the stem. Flowers solitary or up to 12 on a branched
or umbel-like inflorescence, usually bisexual, yellow or white, becoming
green after flowering, usually star-shaped when open in the sun.
Perianth segments 6, more or less equal, without nectaries. Stamens
6, shorter than the perianth, the filaments usually straight. Ovary
superior, with 3 carpels, each with many ovules; style 1, stigma slender
and undivided or divided with 3 branches. Pollination is by insects.
The fruit is a 3-celled capsule with numerous flat or pear-shaped seeds.

Key Recognition Features The starry, generally yellow flowers on
a small plant with narrow leaves.

Ecology and Geography On rocky hills and in woods, scrub, and
meadows from western Europe and North Africa eastwards to central
Asia and the western Himalayas.

Comment A few species are cultivated for their shining, celandine-
like flowers (*Ranunculus ficaria,* see p.47) in early spring. It is
interesting that the woodland and grassland species have pear-shaped
seeds, while the desert species have flat seeds more easily dispersed
by wind. The genus is named after Sir Thomas Gage (1781–1820),
lichenologist of Hengrave Hall, Suffolk. *Lloydia* Salisb. ex Rchb. is
similar, but has flowers with nectaries at the base, usually white or
pink, though yellow-flowered species are found in the Himalayas;
the name *Lloydia* commemorates Edward Lhuyd (1660–1709),
botanist and keeper of the Ashmolean museum, who discovered
L. serotina (L.) Reichenb., the Snowdon lily.

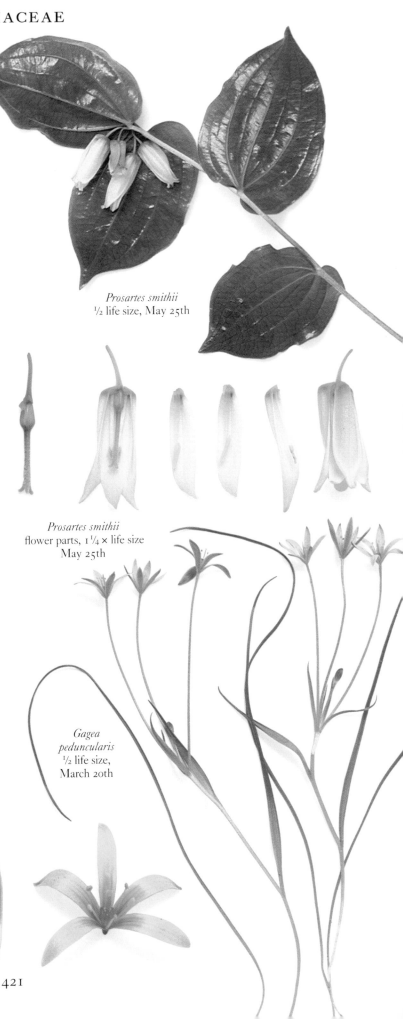

Prosartes smithii
½ life size, May 25th

Prosartes smithii
flower parts, 1¼ × life size
May 25th

Gagea
peduncularis
½ life size,
March 20th

Gagea peduncularis
flower parts, 2 × life size
March 20th

Erythronium

Erythronium L. (1753), dog's tooth violet or adder's tongue, in the family Liliaceae, contains around 26 species, mainly in North America.

Description Perennials to 40cm, with corms with a thin tunic. Leaves ovate to lanceolate, all basal, often mottled with silver or brown. Flowers solitary or up to 5 on a leafless inflorescence, usually bisexual, purple, pink, yellow, or white, sometimes lightly marked near the base inside, usually nodding. Perianth segments 6, more or less equal, rather narrow, often reflexing in warm conditions, usually with inflated appendages and a small nectary at the base. Stamens 6, shorter than the perianth, the filaments usually straight, often swollen. Ovary superior, with 3 carpels, each with many ovules; style 1, stigma slender and undivided or divided with 3 branches. Pollination is by bees. The fruit is a narrowly cylindrical, 3-celled capsule with numerous pear-shaped seeds.

Key Recognition Features The nodding, starry flowers on leafless stems, and usually 2 wide basal leaves.

Ecology and Geography In dry woods and scrub or damp meadows. Most species in western North America, and around 4 in the eastern states; 1 species, *E. dens-canis* L., in Europe, with varieties in northeastern Asia and Japan.

Comment Many species are grown as ornamentals, especially in woodland gardens, as the corms should not become completely dry in summer. The name *dens-canis*, dog's tooth, refers to the pointed corms.

Erythronium californicum
½ life size, April 11th

Erythronium californicum
¾ life size, April 20th

Erythronium tuolumnense
⅔ life size, April 15th

Erythronium californicum
flower parts, life size
April 11th

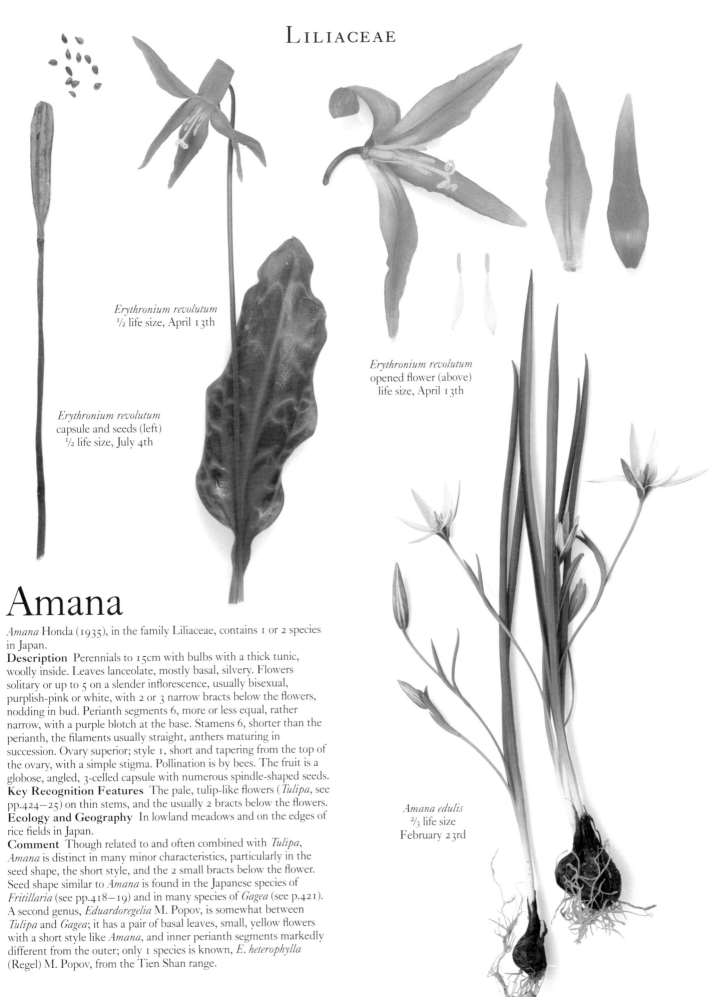

Erythronium revolutum
½ life size, April 13th

Erythronium revolutum
capsule and seeds (left)
½ life size, July 4th

Erythronium revolutum
opened flower (above)
life size, April 13th

Amana

Amana Honda (1935), in the family Liliaceae, contains 1 or 2 species in Japan.

Description Perennials to 15cm with bulbs with a thick tunic, woolly inside. Leaves lanceolate, mostly basal, silvery. Flowers solitary or up to 5 on a slender inflorescence, usually bisexual, purplish-pink or white, with 2 or 3 narrow bracts below the flowers, nodding in bud. Perianth segments 6, more or less equal, rather narrow, with a purple blotch at the base. Stamens 6, shorter than the perianth, the filaments usually straight, anthers maturing in succession. Ovary superior; style 1, short and tapering from the top of the ovary, with a simple stigma. Pollination is by bees. The fruit is a globose, angled, 3-celled capsule with numerous spindle-shaped seeds.

Key Recognition Features The pale, tulip-like flowers (*Tulipa*, see pp.424–25) on thin stems, and the usually 2 bracts below the flowers.

Ecology and Geography In lowland meadows and on the edges of rice fields in Japan.

Comment Though related to and often combined with *Tulipa*, *Amana* is distinct in many minor characteristics, particularly in the seed shape, the short style, and the 2 small bracts below the flower. Seed shape similar to *Amana* is found in the Japanese species of *Fritillaria* (see pp.418–19) and in many species of *Gagea* (see p.421). A second genus, *Eduardoregelia* M. Popov, is somewhat between *Tulipa* and *Gagea*; it has a pair of basal leaves, small, yellow flowers with a short style like *Amana*, and inner perianth segments markedly different from the outer; only 1 species is known, *E. heterophylla* (Regel) M. Popov, from the Tien Shan range.

Amana edulis
⅔ life size
February 23rd

Tulipa

Tulipa L. (1753), tulip, in the family Liliaceae, contains around 100 species in southern Europe and western and central Asia.

Description Perennials to 80cm with bulbs with a thick tunic, woolly inside. Leaves lanceolate, mostly basal, green or greyish. Flowers solitary or up to 7 on a stiff inflorescence, usually bisexual, red, purplish-pink, pink, yellow, or white, often with a different colour at the base, with scattered leaves on the stem. Perianth segments 6, more or less equal, usually pointed. Stamens 6, shorter than the perianth, the filaments usually straight, anthers all together. Ovary superior, with 3 carpels, each with many ovules; style lacking, with the stigma on the tip of the ovary. Pollination is by bees. The fruit is a pointed, angled, 3-celled capsule with numerous flat seeds.

Key Recognition Features The upright flowers, which open in the sun, with 6 equal perianth segments.

Ecology and Geography On dry, grassy, and rocky hillsides and rarely in woods, from Europe, mainly in the southeast, to central Asia (around 64 species) and northwestern China.

Comment Tulips have been among the most popular garden plants in Europe since their introduction from Turkey in the late 16th century. Their great variability and the unpredictable way in which the colours and markings could change (now known to be caused by virus infection), caused their cultivation to become a mania in 17th-century Holland. Apart from *Amana* (see p.423), *Tulipa* is most closely related to *Erythronium* (see pp.422–23).

Tulipa humilis
½ life size, March 13th

Tulipa tarda
½ life size, April 25th

Tulipa linifolia
½ life size, May 10th

Tulipa tarda
1²⁄₃ × life size, April 25th

Tulipa saxatilis, bulbs, life size
September 17th

Tulipa 'Artist'
(right) ²/₃ life size
May 3rd

Tulipa kaufmanniana
(left) ²/₃ life size
March 15th

Tulipa 'West Point'
²/₃ life size
April 28th

Tulipa young capsule
just over life size
May 3rd

Tulipa 'Queen of Night', bulbs just
over life size, September 17th

Tulipa
'Slim Whitman'
²/₃ life size
April 28th

Scoliopus

Scoliopus Torr. (1856), in the family Liliaceae, contains 2 species in western North America.

Description Perennials to 10cm with short rhizomes. Leaves usually 2, obovate, all basal, often spotted with brown. Flowers in an umbel, but with the stem hidden, so appearing numerous and solitary on thin, angled stalks; brownish, smelling of bad meat, to 4cm across. Perianth segments 6, the outer 3 spreading, the inner 3 linear, erect. Stamens 3. Ovary superior, of 3 completely fused carpels, appearing 1-celled, with many ovules; styles 3, recurved. Pollination is probably by flies. The fruit is a 3-angled capsule with oblong, curved seeds.

Key Recognition Features The rosette of leaves at the base and the apparently solitary, brownish, foul-smelling flowers.

Ecology and Geography In wet or moist woods, particularly redwood forests, in western North America.

Comment These are unusual plants for the collector, with flowers in early spring, and broad leaves through the summer. *Scoliopus bigelowii* Torr., from northern California, has spotted leaves; *S. hallii* S. Wats. from Oregon, has unspotted leaves and smaller flowers.

Tricyrtis

Tricyrtis Wall. (1826), toad lily, in the family Liliaceae, contains 20 species, mostly in Japan.

Description Perennials to 1m with short or creeping rhizomes; stems upright or pendulous. Leaves ovate to lanceolate, all alternate and often clasping the stem. Flowers up to 20 in a branched, upright inflorescence, or hanging and solitary in the leaf axils, purple, white, or yellow, often spotted. Perianth segments 6, more or less equal, widely spreading or incurved, with a swollen or spurred nectary at the base. Stamens 6, with the filaments pressed against the ovary. Ovary superior, with 3 carpels, each with several ovules; style 1, with 3 2-fid stigmas, which recurve as they mature. Pollination is by insects. The fruit is a 3-celled capsule with numerous flat seeds in each cell.

Key Recognition Features The clasping stem leaves and the spotted flowers with reflexed stigmas.

Ecology and Geography In moist woods and on wet rocks, mostly in Japan, eastern China, and Siberia, extending westwards to India.

Comment These are attractive plants for the woodland garden, particularly valuable for their unusual colours and late flowering. DNA studies have shown *Tricyrtis* to be related to *Scoliopus*, *Prosartes* (see p.421), and *Streptopus* Michaux, this group forming a subfamily within the Liliaceae.

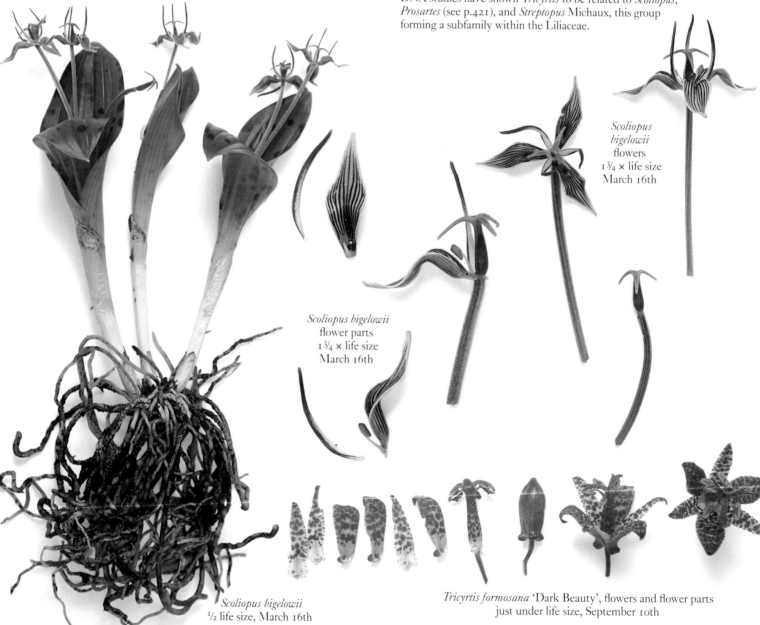

Scoliopus bigelowii
flowers
1¾ × life size
March 16th

Scoliopus bigelowii
flower parts
1¾ × life size
March 16th

Scoliopus bigelowii
½ life size, March 16th

Tricyrtis formosana 'Dark Beauty', flowers and flower parts
just under life size, September 10th

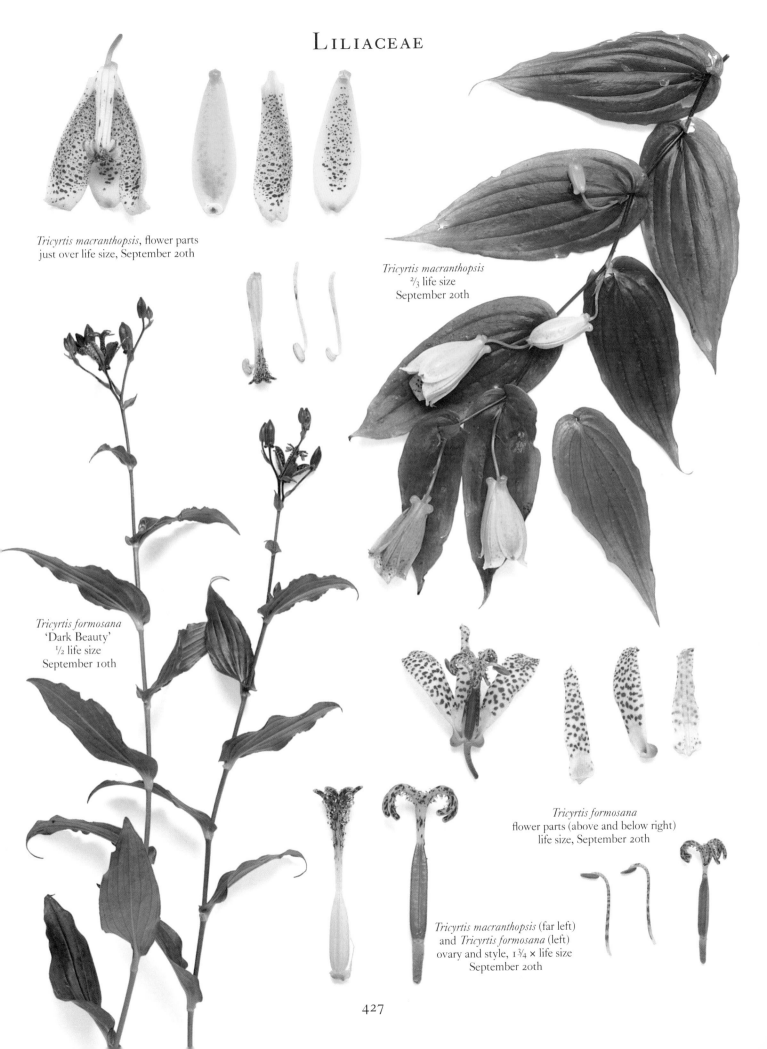

LILIACEAE

Tricyrtis macranthopsis, flower parts
just over life size, September 20th

Tricyrtis macranthopsis
²/₃ life size
September 20th

Tricyrtis formosana
'Dark Beauty'
¹/₂ life size
September 10th

Tricyrtis formosana
flower parts (above and below right)
life size, September 20th

Tricyrtis macranthopsis (far left)
and *Tricyrtis formosana* (left)
ovary and style, 1 ³/₄ × life size
September 20th

427

Calochortus

Calochortus Pursh (1814), mariposa lily, in the family Liliaceae, contains around 60 species, mainly in western North America, extending from Canada to Guatemala.

Description Perennials to 1m with bulbs with a membranous or fibrous tunic. Basal leaves solitary, long and linear or narrowly lanceolate, stem leaves shorter and narrower. Flowers solitary or up to 12 on a branched inflorescence, upright or nodding, usually bisexual, red, purple, pink, orange, yellow, or white, often hairy all over or with a large nectary surrounded by long hairs. Perianth segments 6, unequal, the outer 3 usually coloured and lanceolate, without a nectary, the inner 3 much larger, often hairy, and with an often large and complex nectary. Stamens 6, shorter than the perianth, the filaments usually straight, swollen at the base. Ovary superior, with 3 carpels, each with many ovules in 2 rows; style absent, with a stigma on the tip of the ovary. Pollination is by bees and other insects. The fruit is a pointed, angled, 3-celled, sometimes winged capsule with numerous flat seeds.

Key Recognition Features The inner perianth segments very different from the outer, and usually hairy or with a distinct nectary.

Ecology and Geography On dry, grassy, and rocky hillsides, and in deserts, grassland, and in open woods; from British Columbia eastwards to the Dakotas and southwards to Mexico and Guatemala, with around 40 species in California.

Comment *Calochortus* are some of the most beautiful and interesting of bulbous plants. There are 3 main sections; the largest, the mariposas or butterflies, such as *C. nuttallii* Torr., have upright flowers, sometimes likened to tulips (*Tulipa*, see pp.424–25), with very large inner segments, often beautifully marked and with a hairy gland, and flower in early summer among brown grasses. The fairy lanterns or globe lilies, such as *C. albus* Dougl. ex Benth. and *C. caeruleus* (Kell.) Wats., have smaller, often nodding heads, the whole inner perianth segment often hairy; they belong to section Eucalochortus and are often found in open woods or on shady banks. The third section, Cyclobothra, from southern California and Mexico, have very hairy flowers, often nodding, with the outer perianth segments almost as large as the inner; *C. barbatus* (H.B. & K.) Painter belongs to this section. DNA studies show *Calochortus* to be an isolated genus within the Liliaceae, and it has sometimes been put in its own family, the Calochortaceae.

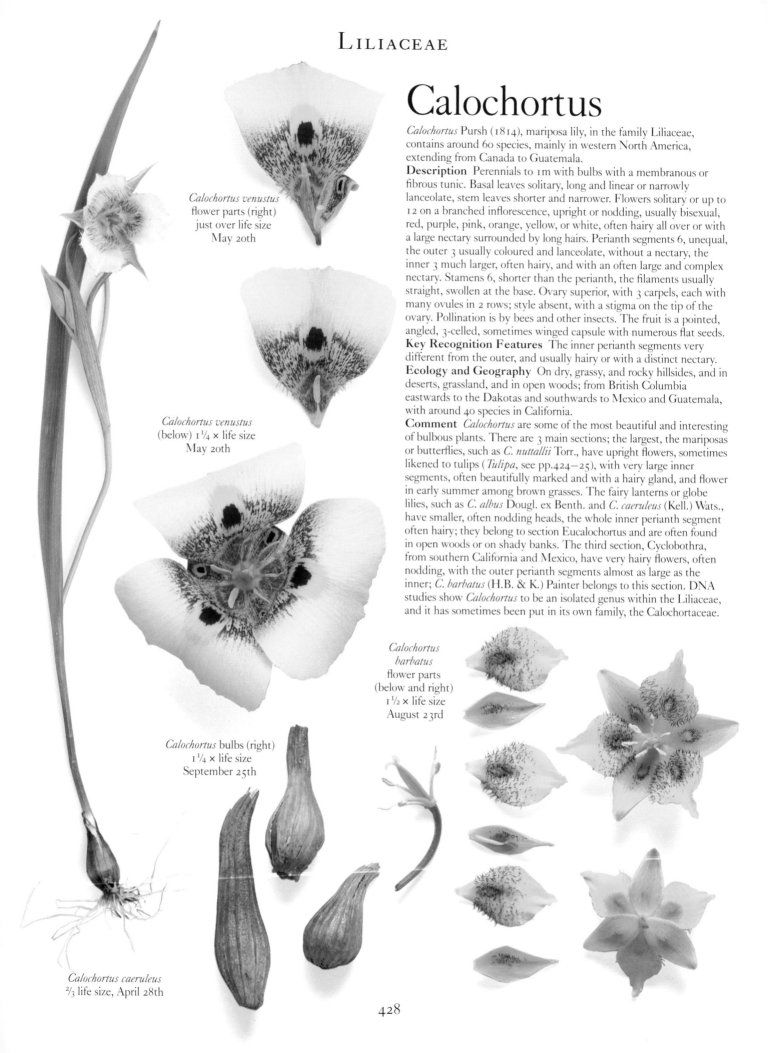

Calochortus venustus
flower parts (right)
just over life size
May 20th

Calochortus venustus
(below) 1¼ × life size
May 20th

Calochortus barbatus
flower parts
(below and right)
1½ × life size
August 23rd

Calochortus bulbs (right)
1¼ × life size
September 25th

Calochortus caeruleus
⅔ life size, April 28th

Calochortus catalinae
flower parts, 1²/₃ × life size
May 20th

Calochortus albus, inner and outer
perianth segments (top) and
stamens, style, and ovary (above)
1²/₃ × life size, June 6th

Calochortus barbatus
²/₃ life size, August 23rd

Calochortus albus
²/₃ life size, June 6th

429

Orchis

Orchis L. (1753), in the family Orchidaceae, contains around 33 species, mainly in Europe and Asia.

Description Perennials to 60cm with 2 or 3 rounded tubers and fleshy roots. Basal leaves several, narrowly to broadly lanceolate, occasionally spotted, stem leaves shorter, narrower, and sheathing. Flowers usually 12 or more on a usually dense, spike-like, upright inflorescence, purple, pink, pale yellow, or white, usually with a spurred nectary, turned through 180°. Bracts narrow, the lowest rather leafy. Perianth segments 6, unequal, the outer 3 usually small and often greenish or dark purple; of the inner, 2 are small and the lowest much larger, forming a lip. Stamens 1, the solid pollinia held in 2 pouches above the stigma. Ovary inferior of 1 carpel with 2 stigmas. Pollination is by bees and other insects. The fruit is a linear capsule with very numerous minute seeds.

Key Recognition Features The spike-like head of flowers with 5 small perianth segments and 1 large one forming a usually lobed lower lip, which is spurred on the back.

Ecology and Geography On dry, grassy hills, in moist grassland, and in open woods and scrub. From Scotland and Ireland to North Africa, and eastwards to central Asia, the Himalayas, and southwestern China.

Comment The orchid family is very large, with over 780 genera and 18 500 species, mainly in forested areas of the tropics. Orchids have always held the attention of botanists, partly because of the rarity of many of the species, partly because of their likeness to bees and their often remarkable (and to Victorians shocking) pollination mechanisms, and partly because of the difficulty of growing them from seed. The minute seeds need infection by a mycorrhizal fungus to begin proper growth, and even then development is slow; tropical orchids were first grown succesfully from seed in the late 19th century, but hardy orchids were not raised successfully until the late 20th century. *Orchis mascula* L., the early purple orchid, is a common species in woods and on grassy banks throughout Europe. In the eastern Mediterranean area, the testicle-like tubers of *Orchis* and *Ophrys* L. are collected and dried to make *salep*, a gruel-like, mucilaginous drink with supposed aphrodisiac properties.

Orchis mascula
flower parts, 2 × life size
May 26th

Orchis mascula
²⁄₃ life size
May 26th

Orchis mascula
flowers side view
2 × life size
May 26th

Orchis mascula
tuber, ²⁄₃ life size
May 10th

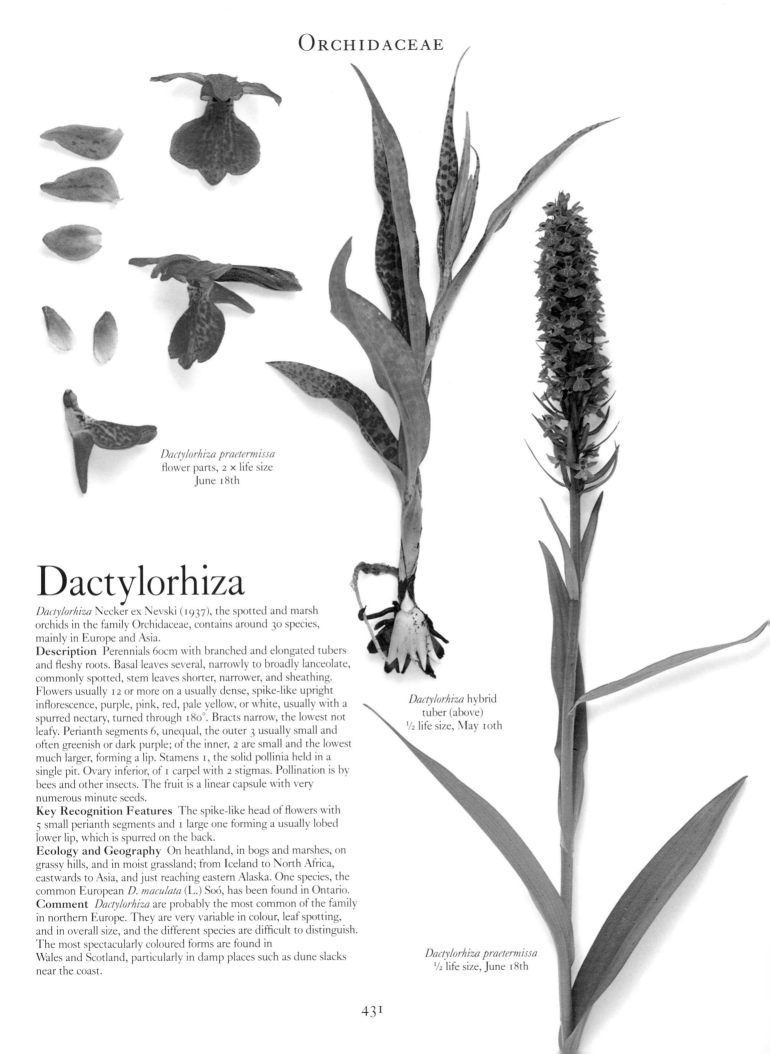

Dactylorhiza praetermissa
flower parts, 2 × life size
June 18th

Dactylorhiza

Dactylorhiza Necker ex Nevski (1937), the spotted and marsh orchids in the family Orchidaceae, contains around 30 species, mainly in Europe and Asia.

Description Perennials 60cm with branched and elongated tubers and fleshy roots. Basal leaves several, narrowly to broadly lanceolate, commonly spotted, stem leaves shorter, narrower, and sheathing. Flowers usually 12 or more on a usually dense, spike-like upright inflorescence, purple, pink, red, pale yellow, or white, usually with a spurred nectary, turned through 180°. Bracts narrow, the lowest not leafy. Perianth segments 6, unequal, the outer 3 usually small and often greenish or dark purple; of the inner, 2 are small and the lowest much larger, forming a lip. Stamens 1, the solid pollinia held in a single pit. Ovary inferior, of 1 carpel with 2 stigmas. Pollination is by bees and other insects. The fruit is a linear capsule with very numerous minute seeds.

Key Recognition Features The spike-like head of flowers with 5 small perianth segments and 1 large one forming a usually lobed lower lip, which is spurred on the back.

Ecology and Geography On heathland, in bogs and marshes, on grassy hills, and in moist grassland; from Iceland to North Africa, eastwards to Asia, and just reaching eastern Alaska. One species, the common European *D. maculata* (L.) Soó, has been found in Ontario.

Comment *Dactylorhiza* are probably the most common of the family in northern Europe. They are very variable in colour, leaf spotting, and in overall size, and the different species are difficult to distinguish. The most spectacularly coloured forms are found in Wales and Scotland, particularly in damp places such as dune slacks near the coast.

Dactylorhiza hybrid
tuber (above)
½ life size, May 10th

Dactylorhiza praetermissa
½ life size, June 18th

431

Epipactis

Epipactis Zinn (1757), helleborine, in the family Orchidaceae, contains around 22 species, mainly in the northern hemisphere.

Description Perennials 75cm without tubers, but with fleshy roots. Basal leaves several or few, narrowly to broadly lanceolate, not spotted, stem leaves shorter, narrower, and sheathing. Flowers usually fewer than 12 in a loose, spike-like, upright inflorescence, dusky purple, pinkish-red, green, brown, or whitish, usually without a spur, turned through 180°. Bracts narrow, the lowest sometimes leafy. Perianth segments 6, unequal, the outer 3 usually small and often greenish or dark purple; of the inner, 2 are small and the lowest slightly larger, forming a hinged lip, the basal part of which contains nectar. Stamen 1. Ovary inferior, of 1 carpel with 2 stigmas. Pollination is by insects, mainly bees, wasps, and flies. The fruit is a linear or ovoid capsule with very numerous minute seeds.

Key Recognition Features The loose spike-like inflorescence of dull-coloured, nodding flowers, with 5 small perianth segments, the lip in 2 parts, the front part hinged.

Ecology and Geography In marshes and dune slacks, on rocky screes, and in woods from Ireland to North Africa and eastwards to Asia and North America.

Comment *Epipactis helleborine* (L.) Crantz, so-called from the similarity of its pleated leaves to those of the hellebore *Veratrum* (see p.404), is found throughout western Asia, Europe, and eastern North America, where it was first found in 1879 near New York, and has since spread in the area round the Great Lakes. *Epipactis gigantea* Dougl. ex Hook. is found throughout western North America, and is often cultivated in Europe.

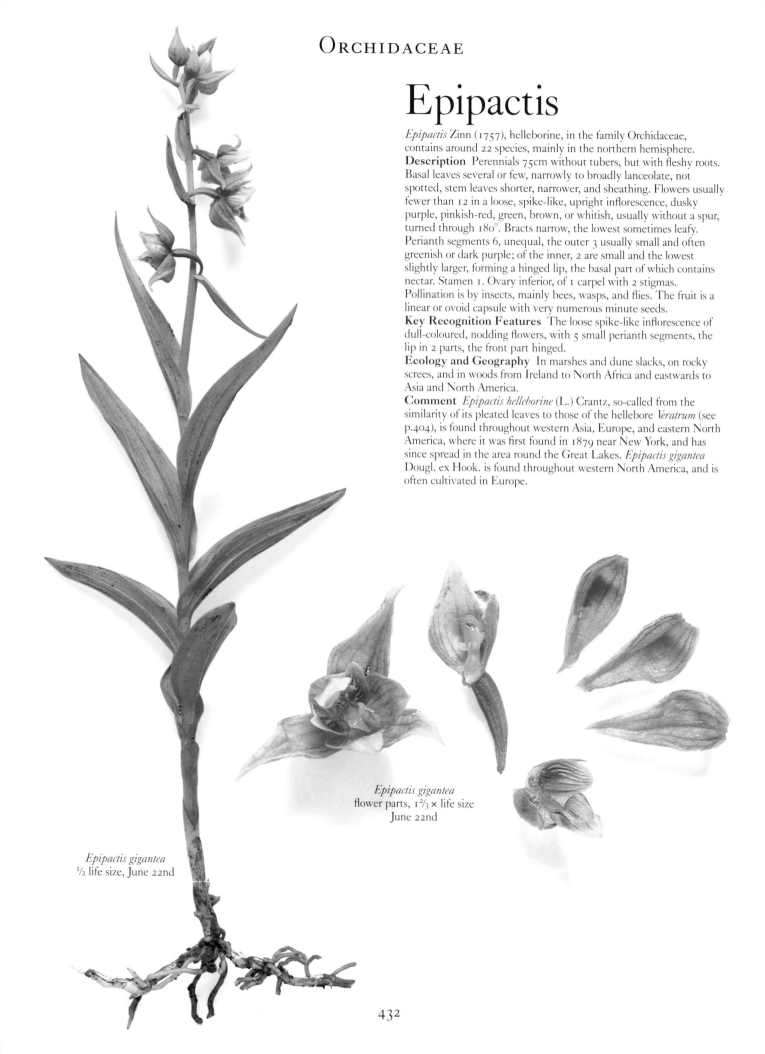

Epipactis gigantea
flower parts, 1²/₃ × life size
June 22nd

Epipactis gigantea
¹/₂ life size, June 22nd

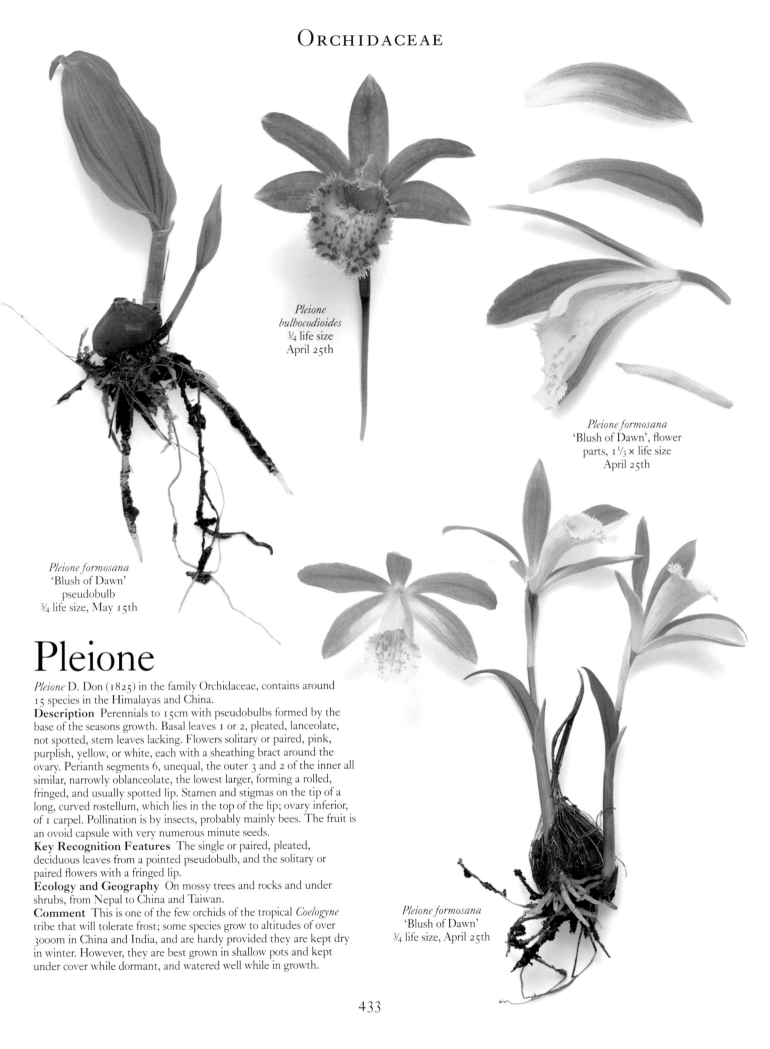

*Pleione
bulbocodioides*
¾ life size
April 25th

Pleione formosana
'Blush of Dawn', flower
parts, 1⅓ × life size
April 25th

Pleione formosana
'Blush of Dawn'
pseudobulb
¾ life size, May 15th

Pleione

Pleione D. Don (1825) in the family Orchidaceae, contains around
15 species in the Himalayas and China.

Description Perennials to 15cm with pseudobulbs formed by the
base of the seasons growth. Basal leaves 1 or 2, pleated, lanceolate,
not spotted, stem leaves lacking. Flowers solitary or paired, pink,
purplish, yellow, or white, each with a sheathing bract around the
ovary. Perianth segments 6, unequal, the outer 3 and 2 of the inner all
similar, narrowly oblanceolate, the lowest larger, forming a rolled,
fringed, and usually spotted lip. Stamen and stigmas on the tip of a
long, curved rostellum, which lies in the top of the lip; ovary inferior,
of 1 carpel. Pollination is by insects, probably mainly bees. The fruit is
an ovoid capsule with very numerous minute seeds.

Key Recognition Features The single or paired, pleated,
deciduous leaves from a pointed pseudobulb, and the solitary or
paired flowers with a fringed lip.

Ecology and Geography On mossy trees and rocks and under
shrubs, from Nepal to China and Taiwan.

Comment This is one of the few orchids of the tropical *Coelogyne*
tribe that will tolerate frost; some species grow to altitudes of over
3000m in China and India, and are hardy provided they are kept dry
in winter. However, they are best grown in shallow pots and kept
under cover while dormant, and watered well while in growth.

Pleione formosana
'Blush of Dawn'
¾ life size, April 25th

433

Rhodohypoxis

Rhodohypoxis Nel (1914), in the family Hypoxidaceae, contains around 6 species in South Africa.

Description Dwarf perennials to 10cm, with corms and grass-like, hairy leaves. Flowers solitary on thin stalks or on a long, narrow tube (see also *Colchicum* pp.412–13), pink, pinkish-purple, or white. Perianth segments 6, all similar and spreading, joined at the base, the inner 3 bent inwards to hide the stamens and style. Stamens 6, very short. Ovary inferior, with 3 fused carpels with many ovules; style absent, stigma feathery, on the tip of the ovary. Pollination is presumed to be by insects. The fruit is a small capsule with small, globose, black seeds.

Key Recognition Features The grassy, hairy leaves and bright, usually pinkish flowers with the inner 3 segments bent inwards to hide the stamens.

Ecology and Geography In wet, stony places on rock sheets and in short turf in the Drakensberg mountains, Natal, and the northeastern Cape in South Africa, and in Lesotho.

Comment These are small and attractive plants, easy to grow in shallow pans or gravelly, bare soil. Ideally they should be kept dry while dormant in winter and watered daily in summer.

Hypoxis

Hypoxis L. (1753), in the family Hypoxidaceae, contains around 150 species mainly in the southern hemisphere.

Description Perennials to 1m, with corms and broadly grass-like, usually hairy leaves. Flowers in a branching inflorescence, starry, usually yellow, rarely pink or white, with a dark spot at the base. Perianth segments 6, all similar and spreading, joined at the base. Stamens 6, conspicuous. Ovary inferior, with 3 fused carpels with many ovules; style absent or very short, stigma feathery, 3-lobed. Pollination is presumed to be by insects. The fruit is a capsule opening by a lid, with black or brown, globose seeds.

Key Recognition Features The broad, grassy, hairy leaves and bright, starry, yellow or rarely pink or white flowers.

Ecology and Geography Wet or dry, grassy places and open woods, often beneath *Eucalyptus* (see Volume 1); in tropical and South Africa, with a few species in India, Australia, and eastern North America.

Comment A few species are cultivated. The very distinct *H. capensis* (L.) Vines & Druce, syn. *Spiloxene capensis* (L.) Garside, and related species have solitary, starry flowers, yellow or white with a dark purple centre; other species have yellow flowers, hairy on the back. DNA studies have shown Hypoxidaceae to be a rather isolated family, related to the Orchidaceae (see pp.430–33).

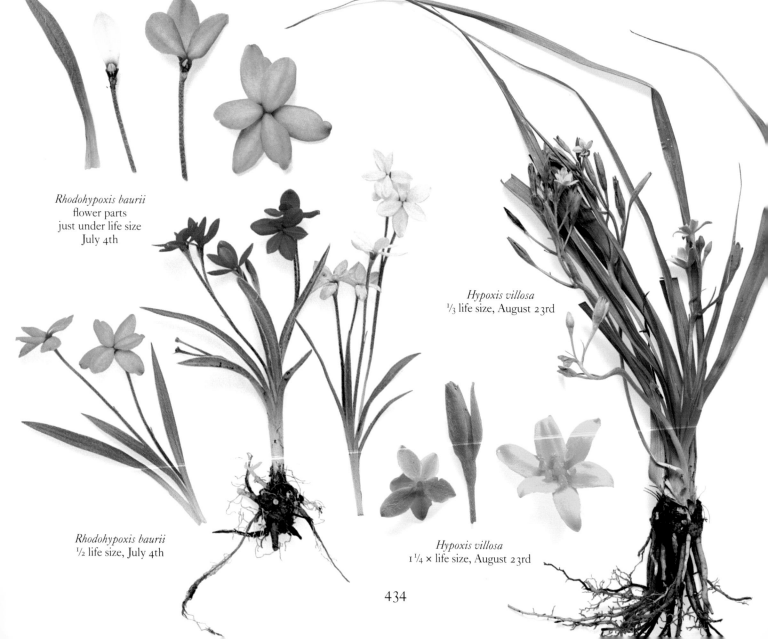

Rhodohypoxis baurii
flower parts
just under life size
July 4th

Hypoxis villosa
⅓ life size, August 23rd

Rhodohypoxis baurii
½ life size, July 4th

Hypoxis villosa
1¼ × life size, August 23rd

Astelia

Astelia Banks & Sol. ex R. Br. (1810), in the family Asteliaceae, contains 25 species, mainly in the Pacific region.

Description Perennials with a tufted rhizome and flowering stems to 75cm. Leaves to 1m, flat or keeled, mostly basal in 3 ranks, covered with silvery scales. Male and female flowers on separate plants, greenish, small, and numerous in a much-branched inflorescence. Perianth segments sometimes joined at the base, all equal. Stamens 6, the filaments straight, usually shorter than the perianth. Ovary superior, of 3 fused carpels with several ovules; style very short or absent. Pollination is presumed to be by insects. The fruit is a red or orange berry, round-pointed or elongated oval, with black, shining, usually angular seeds.

Key Recognition Features Silvery-scaly leaves and branched inflorescence of masses of small, greenish flowers or bright berries.

Ecology and Geography In bogs, often in the mountains, on dry hills, in tussock grassland, and epiphytic on trees. From New Zealand and Australia to New Guinea and Hawaii, with 1 species in Chile.

Comment *Astelia chathamica* (Skottsb.) L. B. Moore, from the Chatham Islands off the coast of New Zealand, is commonly cultivated under the name 'Silver Spear' for its handsome silvery leaves. Asteliaceae is related to the Australian Blandfordiaceae, which includes the showy *Blandfordia* Sm., the Christmas bells, and to the Hypoxidaceae.

Astelia chathamica
flowers, 1¾ × life size
May 24th

Astelia chathamica
½ life size, May 24th

435

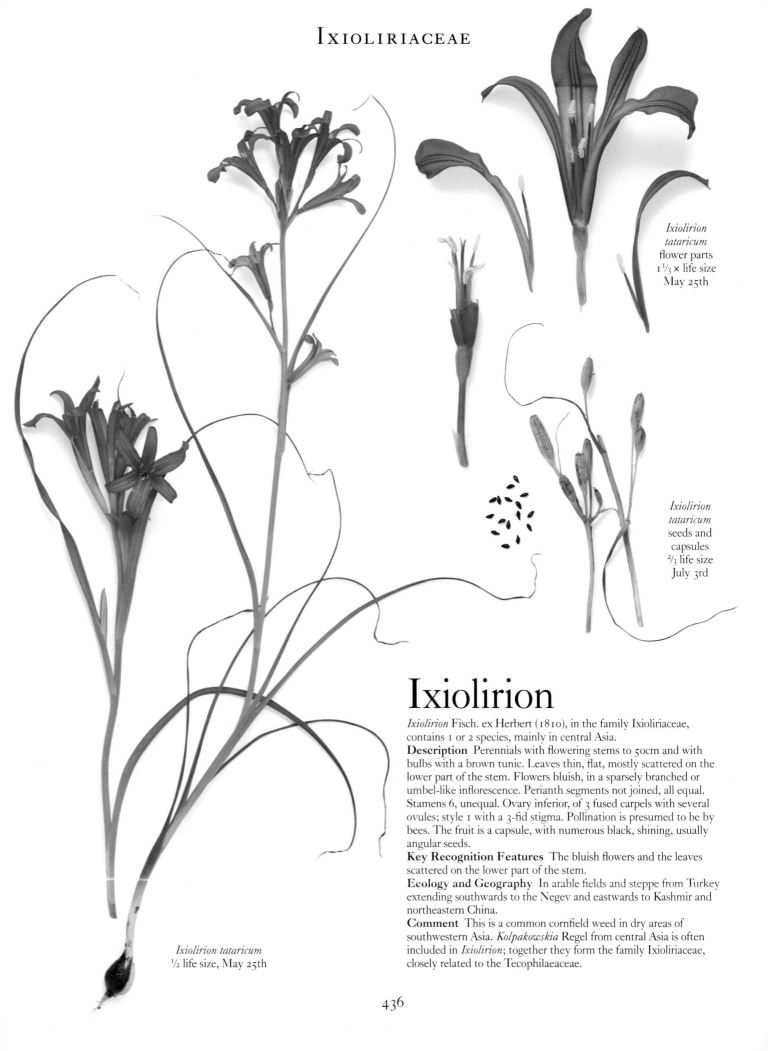

*Ixiolirion
tataricum*
flower parts
1 ⅓ × life size
May 25th

*Ixiolirion
tataricum*
seeds and
capsules
⅔ life size
July 3rd

Ixiolirion

Ixiolirion Fisch. ex Herbert (1810), in the family Ixioliriaceae, contains 1 or 2 species, mainly in central Asia.

Description Perennials with flowering stems to 50cm and with bulbs with a brown tunic. Leaves thin, flat, mostly scattered on the lower part of the stem. Flowers bluish, in a sparsely branched or umbel-like inflorescence. Perianth segments not joined, all equal. Stamens 6, unequal. Ovary inferior, of 3 fused carpels with several ovules; style 1 with a 3-fid stigma. Pollination is presumed to be by bees. The fruit is a capsule, with numerous black, shining, usually angular seeds.

Key Recognition Features The bluish flowers and the leaves scattered on the lower part of the stem.

Ecology and Geography In arable fields and steppe from Turkey extending southwards to the Negev and eastwards to Kashmir and northeastern China.

Comment This is a common cornfield weed in dry areas of southwestern Asia. *Kolpakowskia* Regel from central Asia is often included in *Ixiolirion*; together they form the family Ixioliriaceae, closely related to the Tecophilaeaceae.

Ixiolirion tataricum
½ life size, May 25th

436

Tecophilaea

Tecophilaea Bertero ex Colla (1836), in the family Tecophilaeaceae, contains 2 species from Chile.

Description Perennials to 10cm, with corms rooting from the top, and 2 or 3 narrow, linear leaves. Flowers solitary, bright blue, pale blue and white, or purple. Perianth segments 6, all similar and spreading, rounded at the apex, joined at the base. Stamens 3 fertile, 3 sterile, hidden in the throat of the flower. Ovary half-inferior, of 3 fused carpels with many ovules; style very thin, 3–4mm long, stigma very small. Pollination is presumed to be by insects. The fruit is a capsule opening by a lid, with black or brown, globose seeds.

Key Recognition Features The 2 or 3 folded leaves and the bright blue, purple, or blue-and-white flowers.

Ecology and Geography In grassy hills in the Andes of Chile.

Comment *Tecophilaea cyanocrocus* Leyb., famous for its intense, gentian-blue flowers (*Gentiana*, see p.208), is said to be extinct in the wild, but is commonly cultivated. *Tecophilaea violiflora* Bertero ex Colla, also from the Andes, has smaller flowers on a branching inflorescence. Other genera in the family are from California (*Odontostomum hartwegii* Torr.) and South Africa (*Cyanella* L.), and are related to *Ixiolirion*. The genus is named after Tecofila Billiotti, daughter of Professor Luigi Colla (1766–1848) of Turin: she illustrated most of his *Plantae rarioses in regionibus Chilensibus a M.D. Bertero super detectae* (1834–36) and other books.

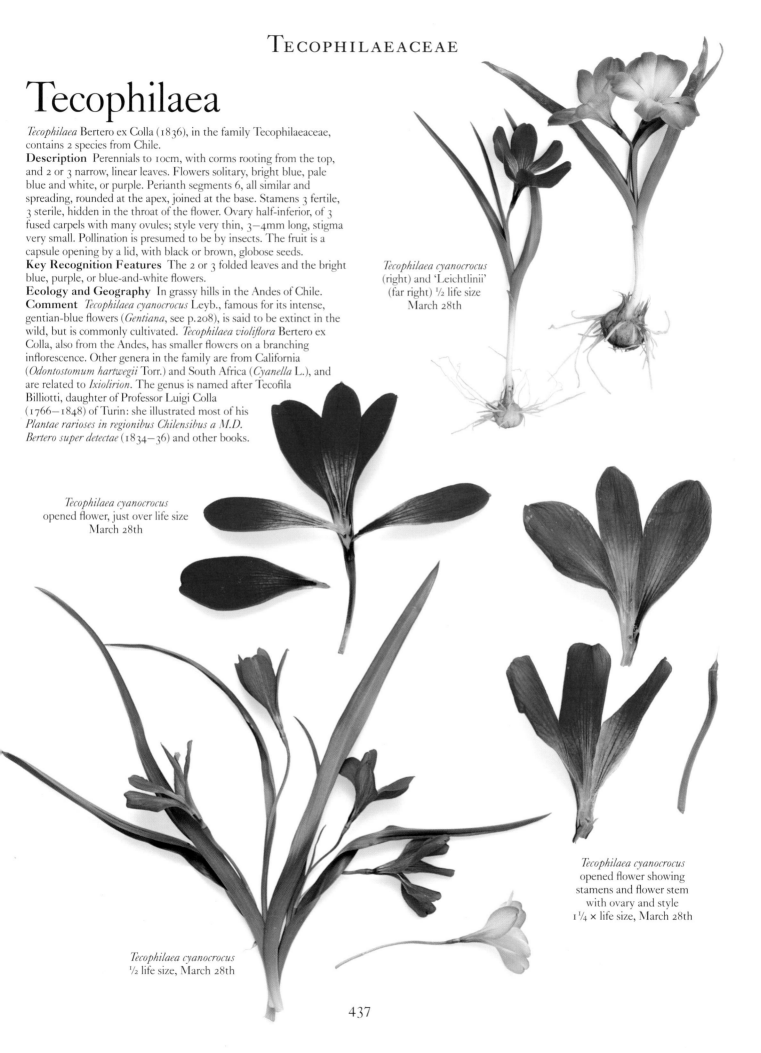

Tecophilaea cyanocrocus (right) and 'Leichtlinii' (far right) ½ life size March 28th

Tecophilaea cyanocrocus opened flower, just over life size March 28th

Tecophilaea cyanocrocus opened flower showing stamens and flower stem with ovary and style 1¼ × life size, March 28th

Tecophilaea cyanocrocus ½ life size, March 28th

437

Iris

Iris L. (1753), in the family Iridaceae, contains around 250 species from the northern hemisphere.

Description Perennials to 2cm, with bulbs or rhizomes. Leaves sword-shaped or linear, flat, folded, or angled in section. Flowers solitary, paired, or several on a branched stem, or stemless, with a subterranean ovary, blue, purple, black, white, yellow, red, orange, or brown, sometimes veined. Perianth segments 6, the outer generally reflexing to form the "falls", which often have a hairy beard, the inner upright and incurved to form the "standards", joined at the base to form a tube. Stamens 3, hidden beneath the flattened styles. Ovary inferior, of 3 fused carpels with many ovules; styles 3, often petaloid, and sometimes with 2 pointed, upright lobes. Pollination is usually by bees, in *I. fulva* Ker-Gawl. by hummingbirds. The fruit is a capsule, usually splitting into 3 brown or sometimes bright orange, globose or thick, flat seeds, which sometimes have a large aril.

Key Recognition Features The hanging falls and usually upright standards.

Ecology and Geography In rivers, lakes, bogs, meadows, flat valleys, open woods, and deserts, and on stony lake shores and rocky hills. Throughout Europe and temperate Asia, in North America, and southwards to the Arabian peninsula, Assam, and southern China.

Comment Many species have long been cultivated for ornament: subdivisions of the genus are detailed on pp.440–41. The blue-flowered *I. germanica* L. was associated with the Virgin Mary in Medieval and Renaissance painting, and the white-flowered *I. germanica* 'Florentina' provides orris root, used in perfumery and for powdering wigs. *Iris albicans* Lange and related species are commonly planted in Muslim cemetaries. The family Iridaceae, with around 80 genera and 1500 species, is very diverse, particularly in southern Africa and in Central and South America. It is recognised primarily by its inferior ovary, much-divided or modified styles, and 3 stamens.

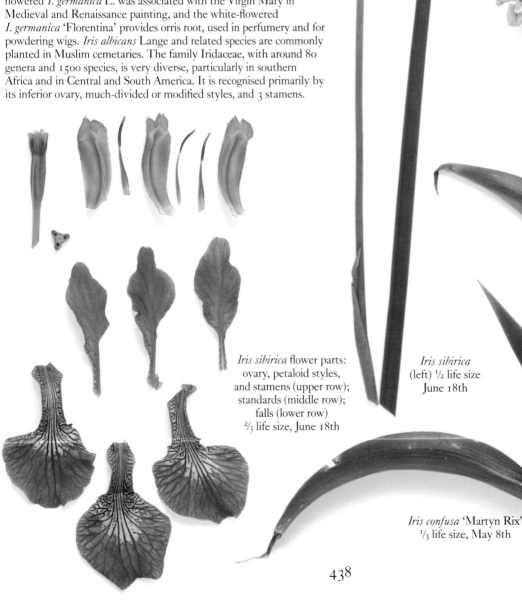

Iris fulva
⅔ life size
June 12th

Iris sibirica flower parts:
ovary, petaloid styles,
and stamens (upper row);
standards (middle row);
falls (lower row)
⅔ life size, June 18th

Iris sibirica
(left) ½ life size
June 18th

Iris confusa 'Martyn Rix'
⅓ life size, May 8th

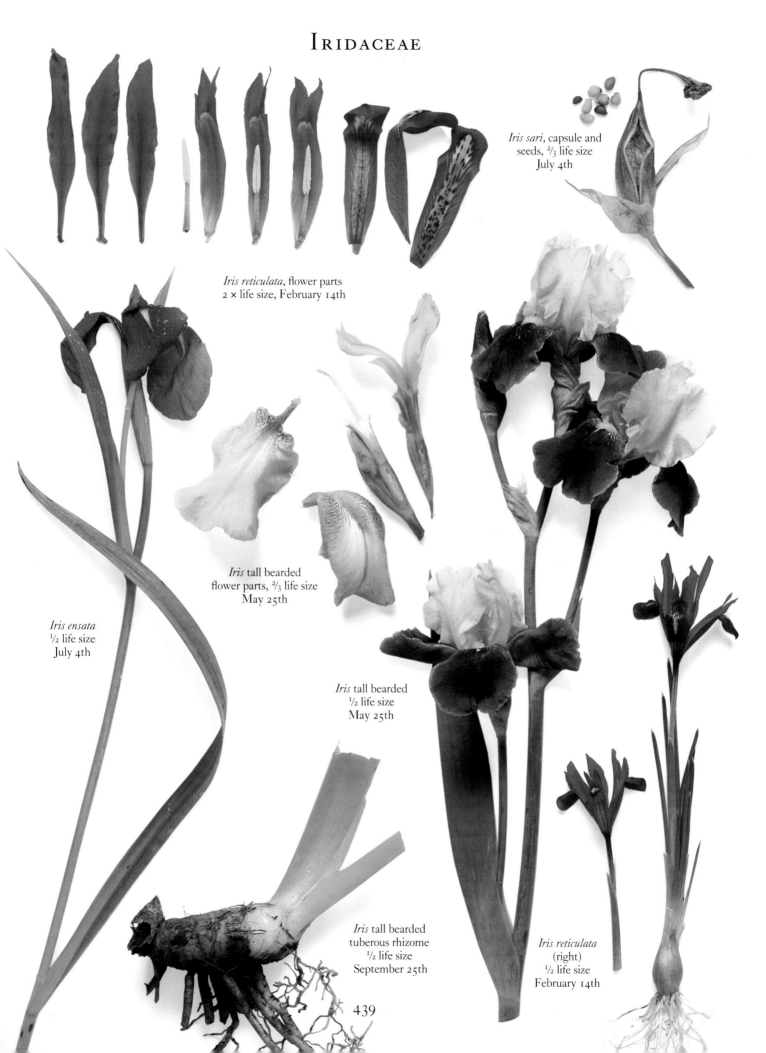

IRIDACEAE

Iris sari, capsule and
seeds, ⅔ life size
July 4th

Iris reticulata, flower parts
2 × life size, February 14th

Iris tall bearded
flower parts, ⅔ life size
May 25th

Iris ensata
½ life size
July 4th

Iris tall bearded
½ life size
May 25th

Iris tall bearded
tuberous rhizome
½ life size
September 25th

Iris reticulata
(right)
½ life size
February 14th

439

Iris subdivisions

The genus *Iris* itself has been divided into 6 subgenera and many sections. The following contain most of the familiar garden plants:

Subgenus Iris These are the bearded irises, with a "beard" of hairs on the inside of the upper part of the falls; this subgenus includes border irises and section Iris, which contains *I. germanica* and all the many cultivars derived from it and related species. Modern border irises have huge, frilled flowers in clear colours, and often have a second period of flowering in late summer, so-called remontant cultivars. This subgenus also includes the aril irises, section Oncocyclus and section Regelia, originating from the eastern Mediterranean as far south as Sinai to central Asia, mostly growing in semi-deserts and mountain areas that are dry in summer. They grow well in climates such as southern California, Arizona, and parts of Australia, where the species and their hybrids are popular garden plants, valued for their solitary or paired, beautifully veined flowers in muted shades of grey, brown, and purple; in wetter areas they need protection from rain during summer.

Subgenus Limniris These are the beardless irises, and the largest subgenus. The species are very varied and have flowers without a beard on the falls. Popular garden plants in this subgenus include the Evansia or Japonica irises, section Lophiris. Also in this subgenus are the water irises and others of the Japanese "Kaempferi" group, *Iris foetidissima* L., with its orange seeds conspicuous in winter, and the winter flowering *I. unguicularis*, all in section Limniris. Also in this section are the American water irises, of which *I. fulva* Ker-Gawl. has the reddest flowers of any species, and is pollinated by hummingbirds.

Subgenus Xiphium The Spanish irises, these are familiar as cut flowers, with long, narrow leaves and blue, white, or yellow flowers.

Subgenus Scorpiris These are the Juno irises, another group from the Middle East and central Asia. Their leaves are usually thin and folded, and their bulbs have papery tunics and thick roots. Shown here is *I. persica* L., difficult to grow, but often illustrated in 17th-century Dutch flower paintings, and *I. cycloglossa* Wendelbo *et al.* from Afghanistan, which has wonderfully scented flowers.

Subgenus Hermodactyloides Reticulata irises, containing the smallest species, which have small bulbs and long, narrow leaves that elongate after the flowers appear in early spring. *Iris reticulata* M. Bieb. and its hybrids are the most common in this section; the bulbs are very hardy, but susceptible to slug damage in mild, moist climates.

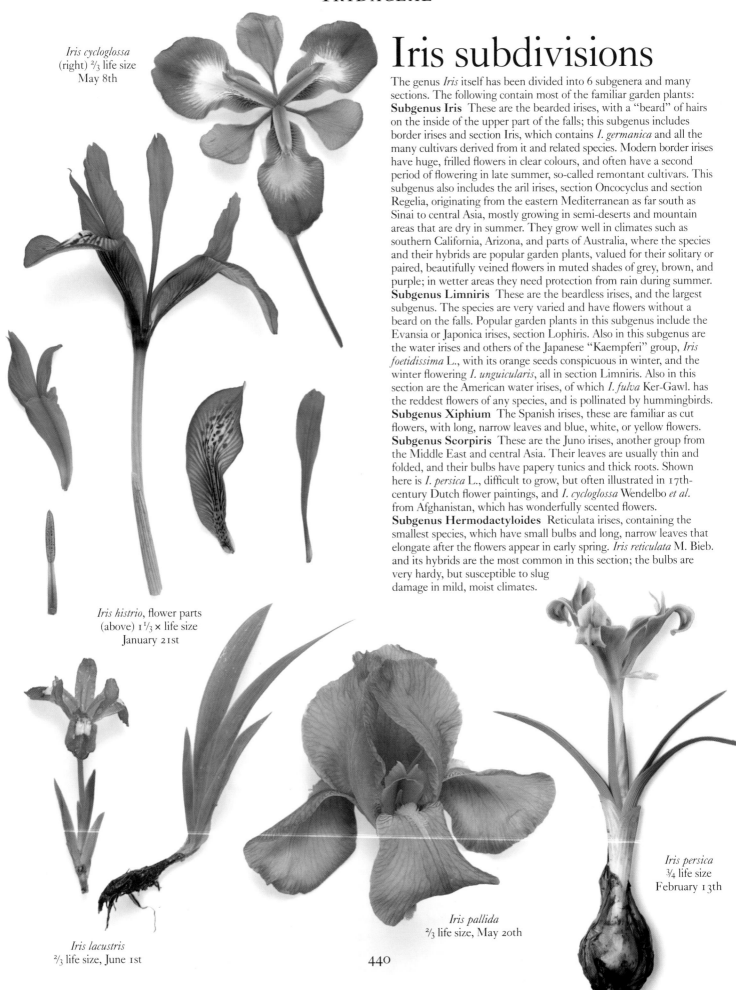

Iris cycloglossa (right) ⅔ life size May 8th

Iris histrio, flower parts (above) 1⅓ × life size January 21st

Iris lacustris ⅔ life size, June 1st

Iris pallida ⅔ life size, May 20th

Iris persica ¾ life size February 13th

IRIDACEAE

Iris helenae, flower parts
²⁄₃ life size, May 8th

Iris korolkowii
(right) ¹⁄₂ life size
May 8th

Iris iberica
subsp. *lycotis*
(left) ¹⁄₃ life size
May 10th

Iris helenae (right)
¹⁄₃ life size, May 8th

Iris foetidissima
(left) ¹⁄₃ life size
June 18th

Iris paradoxa
¹⁄₂ life size, May 20th

Iris foetidissima, fruits
¹⁄₂ life size, October 5th

441

Hermodactylus

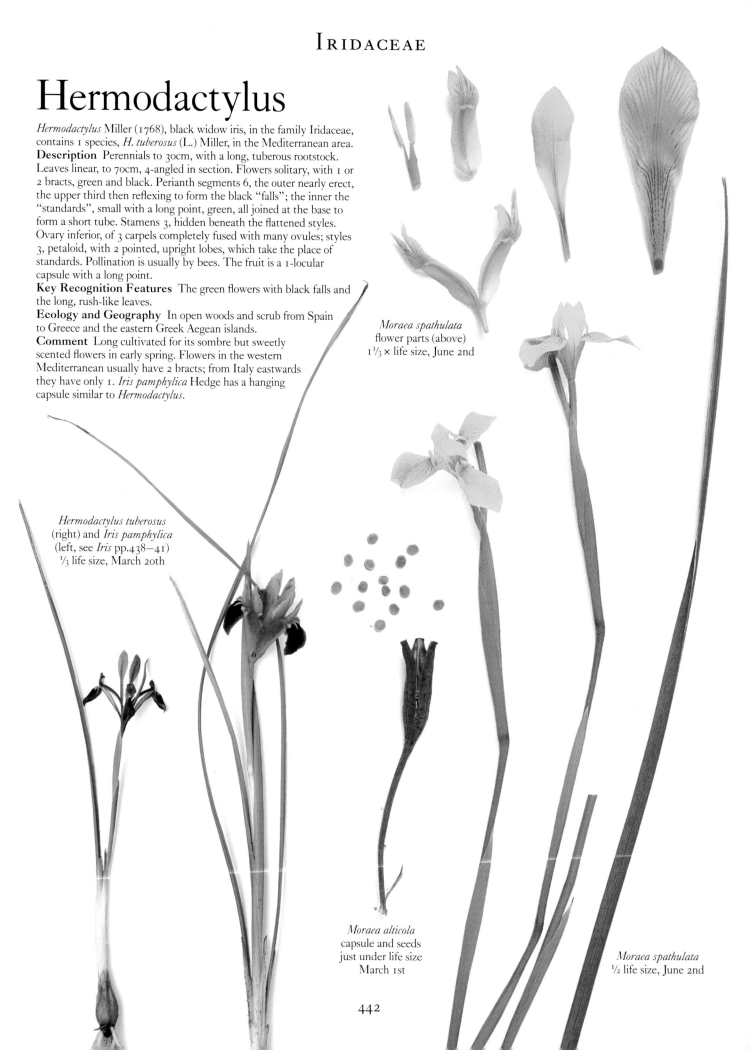

Hermodactylus Miller (1768), black widow iris, in the family Iridaceae, contains 1 species, *H. tuberosus* (L.) Miller, in the Mediterranean area.

Description Perennials to 30cm, with a long, tuberous rootstock. Leaves linear, to 70cm, 4-angled in section. Flowers solitary, with 1 or 2 bracts, green and black. Perianth segments 6, the outer nearly erect, the upper third then reflexing to form the black "falls"; the inner the "standards", small with a long point, green, all joined at the base to form a short tube. Stamens 3, hidden beneath the flattened styles. Ovary inferior, of 3 carpels completely fused with many ovules; styles 3, petaloid, with 2 pointed, upright lobes, which take the place of standards. Pollination is usually by bees. The fruit is a 1-locular capsule with a long point.

Key Recognition Features The green flowers with black falls and the long, rush-like leaves.

Ecology and Geography In open woods and scrub from Spain to Greece and the eastern Greek Aegean islands.

Comment Long cultivated for its sombre but sweetly scented flowers in early spring. Flowers in the western Mediterranean usually have 2 bracts; from Italy eastwards they have only 1. *Iris pamphylica* Hedge has a hanging capsule similar to *Hermodactylus*.

Moraea spathulata
flower parts (above)
1⅓ × life size, June 2nd

Hermodactylus tuberosus
(right) and *Iris pamphylica*
(left, see *Iris* pp.438–41)
⅓ life size, March 20th

Moraea alticola
capsule and seeds
just under life size
March 1st

Moraea spathulata
½ life size, June 2nd

442

Moraea

Moraea Miller (1768), in the family Iridaceae, contains around 120 species, mostly in southern Africa.

Description Perennials to 1.5m, with corms. Leaves to 2m, linear, flat or channelled, sometimes twisted like a corkscrew. Flowers solitary or several in a branched inflorescence, with 2 bracts, yellow, red, blue, white, or brown, sometimes marked with black. Perianth segments 6, the outer nearly erect or spreading, the upper part then reflexing to form falls; the inner, the "standards", usually smaller and often 3-lobed with a long point, not joined at the base. Stamens 3, hidden beneath the flattened styles, the filaments often forming a column around the style. Ovary inferior, of 3 fused carpels with many ovules; styles 3, petaloid, with 2 pointed, upright lobes, which take the place of standards. Pollination is usually by bees, or by flies in the dull-coloured and evil-smelling species. The fruit is a 3-locular capsule, globose to cylindrical, with a blunt apex or short beak, usually flat, but sometimes angular or even with an inflated seed coat.

Key Recognition Features The *Iris*-like flowers (see pp.438–41) with no tube, and the filaments joined around the style. Most species have several flowers emerging from 2 overlapping bracts.

Ecology and Geography In rocky places, deserts, grassy places, veldt, and mountain bogs. In southern Africa from the Cape peninsula to Nigeria and Ethiopia, with most species in the southwestern Cape and Namaqualand.

Comment These are attractive plants, usually with *Iris*-like flowers, but sometimes more like a *Gladiolus* (see pp.444–45), but with a branching inflorescence. Most require a frost-free climate and grow during the winter, but some of the water-loving species from the Drakensberg mountains in South Africa, such as *M. spathulata* (L. fil.) Klatt, are perfectly hardy in southern England, growing and flowering during the summer, and increasing into large clumps. *Homeria* all have orange, pink, or yellow flowers. *Gynandriris* Parl. is also mainly a South African genus, with 2 species in the Mediterranean area, including the afternoon-flowering *G. sisyrinchium* (L.) Parl.; it is very close to *Moraea*, but differs in having a beak on top of the ovary so that the flowers appear to have a perianth tube like an *Iris*.

Melasphaerula

Melasphaerula Ker-Gawler (1805), in the family Iridaceae, contains 1 species, *M. ramosa* (L.) N.E. Br. in South Africa.

Description Perennials to 75cm with corms. Leaves deciduous, in 2 ranks, usually shorter than the stem, flat. Flowers small and numerous, in a much-branched, spike-like inflorescence, with 2 partially papery bracts, pale yellow. Perianth segments 6, the upper 3 slightly shorter than the lower 3, all joined at the base to form a very short tube. Stamens 3. Ovary inferior, of 3 fused carpels with few ovules; style 1, with 3 slender branches. Pollination is perhaps by flies, but self-pollination is probably usual. The fruit is a 3-locular, slightly inflated capsule with round seeds.

Key Recognition Features The branching spikes of small flowers with narrow perianth segments.

Ecology and Geography In rocky places in South Africa, from the southwestern Cape to Namaqualand and Namibia.

Comment *Melasphaerula* is possibly a primitive relative of *Gladiolus* (see pp.444–45), sometimes cultivated as a curiosity, but occasionally becoming a weed by self-seeding. The flowers have a spermatic scent similar to those species of *Fritillaria* (see pp.418–19) that are pollinated by wasps, but I have never observed wasps visiting *Melasphaerula*.

Melasphaerula ramosa
flower parts, 2 × life size, May 3rd

Melasphaerula ramosa,
capsules and seeds
2¼ × life size, May 3rd

Melasphaerula ramosa
⅓ life size, May 3rd

Gladiolus

Gladiolus L. (1753), in the family Iridaceae, contains over 250 species, mostly in southern Africa.

Description Perennials to 1.5m with corms, sometimes with running stolons. Leaves deciduous, mostly in 2 ranks, usually shorter than the stem, flat or very narrow and winged. Flowers few to numerous, in a spike-like inflorescence, rarely branched, with 2 bracts, yellow, orange, red, blue, pink, white, green, or brown. Perianth segments 6, the upper 3 generally a different colour and shape from the lower 3, which are usually spotted or blotched, all joined at the base to form a short or long tube. Stamens 3. Ovary inferior, of 3 fused carpels with many ovules; style 1, with 3 slightly flattened branches, not petaloid. Pollination is usually by bees, but also by flies in the dull-coloured and evil smelling species, by sunbirds in many of the red-flowered, hooded species, and by hawkmoths in the long-tubed, white-flowered species. The fruit is a 3-locular capsule; seeds often winged.

Key Recognition Features The spike of flowers with a curved tube from 2 overlapping bracts, and style with 3 short branches.

Ecology and Geography Rocky places, deserts, grassy places, veldt, and mountain bogs, and in wet, very rocky areas. In southern Africa from the Cape peninsula northwards, with most species in the southwestern Cape and Namaqualand; there are other concentrations of species in Madagascar and the Mediterranean area.

Comment Many species are easily cultivated, including the spectacular red-flowered *G. cardinalis* Curtis, which hangs down by waterfalls in the southwestern Cape and was 1 parent of the hybrid *G.* × *colvillei*. The white-flowered and deliciously-scented *G. murielae* Kelway from tropical East Africa, is easily grown, given ample water in summer; it is typical of the hummingbird-pollinated species. The large-flowered "glads" are complex hybrids between the summer-growing subtropical species, *G. dalenii* van Geel, syn. *G. natalensis* Reinwardt ex Hook. fil., *G. oppositiflorus* Herb., and the red-flowered *G. saundersii* Hook. fil., among other species, and have undergone great development since the first hybrids with *G. dalenii* were made in 1837.

Gladiolus cardinalis
capsules and seeds
1 ½ × life size
September 4th

Gladiolus large flowered
hybrid, flower parts
⅔ life size, August 15th

Gladiolus large flowered
hybrids, ½ life size
August 15th

Gladiolus byzantinus, corms, life size
September 17th

Gladiolus murielae, corm
life size, March 14th

444

Iridaceae

Gladiolus cardinalis
(right) ⅓ life size
July 23rd

Gladiolus murielae
½ life size
September 18th

Gladiolus byzantinus
½ life size, June 6th

Gladiolus cardinalis
flower parts, ⅔ life size
July 23rd

Gladiolus byzantinus
flower parts, 1⅓ × life size
June 6th

445

Cypella

Cypella Herbert (1826), in the family Iridaceae, contains around 15 species, mostly in South America.

Description Perennials to 75cm, with bulbs with pleated tunics. Leaves to 45cm, pleated. Flowers *Iris*-like (see pp.438–41), yellow or blue, several in a much-branched inflorescence, with 2 bracts. Perianth segments 6, the outer large and spreading, the upper part then reflexing to form falls; the inner 3 smaller, erect, and often hairy, sometimes with transverse bands of colour, not joined at the base. Stamens 3, hidden beneath the flattened styles, the filaments free. Ovary inferior, of 3 fused carpels with many ovules; styles 3, sometimes petaloid, longer than the stamens. Pollination is presumed to be by bees. The fruit is a 3-locular capsule with angular seeds.

Key Recognition Features The iris-like flowers with no tube and the filaments free. The pleated leaves distinguish this and most South American Iridaceae from the African ones.

Ecology and Geography In rocky places, damp fields, edges of woods, and by water, in South America from Peru and Brazil to Argentina and Uruguay.

Comment These are attractive plants, similar to *Moraea* (see p.443) but with pleated leaves. The very diverse American genera *Tigridia* Juss. and *Rigidella* Lindl. have pleated leaves and a diversity of flower types. In most species of *Tigridia* the flowers are of subdued colours, except for the well-known *T. pavonia* (L. fil.) DC, which has 3 large, spotted outer perianth segments. *Rigidella* usually has bright red flowers with reflexed petals, adapted for pollination by sunbirds.

Libertia

Libertia Spreng. (1825), in the family Iridaceae, contains around 9 species, mostly in Australia and New Zealand.

Description Perennials to 1.2m, often forming large clumps, with creeping rhizomes and fibrous roots. Leaves to 45cm, flat, mostly basal. Flowers white or pale blue, in loose clusters on usually branching stems. The 3 outer perianth segments smaller than the inner, and usually greenish. Stamens 3, the filaments slightly fused at the base. Ovary inferior, of 3 fused carpels with many ovules; style with 3 spreading branches. Pollination is presumed to be by bees. The fruit is a 3-locular capsule, with many rounded seeds.

Key Recognition Features The small, usually white flowers with 3 conspicuous, rounded perianth segments, and narrow leaves from the base.

Ecology and Geography In damp fields and by water in New Zealand and Australia, with a few species northwards to New Guinea, and in South America in the Andes.

Comment These are modest plants, with small, white flowers, or pale blue in *L. caerulescens* Kunth from Chile. In *L. peregrinans* Ckn. & Allan the stiff leaves are often yellow-edged or all tawny yellow, and appear on the tips of running rhizomes. *Libertia* is the only genus of the Iridaceae in New Zealand. *Diplarrhena* Labill. with 2 species in southeastern Australia and Tasmania, is similar to *Libertia*, but is shorter with larger flowers opening singly at the tips of the stems and the 3 outer perianth segments larger than the inner and pure white.

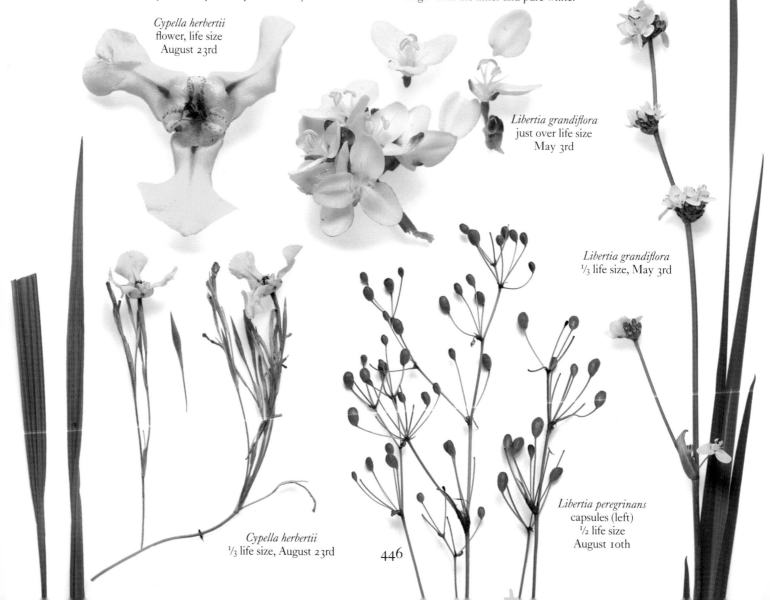

Cypella herbertii
flower, life size
August 23rd

Libertia grandiflora
just over life size
May 3rd

Libertia grandiflora
1/3 life size, May 3rd

Cypella herbertii
1/3 life size, August 23rd

Libertia peregrinans
capsules (left)
1/2 life size
August 10th

Sisyrinchium

Sisyrinchium L. (1753), in the family Iridaceae, contains between 80 and 200 species, mostly in South America.

Description Perennials to 1.5m, often forming large clumps. Leaves to 45cm, flat, often grass-like, mostly basal. Flowers blue, purple, yellow, white, or pale brown, short-stalked, in dense clusters on usually simple stems. Perianth segments 6, usually all equal, often with slender points. Stamens 3, the filaments united into a tube. Ovary inferior, of 3 fused carpels with many ovules; style with 3 branches. Pollination is presumed to be by various insects. The fruit is a 3-locular capsule with many rounded seeds.

Key Recognition Features The small flowers on short stalks, with 6 equal perianth segments with narrow points.

Ecology and Geography In grassy fields, on lake shores, and in open, sandy, and usually damp places; from western Ireland westwards throughout North and South America.

Comment Several species are cultivated. *Sisyrinchium striatum* Smith syn. *Phaiophleps nigricans* (Phil.) R.C. Foster from Argentina and Chile is common, especially in its variegated form 'Aunt May'. The blue-eyed grass, found wild in Ireland, is often called *S. bermudianum* L. but should now be *S. graminoides* Bicknell; though wild in Greenland, there is some doubt as to whether it is native in Ireland; seed could well have travelled there in the gut of a goose. Some species are found under the name *Olsynium* Raf.; these include the attractive *S. douglasii* Dietr. from western North America, with wiry leaves and nodding purple flowers, and *S. junceum* E. Mey. ex K. Presl.. *Sisyrinchium* is most closely related to the South African genus *Bobartia* L. and to *Libertia*.

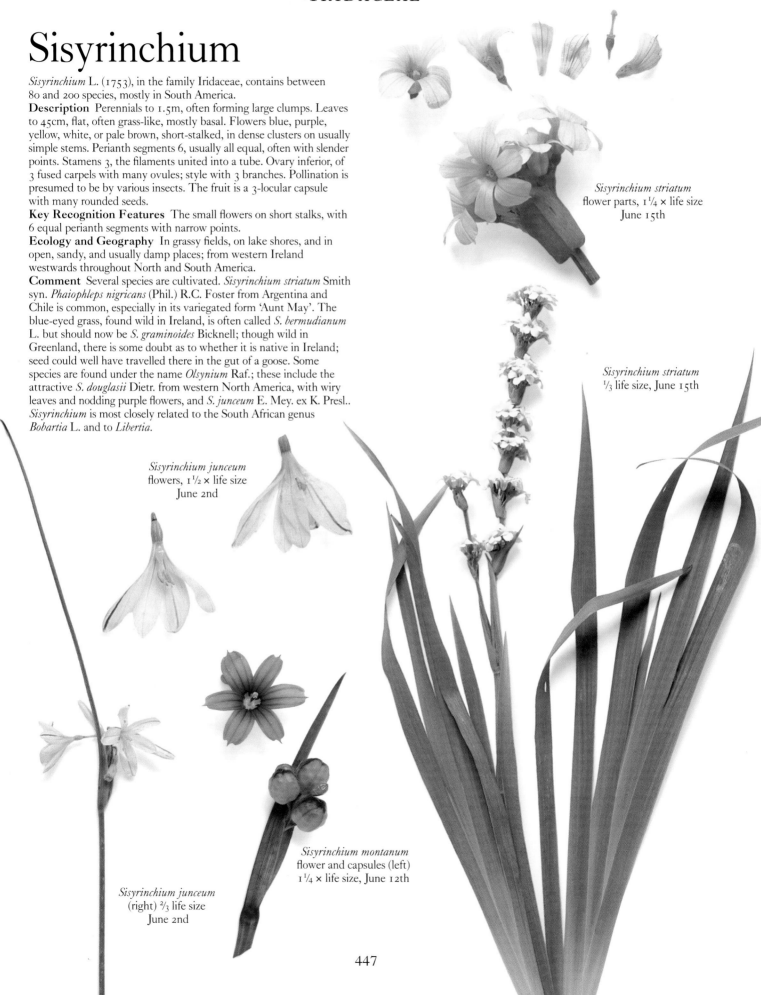

Sisyrinchium striatum
flower parts, 1¼ × life size
June 15th

Sisyrinchium striatum
⅓ life size, June 15th

Sisyrinchium junceum
flowers, 1½ × life size
June 2nd

Sisyrinchium montanum
flower and capsules (left)
1¼ × life size, June 12th

Sisyrinchium junceum
(right) ⅔ life size
June 2nd

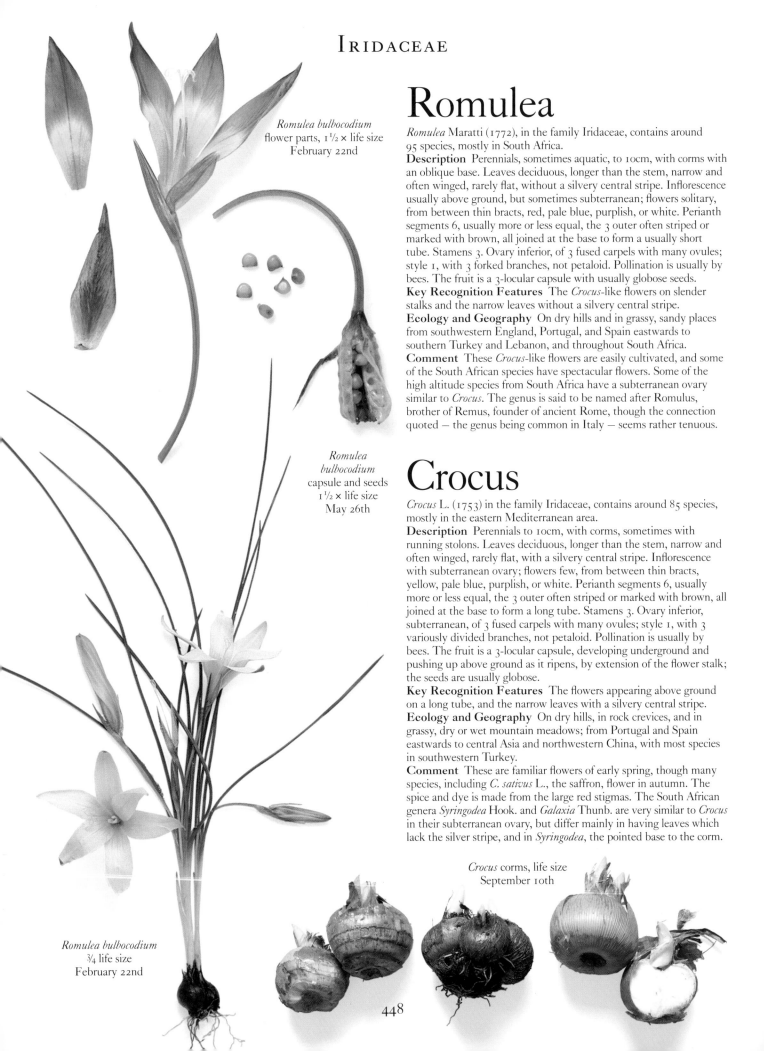

Romulea bulbocodium
flower parts, 1½ × life size
February 22nd

Romulea

Romulea Maratti (1772), in the family Iridaceae, contains around 95 species, mostly in South Africa.

Description Perennials, sometimes aquatic, to 10cm, with corms with an oblique base. Leaves deciduous, longer than the stem, narrow and often winged, rarely flat, without a silvery central stripe. Inflorescence usually above ground, but sometimes subterranean; flowers solitary, from between thin bracts, red, pale blue, purplish, or white. Perianth segments 6, usually more or less equal, the 3 outer often striped or marked with brown, all joined at the base to form a usually short tube. Stamens 3. Ovary inferior, of 3 fused carpels with many ovules; style 1, with 3 forked branches, not petaloid. Pollination is usually by bees. The fruit is a 3-locular capsule with usually globose seeds.

Key Recognition Features The *Crocus*-like flowers on slender stalks and the narrow leaves without a silvery central stripe.

Ecology and Geography On dry hills and in grassy, sandy places from southwestern England, Portugal, and Spain eastwards to southern Turkey and Lebanon, and throughout South Africa.

Comment These *Crocus*-like flowers are easily cultivated, and some of the South African species have spectacular flowers. Some of the high altitude species from South Africa have a subterranean ovary similar to *Crocus*. The genus is said to be named after Romulus, brother of Remus, founder of ancient Rome, though the connection quoted — the genus being common in Italy — seems rather tenuous.

Romulea bulbocodium
capsule and seeds
1½ × life size
May 26th

Crocus

Crocus L. (1753) in the family Iridaceae, contains around 85 species, mostly in the eastern Mediterranean area.

Description Perennials to 10cm, with corms, sometimes with running stolons. Leaves deciduous, longer than the stem, narrow and often winged, rarely flat, with a silvery central stripe. Inflorescence with subterranean ovary; flowers few, from between thin bracts, yellow, pale blue, purplish, or white. Perianth segments 6, usually more or less equal, the 3 outer often striped or marked with brown, all joined at the base to form a long tube. Stamens 3. Ovary inferior, subterranean, of 3 fused carpels with many ovules; style 1, with 3 variously divided branches, not petaloid. Pollination is usually by bees. The fruit is a 3-locular capsule, developing underground and pushing up above ground as it ripens, by extension of the flower stalk; the seeds are usually globose.

Key Recognition Features The flowers appearing above ground on a long tube, and the narrow leaves with a silvery central stripe.

Ecology and Geography On dry hills, in rock crevices, and in grassy, dry or wet mountain meadows; from Portugal and Spain eastwards to central Asia and northwestern China, with most species in southwestern Turkey.

Comment These are familiar flowers of early spring, though many species, including *C. sativus* L., the saffron, flower in autumn. The spice and dye is made from the large red stigmas. The South African genera *Syringodea* Hook. and *Galaxia* Thunb. are very similar to *Crocus* in their subterranean ovary, but differ mainly in having leaves which lack the silver stripe, and in *Syringodea*, the pointed base to the corm.

Crocus corms, life size
September 10th

Romulea bulbocodium
¾ life size
February 22nd

448

IRIDACEAE

Crocus byzantinus (far left)
and *Crocus niveus* (left)
flower parts, 1½ × life size
October 7th

Crocus chrysanthus
'Blue Pearl'
¾ life size
February 25th

Crocus chrysanthus
'Blue Pearl', flower section
1⅓ × life size, February 25th

Crocus niveus
¾ life size
October 7th

Crocus byzantinus
capsule and seeds
1½ × life size
May 26th

Crocus chrysanthus
'E.P. Bowles'
¾ life size
February 14th

Crocus byzantinus
(right) ¾ life size
October 7th

449

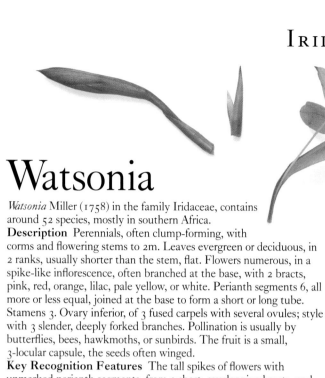

Watsonia

Watsonia Miller (1758) in the family Iridaceae, contains around 52 species, mostly in southern Africa.

Description Perennials, often clump-forming, with corms and flowering stems to 2m. Leaves evergreen or deciduous, in 2 ranks, usually shorter than the stem, flat. Flowers numerous, in a spike-like inflorescence, often branched at the base, with 2 bracts, pink, red, orange, lilac, pale yellow, or white. Perianth segments 6, all more or less equal, joined at the base to form a short or long tube. Stamens 3. Ovary inferior, of 3 fused carpels with several ovules; style with 3 slender, deeply forked branches. Pollination is usually by butterflies, bees, hawkmoths, or sunbirds. The fruit is a small, 3-locular capsule, the seeds often winged.

Key Recognition Features The tall spikes of flowers with unmarked perianth segments, from 2 short, overlapping bracts, and the style with 3 slender, forked branches.

Ecology and Geography In rocky places, grassy plains, veldt, and mountain bogs in southern Africa, from the Cape peninsula northwards to the Transvaal, with most species in the extreme southwestern Cape.

Comment Many species are easily cultivated, long-lived perennials; the summer-growing species are likely to be the most hardy in cold climates, but are seldom cultivated; most evergreen species survive a few degrees of frost. Old plants can be rejuvenated by burning in early spring. In spite of its superficial similarity to *Gladiolus* (see pp.444–45), *Watsonia* is most closely related to *Lapeirousia* Pourret and a group of other small South African genera.

Ixia

Ixia L. (1753), in the family Iridaceae, contains around 50 species, mostly from South Africa.

Description Perennials with corms and flowering stems to 1m. Leaves in 2 ranks, deciduous, usually shorter than the stem, flat. Flowers several in an upright, spike-like inflorescence, with 2 short bracts, red, pink, purple, yellow, pale green, or white. Perianth segments 6, all more or less equal, joined at the base to form a short or long tube. Stamens 3, the filaments free or joined into a short tube. Ovary inferior, of 3 fused carpels with few ovules; style with 3 slender branches. Pollination is presumed to be by insects. The fruit is a small, 3-locular, thin-walled capsule opening by flaps; seeds angular.

Key Recognition Features The upright spikes of flowers on wiry stems, with generally unmarked perianth segments, and the thread-like style with 3 branches.

Ecology and Geography In sandy places and veldt, often in marshy places or open scrub, and on mountain slopes. In the Cape from the Peninsula northwards, with 1 species in tropical Africa.

Comment Many species are cultivated, though as they grow in winter they are not very hardy. The bulbs are inexpensive, and they can be grown as annuals if planted in early spring. *Ixia viridiflora* Lam. has remarkable jade-green flowers with a black centre, and is often cultivated. The genus *Schizostylis* Backh. & Harvey has 1 species, *S. coccinea* Backhouse & Harvey, the kaffir lily, which grows by stony mountain streams in the Drakensberg; it is similar to *Ixia*, but summer-growing, with swollen rhizomes instead of corms and flowers which may be red, pink, or white, with the style divided into 3 slender, red branches. It is especially valuable for its late summer and autumn flowering.

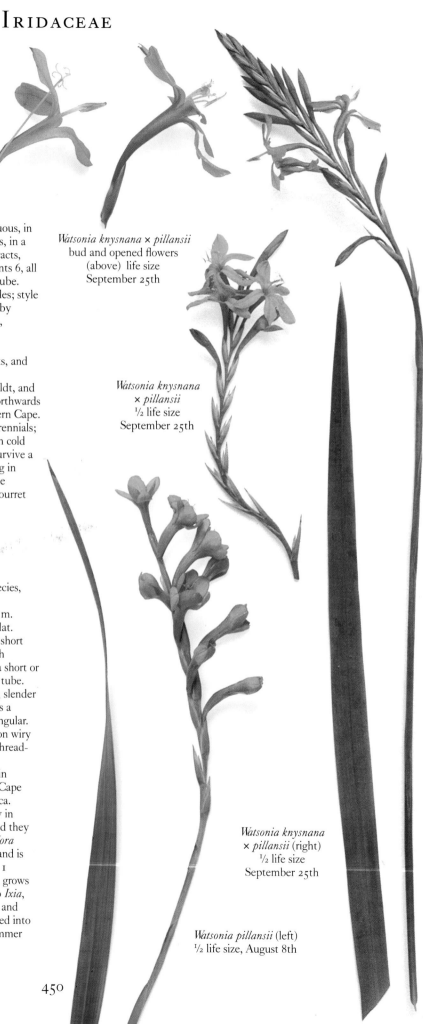

Watsonia knysnana × pillansii
bud and opened flowers
(above) life size
September 25th

Watsonia knysnana × pillansii
½ life size
September 25th

Watsonia knysnana × pillansii (right)
½ life size
September 25th

Watsonia pillansii (left)
½ life size, August 8th

IRIDACEAE

Ixia bellendenii
flower parts
life size
May 25th

Watsonia cultivar
flower and flower section
just under life size
August 14th

Ixia bellendenii
½ life size
May 25th

Schizostylis coccinea
½ life size
November 3rd

Watsonia cultivar
(left) ½ life size
August 14th

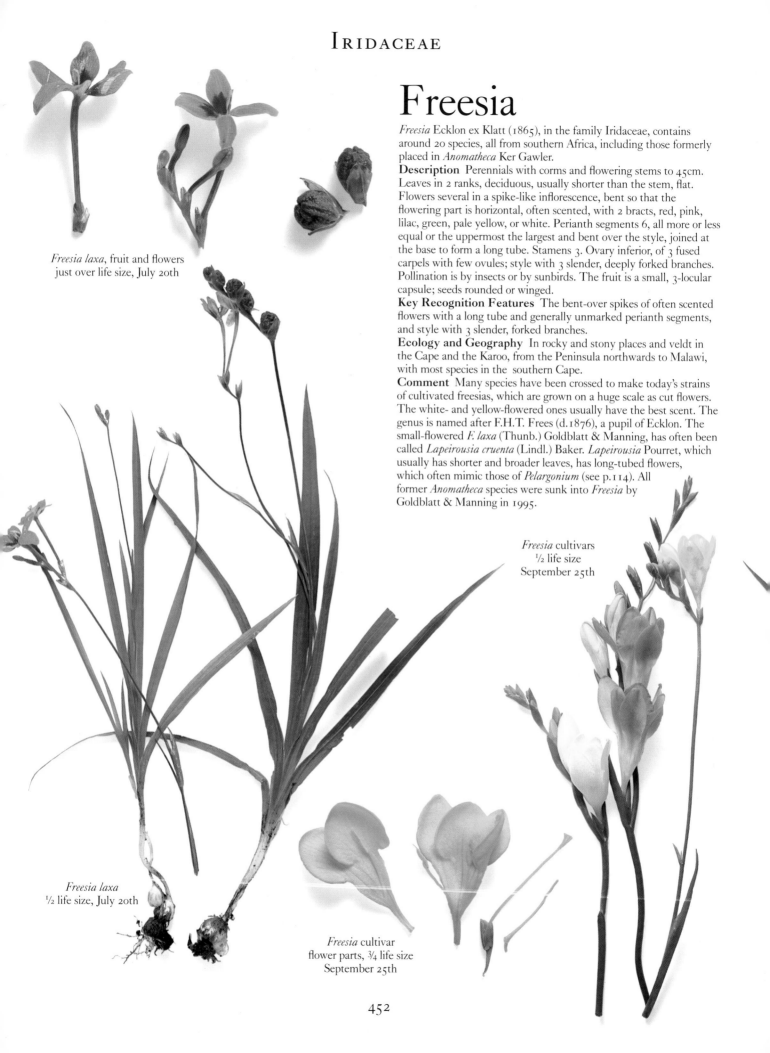

Freesia

Freesia Ecklon ex Klatt (1865), in the family Iridaceae, contains around 20 species, all from southern Africa, including those formerly placed in *Anomatheca* Ker Gawler.

Description Perennials with corms and flowering stems to 45cm. Leaves in 2 ranks, deciduous, usually shorter than the stem, flat. Flowers several in a spike-like inflorescence, bent so that the flowering part is horizontal, often scented, with 2 bracts, red, pink, lilac, green, pale yellow, or white. Perianth segments 6, all more or less equal or the uppermost the largest and bent over the style, joined at the base to form a long tube. Stamens 3. Ovary inferior, of 3 fused carpels with few ovules; style with 3 slender, deeply forked branches. Pollination is by insects or by sunbirds. The fruit is a small, 3-locular capsule; seeds rounded or winged.

Key Recognition Features The bent-over spikes of often scented flowers with a long tube and generally unmarked perianth segments, and style with 3 slender, forked branches.

Ecology and Geography In rocky and stony places and veldt in the Cape and the Karoo, from the Peninsula northwards to Malawi, with most species in the southern Cape.

Comment Many species have been crossed to make today's strains of cultivated freesias, which are grown on a huge scale as cut flowers. The white- and yellow-flowered ones usually have the best scent. The genus is named after F.H.T. Frees (d.1876), a pupil of Ecklon. The small-flowered *F. laxa* (Thunb.) Goldblatt & Manning, has often been called *Lapeirousia cruenta* (Lindl.) Baker. *Lapeirousia* Pourret, which usually has shorter and broader leaves, has long-tubed flowers, which often mimic those of *Pelargonium* (see p.114). All former *Anomatheca* species were sunk into *Freesia* by Goldblatt & Manning in 1995.

Freesia laxa, fruit and flowers just over life size, July 20th

Freesia cultivars
¹⁄₂ life size
September 25th

Freesia laxa
¹⁄₂ life size, July 20th

Freesia cultivar
flower parts, ¾ life size
September 25th

Crocosmia

Crocosmia Planch. (1851), montbretia, in the family Iridaceae, contains around 9 species, all from southern Africa.

Description Perennials with conical corms, usually forming large clumps, sometimes with long stolons. Flowering stems to 1.5m. Leaves in 2 ranks, deciduous, usually shorter than the stem, flat or pleated. Flowers rather few in a spike-like inflorescence, often bent so that the flowering part is horizontal, each with 2 bracts, red, or orange, rarely yellow, not scented. Perianth segments 6, joined at the base to form a long tube. Stamens 3, bent towards the upper side of the flower. Ovary inferior, of 3 fused carpels with few ovules; style with 3 slender, simple branches. Pollination is presumed to be by insects and sunbirds. The fruit is a small, 3-locular capsule; seeds often winged.

Key Recognition Features Clump-forming perennials with arching spikes of red or orange flowers with more or less equal perianth segments and a long tube.

Ecology and Geography In wet places by streams, in woods, and on rock ledges, usually in the mountains, from the eastern Cape northwards to Malawi.

Comment The common montbretia, *C. × crocosmiiflora* (Burbridge & Dean) N.E. Br., which is widely naturalised in Europe, is a hybrid between *C. aurea* (Hook. fil.) Planch. and *C. pottsii* (Baker) N.E. Br.. *Crocosmia pottsii* itself, with smaller, red flowers, is naturalised in western Scotland and on Exmoor in Devon.

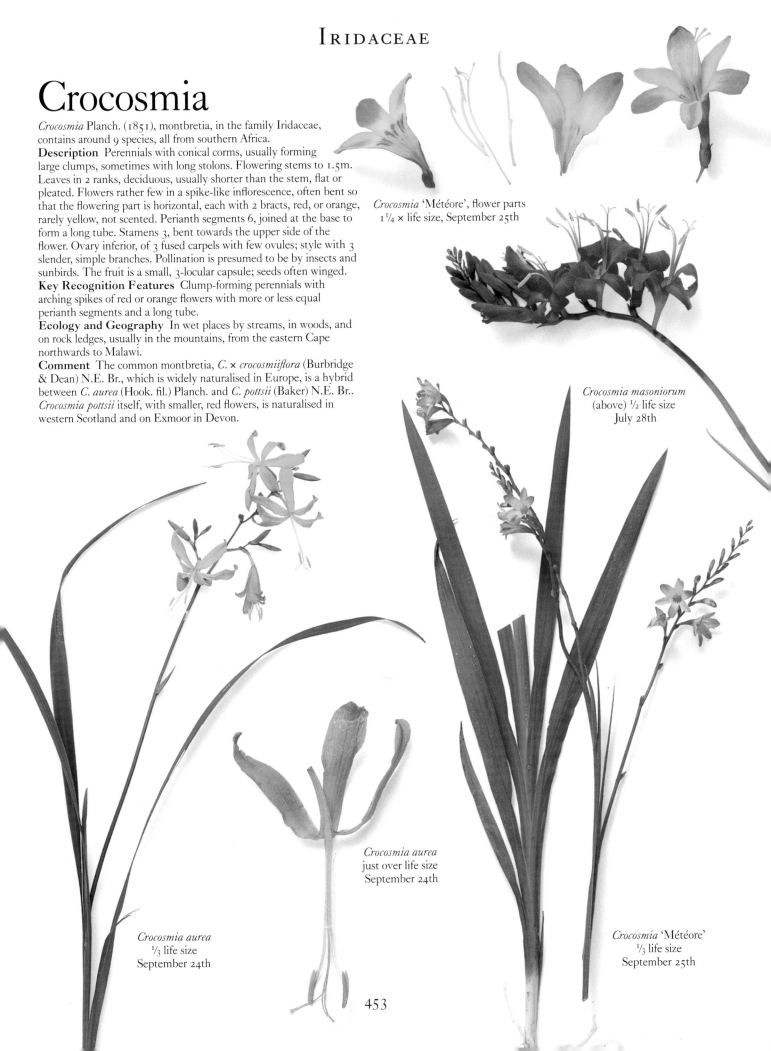

Crocosmia 'Météore', flower parts
1 ¼ × life size, September 25th

Crocosmia masoniorum
(above) ½ life size
July 28th

Crocosmia aurea
just over life size
September 24th

Crocosmia aurea
⅓ life size
September 24th

Crocosmia 'Météore'
⅓ life size
September 25th

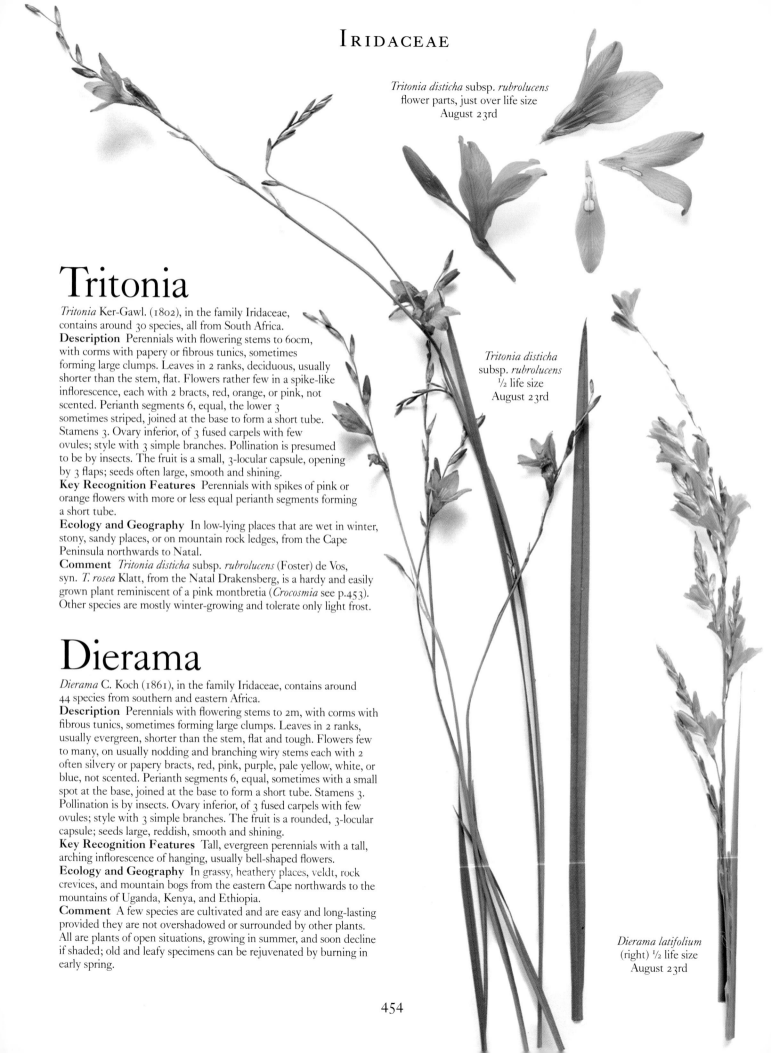

Tritonia disticha subsp. *rubrolucens*
flower parts, just over life size
August 23rd

Tritonia

Tritonia Ker-Gawl. (1802), in the family Iridaceae,
contains around 30 species, all from South Africa.
Description Perennials with flowering stems to 60cm,
with corms with papery or fibrous tunics, sometimes
forming large clumps. Leaves in 2 ranks, deciduous, usually
shorter than the stem, flat. Flowers rather few in a spike-like
inflorescence, each with 2 bracts, red, orange, or pink, not
scented. Perianth segments 6, equal, the lower 3
sometimes striped, joined at the base to form a short tube.
Stamens 3. Ovary inferior, of 3 fused carpels with few
ovules; style with 3 simple branches. Pollination is presumed
to be by insects. The fruit is a small, 3-locular capsule, opening
by 3 flaps; seeds often large, smooth and shining.
Key Recognition Features Perennials with spikes of pink or
orange flowers with more or less equal perianth segments forming
a short tube.
Ecology and Geography In low-lying places that are wet in winter,
stony, sandy places, or on mountain rock ledges, from the Cape
Peninsula northwards to Natal.
Comment *Tritonia disticha* subsp. *rubrolucens* (Foster) de Vos,
syn. *T. rosea* Klatt, from the Natal Drakensberg, is a hardy and easily
grown plant reminiscent of a pink montbretia (*Crocosmia* see p.453).
Other species are mostly winter-growing and tolerate only light frost.

Tritonia disticha
subsp. *rubrolucens*
¹/₂ life size
August 23rd

Dierama

Dierama C. Koch (1861), in the family Iridaceae, contains around
44 species from southern and eastern Africa.
Description Perennials with flowering stems to 2m, with corms with
fibrous tunics, sometimes forming large clumps. Leaves in 2 ranks,
usually evergreen, shorter than the stem, flat and tough. Flowers few
to many, on usually nodding and branching wiry stems each with 2
often silvery or papery bracts, red, pink, purple, pale yellow, white, or
blue, not scented. Perianth segments 6, equal, sometimes with a small
spot at the base, joined at the base to form a short tube. Stamens 3.
Pollination is by insects. Ovary inferior, of 3 fused carpels with few
ovules; style with 3 simple branches. The fruit is a rounded, 3-locular
capsule; seeds large, reddish, smooth and shining.
Key Recognition Features Tall, evergreen perennials with a tall,
arching inflorescence of hanging, usually bell-shaped flowers.
Ecology and Geography In grassy, heathery places, veldt, rock
crevices, and mountain bogs from the eastern Cape northwards to the
mountains of Uganda, Kenya, and Ethiopia.
Comment A few species are cultivated and are easy and long-lasting
provided they are not overshadowed or surrounded by other plants.
All are plants of open situations, growing in summer, and soon decline
if shaded; old and leafy specimens can be rejuvenated by burning in
early spring.

Dierama latifolium
(right) ¹/₂ life size
August 23rd

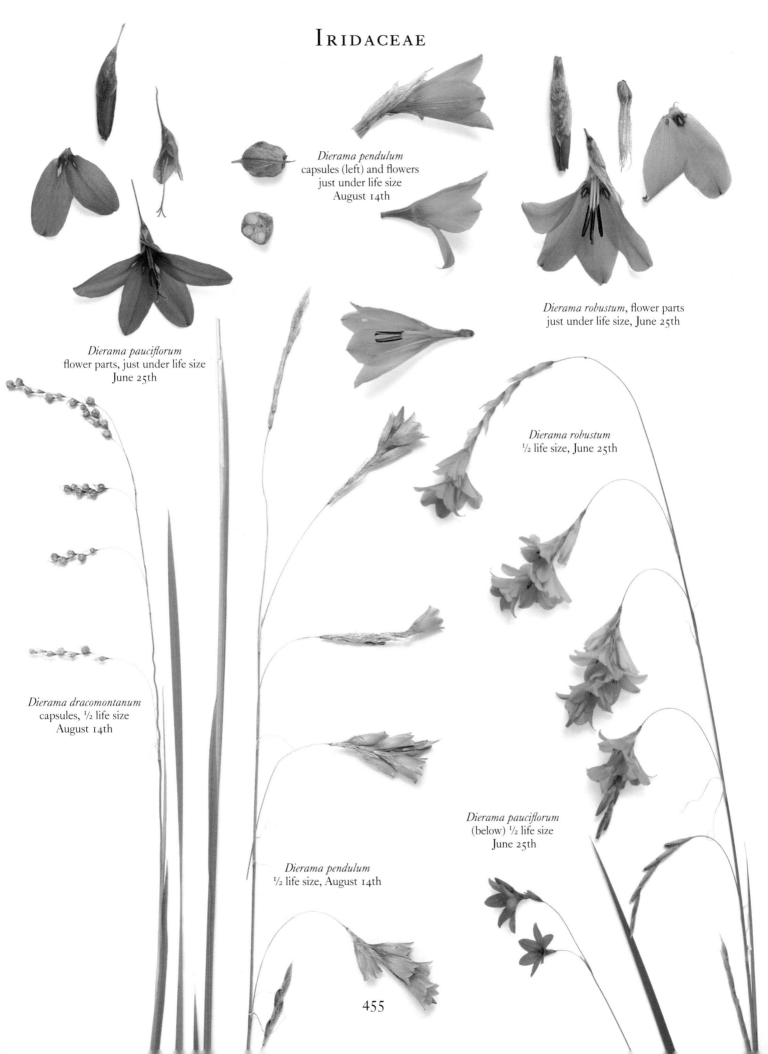

IRIDACEAE

Dierama pendulum
capsules (left) and flowers
just under life size
August 14th

Dierama robustum, flower parts
just under life size, June 25th

Dierama pauciflorum
flower parts, just under life size
June 25th

Dierama robustum
¹/₂ life size, June 25th

Dierama dracomontanum
capsules, ¹/₂ life size
August 14th

Dierama pauciflorum
(below) ¹/₂ life size
June 25th

Dierama pendulum
¹/₂ life size, August 14th

455

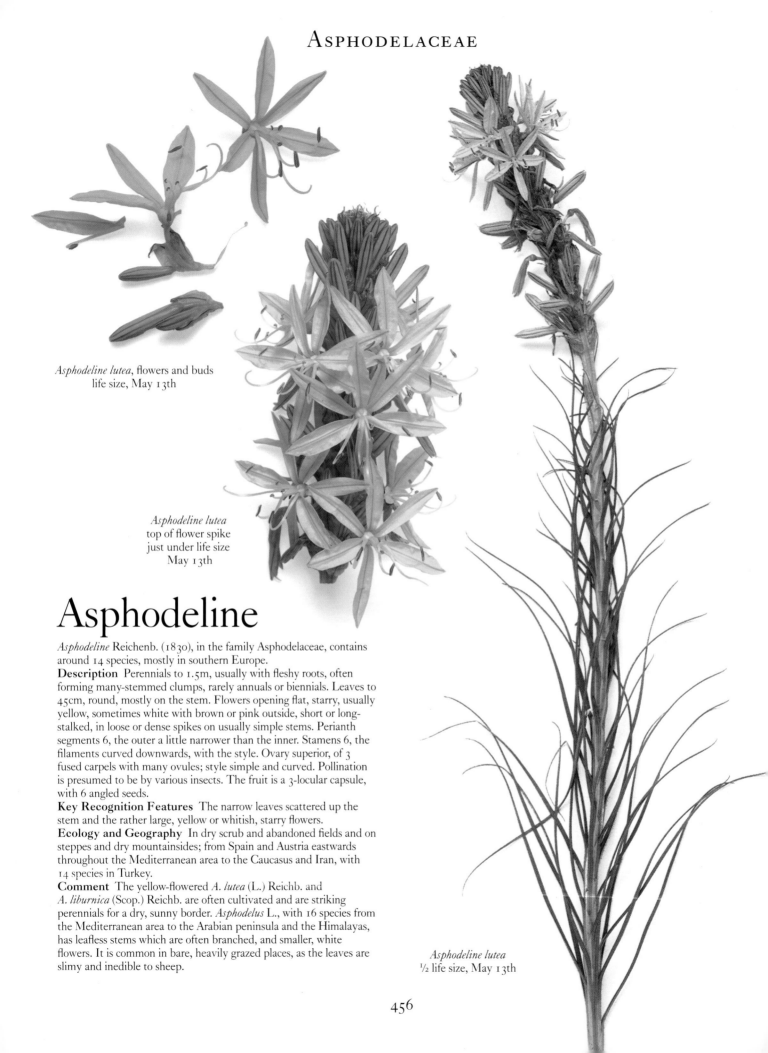

Asphodeline lutea, flowers and buds
life size, May 13th

Asphodeline lutea
top of flower spike
just under life size
May 13th

Asphodeline

Asphodeline Reichenb. (1830), in the family Asphodelaceae, contains around 14 species, mostly in southern Europe.

Description Perennials to 1.5m, usually with fleshy roots, often forming many-stemmed clumps, rarely annuals or biennials. Leaves to 45cm, round, mostly on the stem. Flowers opening flat, starry, usually yellow, sometimes white with brown or pink outside, short or long-stalked, in loose or dense spikes on usually simple stems. Perianth segments 6, the outer a little narrower than the inner. Stamens 6, the filaments curved downwards, with the style. Ovary superior, of 3 fused carpels with many ovules; style simple and curved. Pollination is presumed to be by various insects. The fruit is a 3-locular capsule, with 6 angled seeds.

Key Recognition Features The narrow leaves scattered up the stem and the rather large, yellow or whitish, starry flowers.

Ecology and Geography In dry scrub and abandoned fields and on steppes and dry mountainsides; from Spain and Austria eastwards throughout the Mediterranean area to the Caucasus and Iran, with 14 species in Turkey.

Comment The yellow-flowered *A. lutea* (L.) Reichb. and *A. liburnica* (Scop.) Reichb. are often cultivated and are striking perennials for a dry, sunny border. *Asphodelus* L., with 16 species from the Mediterranean area to the Arabian peninsula and the Himalayas, has leafless stems which are often branched, and smaller, white flowers. It is common in bare, heavily grazed places, as the leaves are slimy and inedible to sheep.

Asphodeline lutea
½ life size, May 13th

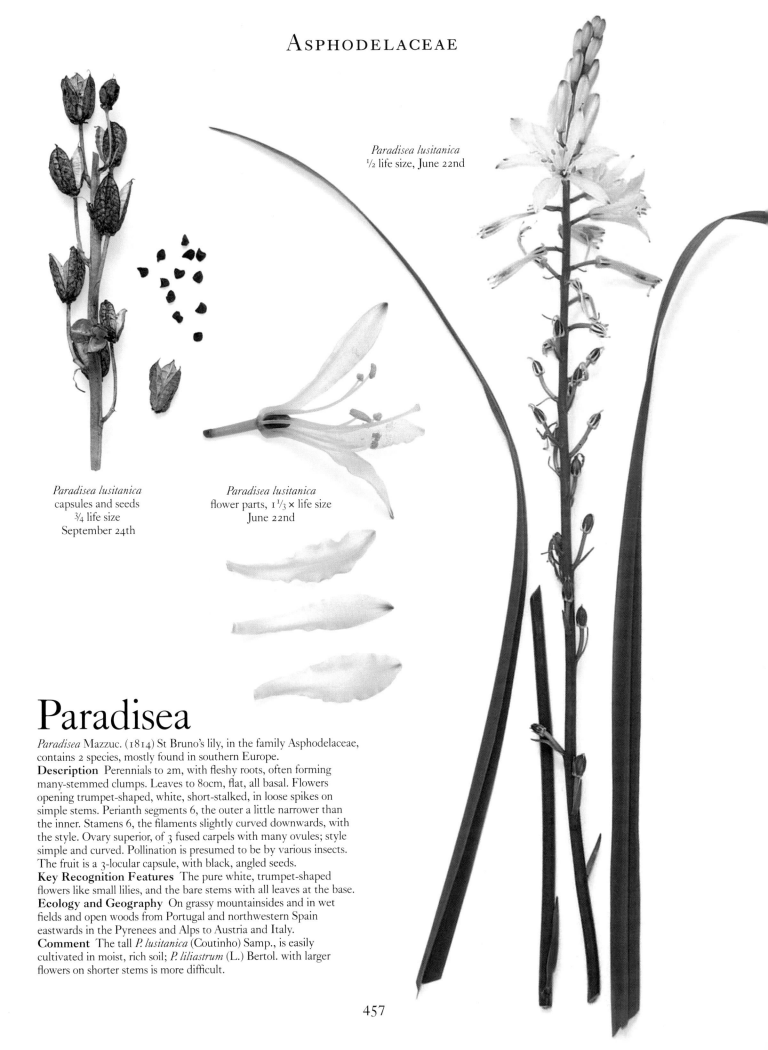

Paradisea lusitanica
½ life size, June 22nd

Paradisea lusitanica
capsules and seeds
¾ life size
September 24th

Paradisea lusitanica
flower parts, 1⅓ × life size
June 22nd

Paradisea

Paradisea Mazzuc. (1814) St Bruno's lily, in the family Asphodelaceae, contains 2 species, mostly found in southern Europe.

Description Perennials to 2m, with fleshy roots, often forming many-stemmed clumps. Leaves to 80cm, flat, all basal. Flowers opening trumpet-shaped, white, short-stalked, in loose spikes on simple stems. Perianth segments 6, the outer a little narrower than the inner. Stamens 6, the filaments slightly curved downwards, with the style. Ovary superior, of 3 fused carpels with many ovules; style simple and curved. Pollination is presumed to be by various insects. The fruit is a 3-locular capsule, with black, angled seeds.

Key Recognition Features The pure white, trumpet-shaped flowers like small lilies, and the bare stems with all leaves at the base.

Ecology and Geography On grassy mountainsides and in wet fields and open woods from Portugal and northwestern Spain eastwards in the Pyrenees and Alps to Austria and Italy.

Comment The tall *P. lusitanica* (Coutinho) Samp., is easily cultivated in moist, rich soil; *P. liliastrum* (L.) Bertol. with larger flowers on shorter stems is more difficult.

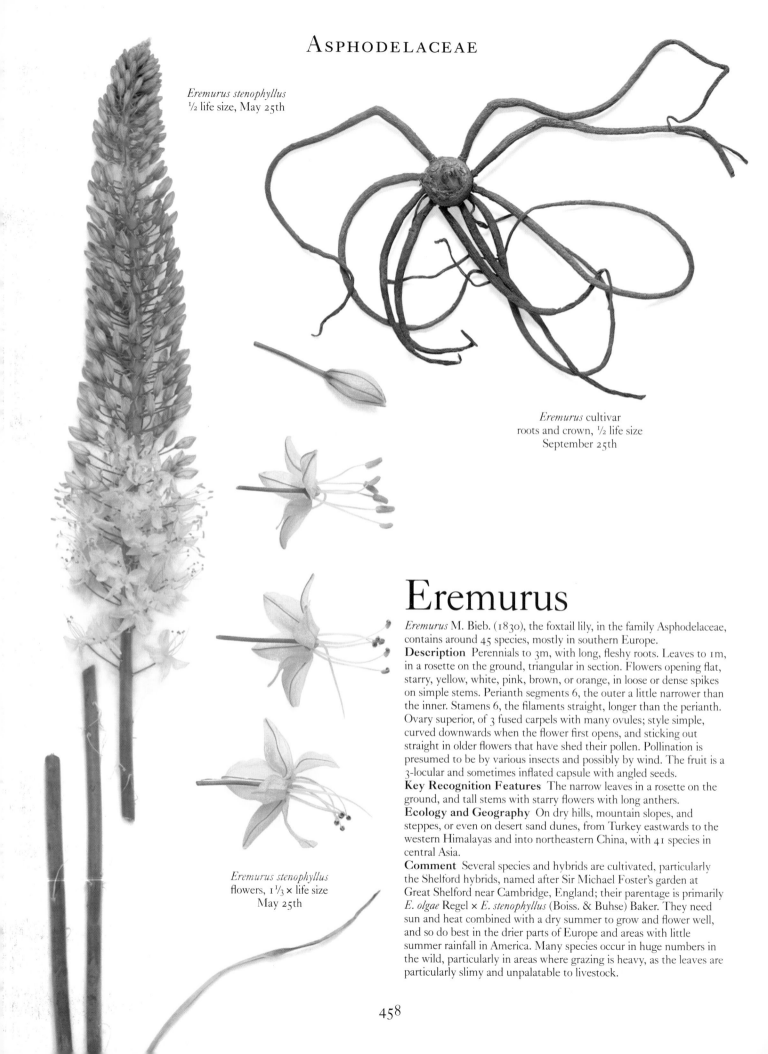

Eremurus stenophyllus
½ life size, May 25th

Eremurus cultivar
roots and crown, ½ life size
September 25th

Eremurus stenophyllus
flowers, 1⅓ × life size
May 25th

Eremurus

Eremurus M. Bieb. (1830), the foxtail lily, in the family Asphodelaceae, contains around 45 species, mostly in southern Europe.

Description Perennials to 3m, with long, fleshy roots. Leaves to 1m, in a rosette on the ground, triangular in section. Flowers opening flat, starry, yellow, white, pink, brown, or orange, in loose or dense spikes on simple stems. Perianth segments 6, the outer a little narrower than the inner. Stamens 6, the filaments straight, longer than the perianth. Ovary superior, of 3 fused carpels with many ovules; style simple, curved downwards when the flower first opens, and sticking out straight in older flowers that have shed their pollen. Pollination is presumed to be by various insects and possibly by wind. The fruit is a 3-locular and sometimes inflated capsule with angled seeds.

Key Recognition Features The narrow leaves in a rosette on the ground, and tall stems with starry flowers with long anthers.

Ecology and Geography On dry hills, mountain slopes, and steppes, or even on desert sand dunes, from Turkey eastwards to the western Himalayas and into northeastern China, with 41 species in central Asia.

Comment Several species and hybrids are cultivated, particularly the Shelford hybrids, named after Sir Michael Foster's garden at Great Shelford near Cambridge, England; their parentage is primarily *E. olgae* Regel × *E. stenophyllus* (Boiss. & Buhse) Baker. They need sun and heat combined with a dry summer to grow and flower well, and so do best in the drier parts of Europe and areas with little summer rainfall in America. Many species occur in huge numbers in the wild, particularly in areas where grazing is heavy, as the leaves are particularly slimy and unpalatable to livestock.

Aloe

Aloe Wolf (1776), in the family Asphodelaceae, contains around 350 species, mostly in Africa and Madagascar.

Description Perennials with flowering stems to 60cm, shrubs, or short, stout trees. Leaves to 30cm, evergreen, mostly basal, thick and fleshy, toothed on the edges, and with a terminal spine. Flowers tubular, red, orange, or yellow, sometimes partly green, short-stalked, in loose or dense spikes on simple or branched stems. Perianth segments 6, joined at the base into a straight or curved tube. Stamens 6, often extending one at a time from the perianth. Ovary superior, of 3 fused carpels with many ovules; style simple and straight. Pollination is mostly by sunbirds, and by various warblers in the north. The fruit is a 3-locular capsule with many seeds.

Key Recognition Features Evergreens with succulent leaves and tubular red, yellow, or partially green flowers.

Ecology and Geography On mountain rocks or in dry, grassy, sandy, or rocky places. Mainly in the dry parts of South Africa (145 species) and Madagascar, with a few species reaching as far north as the Canary Islands and the Arabian peninsula.

Comment Many species are grown in dry, frost-free areas where they are valuable for their winter flowering. In America they attract hummingbirds. A few, such as *A. ciliaris* Haw. from the Cape, will tolerate a few degrees of frost. *Aloe variegata* L. the partridge-breast aloe, is a common houseplant. *Aloe vera* (L.) Burm. fil. from the Canary Islands, is the source of aloes used in cosmetics and particularly against sunburn.

Bulbine

Bulbine Wolf (1776) in the family Asphodelaceae, contains around 50 species, mostly in southern Africa.

Description Perennials to 60cm, often with swollen stem or leaf bases. Leaves to 35cm, mostly basal, usually thick and fleshy. Flowers opening starry, white, yellow, or reddish, short-stalked, in loose spikes on simple stems. Perianth segments 6, the outer a little narrower than the inner. Stamens 6, the filaments often with a tuft of hairs. Ovary superior, of 3 fused carpels with many ovules; style simple and straight. Pollination is presumed to be by various insects. The fruit is a 3-locular capsule with few seeds.

Key Recognition Features The yellow or brownish, starry flowers and the fleshy leaves.

Ecology and Geography On mountain rocks or in dry, sandy or rocky places. Mainly in the dry parts of South Africa, with *B. abyssinica* Rich. extending northwards through East Africa.

Comment A few species are grown as curiosities. The remarkable *B. mesembryanthemoides* Haw. from Namaqualand and the Little Karroo is a window succulent or stone plant, like a *Lithops* N.E. Br. or *Fenestraria* N.E. Br., with only 2 leaves, the tips translucent, the rest underground to escape the intense heat. These plants are found growing on patches of white quartzite pebbles, which make them even harder for grazing animals to spot.

Aloe niebuhriana
flowers, 1 ¹/₂ × life size
June 22nd

Aloe niebuhriana
¹/₂ life size
June 22nd

Bulbine frutescens
¹/₂ life size
September 4th

Bulbine frutescens flowers and stem section
1 ³/₄ × life size, September 4th

459

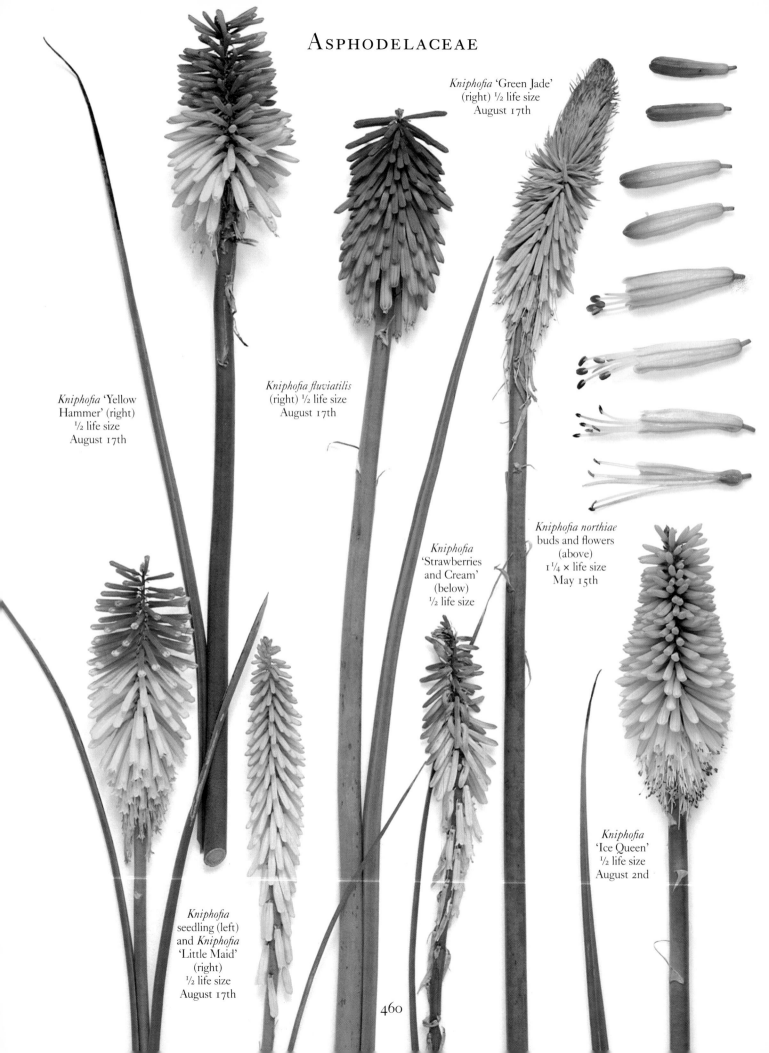

Kniphofia 'Green Jade'
(right) ¹/₂ life size
August 17th

Kniphofia 'Yellow
Hammer' (right)
¹/₂ life size
August 17th

Kniphofia fluviatilis
(right) ¹/₂ life size
August 17th

Kniphofia
'Strawberries
and Cream'
(below)
¹/₂ life size

Kniphofia northiae
buds and flowers
(above)
1¹/₄ × life size
May 15th

Kniphofia
'Ice Queen'
¹/₂ life size
August 2nd

Kniphofia
seedling (left)
and *Kniphofia*
'Little Maid'
(right)
¹/₂ life size
August 17th

460

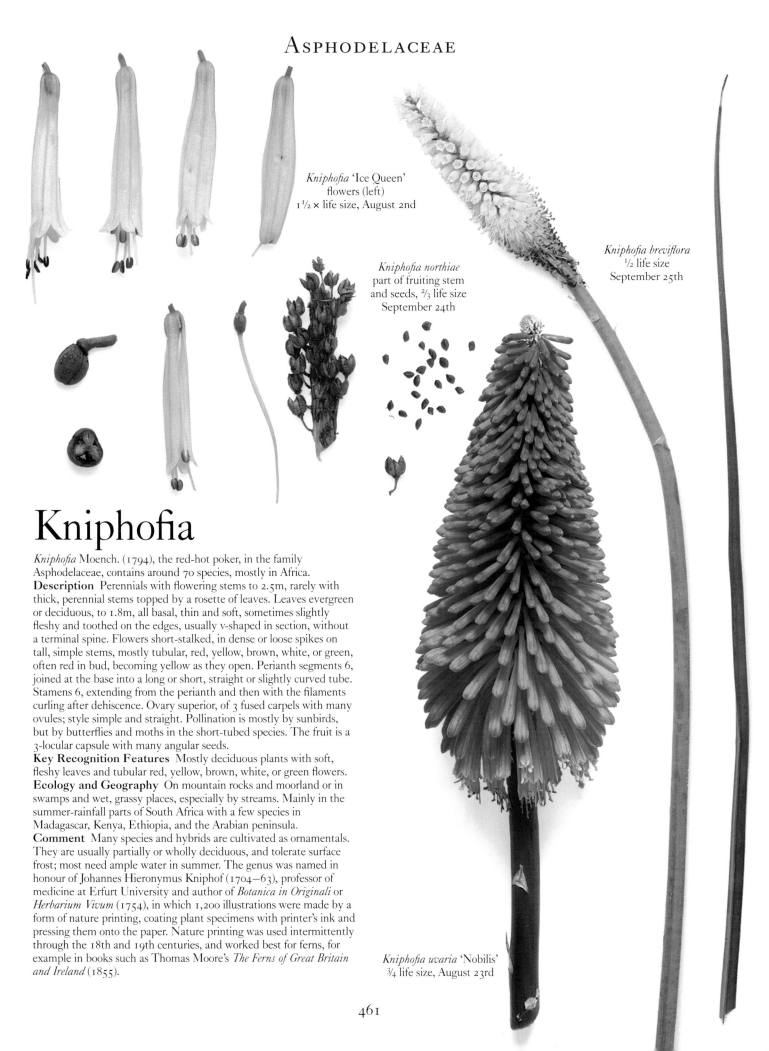

Kniphofia 'Ice Queen'
flowers (left)
1½ × life size, August 2nd

Kniphofia northiae
part of fruiting stem
and seeds, ⅔ life size
September 24th

Kniphofia breviflora
½ life size
September 25th

Kniphofia

Kniphofia Moench. (1794), the red-hot poker, in the family Asphodelaceae, contains around 70 species, mostly in Africa.

Description Perennials with flowering stems to 2.5m, rarely with thick, perennial stems topped by a rosette of leaves. Leaves evergreen or deciduous, to 1.8m, all basal, thin and soft, sometimes slightly fleshy and toothed on the edges, usually v-shaped in section, without a terminal spine. Flowers short-stalked, in dense or loose spikes on tall, simple stems, mostly tubular, red, yellow, brown, white, or green, often red in bud, becoming yellow as they open. Perianth segments 6, joined at the base into a long or short, straight or slightly curved tube. Stamens 6, extending from the perianth and then with the filaments curling after dehiscence. Ovary superior, of 3 fused carpels with many ovules; style simple and straight. Pollination is mostly by sunbirds, but by butterflies and moths in the short-tubed species. The fruit is a 3-locular capsule with many angular seeds.

Key Recognition Features Mostly deciduous plants with soft, fleshy leaves and tubular red, yellow, brown, white, or green flowers.

Ecology and Geography On mountain rocks and moorland or in swamps and wet, grassy places, especially by streams. Mainly in the summer-rainfall parts of South Africa with a few species in Madagascar, Kenya, Ethiopia, and the Arabian peninsula.

Comment Many species and hybrids are cultivated as ornamentals. They are usually partially or wholly deciduous, and tolerate surface frost; most need ample water in summer. The genus was named in honour of Johannes Hieronymus Kniphof (1704–63), professor of medicine at Erfurt University and author of *Botanica in Originali* or *Herbarium Vivum* (1754), in which 1,200 illustrations were made by a form of nature printing, coating plant specimens with printer's ink and pressing them onto the paper. Nature printing was used intermittently through the 18th and 19th centuries, and worked best for ferns, for example in books such as Thomas Moore's *The Ferns of Great Britain and Ireland* (1855).

Kniphofia uvaria 'Nobilis'
¾ life size, August 23rd

Hemerocallis

Hemerocallis L. (1753), daylily, in the family Hemerocallidaceae, contains around 15 species, mostly in eastern Asia.

Description Perennials with fleshy roots and flowering stems to 1.5m, often forming dense clumps. Leaves to 80cm, usually slightly ridged, all basal. Flowers opening trumpet-shaped, yellow or orange, or pink, purple, brown, red, or white in cultivars, short-stalked, opening in succession, in usually branching or umbel-like heads. Perianth segments 6, the outer a little narrower than the inner, joined at the base. Stamens 6, the filaments slightly curved downwards with the style. Ovary superior, of 3 fused carpels with many ovules; style simple and curved. Pollination is presumed to be by various insects. The fruit is a 3-angled or winged capsule with black, angled seeds.

Key Recognition Features The clumps of soft, often pale green leaves, and the trumpet-shaped flowers on bare, branching stems.

Ecology and Geography On grassy mountain slopes and in wet fields and open woods from southwestern China to eastern Siberia and Japan.

Comment Daylilies are popular garden plants, particularly in eastern North America, where they thrive in the hot, humid summers. Here many hundreds of hybrids have been named, with larger flowers and in a much greater range of colours than are found in the wild species. The plants have long been cultivated in China and Japan, where the flowers are eaten.

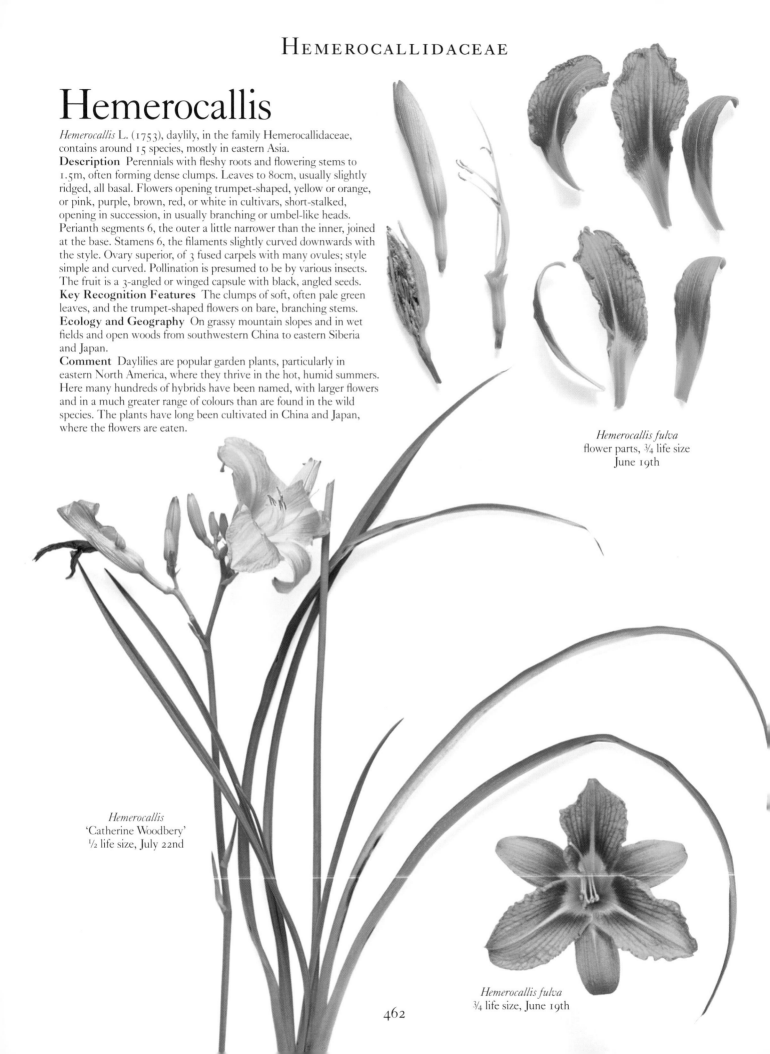

Hemerocallis fulva
flower parts, ¾ life size
June 19th

Hemerocallis
'Catherine Woodbery'
½ life size, July 22nd

Hemerocallis fulva
¾ life size, June 19th

462

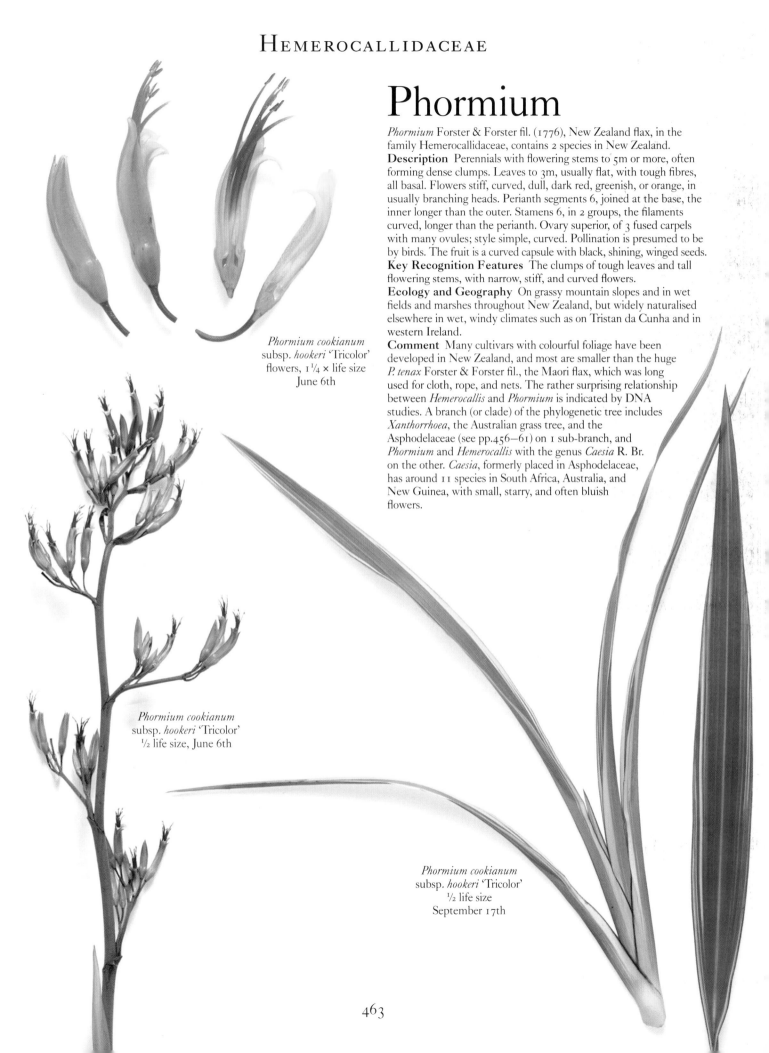

Phormium

Phormium Forster & Forster fil. (1776), New Zealand flax, in the family Hemerocallidaceae, contains 2 species in New Zealand.

Description Perennials with flowering stems to 5m or more, often forming dense clumps. Leaves to 3m, usually flat, with tough fibres, all basal. Flowers stiff, curved, dull, dark red, greenish, or orange, in usually branching heads. Perianth segments 6, joined at the base, the inner longer than the outer. Stamens 6, in 2 groups, the filaments curved, longer than the perianth. Ovary superior, of 3 fused carpels with many ovules; style simple, curved. Pollination is presumed to be by birds. The fruit is a curved capsule with black, shining, winged seeds.

Key Recognition Features The clumps of tough leaves and tall flowering stems, with narrow, stiff, and curved flowers.

Ecology and Geography On grassy mountain slopes and in wet fields and marshes throughout New Zealand, but widely naturalised elsewhere in wet, windy climates such as on Tristan da Cunha and in western Ireland.

Comment Many cultivars with colourful foliage have been developed in New Zealand, and most are smaller than the huge *P. tenax* Forster & Forster fil., the Maori flax, which was long used for cloth, rope, and nets. The rather surprising relationship between *Hemerocallis* and *Phormium* is indicated by DNA studies. A branch (or clade) of the phylogenetic tree includes *Xanthorrhoea*, the Australian grass tree, and the Asphodelaceae (see pp.456–61) on 1 sub-branch, and *Phormium* and *Hemerocallis* with the genus *Caesia* R. Br. on the other. *Caesia*, formerly placed in Asphodelaceae, has around 11 species in South Africa, Australia, and New Guinea, with small, starry, and often bluish flowers.

Phormium cookianum
subsp. *hookeri* 'Tricolor'
flowers, 1¼ × life size
June 6th

Phormium cookianum
subsp. *hookeri* 'Tricolor'
½ life size, June 6th

Phormium cookianum
subsp. *hookeri* 'Tricolor'
½ life size
September 17th

Hippeastrum advenum
½ life size, October 1st

Amaryllis

Amaryllis L. (1753), belladonna lily, in the family Amaryllidaceae, contains 2 species in South Africa.

Description Perennials with large bulbs and flowering stems to 1m. Leaves to 40cm, chanelled, all basal, absent at flowering time. Flowers pink, white, or reddish, sweetly scented, in umbels. Perianth segments 6, joined only at the base, more or less equal. Stamens 6, the filaments curved, shorter than the perianth. Ovary inferior, of 3 fused carpels with many ovules; style simple and curved. Pollination is presumed to be by insects. The fruit is a capsule with few seeds.

Key Recognition Features The pink or reddish, scented flowers in autumn, before the leaves.

Ecology and Geography Wet fields on clay and the edges of *vleis* and marshes in South Africa, in Cape province from near Clanwilliam to George, and in the Richtersveld in the northeastern Cape.

Comment *Amaryllis belladonna* L. is easily grown, but requires good conditions to flower in climates with cold summers; the ideal site is a bed of deep, rich soil at the base of a sunny wall. In some gardens in the south of France and in California it flowers freely in any situation. The name *Amaryllis belladonna* L. has been the subject of some controversy, but the use of *Hippeastrum* for similar large-flowered American Amaryllidaceae seems to have become accepted. A second species has been discovered in the northeastern Cape.

Hippeastrum

Hippeastrum Herb. (1821), in the family Amaryllidaceae, contains around 80 species, in Central and South America, with 1 species, *H. reginae* (L.) Herb., also in West Africa.

Description Perennials with bulbs and with flowering stems to 2m. Leaves to 1m, usually flat, all basal, present at flowering time. Flowers in umbels, red, pink, orange, yellow, white, or pale green, sometimes striped, spotted, or tessellated, occasionally sweetly scented. Perianth segments 6, usually more or less equal, joined at the base, sometimes with a long tube. Stamens 6, the filaments curved, shorter or longer than the perianth. Ovary inferior, of 3 fused carpels with many ovules; style simple and curved, sometimes with 3 short branches at the tip. Pollination is by insects and by hummingbirds. The fruit is a capsule, with black, shining, flat, and winged seeds.

Key Recognition Features The flat leaves and usually large, trumpet-shaped flowers.

Ecology and Geography In stony scrub, on rocky hills, cliffs, and rock ledges, and in mountain meadows from the West Indies to southern Chile and Argentina.

Comment Many species and most cultivars are easily grown in pots, given ample water when they are growing, and kept drier when dormant. Some of the hardier, more southern species, such as *H. bifidum* (Herb.) Baker and *H. advenum* Herb., have been placed in the genus *Rhodophiala* Presl.; they have narrower leaves and flowers 3–7cm long on longer flower stalks. In the subtropical *H. psittacinum* (Ker Gawl.) Herb. from southern Brazil, the upper 3 perianth segments are wide and heavily striped with dark reddish-purple, while the lower 3 are narrower, green with few stripes. In the Mexican *Sprekelia formossisima* (L.) Herb. the lower 3 perianth segments are held together to form a tube around the filaments and style, an adaptation to pollination by hummingbirds.

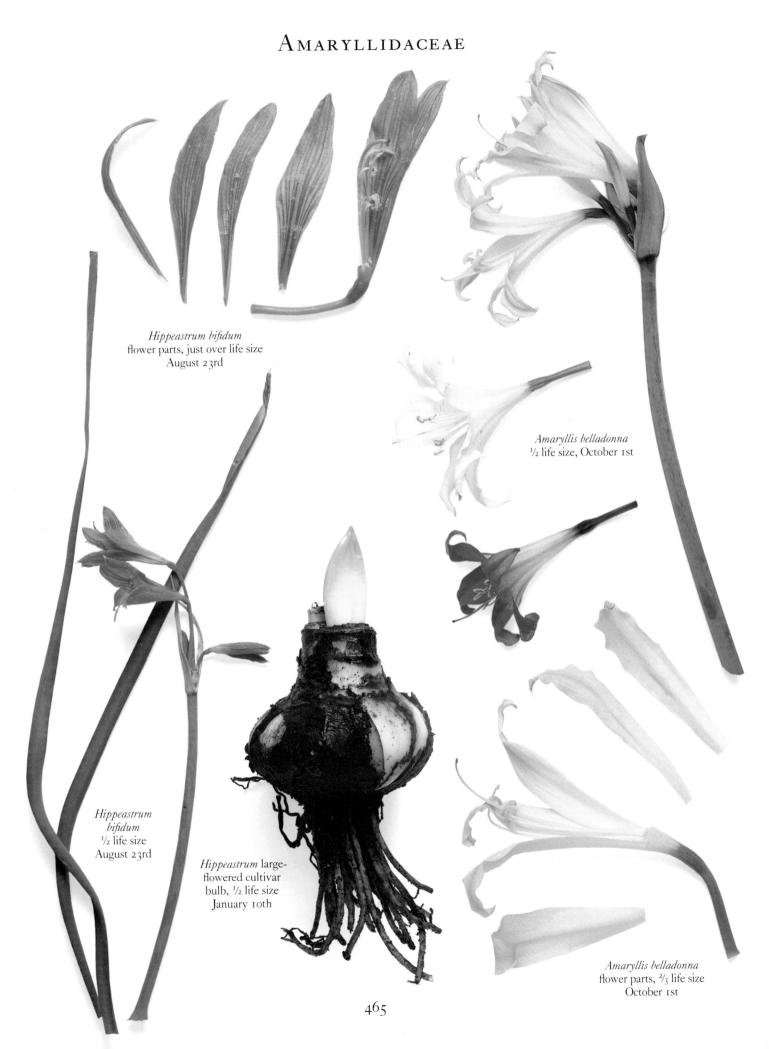

Amaryllidaceae

Hippeastrum bifidum
flower parts, just over life size
August 23rd

Amaryllis belladonna
½ life size, October 1st

*Hippeastrum
bifidum*
½ life size
August 23rd

Hippeastrum large-
flowered cultivar
bulb, ½ life size
January 10th

Amaryllis belladonna
flower parts, ⅔ life size
October 1st

465

Cyrtanthus

Cyrtanthus Herb. (1821), fire lily, in the family Amaryllidaceae, contains around 50 species in southern and eastern Africa.

Description Perennials with hollow flowering stems to 60cm, with bulbs. Leaves to 60cm, parallel-sided, usually flat, occasionally coiled, all basal, present or absent at flowering time. Flowers solitary or in umbels, red, pink, orange, yellow, white, or green, occasionally sweetly scented. Perianth segments 6, usually more or less equal, joined at the base, sometimes with a long tube. Stamens 6, the filaments inserted on the tube, shorter or longer than the perianth. Ovary inferior, of 3 fused carpels with many ovules; style simple and curved, sometimes with 3 short branches at the tip. Pollination is by insects and sunbirds. The fruit is a capsule, with shining black, flat, winged seeds.

Key Recognition Features The flat leaves and usually tubular, nodding flowers in an umbel.

Ecology and Geography On cliffs and rock ledges, in scrub, and on stony or grassy slopes, often flowering soon after a fire. From the Cape Peninsula northwards to Kenya and the Sudan.

Comment Several species are cultivated for their unusual flowers. *Cyrtanthus* now includes *Vallota* and *Anoiganthus,* each with only 1 species. *Vallota purpurea* (Ait.) Herb. the Scarborough or George lily, commonly cultivated but now rare in the wild in the Langkloof around George, is now *Cyrtanthus elatus* (Jacq.) Traub. and *Anoiganthus breviflorus* Harv. is now *Cyrtanthus breviflorus* Harv. Several American genera such as *Eustephia* Cav. have very similar tubular flowers, but have a corona, sometimes reduced to teeth, on which the filaments are inserted.

Cyrtanthus falcatus
½ life size, April 10th

Cyrtanthus falcatus, opened flowers
1¼ × life size, April 10th

Nerine

Nerine Herb. (1820), in the family Amaryllidaceae, contains around 30 species in South Africa.

Description Perennials with solid flowering stems to 60cm, with bulbs. Leaves to 40cm, parallel-sided, usually flat, occasionally filiform, all basal, present or absent at flowering time. Flowers in umbels, red, pink, or white. Perianth segments 6, usually more or less equal, joined at the base, usually narrow with distinctly wavy edges. Stamens 6, the filaments sometimes with appendages at the base, inserted on the tube, usually deflexed and longer than the perianth. Ovary inferior, of 3 fused carpels each with 4 ovules; style simple and curved. Pollination is by insects. The fruit is a capsule with few round, green, and succulent seeds, which split the capsule wall before they are ripe.

Key Recognition Features Autumn-flowering bulbs with narrow, wavy-edged perianth segments, and followed by globose, green, succulent seeds.

Ecology and Geography On cliffs and rock ledges, in marshes and sandy flats, and on low hills in South Africa from the Cape northwards to Natal and Orange Free State.

Comment A few species and numerous hybrids are cultivated for their flowers, which usually appear in autumn before the leaves.

Lycoris

Lycoris Herb. (1821), in the family Amaryllidaceae, contains around 11 species in eastern Asia.

Description Perennials with solid flowering stems to 70cm, with bulbs. Leaves to 60cm, parallel-sided, flat, all basal, usually absent at flowering time. Flowers in umbels, red, pink, or yellow, often scented. Perianth segments 6, usually more or less equal, usually joined at the base, often narrow with distinctly wavy edges, with minute scales. Stamens 6, the filaments sometimes with appendages at the base, inserted on the throat of the tube, often deflexed and longer than the perianth. Ovary inferior, of 3 fused carpels, each with 2 or 3 ovules; style simple and curved. Pollination is by insects. The fruit is an ovoid capsule with blackish-brown seeds.

Key Recognition Features Summer- or autumn-flowering bulbs with usually narrow perianth segments, and blackish-brown seeds.

Ecology and Geography On low hills, in hedges and scrub, and on banks between paddy fields in Japan and eastern China.

Comment These bulbs are not commonly cultivated, but thrive with protection from hard frost and a hot, moist summer. *Lycoris radiata* (L'Hérit.) Herb. has narrow, wavy perianth segments like *Nerine*, but has very long stamens; the other species have trumpet-shaped flowers closer to *Amaryllis* (see pp.464–65).

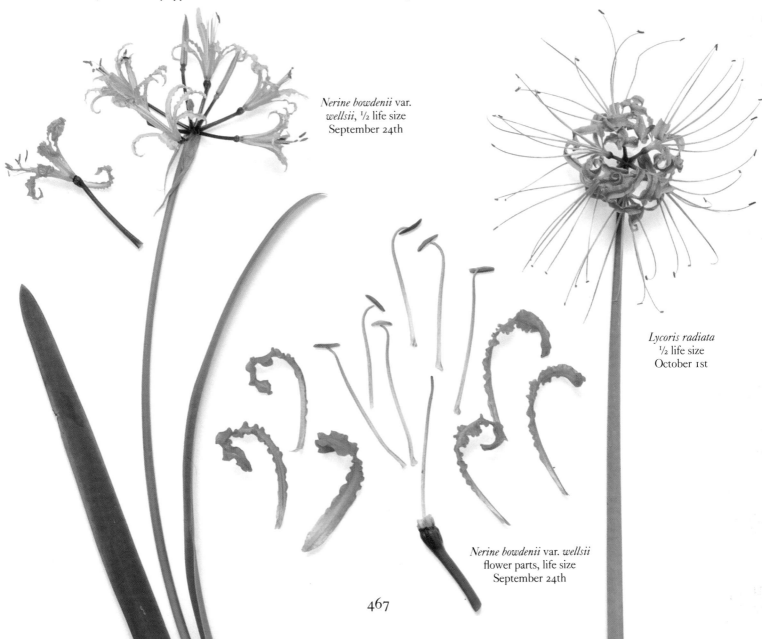

Nerine bowdenii var. *wellsii*, ½ life size
September 24th

Lycoris radiata
½ life size
October 1st

Nerine bowdenii var. *wellsii*
flower parts, life size
September 24th

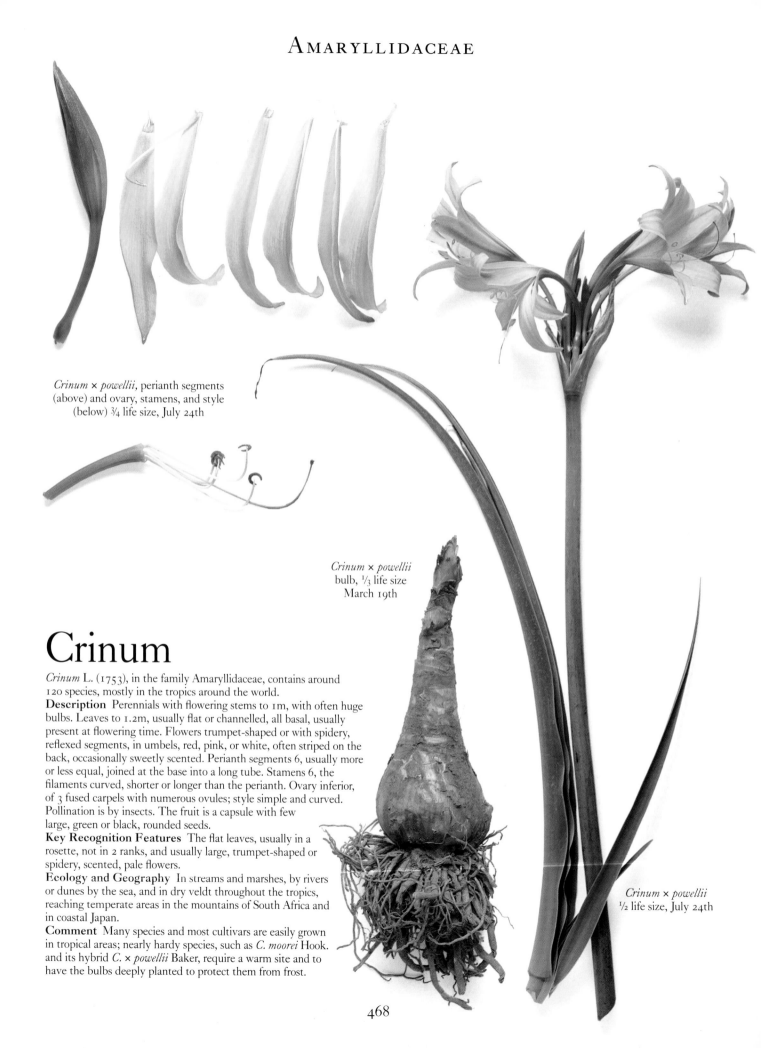

Crinum × *powellii*, perianth segments
(above) and ovary, stamens, and style
(below) ¾ life size, July 24th

Crinum × *powellii*
bulb, ⅓ life size
March 19th

Crinum

Crinum L. (1753), in the family Amaryllidaceae, contains around
120 species, mostly in the tropics around the world.

Description Perennials with flowering stems to 1m, with often huge
bulbs. Leaves to 1.2m, usually flat or channelled, all basal, usually
present at flowering time. Flowers trumpet-shaped or with spidery,
reflexed segments, in umbels, red, pink, or white, often striped on the
back, occasionally sweetly scented. Perianth segments 6, usually more
or less equal, joined at the base into a long tube. Stamens 6, the
filaments curved, shorter or longer than the perianth. Ovary inferior,
of 3 fused carpels with numerous ovules; style simple and curved.
Pollination is by insects. The fruit is a capsule with few
large, green or black, rounded seeds.

Key Recognition Features The flat leaves, usually in a
rosette, not in 2 ranks, and usually large, trumpet-shaped or
spidery, scented, pale flowers.

Ecology and Geography In streams and marshes, by rivers
or dunes by the sea, and in dry veldt throughout the tropics,
reaching temperate areas in the mountains of South Africa and
in coastal Japan.

Comment Many species and most cultivars are easily grown
in tropical areas; nearly hardy species, such as *C. moorei* Hook.
and its hybrid *C.* × *powellii* Baker, require a warm site and to
have the bulbs deeply planted to protect them from frost.

Crinum × *powellii*
½ life size, July 24th

Pancratium illyricum
flower parts, ¾ life size
May 24th

Pancratium

Pancratium L. (1753), in the family Amaryllidaceae, contains around 16 species, from southern Europe to South Africa and tropical Asia.

Description Perennials with flowering stems to 60cm, with often large bulbs. Leaves to 50cm, usually flat, all basal, bluish-green, usually present at flowering time. Flowers in umbels, pure white, sweetly scented, with a trumpet-shaped corona and 6 narrow, equal outer segments. Perianth segments joined at the base into a long tube. Stamens 6, the filaments straight, shorter or longer than the perianth, attached to the corona for much of their length. Ovary inferior, of 3 fused carpels with numerous ovules; style simple and curved. Pollination is probably by hawk moths. The fruit is a capsule with many angular, black seeds.

Key Recognition Features The flat leaves, usually in 2 ranks, and the scented, white flowers with a large corona.

Ecology and Geography In rocky places, in open woods, and on dunes by the sea; 2 species in Europe, the common coastal *P. maritimum* L. and the rare *P. illyricum* L. from Corsica, Sardinia, and Capri. Other species in the Canary Islands, Africa southwards to Namibia, and tropical Asia.

Comment A few species are cultivated. *Pancratium maritimum* is the subject of what must be one of the oldest surviving flower paintings, on frescoes at Thera, and it is also shown on a bronze Mycenaean sword dating from around 1560 BC. The tropical, mainly American genus *Hymenocallis* Salisb. is rather similar, but has ovules basal in each cell, only 1 of which usually develops into a seed; most species are larger-flowered with curling perianth segments.

Pancratium illyricum
½ life size, May 24th

Narcissus

Narcissus L. (1753), daffodil or narcissus, in the family
Amaryllidaceae, contains around 30 species and many subspecies,
mainly in western Europe.

Description Perennials with flowering stems to 60cm, with bulbs.
Leaves to 50cm, flat or filiform, all basal, usually present at flowering
time. Flowers solitary or in umbels, yellow or partly orange, white, or
green, sweetly scented, with a trumpet-shaped to very short corona and
6 equal perianth segments joined at the base into a long or short tube.
Stamens 6, the filaments usually straight, usually shorter than and not
attached to the corona. Ovary inferior, of 3 fused carpels with numerous
ovules; style simple and straight or curved. Pollination is by insects,
mainly bees. The fruit is a capsule with many rounded, black seeds.

Key Recognition Features Familiar daffodil- or narcissus-shaped
flowers with the corona free from the stamens.

Ecology and Geography In rocky places, open woods, and
meadows, with 26 species in Europe; others in North Africa and 1 in
the Canary Islands.

Comment Many species and hundreds of hybrids are cultivated as
garden plants and for the cut-flower market. The genus *Narcissus* is
divided into several sections. Section Tazettae includes the tazettas
and paper-whites, with umbels of small flowers; section Narcissus
includes the pheasant's eye, *N. poeticus* L.; section Jonquillae includes
the jonquils, with several flowers, and the 1-flowered *N. rupicola*
Dufour and its allies, with narrow, solid leaves; section Ganymedes
includes the angel's tears, *N. triandrus* L.; section Bulbocodii includes
the miniature hoop-petticoat daffodils and *N. hedraeanthus* (Webb &
Held.) Colmeiro; section Pseudonarcissi includes the trumpet
daffodils and the miniature *N. cyclamineus* DC. Hybrids both within
and between the groups are common, and have contributed great
diversity to cultivated daffodils.

Narcissus 'Rosy Sunrise'
⅔ life size, April 28th

Narcissus bulbocodium 'Golden Bells'
bulbs, 1⅓ × life size, September 17th

Narcissus pseudonarcissus
capsule section and seeds
1⅔ life size, June 18th

Narcissus 'Rosy Sunrise', bulbs
¾ life size, September 17th

Narcissus
pseudonarcissus
capsule and seeds
1¼ × life size, June 18th

Narcissus
'Soleil d'Or'
life size
March 3rd

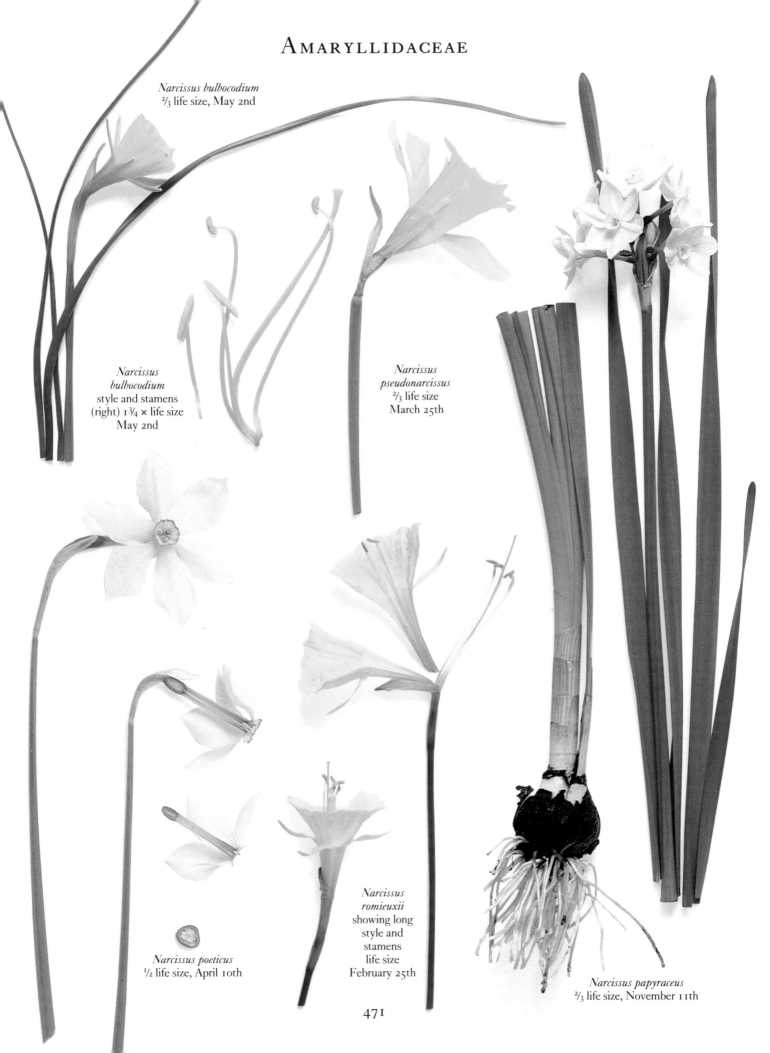

Amaryllidaceae

Narcissus bulbocodium
²/₃ life size, May 2nd

*Narcissus
bulbocodium*
style and stamens
(right) 1 ¾ × life size
May 2nd

*Narcissus
pseudonarcissus*
²/₃ life size
March 25th

Narcissus poeticus
½ life size, April 10th

*Narcissus
romieuxii*
showing long
style and
stamens
life size
February 25th

Narcissus papyraceus
²/₃ life size, November 11th

471

Sternbergia

Sternbergia Waldst. & Kit. (1803), in the family Amaryllidaceae, contains 7 species, mainly in the western Mediterranean area.

Description Perennials with flowering stems to 15cm or absent, with bulbs. Leaves to 20cm, flat, all basal, absent or present at flowering time. Flowers with 6 equal segments, solitary, yellow or white, sometimes scented. Perianth segments joined at the base into a short tube, without a corona. Stamens 6, the filaments straight, usually shorter than the perianth. Ovary inferior, of 3 fused carpels with numerous ovules; style simple, straight or curved. Pollination is by insects, mainly bees. The fruit is a capsule with many rounded seeds, which have a fleshy appendage in some species.

Key Recognition Features Simple, yellow or white, crocus-like flowers, usually on a short stem, but with a subterranean ovary in the small-flowered *S. colchiciflora* Waldst. & Kit..

Ecology and Geography In rocky places, crevices, and open woods, and on dry steppes, from Spain eastwards to central Asia and Kashmir, with 1 species, *S. clusiana* (Ker Gawl.) Spreng. as far south as Jordan.

Comment Most species are cultivated for their crocus-like autumnal flowers. The white-flowered *S. candida* Mathew & Baytop, discovered in cedar forests in southwestern Turkey, was described as recently as 1979. The genus is named after Bohemian botanist Kaspar Graf von Sternberg (1761–1838), author of a monograph on *Saxifraga*.

Galanthus

Galanthus L. (1753), snowdrop, in the family Amaryllidaceae, contains 18 species, mainly in Turkey and the Caucasus.

Description Perennials with flowering stems to 15cm, with bulbs. Leaves to 20cm, flat or ridged, all basal, present or occasionally absent at flowering time. Flowers solitary, hanging on a slender pedicel, with 3 white, equal outer perianth segments, and 3 smaller, green or yellow inner segments; sometimes scented. Perianth segments not joined at the base, without a corona. Stamens 6, the filaments straight, usually shorter than the perianth, the anthers pressed around the slender style. Ovary inferior, of 3 fused carpels with several ovules; style simple, straight. Pollination is by insects, mainly bees. The fruit is a round or oval capsule with few, rounded seeds, which have a fleshy appendage.

Key Recognition Features Hanging flowers in autumn, winter, or early spring, with 3 white outer perianth segments and 3 small, green inner segments.

Ecology and Geography In rock crevices, open woods, and alpine meadows from the Pyrenees eastwards to northern Iran, with most species in northern Turkey and the Caucasus.

Comment Snowdrops are the most common late-winter flowers, and a valuable source of early nectar for bumblebees. The pointed anthers pressed round the narrow style are similar to those of *Cyclamen* (see p.201), which flowers at the same time and comes from the same area.

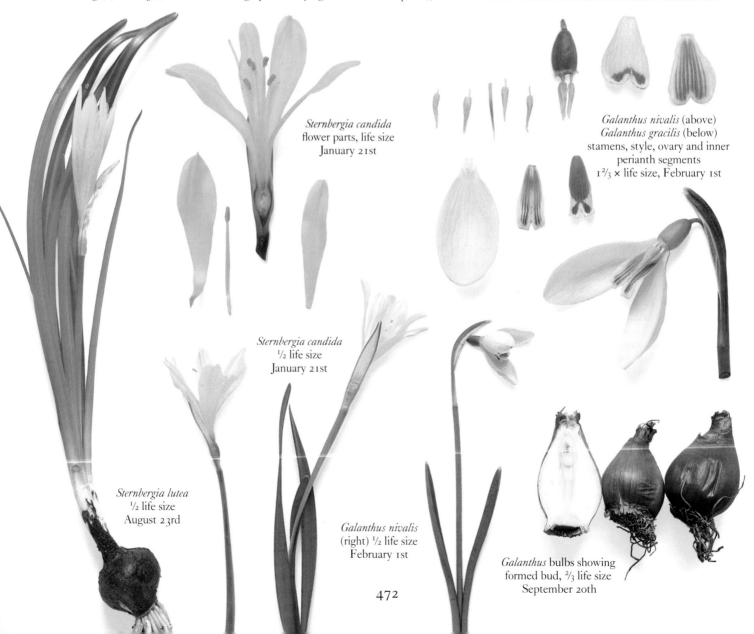

Sternbergia candida
flower parts, life size
January 21st

Galanthus nivalis (above)
Galanthus gracilis (below)
stamens, style, ovary and inner
perianth segments
1⅔ × life size, February 1st

Sternbergia candida
½ life size
January 21st

Sternbergia lutea
½ life size
August 23rd

Galanthus nivalis
(right) ½ life size
February 1st

Galanthus bulbs showing
formed bud, ⅔ life size
September 20th

Leucojum

Leucojum L. (1753), in the family Amaryllidaceae, contains 10 species, mainly in the Mediterranean area.

Description Perennials with flowering stems to 40cm, with bulbs. Leaves to 35cm, flat or filiform, all basal, present or rarely absent at flowering time. Flowers solitary or in an umbel of up to 7, each hanging on a slender pedicel, with 6 white or pink perianth segments, often with a green or yellow tip, sometimes scented. Perianth segments not joined at the base, without a corona. Stamens 6, the filaments straight, usually shorter than the perianth, the anthers sometimes pressed around the slender style. Ovary inferior, of 3 fused carpels with several ovules; style simple, narrowed towards the base. Pollination is by insects, mainly bees. The fruit is a round or sometimes inflated capsule, with few rounded seeds, which have a fleshy appendage or swollen outer layer.

Key Recognition Features Hanging flowers in autumn, winter, or early spring, with 6 white or green-tipped segments.

Ecology and Geography In alpine or riverside meadows, open woods, and sandy places from eastern England to northern Iran, with most species in the southern Mediterranean.

Comment *Leucojum aestivum* L., the summer snowflake, is found in the Thames valley in wet meadows and woods; the swollen green capsules and black seeds with air pockets can be dispersed by water. Other species are generally found in drier places. The dwarf *L. roseum* Martin with pink flowers is common in parts of Corsica and Sardinia, even growing on dunes by the sea.

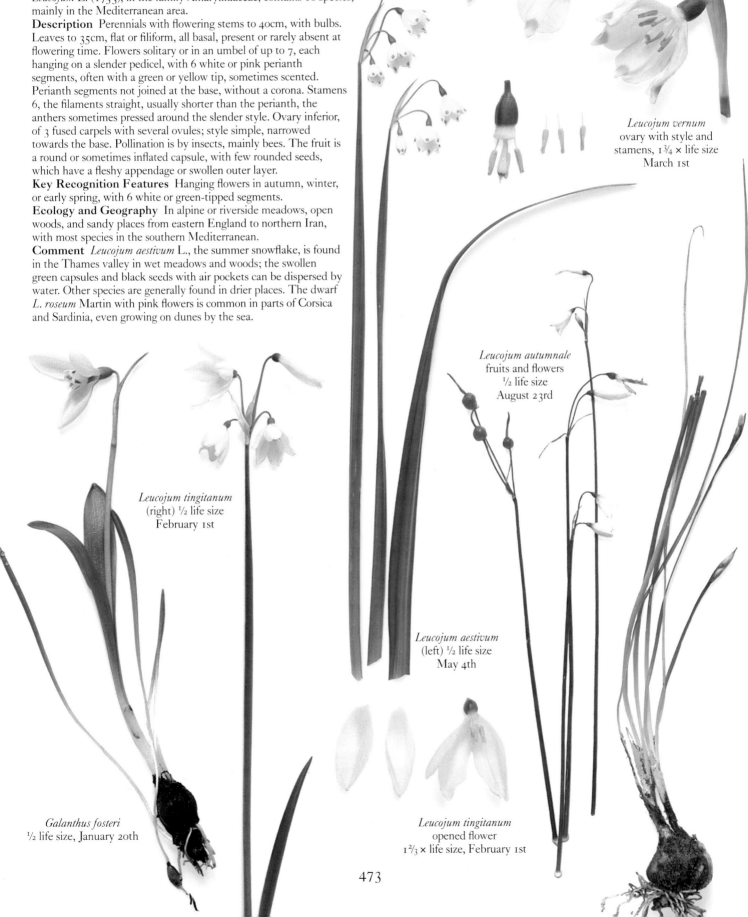

Leucojum vernum
ovary with style and
stamens, 1¾ × life size
March 1st

Leucojum autumnale
fruits and flowers
½ life size
August 23rd

Leucojum tingitanum
(right) ½ life size
February 1st

Leucojum aestivum
(left) ½ life size
May 4th

Galanthus fosteri
½ life size, January 20th

Leucojum tingitanum
opened flower
1⅔ × life size, February 1st

Allium

Allium L. (1753), in the family Alliaceae, contains around 700 species, mainly in central Asia and California.

Description Perennials with flowering stems to 1.8m, usually with bulbs, smelling of onion or garlic. Leaves variable, usually flat, mostly basal. Flowers white, pink, blue, yellow, magenta, purple, or brown, usually starry, sometimes bell-shaped, in an umbel, or rarely in superimposed whorls. Perianth segments not joined, all more or less equal. Stamens 6, equal, the filaments often with long, filiform teeth. Ovary superior or partly inferior, of 3 fused carpels with several ovules; style 1, with a simple stigma emerging from between the carpels (gynobasic). Pollination is mainly by bees. The fruit is a capsule with numerous black, usually angular seeds.

Key Recognition Features The smell of garlic or onion and the separate perianth segments.

Ecology and Geography On steppes and rocky areas, in marshes and damp woods, sometimes on sand dunes or on stony screes; throughout Europe eastwards to China, with around 150 species in Turkey, and in North America, with 38 species in California.

Comment *Allium* is one of the most important vegetable genera, including onions (*A. cepa* L.), leeks (*A. porrum* L.), garlic (*A. sativum* L.), chives (*A. schoenoprasum* L.), and Chinese chives (*A. tuberosum* Rottl. ex Spreng.). The characteristic onion or garlic smell is caused by aliphatic disulphides and many other compounds, which can have powerful anti-bacterial and other beneficial effects, particularly on blood clotting. Cultivation of many species is particularly ancient, garlic being found in deposits near the Dead Sea dating from around 3000 BC. *Allium babingtonii* Borrer, a bulbil-producing variety of wild leek, is known only from promontories and offshore islands on coasts of Ireland and Cornwall, such as the Aran and Scilly islands, where it is often associated with early Christian settlements, who may have used it medicinally and distributed it; reproduction by bulbils is vital for propagation when summers are too cold and wet for seed to ripen. *Allium regelii* Trautr. from the Salang pass in Afghanistan is unique in having the flowers in whorls up the stem. In the desert species *A. schubertii* Zucc. and *A. protensum* Wendelbo and some others such as *A. cristophii* Trautv., the spherical flowerheads become stiff in fruit and blow along in the dry autumn winds, distributing the seeds as they roll along.

DNA studies indicate that the Alliaceae, characterised by the umbel of flowers and superior ovary, is closely related to the Amaryllidaceae, which has an inferior ovary. Some genera of Alliaceae have the characteristic smell, others do not.

Allium ursinum
fruit and flowers
1¾ × life size, May 20th

Allium ursinum
½ life size
May 20th

Allium nigrum
bulbs, life size
September 17th

Allium sativum
garlic cloves, ⅔ life size
September 17th

Allium schoenoprasum
just under life size
May 10th

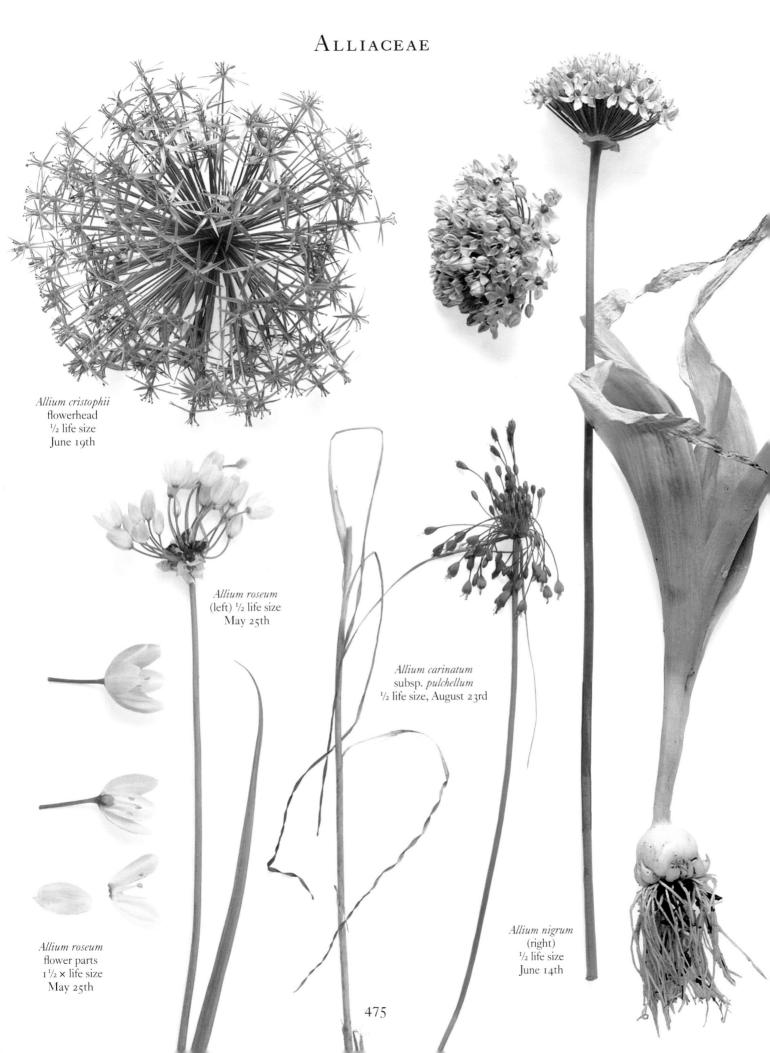

ALLIACEAE

Allium cristophii
flowerhead
½ life size
June 19th

Allium roseum
(left) ½ life size
May 25th

Allium carinatum
subsp. *pulchellum*
½ life size, August 23rd

Allium roseum
flower parts
1½ × life size
May 25th

Allium nigrum
(right)
½ life size
June 14th

475

Nectaroscordum

Nectaroscordum Lindl. (1836), in the family Alliaceae, contains 3 species in eastern Europe and southwestern Asia.

Description Perennials with flowering stems to 1.5m, with bulbs, smelling of particularly rank garlic. Leaves usually 3-winged in section, mostly basal. Flowers white, pink, or brownish, usually shaded with green, bell-shaped, in an umbel, the flower stalks widened into a disc below the flower. Perianth segments not joined, the inner wider than the outer, and narrowed at the base. Stamens 6, equal, filaments flattened and joined to the perianth at the base. Ovary mostly inferior, with 3 nectaries on the top, of 3 fused carpels with several ovules; style 1, with a simple stigma, from the top of the ovary. Pollination is mainly by bees. The fruit is a capsule with numerous black, usually angular seeds.

Key Recognition Features Tall plants, smelling very unpleasant, with umbels of pinkish-green or pale pink bells. It differs from *Allium* (see pp.474–75) in the mainly inferior ovary with 3 nectaries on top.

Ecology and Geography In dry, open woods, on field edges, among rocks, and by streams, from France and Italy to eastern Europe and southeastern Turkey

Comment These are attractive, if smelly, plants for the garden, soon forming a group of stiff stems, with many bell-shaped flowers at the top. They thrive in dry shade.

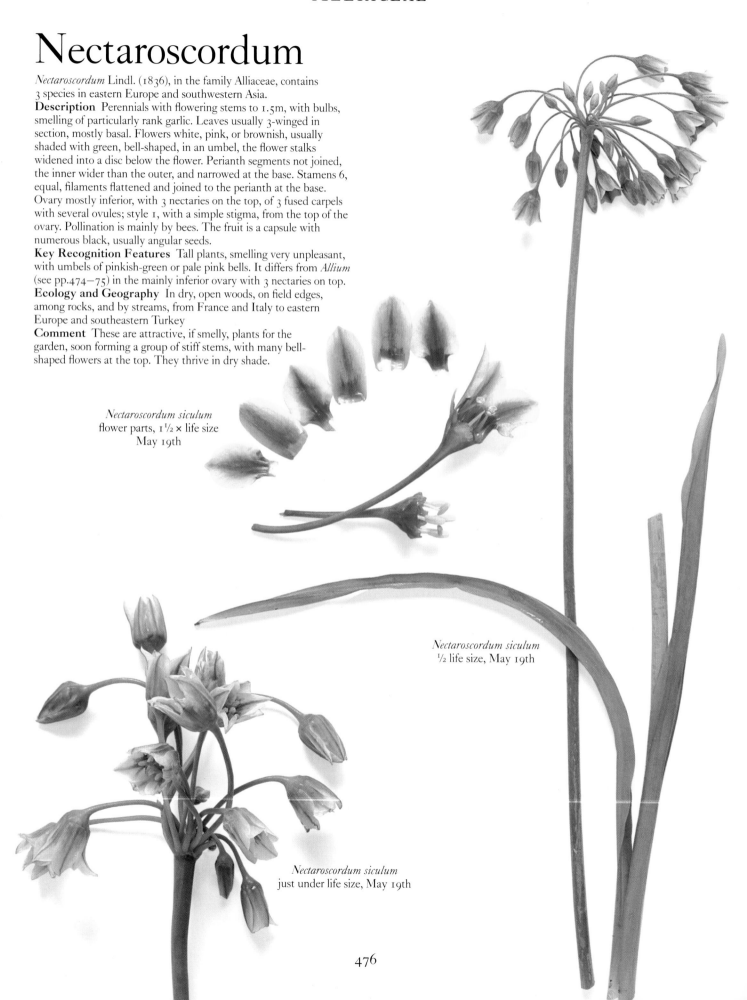

Nectaroscordum siculum
flower parts, 1 ½ × life size
May 19th

Nectaroscordum siculum
½ life size, May 19th

Nectaroscordum siculum
just under life size, May 19th

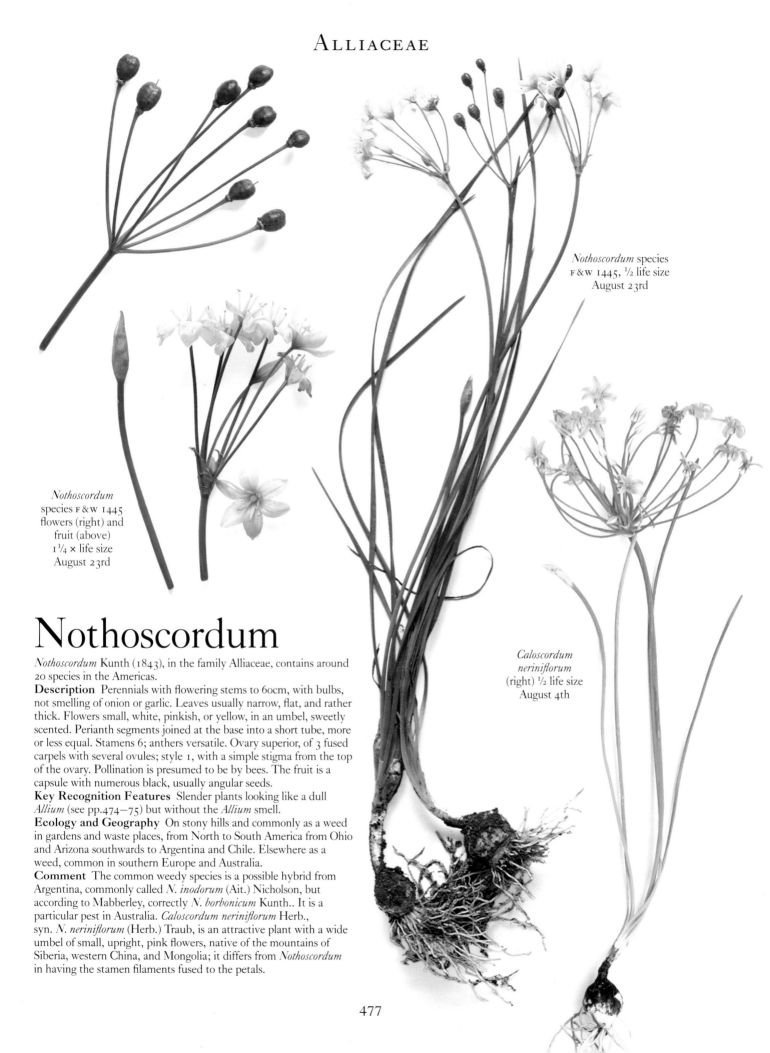

Nothoscordum species
F &W 1445, ½ life size
August 23rd

Nothoscordum
species F &W 1445
flowers (right) and
fruit (above)
1 ¼ × life size
August 23rd

Caloscordum
neriniflorum
(right) ½ life size
August 4th

Nothoscordum

Nothoscordum Kunth (1843), in the family Alliaceae, contains around 20 species in the Americas.

Description Perennials with flowering stems to 60cm, with bulbs, not smelling of onion or garlic. Leaves usually narrow, flat, and rather thick. Flowers small, white, pinkish, or yellow, in an umbel, sweetly scented. Perianth segments joined at the base into a short tube, more or less equal. Stamens 6; anthers versatile. Ovary superior, of 3 fused carpels with several ovules; style 1, with a simple stigma from the top of the ovary. Pollination is presumed to be by bees. The fruit is a capsule with numerous black, usually angular seeds.

Key Recognition Features Slender plants looking like a dull *Allium* (see pp.474–75) but without the *Allium* smell.

Ecology and Geography On stony hills and commonly as a weed in gardens and waste places, from North to South America from Ohio and Arizona southwards to Argentina and Chile. Elsewhere as a weed, common in southern Europe and Australia.

Comment The common weedy species is a possible hybrid from Argentina, commonly called *N. inodorum* (Ait.) Nicholson, but according to Mabberley, correctly *N. borbonicum* Kunth.. It is a particular pest in Australia. *Caloscordum neriniflorum* Herb., syn. *N. neriniflorum* (Herb.) Traub, is an attractive plant with a wide umbel of small, upright, pink flowers, native of the mountains of Siberia, western China, and Mongolia; it differs from *Nothoscordum* in having the stamen filaments fused to the petals.

Ipheion

Ipheion Raf. (1836), in the family Alliaceae, contains around 20 species in South America.

Description Perennials with flowering stems to 15cm, with thin bulbs, smelling faintly of garlic. Leaves usually narrow, flat, and rather fleshy. Flowers large, white, purplish, pale blue, or yellow, usually solitary, sweetly scented. Perianth segments more or less equal, joined at the base into a narrow tube, spreading or reflexed in the sun. Stamens in 2 groups, 3 near the base of the tube, 3 in the throat. Ovary superior, of 3 fused carpels with several ovules; style 1, with a 3-lobed stigma. Pollination is presumed to be by bees. The fruit is a capsule with numerous black, usually angular seeds.

Key Recognition Features Low, tufted plants with a faint *Allium* smell (see pp.474–75), and single, starry flowers.

Ecology and Geography In damp places in southern Brazil, Argentina, Uruaguay, and Chile.

Comment *Ipheion uniflorum* (Graham) Raf. is a popular garden plant with starry flowers in the spring. 'Froyle Mill' has particularly dark-coloured flowers. *Ipheion* is sometimes amalgamated with *Tristagma* Poeppig, a genus usually with smaller, nodding flowers. It is also closely related to the genus *Milla* Cav., which is found in Mexico and Arizona. *Leucocoryne* Lindl. with around 5 species in Chile, has narrow leaves smelling of garlic and beautiful flowers in a small umbel, lilac-blue and white in *L. ixioides* (Hook.) Lindl, and differs from *Ipheion* in having only 3 fertile stamens.

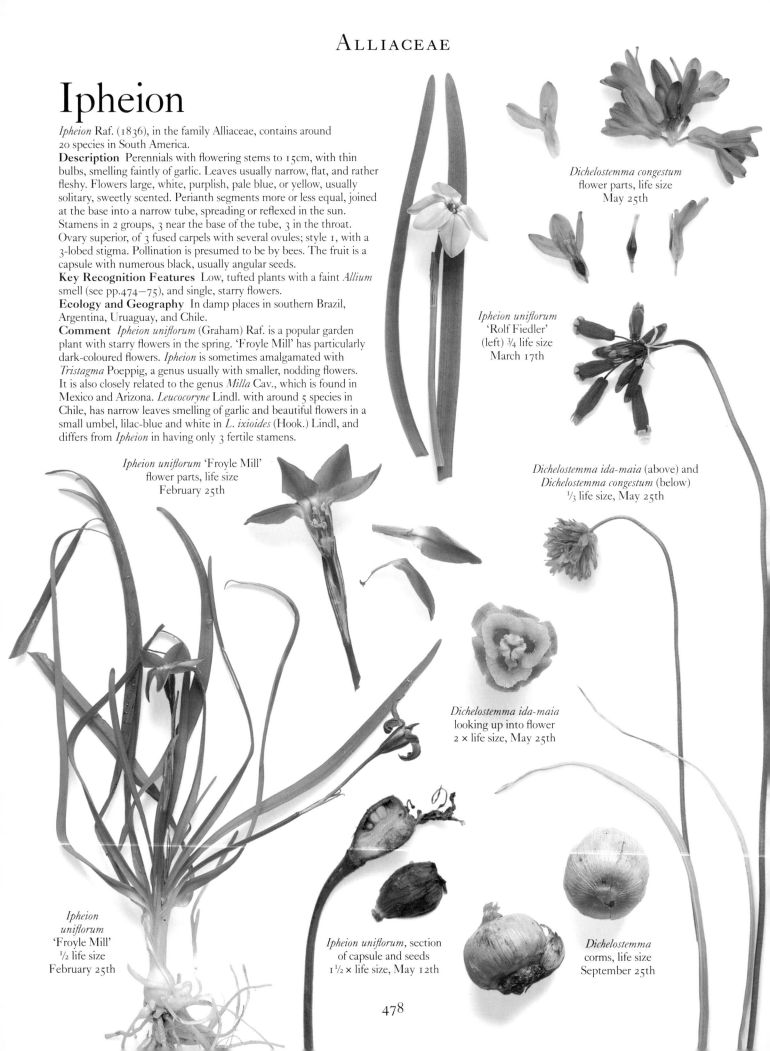

Dichelostemma congestum
flower parts, life size
May 25th

Ipheion uniflorum
'Rolf Fiedler'
(left) ¾ life size
March 17th

Dichelostemma ida-maia (above) and
Dichelostemma congestum (below)
⅓ life size, May 25th

Ipheion uniflorum 'Froyle Mill'
flower parts, life size
February 25th

Dichelostemma ida-maia
looking up into flower
2 × life size, May 25th

*Ipheion
uniflorum*
'Froyle Mill'
½ life size
February 25th

Ipheion uniflorum, section
of capsule and seeds
1½ × life size, May 12th

Dichelostemma
corms, life size
September 25th

Dichelostemma

Dichelostemma Kunth (1843), in the family Alliaceae, contains around 6 species in western North America.

Description Perennials with flowering stems sometimes twining, to 1.5m, with corms, not smelling of garlic. Leaves usually narrow, flat, and rather fleshy, fading by flowering time. Flowers large, purplish, pale blue, rose-red, or crimson and green, in often dense heads, not scented. Perianth segments more or less equal, joined for much of their length into a tube, spreading or reflexed at the tip. Stamens 3, in the throat, with 3 pale staminodes. Ovary superior, of 3 fused carpels with several ovules; style 1, with a simple stigma. Pollination is presumed to be by bees or hummingbirds. The fruit is a capsule with numerous black, sharply angled, and usually elongated seeds.

Key Recognition Features Tall-growing with flowers in a head or umbel. All species of *Dichelostemma* have 3 anthers except *D. pulchella* (Salisb.) A. Heller, which has 6; in all they are all erect and appressed to the style, and the stigma has 3 small lobes.

Ecology and Geography In dry scrub and grassland. Most species in California, a few northwards to Washington and eastwards to Arizona.

Comment The Californian genera described on these 2 pages are very closely related to one another, but differ in stamen number and type of style. *Dichelostemma ida-maia* (Wood) Greene, the firecracker flower, is one of the most spectacular of all Californian monocots, with its crimson, green-tipped tubular flowers adapted to pollination by hummingbirds. In *D. congestum* Kunth the flower stalks are only 1–6mm long.

Triteleia

Triteleia Dougl. ex Lindl. (1830), in the family Alliaceae, contains around 18 species in western North America.

Description Perennials with flowering stems to 70cm, with corms, not smelling of garlic. Leaves usually narrow, flat, rather fleshy, fading by flowering time. Flowers large, blue or purplish, pale blue, or yellow, long-stalked, in umbels, not scented. Perianth segments more or less equal, joined at the base into a tube, not reflexed. Stamens 6, often 3 long and 3 short, with versatile anthers. Ovary superior, of 3 fused carpels with several ovules, held on an extension above the base of the flower; style 1, with a simple stigma. Pollination is presumed to be by bees. The fruit is a capsule with numerous black, very small seeds.

Key Recognition Features Flowers generally trumpet-shaped, in a rather flat-topped umbel. There are 6 anthers and the stigma is not lobed.

Ecology and Geography In dry scrub and grassland, some species in areas where water lies in winter. Most species in California, a few northwards to British Columbia.

Comment These bulbs are frequent throughout California. Of the 2 other closely related genera, *Bloomeria* Kell. has more starry, yellow flowers, with 6 anthers and filaments with cup-shaped, winged appendages, and the stigma is not lobed; *Brodiaea* Sm., with around 15 species in western North America, has 3 anthers, erect and appressed to the style, and a stigma with 3 spreading, recurved lobes.

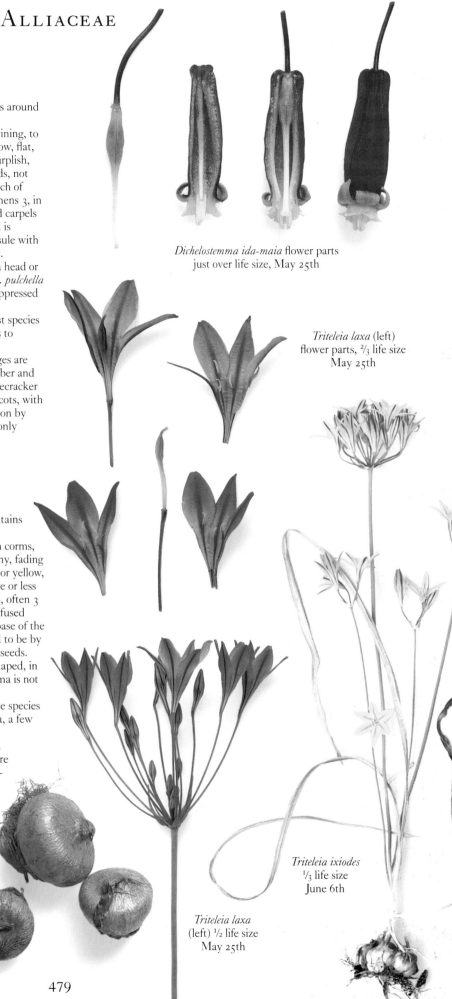

Dichelostemma ida-maia flower parts just over life size, May 25th

Triteleia laxa (left) flower parts, 2/3 life size May 25th

Triteleia ixiodes 1/3 life size June 6th

Triteleia laxa 'Koningin Fabiola' corms, 1 1/4 × life size September 17th

Triteleia laxa (left) 1/2 life size May 25th

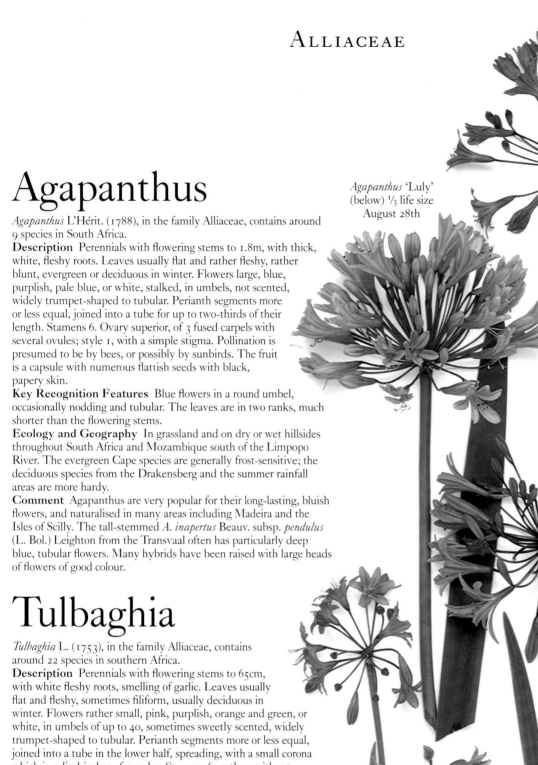

Agapanthus

Agapanthus L'Hérit. (1788), in the family Alliaceae, contains around 9 species in South Africa.

Description Perennials with flowering stems to 1.8m, with thick, white, fleshy roots. Leaves usually flat and rather fleshy, rather blunt, evergreen or deciduous in winter. Flowers large, blue, purplish, pale blue, or white, stalked, in umbels, not scented, widely trumpet-shaped to tubular. Perianth segments more or less equal, joined into a tube for up to two-thirds of their length. Stamens 6. Ovary superior, of 3 fused carpels with several ovules; style 1, with a simple stigma. Pollination is presumed to be by bees, or possibly by sunbirds. The fruit is a capsule with numerous flattish seeds with black, papery skin.

Key Recognition Features Blue flowers in a round umbel, occasionally nodding and tubular. The leaves are in two ranks, much shorter than the flowering stems.

Ecology and Geography In grassland and on dry or wet hillsides throughout South Africa and Mozambique south of the Limpopo River. The evergreen Cape species are generally frost-sensitive; the deciduous species from the Drakensberg and the summer rainfall areas are more hardy.

Comment Agapanthus are very popular for their long-lasting, bluish flowers, and naturalised in many areas including Madeira and the Isles of Scilly. The tall-stemmed *A. inapertus* Beauv. subsp. *pendulus* (L. Bol.) Leighton from the Transvaal often has particularly deep blue, tubular flowers. Many hybrids have been raised with large heads of flowers of good colour.

Tulbaghia

Tulbaghia L. (1753), in the family Alliaceae, contains around 22 species in southern Africa.

Description Perennials with flowering stems to 65cm, with white fleshy roots, smelling of garlic. Leaves usually flat and fleshy, sometimes filiform, usually deciduous in winter. Flowers rather small, pink, purplish, orange and green, or white, in umbels of up to 40, sometimes sweetly scented, widely trumpet-shaped to tubular. Perianth segments more or less equal, joined into a tube in the lower half, spreading, with a small corona which is cylindrical or of 3 scales. Stamens 6; anthers without filaments, in 2 whorls. Ovary superior, of 3 fused carpels with several ovules; style 1, with a simple stigma. Pollination is presumed to be by bees. the fruit is a capsule with numerous black, triangular seeds.

Key Recognition Features Flowers in a loose umbel, mostly nodding, with a small corona. The leaves are in 2 ranks, shorter than the flowering stems and smelling of garlic.

Ecology and Geography In grassland and scrub, on dry or wet hillsides, and on rocks, throughout South Africa northwards to Malawi.

Comment Many of the species are attractive perennials for a sunny, warm situation, with protection from frost in cold winters. *Tulbaghia violacea* Harvey is one of the hardiest. *Tulbaghia cominsii* Vosa has very thin leaves and white, sweetly scented flowers; it is best grown as a pot plant. *Tulbaghia cameronii* Baker from Malawi, has large flowers similar to *Narcissus tazetta* L. (see pp.470–71). The genus was named after Ryk Tulbagh (d. 1771), governor of the Cape.

Agapanthus 'Luly' (below) ⅓ life size August 28th

Agapanthus 'Buckingham Palace' (above) ⅓ life size August 28th

Agapanthus campanulatus subsp. *patens* (left), *Agapanthus* 'Diana' (above), and *Agapanthus campanulatus* subsp. *campanulatus* (right) ⅓ life size, August 28th

ALLIACEAE

Tulbaghia violacea
fruits and flowers
1²/₃ × life size
August 10th

*Agapanthus
campanulatus* subsp.
patens, ½ life size
July 25th

Agapanthus campanulatus
subsp. *patens*, flowers
just under life size, July 25th

Tulbaghia violacea
(left) ½ life size
August 10th

Agapanthus inapertus
subsp. *pendulus* (left)
²/₃ life size
August 23rd

481

Hyacinthus

Hyacinthus L. (1753), hyacinth, in the family Hyacinthaceae, contains 3 species, mainly in the eastern Mediterranean and Iran.

Description Perennials with flowering stems hollow, to 30cm, with bulbs. Leaves basal, flat. Flowers rather pale blue, in cultivars deep blue, purple, pink, pinkish-red, or white, in spikes of up to 40, sweetly scented. Perianth segments more or less equal, joined for the lower two-thirds, the segments reflexed. Stamens 6. Ovary superior, of 3 fused carpels with several ovules; style 1, shorter than the tube, with a simple stigma. Pollination is probably mainly by bees. The fruit is a capsule with black, wrinkled seeds.

Key Recognition Features The usually blue, scented flowers on a thick, hollow, fleshy stalk.

Ecology and Geography Among rocks and low scrub from Turkey, Syria, and Lebanon to Iran and Turkmenia.

Comment Hyacinths were cultivated by the Turks before their introduction to western Europe in the late 16th century. They are now one of the most popular of all bulbs, valuable for their early flowering and wonderful scent, which make them ideal for bringing indoors. The family Hyacinthaceae was formerly part of the Liliaceae (see pp.416–29); it is closest to the Agavaceae (see pp.494–95) and the Anthericaceae (see pp.496–97).

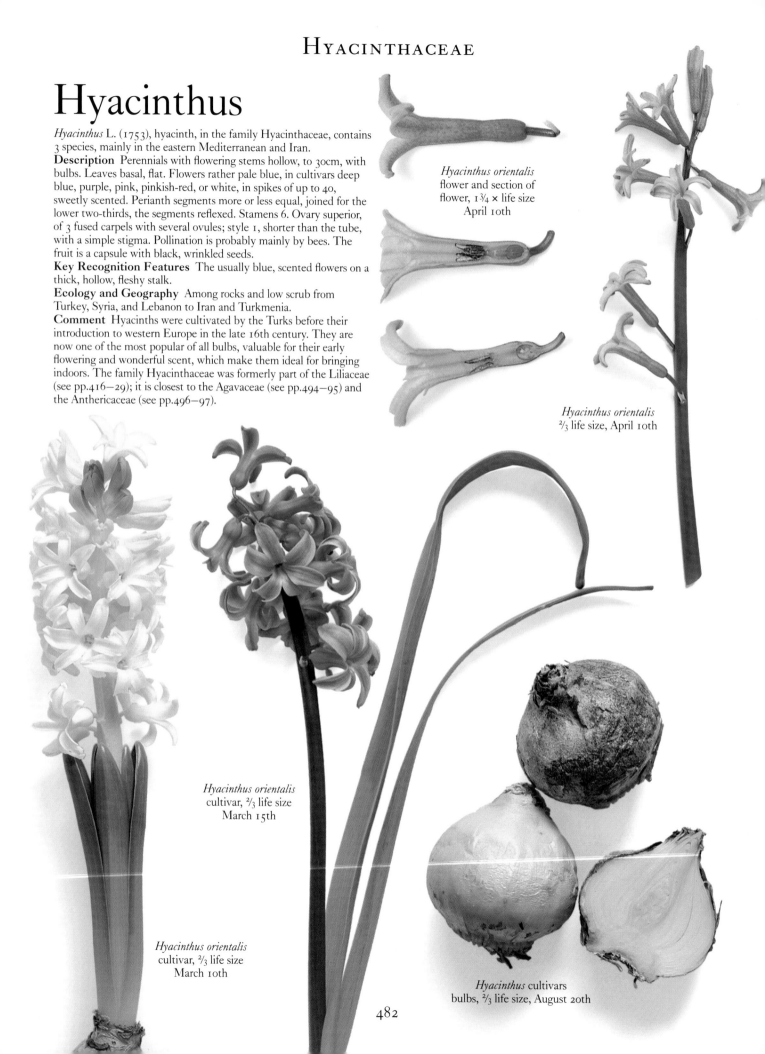

Hyacinthus orientalis
flower and section of
flower, 1¾ × life size
April 10th

Hyacinthus orientalis
⅔ life size, April 10th

Hyacinthus orientalis
cultivar, ⅔ life size
March 15th

Hyacinthus orientalis
cultivar, ⅔ life size
March 10th

Hyacinthus cultivars
bulbs, ⅔ life size, August 20th

Hyacinthoides

Hyacinthoides Medik. (1759), bluebell or wild hyacinth, in the family Hyacinthaceae, contains 3 species, mainly in the eastern Mediterranean and Iran.

Description Perennials with flowering stems solid, to 40cm, usually nodding at the tip, with bulbs that are completely renewed each year. Leaves basal, flat. Flowers hanging down, blue, rarely white, in cultivars pink or purplish, in spikes of up to 30, with pairs of bracts, faintly scented. Perianth segments more or less equal, not joined but often held together with the tips of the segments reflexed. Stamens 6. Ovary superior, of 3 fused carpels with several ovules; style 1, shorter than the tube, with a simple stigma. Pollination is mainly by bees. The fruit is a capsule with black, round, shining seeds.

Key Recognition Features The usually blue, hanging flowers on a thin, tough stalk. Close to *Scilla* (see p.484) but differs in the annually renewed bulb, and the bracts in pairs.

Ecology and Geography In woods, on banks, in meadows, and among rocks and low scrub from Scotland and Ireland to North Africa and eastwards to Italy.

Comment The English bluebell, *H. non-scripta* (L.) Chouard ex Rothm., is one of the most characteristic flowers of the British Isles, in many areas forming blue carpets on the woodland floor, but restricted in mainland Europe to the Atlantic coast, roughly west of Paris, where wood anemones are the common spring flowers in the forest. The bluebell has undergone many name changes, including *Scilla* L. and *Endymion* Dumort.. Endymion was the most beautiful of men, loved by Selene, or in Roman mythology Diana, the moon-goddess and huntress, a suitable name for a woodland plant. The origin of the name *non-scripta* is complex; Hyacinthus was a beautiful youth, loved both by Apollo and Zephyrus; Apollo threw a quoit, and Zephyrus, out of jealousy, blew it so it killed Hyacinthus and from his blood sprang the hyacinth, marked with the cry "AI" (alas!). The bluebell, though a hyacinth, has an unmarked flower, hence *non-scripta*. To complicate the story, there is considerable doubt as to exactly what flower the original classical hyacinth was.

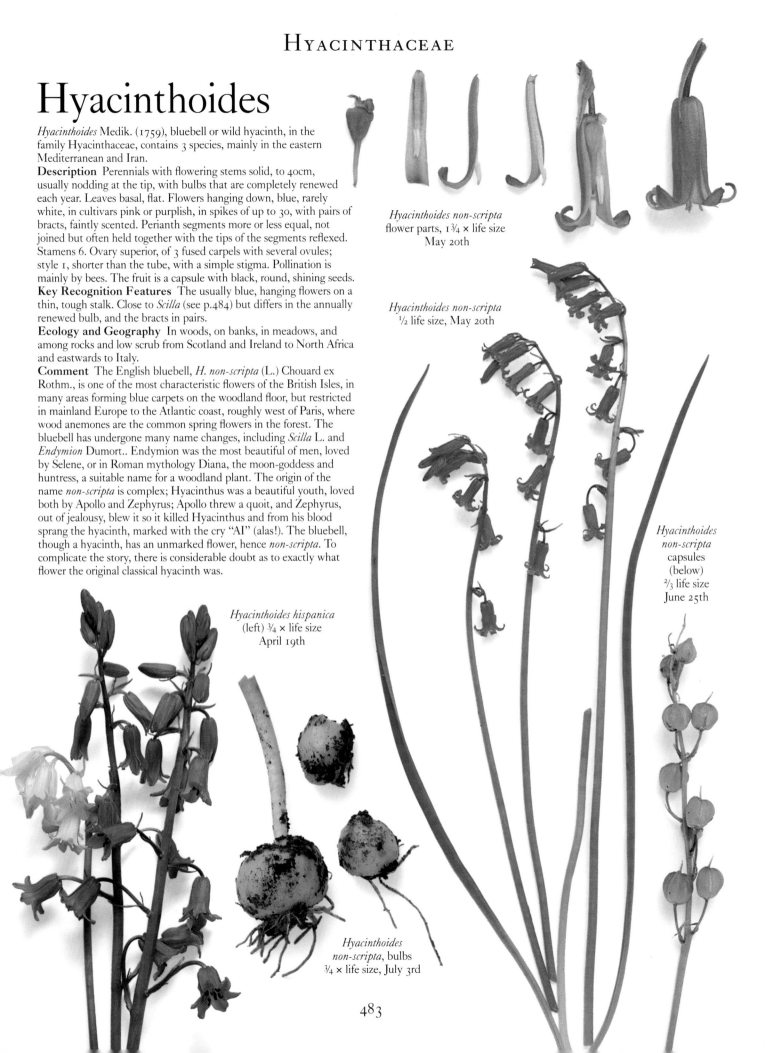

Hyacinthoides non-scripta
flower parts, 1¾ × life size
May 20th

Hyacinthoides non-scripta
½ life size, May 20th

Hyacinthoides non-scripta
capsules (below)
⅔ life size
June 25th

Hyacinthoides hispanica
(left) ¾ × life size
April 19th

Hyacinthoides non-scripta, bulbs
¾ × life size, July 3rd

483

Scilla

Scilla L. (1753), in the family Hyacinthaceae, contains around 40 species, mainly in the eastern Mediterranean and a few in South Africa.

Description Perennials with flowering stems to 50cm, with bulbs. Leaves basal, flat. Flowers in spikes of up to 150, blue, purple, pinkish, white, or green, opening flat and starry or nodding and then often with reflexed segments. Perianth segments more or less equal, not joined at the base. Stamens 6. Ovary superior, of 3 fused carpels with several ovules; style 1, with a simple stigma. Pollination is probably mainly by bees, also by wind and by moths. The fruit is a capsule with numerous black, triangular seeds.

Key Recognition Features The usually blue, starry or hanging flowers in early spring, or the taller plants with masses of small flowers in summer and autumn.

Ecology and Geography In rocky woods, among rocks, in alpine meadows, and on bare hills; from Spain and western Ireland eastwards to China and Japan, with 14 species in Turkey. Most of the species in southern Africa are now put into *Ledebouria*.

Comment Many species are cultivated, especially for their bright blue flowers in early spring. *Scilla peruviana* L. in spite of its name, is found in Spain, North Africa, and the Mediterranean islands. The dwarf *S. verna* Huds. is found in the short grass of Atlantic cliff tops. *Scilla natalensis* Planch. is commonly used as bush medicine in South Africa. *Scilla maritima* L., a large bulb from the coasts of the Mediterranean is now put in the genus *Urginea* Steinh. or *Drimia* Jacq. ex Willd., both largely African genera; it has long been used for rat poison or, in Greece, as a charm to hang over doorways, as well as a heart stimulant to cure dropsy.

Scilla bifolia
(above right)
flower parts
2 × life size
February 22nd

Scilla siberica
just over life size
March 13th

Scilla scilloides
just over life size
(right)
August 23rd

Scilla mischtschenkoana
(left) life size
February 22nd

484

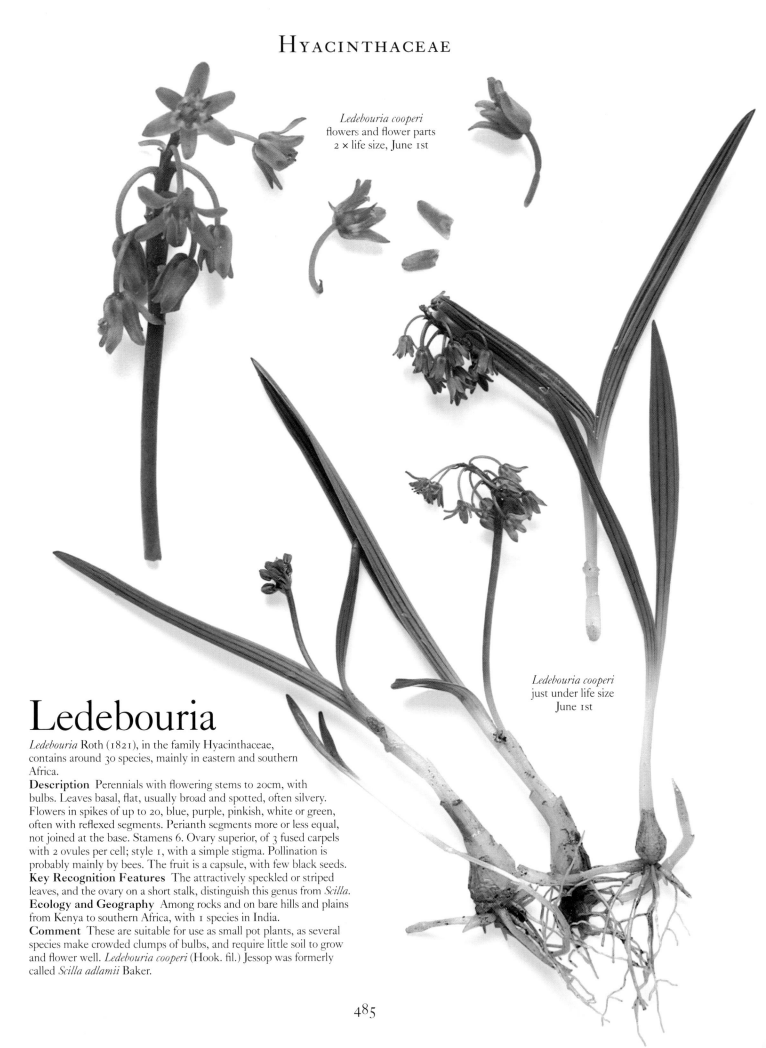

Ledebouria cooperi
flowers and flower parts
2 × life size, June 1st

Ledebouria cooperi
just under life size
June 1st

Ledebouria

Ledebouria Roth (1821), in the family Hyacinthaceae,
contains around 30 species, mainly in eastern and southern
Africa.

Description Perennials with flowering stems to 20cm, with
bulbs. Leaves basal, flat, usually broad and spotted, often silvery.
Flowers in spikes of up to 20, blue, purple, pinkish, white or green,
often with reflexed segments. Perianth segments more or less equal,
not joined at the base. Stamens 6. Ovary superior, of 3 fused carpels
with 2 ovules per cell; style 1, with a simple stigma. Pollination is
probably mainly by bees. The fruit is a capsule, with few black seeds.

Key Recognition Features The attractively speckled or striped
leaves, and the ovary on a short stalk, distinguish this genus from *Scilla*.

Ecology and Geography Among rocks and on bare hills and plains
from Kenya to southern Africa, with 1 species in India.

Comment These are suitable for use as small pot plants, as several
species make crowded clumps of bulbs, and require little soil to grow
and flower well. *Ledebouria cooperi* (Hook. fil.) Jessop was formerly
called *Scilla adlamii* Baker.

485

Chionodoxa

Chionodoxa Boiss. (1844), in the family Hyacinthaceae, contains 6 species, mainly in the eastern Mediterranean region.

Description Perennials with flowering stems to 18cm, with bulbs. Leaves usually 2, basal, flat. Flowers blue, lavender, or pink, rarely white in cultivars, often with a white centre, opening flat and starry or nodding, in spikes of up to 12. Perianth segments more or less equal, joined at the base into a short tube. Stamens 6. Ovary superior, of 3 fused carpels with several ovules; style 1, with a simple stigma. Pollination is probably mainly by bees. The fruit is a capsule with numerous black seeds.

Key Recognition Features The usually blue, starry flowers in early spring with a white centre and a short tube.

Ecology and Geography Mountains, rocky woods, among rocks, or in alpine meadows or screes in western Turkey, Crete, and Cyprus.

Comment Most of the species are cultivated, especially for their bright blue flowers in early spring. *Chionodoxa* is very close to some species of *Scilla* (see p.484), especially *S. bifolia* L., with which it hybridises to form × *Chionoscilla allenii*. The genus *Puschkinia* Adams differs from *Chionodoxa* in its pale blue or green hanging flowers, with a throat with a 6-lobed corona that projects between the anthers. It is widespread in the Caucasus, Iran, Turkey, Iraq, and the Lebanon, growing in stony places in the mountains.

Brimeura

Brimeura Salisb. (1866), in the family Hyacinthaceae, contains 2 species, mainly in the Mediterranean region.

Description Perennials with flowering stems to 18cm, with bulbs. Leaves usually several, all basal, flat. Flowers blue, purple, lilac-pink, or white, in spikes of up to 12, nodding, or upright in a flat-topped head. Perianth segments more or less equal, joined in the lower half into a tube. Stamens 6. Ovary superior of 3 fused carpels with 2–4 ovules in each cell; style 1, with a simple stigma. Pollination is probably mainly by bees. The fruit is a capsule with black seeds.

Key Recognition Features *Brimeura amethystina* (L.) Chouard is like a small and delicate bluebell (*Hyacinthoides*, see p.483) with bracts as long as the pedicels and the flower tube longer than the lobes. *Brimeura fastigiata* (Viv.) Chouard is *Scilla*-like (see p.484) with purplish flowers in a flat-topped head.

Ecology and Geography *Brimeura amethystina* in rocky woods and mountain meadows in the Pyrenees and northeastern Spain and in Croatia; *B. fastigiata* in the Balearic Islands, Corsica, Sardinia, and southern Greece.

Comment *Brimeura amethystina* is often cultivated; there is a form with pure white flowers. These are sometimes found under the name *Hyacinthus* (see p.482).

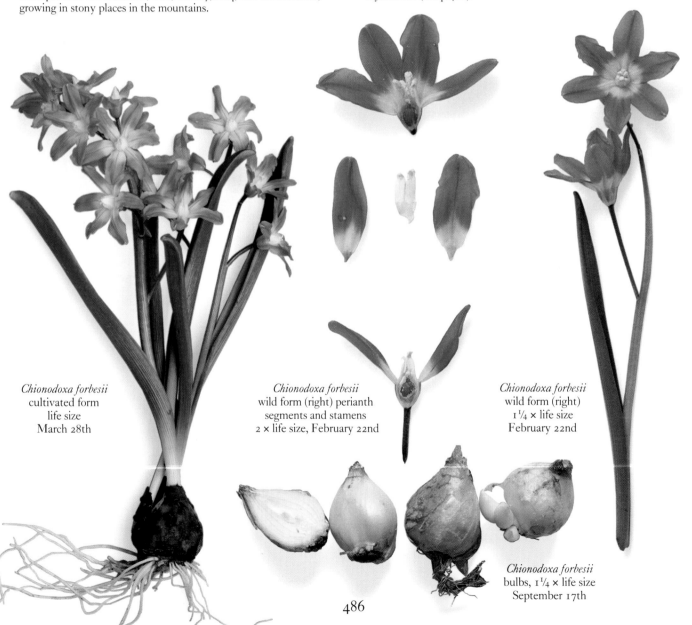

Chionodoxa forbesii
cultivated form
life size
March 28th

Chionodoxa forbesii
wild form (right) perianth
segments and stamens
2 × life size, February 22nd

Chionodoxa forbesii
wild form (right)
1¼ × life size
February 22nd

Chionodoxa forbesii
bulbs, 1¼ × life size
September 17th

Brimeura amethystina
flowers and flower sections
2 × life size, May 20th

Brimeura amethystina
just under life size
May 20th

Puschkinia scilloides
var. *libanotica*
(left) ¾ life size
March 14th

Puschkinia scilloides var. *libanotica*
bulbs, life size, September 17th

Puschkinia scilloides
var. *libanotica* flower
back and section (right)
1²⁄₃ × life size
March 14th

Bellevalia

Bellevalia Lapeyr. (1808), in the family Hyacinthaceae, contains around 20 species, mainly in southwestern Asia.

Description Perennials with flowering stems to 60cm, with bulbs. Bracts minute, bilobed. Leaves usually several, basal, narrow and channelled. Flowers blue, blackish, or greenish-yellow, in spikes of up to 50, shortly or narrowly campanulate. Perianth segments more or less equal, joined into a tube. Stamens 6, with triangular, flattened. Ovary superior, of 3 fused carpels each with 2 ovules; style 1, with a lobed stigma. Pollination is probably mainly by bees. The fruit is a 3-lobed or winged capsule with smooth, black seeds with a grey bloom.

Key Recognition Features Very similar to *Muscari*, but differing in its triangular, flattened filaments and its smooth seeds. The flowers are generally in rather dull colours, and not constricted at the mouth.

Ecology and Geography Among rocks, in alpine meadows or screes, and in abandoned fields,from southern France to Iran, central Asia, and Egypt; 18 species in Turkey.

Comment The genus is named after Pierre Richter de Belleval (1558–1623), who founded the botanic garden in Montpellier in 1593 and was a field botanist who made many drawings of plants. The genus *Hyacinthella* Schur is close to *Bellevalia*, but generally smaller, with broad leaves and small, few-seeded capsules. *Strangweja* Bertol, sometimes included in *Bellevalia*, has 1 species, *S. spicata* (Sibth. & Sm.) Boiss., in Greece. The filaments are winged and toothed, and the lobes are longer than the tube.

Muscari macrocarpum
¾ life size, March 14th

Bellevalia forniculata
½ life size, May 10th

Bellevalia forniculata
flowers, 2 × life size
May 10th

Muscari

Muscari Miller (1754), grape hyacinth, in the family Hyacinthaceae, contains around 30 species, mainly in the eastern Mediterranean region.

Description Perennials with flowering stems to 80cm, with bulbs. Leaves usually several, basal, narrow and channelled. Flowers blue, blackish, lavender, greenish, yellow, or pink, white in cultivars, in spikes of up to 100, globose or campanulate. Perianth segments more or less equal, joined into a tube, the tips often reflexed. Stamens 6, with short, simple filaments. Ovary superior, of 3 fused carpels, each with 2 ovules; style 1, with a simple stigma. Pollination is probably mainly by bees. The fruit is a 3-lobed or winged capsule with black and shiny seeds.

Key Recognition Features The usually blue or purplish flowers with minute bracts and the tube longer than the lobes.

Ecology and Geography In rocky woods, among rocks, in alpine meadows or screes, and in abandoned fields from western Europe and North Africa to Iran and central Asia, with 20 species in Turkey.

Comment Many species are cultivated, especially for their sweetly scented flowers in late spring. The bulbs of some species, such as *M. comosum* L., are collected and eaten in Greece. This and several other species have blue sterile flowers at the top of a long spike, brownish fertile flowers below; pollinating bees are first attracted by the blue flowers and then find the dull but nectar-rich flowers below. *Muscari macrocarpum* Sweet, from cliffs and rocks in the eastern Mediterranean, has particularly sweetly scented yellow flowers, and large, papery capsules. This species and *M. muscarimi* Medik. are sometimes put in the genus *Muscarimia* Kostel ex Los.-Los. Species with bell-shaped rather than globose flowers, such as *M. azureum* Fenzl., are sometimes put in the genus *Pseudomuscari* Garbari & Greuter.

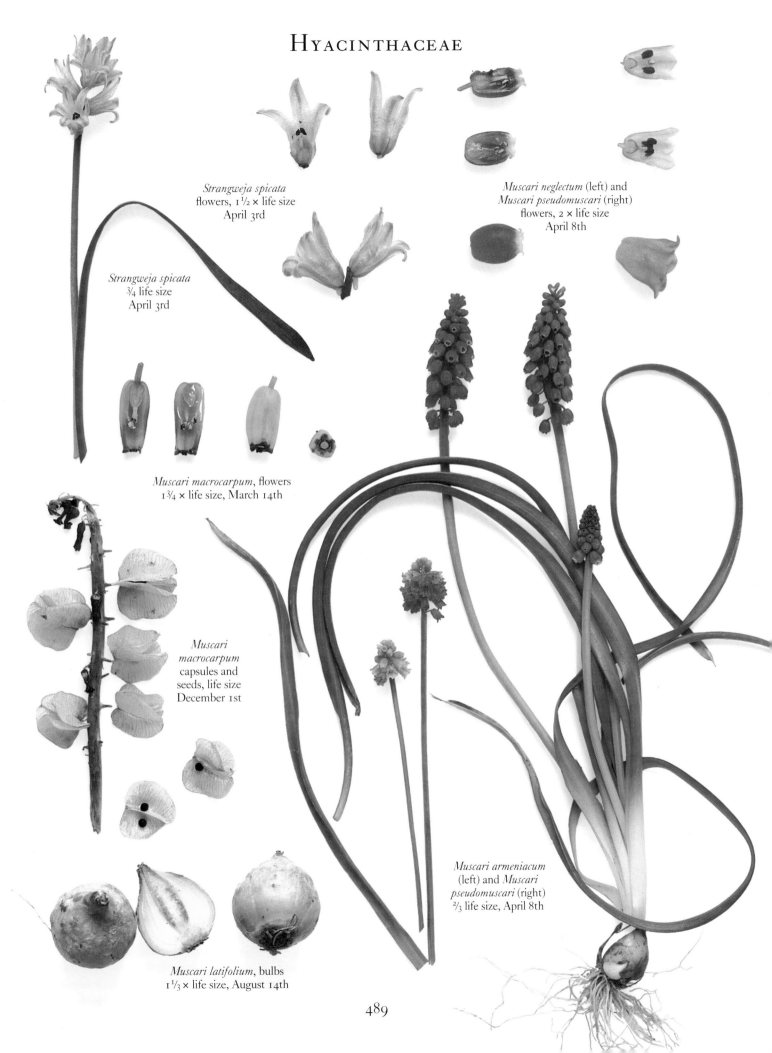

Hyacinthaceae

Strangweja spicata
flowers, 1½ × life size
April 3rd

Muscari neglectum (left) and
Muscari pseudomuscari (right)
flowers, 2 × life size
April 8th

Strangweja spicata
¾ life size
April 3rd

Muscari macrocarpum, flowers
1¾ × life size, March 14th

*Muscari
macrocarpum*
capsules and
seeds, life size
December 1st

Muscari armeniacum
(left) and *Muscari
pseudomuscari* (right)
⅔ life size, April 8th

Muscari latifolium, bulbs
1⅓ × life size, August 14th

489

Ornithogalum

Ornithogalum L. (1753), in the family Hyacinthaceae, contains around 120 species in the Mediterranean area and in southern Africa.

Description Perennials with flowering stems to 1.2m, with bulbs. Leaves basal, flat or channelled, sometimes filiform, often with a white central stripe like a crocus (see pp.448–49). Flowers rather small, usually white, or green, yellow, orange, or red in a few African species, in umbels or spikes of up to 300, usually opening flat and starry in the sun. Perianth segments more or less equal, narrow and pointed or rounded, not joined at the base. Stamens 6. Ovary superior of 3 fused carpels with several ovules; style 1, with a simple stigma. Pollination is presumed to be by bees. The fruit is a capsule with numerous black, triangular seeds.

Key Recognition Features The usually white, starry flowers with a green stripe on the back in a loose umbel-like corymb, or in a spike-like raceme, and the leaves with a white central stripe.

Ecology and Geography In grassland, scrub, and abandoned fields, on dry hillsides and in rock crevices, occasionally in vleis, throughout western and southern Europe and western Asia, with 23 species in Turkey and 31 species in southern Africa.

Comment A few species are cultivated. The chincherinchee, *O. thyrsoides* Jacq., occurs in vast numbers in seasonally wet fields in South Africa, and is exported as a cut flower. Bath asparagus, *O. pyrenaicum* L. has succulent green young flower spikes, and was collected in the woods around Bath, and sold in the market as an asparagus substitute.

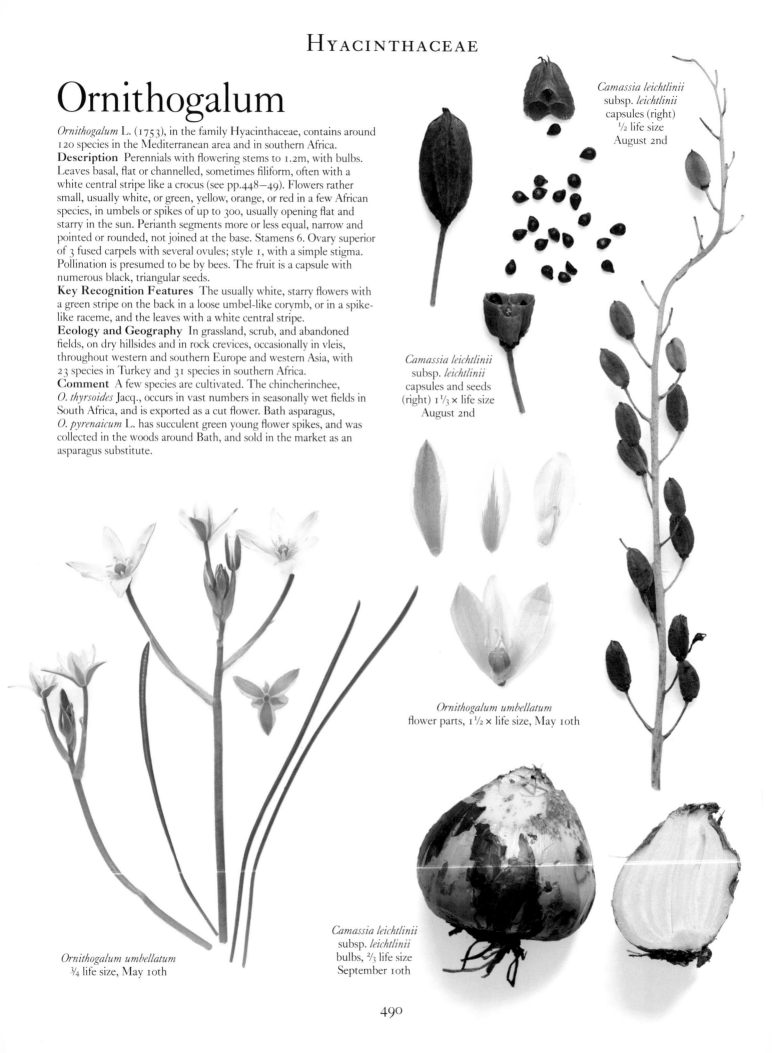

Camassia leichtlinii
subsp. *leichtlinii*
capsules (right)
½ life size
August 2nd

Camassia leichtlinii
subsp. *leichtlinii*
capsules and seeds
(right) 1⅓ × life size
August 2nd

Ornithogalum umbellatum
flower parts, 1½ × life size, May 10th

Ornithogalum umbellatum
¾ life size, May 10th

Camassia leichtlinii
subsp. *leichtlinii*
bulbs, ⅔ life size
September 10th

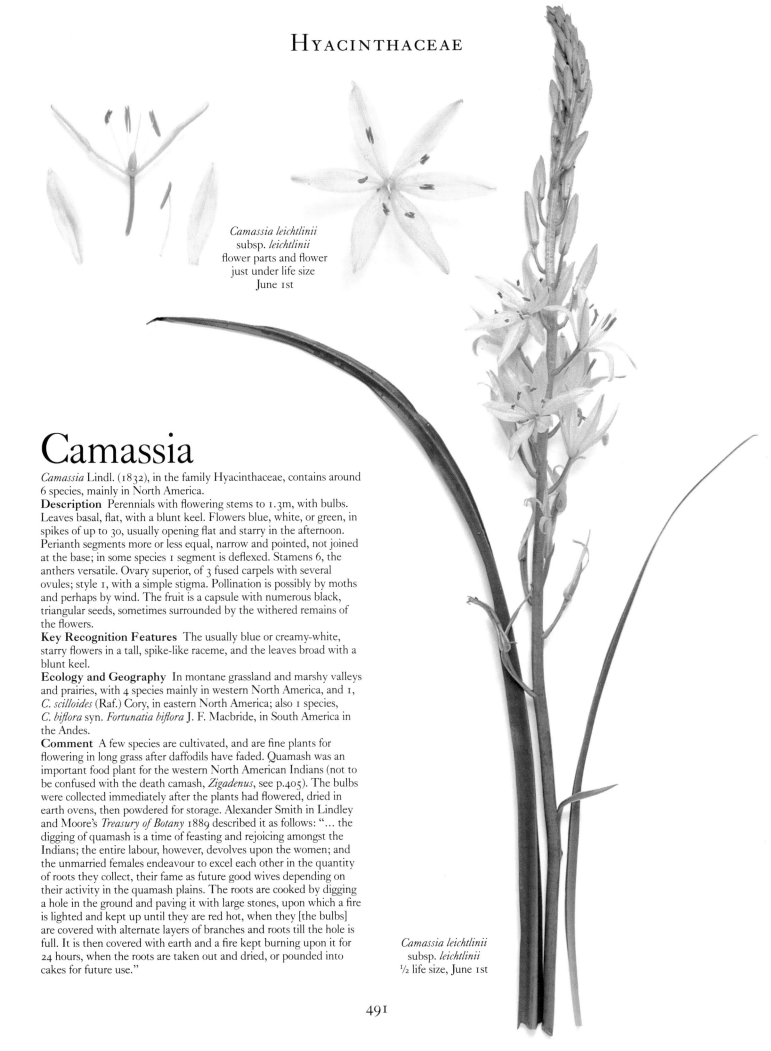

Camassia leichtlinii
subsp. *leichtlinii*
flower parts and flower
just under life size
June 1st

Camassia

Camassia Lindl. (1832), in the family Hyacinthaceae, contains around 6 species, mainly in North America.

Description Perennials with flowering stems to 1.3m, with bulbs. Leaves basal, flat, with a blunt keel. Flowers blue, white, or green, in spikes of up to 30, usually opening flat and starry in the afternoon. Perianth segments more or less equal, narrow and pointed, not joined at the base; in some species 1 segment is deflexed. Stamens 6, the anthers versatile. Ovary superior, of 3 fused carpels with several ovules; style 1, with a simple stigma. Pollination is possibly by moths and perhaps by wind. The fruit is a capsule with numerous black, triangular seeds, sometimes surrounded by the withered remains of the flowers.

Key Recognition Features The usually blue or creamy-white, starry flowers in a tall, spike-like raceme, and the leaves broad with a blunt keel.

Ecology and Geography In montane grassland and marshy valleys and prairies, with 4 species mainly in western North America, and 1, *C. scilloides* (Raf.) Cory, in eastern North America; also 1 species, *C. biflora* syn. *Fortunatia biflora* J. F. Macbride, in South America in the Andes.

Comment A few species are cultivated, and are fine plants for flowering in long grass after daffodils have faded. Quamash was an important food plant for the western North American Indians (not to be confused with the death camash, *Zigadenus*, see p.405). The bulbs were collected immediately after the plants had flowered, dried in earth ovens, then powdered for storage. Alexander Smith in Lindley and Moore's *Treasury of Botany* 1889 described it as follows: "... the digging of quamash is a time of feasting and rejoicing amongst the Indians; the entire labour, however, devolves upon the women; and the unmarried females endeavour to excel each other in the quantity of roots they collect, their fame as future good wives depending on their activity in the quamash plains. The roots are cooked by digging a hole in the ground and paving it with large stones, upon which a fire is lighted and kept up until they are red hot, when they [the bulbs] are covered with alternate layers of branches and roots till the hole is full. It is then covered with earth and a fire kept burning upon it for 24 hours, when the roots are taken out and dried, or pounded into cakes for future use."

Camassia leichtlinii
subsp. *leichtlinii*
½ life size, June 1st

Eucomis

Eucomis L'Hérit. (1788), in the family Hyacinthaceae, contains around 10 species in southern Africa.

Description Perennials with flowering stems to 75cm, with bulbs. Leaves all basal, broad and flat, sometimes spotted beneath or purple. Flowers green, white, reddish, or purplish, in spikes of up to 50, opening flat and starry, with a tuft of leaves on the top of the thick and fleshy stem. Perianth segments more or less equal, not joined at the base. Stamens 6, the anthers versatile, the filaments broad and joined at the base. Ovary often reddish-purple, superior, of 3 fused carpels with several ovules; style 1, with a simple stigma. Pollination is probably by flies and other insects. The fruit is a capsule with numerous black or brown, rounded seeds.

Key Recognition Features The usually green, reddish-purple, or creamy-white starry flowers with a pineapple-like tuft of leaves at the top of the thick stem.

Ecology and Geography In montane grassland and on marshy slopes and rock ledges. Most species in the summer-rainfall area of southern Africa, northwards to Malawi, with 1 species, *E. regia* (L.) L'Hérit., in the winter-rainfall area of the western Cape.

Comment Most species are cultivated by enthusiasts for their late summer flowering and unusual colours and markings.

Eucomis bicolor, flowers
just over life size
August 10th

Eucomis bicolor
½ life size, August 10th

Eucomis bicolor
½ life size, August 10th

492

Galtonia

Galtonia Decne. (1880), in the family Hyacinthaceae, contains 4 species in South Africa.

Description Perennials with flowering stems to 2m, with bulbs. Leaves all basal, broad and flat. Flowers green or white, in spikes of up to 50, nodding and bell-shaped, on a stiff, upright stem. Perianth segments more or less equal, joined at the base. Stamens 6. Ovary often superior, of 3 fused carpels with several ovules; style 1, with a simple stigma. Pollination is probably by bees and other insects. The fruit is a capsule with numerous black or brown, rounded seeds.

Key Recognition Features The tall stems with nodding, green or white, bell-shaped flowers.

Ecology and Geography In montane grassland and on marshy slopes and rock ledges; most species in the summer-rainfall area of South Africa, northwards to the Transvaal.

Comment *Galtonia candicans* Decne., with white bells, is commonly cultivated for its summer flowering. The bulbs will survive a few degrees of frost, especially if kept on the dry side in winter.

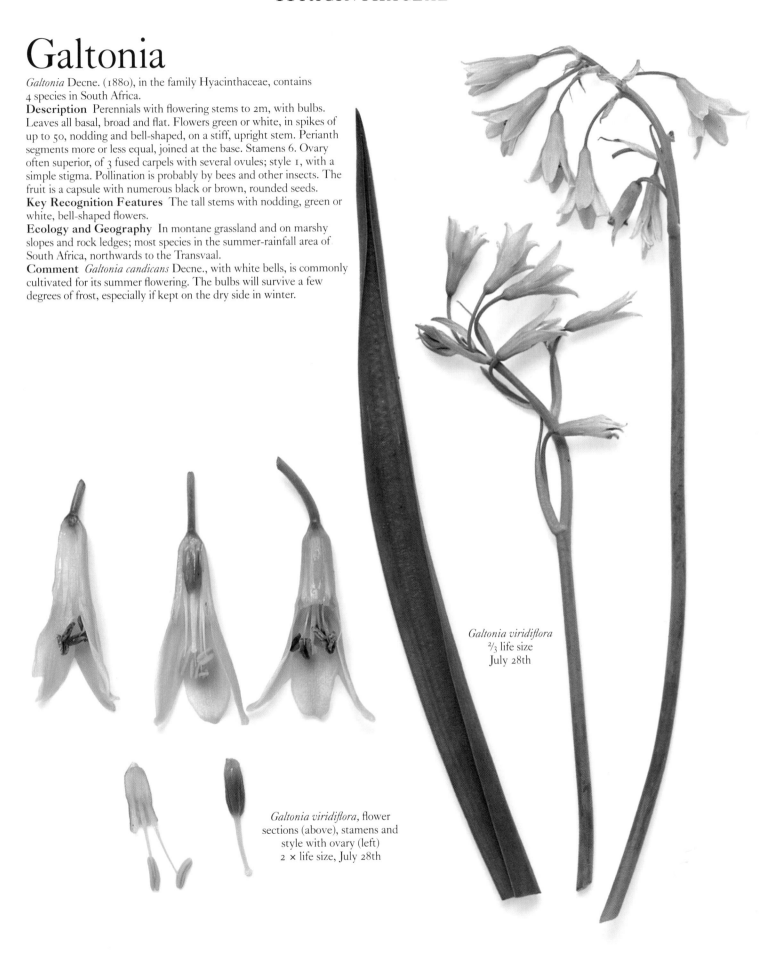

Galtonia viridiflora
²⁄₃ life size
July 28th

Galtonia viridiflora, flower sections (above), stamens and style with ovary (left)
2 × life size, July 28th

Hosta

Hosta Tratt.. (1812), in the family Agavaceae, contains around 25 species in Japan, Korea, and China.

Description Perennials with flowering stems to 1m, with bulbs. Leaves nearly all basal, narrowly lanceolate to broad and heart-shaped, with parallel veins from base to margin. Flowers lilac to white, in spikes of up to 30, nodding and bell-shaped, on a stiff, arching stem. Perianth segments more or less equal, joined at the base. Stamens 6. Ovary often superior, of 3 fused carpels with several ovules; style 1, with a simple stigma. Pollination is probably by bees and other insects. The fruit is an elongated capsule with numerous long, black seeds with a papery wing.

Key Recognition Features Clumps of usually broad, parallel-veined leaves and stems with nodding, lilac or white, bell-shaped flowers.

Ecology and Geography In woods and shady or sunny rocks throughout Japan (15 species), and in Korea, with only a few species in China.

Comment Over 700 cultivars are grown, many with variegated grey or golden-green leaves. Mutations are common, and many so-called species do not come true from seed. Hostas are particularly popular in areas with warm, wet summers and cold winters; slugs and snails are their main enemies. Until the early 20th century, the genus was known as *Funkia* Spreng. DNA studies show *Hosta*, sometimes put in the Hostaceae, to be close to *Agave*.

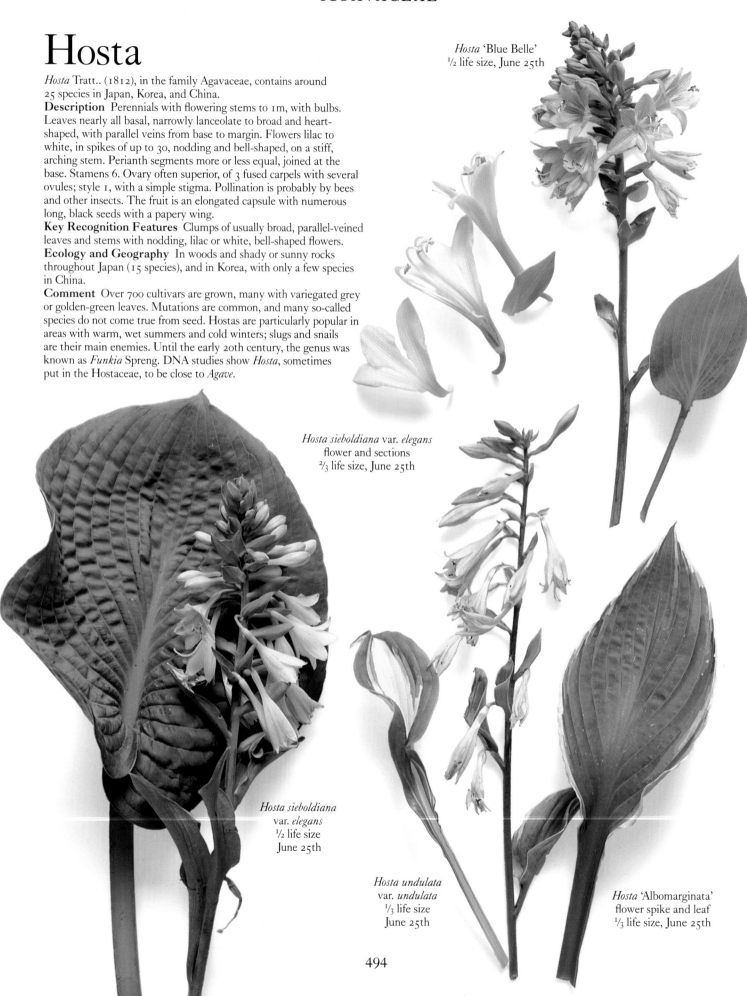

Hosta 'Blue Belle'
½ life size, June 25th

Hosta sieboldiana var. *elegans*
flower and sections
⅔ life size, June 25th

Hosta sieboldiana
var. *elegans*
½ life size
June 25th

Hosta undulata
var. *undulata*
⅓ life size
June 25th

Hosta 'Albomarginata'
flower spike and leaf
⅓ life size, June 25th

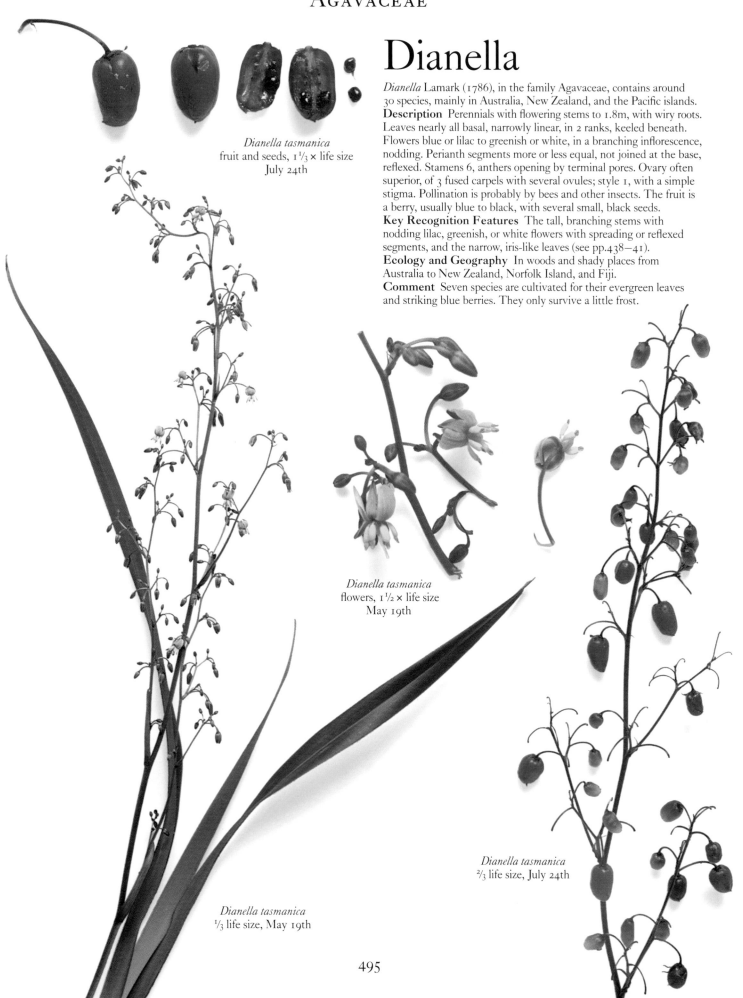

Dianella tasmanica
fruit and seeds, 1⅓ × life size
July 24th

Dianella

Dianella Lamark (1786), in the family Agavaceae, contains around 30 species, mainly in Australia, New Zealand, and the Pacific islands.
Description Perennials with flowering stems to 1.8m, with wiry roots. Leaves nearly all basal, narrowly linear, in 2 ranks, keeled beneath. Flowers blue or lilac to greenish or white, in a branching inflorescence, nodding. Perianth segments more or less equal, not joined at the base, reflexed. Stamens 6, anthers opening by terminal pores. Ovary often superior, of 3 fused carpels with several ovules; style 1, with a simple stigma. Pollination is probably by bees and other insects. The fruit is a berry, usually blue to black, with several small, black seeds.
Key Recognition Features The tall, branching stems with nodding lilac, greenish, or white flowers with spreading or reflexed segments, and the narrow, iris-like leaves (see pp.438–41).
Ecology and Geography In woods and shady places from Australia to New Zealand, Norfolk Island, and Fiji.
Comment Seven species are cultivated for their evergreen leaves and striking blue berries. They only survive a little frost.

Dianella tasmanica
flowers, 1½ × life size
May 19th

Dianella tasmanica
⅔ life size, July 24th

Dianella tasmanica
⅓ life size, May 19th

495

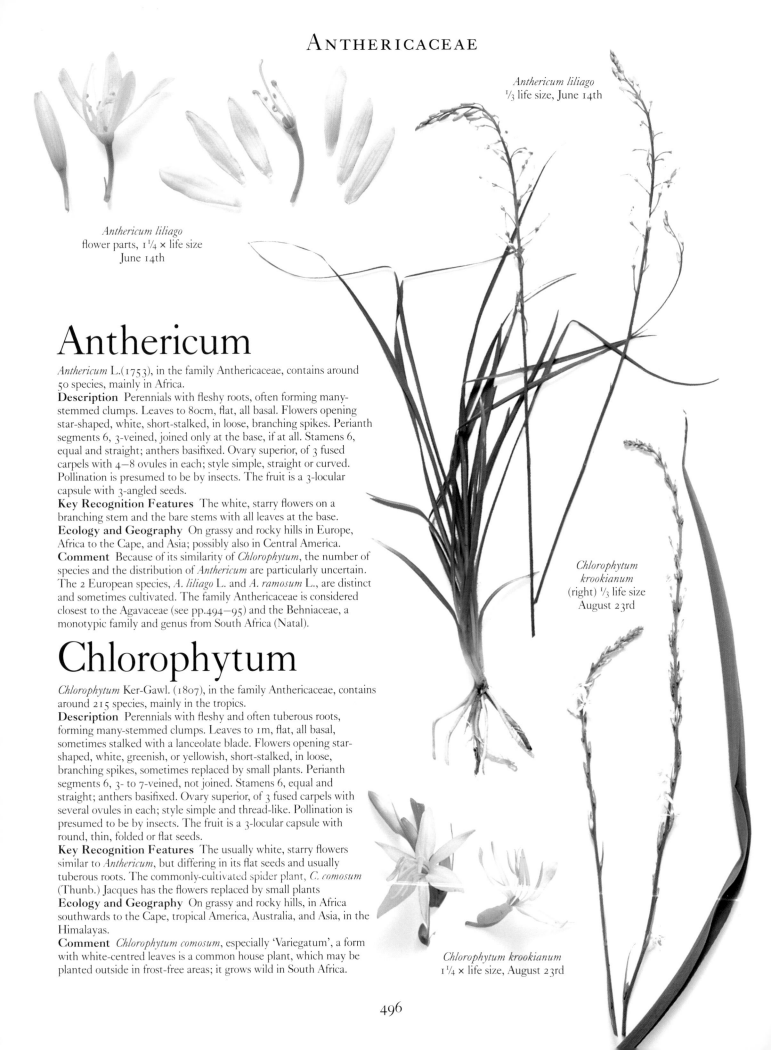

Anthericum liliago
⅓ life size, June 14th

Anthericum liliago
flower parts, 1¼ × life size
June 14th

Anthericum

Anthericum L.(1753), in the family Anthericaceae, contains around 50 species, mainly in Africa.

Description Perennials with fleshy roots, often forming many-stemmed clumps. Leaves to 80cm, flat, all basal. Flowers opening star-shaped, white, short-stalked, in loose, branching spikes. Perianth segments 6, 3-veined, joined only at the base, if at all. Stamens 6, equal and straight; anthers basifixed. Ovary superior, of 3 fused carpels with 4—8 ovules in each; style simple, straight or curved. Pollination is presumed to be by insects. The fruit is a 3-locular capsule with 3-angled seeds.

Key Recognition Features The white, starry flowers on a branching stem and the bare stems with all leaves at the base.

Ecology and Geography On grassy and rocky hills in Europe, Africa to the Cape, and Asia; possibly also in Central America.

Comment Because of its similarity of *Chlorophytum*, the number of species and the distribution of *Anthericum* are particularly uncertain. The 2 European species, *A. liliago* L. and *A. ramosum* L., are distinct and sometimes cultivated. The family Anthericaceae is considered closest to the Agavaceae (see pp.494—95) and the Behniaceae, a monotypic family and genus from South Africa (Natal).

Chlorophytum

Chlorophytum Ker-Gawl. (1807), in the family Anthericaceae, contains around 215 species, mainly in the tropics.

Description Perennials with fleshy and often tuberous roots, forming many-stemmed clumps. Leaves to 1m, flat, all basal, sometimes stalked with a lanceolate blade. Flowers opening star-shaped, white, greenish, or yellowish, short-stalked, in loose, branching spikes, sometimes replaced by small plants. Perianth segments 6, 3- to 7-veined, not joined. Stamens 6, equal and straight; anthers basifixed. Ovary superior, of 3 fused carpels with several ovules in each; style simple and thread-like. Pollination is presumed to be by insects. The fruit is a 3-locular capsule with round, thin, folded or flat seeds.

Key Recognition Features The usually white, starry flowers similar to *Anthericum*, but differing in its flat seeds and usually tuberous roots. The commonly-cultivated spider plant, *C. comosum* (Thunb.) Jacques has the flowers replaced by small plants

Ecology and Geography On grassy and rocky hills, in Africa southwards to the Cape, tropical America, Australia, and Asia, in the Himalayas.

Comment *Chlorophytum comosum*, especially 'Variegatum', a form with white-centred leaves is a common house plant, which may be planted outside in frost-free areas; it grows wild in South Africa.

Chlorophytum krookianum
(right) ⅓ life size
August 23rd

Chlorophytum krookianum
1¼ × life size, August 23rd

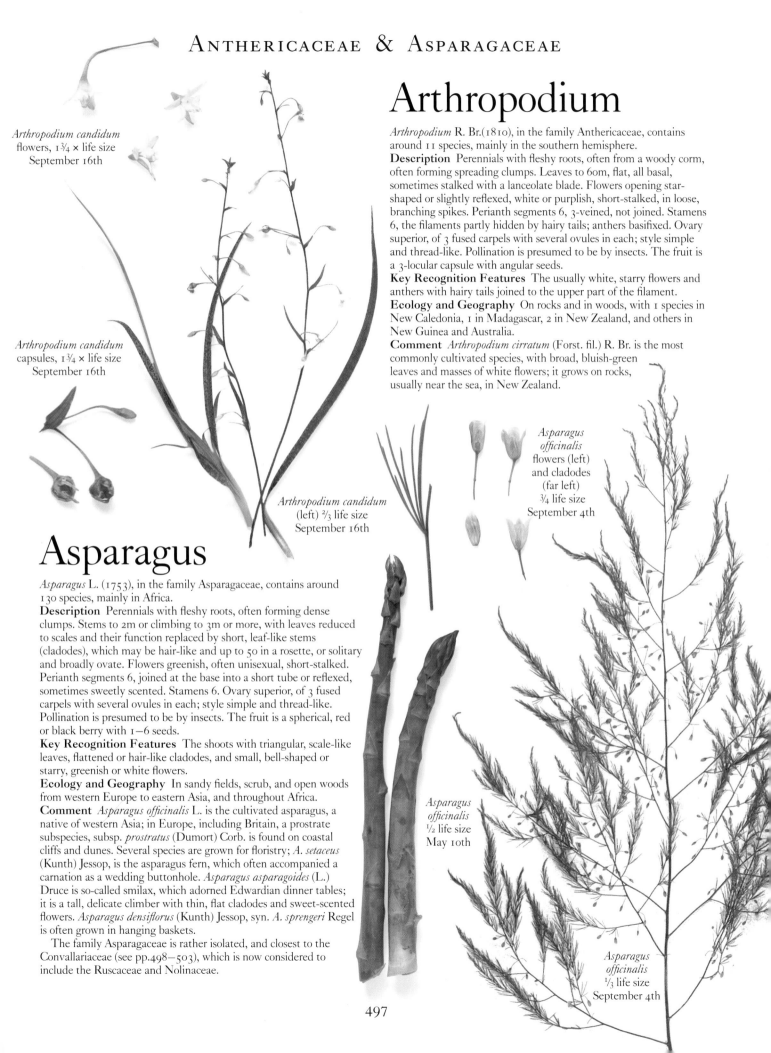

Arthropodium candidum
flowers, 1¾ × life size
September 16th

Arthropodium candidum
capsules, 1¾ × life size
September 16th

Arthropodium candidum
(left) ⅔ life size
September 16th

Arthropodium

Arthropodium R. Br.(1810), in the family Anthericaceae, contains around 11 species, mainly in the southern hemisphere.

Description Perennials with fleshy roots, often from a woody corm, often forming spreading clumps. Leaves to 60m, flat, all basal, sometimes stalked with a lanceolate blade. Flowers opening star-shaped or slightly reflexed, white or purplish, short-stalked, in loose, branching spikes. Perianth segments 6, 3-veined, not joined. Stamens 6, the filaments partly hidden by hairy tails; anthers basifixed. Ovary superior, of 3 fused carpels with several ovules in each; style simple and thread-like. Pollination is presumed to be by insects. The fruit is a 3-locular capsule with angular seeds.

Key Recognition Features The usually white, starry flowers and anthers with hairy tails joined to the upper part of the filament.

Ecology and Geography On rocks and in woods, with 1 species in New Caledonia, 1 in Madagascar, 2 in New Zealand, and others in New Guinea and Australia.

Comment *Arthropodium cirratum* (Forst. fil.) R. Br. is the most commonly cultivated species, with broad, bluish-green leaves and masses of white flowers; it grows on rocks, usually near the sea, in New Zealand.

Asparagus officinalis flowers (left) and cladodes (far left) ¾ life size September 4th

Asparagus

Asparagus L. (1753), in the family Asparagaceae, contains around 130 species, mainly in Africa.

Description Perennials with fleshy roots, often forming dense clumps. Stems to 2m or climbing to 3m or more, with leaves reduced to scales and their function replaced by short, leaf-like stems (cladodes), which may be hair-like and up to 50 in a rosette, or solitary and broadly ovate. Flowers greenish, often unisexual, short-stalked. Perianth segments 6, joined at the base into a short tube or reflexed, sometimes sweetly scented. Stamens 6. Ovary superior, of 3 fused carpels with several ovules in each; style simple and thread-like. Pollination is presumed to be by insects. The fruit is a spherical, red or black berry with 1–6 seeds.

Key Recognition Features The shoots with triangular, scale-like leaves, flattened or hair-like cladodes, and small, bell-shaped or starry, greenish or white flowers.

Ecology and Geography In sandy fields, scrub, and open woods from western Europe to eastern Asia, and throughout Africa.

Comment *Asparagus officinalis* L. is the cultivated asparagus, a native of western Asia; in Europe, including Britain, a prostrate subspecies, subsp. *prostratus* (Dumort) Corb. is found on coastal cliffs and dunes. Several species are grown for floristry; *A. setaceus* (Kunth) Jessop, is the asparagus fern, which often accompanied a carnation as a wedding buttonhole. *Asparagus asparagoides* (L.) Druce is so-called smilax, which adorned Edwardian dinner tables; it is a tall, delicate climber with thin, flat cladodes and sweet-scented flowers. *Asparagus densiflorus* (Kunth) Jessop, syn. *A. sprengeri* Regel is often grown in hanging baskets.

The family Asparagaceae is rather isolated, and closest to the Convallariaceae (see pp.498–503), which is now considered to include the Ruscaceae and Nolinaceae.

Asparagus officinalis ½ life size May 10th

Asparagus officinalis ⅓ life size September 4th

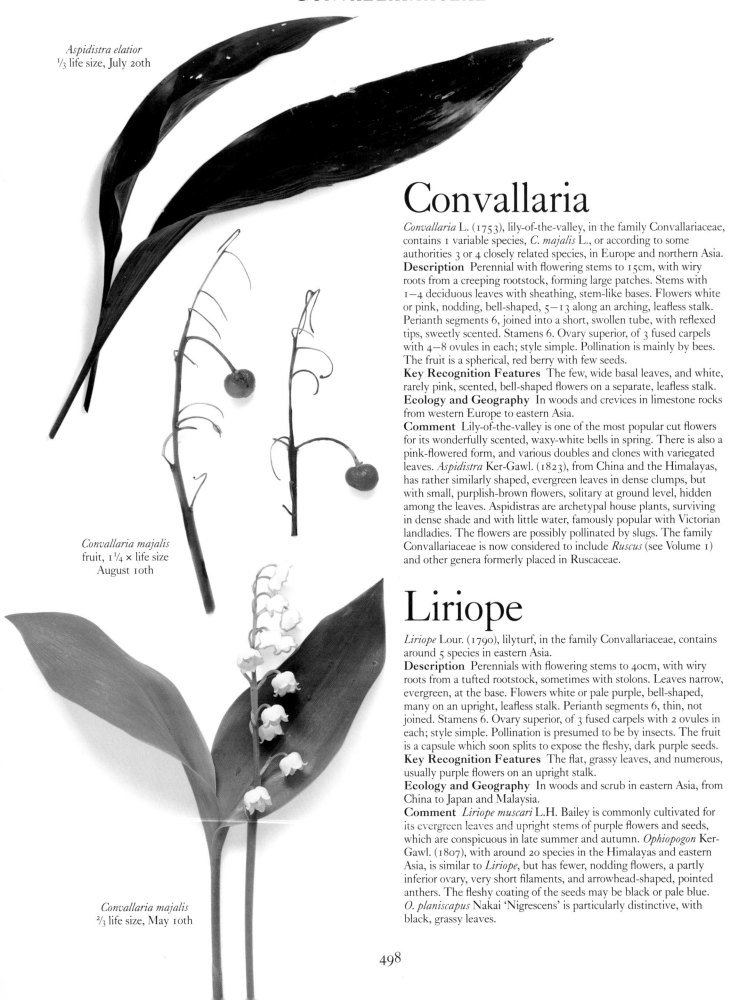

Aspidistra elatior
⅓ life size, July 20th

Convallaria majalis
fruit, 1¼ × life size
August 10th

Convallaria majalis
⅔ life size, May 10th

Convallaria

Convallaria L. (1753), lily-of-the-valley, in the family Convallariaceae, contains 1 variable species, *C. majalis* L., or according to some authorities 3 or 4 closely related species, in Europe and northern Asia.

Description Perennial with flowering stems to 15cm, with wiry roots from a creeping rootstock, forming large patches. Stems with 1–4 deciduous leaves with sheathing, stem-like bases. Flowers white or pink, nodding, bell-shaped, 5–13 along an arching, leafless stalk. Perianth segments 6, joined into a short, swollen tube, with reflexed tips, sweetly scented. Stamens 6. Ovary superior, of 3 fused carpels with 4–8 ovules in each; style simple. Pollination is mainly by bees. The fruit is a spherical, red berry with few seeds.

Key Recognition Features The few, wide basal leaves, and white, rarely pink, scented, bell-shaped flowers on a separate, leafless stalk.

Ecology and Geography In woods and crevices in limestone rocks from western Europe to eastern Asia.

Comment Lily-of-the-valley is one of the most popular cut flowers for its wonderfully scented, waxy-white bells in spring. There is also a pink-flowered form, and various doubles and clones with variegated leaves. *Aspidistra* Ker-Gawl. (1823), from China and the Himalayas, has rather similarly shaped, evergreen leaves in dense clumps, but with small, purplish-brown flowers, solitary at ground level, hidden among the leaves. Aspidistras are archetypal house plants, surviving in dense shade and with little water, famously popular with Victorian landladies. The flowers are possibly pollinated by slugs. The family Convallariaceae is now considered to include *Ruscus* (see Volume 1) and other genera formerly placed in Ruscaceae.

Liriope

Liriope Lour. (1790), lilyturf, in the family Convallariaceae, contains around 5 species in eastern Asia.

Description Perennials with flowering stems to 40cm, with wiry roots from a tufted rootstock, sometimes with stolons. Leaves narrow, evergreen, at the base. Flowers white or pale purple, bell-shaped, many on an upright, leafless stalk. Perianth segments 6, thin, not joined. Stamens 6. Ovary superior, of 3 fused carpels with 2 ovules in each; style simple. Pollination is presumed to be by insects. The fruit is a capsule which soon splits to expose the fleshy, dark purple seeds.

Key Recognition Features The flat, grassy leaves, and numerous, usually purple flowers on an upright stalk.

Ecology and Geography In woods and scrub in eastern Asia, from China to Japan and Malaysia.

Comment *Liriope muscari* L.H. Bailey is commonly cultivated for its evergreen leaves and upright stems of purple flowers and seeds, which are conspicuous in late summer and autumn. *Ophiopogon* Ker-Gawl. (1807), with around 20 species in the Himalayas and eastern Asia, is similar to *Liriope*, but has fewer, nodding flowers, a partly inferior ovary, very short filaments, and arrowhead-shaped, pointed anthers. The fleshy coating of the seeds may be black or pale blue. *O. planiscapus* Nakai 'Nigrescens' is particularly distinctive, with black, grassy leaves.

CONVALLARIACEAE

Liriope muscari
flower buds, 2 × life size
September 25th

Liriope muscari
flower buds, life size
September 25th

Ophiopogon planiscapus
'Nigrescens', ½ life size
July 28th

Ophiopogon planiscapus
'Nigrescens'
flowers, 2 × life size
July 28th

Liriope muscari
½ life size
September 25th

499

Polygonatum

Polygonatum Mill. (1754), Solomon's seal, in the family Convallariaceae, contains around 60 species, in Europe, Asia, and North America.

Description Perennials with deciduous flowering stems, sometimes climbing, from as small as 1cm to 3m, with thick or tuberous rhizomes, sometimes creeping and forming large patches. Leaves alternate or whorled on the stems, often modified into tendrils. Flowers white, green, pinkish-purple or red, nodding, bell-shaped. Perianth segments 6, joined into a short or long, sometimes swollen tube, with reflexed tips. Stamens 6, fixed to the inside of the tube, the anthers opening inwards. Ovary superior, of 3 fused carpels with 2 or more ovules in each; style simple. Pollination is mainly by bees. The fruit is a spherical, pink, red, or blackish berry with few to many seeds.

Key Recognition Features The leafy stems and small groups of white or purplish, tubular flowers on thread-like stems in the leaf axils.

Ecology and Geography In woods, scrub, alpine meadows, and crevices in limestone rocks, from western Europe to eastern Asia, with the largest number of species in southwestern China.

Comment Solomon's seal is so-called because the leaf forms a characteristic neat scar on the rhizome when it has withered. Some species are used medicinally and many species are cultivated as ornamentals; the naming of the Chinese species is very confused, and the 2 species shown here are close to *P. kansuense* Maxim. ex Batal. and *P. cirrhifolium* (Wall.) Royle, both widespread in the eastern Himalayan region. The genus *Disporopsis* Hance, with around 6 species from western China to Taiwan and the Philippines, is superficially similar to *Polygonatum* but has evergreen stems and leaves and thick, fleshy flowers. The stamens, which have flattened and fimbriate appendages longer than the anthers, are joined in a ring, almost blocking the mouth of the flower.

Disporopsis aspera, flower parts
1½ × life size, June 7th

Polygonatum cf.
kansuense, flowers and
flower sections
2 × life size, June 9th

Polygonatum
cf. *kansuense*
½ life size, June 9th

Polygonatum cf. *cirrhifolium*
½ life size, June 9th

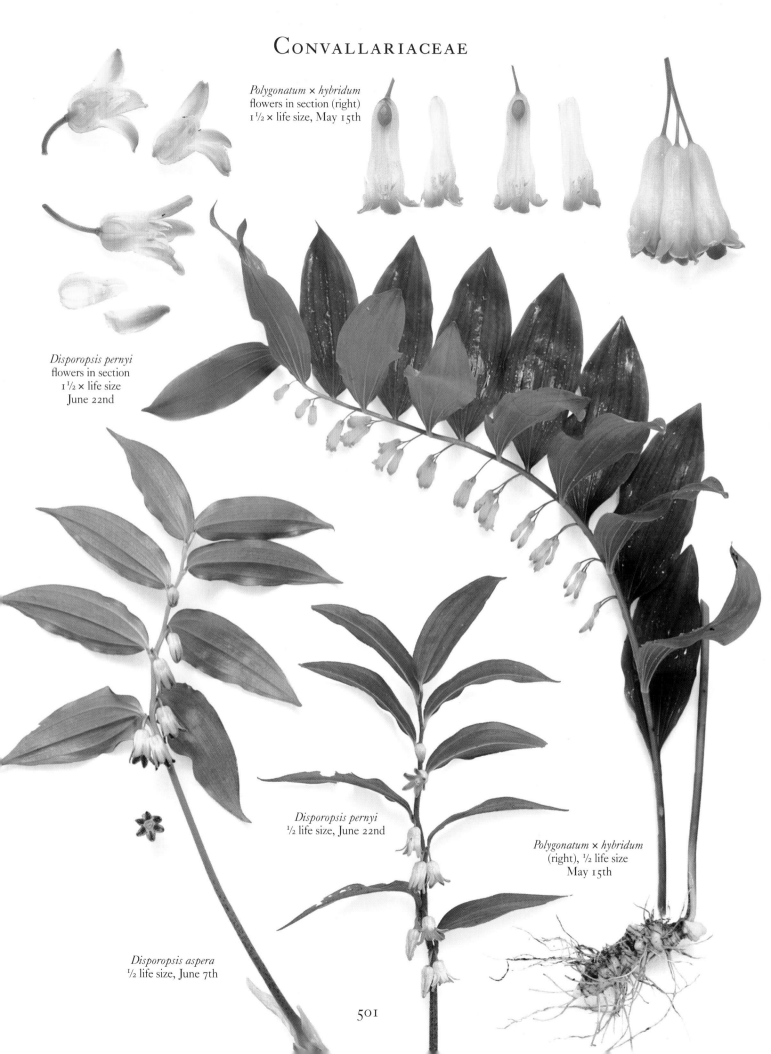

CONVALLARIACEAE

Polygonatum × hybridum
flowers in section (right)
1½ × life size, May 15th

Disporopsis pernyi
flowers in section
1½ × life size
June 22nd

Disporopsis pernyi
½ life size, June 22nd

Polygonatum × hybridum
(right), ½ life size
May 15th

Disporopsis aspera
½ life size, June 7th

Maianthemum

Maianthemum G. Weber ex Wigg. (1780), in the family Convallariaceae, contains around 30 species in Europe, Asia, and North America, including the species formerly separated in *Smilacina* Desf..

Description Perennials with deciduous flowering stems to 1m, with thick or thin rhizomes, sometimes creeping and forming large patches. Leaves alternate, usually broad. Flowers white, green, or purple, star-shaped, rarely tubular, in a simple or much-branched inflorescence. Perianth segments 6, sometimes 4, usually separate, occasionally joined into a tube, with reflexed tips. Stamens 6, separate or fixed to the inside of the tube, the filaments sometimes flattened. Pollination is presumed to be by insects. Ovary superior, of 3 fused carpels with 2 ovules in each; style simple. The fruit is a spherical, pink or red berry with 1 or 2 seeds.

Key Recognition Features The stems with broad, alternate leaves and terminal inflorescence of small flowers, which are followed by showy red fruit.

Ecology and Geography In woods and scrub from northern Europe to eastern Asia and North America, with the largest number of species in southwestern China.

Comment *Maianthemum racemosum* (L.) Link, syn. *Smilacina racemosa* (L.) Desf. from eastern North America, forms stout clumps and has a large, branching head of minute, white flowers with flat filaments, followed by masses of red berries. *Maianthemum stellatum* (L.) Link, is found all across North America and in northern Europe; it has fewer, larger starry flowers and forms large patches in woods. Most of the Chinese and Himalayan species have small, insignificant flowers.

Speirantha

Speirantha Baker (1875), in the family Convallariaceae, contains 1 species, *S. convallarioides* Baker, in China.

Description Perennial with flowering stems to 15cm, with thick rhizomes, spreading by stolons. Leaves evergreen, narrowly lanceolate, 6–8 forming a rosette. Flowering stems leafless, emerging from basal sheaths. Flowers white, star-shaped, sweetly scented, up to 30 on white stalks. Perianth segments 6, separate. Stamens 6, separate. Ovary superior, of 3 fused carpels with 2 ovules in each; style simple. Pollination is presumed to be by insects. Fruit not seen, but presumed to be a spherical red berry with 1 or 2 seeds.

Key Recognition Features The rosette of lanceolate evergreen leaves and the white, starry, scented flowers on white stalks.

Ecology and Geography In woods in southeastern China, in Jiangxi province.

Comment This unusual perennial will survive outside in southern England and the warmer parts of North America.

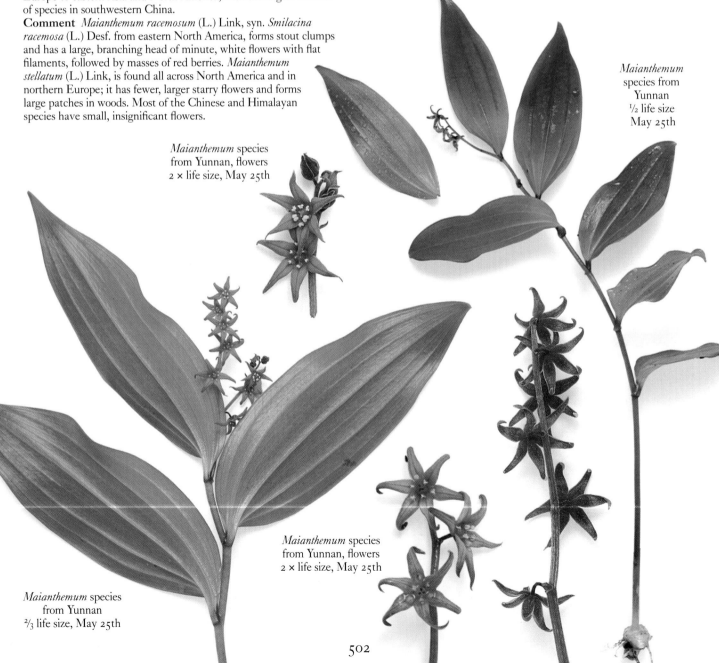

Maianthemum species from Yunnan ½ life size May 25th

Maianthemum species from Yunnan, flowers 2 × life size, May 25th

Maianthemum species from Yunnan, flowers 2 × life size, May 25th

Maianthemum species from Yunnan ⅔ life size, May 25th

*Speirantha
convallarioides*
½ life size
May 15th

Maianthemum racemosum
½ life size, May 25th

Maianthemum species
from China
¾ life size, June 5th

Maianthemum racemosa
flowers, 2 × life size
May 25th

Pontederia cordata, flowers
2 × life size, August 10th

Pontederia cordata
²⁄₃ life size, August 10th

Pontederia

Pontederia L. (1753), in the family Pontederiaceae, contains around 8 species in eastern North America and South America.

Description Perennials with flowering stems to 1.2m, with thick rhizomes. Leaves deciduous, heart-shaped, 1 per stem. Flowering stems with sheathing bracts. Flowers small, blue, star-shaped, 2-lipped, in a dense head. Perianth segments 6, joined at the base into a short tube. Stamens 6, attached at different heights on the inside of the flower. Ovary superior, of 3 fused carpels, of which 1 only ripens; style simple. Pollination is by insects. The fruit is a swollen capsule with 1 seed.

Key Recognition Features Water plants with stalked, heart-shaped leaves and heads of blue flowers.

Ecology and Geography In ponds and slow rivers from Nova Scotia to Minnesota and southwards to South America.

Comment The genus is named after Giulio Pontedera (1688–1757) professor of botany at Padua. Pickerel weed, *P. cordata* L. is the only species in temperate North America; it is pollinated by a particular bee, *Dufourea novae-angliae* Robertson, which emerges at the same time as the *Pontederia* flowers open. Also in the Pontederiaceae is water hyacinth, *Eichhornia crassipes* (Mart.) Solms-Laubach, which is beautiful, but a serious aquatic weed in the tropics; the flowers are fewer and much larger than those of *Pontederia*, and the leaf stalks are swollen and act as floats. The family Pontaderiaceae is closest to the Commelinaceae and Haemodoraceae, and with the rare aquatic Philydraceae forms the Commelinales.

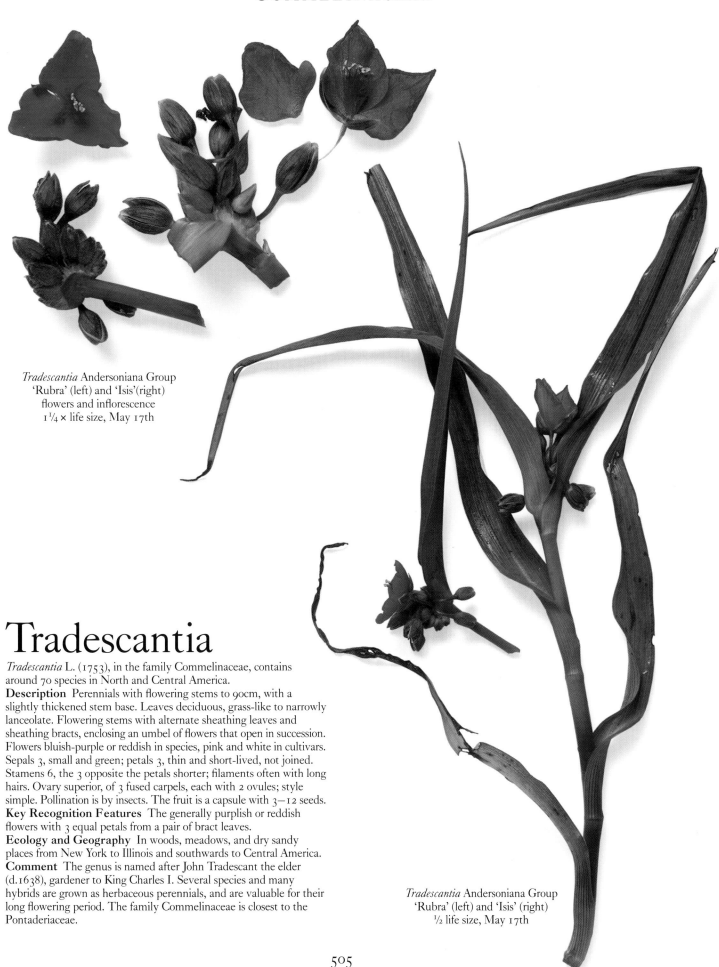

Tradescantia Andersoniana Group
'Rubra' (left) and 'Isis'(right)
flowers and inflorescence
1¹/₄ × life size, May 17th

Tradescantia

Tradescantia L. (1753), in the family Commelinaceae, contains around 70 species in North and Central America.

Description Perennials with flowering stems to 90cm, with a slightly thickened stem base. Leaves deciduous, grass-like to narrowly lanceolate. Flowering stems with alternate sheathing leaves and sheathing bracts, enclosing an umbel of flowers that open in succession. Flowers bluish-purple or reddish in species, pink and white in cultivars. Sepals 3, small and green; petals 3, thin and short-lived, not joined. Stamens 6, the 3 opposite the petals shorter; filaments often with long hairs. Ovary superior, of 3 fused carpels, each with 2 ovules; style simple. Pollination is by insects. The fruit is a capsule with 3–12 seeds.

Key Recognition Features The generally purplish or reddish flowers with 3 equal petals from a pair of bract leaves.

Ecology and Geography In woods, meadows, and dry sandy places from New York to Illinois and southwards to Central America.

Comment The genus is named after John Tradescant the elder (d.1638), gardener to King Charles I. Several species and many hybrids are grown as herbaceous perennials, and are valuable for their long flowering period. The family Commelinaceae is closest to the Pontaderiaceae.

Tradescantia Andersoniana Group
'Rubra' (left) and 'Isis' (right)
¹/₂ life size, May 17th

Anigozanthos

Anigozanthos Labill. (1798), kangaroo paw, in the family Haemodoraceae, contains around 11 species in Western Australia.

Description Perennials with branching rhizomes. Leaves mostly basal, evergreen or deciduous in summer, flat and often curved. Flowering stems to 1m, with alternate, reduced leaves, branched or simple, with dense spikes of flowers. Flowers green, yellow, orange, pink, or reddish, often strikingly bicoloured, stiff and densely woolly outside. Perianth segments 6, all joined at the base into a long tube, which is split on 1 side. Stamens 6. Ovary superior, of 3 fused carpels each with 2 ovules; style simple. Pollination is by birds. The fruit is a capsule with many small, hard, greyish or black seeds.

Key Recognition Features The flat, evergreen leaves, and stiff, hairy flowers with the tube split down 1 side.

Ecology and Geography In dry, sandy places in the southwestern corner of Western Australia.

Comment Several species and hybrids are cultivated, especially in hot areas such as California; some, such as *A. pulcherrimus* Hook. and *A. rufus* Labill., can survive a few degrees of frost. The Haemodoraceae is mainly found in the southern hemisphere, and includes *Wachendorfia* from South Africa; it is closest to the Commelinaceae (see p.505).

Anigozanthos flavidus
⅓ life size, August 23rd

Anigozanthos rufus
(right) ⅓ life size
June 19th

Anigozanthos viridis
(below) ⅓ life size, June 19th

Anigozanthos flavidus
⅓ life size, June 19th

Anigozanthos flavidus
flowers, just under life size
August 23rd

506

Canna

Canna L. (1753), in the family Cannaceae, contains around 10 species in subtropical and tropical America, but widely naturalised elsewhere in the tropics.

Description Perennials with tuberous, branching rhizomes. Leaves deciduous in winter. Flowering stems to 3m, with alternate leaves, simple or a little branched, with loose spikes of flowers. Flowers red or yellow, orange or pink in cultivars. Sepals 3, small, not joined; petals 3, small and narrow, joined into a tube at the base Stamens 4, petal-like, 3 large, 1 smaller with an anther on 1 side, all joined at the base. Ovary inferior, of 3 fused carpels, each with many ovules; style flattened. Pollination is by hummingbirds. The fruit is a capsule, usually warty, with many hard, round, black seeds.

Key Recognition Features The broad, soft leaves and tall stem with irregular-looking flowers with petal-like stamens.

Ecology and Geography In clearings in forest and wet places by streams from South Carolina and Florida to Peru and Argentina.

Comment Several species and hybrids are cultivated, often as summer bedding. Some will survive outside in winter, provided that the rhizomes are protected from frost. Some species are cultivated for their edible rhizomes. The family Cannaceae contains only this genus; it is related to Zingiberaceae (see pp.508–509).

Canna iridiflora
flowers, ¾ life size
October 3rd

Canna iridiflora
flower parts
just under life size
October 3rd

Canna leaves
½ life size, July 11th

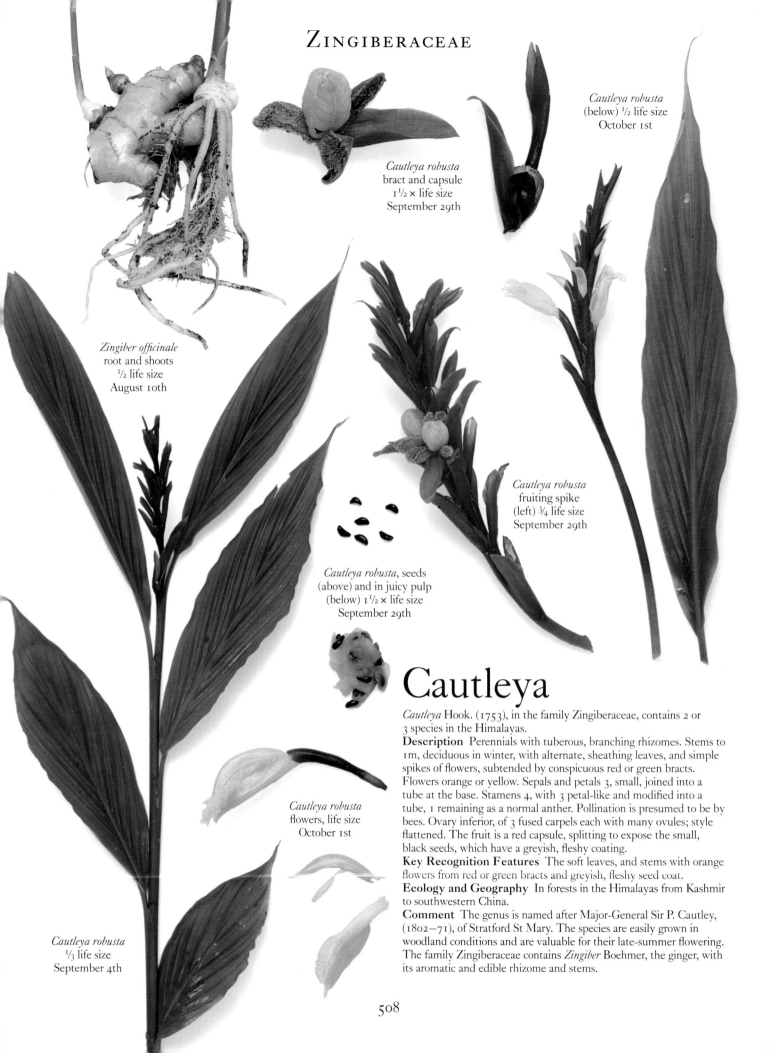

Cautleya robusta
bract and capsule
1¹⁄₂ × life size
September 29th

Cautleya robusta
(below) ¹⁄₂ life size
October 1st

Zingiber officinale
root and shoots
¹⁄₂ life size
August 10th

Cautleya robusta
fruiting spike
(left) ³⁄₄ life size
September 29th

Cautleya robusta, seeds
(above) and in juicy pulp
(below) 1¹⁄₂ × life size
September 29th

Cautleya robusta
flowers, life size
October 1st

Cautleya robusta
¹⁄₃ life size
September 4th

Cautleya

Cautleya Hook. (1753), in the family Zingiberaceae, contains 2 or 3 species in the Himalayas.

Description Perennials with tuberous, branching rhizomes. Stems to 1m, deciduous in winter, with alternate, sheathing leaves, and simple spikes of flowers, subtended by conspicuous red or green bracts. Flowers orange or yellow. Sepals and petals 3, small, joined into a tube at the base. Stamens 4, with 3 petal-like and modified into a tube, 1 remaining as a normal anther. Pollination is presumed to be by bees. Ovary inferior, of 3 fused carpels each with many ovules; style flattened. The fruit is a red capsule, splitting to expose the small, black seeds, which have a greyish, fleshy coating.

Key Recognition Features The soft leaves, and stems with orange flowers from red or green bracts and greyish, fleshy seed coat.

Ecology and Geography In forests in the Himalayas from Kashmir to southwestern China.

Comment The genus is named after Major-General Sir P. Cautley, (1802–71), of Stratford St Mary. The species are easily grown in woodland conditions and are valuable for their late-summer flowering. The family Zingiberaceae contains *Zingiber* Boehmer, the ginger, with its aromatic and edible rhizome and stems.

508

Roscoea

Roscoea Smith (1804), in the family Zingiberaceae, contains around 20 species in the Himalayas and China.

Description Perennials with tuberous roots. Stems to 60cm, deciduous in winter, with alternate, sheathing leaves, and simple spikes of flowers subtended by green bracts. Flowers purple, pink, yellow, white, or red. Sepals 3, joined into a tube. Petals 3, forming a tube at the base, the upper hooded, the lower 2 lateral. Stamens 4, with 1 remaining as a normal stamen, pressed beneath the hooded upper petal, 2 lateral and petal-like, the last forming a large lip. Ovary inferior, of 3 fused carpels each with many ovules; style flattened at the tip, with a papillose margin. Pollination is presumed to be by bees. The fruit is a capsule with small, black seeds.

Key Recognition Features The narrow, soft leaves, and the stems with a head or spike of short-lived, 2-lipped flowers.

Ecology and Geography In forests, in shallow pockets in limestone rocks, on rock ledges, and in alpine meadows in the Himalayas from Pakistan to southwestern China.

Comment The genus is named after William Roscoe (1753–1831), banker and MP for Liverpool, a founder of Liverpool Botanic Garden and author of *Monandrian Plants* 1824–29. Many species are cultivated. The genus *Hedychium* J. Koenig, with 50 species in India, the Himalayas, and China, is the ginger lily; the stems are generally around 2m, the scented flowers emerging from a tight, cone-like head of bracts at the stem apex.

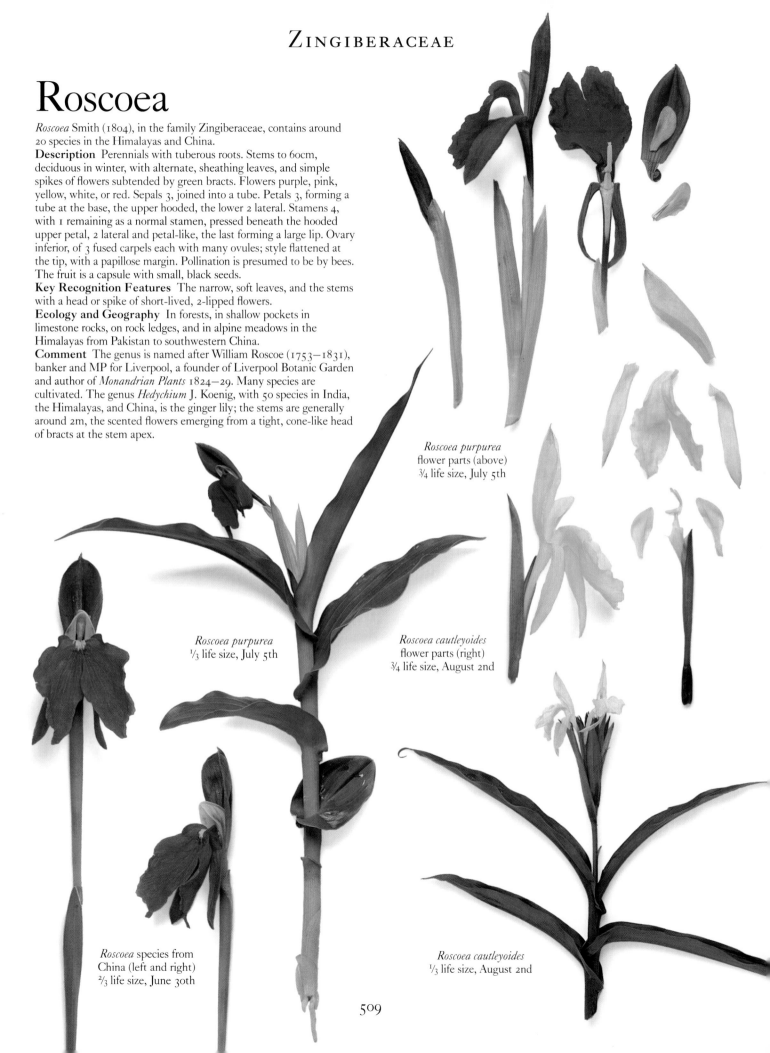

Roscoea purpurea
flower parts (above)
¾ life size, July 5th

Roscoea purpurea
⅓ life size, July 5th

Roscoea cautleyoides
flower parts (right)
¾ life size, August 2nd

Roscoea species from
China (left and right)
⅔ life size, June 30th

Roscoea cautleyoides
⅓ life size, August 2nd

Thalia geniculata
½ life size, June 22nd

Thalia geniculata
flowers, 1²/₃ × life size
June 22nd

Thalia

Thalia L. (1753), in the family Marantaceae, contains around 7 species in tropical and subtropical America.

Description Perennials with tufted rootstocks. Stems to 2m, deciduous in winter, with sheathing leaves with an angled blade, and branching spikes of small flowers subtended by green bracts. Flowers blue to purple. Sepals 3, small, barely joined. Petals 3, joined into a short tube at the base. Stamens 2 or 3, with 1 remaining as a normal stamen, the rest petaloid. Ovary inferior, of 1 carpel with 1 ovule; style flattened at the tip, 2-lipped. Pollination is by insects. The fruit is a capsule with 1 seed.

Key Recognition Features The leaf blade held at an angle and the branching and arching spikes of small flowers.

Ecology and Geography In marshes, lakes, and shallow water from Florida, South Carolina, and Louisiana to southeastern Brazil; 1 species, *T. geniculata* L., is also recorded from western tropical Africa.

Comment These are elegant water plants, which will survive in areas with light frost, provided that the roots are deep enough to remain unfrozen. Mabberley describes the pollination mechanism of *T. geniculata*: the pollen is deposited on the style in bud, and when an insect proboscis touches the style it promotes an explosive S-shaped movement; in 0.03 seconds the style becomes erect, scrapes pollen from the insect's proboscis into the stigmatic hollow, and deposits its own pollen onto the proboscis. Many other species of Marantaceae, particularly from the genera *Calathea* G. Mey., *Ctenanthe* Eichler, and *Maranta* L., are popular house plants, grown for their decorative leaves.

Thalia geniculata
side branch with flowers
¾ life size, June 22nd

Typha latifolia, section of
female (left) and male (right)
parts of the inflorescence
1¾ × life size, July 19th

Typha latifolia
½ life size, July 19th

Typha

Typha L. (1753), reedmace, cattail, or bulrush, in the family Typhaceae, contains around 12 species in Europe, Asia, and the Americas.

Description Perennials with creeping rootstocks. Stems to 3m, deciduous in winter, with flat, linear, upright leaves. Flowers unisexual, very small, crowded onto a dense spike, with the males above the females. Sepals and petals reduced to bristles. Stamens 2–7, the filaments joined. Ovary inferior, of 1 or 2 carpels with 1 ovule; style flattened at the tip, 2-lipped. Pollination is by wind. The fruit is nut-like, with 1 seed.

Key Recognition Features The flat, narrow, upright leaves and brown and cream spikes of minute flowers, followed by fluffy seeds.

Ecology and Geography In shallow water; nearly worldwide.

Comment Common, reed-like plants of shallow water; the pollen is edible, as are the rhizomes. The seeds are transported long distances by wind, and often appear in new bodies of water. DNA studies show Typhaceae to be an isolated family, closest to the Sparganiaceae, which includes *Sparganium* L., the common bur reed.

511

Billbergia

Billbergia Thunb. (1821), in the family Bromeliaceae, contains around 56 species in tropical America.

Description Perennials with tufted rootstocks, the leaves sometimes forming a rosette that holds water, often spiny on the edge and scurfy beneath. Flowering stems to 1m, usually arching, with the flowering part pendulous. Flowers in a loose spike, with ovelapping, pink or reddish bracts. Sepals 3 and petals 3, blue and green, the narrow petals often twisted. Stamens 6, longer than the petals. Ovary inferior, of 3 carpels; style flattened at the tip, 2-lipped. Pollination is by birds and perhaps also by insects. The fruit is nut-like, with 1 seed.

Key Recognition Features The flat leaves and spikes of green or blue flowers with red or pink bracts.

Ecology and Geography Usually epiphytic on trees or rocks, from Mexico to Argentina and Uruguay, with most species in eastern Brazil.

Comment Several species are grown as ornamentals for their showy bracts. *Billbergia nutans* Regel, with narrow leaves 6–10mm wide and petals blue on the edges, will survive light frosts. The family Bromeliaceae contains such diverse plants as *Ananas* Mill., the pineapple, *Puya* Molina, in which some species may reach 8m or more, and the often moss-like *Tillandsia* L., Spanish moss, typical of the warm, southeastern states of North America. Apart from *Billbergia*, nearly hardy species are found in the South American genera *Puya* and *Fascicularia* Mez. DNA studies show it to be an isolated family within the Commelinoid group, which includes gingers, palms, and grasses, as well as the Commelinaceae (see p.505).

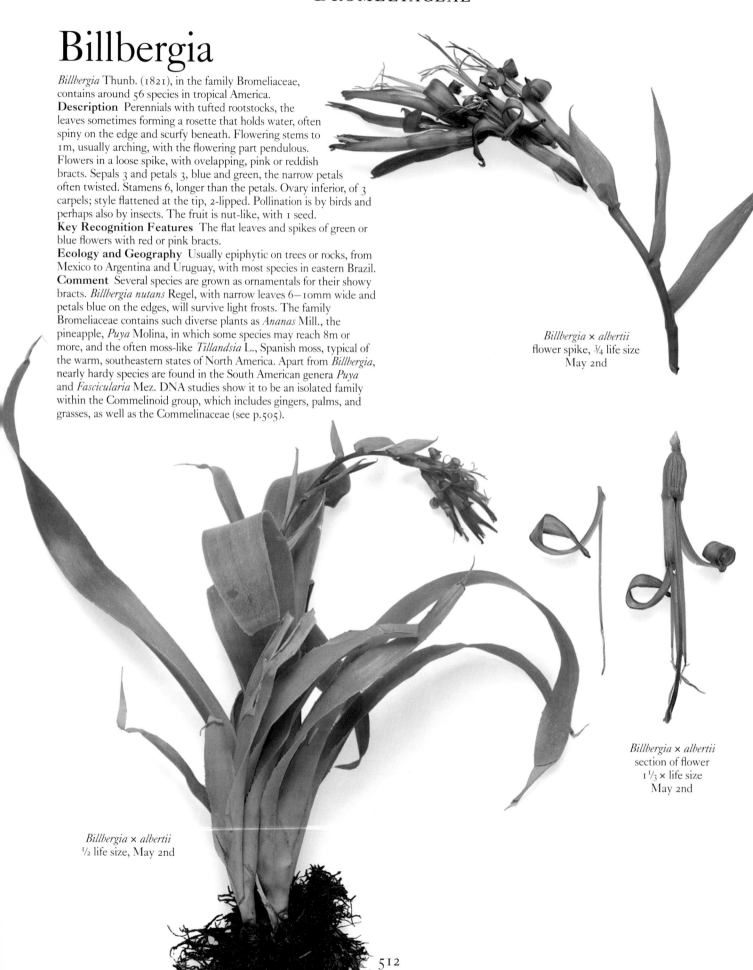

Billbergia × *albertii*
flower spike, ¾ life size
May 2nd

Billbergia × *albertii*
section of flower
1⅓ × life size
May 2nd

Billbergia × *albertii*
½ life size, May 2nd

Luzula

Luzula DC (1805), in the family Juncaceae, contains around 115 species worldwide.

Description Perennials with tufted or sometimes creeping rootstocks, the leaves forming a rosette, usually with scattered white hairs on the surface. Flowering stems to 1m, with the flowered part usually pendulous. Flowers in a widely branching or tight head. Perianth segments 6, brown or green, occasionally white, small. Stamens 3 or 6, longer than the petals. Ovary superior, of 3 carpels; stigmas 3. Pollination is by wind. The fruit is a dark brown, shining, rounded capsule with numerous small seeds.

Key Recognition Features The flat, grass-like leaves, usually with scattered white hairs on the surface, and the small, brownish flowers followed by dark brown, shining capsules.

Ecology and Geography In woods, meadows, bogs, and stony places in the mountains; 31 species in Europe, 15 species in Australia, the rest scattered worldwide.

Comment A few species, especially *L. sylvatica* (Huds.) Gaud. and *L. nivea* (L.) DC with pure white flowers, are grown as ornamentals. *Luzula campestris* (L.) DC is a common weed in damp lawns, flowering in early spring; the seeds are dispersed by ants. The family Juncaceae, which includes the large genus *Juncus* L., the common rush, with 300 species, is found mainly in wet places. DNA studies show it to be closest to Cyperaceae (see pp.514−17) and to Xyridaceae, a mainly southern-hemisphere family, in which the 3 petals are well developed and coloured.

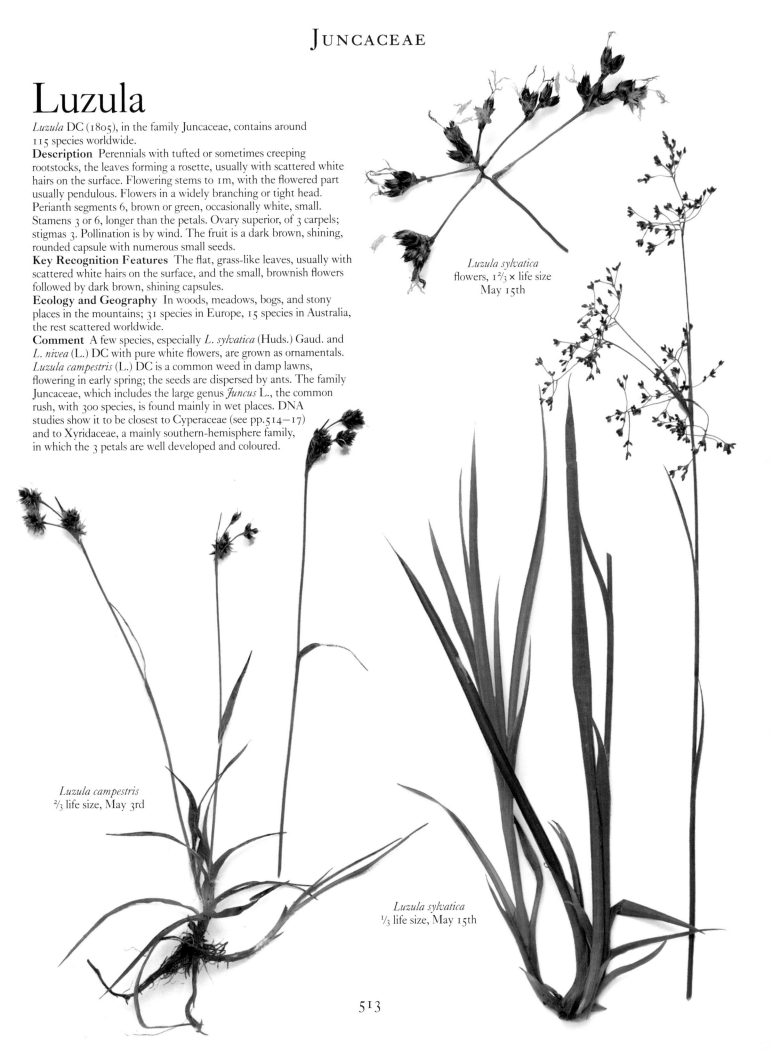

Luzula sylvatica
flowers, 1²/₃ × life size
May 15th

Luzula campestris
²/₃ life size, May 3rd

Luzula sylvatica
¹/₃ life size, May 15th

Carex

Carex L. (1753), sedge, in the family Cyperaceae, contains around 2000 species worldwide.

Description Perennials with tufted or creeping rootstocks, the leaves in 3 ranks, forming a rosette, usually with a sharp edge. Flowering stems to 1.5m, usually triangular in section. Flowers unisexual, in long spikes or short spikelets, the males and females usually on separate stalks, the males usually at the apex of the stem. Perianth segments absent. Male flowers of 2 or 3 stamens, in the axil of a bract. Female flowers of 1 swollen bag, the utricle, with 2 or 3 stigmas and 1 carpel. Pollination is by wind. The fruit has 1 usually triangular seed, held within the sometimes hairy utricle.

Key Recognition Features The flat, grass-like leaves in groups of 3, the triangular flowering stems, and the male and female flowers on separate spikelets.

Ecology and Geography In woods, meadows, stony places, bogs, and shallow water; 180 species in Europe, over 400 in North America, around 500 in China, and the rest scattered worldwide.

Comment A hundred or so species and cultivars are grown as ornamentals, but otherwise few have any economic use.

Carex demissa
male and female
flowering spikelets
1¾ × life size, July 4th

Carex grayi, 5 utricles
(left) and male spike
(right) 1¾ × life size
June 12th

Carex grayi
⅓ life size, June 12th

Carex demissa
½ life size, July 4th

514

Carex riparia 'Variegata' (right)
Carex remota (centre)
Carex pendula (far right)
½ life size, July 4th

Carex pendula utricles (left) and
Carex demissa utricles (right)
2½ × life size, July 4th

Uncinia uncinata
spikelet and flowers
showing hook
2¹/₂ × life size
August 10th

Uncinia

Uncinia Pers. (1807), in the family Cyperaceae, contains around 50 species, mainly in the southern hemisphere.

Description Perennials with tufted or creeping rootstocks, the leaves usually in 3 ranks, often red or brown, forming a rosette, with a sharp edge and a triangular tip. Flowering stems to 90cm, often triangular in section, with 1 terminal spike, with male flowers at the tip, female below. Flowers unisexual, in the axil of a small bract. Perianth segments absent. Stamens 3. Stigmas 3, carpel 1. Pollination is by wind. The fruit is a solitary, triangular nutlet; in the female flowers a long hook protrudes from the tip of the utricle.

Key Recognition Features The grass-like leaves with a triangular tip; the terminal spike with male flowers at the tip, female below; the female flowers with a long hook protruding from the tip of the utricle.

Ecology and Geography In grassland, scrub, and forest, mainly in the colder parts of the southern hemisphere, with 32 species in New Zealand, others in South America, but none in South Africa.

Comment A few species are grown as ornamentals for their often unusually coloured, sedge-like leaves (*Carex*, see pp.514–15).

Uncinia uncinata
(left) ¹/₂ life size
August 10th

Eriophorum angustifolium
¹/₂ life size, May 27th

516

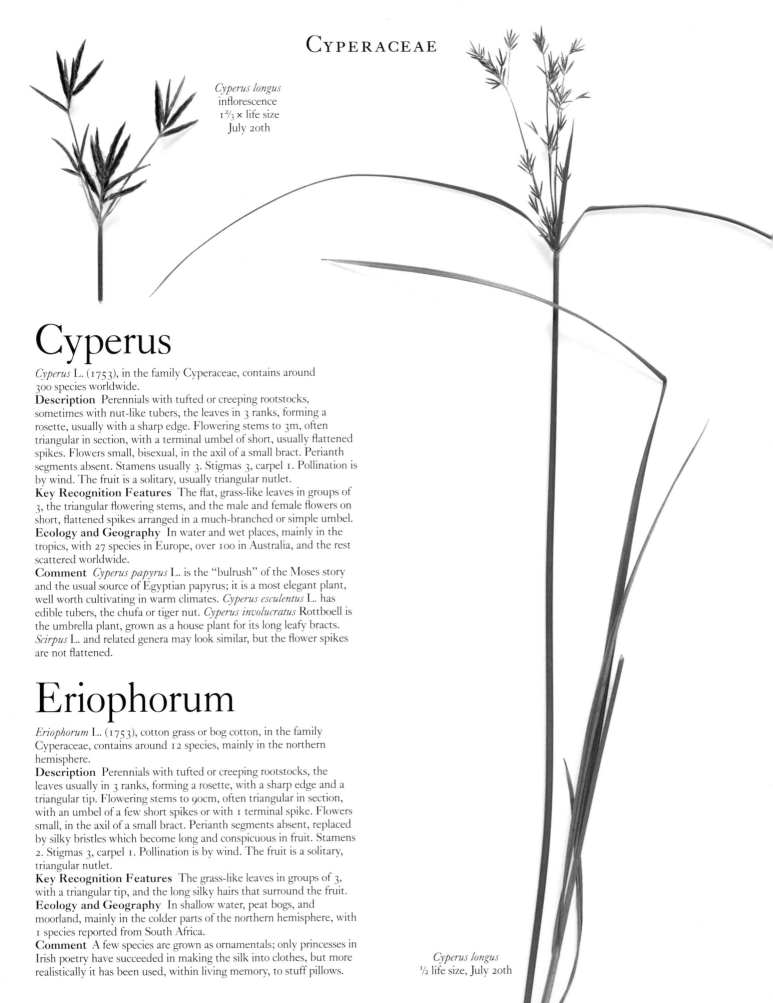

Cyperus longus
inflorescence
1 2/3 × life size
July 20th

Cyperus

Cyperus L. (1753), in the family Cyperaceae, contains around
300 species worldwide.
Description Perennials with tufted or creeping rootstocks,
sometimes with nut-like tubers, the leaves in 3 ranks, forming a
rosette, usually with a sharp edge. Flowering stems to 3m, often
triangular in section, with a terminal umbel of short, usually flattened
spikes. Flowers small, bisexual, in the axil of a small bract. Perianth
segments absent. Stamens usually 3. Stigmas 3, carpel 1. Pollination is
by wind. The fruit is a solitary, usually triangular nutlet.
Key Recognition Features The flat, grass-like leaves in groups of
3, the triangular flowering stems, and the male and female flowers on
short, flattened spikes arranged in a much-branched or simple umbel.
Ecology and Geography In water and wet places, mainly in the
tropics, with 27 species in Europe, over 100 in Australia, and the rest
scattered worldwide.
Comment *Cyperus papyrus* L. is the "bulrush" of the Moses story
and the usual source of Egyptian papyrus; it is a most elegant plant,
well worth cultivating in warm climates. *Cyperus esculentus* L. has
edible tubers, the chufa or tiger nut. *Cyperus involucratus* Rottboell is
the umbrella plant, grown as a house plant for its long leafy bracts.
Scirpus L. and related genera may look similar, but the flower spikes
are not flattened.

Eriophorum

Eriophorum L. (1753), cotton grass or bog cotton, in the family
Cyperaceae, contains around 12 species, mainly in the northern
hemisphere.
Description Perennials with tufted or creeping rootstocks, the
leaves usually in 3 ranks, forming a rosette, with a sharp edge and a
triangular tip. Flowering stems to 90cm, often triangular in section,
with an umbel of a few short spikes or with 1 terminal spike. Flowers
small, in the axil of a small bract. Perianth segments absent, replaced
by silky bristles which become long and conspicuous in fruit. Stamens
2. Stigmas 3, carpel 1. Pollination is by wind. The fruit is a solitary,
triangular nutlet.
Key Recognition Features The grass-like leaves in groups of 3,
with a triangular tip, and the long silky hairs that surround the fruit.
Ecology and Geography In shallow water, peat bogs, and
moorland, mainly in the colder parts of the northern hemisphere, with
1 species reported from South Africa.
Comment A few species are grown as ornamentals; only princesses in
Irish poetry have succeeded in making the silk into clothes, but more
realistically it has been used, within living memory, to stuff pillows.

Cyperus longus
1/2 life size, July 20th

Triticum

Triticum L. (1753), wheat, in the family Gramineae, sometimes called Poaceae, contains around 10 species, mainly in western Asia.

Description Annual grasses with flowering stems to 1.5m. Leaves divided into a flat blade and a sheath curled round the stem. The spikelets of grasses consist of 1–6, or rarely more, unisexual or bisexual flowers. The whole spikelet is surrounded by 2 outer scales, the glumes; within the glumes, each flower is protected by further scales, the lemma, which often has a long awn, and smaller palea; the hanging stamens and usually feathery styles emerge from between the lemma and palea to hang in the wind and release or catch the pollen. Inflorescence a spike of 2- to 6-flowered spikelets. Glumes about equal. Lemma sometimes with an awn. Stamens 3. Pollination is by wind. Styles 3, feathery. Seeds usually large and ovate.

Key Recognition Features The spike of 2- to 6-flowered spikelets, often with awns.

Ecology and Geography Cultivated worldwide, but wild in waste places, particularly in western Asia.

Comment Bread wheat, *T. aestivum* L., is the most common temperate cultivated grass. It is a complex hybrid between wild einkorn, *T. baeoticum* Boiss., with 2 species of *Aegilops*, *A. speltoides* Tausch and *A. tauschii* Cosson, combined with chromosome doubling. Cultivated wheats have the combined characteristics of spikes that do not break into sections, and large seeds that do not fall easily from between the glumes, thus facilitating harvesting. *Triticum durum* Desf., durum wheat, has been cultivated for at least 8000 years; it is now commonly used for pasta and semolina. The Gramineae is most closely related to the Restionaceae, as well as the Juncaceae (see p.513) and Cyperaceae (see pp.514–17).

Aegilops squarrosa, in fruit (left) and *Aegilops speltoides* in flower (right)
½ life size, June 26th

Triticum aestivum spikelets (above)
1 ⅓ × life size, June 10th

Triticum aestivum
½ life size, June 10th

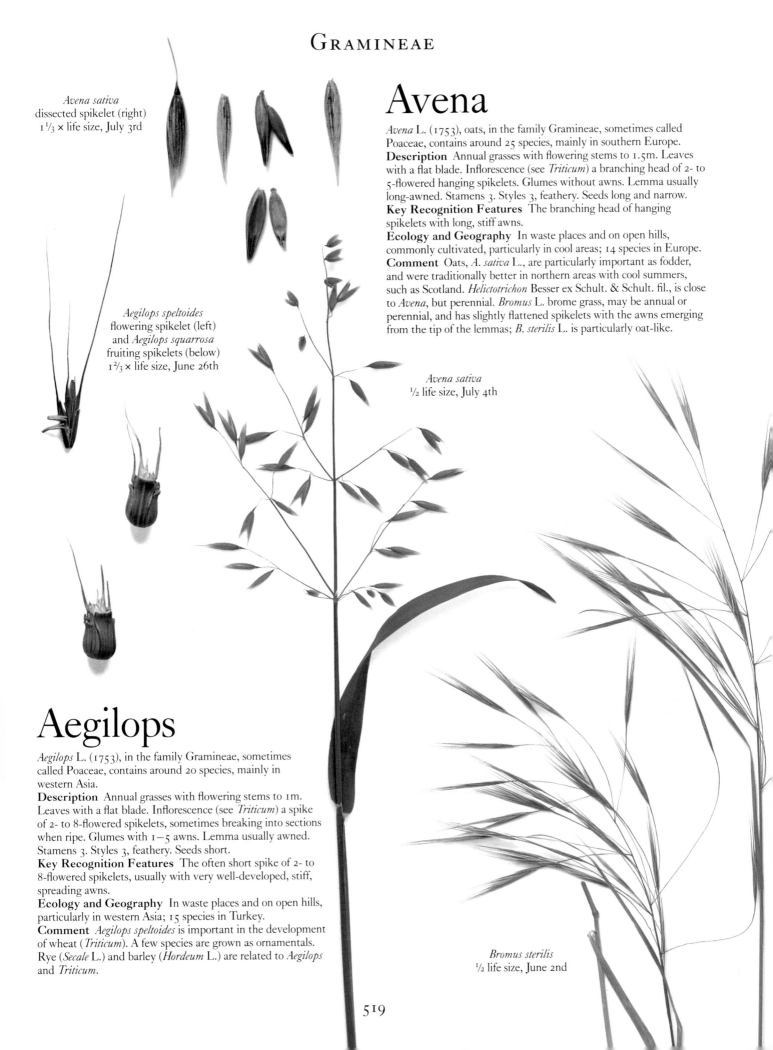

Avena sativa
dissected spikelet (right)
1 ⅓ × life size, July 3rd

Aegilops speltoides
flowering spikelet (left)
and *Aegilops squarrosa*
fruiting spikelets (below)
1 ⅔ × life size, June 26th

Avena

Avena L. (1753), oats, in the family Gramineae, sometimes called Poaceae, contains around 25 species, mainly in southern Europe.
Description Annual grasses with flowering stems to 1.5m. Leaves with a flat blade. Inflorescence (see *Triticum*) a branching head of 2- to 5-flowered hanging spikelets. Glumes without awns. Lemma usually long-awned. Stamens 3. Styles 3, feathery. Seeds long and narrow.
Key Recognition Features The branching head of hanging spikelets with long, stiff awns.
Ecology and Geography In waste places and on open hills, commonly cultivated, particularly in cool areas; 14 species in Europe.
Comment Oats, *A. sativa* L., are particularly important as fodder, and were traditionally better in northern areas with cool summers, such as Scotland. *Helictotrichon* Besser ex Schult. & Schult. fil., is close to *Avena*, but perennial. *Bromus* L. brome grass, may be annual or perennial, and has slightly flattened spikelets with the awns emerging from the tip of the lemmas; *B. sterilis* L. is particularly oat-like.

Avena sativa
½ life size, July 4th

Aegilops

Aegilops L. (1753), in the family Gramineae, sometimes called Poaceae, contains around 20 species, mainly in western Asia.
Description Annual grasses with flowering stems to 1m. Leaves with a flat blade. Inflorescence (see *Triticum*) a spike of 2- to 8-flowered spikelets, sometimes breaking into sections when ripe. Glumes with 1—5 awns. Lemma usually awned. Stamens 3. Styles 3, feathery. Seeds short.
Key Recognition Features The often short spike of 2- to 8-flowered spikelets, usually with very well-developed, stiff, spreading awns.
Ecology and Geography In waste places and on open hills, particularly in western Asia; 15 species in Turkey.
Comment *Aegilops speltoides* is important in the development of wheat (*Triticum*). A few species are grown as ornamentals. Rye (*Secale* L.) and barley (*Hordeum* L.) are related to *Aegilops* and *Triticum*.

Bromus sterilis
½ life size, June 2nd

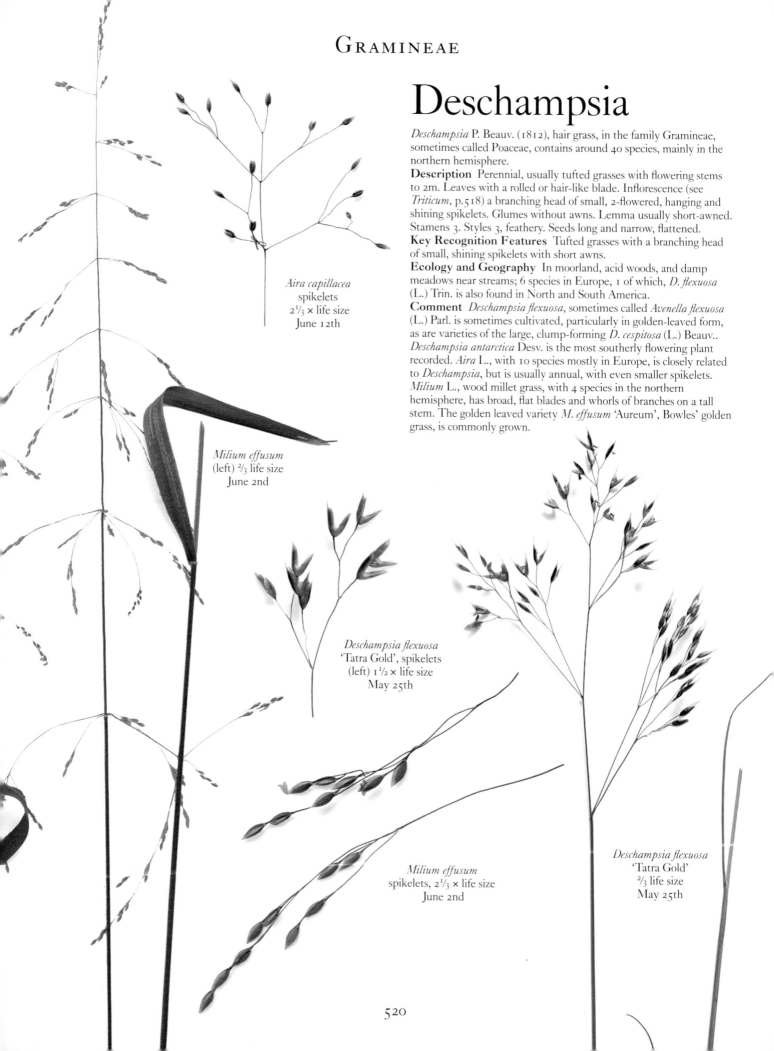

Deschampsia

Deschampsia P. Beauv. (1812), hair grass, in the family Gramineae, sometimes called Poaceae, contains around 40 species, mainly in the northern hemisphere.

Description Perennial, usually tufted grasses with flowering stems to 2m. Leaves with a rolled or hair-like blade. Inflorescence (see *Triticum*, p.518) a branching head of small, 2-flowered, hanging and shining spikelets. Glumes without awns. Lemma usually short-awned. Stamens 3. Styles 3, feathery. Seeds long and narrow, flattened.

Key Recognition Features Tufted grasses with a branching head of small, shining spikelets with short awns.

Ecology and Geography In moorland, acid woods, and damp meadows near streams; 6 species in Europe, 1 of which, *D. flexuosa* (L.) Trin. is also found in North and South America.

Comment *Deschampsia flexuosa*, sometimes called *Avenella flexuosa* (L.) Parl. is sometimes cultivated, particularly in golden-leaved form, as are varieties of the large, clump-forming *D. cespitosa* (L.) Beauv.. *Deschampsia antarctica* Desv. is the most southerly flowering plant recorded. *Aira* L., with 10 species mostly in Europe, is closely related to *Deschampsia*, but is usually annual, with even smaller spikelets. *Milium* L., wood millet grass, with 4 species in the northern hemisphere, has broad, flat blades and whorls of branches on a tall stem. The golden leaved variety *M. effusum* 'Aureum', Bowles' golden grass, is commonly grown.

Aira capillacea
spikelets
2⅓ × life size
June 12th

Milium effusum
(left) ⅔ life size
June 2nd

Deschampsia flexuosa
'Tatra Gold', spikelets
(left) 1½ × life size
May 25th

Milium effusum
spikelets, 2⅓ × life size
June 2nd

Deschampsia flexuosa
'Tatra Gold'
⅔ life size
May 25th

Phalaris

Phalaris L. (1753), in the family Gramineae, sometimes called Poaceae, contains around 20 species, mainly in the northern hemisphere.

Description Perennial or annual, often creeping, with flowering stems to 2m. Leaves with a flat blade, and usually with inflated upper sheath. Inflorescence (see *Triticum*, p.518) a branching or compact head of small, crowded 3-flowered spikelets, only 1 fertile. Glumes without awns, sometimes reduced and hardened. Lemma usually leathery and shiny. Stamens 3. Styles 2, feathery. Seeds ovate, enclosed in the hardened lemma and palea.

Key Recognition Features The branching or compact head of small, crowded, 3-flowered spikelets, 1 only fertile; 1 species, the perennial *P. arundinacea* L., is often grown in its white-striped form 'Picta'. The annual canary grass, *P. canariensis* L. has a rounded head of spikelets.

Ecology and Geography In shallow water, damp meadows, and waste ground, with 8 species in the Mediterranean area, and the rest mainly in Asia and North America.

Comment *Phalaris canariensis* is commonly used for bird seed and is naturalised all over the world.

Anthoxanthum

Anthoxanthum L. (1753), in the family Gramineae, sometimes called Poaceae, contains around 18 species, mainly in Europe and Asia.

Description Perennial or annual, with flowering stems to 1m. Leaves with a flat blade, sweetly scented. Inflorescence (see *Triticum*, p.518) a loose, elongated head of 3-flowered spikelets, only 1 fertile. Glumes without awns, unequal, the upper as long as the spikelet. Lemma of the sterile florets awned, of the fertile floret unawned. Stamens 2. Styles 2, feathery. Seeds elliptic.

Key Recognition Features The short, flat upper leaf blades and loose, elongated heads of spikelets, with 1 fertile floret per spikelet.

Ecology and Geography Moist meadows and dry, open ground, with 6 species in Europe, the rest mainly in Asia and Central America.

Comment *Anthoxanthum odoratum* L., the sweet vernal grass, is an early flowering, low-growing grass with the sweet scent of coumarin, like new-mown hay, and is one of the best for meadow gardens.

Phalaris arundinacea
'Picta', inflorescence
½ life size, June 12th

Phalaris arundinacea 'Picta'
½ life size, September 17th

Anthoxanthum odoratum
(right) ¾ life size
May 20th

Melica

Melica L. (1753), melick grass, in the family Gramineae, sometimes called Poaceae, contains around 80 species, mainly in Europe, Asia, and North America.

Description Perennials with flowering stems to 1m. Leaves with a flat blade. Inflorescence (see *Triticum*, p.518) a narrow or widely branched head of smooth, pointed, often silvery spikelets on thin and delicate stalks, with 2 to many flowers, only the lower 2 fertile. Glumes papery, with transparent margins. Lemmas without awns, sometimes hairy. Stamens 3. Styles 2. Seeds ovoid to ellipsoid.

Key Recognition Features The smooth, often silvery spikelets on very thin and delicate stalks, with only the lower 2 florets fertile.

Ecology and Geography In dry meadows, scrub, woods, and on mountain rock ledges; 8 species and many subspecies in Turkey, the rest mainly in Asia, North America, and South Africa.

Comment *Melica uniflora* (L.) Retz is a very pretty grass for a woodland bank; the purple form of *M. altissima* L. 'Atropurpurea' from eastern Europe and western Asia is often cultivated.

Briza

Briza L. (1753), quaking grass, in the family Gramineae, sometimes called Poaceae, contains around 20 species, mainly in Europe, Asia, and South America.

Description Perennials or annuals, with flowering stems to 80cm. Leaves with a flat blade. Inflorescence (see *Triticum*, p.518) a widely branched head of large, smooth, rounded spikelets, with 4–18 flowers, on very thin and delicate stalks. Glumes without awns, rounded. Lemmas without awns. Stamens 3. Styles 2. Seeds obovoid, flattened on 1 side.

Key Recognition Features The large, smooth, rounded spikelets on very thin and delicate stalks.

Ecology and Geography In dry meadows and open ground, with 5 species in Turkey, the rest mainly in Asia and in South America, with *B. maxima* L. widely naturalised in California.

Comment These very attractive grasses, especially the annual *B. maxima* are often cultivated. The related *Festuca glauca* L. is commonly cultivated for its tufts of thin but very blue-grey leaves; the flowers not significant. Other *Festuca* species such as *F. rubra* L. are common in fine lawns.

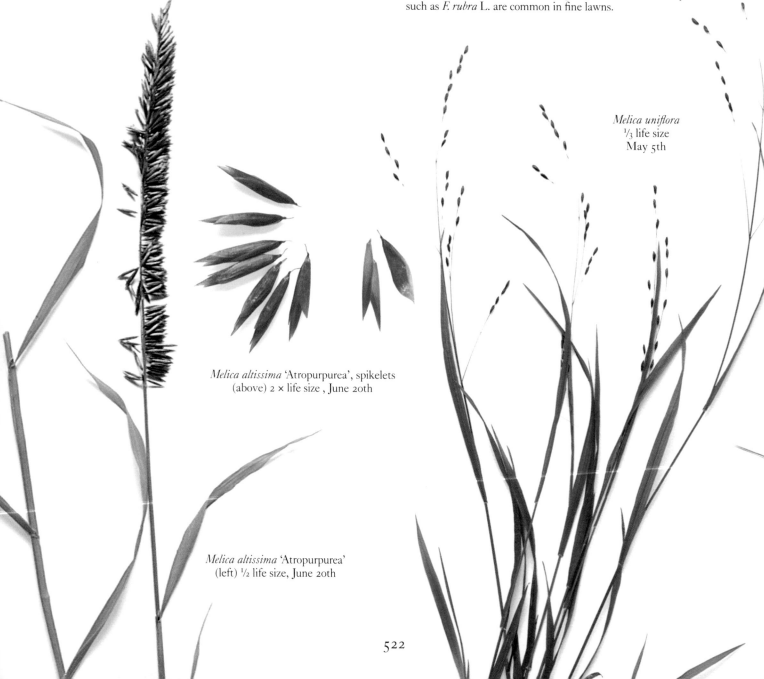

Melica uniflora
⅓ life size
May 5th

Melica altissima 'Atropurpurea', spikelets
(above) 2 × life size , June 20th

Melica altissima 'Atropurpurea'
(left) ½ life size, June 20th

GRAMINEAE

Briza maxima, spikelets
(above and below right)
1²⁄₃ × life size, June 2nd

Melica uniflora
spikelets (above)
2 × life size, May 5th

Festuca rubra
spikelets (left)
2 × life size
June 12th

Festuca glauca
¹⁄₂ life size
September 9th

Briza maxima
(right) ¹⁄₂ life size
June 2nd

Phragmites

Phragmites Adans. (1763), reed, in the family Gramineae, sometimes called Poaceae, contains around 3 species worldwide.

Description Creeping perennials with flowering stems to 3m. Leaves with a flat blade. Inflorescence (see *Triticum*, p.518) a branched head of clusters of 2- to 6-flowered, dark purplish spikelets on a silky-hairy stalk. Glumes shorter than the lemmas. Lemmas without awns, narrowly lanceolate. Stamens 3. Styles 2. Seeds long and narrow.

Key Recognition Features Tall plants forming reed beds, with branching heads of silky spikelets.

Ecology and Geography In swamps or shallow water, rarely on dry land; 1 species, *P. australis* (Cav.) Trin. in Europe and Asia.

Comment The common reed is used for thatching, and in some areas as a source of cellulose and converted into alcohol. The reed *Arundo donax* L. is much larger, with almost woody stems and plumes of whitish flowers.

Stipa

Stipa L.(1753), in the family Gramineae, sometimes called Poaceae, contains around 300 species, mainly in Asia and North America.

Description Tufted perennials with flowering stems to 2.5m. Leaves with a flat or rolled blade. Inflorescence (see *Triticum*, p.518) a narrow or widely branched head of 1-flowered spikelets on thin stalks. Glumes often papery, usually longer than the floret. Lemmas with awns, which often twist at the base and may be 50cm long and densely silky hairy. Stamens 2 or 3. Styles 2. Seeds long and narrow.

Key Recognition Features Large, tufted plants with tall stems and loose heads of awned spikelets, or shorter plants with exceptionally long and silky awns.

Ecology and Geography On dry steppes and mountain slopes among rocks, with 41 species in southern Europe, 15 in Turkey, especially in the east where they may be dominant and particularly beautiful on the steppe-covered hills. Other species mainly in dry areas and in the tropics worldwide.

Comment *Stipa gigantea* Link from Spain and Portugal is a huge, tufted oat-like grass, common in large gardens; *S. pulcherrima* K. Koch has very long, silky awns, to 50cm; it is found as far north as northern Germany.

Phragmites australis
½ life size
September 1st

Phragmites australis
spikelets, 2 × life size
September 1st

Stipa tenuissima spikelets
life size, June 25th

Stipa tenuissima
½ life size
June 25th

Cortaderia

Cortaderia Stapf (1897), in the family Gramineae, sometimes called Poaceae, contains around 24 species, mainly in South America.

Description Huge, tufted perennials with flowering stems to 3m. Leaves mostly basal, long and narrow, with a saw-edged blade. Inflorescence (see *Triticum*, p.518) a narrow or widely branched head of silky-flowered spikelets with 2–7 flowers. Male and female flowers on separate plants. Glumes often papery, unequal. Lemmas silky-hairy, with awns. Stamens 2. Styles 2. Seeds long and narrow.

Key Recognition Features Huge, tufted plants with tall stems and dense heads of silky florets.

Ecology and Geography By streams and in mountain valleys, occasionally in open woods, with 24 species in South America, 4 in New Zealand, and 1 in New Guinea.

Comment Pampas grass, *C. selloana* (Schultes & Schultes fil.) Aschers. & Graebn., is a well-known ornamental, with many cultivars of differing sizes and colours. In male plants the branches of the inflorescence point upwards; in female plants they are more spreading.

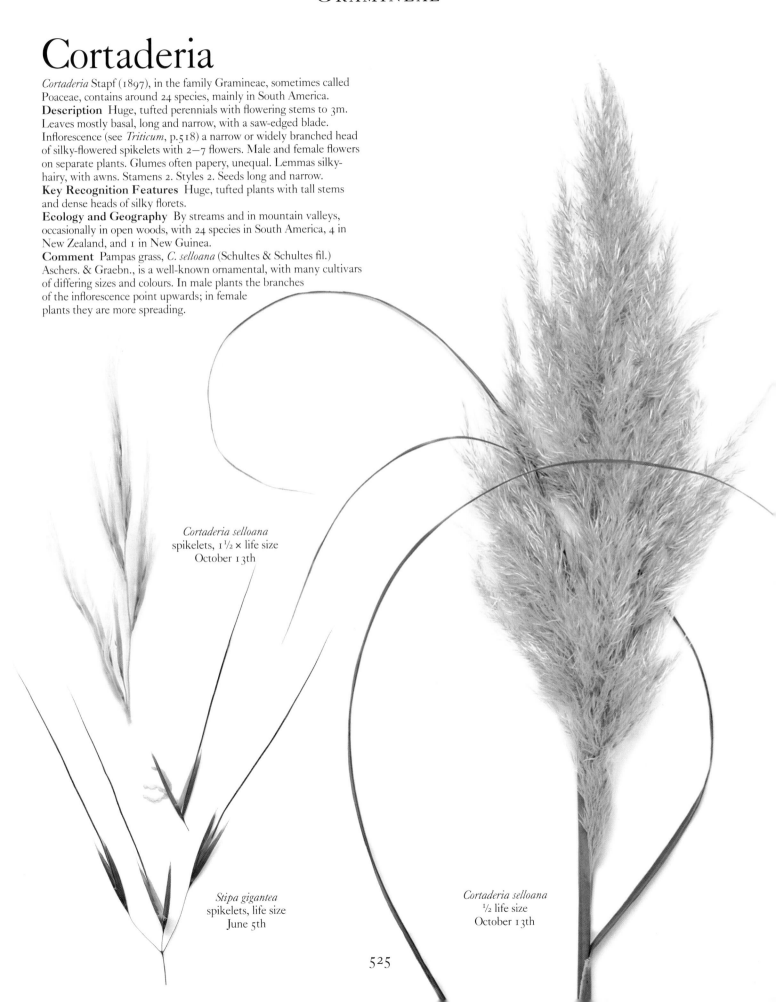

Cortaderia selloana
spikelets, 1 ½ × life size
October 13th

Stipa gigantea
spikelets, life size
June 5th

Cortaderia selloana
½ life size
October 13th

525

Miscanthus

Miscanthus Andersson (1856), in the family Gramineae, sometimes called Poaceae, contains around 20 species, mainly in southern and eastern Asia.

Description Large, usually tufted perennials with flowering stems to 3m. Leaves mostly on the stem. Inflorescence (see *Triticum*, p.518) a head of branches on a short axis, the silky-flowered spikelets with 1 bisexual flower. Glumes often papery, unequal. Lemmas thin and transparent, silky-hairy, with awns. Stamens 2 or 3. Styles 2. Seeds long and narrow.

Key Recognition Features Tufted plants with leaves up the stem and a flat-topped or pyramidal head of branches on a short axis, and silky-flowered spikelets

Ecology and Geography By streams, on the lower slopes of mountains, or in open woods; 6 species in Japan, others in mainland eastern Asia, the Pacific islands, and a few species in South Africa, which are often separated in the genus *Miscanthidium* Stapf.

Comment Several species, especially *M. sinensis* Andersson, are cultivated as ornamentals for their late-flowering, silky heads, which last well into the winter. 'Rotsilber' has leaves with a silver central stripe. Sugar cane, *Saccharum officinarum* L., is closely related to *Miscanthus*, as is *Imperata* Cir., with around 8 species in tropical and warm temperate areas; *I. cylindrica* (L.) Pall. is a serious weed in the tropics, but often cultivated for its red leaves. *Hakonechloa* Mak. ex Honda, has 1 species, *H. macra* (Munro) Mak., which grows on wet rocks in the mountains of Japan; it is often grown for its variously striped leaves. *Setaria* Beauv., with annual species mainly in the tropics of Asia and Africa, is close to *Pennisetum* (see p.528); *S. italica* L., foxtail millet, is commonly cultivated for bird seed.

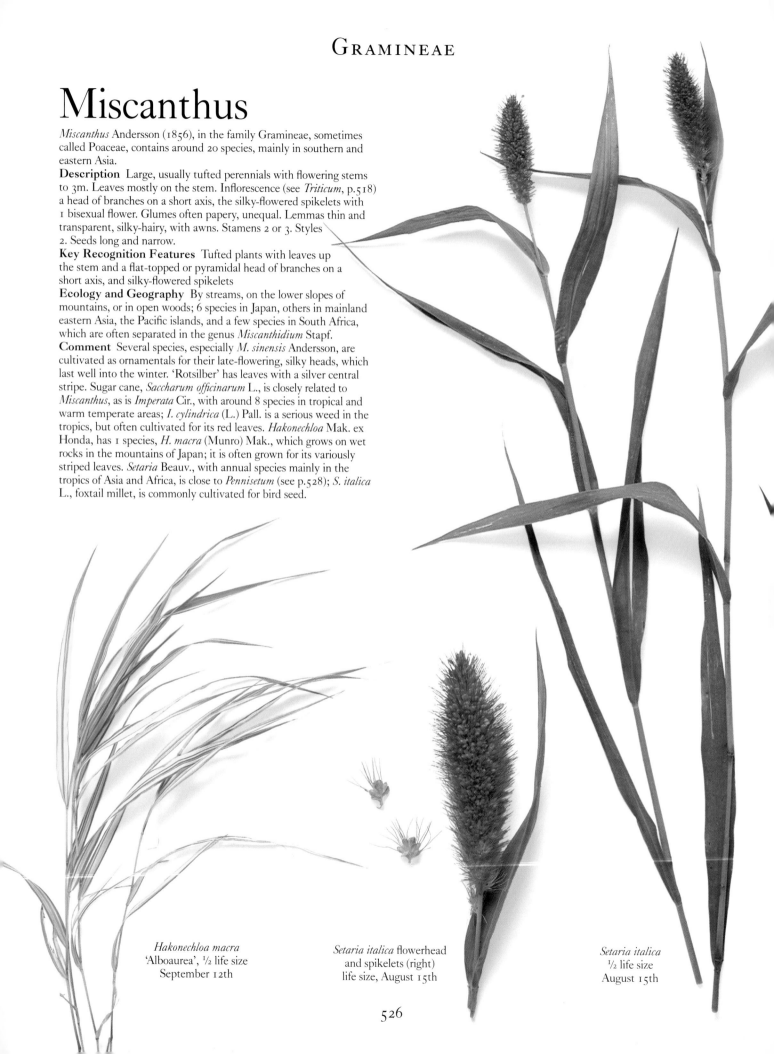

Hakonechloa macra
'Alboaurea', ¹⁄₂ life size
September 12th

Setaria italica flowerhead
and spikelets (right)
life size, August 15th

Setaria italica
¹⁄₂ life size
August 15th

GRAMINEAE

Miscanthus sinensis
'Rotsilber'
⅓ life size , May 17th

Imperata cylindrica
(left) ½ life size
June 22nd

Miscanthus sinensis
'Rotsilber', leaf and
spikelets with anthers
(left) 2 × life size
May 17th

Pennisetum

Pennisetum L.C.M. Rich. (1805), in the family Gramineae, sometimes called Poaceae, contains around 130 species, mainly in the tropics.
Description Annuals or perennials with often branched flowering stems to 1m. Leaves flat or rolled. Inflorescence (see *Triticum*, p.518) a long and narrow head of short branches, the spikelets surrounded by slender bristles, with 2 florets, the lower male or sterile, the upper bisexual. Glumes unequal, the lower often minute. Awns absent. Lemmas thin. Stamens 3. Styles 2.
Seeds flattened.
Key Recognition Features Grasses with long heads of spikelets, each surrounded by slender bristles.
Ecology and Geography In dry and grassy places, with 1 species in Europe, 3 in Japan, others in mainland eastern Asia and the tropics.
Comment *Pennisetum glaucum* (L.) R. Br. is the pearl or spiked millet, grown in Africa and India; *P. alopecuroides* (L.) Spreng., from eastern Asia, is a popular ornamental with several cultivars.

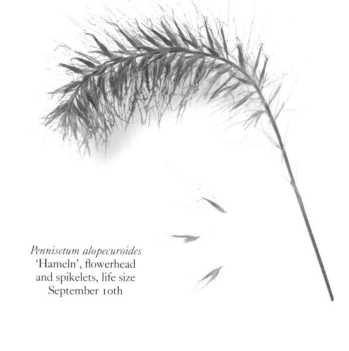

Pennisetum alopecuroides
'Hameln', flowerhead
and spikelets, life size
September 10th

Pennisetum alopecuroides
'Hameln', 1/3 life size
September 10th

Zea

Zea (1856), in the family Gramineae, sometimes called Poaceae, contains 1 cultivated species, *Zea mays* L., maize, corn, or mealies, described here, and possibly 3 wild species, all from Central America.
Description Stout annual with flowering stems to 3m. Leaves mostly on the stem. Male inflorescence (see *Triticum*, p.518) terminal, female inflorescences in the lower leaf axils, with long styles forming the silky tassel, and leaf sheaths covering the seeds. Stamens 3. Style 1, with a forked tip. Seeds short and often flattened.
Key Recognition Features Tall annual grass with male flowers at the top, female in the lower leaf axils.
Ecology and Geography Cultivated throughout the world and often naturalised.
Comment Maize is the third most important grain crop in the world after rice and wheat. Cultivated maize is now thought to have been developed around 6000 years ago by selection from the wild annual teosinte, *Z. mays* subsp. *mexicana* (Schrad.) Iltis. The earliest finds are in the Tehuacan valley in Mexico. The maize shown here is a variety grown particularly in Japan and Thailand, for its miniature cobs, which are eaten soft and before fertilisation. *Sorghum* Moench. and especially *S. bicolor* (L.) Moench., the great millet, is the fourth most important grain crop, originating in Africa, possibly in the Sudan, and more tolerant of poor, dry conditions than maize. The spikelets have 1 fertile floret.

GRAMINEAE

Zea mays, male spikelets
(above) life size
September 25th

Zea mays, section of
young cob, ½ life size
September 25th

Sorghum nigrum
(left) ⅓ life size
August 30th

Sorghum nigrum
spikelets (left)
1 ½ × life size
August 30th

Zea mays
⅓ life size
September 25th

529

Bibliography

General plant books:

The New Royal Horticultural Society Dictionary of Gardening, Macmillan (1992). A new version of the old Dictionary.
The Royal Horticultural Society Dictionary of Gardening, Oxford University Press (1976–77). Old but still valuable.
The European Garden Flora I–VI, Cambridge University Press (1986–2001). Scientific account of cultivated plants.
The Plant Book, A portable dictionary of the vascular plants by D.J. Mabberley, 2nd edition, Cambridge University Press (1997). An excellent account of all known genera, full of interesting or strange facts about plants.
The RHS Plant Finder 2000–2001, Dorling Kindersley. Updated annually, a good source of modern plant names, as well as a source list of nurseries for Great Britain.
Flowering Plants of the World, ed. V.H. Heywood, Batsford (1993). Illustrated account of plant families.
100 Families of Flowering Plants, by M. Hickey and C.J. King, Cambridge University Press (1981). Detailed drawings and explanation of the floral parts of 100 important families.
Wild Flowers of the World by Barbara Everard and Brian Morley, Ebury Press & Michael Joseph (1970). A geographical sample of interesting plants, with excellent and fascinating text.
Flowering Tropical Climbers by Geoffrey Herklots, Dawson (1976). A clear and detailed account of many genera of climbers, with excellent line drawings.
The Pollination of Flowers by Michael Proctor and Peter Yeo, Collins New Naturalist series, no. 54 (1973).

Plant phylogeny and DNA references:

Plant Systematics, a Phylogenetic Approach, by W.S. Judd et al, Sinauer Associates, Inc. (1999).
'Higher-level systematics of the monocotyledons: an assesment of current knowledge and a new classification', by Mark W. Chase, Douglas E. Soltis et al. in *Monocots; Systematics and Evolution* eds K.L. Wilson and D.A. Morrison. CSIRO, Melbourne (2000).
Angiosperm Phylogeny by D.E. Soltis et al in the *Botanical Journal of the Linnaean Society* 39–435 (2000).

Floras and books on different regions of the world:

Europe and southwestern Asia:
Flora Europaea by V.H. Heywood et al, Cambridge University Press (1964–80).
Flora of Turkey by P.H. Davis et al, Edinburgh University Press (1965–87).
Flowers of Greece and the Balkans by Oleg Polunin, Oxford University Press (1980).
Flowers of Southwest Europe by Oleg Polunin, Oxford University Press (1973).

Canary Islands:
Wild Flowers of the Canary Islands by David and Zoë Bramwell, Stanley Thornes (1974).

Africa:
'Plants of the Cape Flora, A Descriptive Catalogue' by Pauline Bond and Peter Goldblatt, in *Journal of South African Botany* suppl. volume 13 (1984).
South African Wild Flower Guides, Botanical Society of South Africa, in association with the the National Botanical Institute:
1. Namaqualand by Annelise Le Roux and Ted Schelpe; photography by Zelda Wahl (1994).
5. Hottentots Holland to Hermanus by Lee Burman and Anne Bean; photography by Jose Burman (1985).
7. West Coast by John Manning and Peter Goldblatt; photography by John Manning (1996).
9. Nieuwoudtville, Bokkeveld Plateau & Hantam by John Manning and Peter Goldblatt (1997).
The Botany of the Southern Natal Drakensberg by O.M. Hilliard and B.L. Burtt, National Botanic Garden (1987).
Wild Flowers of East Africa by Sir Michael Blundell KBE, Collins (1987).

India, China, Japan, and the Himalayas:
Flowers of the Himalaya by Oleg Polunin and Adam Stainton, Oxford University Press (1984); and Supplement, by Adam Stainton Oxford University Press, Delhi (1988).
Flora of Bhutan by A.J.C. Grierson and D.G. Long, Royal Botanic Garden, Edinburgh (1983–94).
Plantae Wilsonianae by J.S. Sargent (1913), reprinted by Dioscorides Press 1988.
Travels in China by Roy Lancaster, Antique Collectors Club (1989).
Flora of Japan by J. Ohwi, Smithsonian (1965).

Australia:
Encyclopaedia of Australian Plants by W. Rodger Elliott and David L. Jones, volumes 1–5, Lothian (1980–90).
Flora of New South Wales ed. Gwen J. Harden, New South Wales University Press, 4 volumes, (1990–93)

New Zealand:
Flora of New Zealand Volume 1 by H.H. Allen, PD Hasselberg (1961)
Flora of New Zealand Volume 2 by L.B. Moore and E. Edgar, PD Hasselberg (1970).

North America:
Flora of North America north of Mexico ed. Flora of North America editorial committee, vols. 1–3, Oxford University Press (1993 and continuing)
A California Flora and Supplement by Philip A. Munz, University of California Press (1973).
Arizona Flora by Thomas H. Kearney, Robert H. Peebles and collaborators, University of California Press (1951).
The Audubon Society Field Guide to Northern American Wild Flowers, western region by R. Spellenberg, Knopf (1979).
Illustrated Flora of the Northern United States and Canada by N.L. Britton and A. Brown, 2nd revised edition (1952).

Glossary

In the text we have tried to avoid obscure technical terms wherever possible, but a few are hard to avoid without resorting to a long explanation.

Achene a small, dry, 1-seeded fruit

Actinomycete generally anaerobic bacteria with a filamentous and branching growth pattern, which help fix atmospheric nitrogen

Acuminate gradually tapering to an elongated point

Amplexicaul with the base of the leaf encircling the stem

Androgynophore extension of the flower that bears both the ovary and the stamens *See also Gynophore*

Anther the part of the male *stamen* that contains the pollen

Aril a fleshy attachment or covering on a seed, which often attracts ants

Auricle, Auriculate ear-like projections at the leaf base

Axil the angle between the leaf stalk and the stem

Basic number (of *chromosomes*) the normal number of chromosome pairs in a species or genus *See also Haploid, Diploid, Polyploid*

Basifixed (of an *anther*) attached by the base *See also Versatile*

Bee-fly Small, fast-flying, bumble-bee-like flies with a long, rigid proboscis, often stout and hairy

Biomass Very fast-growing trees cut about every 5 years and used for cheap wood (such as chipboard) or fuel

Bletting allowing fruit to ripen to the point of decay

Bract a modified leaf below a flower

Calyx the outer parts of a flower, usually green, formed by the often fused sepals

Capitate head-like

Capsule a dry fruit containing seeds

Carpel the part of the flower that produces the seeds

Caruncle a fleshy growth on the end of a seed

Chromosome a rod-like structure in the nucleus of a cell, carrying the genetic information; *species* normally have a constant number of chromosomes *See also Diploid, Haploid*

Ciliate with a fringe of fine hairs on the margin

Cladode a flattened, leaf-like stem *See also Phyllode*

Clavate shaped like a club, narrow at the base, swelling towards the apex

Cleistogamous flowers that never open and are self-pollinated

Clone the vegetatively propagated progeny of a single plant

Connective the tissue that connects the 2 sacs of an anther

Corolla the inner parts of the flower, comprising the petals, usually used when the petals are united into a tube

Corona an appendage or series of united appendages on the inner side of the *corolla* in some flowers (as the daffodil)

Crenate with shallow, rounded teeth

Cultivar a cultivated variety or hybrid, denoted by a name in inverted commas, such as *Hamamelis* 'Diane' *See also Forma, Microspecies, Subspecies, Variant*

Cuneate wedge-shaped

Cyme a more-or-less flat-topped inflorescence, with the central flowers the first to open

Dehiscent opening to shed its seeds

Dentate with sharp, regular teeth

Dichotomous branching in 2 equal parts

Diploid containing the usual complement of *chromosomes*, that is twice the *basic number*, also expressed as 2n *See also Haploid, Polyploid*

Elaiosome a fleshy, edible appendage to a seed that attracts animals, which then disperse the seeds

Erose appearing as if gnawed

Exserted sticking out, usually describing the *style* or *stamens* protruding from the flower

Falcate sickle-shaped

Family A group of related plants, using consisting of several *genera*

-fid split, bifid or 2-fid meaning split in 2, and trifid or 3-fid split in 3

Filament the part of the *stamen* that supports the *anther*

Filiform thread-like

Fl. floruit, given for a date when someone was known to be alive, when their birth or death dates cannot be found

Flagellum the tail on a mobile cell, such as a sperm cell as found in ginkgo, by which it swims (Latin for whip)

Floccose, Flocculose woolly

Forma, f. a minor variant, less different from the basic species than a *Variety See also Cultivar, Microspecies, Subspecies*

Fynbos the South African name for the scrub found on hillsides in the Cape region, a rich community of heathers, pelargoniums, proteas, bulbs etc., which is subject to periodic renewal by fire

Garrigue Vegetation of low, evergreen shrubs, found in the Mediterranean area, usually on thin or shallow soils, the main plants being shrubs of evergreen oak *See also Maquis*

Genome a group of genes, generally a group of *chromosomes* belonging to an ancestral species

Genus, Genera a grouping of related *species* with common features that distinguish them from other plants, such as *Hibiscus, Fuchsia,* or *Pelargonium*

Glabrous without hairs or glands

Glandular with glands, which are usually stalked, like hairs with a sticky blob on the apex

Glaucous with a greyish colour or bloom, especially on the leaves

Globose more or less spherical

Glochid a barbed, often tufted, bristle or spine on a cactus

Glomerule small, crowded, rounded heads of flowers

Gynophore extension of the flower that bears the ovary *See also Androgynophore*

Haploid with a single set of *chromosomes*, the normal state of the reproductive stage of plants, such as pollen or egg cells *See also Basic number, Diploid, Polyploid*

Haustorium a fleshy outgrowth from a parasitic plant, by which it is attached to and receives nourishment from the host

Hispid coarsely and stiffly hairy

Hyaline transparent, often soft or papery

Hybrid the progeny of 2 different *species*

Indusium epidermal tissue covering the spore-bearing parts of a fern frond

Inferior ovary in which the point of insertion of the sepals and petals is above the *ovary See also Superior ovary*

Inflorescence the flowers and flower stalks, especially when grouped

Keeled with a ridge along the lower side, like the keel of a boat

Laciniate deeply and irregularly toothed and divided into narrow lobes

GLOSSARY

Lanceolate shaped like a lance blade, widest below the middle, with a tapering point

Latex white, milky, and rubbery juice

Locule parts of a *capsule*

Loess deep deposits of sandy, wind-blown soil

Lyrate leaf with a broad but pointed apex and lobes becoming smaller towards the leaf base

Mallee, mellee Scrubland vegetation of southern Australia, dominated by shrubby eucalyptus and other shrubs with spiny or leathery leaves

Maquis Scrubland vegetation found on the lower slopes of mountains in the Mediterranean area, the main plants being shrubs or small trees with tough, evergreen leaves *See also Garrigue*

Meiosis cell division producing the halving of the number of *chromosomes* during reproduction *See also Diploid, Haploid*

Mericarp a 1-seeded *carpel*, one of a pair split apart at maturity, as found in many of the Umbelliferae

-merous having parts in groups, for example 3-merous or tri-merous, having parts in groups of 3

Microspecies a *species* that is distinguished from others by very small but constant characteristics *See also Cultivar, Forma, Subspecies, Variety*

Monocarpic usually dying after flowering and fruiting

Mucronate with a short, sharp point

Nectary a gland in the flower that produces nectar

Ochrae or ocrae an inflated or tubular sheath made up of 2 *stipules* found in the Polygonaceae

Ovary the base of the female part of the flower, which contains the *ovules* and develops into the fruit; may be composed of one or several *carpels*

Ovule the female egg cell that develops into a seed

Palmate with lobes or leaflets, spreading like the fingers of a hand

Panicle a branched *raceme*

Papillose with small, elongated projections

Pappus parachute-like ring of fine hairs

Parietal placentation with ovules attached to the walls of the ovary

Pedicel the stalk of a flower

Peduncle the stalk of an *inflorescence*

Peloric regularity in a normally irregular flower

Peltate shaped like a round shield, with the stalk in the centre

Perfoliate a leaf joined right around the stem, thus looking as if pierced by the stem

Phyllary an incurved, usually narrow *bract*, on the base of a daisy-type flowerhead

Phylloclade *See Cladode*

Phyllode a flattened leaf stalk that functions as a leaf

Pilose hairy, with long soft hairs

Pollinium a regular mass of pollen grains that are more-or-less stuck together

Polyploid having more than the usual (*diploid*) number of *chromosomes* for that *genus*, for example triploid, with 3 times the *basic number* of chromosomes, also expressed 3n, or tetraploid, with 4 times the basic number, also expressed 4n

Pome an apple-like fruit

Puberulent with a fine but rather sparse covering of hairs

Pubescent with a fine coating of hairs, denser than *puberulent*

Pyrene a hard-coated seed found within a fruit

Raceme an *inflorescence* with the flowers on a central stem, the oldest at the base

Receptacle part of the stem that bears the flower parts

Reticulate marked with a network, usually of veins

Rhizoids a structure that resembles a root in appearance and function, but is far less specialised and used mainly for anchorage, as in *Selaginella*

Rugose wrinkled

Saccate with a baggy pouch

Samara a winged seed, usually of a maple

Saprophyte a plant that lives on decaying organic matter and usually lacks chlorophyll

Scarious dry and papery, usually also transparent

Section part of (usually) a *genus*, grouping *species* with particular traits that are not necessarily shared by all the species in the genus *See also Subgenus*

Seta, Setose bristle, bristly

Sinus, Sinuate a deep notch between 2 lobes, towards the centre of a leaf

Species, Sp. group of individuals having common characteristics, distinct from other groups; the basic unit of plant classification *See also Genus*

Spicate like a spike

Spinose with weak spines

Stamen the male part of a flower, consisting of a *filament* supporting an *anther*

Stigma the sticky part of a *style* that receives pollen

Stipule leafy lobes along or near the base of a leaf stalk, found especially in roses

Strobilus a cone or cone-like cluster of spore-bearing organs

Style the part of the flower that connects the *stigma* to the *ovary*

Subgenus a major division of a *genus*, grouping *species* with particular traits that are not necessarily shared by all the species in the genus *See also Section*

Suborbicular almost round, but usually slightly narrower

Subspecies, Subsp. a division of a species, with minor and not complete differences from other subspecies, usually distinct either ecologically or geographically *See also Cultivar, Forma, Microspecies, Variety*

Succulent fleshy, storing water in the stems or leaves

Superior ovary in which the point of insertion of the sepals and petals is below the *ovary* *See also Inferior ovary*

Terete not ridged or grooved

Ternate in a group of 3

Tetragonal square in section

Tetraploid *See Polyploid*

Tracheid part of the water-conducting tissue inside a stem

Tribe part of a *family*, usually consisting of several *genera* with common distinguishing characteristics

Triploid *See Polyploid*: triploid plants are usually sterile, but robust growers and good garden plants

Tuberculate warty

Umbel an *inflorescence* in which the branches arise from a single point, usually forming a flat or gently rounded top

Variety, Var., Vars. a group of plants within a *species*, usually differing in one or two minor characteristics, and generally referring to natural variations *See also Cultivar, Forma, Microspecies, Subspecies*

Versatile (of an *anther*) attached in the middle *See also Basifixed*

Vlei seasonal pool in Africa, full of water in winter and drying slowly through the summer, a habitat of many specialised species; vernal pools in California are similar

Index

The entries in roman upper and lower case refer to the main genera covered in this work. The entries in capital letters refer to the families covered, and the entries in italic refer to genera and families only mentioned in the text.

INDEX